D0711291

THE 9/11 EFFECT: COMPARATIVE COUNTER-TERRORISM

This book critically and comparatively examines the responses of the United Nations and a range of countries to the terror attacks on September 11, 2001. It assesses the convergence between the responses of Western democracies, including the United States, the United Kingdom, Australia, and Canada, and those of countries with more experience with terrorism, including Egypt, Syria, Israel, Singapore, and Indonesia. A number of common themes – the use of criminal law and immigration law, the regulation of speech associated with terrorism, the review of the state's whole-of-government counter-terrorism activities, and the development of national security policies – are discussed. The book provides a critical take on how the United Nations promoted terrorism financing laws and listing processes and the regulation of speech associated with terrorism but failed to agree on a definition of terrorism or the importance of respecting human rights while combating terrorism. It also assesses the failures of the American approach of extra-legalism and departures from criminal justice and the challenges of transnational cooperation and accountability for counter-terrorism.

Kent Roach is a professor of law at the University of Toronto, where he holds the Prichard-Wilson Chair in Law and Public Policy. He was elected a Fellow of the Royal Society of Canada in 2002. His 11 books include *Constitutional Remedies in Canada* (winner of the 1997 Owen Prize), *Due Process and Victims' Rights: The New Law and Politics of Criminal Justice* (short-listed for the 1999 Donner Prize), *The Supreme Court on Trial: Judicial Activism or Democratic Dialogue* (short-listed for the 2001 Donner Prize), *September 11: Consequences for Canada* (named one of the five most significant books of 2003 by the *Literary Review of Canada*), and (with Robert J. Sharpe) *Brian Dickson: A Judge's Journey* (winner of the 2004 J. W. Dafoe Prize). He is coeditor of the first and second editions of *Global Anti-Terrorism Law and Policy* and has served with the Commissions of Inquiry into the rendition of Maher Arar and the bombing of Air India Flight 182. He has appeared before working groups and legislative committees in Canada, Indonesia, and the United States and is a member of the International Task Force on Terrorism, Democracy, and the Law.

The 9/11 Effect: Comparative Counter-Terrorism

KENT ROACH

University of Toronto

CAMBRIDGE
UNIVERSITY PRESS

CAMBRIDGE
UNIVERSITY PRESS

32 Avenue of the Americas, New York NY 10013-2473, USA

Cambridge University Press is part of the University of Cambridge.

It furthers the University's mission by disseminating knowledge in the pursuit of education, learning and research at the highest international levels of excellence.

www.cambridge.org
Information on this title: www.cambridge.org/9780521185059

First published 2011

A catalogue record for this publication is available from the British Library

Library of Congress Cataloguing in Publication data
Roach, Kent.
The 9/11 effect : comparative counter-terrorism / Kent Roach.
p. cm.
Includes bibliographical references and index.
ISBN 978-1-107-00616-4 – ISBN 978-0-521-18505-9 (pbk.)
1. September 11 Terrorist Attacks, 2001. 2. Terrorism – United States – Prevention.
3. Terrorism – Great Britain – Prevention. 4. Terrorism – Canada – Prevention.
5. Terrorism – Australia – Prevention. 6. Terrorism – United Nations – Prevention.
7. Terrorism – Egypt – Laws. 8. Terrorism – Syria – Laws. 9. Terrorism – Singapore –
Prevention. 10. Terrorism – Indonesia – Prevention. 11. Terrorism – Law.
12. Terrorism – Prevention. I. Title.
HV6432.7.R57   2011
363.32517 – dc22   2011009190

ISBN 978-1-107-00616-4 Hardback
ISBN 978-0-521-18505-9 Paperback

To Erin and Carey

Brief Contents

1   Introduction 1
2   The United Nations Responds: Security Council Listing
    and Legislation 21
3   Countries That Did Not Immediately Respond 77
4   The United States Responds: Executive Power and
    Extra-Legalism 161
5   The United Kingdom Responds: A Legislative War
    on Terrorism 238
6   Australia Responds: Hyper-Legislation 309
7   Canada Responds: Border and Human Security 361
8   Conclusions 426

Contents

Acknowledgments   *page* xiii

1   Introduction 1
    I   The Post-9/11 Fallout   1
    II   Methodology   5
    III   Outline of the Chapters   14

2   The United Nations Responds: Security Council Listing
    and Legislation 21
    I   Introduction   21
    II   The United Nations   22
    III   Pre-9/11 Experience   25
    IV   The Initial Response to 9/11   28
    V   Security Council Resolution 1373: Panicked Global
          Legislation   31
    VI   Belated Guidance on the Definition of Terrorism: Security
          Council Resolution 1566   51
    VII   Security Council Resolution 1540 and the Dangers of
          Terrorists Using Weapons of Mass Destruction   53
    VIII Security Resolution 1624 and the Emphasis on Speech
          Associated with Terrorism   55
    IX   Attempts to Reform the Security Council's
          Counter-Terrorism Work   59
    X   The Security Council's Post-9/11 Record   63
    XI   The General Assembly's 2006 Counter-Terrorism Strategy   67
    XII   Rights-Protection Bodies   70
    XIII Integrating Whole-of-UN Approaches to Terrorism   72
    XIV   Conclusion   73

3   Countries That Did Not Immediately Respond 77
    I   Introduction   77
    II   Egypt   79

	III	Syria	92
	IV	Israel and the Occupied Territories	100
	V	Singapore	129
	VI	Indonesia	143
	VII	Conclusion	158

4   The United States Responds: Executive Power and
     Extra-Legalism 161
	I	Introduction	161
	II	The Pre-9/11 Experience	167
	III	The Initial Response to 9/11	174
	IV	The USA Patriot Act	175
	V	What the Patriot Act Did Not Authorize	184
	VI	Subsequent Legislation and the Demise of Patriot II	195
	VII	Guantánamo and the Failed Attempt to Preclude	
		Habeas Corpus	198
	VIII	Criminal Prosecutions	214
	IX	Torture	218
	X	Extralegal Conduct and Obstacles to Accountability	223
	XI	Speech Associated with Terrorism	227
	XII	Targeted Killings	229
	XIII	National Security Policies	233
	XIV	Conclusion	235

5   The United Kingdom Responds: A Legislative War
     on Terrorism 238
	I	Introduction	238
	II	Pre-9/11 Experience	244
	III	The Terrorism Act, 2000	255
	IV	The Initial Response to 9/11	262
	V	The Belmarsh Litigation	276
	VI	The Response to the Belmarsh Case	280
	VII	Torture	290
	VIII	Foreign Counter-Terrorism Activities	292
	IX	Stop-and-Search Powers and Discriminatory Profiling	296
	X	Responding to the London Bombings: Terrorism Act, 2006	298
	XI	Counter-Terrorism Act, 2008	301
	XII	National Security Policies	303
	XIII	Conclusion	306

6   Australia Responds: Hyper-Legislation 309
	I	Introduction	309
	II	Pre-9/11 Experience	314
	III	The Initial Response to 9/11	317
	IV	ASIO Questioning Warrants	328

V   Immigration Law as Antiterrorism Law   333
VI   Responding to the London Bombings   334
VII   Criminal Prosecutions   346
VIII Review of National Security Activities   354
IX   National Security Policies   356
X   Conclusion   358

7   Canada Responds: Border and Human Security 361
I   Introduction   361
II   Pre-9/11 Experience   365
III   The Initial Response to 9/11   374
IV   Immigration Law as Antiterrorism Law   395
V   Criminal Prosecutions   406
VI   Foreign Counter-Terrorism Activities   410
VII   Review of National Security Activities   416
VIII National Security Policies   420
IX   Conclusion   423

8   Conclusions 426
I   Some Post-9/11 Mistakes   431
II   The Complexities of the Post-9/11 World   440
III   Some Challenges Going Forward   448
IV   Conclusion   461

Index   463

Acknowledgments

Comparative law is a difficult endeavor, and I have been fortunate to have had much assistance in researching and writing this book over the last decade. I have been able to teach a course on Comparative Antiterrorism Law not only at the University of Toronto's Faculty of Law but also at the Centre for Transnational Legal Studies in London, at the University of New South Wales in Sydney, and at the National University of Singapore. I thank all these institutions for their support as well as the students from many different countries who engaged with my ideas as they developed over the years.

This book also reflects the wonderful experience of coediting two editions of *Global Anti-Terrorism Law and Policy* with Victor V. Ramraj and Michael Hor, and joined by George Williams on the second edition. I am grateful to the National University of Singapore and the Faculty of Law at the University of New South Wales for funding conferences before the publication of each edition and to all the authors in those collections. The work on that book has convinced me of the importance of studying and teaching terrorism law and policy in a comparative fashion that also includes international law and institutions.

I was fortunate enough to have had some hands-on experience that assisted in developing the ideas in this book. I thank the Economic Institutional and Professional Strengthening Group and its then–chief of staff James Agee III for allowing me to work in Jakarta in 2002 with a working group drafting a terrorism law for Indonesia. Back in Canada, I also am grateful to have been included on the research advisory committee for the Commission of Inquiry into the Actions of Canadian Officials in Relation to Maher Arar and to have served as research director (legal studies) for the Commission of Inquiry into the Investigation of Bombing of Air India Flight 182. These experiences allowed me to better understand the difficulties of counter-terrorism and the drastic consequences of overreacting or underreacting to the terrorist threat. The views expressed in this book are, of course, only my own.

The staff of the Bora Laskin Law Library have been exceptionally able, diligent, and cheerful in tracking down material for me; in particular, I thank Sooin Kim and Sufei Xu. A number of research assistants have helped me over the years, including Sabrina Bandalli, Joe Heller, Malcolm Katz, Andrew Martin, and Owen Goddard. John Berger at Cambridge University Press and Brigitte Coulton at Aptara have greatly facilitated the publishing process. I also gratefully acknowledge financial assistance from Canada's Social Sciences and Humanities Research Council and from the Prichard-Wilson Chair in Law and Public Policy endowment. I have tried to keep the book current to the end of 2010, while adding important developments in the first few months of 2011.

A number of colleagues and friends generously read and discussed parts of the manuscript and made helpful suggestions. I thank David Cole, Craig Forcese, Michael Hor, David Jenkins, Mordechai Kremnitzer, Andrew Lynch, Audrey Macklin, Cathy Powell, Victor Ramraj, Rayner Thwaites, Clive Walker, Lynn Welchman, and George Williams for helpful comments.

Last, but definitely not least, I thank my family for all that they do. My parents, Howard and Grace Roach, continue to be a source of encouragement and understanding. This project required me to be on the road for significant periods of time, and my wife, Jan Cox, did much more than keep the home fires burning. Without her, the book and many other things would not be possible. My daughters, Erin and Carey, were small children when 9/11 happened. Now, in the blink of an eye, they are wonderful young adults, and I thank them for helping to keep things in perspective and dedicate this book to them.

1 Introduction

I. THE POST-9/11 FALLOUT

Terrorism was not invented with the September 11, 2001 (9/11), terrorist attacks on the United States. Nevertheless, the coordinated attacks that killed almost 3,000 people were unprecedented as a single act of terrorism. So, too, was the global response to those events. Although individual countries had panicked and reacted to terrorism with repressive and ineffective laws and measures before, the response to 9/11 was an unprecedented global phenomenon. 9/11 produced a horrible natural experiment that allows us to compare how international institutions and different countries responded. Some reacted to 9/11 in novel and disturbing ways; others did very little to respond. All countries responded in a manner that reflected their own particular histories and legal, political, and social cultures.

The United Nations (UN) Security Council had, before 9/11, already used its mandatory powers under Chapter VII of the UN Charter in relation to international peace and security in an attempt to impose an asset freeze and travel and arms bans on all those associated with Osama bin Laden, al Qaeda, and the Taliban. Although the individual sanctions of this process under Security Council Resolution 1267 had failed to stop 9/11, likely the most expensive act of terrorism ever, the Security Council heavily reinvested in attempts to stop terrorism through criminalizing terrorism financing by enacting Security Council Resolution 1373 a few weeks after 9/11. This resolution called on all states to ensure that terrorism and financing of terrorism were serious crimes.

Resolution 1373 constituted a novel form of global legislation imposing permanent and general obligations on all states,[1] but it was also legislation

---

[1] Paul Szasz, "The Security Council Starts Legislating" (2002) 96 American Journal of International Law 901, at 902; Eric Rosand, "The Security Council as 'Global Legislator': Ultra Vires

that had many of the flaws of domestic legislation frequently enacted in an attempt to reassure the public after other acts of terrorism.[2] The Security Council acted quickly with what was at hand,[3] with limited information and time for deliberation. It invested in attempts to prevent terrorism financing even though existing financial sanctions against al Qaeda had failed to prevent 9/11 and subsequent investigations suggested that 9/11 would not have been prevented by even the most robust terrorism financing laws.[4] Resolution 1373 barely mentioned the importance of respecting human rights while countering terrorism and allowed countries with poor human rights records to defend repressive laws as attempts to prevent terrorism.

Although it called on all states to ensure that terrorism and its financing were serious crimes, Resolution 1373 did not provide any guidance about how states should define terrorism. This reflected continued disagreement about the proper definition of terrorism but also a missed opportunity to promote a restrained definition of terrorism that would declare that no motive and no cause justify the murder of civilians to intimidate populations or coerce governments.[5] The lack of a restrained definition of terrorism helped states justify repressive laws that can be used against political opposition in the fashionable garb of antiterrorism.

Resolution 1373 warned states not to allow terrorists to be granted refugee status but provided no advice about how to deal with suspected terrorists who would be tortured if returned to countries like Egypt and Syria. Resolution 1373 called on states to provide more information to each other to prevent terrorism but did not advert to the dangers that intelligence was a very inexact science that might wrongly identify people as terrorists.

Many countries responded to 9/11 and Security Council Resolution 1373 with tough new antiterrorism laws. Most countries did not invoke emergency powers or make formal derogations from human rights, but this raised concerns about permanent emergencies that would limit a variety of rights. In some countries,

---

or Ultra Innovative?" (2004–5) 28 Fordham International Law Journal 542; Marti Koskenniemi, "International Legislation Today: Limits and Possibilities" (2005) 23 Wisconsin International Law Journal 61.

[2] For a defense of legislation designed to reassure a public after large-scale terrorism attacks, including harsh legislation designed to impose large-scale detentions, see Bruce Ackerman, *Before the Next Attack* (New Haven, CT: Yale University Press, 2006).

[3] Mark Tushnet, "The Possibilities of Comparative Constitutional Law" (1999) 108 Yale Law Journal 1225.

[4] National Commission on Terrorist Attacks upon the United States, *The 9/11 Report* (New York: St. Martin's Press, 2004), at 5.4.

[5] Such a definition could be found in Article 2(1)(b) of the International Convention for the Suppression of the Financing of Terrorism, December 9, 1999, UN 54 th Session, UN Document A/RES/54/109 (1999).

post-9/11 laws and practices provoked debates about whether governments were overreacting to 9/11 and sacrificing democratic and due process values in an attempt to prevent terrorism. Indonesia, the world's most populous Muslim country, had a long debate about the appropriate response to 9/11 and Resolution 1373. It refused to enact a draft law that would have brought back some repressive Suharto-era practices. Nevertheless, it quickly enacted an antiterrorism law as an executive regulation less than a week after the October 2002 Bali bombings that killed more than 200 people.

Some countries did not have to do much to respond to 9/11 because they already had tough, if not repressive, laws on the books.[6] Singapore and Malaysia relied on indeterminate detention without trial under their Internal Security Acts. Israel and Egypt also relied on various forms of administrative and military detention of suspected terrorists. The United States was directly implicated in Egyptian antiterrorism policies as the Central Intelligence Agency (CIA) intensified its extraordinary rendition program. A comparison between the way established democracies and other countries with questionable or poor human rights records responded to 9/11 allows for better understanding of how the balance between security and liberty has shifted. In this respect, it is significant that countries that were criticized for abusing the human rights of suspected terrorists before 9/11 were able proudly to report their repressive laws to a new Counter-Terrorism Committee (CTC) created by the UN Security Council without fear of being criticized. Established democracies, most notably the United States, but also Canada and the United Kingdom, were less able to criticize countries with poor human rights records given their own complicity with indeterminate detention and torture.

The differences between the responses of democracies and countries with poor human rights records to terrorism diminished in the wake of 9/11. Australia empowered its intelligence agency to detain and question those with information that would be relevant to terrorism investigations. The United Kingdom derogated from the European Convention on Human Rights to enact a scheme for indeterminate detention on the basis of secret evidence of noncitizens suspected of involvement in terrorism who could not be deported because of concerns that they would be tortured. When this law was declared

---

[6] This is not to say that more repressive regimes did not take advantage of 9/11 to enact new laws. One study has found a correlation between the enactment of new antiterrorism laws in developing countries and high scores on the Freedom House rankings of authoritarianism (14 countries that enacted new laws with minimal debate had a freedom rating of 4.36, whereas 13 countries that engaged in extensive debate had a freedom ranking of 2.54, where 1 is most democratic and 7 is most authoritarian). Beth Whitaker, "Exporting the Patriot Act?" (2007) 28 Third World Quarterly 1017, at 1020.

to be discriminatory and disproportionate by the courts, the United Kingdom responded with new legislation allowing control orders to be imposed on suspected terrorists on the basis of secret evidence. Canada used immigration law as antiterrorism law to impose indeterminate detention on the basis of secret evidence. It even contemplated the possibility of judicially approved deportation of noncitizens to face possible torture. Administrative detention, secret evidence, and control orders in the United Kingdom, Australia, and Canada have some striking similarities to administrative detention schemes that Singapore and Israel inherited from colonial British emergency rule. One difference, however, is that Western democracies were more punitive to suspected terrorists than Singapore, which released the majority of its administrative detainees suspected of involvement in terrorism after imposing a sophisticated rehabilitation program.[7]

The United States was less burdened by a colonial legacy of harsh anti-insurgency and subversion laws, but it famously explored the "dark side"[8] of secret executive counter-terrorism measures in the immediate aftermath of 9/11. Unlike in other democracies, many of these American responses were not initially authorized in legislation and they were mainly directed to external threats. They included harsh interrogation tactics and indeterminate detention without trial at Guantánamo Bay and other venues, the use of extraordinary renditions to countries that notoriously tortured terrorist suspects, and warrantless spying by the National Security Agency. None of these practices were at first authorized by democratically enacted legislation but were purportedly authorized under a dubious doctrine of inherent presidential power to protect national security. The American reaction has evolved in response to media exposés and judicial challenges. Some harsh practices have been repudiated, whereas others have received legislative ratification. Nevertheless, the American response to 9/11, even under President Obama, still differs from that of other democracies in its reliance on executive and warlike powers. The majority of the detainees at Guantánamo have been released, albeit without rehabilitation or compensation, but the United States still asserts its right to indefinitely hold people there without trial before either a court or a military commission. The only legislative authorization for detention without trial is

---

[7] Angel Rabasa et al., *Deradicalizing Islamic Extremists* (Santa Monica, CA: RAND Corporation, 2010), at 104.

[8] The Sunday after 9/11, Vice President Cheney told the press that "we have to work sort of the dark side, if you will. We've got to spend time in the shadows in the intelligence world . . . using sources and methods that are available to our intelligence agencies. . . . It's going to be vital for us to use any means at our disposal basically, to achieve our objectives." Jane Mayer, *The Dark Side* (New York: Anchor Books, 1998), at 9–10.

Congress's bare-bones 2001 Authorization of the Use of Military Force to use force against those who aided 9/11 to prevent future acts. Under President Obama, the extraordinary rendition program reportedly continues, and targeted killings of suspected terrorists have increased without the transparency and judicial review used in Israel.

II. METHODOLOGY

This book is part of the "growing field of comparative and international studies of anti-terrorism law and policy."[9] It examines not only national responses to 9/11 in a number of countries but also the influential response of the UN. It falls between low-N studies, which typically focus on two or perhaps three jurisdictions, and high-N studies, which attempt to provide more comprehensive and often quantitative global coverage.[10] My attempt is to provide both a relatively detailed, nuanced, and contextual examination of antiterrorism law and policy in particular countries and a sense of the global sweep of the 9/11 effect on antiterrorism law and policy, the rule of law, and democracy.

The methodological approach of this book will be to attempt to write what David Garland has called "a history of the present"[11] to reveal many of the forces affecting the framing and development of modern laws and policies, in this case, those countering terrorism. As an academic lawyer, I will take the text of various antiterrorism laws seriously, but I will also attempt to account for historical, political, and organizational factors that have affected the development of antiterrorism laws and policies. Like others, I am conscious that it is impossible to tell the full story of counter-terrorism developments from public sources and that the public record will be skewed to reporting the failures and costs of counter-terrorism policies.[12] Nevertheless, we should not

---

9 Victor Ramraj, Michael Hor, and Kent Roach, introduction to *Global Anti-Terrorism Law and Policy*, ed. Victor Ramraj, Michael Hor, and Kent Roach (New York: Cambridge University Press, 2005), at 1. See also Laura Donohue, *The Cost of Counterterrorism* (New York: Cambridge University Press, 2008) (comparison of the United Kingdom and the United States); Stefan Sottiaux, *Terrorism and the Limitation of Rights: The ECHR and the US Constitution* (Oxford: Hart, 2008); Daniel Moeckli, *Human Rights and Non-Discrimination in the "War on Terror"* (Oxford: Oxford University Press, 2008); and Ian Cram, *Terror and the War on Dissent* (Berlin: Springer, 2009).

10 Ran Hirschl, "The Question of Case Selection in Comparative Constitutional Law" (2005) 53 American Journal of Comparative Law 125, at 132. For an excellent example of a high-N study of 32 jurisdictions, see Stella Burch Elias, "Rethinking 'Preventive Detention' from a Comparative Perspective" (2009) 41 Columbia Human Rights Review 99.

11 David Garland, *The Culture of Control: Crime and Social Order in Contemporary Society* (Chicago: University of Chicago Press, 2001), chap. 1.

12 Donohue, *Cost of Counterterrorism*, at 3.

underestimate the extraordinary amount of new material that has been put into the public domain since 9/11. Some of this material is collected in the multiple country reports that almost every state filed with the UN Security Council's CTC and that, until recently, were publicly posted by that committee. Other valuable sources of information include the monthly bulletins and reports by the International Commission of Jurists and public inquiry reports, including those of the 9/11 Commission in the United States, reports of Parliamentary committees and review bodies in the United Kingdom and Australia, and three Canadian commissions of inquiry that have had access to secret information. Although the benefits of counter-terrorism laws and policies may never be fully known, they must be estimated if the proportionality and necessity of counter-terrorism laws and policies are to be judged by courts and, ultimately, by citizens. An assessment of the proportionality of counter-terrorism measures requires an evaluation of both their propriety and their effectiveness.

One of the great challenges of studying counter-terrorism laws and policies is that they cross traditional disciplinary boundaries within academe and even within law. To begin to understand the global response to 9/11, it is necessary to understand how international law, constitutional law, military and war law, criminal law and procedure, evidence law, immigration law, and various forms of administrative law, including the regulation of financial institutions and charities, have been used to combat terrorism.[13] It is also important to understand the challenges of reviewing both the propriety and efficacy of whole-of-government approaches to terrorism. My approach to these issues is rooted in a new legal process and institutionalist approach to scholarship that focuses on the interplay of multiple forms of law and the dialogues or interchanges that have occurred between courts and other branches of government and society over the legality and proportionality of counter-terrorism measures. The complexities and challenges of such broad-ranging studies are daunting,

---

[13] Leading books on the responses of various countries to 9/11 all span various genres of law, including immigration, criminal, administrative, and international law. See, e.g., David Cole and Jules Lobel, *Less Safe Less Free* (New York: New Press, 2007); Donohue, *Costs of Counterterrorism*; Craig Forcese, *National Security Law* (Toronto, ON, Canada: Irwin Law, 2008); Andrew Lynch and George Williams, *What Price Security?* (Sydney, NSW, Australia: University of New South Wales, 2006); Emmanuel Gross, *The Struggle of Democracy against Terrorism* (Charlottesville: University of Virginia Press, 2006); and Clive Walker, *Guide to Anti-Terrorism Legislation*, 2nd ed. (Oxford: Oxford University Press, 2009). On the legal process and interactional and institutional approaches to legal scholarship, see Kent Roach, "What's Old and New about the Legal Process?" (1997) 47 University of Toronto Law Journal 363, and Jutta Brunee and Stephen Toope, *Legitimacy and Legality in Interactional Law: An Interactional Account* (New York: Cambridge University Press, 2010).

but a comparative approach can be helpful in identifying patterns and discontinuities in the ways various countries and institutions have responded to 9/11.

The book takes a comparative approach that attempts to identify both convergences and divergences in the post-9/11 development of antiterrorism laws and policies. The focus of the book is on in-depth studies of how four established democracies – the United States, the United Kingdom, Australia, and Canada – have responded to 9/11. The book devotes a chapter to each country to allow for a more contextual approach that engages with the pre-9/11 experience and political and legal contexts of each country. A number of common themes – the initial response to 9/11, the use of criminal and immigration law to respond to terrorism, the regulation of speech associated with terrorism, the review of the state's whole-of-government counter-terrorism activities, and the development of national security policies – are discussed in each chapter. These countries have been selected in part because so much information about their laws and practices is available and because they represent how established democracies that profess respect for human rights and the rule of law have responded to the challenges of terrorism. As such, this part of the book follows a "most similar cases logic"[14] that nevertheless can help to isolate differences in how similar countries respond to terrorism such as the effects of judicial review under a bill of rights; differences in governance; differences in history and threat perception, and differences in approaches to multiculturalism, free speech, and law and illegality.

In addition to these countries, I will provide briefer examinations of how five other countries – Egypt, Syria, Israel, Singapore, and Indonesia – responded and, in some cases, had to do little in the way of responding to 9/11. These countries have been chosen in part to allow for comparisons between the responses of established democracies and those with more questionable human rights records. They also allow comparisons between the responses of countries, such as Israel, that have extensive experience with terrorism with those of other democracies, such as the United States, that had minimal experience with terrorism until 9/11. Egypt under Mubarak and Syria are examined as prototypes[15] of countries with poor human rights records. These countries are of particular relevance to the post-9/11 response to al Qaeda because both the United States and Canada have been complicit in some antiterrorism abuses in these countries. Comparisons between these countries and established democracies can

---

[14] Hirschl, "Question of Case Selection," at 133–9.
[15] Ibid., at 142.

help determine if baselines between the state's interests in preventing terrorism and in preserving human rights have shifted post-9/11.

Israel, Singapore, and Indonesia are more difficult cases than Egypt and Syria. As will be seen, Indonesia experienced a similar terrorist threat to its neighbors Malaysia and Singapore but responded in a significantly different manner that did not resort to the use of indeterminate detention or reversion to subversion prosecutions and the militarization of security of the Suharto era. Israel has been included, in part, because of recent interest among Western democracies in Israel's long experience with terrorism and because of the distinctive role that the Israeli Supreme Court has played in reviewing a broad range of antiterrorism measures, including administrative detention, interrogations, and targeted killings. The use of administrative detention in Israel also shares a common British colonial heritage with the Internal Security Acts of Singapore and Malaysia and thus allows for a comparison of the significant transnational British influence on antiterrorism law both before and after 9/11.

The purpose of this book is to provide a critical and comparative assessment of how a number of democracies and some countries with poor human rights records have responded to 9/11. One object of this examination is to assess the degree to which there has been convergence as Western democracies and more repressive regimes have responded to terrorism, often by strengthening the powers of the executive and employing indeterminate administrative or military detention of suspected terrorists without the due process protections generally associated with criminal trials. Led by Security Council Resolution 1624 and British proposals, many democracies also enacted new laws punishing speech that may be associated with terrorism. The United States and Canada, however, resisted this trend to punish speech associated with terrorism, despite facing homegrown and al Qaeda–inspired terrorist threats.

The degree of convergence in counter-terrorism law and policy is striking. Egypt, Syria, Israel, and Singapore have all been better able to justify harsh antiterrorism policies in the new post-9/11 environment. These countries were able to rely on and rehabilitate old antiterrorism laws that had attracted criticism before 9/11. The Security Council's CTC took a nonconfrontational approach that largely ignored questions such as the proper definition of terrorism or human rights. Although none of these countries had to scramble to enact new antiterrorism laws after 9/11, they were also not immune to post-9/11 trends. Israel enacted a new law that built on its prior use of administrative detention on the basis of secret evidence but also followed the Bush administration's practice of focusing on so-called unlawful combatants who were noncitizens. The Egyptian Constitution was amended in 2007 to ensure that an expected new antiterrorism law could not be invalidated for infringing constitutional rights and to entrench the president's powers to refer terrorism cases to special security or military courts. Both Egypt and Israel are discussing enacting new comprehensive antiterrorism laws that will likely seek support from the post-9/11 laws and practices of Western democracies. Singapore enacted new post-9/11 laws on terrorism financing, terrorist bombings, and hostage taking to demonstrate that the country was participating in international efforts to combat terrorism but has relied on its older and constitutionally entrenched Internal Security Act to deal with actual terrorist suspects. The convergence between post-9/11 laws in democracies and those in countries with poor human rights records is telling and disturbing.

Although the convergence between the counter-terrorism practices of democracies and countries with poor human rights records is a matter of serious concern, it would be wrong to conclude that nothing can be learned from the practices of those countries. After decades of repression, a number of important terrorist groups in Egypt have renounced violence in part because of reinterpretations of Islam that were facilitated by the state. Rehabilitation programs in Indonesia and, especially, Singapore that involved religious counseling have resulted in the release of suspected terrorists, apparently with some success in preventing recidivism. There has been very little thinking in the West about the rehabilitation of terrorists or constructive engagement with Islam, but these issues will not go away.

The resignation of President Mubarak in February, 2011 and the approval in a referendum of proposals to repeal Egypt's 2007 constitutional amendments that would shelter anti-terrorism laws from constitutional challenge and entrench emergency rule and exceptional courts suggests that the post-9/11 emphasis on security over liberty can be contested. It remains to be seen whether a more democratic Egypt will also be one with less terrorism. Indonesia's post-9/11 experience reveals some of the challenges that Egypt will face.

The Israeli reaction to Palestinian terrorism remains controversial, but Israel provides an important example of the role that courts can play in the review of a wide range of counter-terrorism activities. The Israeli approach has been to require judicial authorization for counter-terrorism measures, such as targeted killings, that, in the United States, are only authorized in secret by the executive and that resist judicial review. Israel, like the United Kingdom, also had experience with the problems caused by harsh interrogation long before controversies erupted over the issue in the United States.

Although convergence in post-9/11 counter-terrorism laws and policies is the most striking development, divergences in the global reaction to 9/11 are important to understand. Although there has been significant evolution in

American laws and policies since 9/11, the traditional hypothesis of American exceptionalism still needs to be examined. Much of the American response has been rooted in executive action and on the basis of the bare-bones Authorization of Military Force enacted by Congress in the days after 9/11. One thesis I explore is that the United States' advanced degree of legalism may encourage the use of extralegal approaches and those based more on a war model than a crime model. The American descent into illegality was not crude or open: indeed it was almost always supported by dubious claims of legality as symbolized by the infamous torture memos, but also seen by pre-textual use of existing laws against suspected terrorists. The result was extra-legalism – legal resources and arguments employed to support illegal measures. American exceptionalism may also help explain why the United States has not made it an offense to engage in speech that indirectly advocates terrorism, as done by the United Kingdom in the wake of the 2005 London bombings and as encouraged by UN Security Council Resolution 1624. The free press in the United States also helps explain why much misconduct by American officials in the generally secret realm of counter-terrorism activities has come to light. At the same time, however, a blunt state-secrets doctrine has stopped many civil lawsuits arising from illegal conduct. Indeed, there has been almost no individual accountability for illegal American counter-terrorism activities.

Indonesia also provides an interesting case study of divergence from the more repressive approach to terrorism taken in neighboring Singapore and Malaysia. Indonesia resisted an initial attempt to enact a harsh antiterrorism law after 9/11. Indonesia was criticized for not preventing the 2002 Bali bombings that killed more than 200 people but quickly enacted a new antiterrorism law by presidential decree within a week of the bombing. An attempt was made to apply this law retroactively to the Bali bombings, but this was declared unconstitutional by the Indonesian Constitutional Court. The Indonesian law allows for the use of secret intelligence, but only as preliminary evidence. It does not provide for the proscription of terrorist organizations and stresses the importance of nondiscrimination and the use of regular procedures in the administration of the law. The fledging democracy of Indonesia has continued to experience serious acts of terrorism. In response, there have been proposals both for tougher antiterrorism laws and to bring the military back into internal security matters, but so far, Indonesia has resisted such calls.[16] Recent and disturbing reports of extralegal abuses by specialized Indonesian antiterrorism

---

[16] Hikmanto Juwana, "Anti-Terrorism Efforts in Indonesia," in *Global Anti-Terrorism Law and Policy*, 2nd ed., ed. Victor Ramraj et al. (New York: Cambridge University Press, forthcoming 2011).

squads, however, raise the question of the relation between restrained legal approaches to terrorism and unrestrained extralegal responses.

Another potential divergence in the way that countries have responded to terrorism since 9/11 is in the role of courts. Although some have argued that courts should, as in other emergencies, defer to executive and legislative actions after 9/11,[17] there has been a surprising amount of judicial activism with respect to antiterrorism laws and policies since 9/11 in the United States, the United Kingdom, Canada, and Indonesia.[18] In the United Kingdom, the House of Lords and, subsequently, the European Court of Human Rights declared a major part of the legislative response to 9/11 to be both discriminatory and disproportionate. The U.S. Supreme Court extended habeas corpus review to the Guantánamo detentions and held that suspension of the writ was not justified. The Canadian Supreme Court held that the use of secret evidence that was not subject to adversarial challenge to support long-term immigration detention was unconstitutional. The more robust role played by the courts has not, however, been consistent or universal. The Israeli Supreme Court upheld a new administrative detention regime, even though it does not allow for adversarial challenge to secret evidence, and the Australian courts have upheld control orders and legislation that instructs courts to prefer state interests in secrecy over the fair trial rights of the accused. Judicial activism was a nonstarter in Egypt under Mubarak and Singapore, because of the constitutional entrenchment of emergency and security laws.

The courts are not the only or even the most important way to provide accountability for the state's often secret counter-terrorism activities. Many countries are grappling with the difficulties of attempting to ensure accountability for whole-of-government and transnational responses to terrorism. Most domestic accountability mechanisms are siloed to individual organizations, even though police, intelligence, immigration, customs, foreign affairs, and transport agencies now more frequently interact in their efforts to prevent terrorism. In Canada, special public inquiries had to be appointed to review the activities of all Canadian officials in relation to the rendition of Maher Arar and other Canadians held and tortured abroad because of suspicions that they were involved in terrorism. A similar special inquiry into possible British complicity in torture abroad has been established, and the 9/11 Commission

---

[17] Eric Posner and Adrian Vermeule, *Terror in the Balance* (Cambridge, MA: Harvard University Press, 2007); Richard Posner, *Not a Suicide Pact* (Oxford: Oxford University Press, 2006).

[18] David Dyzenhaus, *The Constitution of Law* (Cambridge: Cambridge University Press, 2006); Kent Roach, "Judicial Review of the State's Anti-Terrorism Activities" (2009) 3 Indian Journal of Constitutional Law 138.

reviewed the way multiple agencies failed in the lead-up to 9/11. A great challenge, however, is to move away from reliance on ad hoc inquiries appointed at the discretion of the government and toward permanent review mechanisms that are capable of evaluating the effectiveness and propriety of the often secret and coordinated efforts that are taken by multiple governmental agencies to prevent terrorism.

Even the best domestic accountability mechanisms will fail to cover transnational forms of cooperation. The U.S. and Syrian governments refused to participate in the Canadian inquiries, even though their actions were central to the torture of Canadians held abroad. The UN has a potential to provide international forums of accountability, and its special rapporteurs have done important work since 9/11 on the effects of various counter-terrorism policies on human rights. Nevertheless, the UN is quite fragmented, and its "soft" human rights side is poorly integrated with its "harder" security side.[19] Volunteer nongovernmental organizations such as Human Rights Watch and Amnesty International and investigative journalists have often been forced to attempt to fill the accountability gap for transnational counter-terrorism efforts.

A comparative analysis of post-9/11 antiterrorism law provides an excellent vehicle to assess increasingly complex and global processes of lawmaking. International organizations, most notably the UN Security Council and its Counter-Terrorism and 1267 Sanctioning Committee, have played an important continuing role in the shaping of counter-terrorism policies, leading some to express concerns that these bodies have been the source for a post-9/11 migration of "anticonstitutional ideas" that pay little attention to human rights.[20] The Security Council has struggled with providing judicial remedies for those who may have been wrongly listed as terrorists on the basis of secret intelligence provided by its members.[21] Those who cannot find remedies from the Security Council have sought remedies from various domestic courts and this has raised the possibility of conflicts between domestic constitutionalism and mandatory Security Council mandates – conflicts that may undermine the UN's authority and might have been avoided had the Security Council paid more attention to human rights in its counter-terrorism work.

The Security Council is dominated by its five permanent veto-wielding powers. The United Kingdom and France have colonial antiterrorism experience and have joined with the United States, China, and Russia in adopting

---

[19] Marti Koskenniemi, "The Police in the Temple: Order, Justice and the UN: A Dialectical View" (1995) 6 European Journal of International Law 325.

[20] Kim Lane Scheppele, "The Migration of Anti-Constitutional Ideas," in *The Migration of Constitutional Ideas*, ed. Sujit Choudhry (New York: Cambridge University Press, 2006).

[21] Simon Chesterman, *One Nation under Surveillance* (Oxford: Oxford University Press, 2011), chaps. 6 and 9.

a tough stand against Islamic terrorism after 9/11. In response to the 2005 London bombings, the Security Council supported the Blair's government calls for criminal prohibition on speech that incites terrorism even though the efficacy of such measures are not clear and they may infringe freedom of expression especially given the Security Council's failure to define incitement or terrorism. The UN remains fragmented between the hard and increasingly active power of its Security Council, the softer and more diffuse power of its General Assembly, and the even more diffuse power of its multiplicity of rights-protection bodies. The failure of the UN to agree on a definition of terrorism and the dominance of the Security Council, especially in its initial response to 9/11, had long-lasting and often negative impacts on how the world responded to 9/11.

A comparative study of counter-terrorism law also provides a vehicle to observe and assess the migration of laws among countries. The role of the United Kingdom is very important in this regard and sometimes underappreciated. Emergency rule in former British colonies, such as Malaysia, Singapore, and Palestine, produced regimes of indeterminate detention without criminal trial that persist to this day. These regimes also related the fight against terrorism and insurgency to the control of the press and speech in a manner that has been revived through the United Kingdom's sponsorship of Security Council Resolution 1624 and its own law targeting incitement of terrorism. In addition, the United Kingdom's Terrorism Act, 2000, represented the state of the art in modern antiterrorism laws at the time of 9/11. It influenced the development of many antiterrorism laws enacted in response to 9/11 and Security Council Resolution 1373.[22] Many British innovations, such as control orders, preventive arrests, special advocates to challenge secret evidence and increased regulation of speech associated with terrorism, have migrated to other jurisdictions, most notably Australia.[23] British antiterrorism law has had a much greater effect on other countries than American law, much of which is dauntingly complex and idiosyncratic.

A comparative examination of post-9/11 antiterrorism laws and policies may also make a modest contribution to the discovery of mistakes to be avoided in the crafting of antiterrorism policies. Attempts to develop alternatives to the established laws of war and crime in a number of countries have run into trouble. The most famous example is Guantánamo Bay, but there are also third-model experiments in Canada and the United Kingdom as well as Israel and Singapore. Administrative and military detention of terrorist suspects

---

[22] Kent Roach, "The Post 9/11 Migration of Britain's Terrorism Act, 2000," in Choudhry, *Migration of Constitutional Ideas*.

[23] Andrew Lynch, "Control Orders in Australia: A Further Case Study in the Migration of British Counter-Terrorism Laws" (2008) 8 Oxford University Commonwealth Law Journal 159.

without trial does little to expose and denounce terrorism, and only a few jurisdictions, such as Singapore, have attempted to rehabilitate suspected terrorists
detained without trial. There is a growing appreciation of the virtues of criminal prosecution as a means to incapacitate, punish, and denounce terrorists.
Countries that rely on criminal prosecutions, however, face common challenges with respect to secret intelligence that may have to be used as evidence
or disclosed to the accused in such prosecutions. In the aftermath of 9/11,
there was some attraction to the use of extralegal measures.[24] The post-9/11
experience with extralegal conduct, such as extraordinary rendition, harsh
interrogation, warrantless spying, and targeted killing, however, demonstrates
that the restraining influence of possible prosecutions or civil law suits has often
been illusory and that such activities, absent the extraordinary free American
press, might have always remained secret.

Finally, this book will examine a range of national security policies developed by states and the UN since 9/11. Although such policies can be more
aspirational than operational, they provide an important indication of the values that animate counter-terrorism strategies. American and Australian policies
both tended to define terrorism as the prime threat to national security in the
immediate aftermath of 9/11, whereas a 2004 Canadian policy and more recent
American, Australian, and British policies have adopted an all-risks and general emergency preparedness approach. Events such as Hurricane Katrina and
the 2011 earthquake, tsunami, and nuclear crisis in Japan underline the reality
that terrorism is not the only threat to national security. All-risk human security
policies that help nations recover from natural and man-made disasters as well
as from acts of terrorism can play an important role in limiting damage.[25]

III. OUTLINE OF THE CHAPTERS

Chapter 2 examines the unprecedented role the UN played in responding
to 9/11. The Security Council and its CTC created by Resolution 1373 have
emerged as important new transnational actors in the field of counter-terrorism
law. Through Resolution 1373, the Security Council decided that all countries
should ensure that terrorism and various forms of support for terrorism be
treated as serious crimes, with the 90-day deadline given to report to the
CTC being used by some countries as a virtual deadline for the passage of
new and complex antiterrorism acts. Resolution 1373 offered no guidance on

---

[24] Oren Gross, "Chaos and Rules: Should Responses to Violent Crisis Always Be Constitutional?"
(2003) 112 Yale Law Journal 1011; Posner, *Not A Suicide Pact*, at 154–5.

[25] Kent Roach, *September 11: Consequences for Canada* (Montreal, QC, Canada: McGill Queens
Press, 2003), chap. 7; Cass Sunstein, *Laws of Fear* (New York: Cambridge University Press,
2005); Philip Bobbitt, *Terror and Consent* (New York: Anchor Books, 2008).

the proper definition of terrorism or the role of human rights in countering terrorism. The result was that countries were free to define terrorism often in expansive and overbroad ways, with no resistance from the CTC. The Security Council has also endorsed some forms of antiterrorism measures – laws against financing, denial of refugee status to suspected terrorists, and laws against incitement of terrorism – that are of unproven if not dubious efficacy in actually helping prevent terrorism and furthering human rights. Even before 9/11, the UN was heavily invested in promoting laws against terrorism financing with targeted sanctions against individuals and entities associated with al Qaeda. Terrorist lists fuse executive, legislative, and judicial power to make listed entities virtual outlaws who cannot travel or receive funds from anyone in the world.[26] Despite reform attempts, Security Council listing of outlawed terrorists remains intergovernmental and based on secret intelligence, often forcing those who claim to be wrongly listed to seek indirect domestic remedies.

The Security Council plays something of an executive role within the UN,[27] and its dominance in the counter-terrorism field mirrors the dominance of the domestic executive. The contributions of the General Assembly, representing all nations, are also examined in Chapter 2. It will be seen that the General Assembly's Counter-Terrorism Plan of 2006 significantly differs from the work of the Security Council by placing greater emphasis on respecting rights and the rule of law and responding to conditions conducive to the spread of terrorism. At the same time, the General Assembly cannot effectively challenge the Security Council, especially with respect to mandatory terrorism measures pursued under Chapter VII of the UN Charter relating to international peace and security. The role of the various rights-protection bodies of the UN will also be examined, as will recent attempts to coordinate the many different institutions in the UN that are dealing with terrorism. These challenges of coordination mirror the challenges of coordinating whole-of-government approaches to terrorism.

Chapter 3 focuses on a number of countries that did not immediately respond to Security Council Resolution 1373 because they had robust, if not repressive, existing laws on terrorism. Egypt, Syria, and Israel already had in

---

[26] David Dyzenhaus, "The Rule of (Administrative) Law in International Law" (2005) 68 Law and Contemporary Problems 127.

[27] As Cathleen Powell has argued, the Security Council, without effective checks from courts or the General Assembly, can exercise "untrammeled power in a manner which would be unthinkable in a domestic constitutional system subject to the rule of law" or democratic principles. Powell, "Defining Terrorism: How and Why," in *The Human Rights of Anti-Terrorism*, ed. Nicole LaViolette and Craig Forcese (Toronto, ON, Canada: Irwin Law, 2008), at 138. See also C. H. Powell, "The Legal Authority of the UN Security Council," in *Security and Human Rights*, ed. Benjamin Goold and Liora Lazarus (Oxford: Hart, 2007).

place very broad offenses that could be tried by special military courts and/or result in administrative and indeterminate detention. Similarly, Malaysia and Singapore could rely on their Internal Security Acts as a means to impose indeterminate detention without criminal trial on terrorist suspects and others. To be sure, some of these countries responded to 9/11, but new laws against terrorism financing were at most minor adjustments designed to appease the international community.[28] The United States had a new appreciation for the harsh antiterrorism measures that these countries used after 9/11, and this diminished claims that repressive laws were an expression of "Asian values"[29] or intrinsic to the bloody politics of the Middle East. American support ranged from public praise and financial aid to secret renditions. Not all countries that had used harsh laws in the past, however, embraced such approaches in the aftermath of 9/11, and Chapter 3 concludes with an examination of Indonesia's response to 9/11 and the 2002 Bali bombings as it struggled to maintain its new democracy. The chapter will also reflect on some lessons that Western democracies might learn from countries with extensive experience in terrorism. Lessons from Israel about the dangers of harsh interrogation and the benefits of judicial review were lost on the Bush administration, and many detainees have been released from Guantánamo without any attempts at rehabilitation as practiced in Egypt and Singapore. Indeed, there is a danger that the West is now employing some of the harsh practices examined in this chapter without some of the restraining features of such practices as put into effect in Israel and Singapore.

Chapter 4 examines evolving American responses to 9/11, with a focus on the degree to which they manifest American exceptionalism through both executive and war models and extra-legalism in which illegal acts were masked in dubious claims of legality. The Patriot Act was enacted very quickly after 9/11 and was the subject of much civil libertarian criticism in the United States. Nevertheless, the Patriot Act was a rather mild response to terrorism, particularly when examined in comparison to British antiterrorism laws enacted both before and after 9/11. The relative mildness of the Patriot Act, however, was not found in the response of the American executive to 9/11, including the post-9/11 immigration roundups; abuse of material warrants to impose preventive detentions; and President Bush's attempt to detain those captured in Afghanistan in a law-free zone at Guantánamo, where they were subject to harsh interrogations to collect intelligence. The initial American response to 9/11 was based more

---

[28] Michael Hor, "Terrorism and the Law: Singapore's Solution" (2002) Singapore Journal of Legal Studies 30.

[29] Victor Ramraj, "Terrorism, Security and Rights: A New Dialogue" (2002) Singapore Journal of Legal Studies 1.

on war and extra-legalism than on a legislative and crime-based approach. Accountability for the American extralegal approach with respect to practices like extraordinary rendition and warrantless spying has often been thwarted by its restrictive state-secrets doctrine. The Guantánamo experience will be examined to illustrate the role of the courts and to assess the viability of experimental models that go beyond the established laws of war and crime. Finally, the evolution of American national security policy during this period will be examined, with a focus on the movement from an approach based on a global war against terrorism to one that takes into account other risks to human security such as Hurricane Katrina.

Chapter 5 examines the United Kingdom's evolving response to terrorism. The United Kingdom has extensive experience with terrorism stemming from Northern Ireland and had consolidated and normalized that experience with the enactment of the Terrorism Act, 2000. This act and, in particular, its very broad definition of terrorism provided an influential template for many post-9/11 antiterrorism laws, particularly those enacted in Australia and Canada. Even though the United Kingdom had a tough and recent antiterrorism law in place, it responded to 9/11 with the massive Anti-Terrorism Crime and Security Act, 2001. This legislation derogated from fair trial rights to allow the indeterminate detention of noncitizens suspected of involvement with international terrorism who could not be deported because they would be tortured if returned to countries such as Egypt or Syria. This derogation was ultimately held by the House of Lords to be disproportionate and discriminatory in the most important judicial decision dealing with post-9/11 antiterrorism policies.[30] The government responded by repealing its derogation but enacting new legislation providing for control orders to restrict the movement of both citizens and noncitizens suspected of involvement with terrorism. Control orders and their use of secret evidence have been controversial and repeatedly challenged in the courts. The new U.K. government has agreed to replace them and some other counter-terrorism powers including a 28 day maximum of preventive arrest with less restrictive measures. Chapter 5 also examines controversial provisions targeting the direct and indirect incitement of terrorism enacted after the 2005 London bombings. Finally, the United Kingdom's development of a counter-terrorism strategy and, more recently, of an all-risks national security policy are examined.

Chapter 6 examines the Australian response to 9/11. The Australian government was particularly aggressive in enacting a wide range of antiterrorism laws even before the October 2002 Bali bombings that killed 88 Australians. Much

---

[30] A. v. *Secretary of State* 2004 UKHL 56.

of the Australian legislation is heavily influenced by British law, but Australia forged its own path through controversial laws that augment the powers of Australia's domestic security intelligence agency to detain and question those with information about terrorism. Australia also modernized its treason and sedition laws to target terrorists. Australia provides an interesting case study because of the absence of a national bill of rights and the relatively minor role of the courts as a check on terrorism policy. Perhaps in response to the deficit, Australia has been quite advanced in adapting legislative and watchdog review to respond to the increased integration of whole-of-government responses to terrorism.

Chapter 7 examines Canadian responses to 9/11. Canada's initial response to 9/11 was driven by concerns about keeping its border with the United States open and it relied on immigration law as antiterrorism law in a manner that resulted in long-term administrative detention based on secret evidence. The use of secret evidence in immigration proceedings has been successfully challenged in the courts, and Canada, like the United Kingdom, now allows special advocates to challenge secret evidence. The Canadian experience is also noteworthy with respect to the challenges of ensuring accountability for whole-of-government responses to terrorism with respect to the work of ad hoc commissions of inquiry appointed to review the actions of Canadian policing, intelligence, and foreign affairs officials with respect to Canadian citizens who were detained and tortured in Egypt and Syria before being released and allowed to return to Canada. Finally, Canada provides an early post-9/11 example of an all-risk approach to national security that focuses on the broad range of risks to human security.

The final chapter (Chapter 8) reflects on a number of themes that run throughout the earlier chapters. One theme is the important but problematic role played by the UN since 9/11. The UN has failed, even after the great trauma of 9/11, to produce international agreement on a proper definition of terrorism. The Security Council has promoted policies that are questionable both in terms of their respect for human rights and their efficacy in preventing terrorism. Although the General Assembly produced, in 2006, a more balanced and holistic strategy to combat terrorism while respecting human rights and responding to conditions that cause terrorism, the UN, like the United States, has not recovered from its initial response to 9/11, including its early neglect of human rights.

Another important theme since 9/11 is a loss of faith in the use of criminal law as a main response to terrorism and attempts to use less restrained alternatives to terrorism prosecutions. The United Kingdom and Canada both turned to immigration law as a less restrained alternative to prosecutions in the immediate aftermath of 9/11. The United States used immigration law and the laws of war and even designated a few citizens as enemy combatants. After prolonged legal battles, the Guantánamo detainees finally won access to habeas corpus and some have been released by courts, but this seems only to have legitimated detention of suspected terrorists without criminal trial. Even under President Obama, the United States insists on indefinite detention of some suspected terrorists without a criminal trial or even a trial before a military commission. The United States has moved toward the practices of administrative or military detention without trial used in Egypt, Israel, and Singapore even though criminal terrorism prosecutions in the United States, including of designated "enemy combatants," have generally resulted in convictions and long sentences.

Criminal law itself has changed since 9/11. The enactment of broad new antiterrorism laws has made what previously would have been secret intelligence into potential evidence of new terrorist crimes. This in turn places pressure on criminal courts not to disclose sensitive but unused intelligence to the accused and on intelligence agencies to live up to new evidential and disclosure standards. The twin processes of the judicialization of intelligence and the bringing of preventive intelligence concepts into criminal law provide fundamental challenges to intelligence agencies and criminal law.

Chapter 8 also reflects on a number of challenges going forward from 9/11. Terrorism after 9/11 is undoubtedly transnational, but so, too, is counterterrorism. What the UN Security Council, the United States, and the United Kingdom do on the counter-terrorism front can have unanticipated consequences for what is done in many other countries. Migrating terrorism laws are not simple transplants because each country will modify laws to fit its own political, legal, and social cultures. Countries with poor human rights records have been quick to pick up on cues from Western democracies about tolerance of tough antiterrorism regimes, but Western democracies have not learned much from Singapore and other countries about rehabilitation and have generally only been able to respond to radicalization through blunt measures such as terrorism and speech prosecutions and restrictive immigration measures.

Although whole-of-government and transnational approaches to the prevention of terrorism are necessary, they create dangerous accountability gaps. In some countries, the courts have stepped up and played a surprising but nevertheless welcome role in holding the executive and legislative branches to account for counter-terrorism activities. Judicial performance has not, however, been uniform. In any event, the courts cannot be the prime instrument of accountability for state counter-terrorism actions that are secret and often do not result in prosecutions. Other accountability mechanisms within government have failed to keep pace with whole-of-government and intergovernmental cooperation in counter-terrorism efforts. There is a need to evaluate both the propriety and the efficacy of the many laudable attempts to prevent the horrors and mass deaths of another 9/11. Some countries have responded with ad hoc commissions of inquiry to examine the secret counter-terrorism activities of all parts of government. Nevertheless, accountability efforts, both domestically and internationally, have not caught up to the greater intensity and coordination of attempts to prevent terrorism. Issues of accountability are important because the lack of effective review can threaten both security and human rights.

2 The United Nations Responds: Security Council Listing and Legislation

I. INTRODUCTION

An assessment of the role played by the United Nations (UN) is critical to understanding post-9/11 changes to global antiterrorism law and policy. Although the UN had selectively engaged terrorism issues before 9/11, the role of the Security Council in leading global counter-terrorism efforts after 9/11 was unprecedented. The Security Council and its Counter-Terrorism Committee (CTC) operated without regard to human rights, especially in the first three years after 9/11. Although the UN leaves states a wide of margin of appreciation with respect to the specific details of their counter-terrorism measures, it threw its considerable influence behind a number of counter-terrorism measures – laws against the financing of terrorism, the use of immigration law as antiterrorism law, and laws against the incitement of terrorism – that can limit human rights and may not be very effective in preventing terrorism. Security Council Resolution 1373, enacted on September 28, 2001, called on all states to enact laws against terrorism financing but also required them to report to a newly formed CTC within 90 days. Many states used the 90-day reporting requirement as a virtual deadline for the enactment of new legislation.

The General Assembly failed to agree on a definition of terrorism even after the trauma of 9/11 and belatedly issued its own Counter-Terrorism Policy in 2006. This plan places more emphasis on respect for human rights and responding to the conditions that cause terrorism, but it has had less influence on counter-terrorism policy than earlier Security Council mandates. The various rights-protection bodies in the UN have also evaluated many counter-terrorism policies, but the UN system as a whole remains fragmented, despite recent attempts to coordinate its response to terrorism-related issues. The UN, like many governments, faces challenges in adopting a coherent and coordinated approach to terrorism and there is a danger that the Security

Council will dominate other parts of the UN that are more concerned with human rights.

The role of the UN is sometimes not fully appreciated by those who focus on domestic responses to terrorism.[1] Even before 9/11, the Security Council imposed sanctions on those associated with the Taliban and al Qaeda as a response to the bombing of American embassies in Africa in 1998. The Security Council's listing process has increasingly been challenged as secretive and unfair in domestic courts, but domestic decisions that invalidate 1267 listing place the domestic nation in breach of its supposedly mandatory obligations to comply with that resolution enacted under Chapter VII of the UN Charter relating to international peace and security. The Security Council has responded to these domestic decisions with some reforms, but has been unwilling or unable to give up its decision-making powers over listing or to disclose much of the secret and often U.S.-based intelligence that is said to justify listings.

II. THE UNITED NATIONS

To understand the UN response to 9/11, some basic understanding of the UN is necessary. The lead role, especially after 9/11, has been played by the Security Council, which is a body of 15 countries, including the permanent members of China, France, Russia, the United Kingdom, and the United States. The five permanent members, and only the five permanent members, have a veto. Both the United Kingdom and France have extensive domestic and colonial experience with terrorism before 9/11, and China, Russia, and the United States have all focused on Islamic terrorism, along with France and the United Kingdom since 9/11. The other nonpermanent members of the Security Council are elected for two-year terms and as such have less influence.

The Security Council has responsibility for the maintenance of international peace and security, and for that reason, its smaller membership is permanently on call. As such, the Security Council has some features similar to the domestic executive.[2] It can, if necessary, order the use of force if less drastic

---

[1] My own earlier work discounted the pressure for compliance that Security Council Resolution 1373 placed on Canada to enact new antiterrorism laws. See Kent Roach, "The New Terrorism Offences and the Criminal Law," in *The Security of Freedom: Essays on Canada's Anti-Terrorism Bill*, ed. Ronald Daniels, Patrick Macklem, and Kent Roach (Toronto, ON, Canada: University of Toronto Press, 2001); Roach, *September 11: Consequences for Canada* (Montreal, QC, Canada: McGill Queens Press, 2003), chaps. 2 and 3.

[2] Section 24(1) of the UN Charter provides that "in order to ensure prompt and effective action by the United Nations, its Members confer on the Security Council primary responsibility for

measures, including the use of sanctions, would be inadequate.[3] It can also preempt the work of the General Assembly.[4] During the cold war, the Security Council was often deadlocked by the vetoes held by its permanent members, but it has now emerged as a more powerful force. Although traditionally, it applied sanctions against states, including Libya in relation to the 1988 Pan Am bombing and Sudan in connection with an attempted assassination of Egyptian president Mubarak in 1995,[5] it has also applied sanctions against individuals such as those associated with al Qaeda. This has led to some concern that the Security Council can act as an executive without the judicial, legislative, and civil society checks that are present in most democracies.[6] The post-9/11 dominance of the Security Council as a superexecutive parallels the dominance of domestic executives over security matters. The Security Council has acted quickly and often secretly as an executive body that can list terrorists and require states to comply with asset freezes and travel bans. At the same time, the Security Council has also acted as legislator in the sense of imposing permanent and general obligations on states,[7] most notably in Resolution 1373, with respect to terrorism and terrorism financing, and Resolution 1540, with respect to preventing terrorists from gaining access to weapons of mass destruction.

The General Assembly is composed of all member states of the UN, each with a vote. It has been attempting, without success, to agree on a definition of terrorism since the early 1970s.[8] This continued failure explains why terrorism as such was not included as a crime within the jurisdiction of the International

---

the maintenance of international peace and security, and agree that in carrying out its duties under this responsibility the Security Council acts on their behalf."

[3] Ibid., Section 41.   [4] Ibid., Section 12.

[5] Chantal de Jonge Oudraat, "The Role of the Security Council," in *Terrorism and the UN: Before and After September 11*, ed. Jane Boulden and Thomas G. Weiss (Bloomington : Indiana University Press, 2004).

[6] C. H. Powell, "The Legal Authority of the UN Security Council," in *Security and Human Rights*, ed. Benjamin Goold and Liora Lazarus (Oxford: Hart, 2007); Jeremy Matam Farrall, *The United Nations Sanctions and the Rule of Law* (New York: Cambridge University Press, 2007); Vera Gowland-Debbas, "The Relationship between the International Court of Justice and the Security Council in Light of the Lockerbie Case" (1994) 88 American Journal of International Law. 643; Bernd Martenczuk, "The Security Council and the International Court of Justice: What Lessons from the Lockerbie Case?" (1999) 10 European Journal of International Law 517.

[7] Paul Szasz, "The Security Council Starts Legislating" (2002) 96 American Journal of International Law 901, at 902; Eric Rosand, "The Security Council as 'Global Legislator': Ultra Vires or Ultra Innovative?" (2004–5) 28 Fordham International Law Journal 542; Marti Koskenniemi, "International Legislation Today: Limits and Possibilities" (2005) 23 Wisconsin International Law Journal 61.

[8] Ben Saul, *Defining Terrorism in International Law* (Oxford: Oxford University Press, 2006).

Criminal Court. It might have been thought that the events of 9/11 – especially the initial international solidarity with the victims and the United States – would have persuaded countries to accept that the deliberate mass killing of civilians to compel a government to act or to intimidate a population were acts of terrorism that could not be justified for any reason. As will be seen, however, the General Assembly continued to be unable to agree on a definition of terrorism after 9/11, and the Security Council only provided nation-states with limited guidance on the definition of terrorism in 2004, long after many had reacted to 9/11 and Security Council Resolution 1373 by enacting new antiterrorism laws.

In addition to the Security Council and the General Assembly, there are various rights-protecting bodies within the UN, including the high commissioner for human rights and various special rapporteurs. These persons have often been quite critical of the Security Council's neglect of human rights as well as various domestic abuses of human rights while countering terrorism. There are also various adjudicative bodies such as the Human Rights Committee (now Council) and the Committee against Torture.[9] Not all nations allow individuals direct access to these bodies, and they are not well integrated into the overall UN structure, especially the work of the Security Council.

The UN, like many domestic governments, has taken a whole-of-government approach to terrorism post-9/11, and this raises coordination concerns. In 2005, the secretary general established a Counter-Terrorism Implementation Task Force, which has representation from more than 30 different UN entities. They include committees of the Security Council such as the CTC and the 1267 Taliban and al Qaeda Sanctions Committee; organizations such as the World Bank; atomic energy, civil aviation, customs, and policing agencies; and rights-protection bodies such as the special rapporteur on protecting human rights while countering terrorism.[10] The Counter-Terrorism Implementation Task Force faces some of the challenges of similar domestic bodies in coordinating sprawling whole-of-government approaches to terrorism, with the additional challenge of respecting the sovereignty of all the member states who participate in intergovernmental UN institutions.

---

[9] Kalliopi Koufa, "The UN, Human Rights and Counter-Terrorism," in *International Cooperation in Counter-Terrorism: The UN and Regional Organizations in the Fight against Terrorism,* ed. Giuseppe Nesi (London: Ashgate, 2006).

[10] Report to the Secretary General, *UN Global Counter-Terrorism Strategy: Activities of the UN System in Implementing the Strategy,* A/62/898, July 7, 2008.

III. PRE-9/11 EXPERIENCE

The General Assembly: Definitional Impasse
but Act-Specific Conventions

Consistent with the idea that the General Assembly is the so-called soft UN, whereas the Security Council is the hard UN,[11] much of the 1970s was taken up with a debate in the General Assembly about the causes of terrorism. The General Assembly resisted American proposals for a draft convention on international terrorism; instead, it issued a resolution stating that it was "deeply perturbed over acts of international terrorism" such as the murder of Israeli athletes at the 1972 Munich Olympics. The General Assembly, however, remained fixed on state terrorism and more strongly condemned "the continuation of repressive and terrorist acts by colonial, racist and alien regimes in denying peoples their legitimate rights to self-determination and independence."[12] The Israeli situation was often a focus for continued and bitter disagreements over whether terrorism was a legitimate response to foreign occupation. The role of small states and, in particular, the Arab League has been a factor in preventing the General Assembly from agreeing on a general definition of terrorism.

It would, however, be wrong to conclude that the General Assembly was paralyzed by the definitional issue. It played a role in various conventions that avoided the definitional issue by focusing on various acts of terrorism such as hijacking, bombings, and hostage taking and many states voluntarily ratified these conventions. Even on the definitional issues, progress was made as more and more states experienced terrorism. In 1994, there was a declaration that referred to terrorism as "criminal acts intended or calculated to provoke a state of terror . . . for political purposes" and declared that such actions could not be justified "whatever the considerations of a political, philosophical, ideological, racial, ethnic, religious or any other nature that may be invoked

---

[11] Marti Koskenniemi, "The Police in the Temple: Order, Justice and the UN: A Dialectical View" (1995) 6 European Journal of International Law 325, at 336. He elaborates that "the dichotomy between *hard UN* (political activities for which the Security Council is mainly responsible) and *soft UN* (activities for which the General Assembly . . . is mainly responsible) is functionally and ideologically the most significant structuring feature of the organization. It governs everything from the career options of UN staff members and the specialization of diplomats at permanent missions . . . the permanent tension between Geneva ('soft') and New York ('hard'), to the organization's image in the selective eyes of the mass media."

[12] General Assembly Resolution 3034, para. 4 (1972). See generally Ben Saul, *Defining Terrorism in International Law* (Oxford: Oxford University Press, 2006), at 191ff.

to justify them."[13] This was the start of a criminal law approach that would be based on the idea that no motive or cause could justify violence.

In 1999, a more precise general definition of terrorism was included in the Convention for the Suppression of Terrorism Financing. It referred to the intentional causing of death or serious bodily injury to civilians and others not engaged in armed conflict to intimidate a population or compel a government or international organization to act.[14] This definition dropped the problematic focus on political crimes that invited states both to define terrorism as a crime in their own political interest and to refuse to extradite those charged with terrorism on the basis that terrorism was a political crime. As will be seen, the 1999 Convention on Terrorism Financing was a focal point for the UN's post-9/11 efforts. Unfortunately, however, the UN did very little to promote the general and restrained definition of terrorism contained in that convention, even though it would clearly cover 9/11.[15]

Security Council Resolution 1267

The Security Council acted against terrorism before 9/11, for example, with respect to the levying of sanctions against Libya for its role in the Pan Am bombing over Lockerbie.[16] Although all the permanent members of the Security Council had experience with terrorism, the United States often took the lead even before 9/11, in part because of the increasing number of terrorist attacks against American citizens.[17]

UN Security Council Resolution 1267 was issued on October 15, 1999, under Chapter VII of the UN Charter relating to the maintenance of international peace and security. The resolution recalled that Osama bin Laden and his associates had been indicted in the United States for the 1998 bombings of American embassies in Kenya and Tanzania and demanded that the Taliban, as the de facto government of Afghanistan, hand over bin Laden. It imposed sanctions, including the freezing of funds and travel and arms bans. Countries were required to report to the 1267 committee within 30 days and to make

---

[13] General Assembly Resolution 49/60 (1994), annexed Declaration, para. 3.

[14] International Convention on the Suppression of Terrorism Financing (1999), Article 2(1)(b).

[15] The crashing of American Airlines Flight 77 into the Pentagon would be included in the general definition of terrorism both because the 59 passengers and crew on the airline were civilians and the 125 military personnel killed in the building were non-civilian other persons "not taking an active part in a situation of armed conflict" ibid s.2(1)(b).

[16] Security Council Resolution 748.

[17] Chantal de Jonge Oudraat, "The Role of the Security Council," in *Terrorism and the UN: Before and After September 11*, ed. Jane Boulden and Thomas G. Weiss (Bloomington: Indiana University Press, 2004), at 151–3.

periodic reports to the committee. The resolution also called on states to take proceedings against those who violated the prohibitions in the resolution. In 2000, the Security Council extended the 1267 process from the Taliban to those associated with bin Laden and al Qaeda.[18] It did not define the meaning of what would constitute an association with al Qaeda until 2005, when it defined association as financing, recruiting, supplying arms, or "otherwise supporting acts or activities of Al-Qaeda, Usama bin Laden or the Taliban, or any cell, affiliate, splinter group or derivative thereof."[19] This definition, like many post-9/11 antiterrorism laws, was worded in an extremely broad fashion that imposed little, if any, restraint on law enforcement, in this case, the 1267 committee.

Before 9/11, most of those on the 1267 list were various officials in the Taliban government, with only bin Laden and about nine other al Qaeda members on the consolidated list. The committee's main work seemed to be granting humanitarian exemptions for flights by Taliban-controlled aircraft. This was to change after 9/11 and the invasion of Afghanistan. The number of listed al Qaeda members and affiliated entities expanded dramatically, and the 1267 committee became focused on al Qaeda.[20] The increase in the 1267 list came at the same time as the United States, in the immediate aftermath of 9/11, dramatically and sometimes erroneously increased its own domestic lists of terrorists.[21]

Resolution 1267 did not have the generality of law but rather focused on al Qaeda or any of its broadly defined affiliates or derivatives and thus avoided the thorny issue of the definition of terrorism. By avoiding a general definition of terrorism and by singling out al Qaeda among other terrorist groups, however, Resolution 1267 could be criticized as a form of enemy criminal law that focused on a named adversary without applying general and universal categories. The concept of association with al Qaeda is more of an intelligence concept than a criminal law concept because criminal law requires tangible acts of support and does not generally prohibit open-ended acts of "otherwise supporting" criminals. In contrast, intelligence agencies are often concerned with associations and links that fall short of criminality.

---

[18] UN Security Council Resolution 1333 (2000).

[19] UN Security Council Resolution 1617 (2005), para. 2.

[20] Compare press release, March 8, 2001, SC/7028, listing 10 al Qaeda entities, and press release, November 26, 2001, SC/7222, listing 54 individuals and 66 other entities associated with al Qaeda.

[21] The American process that influenced the 1267 process "departed from the usual procedures to compile and verify evidentiary information about those listed." Sue Eckert, "The US Regulatory Approach to Terrorist Financing," in *Countering the Financing of Terrorism*, ed. Thomas Bierstaker and Sue Eckert (London: Routledge, 2008), at 215.

The 1267 committee prepared a list of terrorists associated with al Qaeda based on information – often secret intelligence – provided by states, often the United States, and without even the necessity for formal meetings of the 1267 committee composed of all 15 members of the Security Council. As will be seen, the secrecy of this intelligence as well as the absence of any judicial body within the UN would result in successful domestic due process challenges to the fairness of the listing process. The Security Council expanded its sanctioning system from states to individuals in part to respond to the challenges of terrorism. At the same time, it retained the same secret and intergovernmental structure used to sanction states for imposing sanctions on individuals. The Security Council defended individual sanctions as preventive measures, but they had punitive effects on the listed individuals who were subject to asset freezes and travel bans.

The 1267 listing and asset freeze process, combined with the 1999 International Convention for the Suppression of Terrorism Financing, meant that the UN was heavily invested in attempting to prevent terrorism through trying to starve terrorists of funds. Both the convention and the 1267 process responded to perceptions that Osama bin Laden was an all powerful financier of terrorism, perceptions that were later found to be exaggerated.[22] In any event, the focus on terrorism financing and the idea that bin Laden was a financier of terrorism would influence how the UN would respond to 9/11. No serious thought was given to disbanding the 1267 regime once its original purpose of forcing the Taliban to hand over bin Laden to face trial in the United States with respect to the 1998 African embassy bombings had become moot after the invasion of Afghanistan in October 2001. By that time, terrorism financing regimes and laws had a momentum of their own.

IV. THE INITIAL RESPONSE TO 9/11

A day after 9/11, President Bush, speaking before the General Assembly, stated that the UN stood "at a difficult and defining moment" and warned that it risked becoming irrelevant if the Security Council's resolutions were not followed.[23] The General Assembly of the UN held a special five-day session in early October 2001, but its only concrete results were calls on states to sign the existing conventions on terrorism. As Peter van Krieken has stated, "it is quite remarkable that the unique 5 day session did not result in a more tangible

---

[22] National Commission on Terrorist Attacks against the United States, *Monograph on Terrorist Financing* (2004), at 4.

[23] Jane Boulden and Thomas G. Weiss, "Whither Terrorism and the United Nations?" in Boulden and Weiss, *Terrorism and the UN*, at 10.

outcome."[24] A subsequent resolution in December 2001 called on states to work on a comprehensive convention (and with it, the thorny definitional issue) as a "matter of urgency" and to take steps to prevent terrorism in accordance with international standards of human rights.[25] In contrast, the Security Council acted much more decisively and without the same concern for human rights. By 2003, Sir Jeremy Greenstock, the first chairman of the Security Council's CTC, could say that counter-terrorism "has gone global, with the United Nations at the centre." Other UN observers, such as Russia's ambassador to the UN, would observe that the Security Council and its CTC were "the leading element in the global anti-terrorist architecture."[26] The Security Council's quick response helped shape the nature of the global response to 9/11.

Security Council Resolution 1368 and the Invasions of Afghanistan and Iraq

The day after 9/11, the Security Council responded with Resolution 1368. This resolution has been interpreted by some as recognizing the right of the United States to use self-defense against the Taliban regime in Afghanistan.[27] It contained an expression of the Security Council's "readiness to take all necessary steps" to respond to 9/11, and its preamble recognized the individual and collective right of self-defense. Ambiguous statements in both this resolution and a subsequent 2003 resolution involving Iraq wavered between the Council's "desire to take matters into its own hands and resignation to the use of unilateral action by the US."[28] At the same time, the bulk of the resolution seemed to favor an enforcement over a war model by calling on all states "to work together urgently to bring to justice" and hold "accountable" those who perpetrated, organized, aided, or harbored those who were responsible for 9/11. As Bardo Fassbender has observed "in these paragraphs the Council continued

---

[24] Peter van Krieken, *Terrorism and the International Legal Order* (The Hague: Asser Press, 2003), at 119.

[25] G.A. Resolution 56/88 (2001), para. 3. This resolution also recalled the rather vague 1994 definition of terrorism as "criminal acts intended or calculated to provoke a state of terror . . . for political purposes." Ibid., para. 2.

[26] As quoted in Alexander Marschik, "The Security Council's Role: Problems and Prospects in the Fight against Terrorism," in Nesi, *International Cooperation in Counter-Terrorism*, at 69.

[27] Boulden and Weiss, "Whither Terrorism and the United Nations?" at 11; de Jonge Oudratt, "Role of the Security Council," at 160.

[28] Antonio Cassese "Terrorism is Also Disrupting Some Crucial Categories of International Law" (2001) 12 European Journal of International Law 993 at 996; Andrea Bianchi "Enforcing International Law Norms Against Terrorism: Achievements and Prospects" in Andrea Bianchi ed *Enforcing International Law Norms Against* Terrorism (Oxford and Portland: Hart Publishing, 2004 at 502–503 commenting on Security Council Resolution 1441 (2002) on Iraq.

to view terrorist acts as primarily criminal offences committed by individuals or groups of individuals who must be brought to justice in accordance with national and international criminal law."[29]

To be sure, Resolution 1368 recognized that 9/11 was a threat to international peace and security, subject to the important caveat that it was a threat "like any act of international terrorism." Before 9/11, it seemed relatively clear that a state had to give directions to or have control of a terrorist group before being held responsible for the acts of terrorism under the international law of self-defense.[30] Although the Taliban supported al Qaeda and expressed approval of 9/11, it is far from clear that they controlled or directed al Qaeda. Thus it appears that subsequent UN ratification of the American- and North Atlantic Treaty Organization–led invasion of Afghanistan has arguably expanded the right of self-defense against states that harbor terrorists. Such an expansion is also consistent with a general broadening of the rules of responsibility for terrorism that is seen in post-9/11 criminal and administrative law. It suggests that the baselines with respect to the use of force against nations in response to terrorist attacks have changed since 9/11.[31]

The Security Council's responses to both the 2001 invasion of Afghanistan and the 2003 invasion of Iraq have been characterized as "'mopping up' operations on behalf of powerful states."[32] Given the veto of the United States and the United Kingdom, the Security Council could not have imposed real restraint on the invasion of either Afghanistan or Iraq, even if it had been prepared to do so. Security Council Resolution 1546 authorized multinational forces in Iraq to use "all necessary measures to contribute to the maintenance of security and stability in Iraq" and annexed a letter from U.S. secretary of state Colin Powell that provided for "internment when this is necessary for

---

[29] Bardo Fassbender "The UN Security Council and International Terrorism" in Andrea Bianchi ed *Enforcing International Law Norms Against* Terrorism (Oxford and Portland: Hart Publishing, 2004) at 86.

[30] Craig Forcese, *National Security Law* (Toronto, ON, Canada: Irwin Law, 2007), at 191–8; Michael Byers, *War Law* (Vancouver, BC, Canada: Douglas and McIntyre, 2005), at 65–7; Jordan Paust, "Use of Armed Force against Terrorists in Iraq, Afghanistan and Beyond" (2002) 35 *Cornell International Law Journal* 533; Jutta Brunee, "Terrorism and Legal Change: An International Law Lesson," in Daniels et al., *Security of Freedom*, at 345; *Nicaragua v. United States* (1986) ICJ Rep. 14.

[31] Jutta Brunee and Stephen Toope, *Legitimacy and Legality in International Law* (New York: Cambridge University Press, 2010), at 296–7, and noting that many accepted Israel's 2006 incursions in Lebanon and its 2009 incursions in Gaza on a similar self-defense against terrorism rationale while also sometimes criticizing the result as disproportionate self-defense. Ibid., at 311.

[32] Ben Saul, *Defining Terrorism in International Law* (Oxford: Oxford University Press, 2006), at 235.

imperative reasons of security."[33] The resolution provided no standards or safeguards for the use of internment, even though it dealt with other matters such as debt relief and investment for Iraq. The only reference to the Geneva Conventions was in Powell's annexed letter. As in other matters, the Security Council seemed unwilling to concern itself with human rights matters that might inconvenience its members. This Security Council resolution was interpreted by the United Kingdom's highest court in 2007 as displacing the right to liberty protected under the European Convention on Human Rights when applied to a British citizen who had been subject to military detention for three years in Iraq without trial or judicial review.[34] The Chapter VII status of the resolution meant that it could displace human rights obligations whether grounded in domestic, supranational, or international law, though the British decision has been appealed to the European Court of Human Rights.

The Security Council asserted a more robust role with respect to various domestic measures taken to combat terrorism than with respect to the invasion of either Afghanistan or Iraq. As Professors Boulden and Weiss have observed, "the Security Council chooses to exercise no control on the use of military force in response to terrorism but is vigilant and arguably intrusive when it comes to dealing with terrorism through national mechanisms and controls."[35] It was easier for the Security Council to sanction and legislate against nonstate actors, such as terrorists, than to control the actions of states, and especially the veto-yielding United States and United Kingdom, with respect to the wars fought in Afghanistan and Iraq in the name of preventing terrorism.

v. SECURITY COUNCIL RESOLUTION 1373: PANICKED GLOBAL LEGISLATION

The Security Council's most influential response to 9/11 was Resolution 1373.[36] It was drafted behind closed doors in just over 48 hours. On September 26, 2001, the United States began informal consultations with the four other permanent members of the Security Council and then circulated a draft resolution the next day. On September 28, 2001, all 15 members of the Security Council approved of the momentous resolution in a five-minute evening meeting. No country explained why it voted for the resolution, and no country outside

---

[33] S/C Resolution 1546 (2004), para. 10 and p. 11, annexing letter for Colin Powell to president of the Security Council.
[34] *R (Al Jedda) v. Secretary of State* (2007) UKHL 58.
[35] Boulden and Weiss, "Wither Terrorism and the United Nations?" at 11.
[36] S/Res/1373 (2001).

the 15-state Security Council was consulted.[37] No dissents or objections were recorded as all relevant ambassadors had been instructed to cooperate with the United States in the wake of 9/11.[38] Although the Security Council acted as a world legislator by proclaiming general, binding, and permanent obligations on states, it functioned with the secrecy and efficiency associated with executive action.

Some commentators have argued that the Security Council's actions in Resolution 1373 were ultra vires its mandate to deal with specific threats to international peace and security.[39] The special rapporteur on the promotion of human rights while countering terrorism reached a similar conclusion in 2010.[40] Others have, however, defended Resolution 1373 as a pragmatic recognition of the limits of consensual treaty making and that terrorism and weapons of mass destruction constitute a manifest threat to international peace and security.[41] In my view, Resolution 1373 constitutes a novel form of legislation by the Security Council because it imposes general and permanent obligations on states about how to respond to terrorism that are not tied to any particular conflict. The arguably illegal character of the Security Council's actions set a bad precedent for what many other nations would do in response to 9/11. At the same time, almost all nations accepted the Security Council's legislative role and cooperated with the 1373 process.

Security Council Resolution 1373 required states to enact legislation to ensure that the funds of all terrorists were frozen. As such, it went beyond the 1267 process that focused on the freezing of funds of the Taliban and al Qaeda[42] without defining the general criteria of terrorism. Resolution 1373 set out a legislative agenda for post-9/11 counter-terrorism law and policy, but this

---

[37] United Nations Security Council Minutes, September 28, 2001, S/PV/4385; "Resolution Requires Members to Act against Terror," New York Times, September 29, 2001, A1; Stefan Talmon, "The Security Council as World Legislature" (2005) 99 American Journal of International Law 175, at 187–8.

[38] Nicholas Rostow, "Before and After: The Changed UN Response to Terrorism since 9/11" (2002) 35 Cornell International Law Journal 475, at 482; Ian Johnstone, "Legislation and Adjudication in the UN Security Council: Bringing Down the Deliberative Deficit" (2008) 102 American Journal of International Law 275, at 284.

[39] Mathew Happold, "Security Council Resolution 1373 and the Constitution of the United Nations" (2003) 16 Leiden Journal of International Law 593; C. H. Powell, "The Legal Authority of the UN Security Council," in *Security and Human Rights*, ed. Benjamin Goold and Liora Lazarus (Oxford: Hart, 2007).

[40] Report of the Special Rapporteur on the Promotion of Human Rights and Fundamental Freedoms While Countering Terrorism, A/65/258, August 6, 2010, at para. 44.

[41] Eric Rosand, "The Security Council as Global Legislator: Ultra Vires or Ultra Innovative" (2005) 28 Fordham International Law Journal 542.

[42] Talmon, "Security Council as World Legislature," at 176–7.

international legislation had many of the shortcomings of panicked domestic laws enacted to respond to particular acts of terrorism.

There is a long history of domestic legislatures enacting laws quickly to respond to acts of terrorism. Bruce Ackerman has defended the need for states to take decisive measures to reassure a panicked public after a traumatic act of terrorism.[43] One problem with quick legislative responses is that they proceed with what is immediately at hand and without full information about why a particular act of terrorism happened. Resolution 1373 decided that all states shall prevent and suppress the financing of terrorist acts and called on them to become parties to the 1999 International Convention for the Suppression of the Financing of Terrorism. The 9/11 Commission Report released in 2004, however, revealed significant limits on the ability of financing laws to prevent even massive acts of terrorism like 9/11, let alone the smaller and less expensive bombings in Bali, Madrid, London, or Mumbai. Resolution 1373 was also influential in drawing a link between immigration and anti-terrorism law by calling on all states to ensure that refugee status was not abused by terrorists. Again, the 9/11 Commission found that the 9/11 hijackers were able to enter the United States in a variety of ways, none of them including claims of asylum.[44] When the Security Council decided to focus on financing of terrorism and the danger that refugee law would be abused by terrorists when drafting Resolution 1373, it was acting with limited information about 9/11. The Security Council, like domestic legislators, worked with what was at hand in responding to 9/11. It also used the methods of the last war by focusing on measures against terrorism financing, despite their failure to prevent the 9/11 atrocity.

The Emphasis on Terrorism Financing

The first paragraph of Resolution 1373 is entirely devoted to the prevention of the financing of terrorist acts. This creates the impression that terrorism is not so much the weapon of the weak but the weapon of those who receive extensive financing. The second paragraph focuses more on the prevention and criminalization of terrorist acts, but even in that paragraph there are repeated references to the financing of terrorism.

Why did the UN place such great emphasis on the prevention of the financing of terrorism in the immediate aftermath of 9/11? One factor may have been suspicions that Osama bin Laden was the mastermind of the 9/11 attacks and

---

[43] Bruce Ackerman, *Before the Next Attack* (New Haven, CT: Yale University Press, 2006).
[44] National Commission on Terrorist Attacks upon the United States, *The 9/11 Report* (New York: St. Martin's Press, 2004).

his exaggerated reputation as a financier of terrorism.[45] As discussed earlier, the Security Council had issued Resolution 1267 in 1999, and its asset freeze and travel ban had been extended to bin Laden and al Qaeda in 2000.[46] Curiously, Resolution 1267 was not mentioned in Resolution 1373, perhaps in recognition of its failure to prevent 9/11.

The initial focus on terrorism financing was also consistent with American priorities in the wake of 9/11. On September 24, 2001, President Bush made a speech announcing a new executive order with respect to terrorism, in which he argued that "we will starve the terrorist of funding" and warned that banks and financial institutions that did not freeze terrorist funds or share information would be kept out of the American market.[47]

Another reason why Resolution 1373 focused on the financing of terrorism is found in paragraph 3(d) of the resolution, which calls on states to "become parties as soon as possible to the relevant international conventions and protocols relating to terrorism, including the International Convention for the Suppression of the Financing of Terrorism of 9 December 1999." This convention was, at the time, the most recent convention on terrorism. Although it had been signed by a number of countries before 9/11, it had only been ratified by a few states.[48] The Security Council had an interest in promoting the Financing Convention and did so despite evidence that attempts to starve al Qaeda of funds had not worked in the past. At the same time as it promoted the 1999 Convention, however, the Security Council did not draw attention to that convention's general definition of terrorism, with its focus on intentional killing and harming of civilians and other persons not taking an active part in hostilities during an armed conflict in order to intimidate populations and coerce governments. As will be suggested later, this was a mistake that allowed many states to draft very broad terrorism laws and that failed to build momentum on reaching international agreement about a definition of terrorism.

The Limited Efficacy of the Terrorism Financing–Money Laundering Model

In its 2004 report, the 9/11 Commission reached some significant conclusions that suggest that the UN and countries following Resolution 1373 may have placed too much faith in measures aimed at the financing of terrorism as a

---

[45] Ibid., at 5.4.   [46] S/Res/1333 (2000), at para. 8(c).
[47] As quoted in Joseph Myers, "Disputing Terrorist Networks: The U.S. and International Regime for Halting Terrorist Funding" (2002) 34 Law and Policy in International Business 17, at 18.
[48] http://untreaty.un.org/partI/chapterXVIII/treaty12.asp.

means to prevent terrorism. The 9/11 Commission found that the 9/11 plotters spent between $400,000 and $500,000 on the plot and that they "moved,
stored, and spent their money in ordinary ways, easily defeating the detection mechanisms at the time. The origins of the funds remain unknown."[49]
It expressed considerable skepticism about the ability of financing laws and
practices of the type contemplated by Resolution 1373 to prevent future acts
of terrorism. It concluded that "if a particular funding source had dried up,
al Qaeda could have easily tapped a different source or diverted funds from
another project"[50] and that "trying to starve the terrorists of money is like
trying to catch one kind of fish by draining the ocean."[51] The 9/11 Commission's pessimism about stopping the financing of terrorism as an effective
means to prevent terrorism is only increased by estimates that the post-9/11
Bali bombings cost between $15,000 and $35,000, the Madrid bombings cost
about $15,000, and the London bombings were even less expensive to carry
out.[52]

Many countries grafted laws against the financing of terrorism onto existing
or new money laundering laws designed to detect large amounts of money
derived from organized crime. This merger of terrorism financing and money
laundering regimes was also promoted by the Financial Action Task Force
(FATF), created in 1989 by the then G-7 group of nations to combat money
laundering but which added terrorism financing to its mandate after 9/11.
FATF wielded considerable power in identifying high-risk and noncompliant
jurisdictions with first its money laundering and later its terrorism financing
recommendations and country evaluations. Many countries responded to Resolution 1373 and the similar FATF 2001 recommendations in part because of
fear of being branded as noncompliant with the new regime, even though
the CTC has not yet identified any country as non-compliant. A fundamental problem with this approach, however, is that it ignores deep differences
between terrorism financing, which may involve the transfer of small amounts
of money from legitimate sources, including charities and alternative remittance systems, and money laundering, which involves large amounts of cash
produced through organized crime.

Even those on the inside of terrorism financing are questioning its effectiveness. Richard Barrett, who serves as the coordinator of the 1267 monitoring
team, has recently written that it is time to rethink terrorism financing schemes

---

[49] National Commission on Terrorist Attacks upon the United States, *9/11 Report*, at 5.4.
[50] Ibid.   [51] Ibid., at 12.3.
[52] "Looking in the Wrong Places," *The Economist*, October 20, 2005, at http://www.economist
.com/displaystory.cfm?story_id=5053373. See also Thomas Biersteker and Sue Eckert, Introduction to *Countering the Financing of Terrorism* (London: Routledge, 2008), at 7.

"that took center stage after 9/11."[53] He notes that suspicious transaction reports from American financial institutions have increased from more than 163,000 in 2000 to 1.25 million in 2007, at the same time as al Qaeda terrorism has become much more decentralized and self-funded. Barrett concludes that as al Qaeda evolves, "financing may become decreasingly relevant to efforts to contain the threat. As the amounts of money used to mount attacks become smaller, they become harder to regulate."[54] Other commentators have warned that a strategic focus on charities and informal money transfer systems has a disproportionate effect on Muslim communities and can even contribute to some of the dislocation that may fuel extremism and terrorism.[55] The Security Council may have made a strategic mistake in focusing on terrorism financing in the aftermath of 9/11.

Terrorism Financing and the Unfairness of Terrorist Lists

In addition to concerns about the effectiveness of laws against the financing of terrorism, there are also concerns about their effects on human rights. Terrorism financing regimes depend on the development of lists of suspected terrorists such as those under the 1267 listing regime. Such lists are necessary to alert countries and financial institutions to freeze assets and prohibit financial transactions involving the listed entities. Lists have been criticized as bills of attainder because they allow individuals to be declared outlaws by a legislative or executive as opposed to a judicial act.[56] As will be seen, domestic implementation of the 1267 list in many countries was at least originally achieved through regulations enacted under the innocuously titled United Nations Act. The U.K. Supreme Court, however, declared in 2010 that such regulations were ultra vires the United Kingdom's United Nations Act because Parliament could not have intended in 1946, when it enacted the act, to authorize permanent and powerful individual sanctions through a Security Council listing process that does not allow any judicial remedy.[57]

---

[53] Richard Barrett, "Time to Reexamine Regulation Designed to Counter the Financing of Terrorism" (2009) 41 Case Western Reserve Journal of International Law 7, at 11.

[54] Ibid., at 18.

[55] Nina Crimm, "The Moral Hazard of Anti-Terrorism Financing Measures: A Potential to Compromise Civil Societies and National Interests" (2008) 43 Wake Forest Law Review 577.

[56] David Dyzenhaus, "The Rule of (Administrative) Law in International Law" (2005) 68 Law and Contemporary Problems 127, at 141–53. See also C. H. Powell, "Terrorism and the Separation of Powers in the National and International Spheres" (2005) 18 South African Journal of Criminal Justice 151, who also makes the point that the listing process augments executive power in both domestic and international politics.

[57] *Treasury v. Ahmed* (2010) UKHL 2, paras. 45–6, 61.

In some cases, individuals have been wrongly added to terrorist lists, which is not surprising given the absence of an adversarial hearing or challenge of evidence before a person is listed either domestically or internationally as a terrorist and the reliance that is placed on secret intelligence when compiling lists.[58] There is a growing number of successful due process challenges to terrorist listings, including decisions by the European Court of Justice, the new U.K. Supreme Court, and the Canadian courts. These challenges typically do not attempt to invalidate UN listing processes under the mandatory Chapter VII provisions of the UN Charter but rather focus on domestic implementation. This provides indirect due process, but due process that, if implemented, would threaten to place states in breach of their Chapter VII obligations. This presents a conundrum for nation-states, which have to choose between obeying domestic due process norms or Chapter VII Security Council mandates enacted without due process norms. This state of affairs will do little for compliance with or public confidence in Security Council resolutions, which are often not enforced.[59]

Domestic judges have not shied away from criticism of the Security Council's secretive listing regime. One Canadian judge, in terms that were endorsed by the U.K. Supreme Court, stated,

> I add my name to those who view the 1267 Committee regime as a denial of basic legal remedies and as untenable under the principles of international human rights. There is nothing in the listing or de-listing procedure that recognizes the principles of natural justice or that provides for basic procedural fairness.... The 1267 Committee listing and de-listing processes do not even include a limited right to a hearing. It can hardly be said that the 1267 Committee process meets the requirement of independence and impartiality when, as appears may be the case involving Mr. Abdelrazik, the nation requesting the listing is one of the members of the body that decides whether to list or, equally as important, to de-list a person. The accuser is also the judge.... The 1267 Committee regime is, as I observed at the hearing, a

---

[58] For an account of how a Canadian man, Liban Hussein, was wrongly placed on both the United Nations' and Canada's lists, see E. Alexander Dosman, "For the Record: Designating 'Listed Entities' for the Purposes of Terrorist Financing Offences at Canadian Law" (2004) 62 University of Toronto Faculty of Law Review. 1. See also Chapter 7.

[59] It has been argued that "inadequate implementation of decisions by the Security Council is a central problem of the UN system. In practice, compliance has become more or less optional. Unless one of the permanent five Security Council Members (P5) brings a case of non-compliance to the attention of the Council and pursues the case, even mandatory sanctions under Chapter VII of the UN Charter are fulfilled only if the States so choose." Alexander Marschik, "The Security Council's Role: Problems and Prospects in the Fight against Terrorism," in Nesi, *International Cooperation in Counter-Terrorism*, at 73–4.

situation for a listed person not unlike that of Josef K. in Kafka's *The Trial*, who awakens one morning and, for reasons never revealed to him or the reader, is arrested and prosecuted for an unspecified crime.[60]

As will be seen, the Security Council has responded to such pointed critiques by appointing an ombudsperson with respect to delisting requests. Nevertheless, such reforms fall short of providing a judicial remedy for those listed as terrorists. The Security Council has, in the past, created courts, such as the tribunals for the former Yugoslavia and Rwanda, but has not done so with respect to the listing of terrorists. One factor is the unwillingness of the states on the Security Council, especially the United States, to disclose the secret intelligence said to justify the listing. Even if a court had the power to review listings, it would still have to confront the difficult issues of protecting intelligence sources and methods and the unfairness produced by the use of secret evidence that is not disclosed to those challenging their listing as terrorists.

In addition to human rights concerns, terrorist lists remain a blunt tool. Lists deliberately simplify complex matters in their unequivocal declaration that an individual, corporation, or group is a terrorist outlaw. The listing of groups and individuals by the Security Council may encourage domestic states to take harsh measures against international outlaws, even though those measures may themselves be counter-productive and generate more terrorism. The listing of a group can preclude both humanitarian aid and negotiations. As Peter Margulies has argued, terrorist-financing regimes can be counter-productive by "wrongly stigmatizing or penalizing organizations that provide legitimate philanthropic support to the international Muslim community."[61] Listings can be quite static and based on old intelligence that fails to detect movements by either individuals or organizations away from violence. They force listed individuals and groups further underground, where they may be difficult to detect. They also encourage parties to eschew negotiation involving "banned groups." Nevertheless, they also fit well into the post-9/11 focus on al Qaeda as a terrorist group that was beyond negotiation. The listing of a group or individual as a terrorist promotes a simplistic belief that the mere act of

---

[60] *Abdelrazik v. Canada* (2009), FC 580, at paras. 51 and 53. See also *Treasury v. Ahmed* (2010) UKSC 2.

[61] Peter Margulies, "Laws of Unintended Consequences: Terrorist Financing Restrictions and Transitions to Democracy" (2007) 20 New York International Law Review 65, at 83. For the adverse effects of overbroad terrorism financing on charities, see Mark Sidel, "Counter-Terrorism and the Enabling Legal and Political Environment for Civil Society: A Comparative Analysis of 'War on Terror' States" (2008) 10(3) International Journal for Not-for-Profit Law 7.

proscription can end terrorism or at least starve the terrorists of funds, even though, unfortunately, all evidence shows that deadly acts of terrorism can be committed very cheaply.

The emphasis placed on preventing the financing of terrorism in Resolution 1373 was not the result of informed analysis of the causes of 9/11 or of the effectiveness of laws prohibiting the financing of terrorism. Indeed, the Security Council enacted Resolution 1373 with a blinding speed that eclipsed the enactment of post-9/11 antiterrorism laws in the United States, United Kingdom, and Canada. The UN had its own institutional reasons for promoting measures against the financing of terrorism. The Security Council, like domestic bodies struggling to do something to reassure the public, worked with what was at hand in terms of the 1999 Convention and the 1267 process. Reliance on what is at hand may result in measures that are not optimal in terms of preventing future acts of terrorism. The consequences of error are particularly great when the Security Council acts under Chapter VII because all member states of the UN will be under pressure to follow its lead down what may be the wrong path. Having started down such a path, both the Security Council and states may be reluctant to retreat.

The CTC, the 1267 committee, and FATF continue to question member states about their terrorism financing efforts, and many states have established extensive laws and institutions to satisfy these mandates. Terrorist-financing laws may require fair trial norms to be violated to the extent that their effective enforcement depends on lists of terrorists that are compiled by the executive within the UN or domestic governments and on the basis of secret intelligence or evidence. That said, it will be difficult for states to cut back on the emphasis given to terrorism financing given that both Resolutions 1267 and 1373 still have binding effect and that many states have now invested heavily in this form of counter-terrorism measure, despite its human rights costs and limited effectiveness.

The Emphasis on the Use of Immigration Law as Antiterrorism Law

In addition to its focus on the financing of terrorism, Resolution 1373 also made specific mention of immigration law. Paragraph 2(g) made reference to the need for "effective border controls" to "prevent the movement of terrorists or terrorist groups." This focus on border controls is understandable given that the 9/11 hijackers entered the United States from abroad. Nevertheless, the Security Council acted without full information about how the 9/11 hijackers entered the United States and singled out problems relating to counterfeit and forged travel documents.[62] It was subsequently found that the hijackers entered the United States on a variety of legitimately obtained visas.[63] In any event, Resolution 1373 signaled a thickening of borders that would occur in the wake of 9/11 but would be overinclusive in excluding and burdening many legitimate migrants and travelers and would be underinclusive with respect to homegrown terrorists.

Paragraphs 3(f) and 3(g) of Resolution 1373 were more problematic than border control because they warned states to make sure "that refugee status is not abused by the perpetrators, organizers or facilitators of terrorist acts." None of the 9/11 hijackers had applied for refugee status, something that would attract increased state scrutiny of a person's history, including the person's involvement in political or terrorist organizations. Although there are some examples of al Qaeda terrorists applying for refugee status,[64] it is far from clear why Resolution 1373 singled out refugee applicants as possible security threats.

The only reference to international human rights law found in Resolution 1373 is in the need to respect human rights while also ensuring that refugee status is not abused by terrorists. The reference to international human rights law in this context refers to the need to ensure that the deportation of a person seeking asylum does not result in that person's torture. The reference to such rights in Resolution 1373 is quite important given the poor human rights records of many of the countries of citizenship of those involved in al Qaeda. As will be seen in the next chapter, the deportation of a suspected terrorist to Syria may very well result in that person's torture. Resolution 1373 thus identified but did not resolve a difficult dilemma that many democracies would face in dealing with suspected terrorists. On one hand, Resolution 1373 instructed countries not to allow terrorists to be granted refugee status, even though they might in other respects satisfy the definition of refugees facing political persecution. On the other hand, Resolution 1373 reminded countries that they should not deport such persons if it would result in their torture.

---

[62] Security Council Resolution 1373, para. 2(g). (2001)

[63] National Commission on Terrorist Attacks upon the United States, *9/11 Report*, chap. 7. Many of the hijackers did, however, acquire new passports before obtaining visas generally from American offices in Saudi Arabia. Some of these passports were fraudulently doctored, some of the visa applications contained false statements, and some visas to potential hijackers were denied, but not for security reasons. Ibid., at 7.3. Some of the hijackers also violated the terms of their visas while in the United States.

[64] An oft cited case is Ahmed Ressam, who applied for but was denied asylum in Canada before being apprehended at the Canadian–American border with a Canadian passport obtained with a stolen baptismal certificate and with plans and materials to bomb the Los Angeles Airport at the Millennium. National Commission on Terrorist Attacks upon the United States, *9/11 Report*, at 6.1.

The deportation-to-torture dilemma does not admit of easy answers and demonstrates the geopolitical complexities of al Qaeda terrorism. The Security Council demanded that states take action, but it did not provide any guidance to nations about how to reconcile the competing demands of security and the protection of human rights. Such an approach can be defended as one that recognizes that international institutions should leave domestic states with a wide margin of appreciation. One problem was that the responses of some states to this dilemma violated human rights. As will be seen in subsequent chapters, the United Kingdom responded by derogating from fair trial rights to allow the indeterminate detention of noncitizens suspected of terrorism who would be tortured if deported. The Canadian courts even contemplated that they might allow a person to be deported to torture, whereas the United States accepted flimsy assurances from states such as Egypt that they would not torture those subject to extraordinary renditions. By requiring states to do what had, before 9/11, proved impossible – to define terrorism and to deny refugee status to terrorists while not deporting them to torture – the Security Council contributed to a state of affairs in which states could take actions that would violate human rights and yet claim that they were implementing Security Council mandates.[65]

As will be seen in subsequent chapters, many democracies picked up on the cues sent by Resolution 1373 and used immigration law as antiterrorism law. Immigration law was attractive for governments because it had broader liability rules, lower burdens of proof, and increased periods of investigative detention than even criminal laws that were amended in the wake of 9/11. Immigration law was particularly attractive because it allowed the state not to disclose intelligence but also to use that intelligence as secret evidence against noncitizens. Democracies generally accepted much lower standards of adjudicative fairness for the detention and deportation of noncitizens than for the criminal prosecution of citizens suspected of involvement in terrorism.[66] Resolution 1373 contributed to this trend to use administrative shortcuts that featured less respect for fair trial rights by signaling to countries that they should use immigration law to deflect, detain, and deport terrorists.

It is particularly disconcerting that the UN should encourage the use of immigration law as antiterrorism law because such an approach allows advantaged countries with sophisticated border controls and immigration law enforcement to deflect potential terrorists back into countries with poor human

---

[65] Craig Forcese, "Hegemonic Federalism: The Democratic Implications of the UN Security Council's 'Legislative' Phase" (2007) 38 Victoria University of Wellington Law Review 175.

[66] Audrey Macklin, "Borderline Security," in Daniels et al., *Security of Freedom*.

rights records and terrorist problems of their own. Although nation-states could possibly justify such actions in their national interests, the UN should have been more concerned about the deflection of terrorists from one country to another. Indeed, for this very reason, some international terrorism conventions developed before 9/11 were based on the principle that states should either criminally prosecute terrorists themselves or extradite them to another state that could prosecute them.[67] The immigration law remedies of removal or deflection seek only to displace terrorism rather than punish it. Some nations eventually accepted the limits of using immigration law as antiterrorism law,[68] but it is disappointing that the UN, which should have had a global perspective, placed such emphasis on using the limited tools of immigration law as a response to international terrorism. The UN, like many other nation-states, seemed to lose confidence in criminal law after 9/11 and encouraged shortcuts around it without adequate thought about the limited remedies that could be achieved by using immigration law as antiterrorism law.

The Emphasis on the Sharing of Intelligence

Resolution 1373 recognized the need for intelligence to flow more freely in an attempt to prevent another 9/11. It decided that all states should take the necessary steps to prevent terrorist acts through "early warning . . . by exchange of information" and called on states to "find ways of intensifying and accelerating the exchange of operational information."[69] This recognized problems in the exchange of information within and among governments that might have prevented 9/11. At the same time, however, it also helped create an environment in which unreliable and speculative intelligence was exchanged too freely, without enough attention paid to the accuracy of the information, how the information would be used, and the consequences of its use for human rights.

---

[67] Van Krieken, *Terrorism and the International Legal Order*, at chap. 3.

[68] In the landmark case of *A v. Secretary of State* (2004) UKHL 56, at para. 43, the House of Lords declared that the United Kingdom's immigration law response to Resolution 1373 was a disproportionate response to terrorism and one that was discriminatory toward noncitizens. Lord Bingham concluded that "the choice of an immigration measure to address a security problem had the inevitable result of failing adequately to address the problem (by allowing non–United Kingdom suspected terrorists to leave the country with impunity and leaving British suspected terrorists at large) while imposing the severe penalty of indefinite detention on persons who, even if reasonably suspected of having links with al Qaeda, may harbour no hostile intentions towards the United Kingdom." On the continued use of immigration law as antiterrorism law in the United Kingdom, see Chapter 5.

[69] Security Council Resolution 1373, paras. 2(b) and 3(a).

The General Assembly was more attentive than the Security Council to the problems that might result in the exchange of intelligence, including with countries with poor human rights records. Like the Security Council, it called for states to intensify the exchange of information, but it also warned that in doing so, they should "avoid the dissemination of inaccurate or unverified information."[70] As will be seen, the General Assembly's warning was prescient as the exchange of inaccurate information in some cases, such as that of Maher Arar, a Canadian falsely suspected of being involved with al Qaeda, led to his detention in the United States and his subsequent transfer to and torture in Syria. In such cases, there was a vicious circle of inaccurate intelligence as false confessions obtained by torture in Syria were recycled back to Canada where they were used as a basis for counter-terrorism activities.[71]

The emphasis on better intelligence sharing in the wake of 9/11 was understandable but created some risks. Intelligence is generally secret information that is designed to inform governments about possible security risks. Intelligence favors the overestimation of risks rather than failures to report possible risks, and intelligence judgments can be made on the basis of associations and ambiguous actions. Although intelligence was more frequently shared after 9/11, the sources and methods used to obtain the intelligence were not, and without such information, the reliability of the intelligence may be difficult to determine. The increased sharing of intelligence encouraged by Resolution 1373 created a risk that some of the intelligence shared would falsely implicate people as terrorist suspects and that the intelligence could be used as the basis for executive action and as secret evidence. Some people were mistreated in a desire to obtain intelligence and by intelligence gatherers who were confident that their methods would never be reviewed by courts.

The sharing of intelligence between countries is generally done pursuant to restrictions on the subsequent distribution and use of intelligence. Intelligence agencies are not generally comfortable with the disclosure of intelligence in open court and, as will be seen, a continued reluctance to disclose intelligence can be a brake on reforms of the 1267 terrorist listing process. Such concerns placed pressures on countries receiving intelligence to use alternatives to the criminal law that allowed the use of secret evidence. The Security Council's

---

[70] GA Res. 56/88 (2001), para. 4.
[71] Commission of Inquiry into the Actions of Canadian Officials in Relation to Maher Arar, *Report of the Events Relating to Maher Arar: Analysis and Recommendations* (Ottawa: Public Works, 2006), at 34–6, 194–200, 271–3. *Internal Inquiry into the Actions of Canadian Officials in Relation to Abdullah Almalki, Ahmad Abou-Elmaati and Muayyed Nureddin* (Ottawa: Public Works, 2008), at 126–30, 271–5, 379–80 (describing how a false confession about a plan to bomb the Canadian Parliament was extracted after beatings in Syria, then was distributed to various agencies and used to obtain a search warrant in Canada). See also Chapter 7.

focus on intelligence was understandable in the wake of 9/11, but it also indirectly promoted the use of alternatives to criminal trials such as administrative, military and immigration detention on the basis of secret evidence. It may also have promoted various forms of mistreatment to obtain intelligence. Finally, the focus on intelligence created an environment that was more conducive to running the risk of false positives, by which people were wrongly identified as terrorists on the basis of their associations, politics, religion, training, travel or past acts, as opposed to false negatives that gave suspects the benefit of reasonable doubt.[72]

The Emphasis on Criminal Law

Although it was drafted mainly by the United States, Resolution 1373 did not endorse the use of a war model against terrorism. Indeed, much of the resolution contemplated the use of criminal law as a main response to terrorism. The resolution decided that states shall "ensure that any person who participates in the financing, planning, preparation or perpetuation of terrorist acts or in supporting terrorists acts is brought to justice and ensure that, in addition to any other measures against them, such terrorist acts are established as serious criminal offences in domestic laws."[73] This provision contemplated that terrorism would be criminalized and that criminal law would be expanded to include preparation and financing of terrorism. The resolution also decided that states should cooperate and assist other states "with criminal investigations or criminal proceedings," including "obtaining evidence" that could be used in such proceedings.[74] As will be seen, many countries did respond to 9/11 by expanding their criminal laws to deal with remote acts of preparation for terrorism and by expanding the scope of accomplice liability. At the same time, many countries did not display full confidence in criminal law and used various forms of military and administrative detention as a less restrained alternative.

Resolution 1373 encouraged countries to expand criminal law in a manner that made what, before 9/11, would only have been secret intelligence about possible terrorist threats into information that was also possible evidence of new terrorist crimes. Resolution 1373 did not, however, provide any guidance about how countries should manage the relation between intelligence and

---

[72] Kent Roach "The Eroding Distinction Between Intelligence and Evidence in Terrorism Investigations" in Nicola McGarrity, Andrew Lynch and George Williams eds. *Counter-Terrorism* (London: Routledge, 2010) at 5—55; Simon Chesterman, *One Nation under Surveillance* (Oxford: Oxford University Press, 2011), at 223—4.

[73] Security Council Resolution 1373, para. 2(e).

[74] Ibid., para. 2(f).

evidence and, with it, the competing demands of secrecy to protect intelligence sources and methods and greater disclosure of intelligence to help prevent and prosecute terrorism. As with similar issues of the definition of terrorism and the deportation of suspected terrorists to torture, the Security Council's approach could be defended as one that allowed states to work out their own solutions to difficult problems. A recurring problem, however, is that the solution to the competing and often irreconcilable demands of intelligence and evidence often resulted in shortcuts that would allow the use of secret evidence and would abandon criminal law, even though Resolution 1373 reaffirmed the traditional notion that terrorism should be a crime and that terrorists should be "brought to justice."

The Creation of the Counter-Terrorism Committee: A Rights-Free Body?

Resolution 1373 also created a committee of the Security Council, the CTC, to monitor its implementation. This followed the precedent of Resolution 1267, which also created its own implementing committee. Resolution 1373 called on all states to report to the newly created CTC no later than 90 days after the resolution. In a number of countries, including Canada and the United Kingdom, this short reporting deadline was taken as a deadline for the enactment of new antiterrorism laws. Although many countries have, at various times, enacted antiterrorism laws in a hurry in response to acts of terrorism, the effects of the 1373 reporting requirement in encouraging rushed enactment of antiterrorism laws in jurisdictions that did not experience acts of terrorism was unprecedented. One study of reports to the CTC concludes that 94 states have defined terrorism as a crime since 9/11.[75] A search of a very useful database of national legislation maintained by the United Nations Office on Drugs and Crime reveals over 500 instances of the phrase "terrorism," "terrorist activity" or "terrorist" being used in legislation including post-9/11 terrorism laws in Afghanistan, Barbados, Belarus, Bulgaria, Cook Islands, Croatia, Cyprus, Denmark, Gambia, Guatemala, India, Ireland, Kazakhstan, Nepal, Malaysia, Mauritis, Myanmar, New Zealand, Philippines, Romania, Saint Kitts and Nevis, South Africa, Sri Lanka, Tanzania, Trinidad and Tobago, Turkmenistan, Ukraine and Vanuatu.[76]

The CTC has emerged as an important player in the formation of counterterrorism laws and policies. In 2003, one commentator characterized the CTC

[75] James Fry, "The Swindle of Fragmented Criminalization: Continuing Piecemeal Responses to International Terrorism and al Qaeda" (2009) 43 New England Law Review 377, at 424.
[76] United Nation Office of Drugs and Crime Terrorist Legislation Database available at https://www.unodc.org/tldb/searchIndex.do?q=terrorism + terrorist + activity + terrorist.

as the "center of global counter-terrorism policy-making" in part because under the leadership of British ambassador Jeremy Greenstock, it took a "consensual, non-confrontational approach."[77] Nico Krisch has recently defended the CTC's non-confrontational approach as one based on non-hierarchical pluralism that lies between international law monism and dualism that simply accepts each country's own sovereignty and its own constitution. Professor Krisch may be correct that the pluralist approach is a practical reconciliation of competing legal orders and a "reflection of underlying problems rather than the problem itself,"[78] but his account underestimates the adverse effects of the CTC's non-confrontational approach on human rights.

The CTC was only able to take a non-confrontational approach because it avoided issues of human rights compliance, the definition of terrorism, and the effectiveness of states' on-the-ground compliance with Resolution 1373.[79] In 2002, Ambassador Greenstock explained the CTC's approach to human rights as follows:

> The CTC is mandated to monitor the implementation of 1373. Monitoring performance against other international conventions, including human rights law, is outside the scope of the CTC's mandate. But as we go forward, the CTC will remain aware of the interaction of its work with human rights concerns, inter alia through the contact the CTC has developed with the OHCHR. And we welcome parallel monitoring of observance of human rights obligations.[80]

The idea that concerns about human rights were outside the CTC's mandate is deeply problematic given that new terrorism laws and enforcement

---

[77] Jane Stromseth, "An Imperial Security Council – Implementing Security Council Resolutions 1373 and 1390" (2003) 97 American Society of International Law Proceedings 41, at 44. See also Eric Rosand, "Security Council Resolution 1373, the Counter-Terrorism Committee, and the Fight against Terrorism" (2003) 97 American Journal of International Law 333, at 336.

[78] Nico Krisch *Beyond Constitutionalism: The Pluralist Structure of Postnational Law* (Oxford: Oxford University Press, 2010) at 181.

[79] Eric Rosand has suggested that "one of the reasons the CTC has maintained such broad support is that it has been able to avoid dealing with the divisive issue of the definition of 'terrorism,'... If the CTC begins to broaden its focus from building technical capacity to monitoring implementation of the laws and the executive machinery designed to deal with terrorism, it may find itself engaged in the same definitional debate that the General Assembly is involved in, and thus run the risk of losing the broad support and cooperation from States it has received to date." Eric Rosand, "Resolution 1373 and the CTC: The Security Council's Capacity-Building," in Nesi, *International Cooperation in Counter-Terrorism*, at 85.

[80] Presentation by Ambassador Greenstock, then chairman of the CTC, at the symposium "Combating International Terrorism: The Contribution of the United Nations," Vienna, June 3–4, 2002, at http://www.un.org/sc/ctc/documents/ViennaNotes.htm.

activities affected human rights and that the CTC interacted with all nation-states, including those with poor human rights records. The CTC's non-confrontational approach on human rights seems more related to a techno-cratic, bureaucratic and narrow interpretation of its mandate than a sophisti-cated pluralistic response to competing sovereignties. To be sure, the CTC might have attracted domestic pushback on some human rights issues, but it did not even appear to try to incorporate human rights into its early work.

The CTC does not act in a transparent manner.[81] Much of what is known about its interaction with states depends on whether the state chose to include the questions that the CTC asked of the state in its follow-up reports to the CTC. As will be seen, however, the available information confirms Ambas-sador Greenstock's statement that the CTC did not monitor the human rights implications of counter-terrorism efforts. It also suggests that the CTC often asked questions without regard to the context of particular countries, including notorious abuses of human rights while countering terrorism in some coun-tries. As will be discussed in the next chapter, the CTC's recorded interactions with Egypt provide some particularly egregious examples of this phenomenon.

Kim Lane Scheppele has documented how the CTC "tried to push coun-tries," such as Mexico, that tried to resist criminalization of terrorism and that wished to rely on existing criminal law. As she has argued, "the CTC also seems to have placed an international imprimatur on definitions of terrorism that sweep up political dissidents, minority religious practitioners, and those who simply hang around with suspicious people, along with those who might actually commit heinous terrorist acts."[82] In later work, Professor Scheppele has stressed how countries responded to the international mandate in a manner that she characterized as the "parallel play" of children.[83] The CTC triggered this "parallel play," but it did not reprimand the states who hit, bullied, and acted out in the course of enacting and implementing their new counter-terrorism laws and policies. Although the CTC has not imposed sanctions on non-compliant states, it has bestowed some degree of legitimacy on their counter-terrorism efforts.

The CTC's approach to human rights was controversial within the UN system. In 2001, the UN high commissioner for human rights called on the

---

[81] Country reports used to be posted on the CTC's Web site, but this practice has stopped without explanation. See http://www.un.org/en/sc/ctc/resources/index.html.

[82] Kim Lane Scheppele, "The Migration of Anti-Constitutional Ideals," in *The Migration of Constitutional Ideas*, ed. Sujit Choudhry (New York: Cambridge University Press, 2006), at 367.

[83] Kim Lane Scheppele, "The International Standardization of National Security Law" (2010) 4 Journal of National Security Law and Policy 437, at 450.

CTC to appoint human rights experts.[84] A few months after Ambassador Greenstock's 2002 declaration that the CTC would not monitor human rights performance, the UN high commissioner for human rights, the late Sergio Viera de Mello, addressed the CTC about his concerns that too many states were "enacting anti-terrorism legislation that is too broad in scope (namely, that allows for the suppression of activities that are, in fact, legitimate), or who are seeking to fight terrorism outside the framework of the court system. In other words, I am concerned that yet one more casualty of the terrorist has been the erosion in some quarters of fundamental civil and political rights." He told the CTC,

> My Office is at your disposal to engage systematically and regularly with you on relevant human rights issues. I say this with full appreciation that yours is not a human rights forum. Our intention is not to turn you into one: rather it is to assist you in encouraging the non-abuse of 1373; in other words, that it is not used for purposes other than those strictly intended by the Security Council or which are not permitted, in any circumstance, by our human rights laws. To that end, I would urge you to consider once more the value of appointing a human rights advisor to the CTC. I for one am convinced that this would only strengthen our collaborative efforts in fighting terrorism.[85]

Despite these calls, a human rights expert would not be added to the CTC until 2005. The addition of this expert was part of a revitalization of the CTC through the creation of an executive directorate that originally had about 25 experts and now has 40 staff, including 20 legal experts focusing on various compliance issues.[86] One human rights expert is better than none;

---

[84] E. J. Flynn, "The Security Council's Counter-Terrorism Committee and Human Rights" (2007) 7 Human Rights Law Review 371, at 376.

[85] Address by the high commissioner on human rights, October 21, 2002, at http://www.un.org/sc/ctc/documents/HC.htm.

[86] E. J. Flynn, "The Security Council's Counter-Terrorism Committee and Human Rights" (2007) 7 Human Rights Law Review 371, at 381. This revitalization was forwarded by Security Council Resolution 1535 (2004), which, in its preamble, reminded states of international human rights obligations but otherwise focused on issues of implementing 1373 and capacity building. In addition, a CTC report calling for its own revitalization mentioned the need for a new executive director to liase with the high commissioner on human rights and human rights organization but did not otherwise focus on human rights issues. *Proposal for the Revitalization of the CTC*, S/2004/124, February 19, 2004. A report by the chair of the CTC to the Security Council in January 2004 did not even mention human rights concerns. *Report of the Chair of the CTC to Security Council*, S/2004/70, 26 January, 2004. A 2008 report on the future of the CTC's executive directorate does not contain the term *human rights*; instead, it focuses on the need for outreach, communication, and technical assistance. See *Organizational Plan for the Counter-Terrorism Committee Executive Directorate*, S/2008/80, February 8, 2008. The work of this committee has been extended to 2013 in Security Council Resolution 1963 (2010).

nevertheless, it hardly amounts to making human rights a priority at the CTC.

Concerns about the CTC's approach to human rights persisted despite some increased emphasis within the CTC and Security Council resolutions on human rights. In 2005, the special rapporteur on respecting human rights while countering terrorism cited many examples of how the CTC had still not given consideration to human rights or the records of countries with poor human rights in its work. He concluded that a review of state reports "reveals that the CTC has shown little, if any, interest in the definition of terrorism at the national level." He warned that some terrorism laws were "designed in bad faith to outlaw political opposition, religious entities, or minority, indigenous or autonomy movements. If the human-rights-conformity of terrorism definitions is not reviewed, then the CTC may end up encouraging the full scope of measures designed to implement resolution 1373 in respect of something that has nothing to do with terrorism."[87] The special rapporteur also noted that the CTC had recommended increased investigative techniques and had neglected distinctions between denial of refugee status and deportation to torture or extradition to face the death penalty.

In 2006, the CTC issued its first human rights guidance, but it was a one-page document providing that the executive directorate should, "as appropriate," provide advice to the CTC on human rights, liase with other bodies, and include human rights in its communication strategies.[88] The CTC's Web site assures that both the CTC and the executive directorate "now routinely take account of relevant human rights concerns in all their activities, including the preparation of preliminary implementation assessments (PIAs) relating to resolution 1373 (2001), country visits and other interactions with Member States."[89] It is, however, difficult to evaluate the CTC's engagement with human rights given the lack of transparency in its work including its unexplained decision to no longer post country reports on its website.

Although some commentators accept that the CTC is becoming more concerned with human rights,[90] there is little concrete evidence that the CTC has

---

[87] Statement by Martin Scheinin, Special Rapporteur on the Promotion and Protection of Human Rights and Fundamental Freedoms while Countering Terrorism, Security Council Counter-Terrorism Committee, New York, October 24, 2005, at http://www.un.org/sc/ctc/pdf/ScheininCTC2005.pdf.

[88] Policy Guidance, PG 2, May 25, 2006, at http://www.un.org/sc/ctc/documents/pg25may06.pdf.

[89] http://www.un.org/sc/ctc/rights.html.

[90] Andrea Bianchi, "Security Council's Anti-Terror Resolutions and Their Implementation by Member States" (2006) 4 Journal of International Criminal Justice 1044; Rosemary Foote, "The United Nations, Counter-Terrorism and Human Rights: Institutional Adaptation and Embedded Ideas" (2007) 29 Human Rights Quarterly 489.

tempered its advice or communication with nations because of human rights concerns. This is especially the case outside the context of Resolution 1624 (2005), which refers to compliance with international human rights law while prohibiting incitement to terrorism.[91] An August 2010 report by the secretary general of the UN responding to a General Assembly resolution stressing the importance of respecting human rights while countering terrorism outlined in detail the many steps taken by the Human Rights Council, treaty bodies, and the Counter-Terrorism Strategy Implementation Task Force on human rights implementation, while simply noting that the CTC will continue to liase with these bodies and respect human rights in its work.[92] The special rapporteur on respecting human rights while countering terrorism remained concerned in 2010 that the publicly available information about the CTC "risks giving the States the impression that turning a blind eye to human rights considerations is acceptable" and may even "risk providing oppressive States with further pretext to crack down on Human Rights defenders."[93] The CTC's mandate and much of its expertise still does not involve human rights. The only specific reference to human rights is found in Resolution 1373, as it relates to the dangers of refugee status being abused by terrorists, and in Resolution 1624, as it relates to laws against the incitement of terrorism. Even assuming that the CTC is now more actively engaged with human rights, however, the initial effects of its lack of concern about human rights will linger as one of the effects of 9/11.

Oren Gross and Fionnuala Ni Aolain observed in 2006 that the CTC now "sits at the apex of the UN's institutional hierarchy" and can "function as a mini–Security Council, with a powerful direct line to the Security Council."[94] The result is executive domination of the type seen in domestic counter-terrorism efforts. An important difference, however, is that neither the Security Council nor the CTC is subject to the same counterweights as the domestic executive, whether from judicial review or from "populist or democratic"

---

[91] The CTC's Web site does assure that both the CTC and the executive directorate "now routinely take account of relevant human rights concerns in all their activities, including the preparation of preliminary implementation assessments (PIAs) relating to resolution 1373 (2001), country visits and other interactions with Member States"; http://www.un.org/sc/ctc/rights.html. The CTC's unexplained decision not to post country reports, however, has taken away even the haphazard transparency provided when countries quote their correspondence with the CTC in subsequent country reports.

[92] Secretary General, *Protecting Human Rights and Fundamental Freedoms While Countering Terrorism*, A/65/224, August 4, 2010, at paras. 8, 37.

[93] *Report of the Special Rapporteur on the Promotion of Human Rights and Fundamental Freedoms While Countering Terrorism*, A/65/258, August 6, 2010, at para. 44.

[94] Oren Gross and Fionnuala Ni Aolain, *Law in Time of Crisis* (New York: Cambridge University Press, 2006) at 404.

forces. Professors Gross and Ni Aolain also express cogent concerns about how Resolution 1373 and the CTC provided "a legitimate basis for illiberal states to act repressively" and to use "the international legal language of anti-terrorism to accomplish anti-democratic domestic goals."[95]

VI. BELATED GUIDANCE ON THE DEFINITION OF TERRORISM: SECURITY COUNCIL RESOLUTION 1566

Resolution 1373 did not provide any guidance about the proper definition of terrorism. Although this lack of guidance reflected a failure to agree on a definition of terrorism, it also ignored resources in international law that could have encouraged states to define terrorism in a restrained manner as they responded to the requirement of Resolution 1373 that terrorism and terrorism financing be treated as serious crimes. Resolution 1373 called on all states to ratify the 1999 Convention on the Suppression of Terrorism Financing but ignored a general definition of terrorism in that convention that focused on intentional killing or causing bodily harm to those not taking an active part in hostilities in an armed conflict in a manner designed to intimidate a population or compel a government to act. This general definition was used by the Supreme Court of Canada in 2002 to define terrorism in Canadian immigration law,[96] but Canada, like many other countries that followed the United Kingdom's Terrorism Act, 2000, defined terrorism much more broadly in its new Anti-Terrorism Act, enacted in time to be featured in Canada's first report to the CTC at the end of 2001.[97]

The reasons for the Security Council's failure to advert to the general definition of terrorism in Resolution 1373 are speculative because of the lack of transparency of the Security Council's hurried deliberations about Resolution 1373. The Security Council may have simply wanted to avoid the controversial definitional issue altogether. The United States, which took the lead in the Resolution 1373 process, may have been concerned that focusing on a definition of terrorism might have suggested that the 9/11 attacks were not an act of armed conflict when, as will be seen in Chapter 4, the idea that the United States was involved in an armed conflict with al Qaeda was and still is a key component of the United States' response to 9/11. For whatever reason, the Security Council delegated the difficult task of defining terrorism to member states and lost an unparalleled opportunity to promote international agreement on a restrained definition of terrorism.

---

[95] Ibid at 398–9.
[97] See Chapter 7.

[96] *Suresh v. Canada* (2002) 1 S.C.R. 3.

The question of the definition of terrorism arose when Resolution 1566 was adopted by the Security Council in October 2004, following killings of more than 320 children and adults by Chechen terrorists in Beslan, Russia. Like Resolution 1373, Resolution 1566 was adopted under Chapter VII of the UN Charter and called on all states to prosecute or extradite those who participate in terrorist acts and to take steps to ensure that terrorism is prevented and punished. The resolution differed from 1373, however, in providing some guidance about the definition of terrorism. It recalled that "criminal acts, including against civilians, committed with the intent to cause death or serious bodily injury, or taking of hostages, with the purpose to provoke a state of terror in the general public . . . intimidate a population or compel a government or an international organization" to act and "which constitute offences" under the international conventions were never justifiable for "political, philosophical, ideological, racial, ethnic, religious,"[98] or other similar reasons. The resolution thus provided some guidance about defining terrorism as a criminal act. It opted for a minimal definition that focused on intentional causing of death and serious injury as well as hostage taking[99] and did not include damage to property or interference with essential services.

Unlike the influential British Terrorism Act, 2000, Resolution 1566 did not define terrorism as acts committed for political or religious motives but rather reaffirmed the traditional criminal law principle that such motives never justified crime. To be sure, the resolution did not address the vexed freedom fighter or state terrorism issues. One reason for this was that Algeria and Pakistan objected to Russian and British proposals to use Resolution 1566 to extend the 1267 listing process to all terrorist groups and not just to al Qaeda. This proposal was rejected because of concerns that Palestinian groups would be listed under the definition proposed in Resolution 1566.[100] Resolution 1566 hardly solved all the definitional problems, but it did provide some guidance.[101]

---

[98] Security Council Resolution 1566, at para. 3.

[99] Michael Scharf has also stressed that the 1566 definition is even more limited as it requires that these acts also be offenses under the existing international conventions. Scharf, "Defining Terrorism as the Peacetime Equivalent of War Crimes: Problems and Prospects" (2004) 36 Case Western Reserve Journal of International Law 359, at 362.

[100] "UN Council Initiates Effort against Terror," New York Times, October 9, 2004.

[101] The 1566 definition and the one adopted later in 2004 by the UN High-Level Panel on Threats, Challenges, and Changes have been criticized for their focus on civilians or noncombatants in part because such definitions "might not include the attack on the Pentagon, but for the fact that it involved the hijacking of a civilian airliner." Adam Roberts, "Countering Terrorism: A Historical Perspective," in *Counterterrorism: Democracy's Challenge*, ed. Andrea Bianchi and Alexis Keller (Oxford: Hart, 2008), at 8. As suggested above, however, even an attack not using civilians could still be classified as terrorism under the general definition because the victims in the Pentagon were not engaged in hostilities in an armed conflict.

Nevertheless, as Ben Saul has concluded, "the definition may be too little, too late"[102] because most states had already responded to Resolution 1373, frequently with much broader and more controversial definitions of terrorism. The committee created by Resolution 1566 has accomplished nothing, in part because of the continued definitional impasse and in part because even the limited 1267 listing of terrorists associated with al Qaeda has increasingly been challenged as an unfair and secret process making it difficult to extend listing to other terrorists.

VII. SECURITY COUNCIL RESOLUTION 1540 AND THE DANGERS OF TERRORISTS USING WEAPONS OF MASS DESTRUCTION

In April 2004, the Security Council enacted Resolution 1540, requiring all states to take steps to ensure that nuclear, chemical, or biological weapons of mass destruction not be developed by or transferred to nonstate actors "in particular for terrorist purposes."[103] This resolution, like Resolutions 1267 and 1373, was enacted as a mandatory measure to protect international peace and security under Chapter VII of the UN Charter, and it imposed permanent and general obligations on all states. Like the two earlier resolutions, Resolution 1540 also created a committee to hear reports from states. The three resolutions are the main pillars in the Security Council's approach to terrorism.

Although the actual threat presented by nuclear, chemical, or biological terrorism is a matter of dispute, even one successful act of such terrorism has the potential to "make 9/11 a footnote."[104] Resolution 1540 directly and constructively addressed the security of material that could be used for the most deadly forms of terrorism. Although some restrictions contemplated in Resolution 1540 were required to be implemented through criminal law restrictions on the sale and possession of chemical, biological, and nuclear material, much of the resolution focused on administrative regulation of such dangerous substances. Such administrative and supply-side strategies may help prevent accidents involving nuclear, chemical, and biological material.[105] Unlike Resolutions 1267 and 1373, Resolution 1540 does not depend on the correct identification

---

[102] Ben Saul, *Defining Terrorism in International Law* (Oxford: Oxford University Press, 2006), at 248.

[103] Security Council Resolution 1540, para. 2.

[104] Graham Allison, *Nuclear Terrorism: The Ultimate Preventable Catastrophe* (New York: Owl Books, 2005), at 203.

[105] For an application of epidemiological principles stressing harm prevention and reduction rather than causal agents to terrorism, see Kent Roach, *September 11: Consequences for Canada* (Montreal: McGill/Queens Press, 2003), chap. 7.

and deterrence of actual terrorists. As such, it presents much less danger to human rights than Resolutions 1267 or 1373, which ran a risk of false positives by making listed terrorists outlaws on the basis of secret evidence and by inviting states to take a variety of criminal, immigration, and intelligence measures to prevent terrorism. In addition, Resolution 1540 is based on a sounder and less risky regulatory approach than Resolutions 1267 and 1373 because it addresses the danger of false negatives – terrorists who were not identified or deterred – by attempting to deprive terrorists of their most deadly weapons.

Unfortunately, Resolution 1540 came after false claims about weapons of mass destruction were used to justify the American-led invasion of Iraq and in the midst of growing pushback in the General Assembly against the new legislative role that the Security Council had assumed in Resolutions 1267 and 1373. The result was that Resolution 1540, which was initiated by the United Kingdom and supported by the United States, enjoyed less support than the previous Chapter VII resolutions on terrorism. Resolution 1540 was unanimously adopted, but only after robust debate, including participation from states that were not members of the Security Council. "Several states, especially in the developing world, expressed substantial doubt as to the legality and legitimacy of the Council's lawmaking."[106] Although 128 states had reported to the 1540 committee by 2006, 62 member states had yet to submit their first reports, and many of these states had capacity problems both with respect to compliance and reporting.[107]

The Security Council responded by expanding the committee's mandate, and in 2008, the committee stated that 155 states had reported.[108] The committee's most recent report, however, continued to emphasize that full compliance with Resolution 1540 would require more time and capacity building. The theme of capacity building has dominated the work of the 1540 committee much more than the work of either the 1267 or 1373 committees. The emphasis on capacity building may well be appropriate, but it should also be similarly reflected in the work of the other committees, which, with respect to terrorism financing, require sophisticated regulation of all forms of financial institutions. To be sure, the CTC made countries aware that donor states could be of technical assistance in capacity building, but it, as well as FATF, insisted that states develop terrorism financing regimes regardless of the sophistication of their financial institutions.

---

[106] Alexander Marschik, "The Security Council's Role: Problems and Prospects in the Fight against Terrorism," in Nesi, *International Cooperation in Counter-Terrorism*, at 78; Johnstone, "Legislation and Adjudication in the UN Security Council," at 290–4.

[107] *Report of the 1540 Committee*, S/2006/257, 2006.

[108] *Report of the 1540 Committee*, S/2008/493, 2008, at para. 17.

The 1540 process of controlling substances that could make terrorism much more deadly is a promising strategy that does not threaten human rights as much as Resolution 1267 or 1373 does. For example, reports that countries with poor human rights records file with the 1540 committee generally focus on matters such as security surrounding plants and warehouses that may contain chemical or biological matters as opposed to police powers and laws that may be used to detain and mistreat terrorist suspects.[109] Despite this promise, the implementation of Resolution 1540 seems much more modest and tentative than the implementation of Resolutions 1267 and 1373. The resistance to Resolution 1540 as legislation by the Security Council may be overcome, at least with respect to nuclear terrorism, by countries ratifying and implementing the 2005 International Convention for the Suppression of Acts of Nuclear Terrorism. That convention requires states to punish offenses relating to nuclear terrorism, but like Resolution 1540, it focuses on nonstate actors and exempts the use of nuclear weapons by states from its terms.[110] The Security Council has focused on terrorism by nonstate actors because it is easier to take tough measures against them than against state actions, including those that may contribute to terrorism or result in non-terrorist nuclear disasters that threaten human security.

VIII. SECURITY RESOLUTION 1624 AND THE EMPHASIS ON SPEECH ASSOCIATED WITH TERRORISM

Security Council Resolution 1624, adopted on September 14, 2005,[111] called on all states to enact offenses against the incitement of terrorism. Enacted two months after the London bombings, the resolution was sponsored by the United Kingdom and defended by Prime Minister Blair. At the enactment of the resolution, Blair defended the invasion of Iraq and declared that "the root cause of terrorism was not a decision on foreign policy, however contentious, but a doctrine of fanaticism." He stressed that it was necessary to respond not only to the methods of terrorists but also to "their motivation, their twisted reasoning, wretched excuses for terror . . . [and their] poisonous propaganda."[112] Because it did not define either terrorism or incitement, Resolution 1624 meant that states that already had broad definitions of terrorism

---

[109] See, e.g., Egypt County Report, December 29, 2004, and supplementary report, March 29, 2010.

[110] International Convention on the Suppression of Nuclear Terrorism, 2005, Article 4.

[111] S/Res/1624 (2005).

[112] United Nations Security Council press release, September 14, 2005, at http://www.un.org/News/Press/docs/2005/sc8496.doc.htm.

could enact new offenses criminalizing the incitement of terrorism and that such offenses could be used selectively or against legitimate dissent. Another danger was that such laws would be used to target speakers who might not share Prime Minister Blair's strongly held views that terrorism was not caused by foreign policy decisions.

In its focus on speech and extremism, Resolution 1624 was motivated by Karl Lowenstein's theory of militant democracy, which suggests that democracies need to be more aggressive toward those who do not believe in democracy.[113] Prime Minister Blair appealed to militant democracy when he warned, at the enactment of Resolution 1624, that "terrorism was a movement with an ideology and strategy. That strategy was not just to kill, but also to cause chaos and instability, to divide and confuse. Terrorism would not be defeated until the Council's determination was as complete as theirs and until its defence of freedom was as absolute as their fanaticism, and until its passion for democracy was as great as their passion for tyranny."[114] Even leaving aside the debate about whether militant democracy is justified, Resolution 1624 invited many non-democratic states to use the speech regulation techniques of militant democracy.

Even the softer third paragraph of Resolution 1624 perhaps unconsciously echoed a simplistic and dangerous "clash of civilianizations"[115] thesis by calling on states "to enhance dialogue and broaden understanding among civilizations" before stressing the need "to take all measures as may be necessary and appropriate in accordance with their obligations under international law to counter incitement of terrorist acts motivated by extremism and intolerance and to prevent the subversion of educational, cultural and religious institutions by terrorists and their supporters."[116] Such sentiments would mean one thing when played out in London and the rest of Europe but quite another when implemented in Cairo under Hosni Mubarak or Damascus under Bashar al-Assad, where they could be taken as an international invitation to continue crushing dissent, especially that associated with the Muslim Brotherhood or other Islamic parties. Resolution 1624 received more debate and deliberation within the Security Council than Resolution 1373, but it was also paired or logrolled with another resolution on humanitarian intervention in Africa in a

---

[113] Karl Lowenstein, "Militant Democracy and Fundamental Rights" (1937) 31 American Political Science Review 417, at 638. See generally Andras Sajo, ed., *Militant Democracy* (Amsterdam, Netherlands: Eleven, 2004).

[114] United Nations Security Council press release, September 14, 2005, at http://www.un.org/News/Press/docs/2005/sc8496.doc.htm.

[115] Samuel Huntington, *The Clash of Civilizations and the Making of a New World Order* (New York; Touchstone, 1997).

[116] S/Res/1625 (2005), para. 3.

successful attempt to gain unanimous approval by the 15 states on the Security Council.[117]

The United Kingdom's sponsorship of Resolution 1624 is significant. The regulation of speech was an important part of British colonial emergency rule that, as will be seen in the next chapter, still makes its influence felt in countries such as Singapore and Israel. The United Kingdom itself had a long history of regulating speech associated with terrorism in Northern Ireland: broadcast bans were used by the British government against the Irish Republican Army. Section 59 of the Terrorism Act, 2000, made it an offense to incite terrorism overseas, and Section 11 made it an offense to be a member of or to profess membership in a terrorist group. The House of Lords has held this latter offense to be a proportionate restriction on freedom of expression simply by concluding that "the necessity of attacking terrorist organizations is . . . clear" and without any sustained analysis of how such crimes will prevent terrorism or whether there are effective alternatives that constitute a less drastic infringement of freedom of association and freedom of expression.[118] The theory of militant democracy also finds some support in Article 17 of the European Convention on Human Rights, which recognizes that people should not be able to abuse their rights for purposes inconsistent with those rights. As will be seen, speech regulation is a harder sell in the United States which has a more libertarian constitutional culture than Europe.

The Blair government encountered more resistance in Parliament than in the Security Council in producing legislation aimed at speech association with terrorism, again underlining the failure of the Security Council to work as a deliberative body that tested and resisted proposals. As examined in chapter 5, the Blair government had to retreat in Parliament from its original proposals to criminalize the glorification of terrorism. Resolution 1624 was also a bit of a retreat for the Security Council because unlike Resolutions 1267, 1373, and 1540, it was not enacted under Chapter VII of the UN Charter. Nevertheless, it placed pressure on states to consider the adequacy of their existing laws against incitement of terrorism. Resolution 1624 differs from Resolution 1373 in specifically reminding states of their obligations concerning international human rights. The CTC has paid more attention to international human rights in monitoring the response of countries to Resolution 1624 than to Resolution 1373. It has issued two reports on how states have complied with Resolution 1624. Both reports have noted that a number of states have stressed concerns about freedom of expression, and a few even require some degree of

---

[117] S/Res/1624 (2005) .
[118] *Sheldrake v. DPP; Attorney General's Reference (No. 4 of 2002)* (2005) 1 A.C. 264, at para. 54.

probability that the incitement will result in a terrorist act, while most do not. The CTC's reports, however, follow its original nonconfrontational approach by being written in a neutral tone, with no specific country being identified and no explicit criticism of any particular country.[119] To be sure, these reports feature discussion of human rights, but more as a bureaucratic checkoff. As Yael Ronen has noted in an article otherwise supportive of criminalizing incitement to terrorism, the reports do not demonstrate "any engagement by the CTC with the various States to promote best practices" and raise the question of whether the CTC's role with respect to human rights is credible or whether it "operates as a tool only for strengthening counter-terrorism measures."[120]

It is also striking that far fewer states have reported back to the CTC about Resolution 1624 than about Resolution 1373. Of the 88 states that have reported back to the CTC on Resolution 1624, less than half have enacted new laws. This undoubtedly reflects that 1624 was not enacted under Chapter VII, but may also suggest that states have been influenced by some of the criticisms of the CTC. At the same time, some of the states that have issued reports under Resolution 1624 have sought to justify very broad and repressive laws under the guise of compliance with the resolution. Algeria, for example, has cited a 1995 law that criminalizes the justification and encouragement of terrorism and a 2001 law that prohibits speech "contrary to the noble mission or the mosque or likely to undermine social cohesion."[121] Russia similarly cited a broad 2006 law that applies not only to incitement to commit a terrorist act but also to "advocacy of the idea of terrorism" or information "supporting or justifying" terrorism as evidence of its compliance with Resolution 1624.[122]

The United States explained that the First Amendment, as interpreted in *Brandenburg v. Ohio*,[123] meant that "most terrorist propaganda" and even calls for terrorist violence could not be criminalized in the absence of proof of some probability that unlawful activity would result. At the same time, the United States held open the possibility of using seditious conspiracy law to criminalize some speech as well as the use of immigration law excluding individuals and

---

[119] *Report of the CTC on the Implementation of Resolution 1624*, S/2006/737, September 15, 2006; *Report of the CTC on the Implementation of Resolution 1624*, S/2008/29, January 21, 2008. The 2008 reports observes that less than half of the 88 states that have reported have enacted specific incitement laws and instead view existing laws as sufficient to comply with the resolution. Ibid., at para. 6.

[120] Yael Ronen, "Incitement to Terrorist Acts under International Law" (2010) 23 Leiden Journal of International Law 645.

[121] *Algeria Report to the CTC*, S/2007/138, March 12, 2007.

[122] *Russia Report to the CTC*, S/2006/446, June 30, 2006.

[123] 395 U.S. 444 (1969).

designating groups as terrorist organizations on the basis of speech.[124] Countries that may be constitutionally unable to implement Resolution 1624 directly can indirectly implement it through the shortcut of immigration law.

Resolution 1624 endorses laws that incite terrorism, despite a lack of clarity about the effectiveness of such laws in preventing terrorism.[125] The possibility that terrorist speech prosecutions could counter-productively result in greater attention and sympathy for those who glorify and incite terrorism should not be dismissed, nor should the possibility that driving extremism underground and onto the diffuse Internet may make it more difficult to identify and monitor terrorist suspects. Although Tony Blair and the Security Council were confident that there is a causal relation between extremist speech and terrorism, not enough is known about why people commit acts of terrorism, and extremist beliefs and even incitement are not necessarily related to actual preparation to commit acts of violence. As with terrorism financing, the Security Council promoted a counter-terrorism instrument that may not be effective and that will harm human rights.

IX. ATTEMPTS TO REFORM THE SECURITY COUNCIL'S COUNTER-TERRORISM WORK

Reform of the 1267 Listing Process

Just as the CTC has, especially in relation to Resolution 1624, attempted to respond to criticism that it has ignored human rights in its work, attempts have been made to reform the 1267 listing process to respond to growing criticism. In 2006, Resolution 1735 decided that all states, when proposing names to be added to the list, should provide as much supporting information as possible in an attempt to increase the transparency, effectiveness, and fairness of the listing process. At the same time, however, the resolution confirmed the traditional intelligence rule of control over the information by providing that no information should be released without the originating state's permission.[126]

Resolution 1730 adopted a delisting procedure that created a focal point to receive requests for delisting from entities on the consolidated list. This process was in addition to the process by which a listed person could approach his or her

---

[124] *United States Report to the CTC*, S/2006/397, June 16, 2006.

[125] Experts in terrorism do not agree on basic information such as the nature and role of al Qaeda let alone the motivating triggers of terrorism. See Bruce Hoffman "The Myth of Grass-Roots Terrorism" *Foreign Affairs* May/June 2008; Marc Sageman "Does Osama Still Call the Shots?" *Foreign Affairs* July/August 2008.

[126] Security Council Resolution 1735, paras. 5 and 6.

state of citizenship or residence and the state could hold bilateral consultations with the state that had first proposed that the entity be listed. Resolution 1730, however, affirmed the intergovernmental nature of the delisting process by providing that once a delisting request had gone before the 1267 committee, the request for delisting should be deemed rejected if no committee member recommended delisting.

Resolution 1822 (2008) directed the 1267 committee to provide a narrative summary of the reasons for the listing and make these available on the committee's Web site. Narrative summaries attempt to provide public reasons for the listing, but they invariably protect the sources and methods used to obtain the intelligence. The result is that most narrative summaries contain only bald and unsourced allegations that a named person has various associations with al Qaeda and played various roles within al Qaeda. There is no way to know under what conditions and from whom this information was obtained. The narrative summaries may include information confirmed from multiple reliable sources, but they may also include information obtained under duress and even torture. Some narrative summaries are infected by reasonable suspicions that some of the information may have been derived from torture. The narrative summary supporting a 1267 listing of a Canadian for example features his association with abu Zabaydah but does not reveal if this information comes from abu Zabaydah and if so before or after he was subject to multiple waterboardings.[127] Even with respect to information that is confirmed from multiple sources, the information may simply be unreliable intelligence that has been shared and recycled by multiple agencies. The desire of countries to protect the sources and methods used to obtain the intelligence will often prevent effective challenge to the narrative summaries.

Resolution 1904 (2009) replaced the focal point with a new process whereby an ombudsperson will be involved in delisting requests. The ombudsperson is instructed to interact with the 1267 committee and relevant states and UN bodies as well as the entity requesting delisting and then prepare a report for the 1267 committee laying out the information obtained and the "principal arguments concerning the delisting request."[128] In the end, however, the 1267 committee decides the delisting request through its normal procedures, which include working in closed sessions on the basis of consensus, with any disputes being referred to the Security Council, where, presumably, at least

---

[127] Narrative Summary Listing of . A.220.06. ABU SUFIAN AL-SALAMABI MUHAMMED AHMED ABD AL-RAZZIQ June 22, 2009 available at http://www.un.org/sc/committees/1267/ NSQI22006E.shtml.

[128] Security Council Resolution 1904, at Annex 2, para. 7(c).

nine members would have to agree and the five permanent members would have a veto.[129]

The ombudsperson then informs the petitioner of the delisting decision, providing to the extent possible publicly releasable information but also respecting "the confidentiality of Committee deliberations and confidential communications between the Ombudsperson and Member States."[130] Although the ombudsperson can interact with the listed person, he or she is not the ultimate decision maker and cannot provide a judicial remedy. Ombudsperson Kimberly Prost has engaged in energetic outreach and reported that she has accepted 6 petitions for delisting as of January, 2011 and has made 25 requests for information to 17 states in relation to these petitions. To her credit, she has recognized that one of the major challenges will be "access to classified or confidential information" possessed by states. At present, she is dealing with such issues on a case-by-case basis, but has expressed a desire to develop a broader based approach based on agreement or assurances.[131] Even if the Ombudsperson does obtain access to secret information, this will only present problems about how this information can be subject to effective challenge by the petitioner. At present, the Ombudsperson cannot even reveal to a petitioner the identity of the designating state without the state's permission.[132]

A number of domestic courts continue to have problems with the fairness of the 1267 listing process. Although these courts generally eschew any powers directly to review the legality of the Security Council's exercise of its Chapter VII powers, they have generally insisted that such powers should respond to domestic constitutional norms relating to a fair hearing and access to a judicial remedy. In *Kadi and Al Barakaat International Foundation v. Council of the EU and Commission of the EC*,[133] the European Court of Justice invalidated European Union regulations implementing a 1267 listing on the basis that at no time were the listed applicants informed "of the evidence adduced against them that allegedly justified the inclusion of their names"[134] on a list that would freeze their assets and prevent their travel. In response to this ruling, a narrative summary of reasons about Kadi's listing was released by the 1267 committee but was found to be unsatisfactory in follow-up litigation. The European Court was

---

[129] *1267 Committee Guidelines*, at http://www.un.org/sc/committees/1267/pdf/1267_guidelines.pdf.
[130] Ibid., at Annex 2, para. 14.
[131] *Report of the Ombudsperson pursuant to Security Council Resolution 1904* January 24, 2011 S/2001/29 at para 33–35.
[132] Ibid., at para 51.
[133] Joined Cases C-402/05 P and C-415/05 P, *Yassin Abdullah Kadi and Al Barakaat International Foundation v. Council of the EU and Commission of the EC* (ECJ Judgment), September 3, 2008.
[134] Ibid., at para. 346.

not impressed with the addition of an ombudsperson, concluding that "the removal of person from the Sanctions Committee's list requires consensus within the committee. Moreover, the evidence which may be disclosed to the person concerned continues to be a matter entirely at the discretion of the State which proposed that he be included on the Sanctions Committee's list and there is no mechanism to ensure that sufficient information be made available to the person concerned in order to allow him to defend himself effectively."[135] It noted the open-ended nature of the listing and that Kadi had been listed for 10 years. It also found that the "few pieces of information and imprecise allegations"[136] in the narrative summary were insufficient to provide a fair hearing to Kadi.

These and similar challenges to terrorist lists provide a fundamental challenge to a central pillar of terrorism financing regulation that the Security Council has promoted under Resolutions 1267 and 1373. Lists are prepared by international and domestic executives, often on the basis of secret intelligence that will not be disclosed to the listed entity or subject to any adversarial challenge. Listing can be based on vague and politicized intelligence that lumps together very different groups and groups with very different connections to terrorist violence.[137] Lists challenge the separation of powers by fusing legislative, executive, and judicial powers.

Although the Security Council has appointed an ombudsperson to assist applicants with delisting requests, the ombudsperson may not necessarily have access to all the underlying intelligence. Moreover, the ultimate decision whether to delist remains a consensual and intergovernmental one made by those represented on the Security Council and including the veto of the permanent members, who also control the bulk of the intelligence used in listing. A report issued at the end of 2010 outlined how the listing process, even as reformed by the creation of an ombudsperson, still violates various human rights, such as the right to a hearing and a judicial remedy, and called for its abolition. A preface by Professor Martin Scheinin, the UN special rapporteur on the promotion of human rights while countering terrorism, stresses that the reasons given by the 1267 committee for listing are "something quite different from actual evidence of links with terrorism. In fact, it appears that listing

---

[135] *Kadi v. European Commission (Judgment of the General Court, Seventh Chamber)*, September 30, 2010, at para. 128; http://eur-lex.europa.eu/LexUriServ/LexUriServ.do?uri=CELEX: 62009A0085:EN:HTML.

[136] Ibid., at para. 174.

[137] Chantal De Jonge Oudraat and Jean-Luc Marret, "The Uses and Abuses of Terrorist Designation Lists," in *The Consequences of Counterterrorism*, ed Martha. Crenshaw (New York: Russell Sage, 2010).

decisions can be made on the basis of assertions by some states that they possess intelligence information, rather than through sharing the evidence with others. Just one look at the composition of the Security Council at any given time will be enough . . . to realize that the 15 states running the show are not willing to share their intelligence with each other."[138]

The human rights costs of listings are being revealed by the growing numbers of domestic challenges. The effectiveness of listing and terrorism financing regulation in general remains in doubt, especially as al Qaeda evolves into an ideology that inspires acts of terrorism as well as an organization that funds terrorism. Listing may be an inefficacious example of fighting the last war when it was still possible to imagine identifying all the associates of al Qaeda central. The report of the 1267 monitoring team issued in September 2010 suggests that many states support listing, but more as a symbolic gesture of disapproval than as an actual legal resource that can be used to prevent terrorism.[139] Similar defenses have been made of domestic proscription, especially in the United Kingdom.[140] Listing may continue as a symbolic gesture, even though it has failed to keep pace with the post-9/11 diffusion of al Qaeda, and it has failed to provide the listed outlaw with a judicial remedy.

X. THE SECURITY COUNCIL'S POST-9/11 RECORD

The Security Council's post-9/11 performance leaves much to be desired. Resolution 1373 only paid scant attention to human rights and offered states no guidance about how to define terrorism or how to deal with suspected terrorists who would be tortured if returned to their country of citizenship. The Security Council has attempted to reform the 1267 listing process, but indirect domestic challenges to the listing process provide the only judicial remedy and one that will often not produce true merit-based review, given the refusal of states to disclose the grounds or the intelligence behind the listing.[141]

Resolution 1540 used an alternative strategy by focusing on nuclear, chemical, and biological materials that could be used by terrorists. Although the

---

[138] European Center for Constitutional and Human Rights, *Blacklisted: Targeted Sanctions, Preemptive Security and Fundamental Rights* (Berlin: European Center for Constitutional and Human Rights, 2010), at 4.

[139] The committee concluded that "states see the value of listing as much in the symbolic and awareness-raising aspects of the regime as in its restrictive effect" and noted support for listing of those who are imprisoned or who provided ideological as opposed to financial support to al Qaeda. *Report of the 1267 Monitoring Team*, S/2010/497, September 29, 2010, at paras. 62–3.

[140] See Chapter 5.

[141] Craig Forcese and Kent Roach, "Limping into the Future: The 1267 Committee at the Cross Roads" (2011) 42(2) George Washington International Law Review (forthcoming).

1540 process presents less of a danger to human rights than the processes contemplated by Resolutions 1267 and 1373, there was much less support for its work. The council's constructive focus on the dangers of terrorists gaining access to nuclear, biological, or chemical materials was, unfortunately, a victim of bad timing coming after the Iraqi weapons of mass destruction debacle and growing resistance to the legislative role of the Security Council.

The Security Council has flexed its Chapter VII muscles, but it has lurched from trend to trend with respect to its new legislative role over counterterrorism. It started with the asset freeze and travel ban of 1267 and continued to invest heavily in terrorism financing regulation even after the 1267 bans failed to prevent 9/11, the most expensive act of terrorism in history. Resolution 1373 encouraged states to use immigration law as antiterrorism law, even though subsequent events underlined the dangers of ignoring homegrown terrorism and immigration law may simply export terrorists to states with less developed controls. It then responded to the London bombings through the blunt instrument of promoting offenses that criminalized the incitement of terrorism. This approach follows some European concepts of militant democracy and Prime Minister Blair's strong beliefs that the cause of terrorism is a cancerous fanaticism but plays less well in many other parts of the world. Resolution 1624 includes references to the need to respect international human rights norms, but the role played by the CTC in these matters is uncertain. In any event, the efficacy of Resolution 1624 remains speculative as the links between ideas and incitement and actual preparation and commission of violence are not clear.

Trends in antiterrorism laws promoted by the Security Council, unlike trends in fashions, do not fade away; rather they build and feed on each other. The emphasis in Resolution 1624 on speech and extremism reflects the failure of past initiatives, including the focus on the financing of terrorism and the use of immigration law as antiterrorism law in Resolution 1373. In other words, laws against the financing of terrorism and the use of immigration law as antiterrorism law were unable to stop low-cost acts of terrorism by citizens such as the 2005 London bombings. Resolution 1624 added incitement to the Security Council's arsenal of antiterrorism instruments while not rethinking the previous strategies that failed to prevent terrorism. Offenses of incitement or encouragement of terrorism can aggravate the danger of overbroad definitions of terrorism that were crafted in part because the Security Council failed to provide guidance on the proper definition of terrorism. They will also be applied in a context in which many Western states have, through the use of immigration law and other measures, focused on Arab and Muslim communities as likely sources of terrorism. They could even be counter-productive in convincing some people that states are attacking Islam and ignoring Muslim grievances.

What can be done to improve the Security Council's performance on terrorism issues? Even the best policy making in the terrorism context may often lag behind the constantly changing nature of terrorism. The Security Council should not be criticized too harshly for not anticipating the changing nature of al Qaeda. In addition, some of the blame for the Security Council's performance must be placed on the General Assembly for its continued failure to reach a consensus on the definition of terrorism and for not agreeing on a comprehensive antiterrorism strategy until 2006, after the Security Council had established the main pillars of its problematic approach to terrorism. In the future, however, the Security Council should take its cues from the General Assembly's strategy, which, as will be seen, is a balanced and comprehensive strategy.

A case can be made for both increasing and consolidating the resources of the various Security Council counter-terrorism committees. The executive directorate of the CTC was not in place until the fall of 2005 and this may have adversely affected the CTC's work. Even if the experts in the CTC were combined with experts on the other Security Council committees and the counter-terrorism experts in the United Nations office on Drugs and Crime, they would still only amount to about 60 experts with a budget between $17-18 million US. Proposals to move the committees from New York to the less political and more technical drugs and crime office in Vienna have been made,[142] but they beg the question of whether a consolidated committee would be any more concerned about the human rights implications of counter-terrorism work or better able to integrate counter-terrorism into good governance reforms.

There are serious arguments that the Security Council lacks the power to legislate and that it should have relied more on consensual treaty making. Although the council, with Resolution 1373, urged countries to ratify the 1999 Financing Convention, and many did so, it did not promote its general definition of terrorism as a precursor to a general international convention on terrorism. Such an approach would have produced a more consensual and sustainable international framework for combating terrorism. Many countries in the wake of the international condemnation of 9/11 might have agreed to a general convention based on such a definition while deferring many other difficult issues relating to national liberation movements and state terrorism

---

[142] Eric Rosand and in *Uniting Against Terror* ed David Cortright and George Lopez eds (Cambridge: MA: MIT Press, 2007) at 70-71; David Cortright et al "Global Cooperation Against Terror Evaluating the United Nations Counter-Terrorism Committee" in ibid at 27.

to the evolving laws of war. The Security Council missed an opportunity to push the consensual development of a better international counter-terrorism framework.

If the Security Council is going to continue to legislate, it should at least borrow some of the checks and balances of democratic domestic legislative processes. Attempts should be made to increase deliberation both within the 15-member Security Council and outside the council. In this respect, the 1540 process, which included months of deliberation and involvement of non–Security Council members, was much to be preferred to the rushed and U.S.–dominated process that led to Resolution 1373.[143] It might be helpful to ask the human rights commissioner or some other body with expertise in human rights to prepare reports on the implications of proposed Security Council antiterrorism resolutions and to allow countries outside the Security Council to comment on proposed Chapter VII resolutions. There is also a need to allow individuals affected by the Security Council to seek meaningful judicial remedies against the council from within the UN system. Failure to provide such remedies will, as has occurred with respect to terrorist listing under Resolution 1267, require individuals to seek indirect domestic remedies and place states in the impossible position of either complying with domestic due process or Chapter VII mandates from the Security Council.

One of the defining features of legislation by the Security Council is its permanent nature and that it is not limited to specific wars or conflicts. Resolutions 1267, 1373, and 1540 all impose perpetual obligations on states. Some form of review and sunset is required. The 1267 process, in particular, is a prime candidate for such review, given that much of the intelligence said to justify the listings may be dated. The changing nature of al Qaeda, including the death of bin Laden, threatens to render the idea of an al Qaeda consolidated list somewhat quaint. The Security Council needs to be able to exit or ramp down counter-terrorism strategies that may no longer be effective and/or have received widespread criticism for their effects on human rights.

The Security Council and the 1267, counter-terrorism, and 1540 committees might benefit from having a membership that goes beyond the council and includes representatives of other parts of the UN system, including more direct representation from the various rights-protection bodies of the UN. In addition, there should be independent human rights reviews and audits of the work of the CTC, the 1267 committee, and the 1540 committee, including country reports submitted to those committees. Those committees, particularly the

---

[143] Roberto Lavalle, "A Novel, If Awkward, Exercise in International Law-Making – Security Council Resolution 1540" (2004) Netherlands International Law Review 411; Johnstone, "Legislation and Adjudication in the UN Security Council."

CTC, must work harder to be more transparent about their interactions with countries and should conduct joint country visits along with those from the rights-protection wing of the UN.

The Security Council should be more concerned with the danger that countries with poor human rights records will seek to justify repressive practices and laws under Security Council mandates. It should recognize that shortcuts, such as the use of immigration law as antiterrorism law, long-term administrative detention, and the abuse and torture of terrorist suspects, not only violate human rights but are not sustainable or effective security policies, especially from a global perspective. The Security Council and its committees will have to continue, as in the 1267 process, to be responsive to domestic due process challenges. It should recognize that the Security Council, like domestic legislators, has made some mistakes in responding to 9/11, especially in underestimating the value of respecting human rights and overestimating the importance of lists and other laws aimed at terrorism financing. Reviews should evaluate both the effectiveness of the various counter-terrorism measures that the Security Council has promoted and mandated as well as their effects on human rights. As will be seen, the General Assembly has taken a more integrated and holistic approach to counter-terrorism.

XI. THE GENERAL ASSEMBLY'S 2006 COUNTER-TERRORISM STRATEGY

In September 2006, all 191 member states of the UN unanimously adopted the UN Global Counter-Terrorism Strategy. Groundwork for this strategy was laid in 2005 and 2006 by the work of Secretary General Kofi Annan, who stressed the need to respect human rights as a key and integral element of counter-terrorism strategies.[144] The strategy was the first tangible intervention by the General

---

[144] In a 2006 report, the secretary general stressed that "effective counter-terrorism measures and the protection of human rights are not conflicting goals, but complementary and mutually reinforcing ones. Accordingly, the defence of human rights is essential to the fulfilment of all aspects of a counter-terrorism strategy. The central role of human rights is therefore highlighted in every substantive section of this report, in addition to a section on human rights per se." Secretary General, *Uniting against Terrorism: Recommendations for a Global Counter-Terrorism Strategy*, A/60/825, April 27, 2006, at para. 5. In 2006, Secretary General Annan wrote a letter to the president of the Security Council, never released but subsequently read into the record, that stressed that those subject to 1267 listing "[have] a right to review by an effective review mechanism. The effectiveness of that mechanism will depend on its impartiality, degree of independence, and ability to provide an effective remedy, including lifting of the measure and/or, under specific conditions to be determined, compensation." As quoted in Carmen Cheung, *The UN Security Council's 1267 Regime and the Rule of Law in Canada* (Vancouver, BC, Canada: British Columbia Civil Liberties Association, 2010), at 18.

Assembly since 9/11 as the Assembly continued to be bogged down in the problems of defining terrorism. The strategy is a balanced and comprehensive framework based on four planks: (1) measures to address conditions conducive to terrorism, (2) measures to prevent and combat terrorism, (3) measures to build capacity to prevent and combat terrorism, and (4) measures to ensure respect for human rights and the rule of law. Like Resolution 1373, the General Assembly's strategy avoided a definition of terrorism. The preamble, however, adverted to some of the definitional issues by recalling "the right to self-determination by peoples which remain under colonial domination or foreign occupation."[145]

The General Assembly's Global Counter-Terrorism Strategy departed from the work of the Security Council and its CTC in its emphasis on both the causes of terrorism and the need to respect human rights while countering terrorism. With respect to the causes of terrorism, the strategy recognizes how unresolved conflicts; dehumanization of victims of terrorism; lack of rule of law and good governance; violation of human rights; and discrimination, including political exclusion and socioeconomic marginalization, contribute to terrorism while, at the same time, do not excuse or justify it. This approach takes a more contextual approach than that taken by the CTC and the Security Council, which, in its follow-up inquiries to states, tended to stress technical issues of compliance without apparent regard for the capacity of the particular state or its history and human rights record in combating terrorism. The General Assembly also took a more nuanced approach to the causes of terrorism than Security Council Resolution 1624, which, following the views of Prime Minister Blair, ascribes terrorism simply to the "extremism and intolerance" of those who would incite terrorism.

The General Assembly placed more emphasis on respecting human rights than the Security Council. It stressed that effective counter-terrorism measures and respect for human rights "are not conflicting goals" but are "complementary and mutually reinforcing." It emphasized the important role played by the rights-protection bodies of the UN such as the high commissioner for human rights, who had, at various times, pleaded to be included more in the work of the CTC. The preamble to the plan looked beyond a post-9/11 focus on Islamic terrorism by stating that terrorism cannot and should not be associated with "any religion, nationality, civilianization or ethnic group."

At the same time, the General Assembly's plan should not be dismissed as being soft on terrorism or dismissive of the actions taken by the Security Council. It echoed many of the themes found in the Security Council's

---

[145] A/Res/60/288.

counter-terrorism work, including enhanced international cooperation, laws against terrorism financing, assurance that refugee status is not abused, weapons control, and the principles of prosecute or extradite. There were, however, some important nuances even with respect to these strategies that distinguished the General Assembly's approach from that of the Security Council. For example, the General Assembly's strategy stressed the need to ensure that the information exchanged be "accurate"; that prosecutions and extraditions respect "human rights law, refugee law and international humanitarian law"; and that the listing of terrorists use "fair and transparent procedures."[46] This latter reference, in 2006, predated much of the Security Council's more recent concerns with attempting to reform the 1267 listing procedure. The strategy also endorsed some new measures that have not been promoted by the Security Council such as the protection of vital infrastructure "as well as the response to terrorist attacks and other disasters."[47] This part of the strategy recognizes that terrorism is not the only threat to security and that some measures, such as emergency preparedness, can respond to a variety of risks, including terrorism. More work, however, can be done in integrating the threat of terrorism with other threats to human security.

The strategy also recognized the whole-of-government response to terrorism that has become prevalent in developed democracies but stressed the need for capacity building to allow all states to participate in such a complex project. The strategy recognized the need for capacity building with respect to intelligence or the exchange of information; policing; border control; aviation and maritime security; banking; control of nuclear, chemical, or radiological materials; and public health systems. It also recognized that the prosecute-or-extradite principle will require states to have assistance in developing and maintaining "effective and rule of law–based national criminal justice systems."[48] In 2008, the General Assembly affirmed this strategy and stressed the role of a Counter-Terrorism Implementation Task Force run out of the Secretary General's Office.[49] It remains to be seen whether this task force can counter-balance the dominance of the Security Council and its committees in the counter-terrorism field and whether the General Assembly's strategy will give greater force to the diffuse but important work done by many UN bodies concerned with rights protection.

Although they have called on the CTC to become involved in implementing the General Assembly's Global Counter-Terrorism Strategy, Millar and Rosand recognize that the CTC is seen by many as a "policeman" with

---

[46] Ibid., at II, paras. 3, 4, 15.
[48] Ibid., at IV, para. 4.

[47] Ibid., at II, para. 18.
[49] A/Res/62/272; also Resolution 60/288.

"questionable 'legislative' authority" wielded by the Security Council as opposed to a "social worker" that is interested in capacity building, human rights,
and the underlying causes of terrorism.[150] Some of the work on bridging the
gaps in the UN system has started with the Security Council and the CTC
becoming more conscious of human rights. In turn, the General Assembly
accepted most of the Security Council's harder strategies, while placing them
in a broader context that includes human rights and the causes of terrorism.
In September 2010, the president of the Security Council implicitly endorsed
many aspects of the General Assembly's approach that had not been traditionally stressed by the Security Council when he addressed the need to examine
the conditions that cause terrorism and the relationship between security,
peace, development, and human rights and the need for capacity building
and respect for good governance and the rule of law.[151] The president's statement, however, needs to be backed by concrete action and better coordination
between the Security Council and other parts of the UN. One possible example would be to include appropriate special rapporteurs in country visits and
reports to ensure that the CTC has a fuller appreciation of the context in a
particular country. Both thematic and country special rapporteurs could assist
the work of the Security Council and its committees and the CTC should
be more transparent about its work. The UN cannot afford to maintain a
bureaucratic and segmented approach in which the human rights implications of antiterrorism measures are left to human rights bodies and in which
the Security Council and CTC act as if human rights were outside their
mandates.

XII. RIGHTS-PROTECTION BODIES

Writing in 2006, Oren Gross and Fionnuala Ni Aolain observed that "specialist
UN human rights institutions have just started to flex some consistent institutional muscle in the post–September 11 context. Increased visibility by these
bodies is an imperative so that some institutional balance can be regained"[152]
from the domination of the Security Council. Much work has been done by
the UN high commissioner for human rights, the Human Rights Commit-
tee/Council, and various special rapporteurs. One of the strengths of the UN
system is its ability to accommodate fairly fundamental disagreements within
its large and fragmented structure. As seen earlier, the special rapporteur on

---

[150] Alistair Millar and Eric Rosand, "Implementing the General Assembly's Global Counter-
Terrorism Strategy in the Asia Pacific" (2007) 3 Asian Security 181, at 193.
[151] *Statement of the President of the Security Council,* S/PRST/2010/19, September 27, 2010.
[152] Gross and Ni Aolain, *Law in Times of Crisis,* at 407.

the promotion of human rights and fundamental freedoms while countering terrorism has not hesitated to criticize the work of the CTC for not giving enough weight to human rights. In 2010, he made an even more fundamental critique of the Security Council's work by arguing that Resolutions 1267 and 1373 should not have been enacted under the mandatory provisions of Chapter VII of the UN Charter relating to international peace and security and recommending that they be reformulated with greater attention to human rights and the treaty-making process.[153]

A joint study by the special rapporteur on the promotion of human rights and fundamental freedoms while countering terrorism, the special rapporteur on torture, and the Working Group on Arbitrary Detention examined global practices involving secret detentions while countering terrorism in 66 different states.[154] As will be discussed in greater detail in Chapter 8, such coordinated transnational studies are important if the accountability gap between domestic systems and transnational cooperation in the countering of terrorism is to be overcome. Various rights-protection bodies have examined topical issues such as privacy rights, the practices of intelligence agencies, equality rights, freedom of religion, the role of human rights defenders, migrants, and targeted killings in the context of post-9/11 terrorism policies. Special rapporteurs concerned with human rights have also made important country visits and issued public reports that are much more transparent than the country visits conducted by the CTC. For example, the special rapporteur on the promotion of human rights and fundamental freedoms while countering terrorism has published extensive reports on country visits to Tunisia, Peru, Egypt, Spain, South Africa, the United States, and Turkey.[155]

The Human Rights Committee indirectly reviewed 1267 listings in a 2008 case in which it held that Belgium had violated articles of the International Covenant on Civil and Political Rights by enforcing a 1267 listing. There were a number of dissenters on the committee, who argued that its decision placed Belgium in an untenable position of complying with the Human Rights Committee but disobeying the Chapter VII obligations of the 1267 regime.

---

[153] *Report of the Special Rapporteur on the Promotion of Human Rights and Fundamental Freedoms While Countering Terrorism*, A/65/258, August 6, 2010, at para. 44.

[154] Joint study on global practices in relation to secret detention in the context of countering terrorism of the Special Rapporteur on the promotion and protection of human rights and fundamental freedoms while countering terrorism, the Special Rapporteur on torture and other cruel, inhuman, or degrading treatment or punishment, the Working Group on Arbitrary Detention, and the Working Group on Enforced or Involuntary Disappearances, A/HRC/13/42.

[155] These reports are all available at http://www2.ohchr.org/english/issues/terrorism/rapporteur/reports.htm.

Fortunately, the successful petitioners in this case were subsequently delisted by the 1267 committee,[156] but there is a judicial as well as democratic deficit in the counter-terrorism work of the Security Council.

The various rights-protection bodies of the UN as well as regional bodies, such as the European Union, and transnational civil society groups, such as the International Commission of Jurists, Human Rights Watch, and Amnesty International, have played important roles in providing some sense of how transnational antiterrorism policies affect human rights. Only transnational bodies such as those in the UN and regional systems can hope to fill fundamental accountability gaps that have emerged with increased and necessary transnational cooperation in the prevention of terrorism.

XIII. INTEGRATING WHOLE-OF-UN APPROACHES TO TERRORISM

The UN, like domestic governments, faces formidable challenges in coordinating the manner in which multiple agencies with different mandates and interests approach the terrorism issue. The challenge is great for the UN because of its extreme fragmentation between the General Assembly, the Security Council, and the various rights-protection bodies. In addition, the rights-protection bodies are themselves fragmented with the overlapping mandates and work of many special rapporteurs, the Human Rights Council, treaty bodies such as the Committee against Torture, and the high commissioner for human rights.

The hard UN, in the form of the Security Council and its committees, has mainly been concerned with ensuring that tough measures are in place with respect to terrorism, whereas the softer UN, in the form of the General Assembly, has also addressed broader issues related to conditions that cause terrorism and promote good governance and the rule of law. The rights-protection side of the UN has been very active since 9/11 and has frequently criticized the antiterrorism actions of governments and the Security Council for infringing on human rights. These criticisms have had some effect, but there is a danger when one side of the UN focuses on human rights and the other side focuses on security. There is a need for better integration that will allow the effectiveness and propriety of counter-terrorism measures to be considered together.

One possible mechanism for coordination of the UN's approach is the Counter-Terrorism Implementation Task Force. It was created in July 2005 and now has representatives from 30 different UN entities, including the CTC and its executive directorate, the 1267 committee, the International Atomic

---

[156] *Sayadi and Vinck v. Belgium* (1472/2006) (2008) CCPR/C/94/D/1472/2006.

Energy Agency, INTERPOL, the World Bank, the World Customs Organization, the International Civil Aviation Organization, the World Health Organization, the UN Office on Drugs and Crime, and the special rapporteur on the promotion and protection of human rights while countering terrorism. This coordinating body has formed several working groups on a variety of issues relating to terrorism financing, use of the Internet for terrorist purposes, preventing and resolving conflict, supporting victims of terrorism, responding to weapons of mass destruction of terrorist attacks, the protection of human rights, and the protection of vulnerable targets. All these working groups address important topics, and they blend some of the priorities of the Security Council (terrorism financing, weapons of mass destruction) with those of the General Assembly (conflict, victims of terrorism) and, furthermore, with those of the rights-protection bodies (human rights). Nevertheless, there is a danger that attempts at coordination will suffer the same fragmentation and diffuseness as the activities being coordinated. It may be better to use the four pillars of the General Assembly's 2006 strategy – (1) conditions or causes of terrorism, (2) measures to prevent terrorism, (3) state and UN capacity to prevent and combat terrorism, and (4) respect for human rights and the rule of law – as the organizing basis for coordination. This strategy would provide a sound basis for organizing counter-terrorism efforts that, unfortunately, were not in place until 2006.

A divide within the UN was also apparent with respect to the American killing of Osama bin Laden. UN Secretary General Ban Ki-moon praised the killing as a "watershed moment in our global fight against terrorism" and the President of the Security Council welcomed news of bin Laden's death. In contrast, the High Commissioner for Human Rights and the special rapporteur on extra judicial executions and protecting human rights while countering terrorism, however, called for more facts to be revealed about the killing to ensure that it complied with international law.[157] There remains a need to integrate the hard side of the UN with its softer rights protection side if the UN's important counter-terrorism work is to be integrated and guided by both concerns about effectively preventing terrorism while also respecting human rights.

xiv. CONCLUSION

The UN has emerged as a very important actor in counter-terrorism since 9/11, but the Security Council's performance has been disappointing. Given the global revulsion at 9/11, it was possible to imagine substantial progress being made on a minimal definition of terrorism, a comprehensive international

---

[157] Steven Edwards, "UN human rights boss questions US on legality of bin Laden killing," *Vancouver Sun*, May 4, 2011; "Statement by the President of the Security Council," May 2, 2011; "Statement by the UN special rapporteurs on Osama bin Laden," May 6, 2011.

convention, and even inclusion of terrorism as a crime that could be prosecuted in the International Criminal Court. Such an approach could have built on the general definition of terrorism in the 1999 Financing Convention as the intentional killing and wounding of those not taking part in hostilities in armed conflict in order to compel governments or intimidate populations. Such an approach would have reaffirmed and strengthened the basic criminal law principle that no political or religious motive or cause justifies the murder of civilians while also delegating some of the more vexed issues of state terrorism and freedom fighting to the evolving laws of war. After years of international disagreement over freedom fighter and state terrorism issues, terrorism could have been seen as a crime equivalent to war crimes, crimes against humanity, and torture.[158] At the very least, 9/11 should have strengthened the traditional principle that states should prosecute or extradite terrorists and terrorist supporters found in their jurisdictions. It also should have led to even greater support for all reasonable measures to ensure that weapons of mass destruction would not fall into the hands of terrorists who, as 9/11 revealed, would not hesitate to use such weapons to inflict great mass casualties.

Instead of this admittedly optimistic picture of what the UN and the international community might have achieved, we have the reality of the Security Council enacting global legislation on counter-terrorism without much regard for either human rights or the effectiveness of the policy instruments that it promoted under its Chapter VII powers relating to international peace and security. Resolution 1373 was, like much domestic legislation enacted in response to horrific acts of terrorism, formulated without full information or adequate time for deliberation. Institutional interests within the UN, including the desire to promote the Financing Convention and the 1267 listing process, explain the emphasis that Resolution 1373 placed on laws against the financing of terrorism. The Security Council focused on what was at hand – measures against terrorism financing – even though those measures failed to prevent 9/11, the most expensive act of terrorism in history.

The Security Council, like domestic executives, acted decisively, but it is not subject to the same legislative, judicial, or democratic checks as the domestic executive. The inability to reform the 1267 listing process to provide those listed with a judicial remedy underlines structural difficulties within the UN that have made it impossible for individuals seeking delisting to obtain a judicial remedy within the UN system. Attempts to reform the listing process will also encounter a reluctance among states, especially the United States which

---

[158] For a pre-9/11 articulation of terrorism as a "'Nuremberg crime' akin to a crime against humanity" and one that would be subject to international regulation, see Irwin Cotler, "Towards a Counter-Terrorism Law and Policy" (1998) 10 Terrorism and Political Violence 1, at 5.

supplies the most intelligence and domestically enjoys very broad state secrets protection, to disclose intelligence that may support the listing. Without such disclosure, the intelligence will not be subject to adversarial challenge. As will be seen, a reluctance to disclose intelligence to judicial processes is a common theme that affects domestic as well as international responses to terrorism. Even leaving aside its due process deficit, terrorism financing laws and related lists do not seem that effective in light of the low costs of much post-9/11 terrorism and the diffusion of al Qaeda. Nevertheless, Resolutions 1267 and 1373 remain permanent Chapter VII measures, and terrorist-financing laws and institutions are now solidly entrenched in most countries and unhelpfully merged with money-laundering laws. Although a critical reevaluation of these international mandates is long overdue, it may be impossible to roll back such laws.

Resolution 1373 also singled out immigration law, especially refugee law, as a focus for antiterrorism efforts, despite that not one of the 9/11 plotters had applied for asylum. Many countries followed the lead of the Security Council and used immigration law as antiterrorism law. This has had adverse effects on human rights because immigration proceedings typically offer less procedural protection for detainees than criminal proceedings and because a number of countries reevaluated detainees' right not to be deported to torture. The focus on immigration law can also have adverse effects on security because it provides no remedy for terrorism by a country's own citizens and because deportation can export terrorism. It is particularly disappointing that the UN promoted the use of immigration law as antiterrorism law because it, unlike nation-states, should have an interest in not deflecting terrorists from country to country and thickening borders. The immigration law approach to terrorism is the antithesis to one in which nations agree on a definition of terrorism and operate under a prosecute-or-extradite principle backstopped by the International Criminal Court.

Unfortunately, Resolution 1373 made no attempt to define terrorism or even to promote the general definition of terrorism found in the 1999 Financing Convention. The Security Council finally addressed this issue in 2004 in Resolution 1566, but its guidance came too late for most countries and did not really advance work on an internationally agreed definition of terrorism because of its reliance on the existing conventions that target particular acts. The General Assembly still remains unable to reach agreement on a definition of terrorism, and many countries have opted for definitions of terrorism much broader than the restrained general definition of the 1999 Financing Convention. The Security Council and its CTC paid inadequate attention to the dangers of broad definitions of terrorism, especially when, in Resolution 1624, it called on states to enact laws prohibiting the incitement of terrorism. Broad definitions of terrorism could have adverse effects on security as well as human rights if they result in a misallocation of limited law enforcement and security intelligence resources.

One potential bright spot in the UN's performance has been Resolution 1540, to control chemical, biological, and nuclear material that might fall into the hands of terrorists, and the 2005 Convention on the Suppression of Nuclear Terrorism. Even if the risks of such forms of terrorism are small, they are worth addressing, especially in light of 9/11. The 1540 committee deserves credit for recognizing that effective controls in this area will require not the simple expedient of enacting new offenses but also capacity building in the relevant states. The 1540 process, however, seems to have been hampered by a belated backlash to the Security Council's novel legislative role pioneered in Resolutions 1267 and 1373. Resistance to the Security Council's legislative role and its challenge to the consensual treaty-making process is justified, but it is unfortunate that this backlash affected regulations that could do more good than Resolutions 1267 and 1373 and certainly less harm.

The failings of the UN's post-9/11 regime underline the need to be concerned about both the effectiveness and the propriety of counter-terrorism measures. Terrorism financing laws and lists undermine the right to a fair trial and a judicial remedy but also seem unable to stop low-cost terrorism by diffuse groups who see al Qaeda more as an ideology than as a central financier. The use of immigration law as antiterrorism law harms human rights, but it also fails to address terrorism by citizens. The ineffectiveness of financing and immigration law in preventing the 2005 London bombings prompted another trend in Resolution 1624 of laws against speech associated with terrorism. The trendy nature of antiterrorism law may result in the exponential growth of antiterrorism law as each new trend is discredited, without hard decisions being made to discard or revise prior policies that have not been effective. Incitement laws produced by Resolution 1624 will build on existing broad definitions of terrorism as well as the focus on newcomer communities that is encouraged by the use of immigration law as antiterrorism law. The cumulative effects of Security Council actions are aggravated by the permanent nature of the legislative obligations that they impose and the lack of sunset or review provisions. Fortunately, there are some signs that domestic courts are forcing the Security Council to reevaluate the 1267 listing process, but this review should extend beyond real due process deficiencies to include a clear-minded evaluation of the efficacy of listing and terrorism financing regulation in light of the evolution of al Qaeda and the low cost of deadly terrorist acts.

3 Countries That Did Not Immediately Respond

I. INTRODUCTION

The 9/11 terrorist attacks came as a shock to many. As discussed in the previous chapter, they resulted in an unprecedented amount of counter-terrorism activity by the United Nations (UN) Security Council, with little attention paid to human rights. A common narrative that emerged from 9/11 was that terrorism was taken more seriously when it came to the West. This narrative underestimated the degree of terrorism experienced in the West and, in particular, in the United Kingdom, where more than 3,000 people also died, albeit over a much longer period, in Northern Ireland. At the same time, however, the narrative was a powerful one because many democracies and the UN were prepared to enact much harsher laws in response to 9/11 than they had enacted in response to previous acts of terrorism. In his pre-9/11 comparative survey, David Charters has found that democracies were more likely to react harshly to prolonged domestic terrorism than international terrorism but that "democratic checks and balances worked" with the harshest states, Britain and Israel, limiting their response to geographically contained areas.[1] As will be seen, the same cannot be said of the post-9/11 democratic experience as even democracies, such as Australia, that had experienced very little terrorism dramatically and quickly expanded their antiterrorism laws.

In this chapter, the focus will be on a number of countries that did not enact massive new antiterrorism laws and programs in response to 9/11 because they already had in place strong antiterrorism measures. The countries examined in this chapter include those with tenuous claims to be democracies and those that had been almost universally criticized before 9/11 for their poor

---

[1] David Charters, "Conclusions: Security and Liberty in the Balance: Countering Terrorism in the Democratic Context," in *The Deadly Sin of Terrorism*, ed. David Charters (Westport, CT: Greenwood Press, 1994), at 223.

human rights records. Egypt under Mubarak and Syria are prototypes of this type of regime. Egyptian president Hosni Mubarak boasted that American renditions revealed the wisdom of his country's harsh approach to terrorism. Such claims need to be critically examined because there are many important legal and practical differences between the counter-terrorism practiced in Egypt or Syria and even the most excessive laws or practices of the United States. Nevertheless, claims that 9/11 revealed Western hypocrisy with respect to human rights should be taken seriously. The United States, in particular, could not effectively criticize human rights abuses in Egypt when, through its foreign aid and its extraordinary rendition program, it supported Egypt's brutal approach to terrorism. The Western example is not lost on countries with poor human rights records. Egypt eventually responded to 9/11 both by prolonging emergency rule and by enacting constitutional amendments in 2007 designed to make the emergency permanent by ensuring that many constitutional rights would not apply to any new antiterrorism law and that the Egyptian president would have explicit constitutional powers to transfer terrorism cases to special security and military courts. After the overthrow of President Mubarak in February 2011, however, constitutional reform proposals that include the abolition of these amendments and much tighter restrictions on emergency rule were approved in a popular referendum in Egypt.

This chapter will also examine a number of other countries where countries initially concluded that they did not have to respond to 9/11 with massive new state powers. Singapore is a very advanced city-state, but one that is dominated by one party and that is well known for its harsh approach to crime. Singapore enacted laws in response to post-9/11 UN mandates, but these laws have played a negligible role in Singapore's response to a real terrorist threat in Southeast Asia. Singapore, like Malaysia, relied on indeterminate detention under an Internal Security Act (ISA) inherited from British colonial emergency rule. The approach in Singapore will be compared with Indonesia's struggle to deal with both terrorism and post-9/11 demands for tougher terrorism laws. As will be seen, Indonesia resisted the temptation to return to the military trials and harsh antisubversion laws of the Suharto era. Nevertheless, this refusal has made Indonesia vulnerable to criticisms that it has not responded effectively to multiple acts of terrorism. A democratic Egypt that suspended long-time emergency rule might face similar criticisms should future acts of terrorism occur or be launched from that country.

The Israeli experience is also examined in this chapter. Like Singapore, Israel has relied on harsh older laws originally inherited from British colonial emergency rule, but only in its Occupied Territories. The Israel situation is also affected by the existence of armed conflict and application of the laws of war. It has stressed a war and administrative detention approach to terrorism over a crime-based approach. As such, its experience has considerable appeal to those who supported the Bush Administration's global war against terror. At the same time, Israel employs both legislative and judicial regulation[2] of executive counter-terrorism powers more than the United States. A willingness by Israeli courts to apply international law and legal rules of proportionality even to targeted killing stands in contrast to the Obama administration's successful defense of targeted killings as not subject to judicial review.[3]

Although Israel had old and strong laws to deal with terrorism and it did not need initially to respond to 9/11, it has also been affected by 9/11. In 2002, it enacted a new administrative detention law that following the Bush administration's practice, limited detention to noncitizens classified as "unlawful combatants." The law was upheld by the Israeli Supreme Court in 2008, even though it allows the use of intelligence as secret evidence that is not subject to any adversarial challenge, as required in both the United Kingdom and Canada.

Recent proposals for new comprehensive antiterrorism laws in both Israel and Egypt suggest that it may be possible for both countries to rationalize and modernize their old laws by enacting new laws that reflect many of the features of post-9/11 legislation. If adopted, such laws would still be subject to local differences in administration, but they would also underline a growing convergence in antiterrorism legislation between Western democracies and countries that have traditionally responded more forcefully to terrorism. This would be another sign of the 9/11 effect in shifting baselines between the state's security interests and human rights.

II. EGYPT

Egypt has a long experience with terrorism, including attacks in Luxor in 1997 that killed 62 people and post-9/11 attacks such as the 2004 Sinai bombings, the 2005 Sharm-el-Sheikh attacks, and the 2010 bombing of a Christian church in Alexandria. Egypt was in a seemingly endless state of emergency since the 1981 assassination of President Sadat. In the wake of 9/11, the Egyptian prime minister suggested that "maybe Western countries should begin to think of Egypt's own fight against terrorism as their new model," and then U.S. secretary of state Colin Powell agreed that the United States "had much

---

[2] Aharon Barak, "Human Rights in Times of Terror – A Judicial Point of View" (2008) 28 Legal Studies 493.
[3] See Chapter 4.

to learn" from Egypt's antiterrorist tactics.[4] Similarly, former Egyptian president Mubarak declared that American post-9/11 policy proves "that we were right from the beginning in using all means, including military tribunals, to combat terrorism."[5] These statements demonstrate some of the legitimizing effects of American participation and complicity in Egyptian antiterrorism practices.

The growing convergence between the post-9/11 responses of democracies to terrorism and the practices of repressive regimes has not been lost on those struggling for reforms. A Yemeni human rights activist observed that the West is learning "from the developing countries in a negative way: they have learned how to violate human rights."[6] Egyptian Mohamed el-Baradei, who won the Nobel Prize for his work as head of the UN Nuclear Watchdog, criticized Western governments for their support of authoritarian regimes in the Middle East and argued that "the idea that the only alternative to authoritarian regimes is bin Laden and co is a fake one."[7] This idea, however, hung on as witnessed by concerns about the release of members of terrorist groups in Egypt after the resignation of Hosni Mubarak.

Extraordinary Renditions

The most direct connection between antiterrorism laws and practices in Egypt and Western democracies is the use of extraordinary renditions, in which American authorities transfer terrorist suspects into Egyptian custody. This practice started before 9/11 and included the Central Intelligence Agency's (CIA) 1998 rendition of four Egyptian terrorist suspects from Albania to Egypt. One of these men, Ahmed Saleb, was given electric shocks before he was eventually hanged after being convicted of an offense for which he had been tried in absentia.[8] The American rendition program increased in intensity after 9/11, and in 2005, the Egyptian prime minister admitted that 60–70 people had

---

[4] As quoted in Lynn Welchman, "Rocks, Hard Places and Human Rights: Anti-Terrorism Law and Policy in Arab States," in *Global Anti-Terrorism Law and Policy*, ed. Victor Ramraj, Michael Hor, and Kent Roach (New York: Cambridge University Press, 2005), at 582, 584.

[5] As quoted in Aziz Huq, "Extraordinary Rendition and the Wages of Hypocrisy" (2006) World Policy Journal 25, at 36.

[6] Shadi Mokhtari, *After Abu Ghraib: Exploring Human Rights in America and the Middle East* (New York: Cambridge University Press, 2009), at 12.

[7] "El Bardei Hits Out at the West's Support for Repressive Regimes," The Guardian, March 31, 2010, at http://www.guardian.co.uk/world/2010/mar/31/mohamed-elbaradei-tyrants-support-militants.

[8] Stephen Grey, *Ghost Plane: The True Story of the CIA Rendition and Torture Program* (New York: St. Martin's Press, 2006), at 143–4.

been transferred by American intelligence to Egyptian custody since 9/11.[9] One of those rendered to Cairo was Osama Mustafa Hassan Nasr, also known as Abu Omar, who was forcibly taken from Milan, where he had been granted refugee status, and returned to Egypt, his country of citizenship, in February 2003. The Italian courts have convicted a number of CIA operatives for kidnapping and other offenses in relation to these actions. Once in Egypt, Abu Omar was tortured by being hung upside down and having electric shocks administered to his genitals. He was released from an Egyptian prison 14 months later, only to be rearrested and detained after he contacted Italian authorities. He was held under an emergency law and eventually released in February 2007.[10]

Another notorious case included two Egyptians, Ahmed Agiza and Mohamed Alzery, who were denied asylum in Sweden on security grounds. On December 18, 2001, they were transported by the CIA from Stockholm to Cairo. Sweden had obtained assurances from Egypt that the men would not be tortured or treated unfairly, including provisions for monitoring by the Swedish embassy, but the UN Committee against Torture subsequently criticized Sweden's action, as did its own parliamentary ombudsman.[11] Alzery was released in October 2003 but was not allowed to leave his village without the permission of authorities, and Agiza was sentenced to 25 years' imprisonment with hard labor for membership in an organization with the aim of overthrowing the Egyptian government by violence. The trial was held before a military court that heard secret evidence and refused to investigate Agiza's claims, corroborated by a prison doctor, that he had been tortured while in custody. The court also refused to allow Agiza to call witnesses in his defense.[12]

The Counter-Terrorism Committee (CTC) created by UN Security Council Resolution 1373 seemed to turn a blind eye to Egypt's notorious practices

---

[9] *Report of the Special Rapporteur on the Promotion and Protection of Human Rights and Fundamental Freedoms While Countering Terrorism*, A/HRC/13/37/add 2, October 14, 2009, at para. 44.

[10] Margaret Satterthwaite, "Rendered Meaningless: Extraordinary Renditions and the Rule of Law" (2007) 75 George Washington Law Review 1333, at 1342.

[11] United Nations Committee against Torture, decision of May 20, 2005, CAT/C/34/D/233/2003; see also United Nations Committee against Torture, *Conclusions and Recommendations of the Committee against Torture: Sweden*, 06/06/2002, CAT/C/CR/28/6 (Concluding Observations/Comments), and the Swedish reply (*Comments by the Government of Sweden on the Concluding Observations of the Human Rights Committee*, CCPR/CO/74/SWE, May 14, 2003).

[12] Dick Marty, *Alleged Secret Detentions and Unlawful Inter-State Transfers of Detainees Involving Council of Europe Member States*, June 12, 2007, at para. 158; http://assembly.coe.int/Documents/WorkingDocs/doc06/edoc10957.pdf; Human Rights Watch, "Sweden Implicated in Egypt's Abuse of Suspected Militant," May 5, 2004, at http://www.hrw.org/english/docs/2004/05/05/egypt8530_txt.htm.

of torturing terrorist suspects and even pressed Egypt on the adequacy of its bilateral arrangements with other countries with respect to the exchange of "operational information," without noting that some of this information is likely obtained from torture. This allowed Egypt, in its second report to the CTC, to enumerate its extensive bilateral agreements with many countries on terrorism matters.[13] In 2004, the CTC asked whether Egypt had encountered "any difficulties . . . in gathering intelligence," with Egypt replying that it had not.[14] As suggested in the previous chapter, the CTC's practice of interacting with countries with poor human rights records on matters involving terrorism raises concerns that human rights violations, revealed and deplored by other parts of the UN system, have not been given adequate consideration.

Emergency Law and Administrative Detention

Egypt has a long history of martial law and emergency rule stemming from British colonial times.[15] Under the 1958 Emergency Law, the declaration of an emergency by the president triggered extremely broad powers, including the ability to conduct searches without adhering to criminal law, to practice censorship, and to confiscate property.[16] Article 3(1) of the Emergency Law allowed for the arrest and indeterminate detention of "persons who are dangerous to public security and order" without charge or trial. A person subject to such a detention order does not have to be brought before a court for 30 days.[17] In addition, the court that makes decisions about detentions under this law is a state security court that includes military court judges appointed by the president and whose final verdicts are subject to ratification by the president. The use of such courts "seriously undermine[s] the strict distinction between the judiciary and the executive, therefore unavoidably putting at least into question the appearance of impartiality and independence of these tribunals."[18]

Between 1992 and 2000, more than 1,000 civilians were prosecuted in military courts, resulting in 92 death sentences and 644 prison terms.[19] Military

---

[13] Egypt Country Report, S/2002/601.   [14] Egypt Country Report, S/2004/343, at 10.

[15] Sadiq Reza, "Endless Emergency: The Case of Egypt" (2007) 10 New Criminal Law Review 532.

[16] Ibid., at 538.

[17] *Report of the Special Rapporteur on the Promotion and Protection of Human Rights and Fundamental Freedoms While Countering Terrorism*, A/HRC/13/37/add 2, October 14, 2009, at paras. 19–21.

[18] Ibid., at para. 35.

[19] Sadiq Reza, "Endless Emergency: The Case of Egypt" (2007) 10 New Criminal Law Review 532, at 541.

and state security courts were used against Islamists, including the Muslim Brotherhood, opposition Labor Party leaders, and other dissenters. They were also used against terrorists such as Ayman al-Zawahiri, who was detained and tortured for three years before being released and going to Afghanistan, where he became a top figure in al Qaeda.[20] Zawahiri was tortured in prison and told another prisoner that he confessed to involvement in the assassination of Sadat because "the death penalty is more merciful than torture." At his trial, he alleged that his captors "shocked us with electricity! And they used wild dogs," leading some to conclude that 9/11 "was born in the prisons of Egypt."[21]

In 2010, 26 men alleged to be connected with Hezbollah were convicted of terrorism in the Egyptian State Security Court, despite claims that their convictions were based on confessions obtained by torture when they were subject to incommunicado detention in 2008 and 2009, and despite that involuntary confessions are supposed to be inadmissible under Egyptian law.[22] The Egyptian Supreme Constitutional Court upheld the state's ability to transfer cases to both security and military courts. The court deferred to the government in these national security cases to avoid "a futile confrontation with the regime,"[23] even while it opposed other state initiatives. The Egyptian government did not provide the UN special rapporteur on protecting human rights while countering terrorism with exact numbers of those detained under emergency powers,[24] but it has been estimated that there were about 18,000 security detainees.[25] In 2010, the emergency law was extended by the Egyptian government for another two years, with the government stating that it would only use it with respect to terrorism and narcotics. The White House expressed regret at this decision and called "on the Egyptian government to fulfill its pledge to the

---

[20] Ibid., at 550.

[21] Lawrence Wright, *The Looming Tower: Al-Qaeda's Road to 9/11* (London: Penguin, 2006), at 52–3.

[22] Amnesty International, "Egypt Hizbullah Conviction Marred by Torture Allegation," April 30, 2010, at http://www.amnesty.org/en/news-and-updates/egypt-hizbullah-cell-convictions-marred-torture-allegations-2010-04-30; Sadiq Reza, "Egypt," in *Criminal Procedure: A Worldwide Study*, 2nd ed., ed. Craig Bradley (Durham, NC: Carolina Academic Press, 2007), at 127.

[23] Tamir Moustafa, "Law and Resistance in Authoritarian States: The Judicialization of Politics in Egypt," in *Rule by Law: The Politics of Courts in Authoritarian Regimes*, ed. Tom Ginsburg and Tamir Moustafa (New York: Cambridge University Press, 2008), at 154. Moustafa has noted that "ironically, the regime's ability to transfer cases to exceptional courts and even to detain political opponents indefinitely . . . facilitated the independence of the regular judiciary." Ibid., at 154–5.

[24] *Report of the Special Rapporteur on the Promotion and Protection of Human Rights and Fundamental Freedoms While Countering Terrorism*, A/HRC/13/37/add 2, October 14, 2009, at para. 19.

[25] Reza, "Endless Emergency," at 551.

Egyptian people to replace the emergency law with a counter-terrorism law that protects the civil liberties and dignity of Egyptian citizens."[26] As will be seen, however, any new counter-terrorism law enacted under Mubarak would likely have drawn on the harshest aspects of post-9/11 antiterrorism laws. As a result of 2007 amendments to the Egyptian Constitution, any new antiterrorism law would also have been sheltered from most judicial review designed to protect civil liberties or human dignity. Now with the overthrow of Mubarak and the popular approval of constitutional proposals to restrict emergency laws and to repeal the 2007 constitutional amendments relating to security, there is a potential that a new antiterrorism law in Egypt might be more restrained and precise than earlier terrorism and emergency laws and in any event would be subject to judicial review.

Reliance on Old Laws

In its first report to the CTC under Security Council Resolution 1373, Egypt did not rely on administrative detention under the Emergency Law but instead focused on a 1992 law enacted against terrorism. It stressed that Egypt was "among the first states to deal with the phenomenon of terrorism and its causes, owing to the extremely serious impact of terrorism on the country's social, economic and political interests."[27] This law featured an extremely broad definition of terrorism that had influenced the 1999 Arab Convention for the Suppression of Terrorism. Section 86 of the Egyptian Penal Code defines terrorism as

> all use of force, violence, threatening, or frightening, to which a felon resorts in execution of an individual or collective criminal scheme, with the aim of disturbing public order, or exposing the safety and security of society to danger, if this is liable to harm the persons, or throw horror among them, expose their life, freedom or security to danger, damage the environment, causes detriments to communications, transport, property and funds, buildings, public or private properties, occupying or taking possession of them, preventing or obstructing the work of public authorities, worship houses, or educational institutions, or interrupting the application of the constitution, laws, or statutes.[28]

---

[26] "Egypt Extends Emergency Law, US Calls for New Anti-Terror Law," Bloomberg Business Week, May 11, 2010, at http://www.businessweek.com/news/2010-05-11/egypt-extends-emergency-law-u-s-calls-for-new-anti-terror-law.html.

[27] Egypt Country Report, S/2001/1237, at para. 4.

[28] Egyptian Penal Code, Article 86. The English translation is taken from a UN database at https://www.unodc.org/tldb/showDocument.do?documentUid=6605.

This definition of terrorism is similar to many post-9/11 definitions of terrorism in Western democracies in including not only murder and violence but actions that disturb essential services, property damage, and the threats[29] of such actions. It goes beyond those definitions, though, in its reference to vague concepts such as "disturbing public order" and "obstructing the work of public authorities, worship houses or educational institutions, or interrupting the application of the constitution, laws, or statutes." At the same time, the idea that terrorism is an affront to the constitution and that educational and religious institutions should be protected from fundamentalist ideas could be seen as an appeal to militant democracy,[30] even though Egypt's claims to be a democracy were tenuous. Nevertheless, Egypt's broad definition of terrorism is consistent with many post-9/11 antiterrorism laws.

In 1992, the UN Human Rights Committee criticized the above definition of terrorism as overbroad and asked Egypt to review it.[31] By 2001, however, Egypt was able to report to the CTC that it had taken "pains to define terrorism in such a way that the range and scope of the definition would ensure that the objectives sought in dealing with the phenomenon of terrorism and its forms, means, etc., were attained."[32] The public record does not suggest that the CTC objected in any way to Egypt's defense of its broad definition to terrorism. Given the CTC's nonconfrontational approach to these issues, it is unlikely that the CTC raised any objection. Thus an overbroad definition of terrorism that was criticized by the UN before 9/11 was accepted by it after 9/11.[33]

---

[29] In its critique of a similar definition in the Arab Convention, Amnesty International warns that reference to threats could be interpreted to criminalize "alleged affiliation with certain political opposition parties that use violence." Amnesty International fails to note, however, that Section 1 of the United Kingdom's influential Terrorism Act, 2000, also criminalizes threats of terrorist actions. Amnesty International, *The Arab Convention for the Suppression of Terrorism* (2002), at 19. The Egyptian law, like the U.K. law, does not provide an exemption for protests and strikes. Lynn Welchman, "Rocks, Hard Places and Human Rights: Anti-Terrorism Law and Policy in Arab States," in Ramraj et al., *Global Anti-Terrorism Law and Policy*, at 588.

[30] For a suggestion that harsh measures in Egypt are designed to "prevent a fundamentalist takeover" and that "this is clearly a militant democracy argument and as such is quite acceptable," see Andras Sajo, "From Militant Democracy to the Preventive State?" (2006) 27 Cardozo Law Review 2255, at 2278n72.

[31] Welchman "Rocks, Hard Places and Human Rights," at 591.

[32] Egypt Country Report, S/2001/1237, at para. 7.

[33] The CTC's most recent review, however, does note that North African "measures often lack the precise definition of criminal behavior set forth in the international counter-terrorism instruments. This might raise concerns in relation to human rights and the rule of law." Nevertheless, definitional reform is not identified as a priority area for reform. CTC, *Survey of the Implementation of Resolution 1373 by Member States*, S/2009/620, at 6.

The broad definition of terrorism in Egypt's 1992 terrorism law was accompanied by equally as broad offenses. Joining a group that engages in terrorism as defined earlier was subject to five years' imprisonment, with higher penalties for those who established, organized, founded, or directed such a group.[34] If terrorism was used as a means to accomplish the aims prohibited by the broad definition of terrorism, the penalty was death or hard labor for life.[35] The same penalty would apply to those who supply terrorist groups with arms, explosives, funds, property, or information.[36] As in Israel, Egypt's existing broad terrorism law already covered acts of assisting terrorism, including terrorism financing, that would be criminalized by other countries in response to Security Council Resolution 1373. To a generally underappreciated extent, broad post-9/11 antiterrorism laws have roots in the harsh antiterrorism laws and internal security regimes of repressive states. This, of course, does not mean that democracies will use their broad new post-9/11 laws in the same way as Egypt did to stifle dissent, but it does mean that democracies can no longer, without hypocrisy, criticize such laws.

In 2009, the special rapporteur on protecting human rights while countering terrorism continued to express concerns about the breadth of the definition of terrorism in Egypt. He urged Egypt to draft a new antiterrorism law that focuses on specific acts of violence and does not include damage to or occupation of property. Such criticisms, however, are much less persuasive in light of broad definitions of terrorism contained in the post-9/11 laws of many democracies. For example, it would be difficult to criticize Egyptians for including threats to property, vital infrastructure or essential services in any new definition of terrorism when British laws and laws inspired by the British laws including a new Israeli law to be examined below also defined the harms of terrorism in such a broad fashion. The existence of similar Western laws can be used to legitimate repressive practices. For example, the draft Egyptian antiterrorism law apparently proposed that authorities have powers to detain terrorist suspects for 29 days without charge. The special rapporteur articulated concerns about such a scheme and stressed the importance of providing detainees with access to a judge within 24 hours.[37] There are merits to these concerns, but it is likely that 29 days has been deliberately selected by the Egyptian drafters in part because of the precedent of 28 days' detention without charge

---

[34] Egyptian Penal Code, Section 86. The English translation is taken from a UN database at https://www.unodc.org/tldb/showDocument.do?documentUid=6605.

[35] Ibid.   [36] Ibid.

[37] *Report of the Special Rapporteur on the Promotion and Protection of Human Rights and Fundamental Freedoms While Countering Terrorism*, A/HRC/13/37/add 2, at para. 17.

set by the United Kingdom at that time.[38] Any defense of the proposed 29-day period by Egypt could be rebutted by valid arguments that there would be judicial review in the United Kingdom long before 28 days and that detention in London is different than detention in Cairo. Moreover, the British government has now proposed to lower the maximum period of detention upon preventive arrest to 14 days while also proposing to reinstate the maximum 28 day period in an emergency.[39] Nevertheless, as suggested at the outset, developing countries like Egypt are sensitive to the example set by leading Western democracies. They are also understandably resistant to Western claims that laws that are acceptable in the West are not acceptable in the developing world.

Egyptian authorities claimed that the unreleased draft antiterrorism law is influenced by post-9/11 antiterrorism laws enacted in Western democracies. As will be seen, Israel is similarly attempting to update and modernize its antiterrorism law, which was first enacted in 1948. The details of both new laws will need to be examined when they are released and the details of the Egyptian bill may change given the fall of Mubarak. Nevertheless both countries may try to forestall human rights criticisms of their new laws by relying on the examples set by post-9/11 laws in the United Kingdom and elsewhere. Indeed, it may be that the West has caught up with terrorism so that Western laws can now migrate to Egypt and Israel. At the same time, even similar laws would be subject to local culture and administration. In this vein, it is significant that the special rapporteur criticized Egypt for not investigating many claims that its officials have tortured security detainees. Western criticisms of Egypt for engaging in torture, however, carried less weight given the complicity of the United States and other countries that rendered terrorist suspects to Egypt and accepted their assurances that such detainees would not be tortured or mistreated.

Laws against Speech Associated with Terrorism

Egypt did not have to enact new laws to comply with the UN Security Council's call in Resolution 1624 that countries prohibit speech that incites terrorism. It was able to reply to the CTC that Article 86 of the 1992 terrorism law provided that "any person who promotes by speech, writing or any other means . . . or any person directly or indirectly possessing or acquiring writings, printed materials

---

[38] See Chapter 5. As will be discussed later, there is a similar current proposal in Indonesia to allow preventive arrest for a 30-day period.

[39] *Protection of Freedoms Bill* (UK) part 4; *Draft Detention of Terrorist Suspects (Temporary Extension) Bill* February, 2011.

or recordings . . . that promote or advocate" the broadly defined purposes of terrorism shall be subject to imprisonment for five years.[40] In this way, Egypt was able to again sanitize its broad definition of terrorism through reporting to the CTC, which again voiced no apparent concerns about the human rights implications of laws against speech associated with terrorism and their use to stifle opposition to the Mubarak regime.

Pursuant to Resolution 1624, the CTC asked Egypt what steps it had taken to ensure that its implementation of the resolution would comply with international law, including international human rights law. As discussed in the preceding chapter, reference to international human rights law was included in Resolution 1624 in an attempt to respond to criticisms that the Security Council and its CTC had neglected human rights in the aftermath of 9/11. Egypt tersely replied that it had ratified all international agreements on human rights and that "all levels and types of courts are obligated to apply and implement, particularly those provisions that pertain to a fair trial in criminal proceedings for crimes of terrorism."[41] Although the reference to international human rights in Resolution 1624 was designed to make the CTC process more rights friendly, it allowed Egypt to make false and apparently unchallenged claims that its harsh and repressive antiterrorism efforts complied with human rights and that even its military courts complied with fair trial rights.

A New Money Laundering Law

Although Egypt largely relied on existing emergency powers and its harsh and broad 1992 terrorism law, this did not mean that it made no response to 9/11. It enacted a new money laundering law that included terrorism financing both to comply with Resolution 1373 and in a successful attempt to remove itself from the Financial Action Task Force's (FATF) list of noncooperative countries. Article 2 of the new law included terrorist offenses with other criminal offenses that produced proceeds of crime. The law followed FATF recommendations by creating a financial intelligence unit to consider reports about suspected money laundering from financial institutions. It also features "know your customer" provisions and requirements for reporting suspicious transactions.[42] The law has a generic quality that suggests that it was enacted more to respond to external pressures than to the Egyptian context. The CTC generally accepted Egypt's reforms but also questioned its omission of

---

[40] Egypt Country Report, S/2006/351, at para. 2.1.

[41] Ibid., at para. 2.6

[42] Anti-Money Laundering Law, no. 80 of 2002, available at https://www.unodc.org/tldb/pdf/ Egypt_Promulgating_Anti-_Money_Laundering_Law_Amended_by_Law_No._78_for_2003.pdf.

informal money transfer systems and lawyers as entities that had to report sus-pected money laundering offenses and sought reassurance that the law could be applied even if no actual terrorist act was committed or attempted and that Egypt was complying with FATF's recommendations.[43] The CTC's bureau-cratic checklist questions to Egypt were devoid of context and could have been asked of any country.

Not surprisingly, given its nature as an external transplant designed to respond to international mandates, the new law does not seem to have been effective or even used to prevent terrorism. In 2006, Egypt reported that no terrorist assets had yet been frozen under the new law.[44] As Victor V. Ramraj has argued, the CTC appears to proceed under the assumption that there could be one global antiterrorism law and that any failure to achieve this end is simply a matter of lack of capacity that can be addressed through technical assistance. Similar laws such as the money laundering and terrorism financing laws enacted since 9/11 in all five countries examined in this chapter will be administered in very different legal, political, and social contexts. In the terror-ism financing context especially, "the superficial penetration of international legal norms into particular legal systems might also be a matter of the relative unimportance of formal law in particular societies."[45]

The Constitutional Amendments of 2007

The most significant post-9/11 development in Egypt was not the addition of a money laundering/terrorism financing law but a set of 2007 constitutional amendments that exempted antiterrorism laws from constitutional provisions that provide for judicial oversight of detention, home searches, and surveil-lance or seizure of communications. The amendments also entrenched the power of the president to refer terrorism cases to special security or military courts.[46]

The special rapporteur expressed concerns about the 2007 amendments and warned that though they may render any antiterrorism law technically

---

[43] Egypt Country Report, S/2003/7, at para. 5. Egypt Country Report, S/2004/343, at paras. 3–6. In some questions to Egypt, the CTC blurred the response to money laundering and terrorism financing, whereas in others, it distinguished between the two phenomena. Compare Egypt Country Report S/2005/288, at paras. 10–11, and Egypt Country Report S/2006/351, at para. 3.

[44] Egypt Country Report, S/2006/351, at para. 5.

[45] Victor V. Ramraj "The Impossibility of Global Anti-Terrorism Law?" in Victor V. Ramraj et al. *Global Anti-Terrorism Law and Policy* 2nd ed (Cambridge: Cambridge University Press, forthcoming 2011).

[46] Carnegie Endowment for International Peace, "Egypt's Controversial Constitutional Amend-ments," at 13; http://www.carnegieendowment.org/files/egypt_constitution_webcommentary01 .pdf/. See also Reza, "Endless Emergency," at 541.

constitutional, such proceedings may still violate international human rights norms.[47] As Sadiq Reza has argued, the 2007 amendment was designed to make emergency rule permanent in Egypt.[48] Nevertheless, it would be difficult for the United States to criticize the idea that the Egyptian president could refer any terrorism case to military courts when both presidents Bush and Obama have claimed and exercised that right since 9/11, at least with respect to noncitizens, with President Bush for a time claiming that he could subject American citizens suspected of terrorism to military detention.[49] Even President Obama in his criticisms of Egypt focused on the need to end the emergency, even though the 2007 amendments would have allowed the main elements of the emergency to continue under the guise of normal antiterrorism measures. The 2007 amendments provided some support for the idea that harsh antiterrorism laws and practices have received a new legitimacy in the post- 9/11 era that will make reform in repressive regimes more difficult to achieve.

Egypt after the Fall of Mubarak

The protests that led to the fall of President Mubarak in February, 2011 will undoubtedly influence the Egyptian approach to countering terrorism. In response to the growing protests in early February, 2011, President Mubarak announced that he was prepared to propose the cancellation of the 2007 constitutional amendments that sheltered terrorism laws from much constitutional review and gave him as President powers to refer security cases to special courts. Subsequent to his resignation, a constitutional reform committee of legal experts appointed by the Supreme Council of the Armed Forces proposed constitutional changes that also included the repeal of the 2007 amendment relating to security laws and cases. The committee proposed that any subsequent Presidential declaration of a state of emergency would have to be approved by the legislature after 7 days and by the people in a referendum after six months. These proposals for constitutional changes were the subject of a referendum that was supported by the Army and the Muslim Brotherhood, but opposed by others in Egypt on the grounds that the electoral reforms especially did not go far enough.[50] The referendum and the proposals

---

[47] *Report of the Special Rapporteur on the Promotion and Protection of Human Rights and Fundamental Freedoms While Countering Terrorism*, A/HRC/13/37/add 2, at para. 12.

[48] Reza, "Endless Emergency."

[49] See the discussion in Chapter 4 of the Hamdi and Padilla cases.

[50] Other proposed constitutional changes include term limits on the President and Vice President and the restoration of judicial supervision of elections. Reuters "Factbox: Egypt's Constitution" 10 February 2011; Reuters "Factbox: Proposed Changes to Egypt's Constitution" 26 February 2011.

were approved by a 77% vote with participation by 41% of eligible voters.[51] Emergency rule will likely end in Egypt and there will be freer elections and new restrictions on the declarations of emergencies.

A new Interior Minister has apologized for the actions of the security agency under the emergency and during the protests that ousted Mubarak. The agency has been abolished to be replaced with a new one restricted to combating terrorism and espionage.[52] Such an approach makes it very important that any new antiterrorism law introduced in Egypt contain more precise definitions of terrorism that cannot easily be applied to dissent and that terrorism cases be decided in regular courts subject to ordinary rules of criminal procedure and evidence as opposed to in security or military courts. As will be seen later in this chapter with respect to Indonesia, a restrained terrorism law can be a vehicle for advancing the rule of law and democracy especially in emerging democracies that have abused broad security laws in the past. Formal legal change will, however, have to be accompanied by increased accountability for human rights abuses.

There will also need to be a reckoning with Egypt's past. There are calls within Egypt for a review of convictions obtained in security courts on the basis of coerced and probably tortured confessions. This process has started somewhat haphazardly with the escape of many prisoners during the February, 2011 uprising and the subsequent release of additional prisoners with links to groups that had been involved with terrorism in the past including two people convicted in relation to the assassination of President Sadat in 1981 and the younger brother of al Qaeda's second in command Ayman al-Zawahiri with reports that the latter was subsequently re-arrested.[53] As will be seen, even before the overthrow of Mubarak, Egypt was prepared to release those detained under its broad security laws and there is a danger that Western democracies will ignore the prospects of rehabilitating those who were in the past prepared to engage in terrorist violence.

Deradicalization and Renunciations of Violence?

Although the Egyptian experience was quite bleak, one possible bright spot even under Mubarak was a number of prominent repudiations of terrorism by Egyptian terrorist groups. Egyptian authorities have allowed some prisoners to

---

[51] "Constitutional changes pass in Egypt referendum" *The New York Times* March 20, 2011.

[52] "Men tied to Sadat death to be freed" *The Australian* 12 March 2011; "Egypt Ends Domestic Spying Agency, but creates a new one" *The New York Times* March 15, 2011.

[53] "Egypt Amends Views of Islamists" *The Wall Street Journal* 11 March 2011; "Egypt Releases Brother of al Qaeda's al-Zawahiri" *The New York Times* March 17, 2011; "Militant is re-arrested days after release from prison" *The New York Times* March 21, 2011.

meet with religious scholars, and in some cases, this has led to public statements that previous acts of violence have been based on a misinterpretation of Islam. A RAND study has suggested that the 9/11 attacks helped convince an initially skeptical Egyptian government to facilitate deradicalization by a group that had previously renounced violence against the Egyptian state in 1999 and to release thousands of such prisoners in 2003.[54] These efforts were subsequently extended to members of the Egyptian Islamic Jihad group.[55] The Egyptian state allowed leaders of these groups to meet in prison with their followers and subsequently released as many as 20,000 members from its prisons.[56] The authors of these recantations have not become "secular nor liberal: their self-criticism includes observations that the wrong path to jihad benefits only the Jews, the United States and Egypt's Christian minority."[57] It is possible that some of their statements might even qualify as hate speech or incitement of terrorism abroad, even though they appear to have renounced violence at home. It is difficult to determine how genuine such renunciations of violence are as they may also reflect attempts to escape detention in Egypt's prisons or a recognition that some of the prior terrorist attacks within Egypt, notably the Luxor attacks, caused widespread revulsion. That said, the groups that have renounced violence in Egypt have not returned to violence, though there was violence directed against the Coptic Christian minority in Egypt in early 2011. In any event, Western democracies have not yet begun to struggle with rehabilitation of terrorists or engagement with Islam to encourage renunciation of violence.

III. SYRIA

Syria felt no immediate need to enact new laws to respond to 9/11 and Security Council Resolution 1373. Like Egypt, Syria's pre-9/11 responses to terrorism demonstrated some of the colonial origins of repression. In the years leading up to independence in 1946, France attempted to repress nationalist movements in Syria. In what has been described as "a tragic dress rehearsal for present-day abuses," the French occupiers "imposed heavy censorship, confiscated presses,

---

[54] Angel Rabsas et al., *Deradicalizing Islamic Extremists* (Santa Monica, CA: RAND Corporation, 2010), at 82. See also Omar Ahsour, "Lions Tamed? An Inquiry into the Causes of De-Radicalization of Armed Islamist Movements: The Case of the Egyptian Islamic Group," 61 Middle East Journal 622.

[55] Rabsas et al., *Deradicalizing Islamic Extremists*, at 84.

[56] Diaa Rashwan, "The Renunciation of Violence by Egyptian Jihadi Organizations," in *Leaving Terrorism Behind*, ed. Tore Bjorgo and John Horgan (London: Routledge, 2009), at 121, 124.

[57] Rohan Gunaratna and Mohamed Bin Ali, "Deradicalization Initiatives in Egypt: A Preliminary Insight" (2009) 32 Studies in Conflict and Terrorism 277, at 280.

closed theatres, and set up . . . a large intelligence apparatus."[58] These traditions continued and intensified so that "every lecture, book and magazine –
even Friday sermons in the mosque – must be approved in advance."[59] As in
Egypt, and as also seen in Israel and Singapore, colonial emergency rule gave
Syria a leg up in responding to 9/11.

Syria has been in a constant state of emergency since a Baathist military coup in 1963. At the height of repression of the opposition, a law was
enacted in 1980 that made membership, even past membership, in the Muslim
Brotherhood a capital offense.[60] Security laws were enforced by a number of
special military courts. A study published in 1991 estimated that 1 in 240 persons in Syria worked in various security services, or *mukhabarat*, and that
these services had a budget equivalent to $750 million a year or 5 percent of
gross domestic product.[61] This allowed for widespread surveillance and use
of informers. The same 1991 study cited the Palestine branch of the military
intelligence agency as one that "has been responsible for more deaths under
torture than any other agency in recent years."[62] As will be seen, several Canadians suspected of terrorism would be detained and tortured at that prison
after 9/11.

Problematic Definitions of Terrorism and Exemptions for Freedom Fighters

In its first report to the CTC, Syria pointedly noted that because Resolution
1373 did not define terrorism, it would define terrorism in accordance with the
1999 Arab Convention for the Suppression of Terrorism, "which distinguishes
between terrorism and legitimate struggle against foreign occupation."[63] Thus,
for Syria, compliance with Resolution 1373 was not necessarily incompatible with state sponsorship of terrorism against Israeli citizens if such actions
could be characterized as a legitimate struggle against foreign occupation.
The Security Council's failure to give guidance on the definition of terrorism gave states the freedom to define terrorism in vague and overbroad ways
but also to exempt terrorist violence against civilians committed in the name
of self-determination. As argued in the previous chapter, the UN's failure
to define terrorism was unfortunate because 9/11 provided the world with

---

[58] Middle East Watch, *Syria Unmasked: The Suppression of Hunan Rights by the Asad Regime*
(New Haven, CT: Yale University Press, 1991), at 3.
[59] Ibid., at 111.   [60] Ibid., at 35.
[61] Ibid., at 41.   [62] Ibid., at 50.
[63] Syria Country Report, S/2001/1204, at para. 1.

an unprecedented opportunity to agree that the intentional killing of civilians and others not taking part in hostilities in an armed conflict was always unacceptable.

Reliance on Old Laws

Although it followed the Arab Convention in exempting freedom fighters from its definition of terrorism, in other respects, Syria defined terrorism very broadly. This approach was also consistent with the Arab Convention, which featured both a broad definition of terrorism based on Egyptian law as well as a provision that hypocritically stated that its broad freedom fighter exemption would not exempt from the definition of terrorism "any act prejudicing the territorial integrity of any Arab state."[64] This approach could be used to deny rights to Syria's Kurdish minority. The Syrian Penal Code broadly defined terrorism as "all acts intended to create a state of fear which are committed by means . . . likely to cause public danger."[65] Syria noted in its report to the CTC that this terrorism offense had been a crime punishable by death since 1949. Article 306 of its penal code provided that "all associations established for the purpose of changing the economic or social character of the State or the basic conditions of society" using terrorist means "shall be dissolved and their members shall be sentenced to a term of hard labour."[66] As with Egypt, Syria was able proudly to report the existence of offenses to the CTC that before 9/11 would have been widely regarded within the UN and elsewhere as repressing political freedoms.

Syria also reported how "political offenses" defined as those committed with "political motives"[67] received augmented penalties under the Syrian Penal Code. As will be seen, the United Kingdom and other states would be attracted to the idea that a militant democracy needed to be more vigilant about political offenses committed through undemocratic means, and this theory was implicitly endorsed in Security Council Resolution 1624. Repressive and brutal regimes such as Syria, however, were prepared to use some of the rhetoric of militant democracy for their own ends. As will be seen, Syria did not require much prompting from the Security Council to prosecute speech that it associated with terrorism.

[64] Arab Convention for the Suppression of Terrorism, Article 2(2).

[65] Syrian Penal Code, Article 304; english translation available at www.unodc.org/tldb/showDocument.do?documentUid=1480&node=docs&cmd=add&country=SYR.

[66] Syria Country Report, S/2002/1046, at para. 5.

[67] Ibid., at para. 15.

Laws against Speech Associated with Terrorism

In its 2002 report to the CTC, Syria linked terrorism and speech by noting that Article 278 of its penal code had long made it an offense punishable by imprisonment to engage in "writings or speeches for which permission has not been granted by the Government" and "which expose Syria to the risk of acts of aggression, disturb its relations with other States or expose Syrians to acts of retaliation against their persons or property."[68] In response to Resolution 1624 and the CTC's inquiry into what steps Syria was taking to counter incitement of terrorist acts motivated by extremism and intolerance and to prevent its subversion of educational, cultural, and religious institutions, Syria was able to reply that the government supervised and controlled "all educational, cultural and religious institutions" and directed all imams "to adopt a balanced and moderate approach in their teaching and to repudiate all forms of extremism and intolerance."[69] What was unspoken but understood is that anyone perceived by the state as going beyond such a "balanced and moderate" approach to religion would be liable to detention and prosecution under Syria's broad terrorism laws. Although repression may have persisted in any event, Resolution 1624 gave Syria additional resources to repress Islamic groups and dissenters and characterize them as terrorists. Resolution 1624 may have been motivated by Prime Minister Blair's strong belief in the necessity of militant democracy, but in Syria, it helped legitimate the totalitarianism that kept all aspects of political and religious life under surveillance and control.

Special Courts and Speech Prosecutions

Like Egypt, Syria was able to draw on an established tradition of using special courts to deal with those suspected of terrorism. Syria's Supreme State Security Court had its origins in a 1963 state of emergency. The court is composed of a military judge and two civilian judges appointed by the martial law governor. It has a history of trying Communists and members of the Muslim Brotherhood.[70] There is no appeal, except to the executive, and hearings are not open to the public.[71] Lawyers can be present but do not have access to

---

[68] Syria Country Report, S/2002/1046, at para. 3.
[69] Syria Country Report, S/2005/265, at para. 21.
[70] Human Rights Watch, *Far from Justice: Syria's Supreme State Security Court* (New York: Human Rights Watch, 2009), at 10.
[71] Ibid., at 11.

the dossier prepared by the intelligence agency. In the words of one accused, this makes it impossible for the accused even to know or address "the heart of the accusations against me."[72] The court is exempt from rules of procedure that apply in Syria's criminal courts, but it does apply the broad offenses found in Syria's penal code.[73] The operation of these courts casts doubt on the wisdom of statements made by Canada's minister of foreign affairs, Bill Graham, that Maher Arar, a Canadian detained on suspicion of terrorism in Syria and tortured there after 9/11, could receive a fair and open public trial in Syria.[74]

A Human Rights Watch report on the operation of the security court between January 2007 and July 2008 found that 153 of the 237 cases decided during that period were for broad offenses that targeted speech. In more than 100 cases, convictions were issued under Article 285 of the penal code, which prohibits statements that "weaken national sentiment or awaken racial or sectarian tensions while Syria is at war or expecting a war."[75] This provision has been applied to Kurdish activists as well as alleged members of the Kurdish Workers Party, now widely listed as a terrorist group. In addition, the Syrian Penal Code also makes it a crime to engage in speech in favor of separatism of part of the country, and this provision has been applied to peaceful Kurdish protesters seeking more autonomy for the Kurdish minority in Syria.[76]

The study also found that Article 306 of the penal code, which prohibits membership in an organization that has "the intention of changing the social or economic character of the state" by "terrorist means," was also used to convict at least 106 defendants during this period. Many of these people were designated as "Salfafis" because of their desire to establish an Islamic state or were alleged to be members of the Muslim Brotherhood, an illegal organization in Syria.[77] A Western diplomat in Damascus who observed many of these proceedings reported that convictions were registered in many cases because the accused possessed material from "apparently radical Imams" and not on evidence relating to preparation for terrorist violence.[78] Another 34 cases in the study involved Article 278 of the penal code, which as discussed above prohibits speech that has not been authorized by the government or that disturbs Syria's relations with other governments or exposes Syrians to retaliation against their

---

[72] Ibid., at 16.　　　　　　　　　　　　[73] Ibid., at 2.

[74] Commission of Inquiry into the Activities of Canadian Officials in Relation to Maher Arar, *Analysis and Recommendations* (Ottawa: Public Works, 2006), at 246.

[75] Human Rights Watch, *Far From Justice*, at 3.

[76] Ibid., at 5, 43, 48.　　　　　　　　　[77] Ibid., at 4.

[78] Ibid., at 5.

persons or property.[79] Syria has defended this vague and overbroad offense as a response to international terrorism in various reports to the CTC.[80]

Torture

The Human Rights Watch report was able to document that in at least 38 of the 237 cases it examined, defendants claimed that their confessions were obtained through the use of torture by the Syrian security service. At the same time, it found no evidence of the court taking steps to investigate these serious allegations.[81] Defense lawyers have reported of cases in which the court has ignored physical evidence of torture.[82] As in Mubarak's Egypt, there was a lack of accountability in Syria for officials who engaged in torture in domestic security cases.

After 9/11, torture by Syrian security officials gained increased attention in the West. Four Canadians who were suspected of terrorism in Canada after 9/11 were detained by Syrian military intelligence at the Palestine branch in Damascus, Syria.[83] Maher Arar was rendered to Syria from the United States, but three other less well known Canadians – Abdullah Almalki, Ahmad Abou-Elmaati, and Muayeed Nureddin – traveled to Syria, where they were detained and tortured. Maher Arar was beaten and lashed with an electrical cable. Abdullah Almalki was severely beaten and forced into stress positions. Ahmad Elmaati was repeatedly beaten with fists and a braided electric cable and threats were made that his wife would be raped until he made a false confession that he was planning to bomb Canada's Parliament. He was also tortured with electric shocks when he was subsequently transferred to Egypt. Muayeed Nureddin was beaten and placed in stress positions. All four men were kept in coffin-like and rat infested cells in solitary confinement at the Far Falestin detention centre also called the Palestine Branch.[84]

---

[79] As translated in Welchman "Rocks, Hard Places and Human Rights," at 596.

[80] In its 2006 report, the offense was translated as stating that "any person who engages in actions or who utters words, in either written or spoken form, that are not permitted by the Government and who thereby subject Syria to the danger of hostile action, or impairs its relations with a foreign State, or subjects Syrian citizens to acts of reprisal that affect their persons or property" shall be liable to a term of imprisonment. Syria Country Report, S/2006/612.

[81] Human Rights Watch, *Far from Justice*, at 27.

[82] Ibid., at 29.

[83] A UN report concluded that eight others were rendered by the CIA to Syria, including four people captured with Abu Zubaydah in Pakistan in 2002. *Joint Study on Global Practices in Relation to Secret Detention*, A/HRC/13/42, January 26, 2010, at para. 147.

[84] Commission of Inquiry into the Activities of Canadian Officials in Relation to Maher Arar, *Analysis and Recommendations* ch 2; *Internal Inquiry into the Actions of Canadian Officials in*

Two official inquiries in Canada have established that Canadian officials were indirectly responsible for the torture of these Canadians through their sharing of information and the sending of questions for Syrian intelligence to ask. In addition, the inquiries documented a November 2002 visit by Canada's security intelligence agency to meet with Syrian intelligence in Damascus, where Canada's intelligence agency incredibly maintained that it did not consider whether the intelligence it obtained from Syria and subsequently shared with others was derived from torture.[85] The inquiries did not recommend that Canada not share intelligence with Syria but rather that it do so in a way that acknowledged the risk of torture. The United Kingdom has recently reinitiated intelligence sharing with Syria.[86] One of the most important 9/11 effects examined in this book is how international terrorism investigations connect Western democracies with countries with poor human rights records. Complicity with torture has been investigated by commissions of inquiry in Canada and is presently being investigated by a commission in the United Kingdom. Transnational cooperation in counter-terrorism has increased awareness of the use of torture and other human rights abuses by Syria and other repressive states.

A New Money Laundering Law

Although the CTC did not apparently criticize Syria's old-style, broad terrorism offenses and accepted its regulation of speech as a response to Resolution 1624, it was not satisfied with Syria's argument that those who financed terrorism could be prosecuted as accessories to crimes of terrorism. It requested that Syria enact a new law against terrorist financing.[87] Syria responded with the 2005 enactment of new money laundering legislation that provides for the freezing of terrorist funds. The law also purports to outlaw alternative remittance systems and established a financial intelligence agency. As in Egypt, however, such new laws promoted by the CTC and FATF were rather peripheral to older and harsher laws used to detain suspected terrorists. Attempts to outlaw alternative remittance systems widely used in Islamic countries seem destined to fail.

Relation to Abdullah Almalki, Ahmad Abou-Elmaati and Muayeed Nureddin (Ottawa: Public Works, 2008) chs 7–9.

[85] Commission of Inquiry into the Activities of Canadian Officials in Relation to Maher Arar, *Analysis and Recommendations*, at 198; *Internal Inquiry into the Actions of Canadian Officials in Relation to Abdullah Almalki, Ahmad Abou-Elmaati and Muayeed Nureddin* (Ottawa: Public Works, 2008), at 379.

[86] "Syria and UK Share Intelligence," November 19, 2008, at http://news.bbc.co.uk/2/hi/middle_east/7738348.stm.

[87] Syria Country Report, S/2005/265, at para. 3.

They highlight a disjunction between the law as written and the law as applied that can be especially corrosive in countries without a rule of law tradition. In addition, the new terrorism financing law would not target Syria's frequent involvement in state-sponsored terrorism. Although Resolution 1373 called on states not to provide support for terrorism, its many terrorism financing provisions focused on nonstate actors. The same is true with Resolution 1540, which focused on the dangers of nonstate actors and not states obtaining access to weapons of mass destruction. It was easier for the UN to focus on nonstate actors than to take on state actors, even when they were involved in supporting terrorism.

In its subsequent published interactions with Syria, the CTC doggedly focused on the details of terrorism financing. It made repeated inquiries to Syria about its compliance with terrorism financing and whether there had been successful prosecutions for terrorism financing. These inquiries, which only are public because Syria published them in its country reports, are so generic and devoid of context that they seem otherworldly when compared to the available information about counter-terrorism and torture in Syria. In any event, a CTC question about whether Syrian officials were adequately trained in terrorism financing gave Syria the opportunity to reply that "all branches of the security bodies . . . have the means necessary for the investigation of crimes connected with terrorist acts and terrorist financing."[88] Too often in Syria, "the means necessary" were brutal forms of torture.

Summary

It is far from clear that there would have been extensive reform and commitment to rule of law, free speech, and democracy in Syria without 9/11. Even after the uprisings in Tunisia, Egypt and Libya in early 2011, the Syrian regime seemed relatively stable. Nevertheless, the legitimating effects of Security Council actions and other forms of Western approval of repression, such as extraordinary renditions and increased intelligence cooperation in the Middle East, should not be ignored. They are well represented by reports by a Canadian detained on suspicion of terrorism and tortured in Syria. He recalled that one of his Syrian interrogators, who had been provided questions by Canada to ask, explained to him, "We were the first people to face terrorism in the '80's. We fought it with iron and fire, and everyone in the West criticized us. But now when they are faced with terrorism, they come to us for

---

[88] Ibid., at para. 11.

help."[89] Many in the West came to Egypt and Syria for help after 9/11, and too often, they turned a blind eye to the brutal ways that those countries combated terrorism.

The Egyptian people in 2011 were able to overthrow the Mubarak regime, but the Syrian people remain subject to authoritarian rule. Even in Syria, however, there were some signs of change. In early March, 2011, an 80 year old human rights lawyer who had been convicted by a security court of spreading false news was released.[90] Protests continued during that month with reports of over 60 protesters being killed. President Assad initially apologized for some of the deaths and announced a plan to study the ending of the emergency started in 1963 and allowing other political parties.[91] At the end of March, 2011, however, he refused to lift the state of emergency justifying it as medicine administered to a sick child and blaming the protests on foreign agitation.[92] By mid April 2011, however, with reports of more protests and up to 200 protesters killed, President Assad promised to repeal the emergency law while at the same time warning that once the emergency was ended "there will no longer be a need to organize demonstrations in Syria."[93] Many more protesters were killed and tortured after the emergency was ended, underlining the lack of rule of law. Should Syria move towards reform as in Egypt, a restrained terrorism law that could be administered in the ordinary courts would be critical as would reforms to emergency laws and the security apparatus.

iv. ISRAEL AND THE OCCUPIED TERRITORIES

Few, if any, countries have more experience with terrorism than Israel. Terrorism played a role in the creation of the Jewish and democratic state in 1948 out of the colonial British mandate period. Terrorism against Israeli targets intensified in various waves, with more than 300 deaths recorded in the 1990s and over 1,000 deaths since 2000, with 220 deaths in 55 suicide attacks during the height of the second intifada in 2002.[94] From 2000 to 2007, the UN has estimated that more than 4,000 Palestinians have died, with more than 1,000

---

[89] Kerry Pither, *Dark Days: The Story of Four Canadians Tortured in the Name of Fighting Terror* (Toronto, ON, Canada: Viking, 2008), at 222.

[90] "Syrian human rights lawyer freed among discontent" March 8 2011 CNN News at http://www.cnn.com/2011/WORLD/meast/03/08/syria.attorney.freed/.

[91] "In Syria, crackdown after protests" *The New York Times* March 18, 2011; "Syria struggles to end protest" *The Toronto Star* March 25, 2011.

[92] "Syrian President blames 'conspirators' for unrest" *The Wall Street Journal* March 30, 2011.

[93] Patrick Martin "Syrian President's pledge to repeal emergency law falls on deaf ears" *Globe and Mail* April 18, 2011.

[94] Israel Ministry of Foreign Affairs, "Victims of Palestinian Violence and Terrorism since September 2000," at http://www.mfa.gov.il/MFA/Terrorism-+Obstacle+to+Peace/Palestinian+terror+since+2000/Victims+of+Palestinian+Violence+and+Terrorism+sinc.htm.

in 2002.[95] As Aharon Barak, the retired president of the Israeli Supreme Court, has written, "in Israel we had not only September 11, but also September 10 and September 12."[96]

As with Northern Ireland and the initial U.S. approach to Guantánamo, there are important spatial distinctions in Israel between terrorism law in the Occupied Territories and in Israel proper, with the law of war increasingly being applied in the Occupied Territories. At the same time, such distinctions are permeable, as suggested by Oren Gross and Fionnuala Ni Aolain.[97] The Israeli approach is closer to a war than a criminal justice model, especially in the Occupied Territories. Nevertheless, the Israeli approach is rooted in legality, transparency, and frequent judicial review, even over matters, such as targeted killing, that, in the United States, remain resistant to judicial review.

Reliance on Old Laws and British Colonial Emergency Regulations

Israel's first report to the CTC established by Security Council Resolution 1373 sounded similar themes in relying on old laws and extensive experience with terrorism, as seen in Egypt's and Syria's reports. Israel's report noted that it had been "threatened by terrorism since its independence" and that 66 men, women, and children had been killed by acts of terrorism in Israel, including suicide bombings in the three months since 9/11.[98] Although the report noted some new initiatives with respect to terrorism financing and money laundering and the declaration of al Qaeda as an unlawful organization in October 2001,[99] much of it focused on older laws that already provided Israel with strong measures to combat terrorism.

Israeli's older measures included the Defence Regulations (State of Emergency) (1945), which were inherited from colonial rule during the British mandate rule in Palestine. These measures applied in the West Bank and the Gaza Strip. They established military courts to try offenses. In addition to military offenses, the Defence Regulations authorized indeterminate detention without trial in the form of renewable, six-month periods of detention, with appeals to an advisory committee that provided advice to the military commander about release.[100] These powers are quite similar to those of the ISAs

95 United Nations Office for the Co-ordination of Humanitarian Affairs, "Israeli-Palestinian Fatalities Key Trends," at http://domino.un.org/unispal.nsf/d9d90d845776b7af85256d08006f3ae9/beo7c8ocda45794685257348005002?2?OpenDocument&Click=.
96 Barak, "Human Right in Times of Terror," at 499.
97 Oren Gross and Fionnuala Ni Aolain, *Law in Times of Crisis* (New York: Cambridge University Press, 2006), at 181.
98 Israel Country Report, S/2001/1312, at para. 4.
99 Ibid., at 10.
100 Defence Regulations (State of Emergency) (1945), Section 111.

used in Singapore and Malaysia, as well as those used in the early 1970's in Northern Ireland, and they provide a reminder that colonial powers imposed harsh measures against insurgents and terrorists long before 9/11.[101] Part of the 9/11 effect has been increased legitimacy of old powers of administrative detention on the basis of secret evidence.

The 1945 Defence Regulations allowed the minister of defense to declare organizations to be unlawful and criminalized membership and support in such associations. The regulations provided for what today would be called control orders in the form of curfews and restrictions on the residence of persons.[102] They also contained provisions to prohibit immigration and sub-ject illegal immigrants to detention.[103] The use of immigration law as anti-terrorism law did not start with 9/11 and as will be seen deportations were a frequently used anti-terrorism device during the Malaya emergency. It is striking how much of post-9/11 antiterrorism law has roots in British colonial emergency rule.[104] Another of the 9/11 effects seen throughout this book is the ability of 9/11 to revive and relegitimize harsh older measures used in colonial emergencies.

Israel's 1948 Prevention of Terrorism Ordinance made membership in a terrorist organization, "even if not accompanied by active participation,"[105] an offense punishable by up to five years' imprisonment. Section 2 of the 1948 act made participation in a terrorist organization a crime punishable by up to 20 years' imprisonment.[106] As will be seen, many forms of membership and participation in terrorist group offenses were featured in post-9/11 antiterrorism laws in Australia and Canada. The 1948 Israeli law also provided for an early form of terrorism financing law by prohibiting fund-raising or the giving of property to terrorist groups and providing for the confiscation of their prop-erty. Prosecutions were assisted by a number of presumptions, including a presumption that a person who had once been a member continued to be a member and that government listing of a terrorist organization meant that the organization was a terrorist organization. Israel already had the benefit of

---

[101] For an examination of the role of British colonial emergency regulations in India, see Anil Kalhan et al., "Colonial Continuities: Human Rights, Terrorism and Security in India" (2006) 20 Columbia Journal of Asian Law 93, at 128ff.; A. W. B. Simpson, "Round Up the Usual Suspects: The Legacy of British Colonialism and the European Convention of Human Rights" (1996) 41 Loyola Law Review 629; Simpson, "Colonialism, Emergencies and the Rule of Law" (2002) 22 Oxford Journal of Legal Studies 17.

[102] Defence Regulations (State of Emergency) (1945), Section 110.

[103] Claude Klein, "Israel's Legal Arsenal in Its Struggle against Terrorism" (2006) 27 Cardozo Law Review 2223, at 2227–8.

[104] Gross and Ni Aolain, *Law in Times of Crisis*, at 181–90.

[105] Ibid., at 13.   [106] Ibid.

broadly worded laws prohibiting direct or indirect support of terrorist groups even while many other democracies were drafting similar laws in response to 9/11 and Resolution 1373.

New Laws and Expanded Definitions of Terrorism

Despite its broad offenses, Israel's 1948 Prevention of Terrorism Ordinance used a minimalist definition of terrorism that focused on "acts of violence calculated to cause death or injury to a person" or "threats of such acts of violence."[107] As will be seen, such narrow definitions of terrorism were out of fashion in the post-9/11 era. In 2004, Israel enacted a new law against terrorism financing that had a broader and more modern definition of terrorism. This definition of terrorism is also contained in new draft Israeli legislation to consolidate terrorism laws. The 2004 Prohibition on Terrorist Financing Law[108] defines an act of terrorism as an act or threat committed or planned "in order to influence a matter of policy, ideology or religion" to cause fear or panic or to coerce a government, if the act included the following:

1. actual injury to a person's body or his freedom, or placing a person in danger of death or danger of grievous bodily injury;
2. the creation of actual danger to the health or security of the public;
3. serious damage to property;
4. serious disruption of vital infrastructures, systems or services.[109]

This definition of terrorism, like many other post-9/11 acts, relies heavily on the broad definition of terrorism found in Section 1 of the United Kingdom's Terrorism Act, 2000. The influential British definition similarly applies to threats of actions and actions designed to influence governments and advancing a political, religious or ideological goal and covers not only violence but also serious property damage and serious disruption of important systems.[110]

---

[107] Prevention of Terrorism Ordinance (1948), Sections 1, 7. A translated version of the 1948 law is available at http://www.unodc.org/tldb/showDocument.do?documentUid=2183&node= docs&cmd=add&country=ISR.

[108] Prohibition on Terrorist Financing Law, 5765–2004; unofficial English translation available at http://www.unodc.org/tldb/pdf/Israel_ProhibitionTerroristFinancing-5765-2004.pdf.

[109] Ibid., Section 1.

[110] As in Australia and Canada, Israel expanded the reference in Section 1 of the Terrorism Act, 2000, c.11, to disruption of an electronic system to include serious disruptions of all vital infrastructure, systems, or services and to require that acts of terrorism be designed to coerce foreign or domestic governments, as opposed to the British use of the broader concept of simply influencing governments.

It is striking how much transnational borrowing has occurred with respect to the definition of terrorism. Defenders of the broad British definition of terrorism argue with some justification that it simply mirrors the nature of modern terrorism and the vulnerabilities of modern societies.[111] At the same time, however, it also increases the risk that terrorism laws and powers will be used to target unlawful but nonviolent dissent.[112] The use of a broad new definition of terrorism in Israel's 2004 terrorism financing law may make it difficult for Israel to adopt a more limited definition either in its own laws or in the international arena. Broader definitions of terrorism may prevail, despite Israel's s 1948 law having a minimal definition of terrorism that, like earlier British versions,[113] focused on violence. One important 9/11 effect is the trend toward broader definitions of terrorism.

House Demolitions and Forfeiture of Terrorist Property Compared: The Question of Collective Punishment

Israel's 2004 terrorism financing law is fairly typical of such laws and relies on the listing of terrorist groups and individuals. It provides for executive proscription of international terrorist groups under a new procedure for groups listed by the UN Security Council and foreign governments while also not derogating from old Israeli listing provisions provided by the 1945 and 1948 laws. It includes various offenses against dealings with terrorist property, imposes duties on people to report reasonable suspicions about such transactions, and provides for the forfeiture of terrorist property both on conviction and in separate civil proceedings. Section 26(b) of the 2004 law, however, provides that judges should not order forfeiture of property under the act "unless it has found that the owner of the property to be forfeited and his family members residing with him shall have reasonable means of subsistence and a reasonable place of residence."[114] This humanitarian standard seems designed to ensure that families affected by forfeitures still have a roof over their heads. It can be contrasted with a harsher approach to the demolitions of houses of terrorists under the 1945 Emergency Regulations.

---

[111] Emmanuel Gross, *The Struggle of Democracy against Terrorism* (Charlottesville: University of Virginia Press, 2006), at 17; Lord Carlile, *Report on the Definition of Terrorism* (2007).

[112] Special rapporteur on protecting human rights while countering terrorism has criticized the breadth of Israel's new definition. Israel Country Report, A/HRC/6/17/add.4, at para. 16. This criticism, however, discounts how much Israel closely followed the United Kingdom's definition.

[113] See Chapter 5.

[114] Prohibition on Terrorist Financing Law, 5765–2004; unofficial English translation available at http://www.unodc.org/tldb/pdf/Israel_ProhibitionTerroristFinancing-5765-2004.pdf.

In 1997, a divided Israeli Supreme Court upheld Section 119 of the 1945 regulations used to demolish the house of a suicide bomber. In the majority judgment, President Barak concluded,

> We are aware that the demolition will leave petitioner 1 and her children without the roof over their heads, but this is not the aim of the demolition. It is not a punitive measure. It aims, rather, to deter. Its outcome does pose difficulties for the family, but respondent believes that this measure is essential in order to prevent further attacks on innocent people. He maintains that family pressure does discourage terrorists. There is no absolute assurance that this measure will be effective. But considering the very few measures left to the state to defend itself against these "human bombs," we should not despise them.[115]

Justice Cheshin, in a strong dissent, emphasized that the woman and children were innocent and did not know about and were not accomplices in the suicide bombing, which killed three persons.

In subsequent cases, the Israeli Supreme Court upheld house demolitions and deferred to the security authorities in determining what was necessary to deter suicide bombers. It also stressed the preventive and deterrent purposes of the demolitions, as opposed to their punitive effects. The courts applied a shallow proportionality principle that focused on whether less restrictive measures, such as sealing or destroying only part of the house, would suffice, without really probing the assertions of security officials that demolitions were rationally connected to the deterrence of terrorism. The shallowness of the court's proportionality analysis in these cases is revealed by its reliance on the language of balancing.[116] In one case, the Israeli Supreme Court concluded

---

[115] *Janimat v. IDF Military Commander HCJ* (2006/97); English translation in *Judgments of the Israel Supreme Court: Fighting Terrorism within the Law* (Jerusalem: Israel Supreme Court, 2005), at 63.

[116] In one case, the court stressed that "the reasonability of a decision under Regulation 119 is the outcome of the balancing and weighing up" of multiple criteria. In another case, the court stressed that "both the scope and the reasonableness of measures adopted by competent authorities for the maintenance of security can only be measured against the background of changing circumstances. . . . We are all aware and sense the extreme increase of late in the readiness of terrorist organizations to commit murderous attacks against all Israelis, soldiers and citizens alike, with the perpetrators undertaking to execute the attack by becoming suicide bombers. This is an entirely new dimension of crazy fanaticism." As quoted and translated in Gross, *Struggle of Democracy*, at 98, 100. For defense of the decisions as a form of balancing the demands of security and rights and stressing the role of judicial review, see Aharon Barak, "A Judge on Judging: The Role of a Supreme Court in a Democracy" (2002) 116 Harvard Law Review 19, at 154–5. For criticisms of balancing as opposed to more rigorous proportionality analysis, see Jeremy Waldron, "Security and Liberty: The Image of Balance" (2005) 11 Journal of Political Philosophy 191; Lucia Zedner, "Securing Liberty in the Face of Terror" (2005)

that house demolitions are not collective punishment because "the power is administrative" even while recognizing that "the harsh result" of destroying the family's home is "intended to deter potential perpetrators...who must understand that by their own actions, not only do they endanger public peace and security and the lives of innocent people, but also the welfare of their own relatives."[117] Such conclusions ignore the punitive effects of house demolitions.

Even when the focus is on the state's purposes, the idea that house demolitions are designed to deter suggests that they are a form of collective punishment because deterrence is one of the long-accepted purposes of punishment.[118] The idea of collective culpability for terrorism is more of a war model or a form of enemy criminal law than a crime model based on individual responsibility. It also arguably violates Article 33 of the Fourth Geneva Convention, providing that "no protected person may be punished for an offence he or she has not personally committed. Collective penalties and likewise all measures of intimidation or of terrorism is prohibited."[119] A democracy

---

32 Journal of Law and Society; Kent Roach, "Must We Trade Rights for Security?" (2006) 27 Cardozo Law Review 2151.

[117] *Shukri v. Minister of Defence* (HC 798/98), as translated in Gross, *Struggle of Democracy*, at 97.

[118] Defenders of house demolitions seem to concede that they are a form of collective punishment. Professor Emmanuel Gross argues that house demolitions "may lead other potential terrorists to reconsider whether to undertake terrorist activities. They are made aware that in doing so they are endangering not only themselves but also the domicile of their families. *This is a just punitive measure, if indeed it proves to be a deterrent.*" Gross, *Struggle of Democracy*, at 107. Professor Alan Dershowitz goes further and asserts that by encouraging suicide bombers, Palestinians "share culpability for the murder of civilians" and concludes that "any effective attack calculated to reduce terrorism – especially suicide bombers – *must* include an element of collective accountability and punishment for those supporting terrorism." Alan Dershowitz, *Why Terrorism Works* (New Haven, CT: Yale University Press, 2002), at 177, 181.

[119] The Red Cross commentary to this provision explains that a "great step forward has been taken. Responsibility is personal and it will no longer be possible to inflict penalties on persons who have themselves not committed the acts complained of." The commentary also notes the often counterproductive effects of collective punishment by stating that "during past conflicts, the infliction of collective penalties has been intended to forestall breaches of the law rather than to repress them; in resorting to intimidatory measures to terrorise the population, the belligerents hoped to prevent hostile acts. Far from achieving the desired effect, however, such practices, by reason of their excessive severity and cruelty, kept alive and strengthened the spirit of resistance. They strike at guilty and innocent alike. They are opposed to all principles based on humanity and justice and it is for that reason that the prohibition of collective penalties is followed formally by the prohibition of all measures of intimidation or terrorism with regard to protected persons, wherever they may be." Convention (IV) Relative to the Protection of Civilian Persons in Time of War, Geneva, August 12, 1949. Commentaries at 225–6, available at http://www.icrc.org/ihl.nsf/WebList?ReadForm&id=380&t=com. There is much critical literature on house demolitions that stress their punitive effects and conclude that they violate international law, including Dan Simon, "The Demolition of Homes in Israel's Occupied Territories" (1994) 19 Yale Journal of International Law 1; Martin Carroll,

that resorts to collective punishment when combating terrorism loses its upper hand by accepting the way of the terrorist by punishing the innocent.

Although the Israeli Supreme Court accepted that house demolitions were legal in the vast majority of the cases it heard, the Israeli Defence Force eventually concluded that they were ineffective after having engaged in a reported 675 dwelling demolitions between 2000 and 2005.[120] It is striking that the security professionals eventually decided that legally approved harsh tactics were counter-productive. This is a pattern that will be seen in other chapters. Internment was abandoned by the British in Northern Ireland because of a sense that it was the "terrorist's best friend," and the Obama administration has (unsuccessfully) attempted to close Guantánamo on the basis of similar instrumental reasoning. We will also see that instrumental concerns about the effectiveness of counter-terrorism measures are not simply the preserve of executive and political actors.[121] In the United Kingdom, the House of Lords declared indeterminate detention of international terrorists who were noncitizens to be disproportionate and discriminatory, in large part on the basis that such measures are not an effective response to the terrorist threat. It stressed that the measures did not match the terrorist threat, which also came from citizens, and that it allowed the release of an alien if another country was prepared to accept the person.[122] In many cases, full proportionality analysis of counter-terrorism measures will evaluate the effectiveness of the proposed measures and conclude that disproportionate measures are both unfair and counter-productive.[123]

The policy of house demolitions has been revived and approved in two cases in 2009, involving the houses of terrorists in East Jerusalem. The Israeli Supreme Court, consistent with earlier cases, held that the demolitions were legal and did not constitute collective punishment. It stated that the issue of

"The Israeli Demolition of Palestinian Homes" (1990) 11 Michigan Journal of International Law 1195.

[120] Amos Guiora, *Global Perspectives on Counterterrorism* (New York: Aspen, 2007), at 32; Ami Pedahzur and Arie Perliger, "The Consequences of Counterterrorist Policies in Israel," *The Consequences of Counterterrorism*, ed. Martha Crenshaw (New York: Russell Sage, 2010), at 343; Menachem Hofnung and Keren Weinshall-Margel "Judicial Rejection as Substantial Relief: The Israel Supreme Court and the 'War on Terror'" in Mary Volcansek and John Stack eds. *Courts and Terrorism* (New York: Cambridge University Press, 2011) at 159.

[121] Aharon Barak has, however, argued that "the court should not adopt a position on the efficient security measures for fighting terrorism." Barak, "A Judge on Judging," at 157.

[122] A v. *Secretary of State* (2004) UKHL 56.

[123] In some cases, harsh policies can be excluded on the basis that they are an emotive response that is not even rationally connected to their purported aim in preventing terrorism. See Roach, "Must We Trade Rights for Security?"

the effectiveness and wisdom of the policy should be left to other authorities.[124] The old policy of house demolitions has been revived even though the 2004 terrorism financing law prohibits forfeiture of terrorist property that would leave people homeless. In this respect, a post-9/11 antiterrorism is more restrained and consistent with the rule of law than the older antiterrorism measure of house demolition authorized under the 1945 emergency regulations. In Israel the older regulation would be sheltered from judicial challenge under the 1992 Basic Law on Human Dignity and Liberty. Although this Basic Law protects the right to property, it does not affect the validity of laws enacted before 1992.

The revival of house demolitions raises the possibility that such measures will be counter-productive even though they have been upheld by the courts. Some harsh counter-terrorism measures, particularly those that harm the innocent, may simply inspire more acts of terrorism than they deter. As suggested earlier, some forms of proportionality analysis allow courts to evaluate the effectiveness of an impugned measure and to suggest to governments that the same security objectives can be achieved through less drastic measures. Courts may, however, be reluctant to draw such conclusions, and as is the case with house demolitions, they may leave such issues to the executive. One study of 462 rulings made by the Israeli Supreme Court in security cases between 2000 and 2008 including those concerning house demolitions, administrative detention, the separation wall between Israel and the West Bank and military operations in the Occupied Territories found that the Court rejected petitions in 63% of cases and only fully accepted the petition in 8% of cases.[125] Although this study stresses that these success rates are higher than in previous studies and that Court can place restraints on security policies even when they do not invalidate them, these findings suggest that judicial review of many security measures in Israel frequently results in judicial deference to state measures.

Laws against Speech Associated with Terrorism

Although the UN Security Council would not focus on the incitement of terrorism until after the London bombings in 2005, Israel's first report to

---

[124] Ido Rozenzweig and Yuval Shany, "H.C.J. [Israeli High Court of Justice] 9353/08 Abu-Dahim v. Aluf Pikud HaOref Regarding a House Demolition in East Jerusalem," at http://www.idi.org.il/sites/english/ResearchAndPrograms/NationalSecurityandDemocracy/Terrorism_and_Democracy/Newsletters/Pages/1st%20Newsletter/3/first_3.aspx.

[125] Menachem Hofnung and Keren Weinshall-Margel "Judicial Rejection as Substantial Relief: The Israel Supreme Court and the 'War on Terror'" in Mary Volcansek and John Stack eds. *Courts and Terrorism* (New York: Cambridge University Press, 2011) at 163.

the CTC stressed how its 1945 and 1948 laws responded to the dangers of recruiting terrorists "via incitement and propaganda."[126] Section 2 of the 1948 law made delivering a propaganda speech at a public meeting or over the airwaves punishable by up to 20 years' imprisonment, whereas Section 4 made publishing "words of praise, sympathy or encouragement" of acts of violence or appeals to support a terrorist organization punishable by up to 3 years' imprisonment. Regulation 85 of the 1945 Emergency Regulations also established "a number of offences relating to unlawful associations, including membership, holding an office, performing services, attending meetings, providing a place for meeting to be held, possessing propaganda or acting as a representative of such an organization."[127] The 1948 law went on to make it an offense to express "identification with a terrorist organization or sympathy with a terrorist organization" by display of symbols such as flags or slogans or to suggest that one "acts on behalf, or as representative of an unlawful organization."[128] These offenses bear some resemblance to the broad proscription offenses found in Section 11-13 of the United Kingdom's Terrorism Act, 2000, which similarly targets speech and associations with proscribed organizations. They embrace an anti-insurgency model of counter-terrorism that prohibits not only violence but any expression of support or sympathy for terrorists.

The 1948 Israeli law resembles Singapore's ISA in its focus on expression associated with terrorism, including provisions directed at the possession of propaganda for a terrorist organization. To the extent the 1948 law went beyond punishing terrorist acts, it can be seen "as the first instance in which the new state applied the principle of self-defending democracy"[129] or militant democracy. The speech provisions of the 1948 ordinance had largely not been enforced because of concerns about interference with free speech, but prosecutions increased with concerns about violent rhetoric in the wake of the 1995 assassination of Prime Minister Rabin and the 1994 killing of 29 Muslim worshippers in Hebron.[130]

When the UN encouraged states to enact laws against the incitement of terrorism in Resolution 1624, Israel was able to reply that the work was already done. Israel relied not on the 1948 law but on 2002 criminal code amendments that prohibited both calls to commit acts of terrorism and also words of

---

[126] Israel Country Report, S/2001/1312, at para. 10.
[127] Ibid., at para. 14.   [128] Ibid., at para. 9.
[129] Benjamin Neuberger, "Israel," in *The "Militant Democracy" Principle in Modern Democracies*, ed. Markus Thiele (London: Ashgate, 2009), at 188. For the related idea that Israel is a defensive democracy, see Barak, "A Judge on Judging," at 21, 37.
[130] Miriam Gur-Ayre, "Can Freedom of Expression Survive Social Trauma?" (2003) 13 Duke Journal of Comparative and International Law 155.

"praise, sympathy or encouragement" if there was a "real possibility" that acts of terrorism or violence would occur as a result of the incitement.[131] The 2002 Israeli law was enacted in part because the 1948 law was interpreted to apply only to the praise of violence by terrorist organizations and not by individuals.[132] Nevertheless, the 2002 law was more protective of free expression than the speech provisions of Israel's 1948 law or even 2006 British laws against indirect advocacy of terrorism because it required a real possibility that the speech would cause an act of violence or terrorism.

The Criminal Law Model

Israel has a number of criminal offenses against terrorism, including offenses against assisting the "enemy" or having contact with a "foreign agent," with both terms being defined to include terrorist organizations and their members. As in the United Kingdom, there is also an offense of failing to inform authorities of a terrorist act. In addition, Israel also asserted extraterritorial jurisdiction over terrorist crimes directed at Israel or Jews before many states enacted post-9/11 laws asserting universal jurisdiction over terrorist crimes.[133] Even with respect to these criminal laws, however, Israel moved in the direction of a war model, with its emphasis on assisting the enemy and protecting Israeli interests abroad.

Most acts of terrorism in the Occupied Territories are tried in military courts, where the state must prove guilt and the use of secret evidence is not allowed.[134] The suspects can, however, be denied access to defense lawyers for significant periods, and they are generally first interrogated by the security service in an attempt to develop intelligence.[135] Concerns have been raised about incommunicado detention during this period.[136] In 2002, an Israeli civilian criminal court affirmed its ability to try Marwan Barghouti, a resident

---

[131] Israel Country Report, S/2006/183, at para. 7.

[132] Gur-Ayre, "Can Freedom of Expression Survive Social Trauma," at 198–9; Mordechai Kremnitzer and Liat Levanon-Morag, "Limiting Freedom of Speech for the Prevention of Terrorism" (2004) 7 Law and Government 305.

[133] The Israeli offense, unlike the U.K. offense, however, exempts close relatives from prosecutions. At the same time, defenses of necessity and duress are precluded in Israel as defenses to terrorist crimes. See Mordechai Kremnitzer, "Israeli Substantive Criminal Law Dealing with Terrorism," forthcoming.

[134] Amos N. Guiora, *Global Perspectives on Counterterrorism* (Austin, TX: Aspen, 2007), at 335.

[135] Ibid., at 289.

[136] Public Committee against Torture in Israel, *When the Exception Becomes the Rule*, November 2010.

of the West Bank, on criminal terrorist charges and rejected arguments that the accused was entitled to prisoner of war status or to employ force against Israel.[137] This decision to use the criminal courts, however, has been described as a political one, based on the high profile of the accused, and one that was resisted by the "security apparatus,"[138] who believed that it was better to continue to rely on military judges. In the end, however, Barghouti was convicted of five murders and other crimes.[139] Nevertheless, security offenses make up fewer than 1 percent of convictions in Israeli courts, whereas offenses of "hostile terrorist activity" make up about one-third of indictments in military courts in the Occupied Territories.[140]

The UN response to 9/11 has encouraged Israel to enact more criminal offenses against terrorism and terrorism financing. In its first report to the CTC, Israel reported that providing money to terrorist organizations was illegal under the 1948 Prevention of Terrorism Ordinance, which, as discussed earlier, featured a minimal definition of terrorism. In 2004, however, Israel enacted a new terrorist financing law that included a broad definition of terrorism. This new definition was also included in a new draft terrorism bill circulated in Israel in 2010. The new law is designed to update and replace the 1948 Prevention of Terrorism Ordinance. Consistent with post-9/11 trends to expand terrorism laws, the draft bill features broader definitions of both terrorism and terrorist organizations than found in the 1948 law. For example, a terrorist organization is defined not only as a group that commits a terrorist act but also as "an association of people which promotes or enables the activity of a terrorist organization."[141] Such a broad definition would apply to the Dahwah organization, which provides medical and social services for Hamas.[142] The rationale for such a broad definition is that money and energy

---

[137] *Israel v. Barghouti* (Criminal Case no. 092134, 2002), District Court of Tel Aviv, and Jaffa, as translated in ibid., at 338–41.

[138] Ibid., at 338n78.

[139] Daphne Barak Erez, "Israel's Anti-Terrorism Law: Past, Present and Future," in *Global Anti-Terrorism Law and Policy*, 2nd ed., ed. Victor Ramraj (New York: Cambridge University Press, forthcoming).

[140] Public Committee against Torture in Israel, *When the Exception Becomes the Rule*, at 18–19.

[141] Ibid.

[142] Ido Rozenzweig and Yuval Shany, "New Comprehensive Counter-Terrorism Memorandum Bill" (2010) 17 Terrorism and Democracy Newsletter, at http://www.idi.org.il/sites/english/ResearchAndPrograms/NationalSecurityandDemocracy/Terrorism_and_Democracy/Newsletters/Pages/17th%20newsletter/1/1.aspx.

spent on humanitarian objectives frees up money for violence. A similar rationale has been approved by the majority of the U.S. Supreme Court in its 2010
decision in *Holder v. Humanitarian Law Project*.[143]

The new bill also provides expanded offenses against providing services,
recruiting terrorists, providing or receiving training, preparation for a terrorist
act, and failing to prevent a terrorist act. It also provides for some special
procedures for terrorist trials, including provisions relating to denial of access to
counsel, preventive arrests and the deeming of statements by absent witnesses
to be evidence. Following the British example, it also provides for control
orders. All these provisions seem generally to be consistent with the expansion
of post-9/11 terrorism law seen in other democracies. That the new bill will, in
many respects, be broader than the 1948 law underlines the post-9/11 expansion
ambit of state powers to prevent and prosecute terrorism. The new bill, unlike
the 1948 law, is no longer tied to a declaration of emergency and as such would
represent a normalization of strong antiterrorism measures.

It remains to be seen whether the proposed bill will be enacted and whether
it will encourage Israel to rely more on criminal law than on military or administrative detention when responding to terrorism. Israeli criminal procedure
gives the accused broad rights to disclosure of all material held or in the
control of the state.[144] This approach helps promote fairness in the criminal
courts, but it also gives the state incentive to rely on administrative detention,
which, as will be seen, allows the use of secret evidence. In addition, the use of
criminal prosecutions would subject the gathering of intelligence, including
harsh interrogations, to more intense judicial review because Israeli criminal
courts apply voluntariness and other exclusionary rules.[145] Security intelligence
agencies in Israel and elsewhere see advantages in relying on alternatives to
criminal prosecutions that allow the use of secret evidence, thus protecting
the state's interests in secret intelligence and minimizing the scrutiny of its
intelligence-gathering practices. The choice between administrative detention and criminal prosecution is not zero sum because, as will be seen, Israel
allows administrative detention after offenders have served prison sentences
under the criminal law. Both the United Kingdom and Australia would take a

---

[143] 130 S.Ct. 2705 (2010). As Rozenzweig and Shany write, "the philosophy underlying such a
broad definition is that auxiliary organizations are meant to generate public support for terrorist
organizations, such as Hamas, through the humanitarian activities they conduct. Moreover,
the bill assumes that auxiliary organizations can also be used to channel money for the purpose
of financing the terrorist activity of the terrorist organizations and recruiting new members for
terrorist activity." Ibid.

[144] Rinat Kitai-Sangero, "Israel," in *Criminal Procedure: A Worldwide Study*, 2nd ed., ed. Craig
Bradley (Durham: Carolina Academic Press, 2007), at 292.

[145] Ibid., at 286.

somewhat similar approach after 9/11 by allowing the use of control orders in cases in which criminal convictions failed or were overturned.[146]

Harsh Interrogation and Torture: From the Landau Commission to the Public Committee against Torture Cases

As will be examined in the next chapter, debates about harsh interrogation and torture of terrorist suspects to gain intelligence are probably the best known and most controversial feature of the American response to 9/11. In many of these debates, however, the Israeli (as well as the British) experience with these issues was not adequately considered. In 1987, the Landau Commission found that the Israeli General Security Service (GSS) was at fault for lying to criminal courts about the harsh nature of its interrogation practices. The commission did not accept the agents' attempts to justify their actions as necessary to secure convictions or to protect their methods of interrogation from disclosure or their assurance that other intelligence confirmed the guilt of the accused.[147] In this respect, the Landau Commission set strict standards for criminal prosecutions that did not tolerate the use of torture to obtain involuntary confessions or perjury.

Although it repudiated the use of the torture to obtain confessions, the Landau Commission concluded that a "moderate measure of physical pressure"[148] was nevertheless justified in interrogations by the necessity defense in criminal law. The commission concluded, "Are we to accept the offence of assault in slapping a suspect's face or threatening him, in order to induce him to talk and to reveal a cache of explosive materials meant for use in carrying out an act of mass terror against a civilian population, and thereby prevent the greater evil which is about to occur? The answer is self-evident."[149] The commission warned that "the pressure must never reach the level of physical torture or maltreatment of the suspect or grievous harm to his honour which deprives him of his human dignity."[150] Nevertheless, it concluded that interrogations using "a moderate measure of physical pressure"[151] were lawful and could even produce confessions that would be admissible in court. The voluntariness rule applied by civil and military courts in Israel would be tempered by factors such as the seriousness of the offense charged and the need for public safety.[152]

---

[146] See Chapters 5 and 6.
[147] Landau Commission Report (1989) 23 Israel Law Review 141, at 164.
[148] Ibid., at 141.
[149] Ibid., at 174.
[150] Ibid., at 175.
[151] Ibid., at 184.
[152] Ibid., at 178.

The commission proposed not legislation but internal and secret regulations within the GSS to regulate how much force could be used in interrogations. A secret part of the report provided "detailed guidelines" about interrogation methods to be reviewed annually by ministers.[153] The commission also recommended against prosecution or disciplinary action of GSS agents who had applied physical pressure in their interrogations and lied about it to the courts, thus accepting the extralegal actions of the security service.

There was much negative reaction to the Landau Commission's proposals. Professor Dershowitz argued that allowing an intelligence agency to claim necessity on an ad hoc basis was "essentially lawless and undemocratic."[154] Professor Kremnitzer argued that the commission had misinterpreted the necessity defense as an authorization of governmental actions and that the use of physical pressure would violate the human dignity of those interrogated and could spiral into torture.[155] Professor Feller also criticized reliance on the necessity defense and concluded that the legislature would never enact a law authorizing the use of physical force because it "would constitute an affront to the values of all civilized people."[156] In the wake of the Landau Commission, unsuccessful attempts were made to challenge the legality of the GSS directives, and the Israeli courts refused to prohibit the use of physical force in interrogations. There were widespread reports of torture and abuse by the GSS, and the UN criticized Israel for its practices.[157] There were also concerns that GSS interrogators continued to lie to the courts about harsh interrogation techniques, even though some of them might have been authorized by the Landau Commission recommendations.[158]

In 1999, the Israeli Supreme Court decided perhaps its most famous case involving terrorism. An unusual nine-judge panel found that neither the necessity defense nor the GSS directives authorized the use of physical pressure, including shaking, various stress positions, sacking, and sleep deprivation.

---

[153] Ibid., at 185.

[154] Alan Dershowitz, "Is It Necessary to Apply Physical Pressure to Terrorists and to Lie about It?" (1989) 23 Israel Law Review 192, at 200.

[155] Mordechai Kremnitzer, "Was the Security Service Subordinated to the Law or the Law to the Needs of the Security Service?" (1989) 23 Israel Law Review 216, at 251, 263.

[156] S. Z. Feller, "Not Actual Necessity but Possible Justification" (1989) 23 Israel Law Review 201, at 213.

[157] Ardi Imseis, "Moderate Torture on Trial: Critical Reflections on the Israeli Supreme Court" (2001) 5 International Journal of Human Rights 71, at 78–9; Catherine Grosso, "International Law in the Domestic Arena: The Case of Torture in Israel" (2000) 86 Iowa Law Review 305.

[158] Mordechai Kremnitzer and Re'em Segev, "The Legality of Interrogational Torture: A Question of Proper Authorization or a Substantive Moral Issue?" (2000) 34 Israel Law Review 509, at 513–14.

The case involved several petitions, including those brought by public interest groups, such as the Public Committee against Torture in Israel, but also by individuals detained, charged, and sometimes subsequently convicted of terrorism offenses. In two of the cases, the state told the court that the interrogations had resulted in the discovery of a bomb and the thwarting of other terrorist attacks. Nevertheless, President Barak concluded that it is the "destiny of a democracy ... [to] fight with one hand tied behind its back. Even so, a democracy has the upper hand. The rule of law and the liberty of an individual constitute important components in its understanding of security."[159]

President Barak concluded that "if the state wishes to enable GSS investigators to utilize physical means in interrogations, it must enact legislation for this purpose"[160] and that the legislation would have to stand up to constitutional scrutiny under Israel's 1992 Basic Law on Human Dignity and Liberty. This was a call for much more transparency than contemplated by the Landau Commission, and it demonstrates how courts in the counter-terrorism field can force the legislature, by invalidating illegal executive action, to take responsibility and to regulate the otherwise secret activities of the security executive. In this way, judges can force increased democratic debate about security measures while not accepting final responsibility for the measures taken or, indeed, for the failure to prevent acts of terrorism.

The court's judgment also addressed the issue of torture, albeit in a somewhat ambiguous manner. On one hand, President Barak stated that "a reasonable investigation is necessarily one free of torture, free of cruel, inhuman treatment and free of any degrading conduct whatsoever," with "no exceptions" and "no room for balancing."[161] At the same time, the judgment did not rule out that the necessity defense might be available after the fact in a ticking-bomb case.[162] The judgment has been criticized for leaving the door open to the use of torture in vaguely defined ticking-bomb situations and for failing to focus on the absolute nature of the right against torture in international law.[163]

In response to the decision, some opposition members, including Ariel Sharon, drafted a law that would have allowed the director of the GSS to authorize "special measures" and "physical pressure" in ticking-bomb situations.[164] These controversial provisions were dropped, and a 2002 law on the GSS remained silent on interrogation. The GSS directives were not made public

---

[159] *Public Committee against Torture v. Israel* (HCJ 5100/94), at para. 39, in *Judgments of the Israel Supreme Court.*

[160] Ibid., at para. 37.   [161] Ibid., at 43, para. 23.

[162] Ibid., at 50, para. 34.

[163] Kremnitzer and Segev, "Legality of Interrogational Torture."

[164] Michael L. Gross, "Regulating Torture in a Democracy" (2004) 36 Polity 367, at 375.

in the 1999 Public Committee against Torture case because the court accepted the government's claim that they could only be presented in secret, and the petitioner objected to the procedure.[165] Unfortunately, interrogation in Israel remains, as it did under the Landau Commission, in the less transparent executive realm as opposed to the legislative realm,[166] despite the court's efforts to encourage interrogation policy to be legislated.

The lead petitioner in the 1999 case, the Public Committee against Torture in Israel, requested that the supreme court reopen the case in 2009 after documenting 600 complaints of torture against the GSS since 2001 and refusals by authorities to investigate them or to videotape security interrogations, as is done for police investigations.[167] The case was rejected by the supreme court, uncharacteristically on procedural grounds relating to a conclusion that an application for contempt could not be used to enforce the declarations in the 1999 judgment.[168] In 2009, the UN's Committee against Torture expressed concerns about the continued possibility of necessity being used as a defense to torture. It also expressed concerns about a 2006 law that allows up to 96 hours before a detainee is brought before a judge and up to 21 days without access to a lawyer, exemptions of security interrogations from video-recording requirements, the use of administrative detention, and the lack of criminal investigation into the 600 complaints of ill treatment by intelligence investigators.[169] The UN special rapporteur on protecting human rights while countering terrorism expressed concerns that no interrogator has been criminally charged since the 1999 decision and that they can obtain advance approval for physical interrogation in so-called ticking-bomb cases.[170]

---

[165] Imseis, "Moderate Torture on Trial," at 81.

[166] Daphne Barak-Erez, "Terrorism Law between the Executive and the Legislative Models" (2009) 57 American Journal of Comparative Law 877.

[167] Public Committee against Torture in Israel, *Accountability Denied: The Absence of Investigation and Punishment of Torture in Israel*, December 2009, at http://www.stoptorture .org.il/files/Accountability_Denied_Eng.pdf.

[168] The court also noted that the factual basis for the proceedings was incomplete and would have to be determined in individual proceedings. Ido Rozenzweig and Yuval Shany have commented that "although the factual basis presented by the applicant NGOs may indeed be incomplete, it at the very least raises concerns about the degree of compliance of the Israeli authorities with the 1999 HCJ judgment." "Israel High Court Rejects Contempt of Court of Motion on the Use of Torture," at http://www.idi.org.il/sites/english/ ResearchAndPrograms/NationalSecurityandDemocracy/Terrorism_and_ Democracy/Newsletters/Pages/7th%20Newsletter/3/ContemptCourtMotionTorture.aspx.

[169] *Concluding Observations of the Committee against Torture: Israel*, CAT/C/ISR/CO/4, June 23, 2009. See also Yuval Ginbar, *Why Not Torture Terrorists?* (Oxford: Oxford University Press, 2008), chap. 13, for a critique of the supreme court's decision on the basis that it contemplates that torture in a ticking bomb situation could be excused on the basis of necessity.

[170] Israel Country Report, A/HRC/6/17/add.4, at paras. 19–21.

The Israeli experience with harsh interrogation is significant for post-9/11 developments in other democracies. It suggests that legislatures will be reluctant to attempt to authorize or regulate harsh interrogation and that such practices will generally remain in the secret executive realm. Although the Israeli Supreme Court condemned both torture and degrading treatment, it also left the door open for security service personnel in undefined ticking-bomb cases to break the law and engage in torture and claim the necessity defense afterward. This approach is consistent with an extralegal approach because it suggests that the prohibitions on mistreatment may restrain officials even if they are at times broken.[171] Nevertheless, the benefits of such restraints remain doubtful if only because of the lack of subsequent enforcement, even in the face of many complaints of mistreatment and attempts to relitigate the issue.

Administrative Detention

Israel used administrative detention extensively before 9/11 and has expanded its use afterward. As in Singapore and Malaysia, administrative detention was inherited from British colonial emergency rule. The Defence Emergency Regulations (1945) allowed for detention without trial by order of military commanders for renewable six-month periods with limited appeals to an advisory committee. In 1979, this power was reformed in the Emergency Powers (Detention) Law to provide for judicial review within the first 48 hours of administrative detention.[172] As in the original emergency regulations, detention could still be imposed by the executive when deemed necessary for state or public security for renewable six-month increments, and the law allowed the use of secret evidence and deviations from the rules of evidence. The 1979 law is only effective in an emergency situation, but Israel has been in a constant declared state of emergency since its creation.[173] The 1979 law can be applied against citizens and was used against Jewish extremists suspected of being involved in preparing for acts of terrorism against Arabs.[174]

---

[171] Oren Gross, "The Prohibition on Torture and the Limits of the Law," in *Torture*, ed. Sandford Levinson (Oxford: Oxford University Press, 2004).

[172] Section 4(c) allowed the district court to set aside the detention order "if it has been proven to him that the reasons for which it was made were not objective reasons of state security or public security or that it was made in bad faith or from irrelevant considerations." *Emergency Powers (Detention) Law, 1979*, as translated at 21 Columbia Human Rights Law Review 469, at 511.

[173] Gross, *Struggle of Democracy*, at 124.

[174] For criticisms of the use of the law in this context, see Raphael Cohen-Almagor, "Administrative Detention in Israel and Its Employment as a Means of Combating Political Extremism" (1996) 9 New York International Law Review 1.

Administrative detention has been justified as a device both to prevent terrorism and to gather intelligence. Its use of secret evidence allows the state to detain people without exposing intelligence sources and methods to disclosure.[175] Professors Barak-Erez and Waxman have observed that the 1979 law "is quite deferential to the security interests of the state" because it requires evidence to remain secret if its disclosure "may impair state security or public security"[176] without balancing the state's interests in secrecy against those of the detainee. They also note, however, that judges will examine the secret evidence and have recently been insisting that the state disclose the gist of the allegations against the detainee. As will be seen, a number of other countries, including the United Kingdom and Canada, also engaged in administrative detentions on the basis of secret evidence of suspected terrorists after 9/11, though these schemes were subject to successful legal challenges, with the Canadian court stressing the need for adversarial challenge of the secret evidence. In Israel, neither the 1945 nor the 1979 law could be invalidated under the 1992 Basic Law on Human Rights that only applies prospectively. In addition, Israel issued a reservation to Article 9 of the International Covenant on Civil and Political Rights that gives a detainee the right to be informed of the reasons for his or her detention.[177]

The state has many incentives to use administrative detention as a less restrained alternative to criminal prosecutions. In 2003, the Israeli Supreme Court stated that though criminal prosecutions were generally preferable, "for reasons of protecting intelligence sources, it is not always possible to use criminal proceedings."[178] In late 2005, the court upheld the administrative detention of a man apprehended in 2001 in the West Bank, allegedly on his way to commit a suicide bombing. President Barak stressed that "administrative detention is forward-looking, toward future danger. At its foundation, it is not a punitive measure, rather a preventive measure."[179] After reviewing the classified information, which dated from 2001 and 2002, when the person

---

[175] The Landau Commission suggested that administrative detention was an alternative to criminal prosecutions in cases where the state decided that it was necessary to ensure the secrecy of their interrogation techniques. This recommendation revealed the possibility of administrative detention being used as a shortcut that would avoid both disclosure of information and scrutiny of intelligence-gathering techniques. Landau Commission Report (1989) 23 Israel Law Review 141, at 188.

[176] Daphne Barak-Erez and Mathew Waxman, "Secret Evidence and the Due Process of Terrorist Detentions" (2009) 48 Columbia Journal of Transnational Law 3, at 21.

[177] Ibid., at 128–9.

[178] *Salama v. Commander* (IDF HCJ 5784/03), as quoted in Barak-Erez and Waxman "Secret Evidence," at 8–9.

[179] A. v. *Commander of the IDF* (HCJ 11026/05), at para. 7, in *Judgments of the Israel Supreme Court*, at 221.

was first detained, and considering that the burden of justifying the detention would increase with the duration of the detention, President Barak concluded that the petitioner's "release from administrative detention in these times of bloody struggle between the terrorist organizations and the State of Israel would be like the release of a 'ticking bomb' waiting to explode."[180] Unfortunately, the judgment does not examine other alternatives such as prosecution for the alleged attempt at suicide bombing. Such decisions provide intelligence agencies with great incentives to claim that intelligence sources and methods can never be disclosed and subject to adversarial challenge. They also result in long-term administrative detention without clear findings of guilt or innocence.

In 2002, the Knesset expanded the use of administrative detention through the enactment of an Internment of Unlawful Combatants Law. The 2002 law authorizes the chief of staff of the Israeli Defence Force to detain unlawful combatants whose release would harm state security. Unlawful combatants are defined as noncitizens who have directly or indirectly participated in hostilities against Israel or are members of forces that do so and who are not, as regular soldiers, entitled to prisoner of war status. The law's focus on unlawful combatants rejects the dichotomy in the Geneva Conventions that divides persons into civilians or lawful combatants. As with the Bush administration's approach in Guantánamo, this third category approach presents a danger that unlawful combatants, like prisoners of war, will be detained until the end of hostilities, something that given the nature of terrorism may never occur, but also not enjoy the protections that prisoners of war would normally receive against interrogation and intelligence gathering. As in Guantánamo, the 2002 Israeli law is based on the idea that a third way that does not follow the traditional laws of war or crime is necessary to deal with terrorists who are not citizens.

There is still judicial review of administrative detention under the 2002 law, but the standards are less generous than under the 1979 law. Whereas the 1979 law requires a detainee to be brought before a judge in 48 hours, the 2002 law allows a maximum of 14 days' detention without access to a judge. Sections 7 and 8 of the 2002 law provide double presumptions that the release of an unlawful combatant will harm state security and that forces designated by the minister of defense are still pursuing hostilities. Secret evidence that would not be admissible under the ordinary laws of evidence is also allowed, and such evidence or intelligence cannot be disclosed to the detainee if its release would harm state or public security.

---

[180] Ibid., at para. 9.

The immediate impetus for the 2002 law was a controversial decision by the Israeli Supreme Court that maintained that Lebanese citizens held under the 1979 law could not be used as "bargaining counters" for prisoner exchanges.[181] This raises a recurring issue of how legislatures respond to judicial decisions in the security field. As will be seen, rights protecting judicial decisions in both the United Kingdom and the United States have provoked legislative replies such as the enactment of control orders and legislation depriving courts of habeas corpus jurisdiction over the Guantánamo Bay detainees. Professors Ewing and Tham argue that such cases reveal the futility of judicial review in the face of the state's security interests.[182] Although their thesis discounts the role of unelected judges in defending unpopular minorities and forcing the state to justify its counter-terrorism activities,[183] it highlights dangers that legislatures may respond aggressively to adverse judicial decisions and that courts may defer to legislation enacted in reply to their decisions. As will be seen, the Israeli Supreme Court upheld the 2002 law, despite strong arguments that it violated the Basic Law.[184]

In 2008, the Israeli Supreme Court upheld the 2002 law from a challenge brought by two Palestinian residents of Gaza who were alleged to be members of Hezbollah.[185] In upholding the law, President Beinisch stressed that the law was not designed to allow detainees to be held as bargaining chips but rather "to remove from the cycle of hostilities someone who belongs to a terrorist organization or who takes part in hostilities against the state of Israel."[186] This holding characterized the state as complying with the court's earlier judgment. In upholding the law, the court stressed that it would only apply to foreigners and that it was entitled to "a relatively broad margin of appreciation," even though its effects on the constitutional right to liberty were "significant and

---

[181] Gross, *Struggle of Democracy*, at 147–8. An early 1997 decision had held the opposite, concluding "that the return of the Israeli soldiers is an integral part of the security of the state and fulfills an important function in relation to the morale of the army and its values." Ibid., at 148.

[182] K. D. Ewing and Joo-Cheong Tham, "The Continuing Futility of the Human Rights Act" (2008) Public Law 668.

[183] Kent Roach, "Judicial Review of the State's Anti-Terrorism Activities" (2009) 3 Indian Journal of Constitutional Law 138. See also Chapter 8 for a defense of the utility of judicial review in the counter-terrorism context.

[184] Hilly Moodrick-Even Khen, *Unlawful Combatants or Unlawful Legislation?* Research Paper 3-06, Hebrew University Faculty of Law, May 2006. In Chapter 5, we will see that the British courts have not declared control orders enacted in response to the Belmarsh case to be incompatible with the European Convention, and in Chapter 7, we will see that lower courts have upheld reply legislation enacted in response to the court's invalidation of the use of secret evidence without adversarial challenge in *Charkaoui v. Canada* (2007) 1 S.C.R. 350.

[185] *Iyyad v. Israel*, in *Judgments of the Israel Supreme Court*, vol. 3, at 250.

[186] Ibid., at 259.

even severe."[187] It is difficult to escape the conclusion that the law would not likely have been upheld if applied within Israel proper or to Israeli citizens. The court's deferential approach retreats from the important anti-majoritarian role of non-elected courts in defending unpopular minorities, the most unpopular of which must be non-citizens accused of terrorism. The court also saved the law in part by engaging in a form of "constitutional minimalism"[188] by not relying on the presumptions contained in the 2002 law.

The court did not endorse the Knesset's use of the concept of "unlawful combatants" as an alternative to traditional distinctions between combatants and civilians. As in the targeted killing case to be examined subsequently, the court rejected the idea that unlawful combatants enjoyed a status less than civilians under the Geneva Conventions. In both cases, however, the court also held that civilians would not be immune from aggressive state actions if they played a significant role in activities leading to terrorism.[189] The court thus stayed within the international mainstream that rejects the concept of unlawful combatant while at the same time following the post-9/11 trend of allowing the state to intervene against suspected terrorists long before any specific act of terrorism.

In upholding the law, the court stressed that administrative detention was not intended to punish or deter but to "prevent the tangible risk of the detainee to the security of the state" and to prevent their return "to the cycle of hostilities."[190] This approach seems to merge a war paradigm that focuses on the state's enemies with an emphasis on membership in a terrorist organization found in many counter-terrorism laws. The court accepted that the use of secret evidence was a principal feature of administrative detention when it stated that "reliance on inadmissible administrative evidence and on privileged material for reasons of state security lie at the heart of administrative detention."[191] It stressed the need for the judge to examine the secret evidence "with caution and care"[192] but did not advert to other alternatives such as the use of security-cleared counsel who could challenge the intelligence offered by the state. In this respect, the court used shallow proportionality reasoning that did not really explore the availability of less rights invasive alternatives. The court rejected the idea that criminal trials were a more proportionate and less rights-restrictive alternative on the basis that criminal trials would be impossible "because of

---

[187] Ibid., at 286.

[188] See Cass Sunstein, "Constitutional Minimalism at War," 2004 Supreme Court Law Review 47.

[189] *Iyyad v. Israel*, in *Judgments of the Israel Supreme Court*, vol. 3, at 271, para. 16.

[190] Ibid., at 273.   [191] Ibid., at 300.

[192] Ibid., at 302.

the absence of sufficient admissible evidence or the impossibility of revealing privileged sources."[193] As mentioned earlier, however, this approach discounts the incentives that the state and, in particular, intelligence agencies will
have to claim that intelligence sources and methods should never be revealed
if they can simply be used to produce secret evidence that will result in security
threats being subject to long-term administrative detention.

One of the most corrosive 9/11 effects is a widespread loss of faith in the ability of criminal trials to respond to terrorism. President Beinisch revealed such
skepticism when she suggested that administrative detention was also necessary because "holding a criminal trial" may not "provide a satisfactory solution
to averting the threat presented to the security of the state in circumstances
where after serving the sentence the person concerned is likely to become
a security danger once again."[194] In a subsequent case, the court affirmed
that indeterminate administrative detention could be imposed immediately
after a person had served his or her criminal sentence for being a member
of an unlawful terrorist group.[195] This approach reveals a profound lack of
confidence in the criminal justice system and may produce bitter cynicism
that the state will simply use an endless stream of instruments to ensure that
those it determines are enemy security threats are detained indefinitely. As
will be seen, similar reasoning has motivated those who argue that suspected
terrorists should be indefinitely detained at Guantánamo[196] and the imposition of administrative control orders in the United Kingdom and Australia in

---

[193] Ibid., at 303.   [194] Ibid., at 288.

[195] In August 2009, the Israeli Supreme Court rejected an appeal by a Gaza resident who was
detained under the 2002 administrative detention law after he had completed a term of imprisonment for being a member of an unlawful association, the Popular Front for the Liberation
of Palestine, and for attempted murder. The court reviewed secret evidence that indicated that
the man had not truly renounced terrorism, as he claimed. It affirmed that the person's release
and return to Gaza would constitute a security risk and that his detention would be reviewed at
six-month intervals, and that with the passage of time and the change of conditions in Gaza, his
release in the future might not harm state security. Library of Congress, "Israel Review of Internment of Unlawful Combatant," September 10, 2009, at http://www.loc.gov/lawweb/servlet/lloc_
news?disp3_l205401559_text.

[196] Jack Goldsmith makes this argument when he states that "a final problem with using any trial
system, civilian or military, as the sole lawful basis for terrorist detention is that trials can result in
short sentences (as the first military commission did) or even acquittal of a dangerous terrorist.
In criminal trials, defendants often go free because of legal technicalities, government inability
to introduce probative evidence, and other factors beside the defendant's innocence. These
factors are all exacerbated in terrorist trials by the difficulty of getting information from the place
of capture, by restrictions on access to classified information and by stale or tainted evidence."
Jack Goldsmith, "Long-Term Detention and a National Security Court," in *Legislating the
War against Terror*, ed. Benjamin Wittes (Washington, DC: Brookings Institution Press, 2009),
at 79.

response to failed criminal prosecutions.[197] Many states seem prepared to use the less restrained alternative of administrative detention if criminal law does not produce the desired result.

The Israeli Supreme Court recognized that there were no time limits on detention under the 2002 law. The petitioners had been detained since 2002 and 2003. The court, however, stated that the detention could not continue "indefinitely"[198] and that the state's burden of justifying detention would increase with passing time. As will be seen in Chapter 7, the Supreme Court of Canada used similar reasoning a year earlier.[199] In both cases, however, the courts can be criticized for downplaying the long-term and indeterminate nature of detention. Continued judicial review of the detention requires the state to justify the detention, often on the basis of secret intelligence. Judicial review of secret intelligence can take on an intelligence mind-set that focuses on a person's past status as a member of a terrorist group, past bad acts, associations, and political beliefs as well as strategic information about the threat environment. Intelligence of this sort is used as evidence in administrative detention cases, but it is very different from the evidence about a person's actions and intent required in a criminal trial and that must be proven beyond a reasonable doubt. Judges may also not know all the circumstances and perhaps not the identity of the sources of intelligence that is used as secret evidence in administrative detention cases. A person once viewed as a security threat (perhaps on the basis of ambiguous or unreliable information) may always be viewed as a threat. Detention decisions may also be made based on perceptions of the external threat environment-factors over which the detained person has no control or responsibility. There is a danger that deferential judicial decisions will help legitimate indeterminate detention on the basis of secret evidence that has not been subject to adversarial challenge.

The 2002 Internment of Unlawful Combatants Law only applies to those who are not Israeli citizens. Attempts to distinguish between the rights of citizens and the rights of noncitizens were a critical feature of the Bush administration's approach to Guantánamo and were subsequently accepted by Congress but rejected by the U.S. Supreme Court to the extent that they deprived noncitizens detained at Guantánamo of habeas corpus.[200] A focus on noncitizens emphasizes a war paradigm in the battle against terrorism that stresses different treatment of citizens and noncitizens as opposed to a criminal law paradigm

---

[197] *Secretary of State v. AY* (2009) EWCA 3053, at para. 196, as discussed in Chapter 5, and *Thomas v. Mowbry* (2007) HCA 33, as discussed in Chapter 6.

[198] *Iyyad v. Israel*, in *Judgments of the Israel Supreme Court*, vol. 3, at 271, 308.

[199] *Charkaoui v. Canada* (2007) 1 S.C.R. 350.   [200] See Chapter 4.

that stresses the equality of all individuals. It also conceptualizes the threat of terrorism as an external threat and not one that can come from a country's own citizens. The courts, as unelected institutions, have a special obligation to protect the rights of the unpopular and the disenfranchised, including noncitizens, and the Israeli Supreme Court's deferential approach to the 2002 law failed to discharge this responsibility.

Stephanie Cooper-Blum has argued that though Israel's systems of administrative detention have problems, given their reliance on secret evidence and indeterminate detention, they nevertheless have "more transparency" and "due process" than the American system of detention of enemy combatants at Guantánamo.[201] The Israeli system certainly has a legislative basis that is not present in the United States apart from the Military Commissions Act, which regulates military commission trials as opposed to military detention. In addition, the Israeli courts play an active role in judicial review. Nevertheless, the activism of the Israeli courts can be overstated, especially given the court's most recent decision to uphold the Internment of Unlawful Combatants and its willingness to accept the need for secret evidence. Israeli courts have shown little interest in devising means to allow the intelligence to be subject to adversarial challenge. Although they have stressed the preventive motives of administrative detention, such detention is likely experienced as punishment by those who are detained. Administrative detention, with its use of secret evidence and indeterminate detention, provides an important challenge to the use of criminal law as a means to respond to terrorism.

Targeted Killings

Targeted killings have a long history in Israel. The assassination of a Palestine Liberation Organization leader in Tunis in 1988 resulted in a Security Council resolution condemning the killing as a flagrant violation of international law.[202] Israel's policy of targeted killing became more public during the second intifada, with the Israeli defense minister stating, in February 2001, that "we will continue our policy of liquidating those who plan or carry out attacks, and no one can give us lessons in morality because we have unfortunately one

---

[201] Stephanie Cooper-Blum, "Preventive Detention in the War against Terror: A Comparison of How the United States, Britain and Israel Detain and Incapacitate Terrorist Suspects" (2008) 4(3) Homeland Security Affairs 1, at 13; Stephanie Cooper-Blum, *The Necessary Evil of Preventive Detention in the War on Terror* (Amherst, MA: Cambria Press, 2008).

[202] Security Council Resolution 611.

hundred years of fighting terrorism."[203] A Security Council resolution in 2004 condemning targeted killings and calling for their cessation was vetoed by the United States, though General Assembly resolutions and a special rapporteur on extrajudicial, summary, or arbitrary executions condemned many of Israel's targeted killings.[204]

After a 2002 decision that held that the tactics used by the state in warfare were not justiciable,[205] the Israeli Supreme Court took on the question of targeted killing in a 2006 decision.[206] The court took notice that from the start of the second intifada to the end of 2005, almost 300 terrorists were killed by targeted killings, along with 150 civilians who were near the targets.[207] The case was brought by the Public Committee against Torture, the same group that had brought the 1999 case on harsh interrogations. The committee argued that targeted killings of terrorists were illegal because terrorists are civilians under international humanitarian law and should be prosecuted under criminal law, at least when they were not directly involved in hostilities.

The Israeli Supreme Court accepted that in international law, there are only lawful combatants and civilians, and that terrorists fall into the civilian category. In this way, the court did not follow the Bush administration's approach or, indeed, the Knesset's own approach in the 2002 Internment of Unlawful Combatants Law of creating a new category of unlawful combatants for terrorists. The court did, however, rule that targeted killing of civilian terrorists during an armed conflict could be justified if there was reliable information that they were involved in direct hostilities, arrests were not possible, and collateral harm to nonterrorist civilians was proportionate to the military advantage in protecting combatants and civilians. This approach indirectly recognized the concept of the terrorist as an unlawful combatant who could be attacked as if he or she were a soldier but, if captured, could be interrogated as if he or she

---

[203] As quoted in Nils Melzer, *Targeted Killing in International Law* (Oxford: Oxford University Press, 2008), at 29.

[204] Ibid., at 31.

[205] The panel composed of Justice Matza, Cheshin and Levy ruled that "the choice of weaponry used by the respondents with the objective of putting a stop to murderous terror attacks, is not among the matters that this Court sees as its authority to intervene with" *Barakhe v. The Prime Minister* HCJ 5872/10 as quoted in Menachem Hofnung and Keren Weinshall-Margel "Judicial Rejection as Substantial Relief: The Israel Supreme Court and the 'War on Terror'" in Mary Volcansek and John Stack eds. *Courts and Terrorism* (New York: Cambridge University Press, 2011) at 167.

[206] *Public Committee against Torture v. Israel* (HCJ 769/02), in *Judgments of the Israel Supreme Court*, vol. 3, at 88.

[207] Ibid., at 93, para. 2.

were a civilian and did not have prisoner of war status.[208] Indeed, a concurring opinion acknowledged that the court had created a third category, "and rightly so," namely, a group of civilians "who are international lawbreakers whom I would call 'uncivilized civilians.'"[209]

Following the tendency of post-9/11 antiterrorism law to focus on participation in terrorist groups, the court defined involvement in direct hostilities broadly to include those who not only commit acts of terrorism but also plan such acts or direct others to do so. This part of the judgment has been criticized for limiting the protections offered under international law to civilians.[210] At the same time, the scope of those involved in direct hostilities was not unlimited and did not include those who only finance or deliver propaganda for the organization. The court's decision demonstrates how the concepts of crime and war are blurred in the targeted killing debates. The court determines that a target is guilty of being directly involved in hostilities but not on the basis of traditional evidence presented in an open and adversarial process; rather the judgment that a person is involved in direct hostilities is made on the basis of intelligence. As in the administrative detention cases, this intelligence is presented in secret to the court. At the same time, the court authorizes a violent response that, following laws of war, accepts the inevitability of collateral damage. The use of force is restrained by the requirement of proportionality between the collateral damage and the "military advantage" secured.

Consistent with its expansive views of justiciability, the court stressed that there was no black hole where laws did not apply and suggested the need for careful examination of the proportionality of targeted killings both before and after the killings.[211] It invoked the language of balancing between the demands of military necessity and human rights,[212] concluding in some cases that targeted killings would be justified and in some cases that they would not

---

[208] President Emeritus Barak stated that "guerrillas and terrorists who carry out hostilities are not entitled to the protection given to civilians. Admittedly, terrorists who carry out hostilities do not cease to be civilians, but by their actions they have deprived themselves of the benefit of being civilians that grants them protection from military attack. They also do not enjoy the rights of combatants, such as the status of prisoners of war." Ibid., at 124, para. 31.

[209] Ibid., at 155, para. 2, per Vice President Rivlin. This judge recognized the human dignity of innocent civilians "on the other side," ibid., at para. 4, while also placing "the main emphasis on the right of the state of Israel to protect itself and the lives of its citizens," ibid., at para. 7. This indicates how concepts of war can seep into the legal analysis, particularly one in which proportionality is defined as a general balancing exercise.

[210] Comment "On Target? The Israeli Supreme Court and Targeted Killings" (2007) 116 Yale Law Journal 1873.

[211] *Public Committee against Torture v. Israel* (HCJ 769/02), in *Judgments of the Israel Supreme Court*, vol. 3, at 149, para. 61.

[212] Ibid., at 112, para. 22.

be justified. President Barak proceeded by articulating clear cases in which targeted killing would or would not be justified, but he also noted that there was a gray zone in the middle that would depend on all the circumstances. The court's approach can be defended as more transparent than its prior approach (and the current American one) of holding that targeted killings are nonjusticiable. Nevertheless, it also raises the danger of what David Dyzenhaus has criticized as "gray holes," which provide only a thin facade of legality and legitimacy for what is, in essence, unlawful behavior.[213] At the same time, the emphasis in the court's judgment on the need for both ex ante and ex post review of targeting decisions can be seen as the adoption of new institutions to respond to the challenges of using the inexact science of intelligence as evidence.[214]

In determining the legality of targeted killing, the court relied on the concept of proportionality, which is also used in established human rights jurisprudence. Proportionality helps establish the important principle that less drastic means, such as arrest and prosecution, should be used when possible. As will be seen, this emphasis on criminal justice alternatives is absent from the Obama administration's defense of its targeted killing policy.[215] Nevertheless, once it is concluded that use of criminal law is not possible, the proportionality concept is difficult to apply in cases in which the strategic and military value of a killing is being compared to the collateral damage of a loss of innocent lives.[216] Although the court's use of proportionality has been praised by some international law experts,[217] it also invites a difficult weighing of the costs of Israeli and Palestinian lives and accepts notions of collateral damage that would be abhorrent in a criminal justice paradigm that insists on public evidence of guilt and despises the notion of punishing the innocent. As Ronald Dworkin has reminded us, much post-9/11 talk of

---

[213] David Dyzenhaus, *The Constitution of Law* (Cambridge: Cambridge University Press, 2006).

[214] Although not writing in the extreme context of targeted killings, Dyzenhaus argues that institutional innovation that blurs traditional lines between the executive, judiciary, and legislature is necessary "for the rule of law to approach its ideals." Ibid., at 230. For praise of the targeted killing decision for stressing the need for ex ante and ex post review of targeting decisions, see Amichai Cohen and Yuval Shany, "A Development of Modest Proportions" (2007) 5 International Journal of Criminal Justice 310. The special rapporteur on protecting human rights while countering terrorism has, however, raised concerns that the reviews of targeted killings are not being conducted by those independent of the Israel Defence Force, nor are they being made public. Israel Country Report, A/HRC/6/17/add.4, at para. 52.

[215] See Chapter 4.

[216] Cohen and Shany, "A Development of Modest Proportions," at 316.

[217] Antonio Cassese, "On Some of the Merits of the Israeli Judgment on Targeted Killings" (2007) 5 International Journal of Criminal Justice 339.

balancing ignores equality concerns about whose security is being traded for whose rights.[218]

It is also noteworthy that after first indicating that targeted killing was non-justiciable that the court has now held that it should be judicially reviewed. The judicialization of targeted killing in Israel has been seen by some as an attempt to head off possible war crime prosecutions.[219] At the same time, however, the UN Human Rights Committee has expressed concerns about targeted killings by Israel, noting the unintended deaths of 155 individuals and calling for an independent body to investigate complaints about the disproportionate use of force.[220]

Summary

Although the Israeli response to terrorism is unique, much can be learned from it. Israel provides an example of a country that did not initially respond to 9/11 with comprehensive new antiterrorism measures; instead, it relied on older measures, including those directly inherited from British colonial emergency rule. This reliance is consistent with the idea that democracies like the United States, with less experience with terrorism, struggled to catch up after 9/11. The Israeli Supreme Court's decision on targeted killing has been much discussed in the United States as targeted killings of terrorists have increased under the Obama administration.[221] The United States has followed the Israeli example with respect to the targeted killing of terrorists, but in a manner that has been resistant to judicial review and has elements of the extralegal that are not present in Israel. The American experience with harsh interrogations could also have benefited from an examination of the Israeli experience and, in particular, the court's 1999 ruling that necessity and self-defense did not provide a before-the-fact justification for harsh interrogations or torture. At the same time, the 1999 decision left the door open to torture in undefined exceptional circumstances, and concerns about the continued conduct of interrogations reveal some of the shortcomings of relying on publicity and prosecutions to deter secret and possibly illegal state actions in so-called ticking-bomb cases.

---

[218] Ronald Dworkin, "The Threat to Patriotism," New York Times Review of Books, February 28, 2002.

[219] Cohen and Shany, "A Development of Modest Proportions."

[220] *Concluding Observations of the Human Rights Committee*, CCPR/C/ISR/Co/3, July 29, 2010, at para. 10.

[221] See, e.g., Richard Murphy and Afsheen Radsan, "Due Process and Targeted Killing of Terrorists" (2009) 31 Cardozo Law Review 405; Gabriella Blum and Philip Heymann, "Law and Policy of Targeted Killing" (2010) 1 Harvard National Security Journal 145.

There are some interesting similarities between the Knesset's use of the concept of unlawful combatants in its 2002 administrative detention law and the Bush administration's use of the concept at Guantánamo. At the same time, the Israeli Supreme Court has rejected the idea that unlawful combatants are a valid category under international law and has instead worked within the traditional law of war categories of combatants and civilians, while at the same time also accepting that civilian terrorists who participate in terrorist activities may, in some cases, be subject to administrative detention and targeted killing.

Although Israel did not need to respond immediately to 9/11, it has been influenced by the post-9/11 environment, with its greater stress on preventing terrorism and acceptance in some quarters of the need for a war on terrorism. Israel's 2004 law on terrorism financing follows the trend in post-9/11 law for broader definitions of terrorism, and its proposed counter-terrorism bill, if enacted, will accelerate this trend. Israel's 2002 Internment of Unlawful Combatants Law is also consistent with revived post-9/11 interest and acceptance of administrative detention of noncitizens suspected of terrorism. The 2008 supreme court decision upholding this law from challenge, however, can be contrasted with more aggressive judicial resistance to administrative detention in the United Kingdom, the United States, and Canada. The validation of both administrative detention and targeted killings is consistent with post-9/11 challenges to reliance on criminal law to deal with terrorists. The new Israeli offense of praise and celebration of terrorism is consistent with a renewed emphasis on speech regulation in Resolution 1624. Unlike new British and Australian speech offenses however, the Israeli law insists that speech praising or advocating terrorism create a real possibility of terrorist violence.

v. SINGAPORE

Singapore did not drastically adjust its laws to respond to 9/11. As Michael Hor observed in 2002, "while the rest of the liberal democratic world scrambled to enact massive new anti-terrorism legislation, Singapore had only to perform a relatively minor tweaking of its laws."[222] Singapore did not need to do much to respond to 9/11 because of its inheritance of British colonial emergency powers.

---

[222] Michael Hor, "Terrorism and the Criminal Law: Singapore's Solution" (2002) Singapore Journal of Legal Studies 30, at 31.

British Colonial Emergency Rule: Antecedents to the Internal Security Act

There are some interesting links between British colonial emergency rule in Israel and in Singapore and Malaysia. Sir Henry Gurney served as a high colonial official in Palestine before becoming high commissioner of Malaya, where he was killed by terrorists in 1951. He described the emergency regulations that he helped develop in Palestine and that were later transferred to Malaya as being so strong that "at the end it might almost have been said that the whole book of regulations could have been expressed in a simple provision empowering the High Commissioner to take any action that he wished."[223] These colonial emergency regulations provided the basis for Singapore's and Malaysia's ISAs, which provide the government with broad powers to impose indeterminate detention without trial. The ISAs are protected under both countries' constitutions[224] in a manner somewhat similar to that achieved by Egypt's 2007 constitutional amendments. Egyptians have, however, voted to repeal such constitutional shelters, but there is no serious discussion of ISA reform in Singapore or Malaysia. Singapore's ISA allows administrative detention on the basis of secret evidence, release on conditions, and extensive regulation of speech. As such, it provides some precedent for post-9/11 laws and suggests that one 9/11 effect was to revive and relegitimate some older techniques of colonial emergency rule.

The origins of the ISA are found in British emergency regulations enacted in 1948 pursuant to an Emergency Regulations Ordinance[225] that provided for regulations designed to respond to an emergency, defined as a threat that would deprive the community of the "essentials of life," including supplies of food, water, fuel, light, or health services.[226] The ordinance also provided that the regulations could allow detention of persons for a renewable two-year period, subject to "periodic review of the case of each individual under detention."[227] The emergency regulations provided indeterminate detention subject to review every six months by an advisory committee consisting of a judge and two others.[228] Thus the core of the ISA – indeterminate detention subject to periodic review by a quasi-judicial body – had been put in place by British colonial officials by 1948.

---

[223] As quoted in Simpson, "Round Up the Usual Suspects," at 640, 660.
[224] Malaysian Constitution, Article 149; Singapore Constitution, Article 151.
[225] No. 17 of 1948, Colony of Singapore.   [226] Ibid., Section 3.
[227] Ibid., Section 4(3).
[228] Emergency Regulations, 1948, Section 20 (Singapore Supplement to the Government Gazette, July 28, 1948).

The emergency regulations provided broad offenses that have some similarity to post-9/11 terrorism offenses. One offense applied to those who consorted with or were found in the company of a person with a firearm "in circumstances, which raise a reasonable presumption that he intends to or is about to act or has recently acted with such other person in a manner prejudicial to public safety or the maintenance of public order."[229] In addition, it was an offense to fail to report such an offense when a person knew or had reasonable cause to believe that another was committing a firearm offense, with the onus being on the accused to demonstrate that he or she reported the offense "at the earliest possible opportunity."[230] The emergency regulations departed from the regular law by allowing confessions taken by the police to be admissible. The regular law was designed to protect against harsh interrogations and unreliable statements, but the precedent established by the emergency regulations eventually was to make its way into ordinary law.[231] This provided another example of the ability of exceptions made during emergencies to become part of ordinary law.

The emergency regulations also outlawed the Malayan Communist Party and provided for strict censorship and offenses of making or possessing insurgent propaganda. Prohibitions on the public wearing of military uniforms were also imported from British regulations.[232] Censorship powers applied to speech that, in the opinion of the commissioner of the police incited violence, counseled disobedience to laws and lawful orders, or was likely to lead to a breach of the peace. In addition, the powers also applied to speech that would "promote feelings of ill-will or hostility between different races or classes of the population."[233] This foreshadowed post-9/11 speech regulations, which would combine concerns about hate speech with concerns about the prevention of terrorism.

The emergency regulations also featured the use of immigration measures as antiterrorism measures. Although the regulations were used to detain thousands, even more people were deported to China before the Communists took

---

[229] Emergency Regulations, 1948, Section 4 (Singapore Supplement to the Government Gazette, July 28, 1948).

[230] Ibid., Section 5.

[231] Michael Hor, "Constitutionalism and Subversion: An Exploration," in *Evolution of a Revolution: Forty Years of the Singapore Constitution*, ed. Li-ann Thio and Kevin Tan (London: Routledge, 2009), at 276.

[232] A. W. B. Simpson, *Human Rights and the End of Empire* (Oxford: Oxford University Press, 2004), at 831.

[233] Emergency Regulations, 1948, Section 20 (Singapore Supplement to the Government Gazette, July 28, 1948), Section 16.

over that country.[234] Such expulsions were achieved under a law that allowed "banishment from the Colony of any person, not being a natural born subject of His Majesty" when it was "conducive to the public good."[235] As will be seen, the United Kingdom returned to such a broad formulation in removing citizenship after it experienced problems in depriving Guantánamo detainee David Hicks of his British citizenship.[236]

Britain provided a notice of derogation from the European Convention of Human Rights in relation to the emergency in the Federation of Malaya and Singapore in 1954.[237] As will be seen in Chapter 5, the United Kingdom was prepared to derogate from the convention in relation to terrorism in Northern Ireland before 9/11 and then again in response to 9/11. Despite the forceful response to the Malaya insurgency, in which close to 7,000 insurgents and 2,000 security forces were killed,[238] it was eventually resolved through an amnesty, the granting of self-government to the Malayans, the use of rewards, and a heart-and-minds approach, albeit one backed by harsh laws and military force. As will be seen in Chapter 5, a somewhat similar approach led to a deescalation of terrorism in Northern Ireland.

Singapore enacted a Preservation of Public Security Ordinance in 1955 that provided for preventive detention but allowed review by a special court of three judges.[239] The 1957 Reid Commission stipulated that a person should not be detained in an emergency for more than three months without review by an advisory board but also that the government could, in such proceedings, "refuse to disclose facts whose disclosure would in its opinion be against the national interest."[240] The ISA was enacted in 1960 by Malaysia to preserve emergency powers even after the formal emergency was ended. It was extended to Singapore when it became part of Malaysia and was retained by Singapore when that country obtained independence in 1965.

---

[234] Simpson, "Round Up the Usual Suspects," at 661.

[235] An Ordinance to Amend the Banishment Ordinance, No. 52 of 1941, Section 2. The present law of Singapore retains the power of banishment. Banishment Ordinance, Revised Statues of Singapore 1985, chap. 18, Section 4.

[236] Immigration, Asylum and Nationality Act, 2006 (UK), c.13, Section 56; discussed in Chapter 5.

[237] Simpson, "Round Up the Usual Suspects," at 688–9.

[238] Therese Lee, "Malaysia and the Internal Security Act: The Insecurity of Human Rights after September 11" (2002) Singapore Journal of Legal Studies 56, at 57.

[239] A. J. Harding, "Singapore," in *Preventive Detention and Security Law: A Comparative Survey*, ed. Andrew Harding and John Hatchard (Dordrecht, Netherlands: Martinus Nijhoff, 1993), at 193.

[240] Lord Reid, *Report of the Federation of Malaya Constitutional Commission* (1957), at para. 176, as quoted and discussed in Kevin Y. L. Tan, "From Myanmar to Manila: A Brief Study of Emergency Powers in Southeast Asia," in *Emergency Powers in Asia*, ed. V. Ramraj and A. Thiruvengadem (New York: Cambridge University Press, 2010), at 159.

The Internal Security Act

As Michael Hor has suggested, the ISA is "not a criminal law at all" but "super criminal law, swooping down and dealing with those suspected of criminal activity when the Executive perceives that the normal processes of the criminal law are likely to fail or to create more problems than they solve."[241] Section 8 of the ISA allows preventive detention for renewable two-year periods on the basis that the president is subjectively satisfied that detention is necessary, "with a view to preventing that person from acting in any manner prejudicial to the security of Singapore . . . or to the maintenance of public order or essential services."[242] This power resembles many post-9/11 antiterrorism laws in its emphasis on preventing terrorist acts before they occur and on protecting essential services.

The ISA also contemplates less drastic measures than preventive detention. Section 8(b) allows the executive to impose restrictions on a person's activities, including the imposition of a curfew, residence and employment restrictions, and requirements to notify authorities of his or her movements. In this way, the ISA provides a precedent for the use of control orders in Britain and Australia. The ISA, however, goes beyond control orders in contemplating that a person can be restricted "from addressing public meetings . . . or from taking part in any political activities."[243] The ISA also acknowledges the frequent link between antiterrorism and immigration seen in the post-9/11 environment by allowing a detention or restriction order to be suspended to allow detainees to return to their countries of citizenship or another country.[244] In some cases, it is best that security threats be expelled to another country. As will be seen in the next chapter, the United States would eventually pursue a similar expulsion strategy with Yaser Hamdi.

There is a "semblance of due process"[245] under the ISA. Detainees must be informed of the allegations against them and can make representations to an advisory board chaired by a judge, which will periodically review the detention at least every year. At the same time, these proceedings contemplate the use of secret evidence against the detainee. The ISA provides little challenge to the state's secrecy claims by making it clear that neither the executive nor the advisory board is required to disclose facts or documents that they consider "to be against the national interest."[246] In addition, the proceedings before the

---

[241] Hor, "Terrorism and the Criminal Law," at 43.
[242] Internal Security Act, chap. 143, Section 8.   [243] Ibid., Section 7. See also Section 10.
[244] Ibid., Section 10(f).
[245] Hor, "Terrorism and the Criminal Law," at 43.
[246] Internal Security Act, chap. 143, Sections 11, 16.

advisory board are held in camera. As Professor Hor has observed, "perhaps the feature most disturbing to a criminal lawyer is the secrecy of it all."[247]

The ISA also contains a focus on speech found in some post-9/11 terrorism laws. Section 20 allows the executive to prohibit material that "contains any incitement to violence" or is calculated to lead to a breach of peace or "to promote feelings of hostility between different races or classes of the population." The latter concept reflects the diverse races and religions in Singapore but also merges state interests against hate speech and the security interests of the state in a manner seen in some post-9/11 terrorism laws most notably in Australia. There are also offenses of failing to report offenses or to give information about a terrorist[248] and powers to transfer prisoners notwithstanding court orders[249] and to impose investigative detention for up to 28 days.[250]

The Use of the Internal Security Act

The ISA was used long after the emergency passed. In Malaysia, it was used against labor leaders, students, Islamic groups, and political opponents, among others. For example, in 1997, three individuals, including a professor from the Islamic studies faculty of the University of Malaya, were detained under the ISA for spreading the teaching of Sharia law.[251] In Singapore, the ISA was used against political opponents.[252]

Singapore's ISA was used in 1987 against 22 persons in the so-called Marxist conspiracy case. These arrests extended to lawyers, who represented some of the original detainees, but by the end of the year, all but one had been released.[253] Nine of the detainees were, however, rearrested in 1988, along with their lawyer, Patrick Seong, after they made public statements alleging mistreatment such as face slapping, sleep deprivation, and prolonged standing. They also stated that they were discouraged from engaging legal counsel and were threatened with long-term detention if they did not cooperate with authorities to make scripted and edited public confessions.[254] All but two were released by May 1989 but were subject to restrictions on their movement

[247] Hor, "Terrorism and the Criminal Law," at 44.
[248] Ibid., Section 61 (these offenses only apply in defined security areas).
[249] Ibid., Section 19.   [250] Ibid., Section 74.
[251] Koh Swe Yong, *Malaysia: 45 Years under the Internal Security Act* (Petaling Jaya, Malaysia: Strategic Information Research Development, 2004), at 156.
[252] Asia Watch, *Silencing All Critics: Human Rights Violations in Singapore* (New York: Asia Watch, 1989), at 16. See also *Report of the International Mission of Jurists to Singapore*, ICJ, October 1987.
[253] Ibid., at 21.
[254] The statements are contained in Asia Watch, *Silencing All Critics*, at appendix B-4.

and associations.[255] One of those detained has recently published a harrowing account of her detention and solitary confinement and how she was rearrested immediately after a court victory. A lawyer herself, she experienced the arrest of her own lawyers and the exclusion of a British Queens Counsel, now Lord Lester, who represented her. She was only released when she abandoned a number of legal actions against the state, including one in relation to alleged assaults against her in the first few days of her detention.[256] The restrictions imposed on the released detainees prevented them from knowingly associating with others detained under the ISA and from issuing public statements or participating in the activities of an organization "without the prior written approval of the Director, Internal Security Department, Singapore."[257]

In 1988, Singapore's court of appeal ordered the release of four of these detainees on the basis that the grounds for detention under the ISA had not been established in part because the recitals constituted hearsay because they were signed by the wrong person.[258] The court of appeal also expressed support for Lord Atkin's famous dissent in the wartime detention of *Liversidge v. Anderson*[259] when he had stressed that courts should concern themselves not only with the executive's subjective views but also with their own judgment of the objective circumstances said to justify detention. The decision left much discretion to the executive about what was required for national security but asserted some judicial power to determine whether the state had acted illegally, irrationally, or on the basis of procedural impropriety.

The government's response to the case was swift and drastic. The detainees were released by court order but were immediately rearrested and redetained under a new ISA order. Unlike under the criminal law, there are no double jeopardy protections when administrative detention is used. Both the constitution and the ISA were amended to restore the prior law that followed the majority in *Liversidge*, which held that the only issue for the court was whether the executive subjectively desired detention and not whether there was an objective basis for the detention. The constitution was amended to make clear that the ISA would apply notwithstanding various constitutional protections, including those of liberty, freedom of movement, freedom of association, access to habeas corpus, rights against retroactive criminal laws, and equal protection of the law, including access to habeas corpus. Appeals to

---

[255] Ibid., at 25.
[256] Teo Soh Lung, *Beyond the Blue Gate: Recollections of a Political Prisoner* (Petaling Jaya, Malaysia: Strategic Information and Research Centre, 2010).
[257] As quoted in Asia Watch, *Silencing All Critics*, at appendix C-2.
[258] *Chng Suan Tze v. Minister of Home Affairs* (1989) 2 MLJ 69; (1988) SGCA 16.
[259] (1942) AC 206.

the privy council were also abolished to prevent an appeal that likely would have vindicated the court of appeal.[260] Andrew Harding commented that the result was more extreme than in other countries, such as India, which faced more serious security threats.[261] A subsequent constitutional challenge to the amendments was denied.[262] As Reuban Balasubramanian has suggested, Singapore's drastic response (and similar ones in response to judicial decisions in Malaysia) revealed the state as committed to authoritarian rule by law and undermined its claim to "rule of law legitimacy."[263] At the same time, however, he warns that 9/11 has allowed Singapore and Malaysia to rehabilitate indeterminate detention without making problematic appeals to either the need to maintain social order or Asian values;[264] rather they can point to the use of indeterminate detention and secret evidence by established Western democracies.

The Initial Response to 9/11

Singapore responded to 9/11 by ratifying the Convention on the Suppression of the Financing of Terrorism and enacting the United Nations Act, 2001, that allowed the government to enact regulations to give effect to Security Council measures under Chapter VII of the UN Charter, including the creation of criminal offenses punishable by up to five years' imprisonment. Most of the immediate work in ensuring compliance with Resolution 1373 was then done through the creation of new offenses in the UN (Anti-Terrorism Measures) Regulations. As in many other countries, the quickest and most efficient means to comply with Resolution 1373 was through regulations proclaimed by the executive.

The regulations drew from the United Kingdom's Terrorism Act, 2000, to define terrorism broadly to include the use or threat of an action that involves serious damage to property and serious risk to health or safety as well as serious violence. The definition also borrowed from the ISA by including disruption of essential services, the use of firearms or explosives, and "prejudice to public security or national defence."[265] An interesting departure from the British

---

[260] Hor, "Constitutionalism and Subversion," at 288–93.
[261] Harding "Singapore," at 206.
[262] *Teo Soh Lung v. Minister of Home Affairs* (1989) 2 MLJ 449.
[263] R. Rueban Balasubramanian, "Indefinite Detention: Rule by Law or Rule of Law?" in *Emergencies and the Limits of Legality*, ed. Victor Ramraj (New York: Cambridge University Press, 2008), at 129.
[264] Ibid., at 135.
[265] UN (Anti-Terrorism Measures) Regulations 2001, Section 4.

definition of terrorism, however, was the failure to include proof of religious or political motive as a defining feature of terrorism. This omission likely responded to Singaporean sensitivities on religious issues given its sizeable 15% Muslim minority. The end result of Singapore's selective use of the British definition and ISA concepts was a very broad definition of terrorism. This did not, however, stop the CTC from asking Singapore whether the definition covered "all persons or entities which may be proceeded against for acts criminalized under the Resolution."[266] Singapore could confidently reply that its definition had done the job, in part because, as discussed in the previous chapter, Resolution 1373 provided no guidance on how terrorism should be defined.

Singapore's UN (Anti-Terrorism Measures) Regulations also incorporated the 1267 list of persons associated with the Taliban and al Qaeda and imposed broad prohibitions against the provision or collection of funds to terrorists and a broad duty on all persons to provide the police with information relating to terrorist property. The regulation went beyond Security Council Resolution 1373 by also criminalizing false threats of terrorism. At the same time, the regulations were only subject to a maximum of five years' imprisonment, which was a very light maximum sentence, especially by Singapore's standards. Singapore's initial response to 9/11 "look[ed] like a slap on the wrist, but a slap which is meant for the world to see nevertheless."[267]

In 2002, the regulation was replaced by legislation that contained a definition of terrorist activity based in part on the United Kingdom's Terrorism Act, 2000, and the ISA. The maximum penalty for terrorism financing was increased from 5 to 10 years. The statutory offense went beyond the 1999 Terrorist Financing Convention by applying not only to those who intentionally or knowingly fund terrorism but also to those who have reasonable grounds to believe that they are providing property or funds to terrorists.[268] This created the possibility that someone could negligently commit a serious terrorism offense in relation to terrorism financing. In subsequent years, Singapore enacted offenses against terrorist bombing and hostage taking to demonstrate compliance with international battles against terrorism.[269] At the same time, however, Singapore has not relied on any of these new laws when it has been confronted with suspected terrorists.

---

[266] S/2002/690, at 4.
[267] Hor, "Terrorism and the Criminal Law," at 50.
[268] Terrorism (Suppression of Financing Act), 2002, Act 16 of 2002, Sections 3–7.
[269] Terrorism (Suppression of Bombings) Act, 2007, Act 50 of 2002; Hostage Taking Act, 2010, Act 19 of 2010.

The Jemaah Islamiyah Arrests

In December 2001, the ISA was used to arrest 15 members of Jemaah Islamiyah (JI) who were alleged to have been planning to bomb a number of targets in Singapore, including the public transit system and the American embassy. The JI had roots in Darul Islam, a group that had fought against the Dutch in gaining Indonesia's independence in 1949. Many JI members fled to Malaysia to avoid arrest by Suharto in Indonesia, though many returned after the overthrow of Suharto and desired a pan-Islamic state in the region. In August 2002, another 21 members were arrested, including two with links to the Moro Islamic Liberation Front in the Philippines. Although Singapore, unlike Malaysia, had not stressed the ISA in its first report to the CTC, it explained in its second report that the ISA arrests were "a demonstration of the Singapore Government's commitment to take firm action against terrorists and supporters of terrorism."[270] It also cited the "swift and decisive steps" it had taken under the ISA when asked by the CTC what steps it was taking to prevent the recruitment of terrorists. As in Egypt and Syria, the CTC reports provided Singapore with an opportunity to attempt to legitimize laws and practices that had been criticized before 9/11 for a lack of due process and respect for human rights.

Singapore's attempt to build support for the ISA as an effective antiterrorism law went beyond its reports to the CTC. In the wake of the arrests, the government engaged in a "promotional campaign aimed to recast the ISA as anti-terrorism legislation."[271] As other politicians would do in the aftermath of 9/11, there were inaccurate suggestions that the criminal law was inadequate because it could only be applied after a terrorist act. The prime minister stressed the need for an intelligence-based preventive approach because "you can't work like the police – let the bomb go off first and then catch them and put them on trial."[272] A more sophisticated defense of the ISA came in a 28-page pamphlet issued by the government in November 2002. It stressed that the ISA is used as a last resort in cases "when prosecution is not practical" because of threats to the safety of witnesses, "secret sources of intelligence or undercover investigations. . . . Relationships with other countries may be affected or racial and religious feelings may be provoked in a prolonged trial."[273] It stated that restriction orders would be used as a less drastic alternative under the ISA and that by November 2002, five of the persons detained in the JI arrests had

---

[270] Singapore Country Report, S/2002/690, at para. 2.
[271] Damien Cheong, "Selling Security: The War on Terrorism and the Internal Security Act of Singapore" (2006) 23 Copenhagen Journal of Asian Studies 28, at 46.
[272] Ibid., at 30.
[273] Ministry of Home Affairs, *Why the ISA?* November 2002.

already been released under restriction orders.[274] It also stressed that detainees had their religion respected and were examined by doctors before and after each interview and that the government and the president were ultimately responsible to the people of Singapore for the use of the ISA.[275] The *Straits Times* newspaper concluded, "Whatever qualms some Singaporeans and foreigners may have had before about the use of the Internal Security Act to detain people without trial, few would entertain such qualms now."[276]

It is not known whether consideration was given to applying the regular criminal law to the JI arrests. Professor Hor has suggested that criminal convictions may well have been possible but that the government wanted to avoid a public trial that could have allowed the detainees, who were part of the Muslim and Malay minority that makes up 15 percent of Singaporean citizens, to claim that they were religious martyrs and to exacerbate social and religious tensions.[277] Another factor was that a criminal trial would not have allowed the use of secret evidence and might have risked disclosure of informers within Singapore's Muslim community.[278] In any event, the government avoided an unpredictable public trial but also took steps to deliver a controlled message to the public about the dangers behind the arrests. As will be seen, the end result for many of those detained was much more lenient than if they had been convicted under Singapore's harsh criminal laws, including new bombing and hostage taking offenses that provide for the death penalty.[279]

The White Paper

The government released a white paper in 2003 to explain the terrorist threat in Singapore. It outlined links between JI and al Qaeda and other terrorist groups. It stated that the detainees were all educated and employed and were not "ignorant, destitute or disenfranchised outcasts."[280] It outlined the evidence heard by the advisory board and its conclusion that the detainees

---

[274] Ibid., at 23.   [275] Ibid., at 27.

[276] As quoted in Senia Febrica, "Securitizing Terrorism in Southeast Asia" (2010) 50 Asian Survey 569, at 577.

[277] Hor, "Terrorism and the Criminal Law," at 48–9.

[278] A 2010 law creating offenses against hostage taking, however, does have special protections for the identity of informers but also provides that their identity can be disclosed, if necessary, to ensure that justice is done. Hostage Taking Act, Section 10.

[279] Section 3 of the Terrorism (Suppression of Terrorist Bombings) Act, 2007, provides for a mandatory death penalty if death is intended or if death or serious bodily injury is caused and mandatory life imprisonment in other cases. Section 3 of the Hostage Taking Act, 2010, provides for the death penalty or life imprisonment supplemented by fines and caning.

[280] *The JI Arrests and the Threat of Terrorism in Singapore*, Cmnd 2 of 2003, at 15.

were still dangerous because of their training and capability of engaging in violence. It also suggested that continued detentions were necessary to allow "investigations to ferret out" all others in the terrorist network.[281] The reasoning of the advisory board focused more on the future in terms of danger and investigations than on the past in terms of what the detainees actually did. This followed a logic of preventive detention that looked to the future, including whether the detainees had been rehabilitated. As will be seen, the majority of these JI detainees have now been released after a sophisticated rehabilitation program has convinced the authorities that they no longer present a security threat. Although some detainees are still detained, the main response to the JI arrests has been characterized as a "therapeutic" one in which "the government did not want to treat the detainees as criminals-bad people who chose to do evil-but as misguided people who could be salvaged by right teaching."[282]

The white paper warned that "Singaporeans must remain committed to the ideal of a harmonious and tolerant multi-ethnic and multi-religious society, in order to prevent dangerous, radical ideas from taking root in Singapore."[283] It listed various security precautions that all should take and placed responsibility on Singapore's Muslim community to "develop a comprehensive, self-regulatory system to monitor religious education. Such a system will help the Muslim community to detect dangerous extremist teachings, especially those from abroad, before they take root here."[284] The white paper also reminded citizens that the Muslim minority in Singapore had condemned both 9/11 and the JI. The government stressed the need for social cohesion and religious harmony.

Rehabilitation Programs

The Singapore government responded to the JI arrests with a variety of "soft-law" responses.[285] They included a 2003 declaration of religious harmony and a community engagement program that featured interracial harmony circles. The effect of these programs is controversial, and there are dangers that they may affirm divisions in Singaporean society. At the same time, they do result

---

[281] Ibid., at 20.

[282] Michael Hor "Singapore's Anti-Terrorism Laws: Reality and Rhetoric" in Victor Ramraj et al., *Global Anti-Terrorism Law and Policy* 2nd ed. (Cambridge: Cambridge University Press, forthcoming, 2011).

[283] *The JI Arrests and the Threat of Terrorism in Singapore*, Cmnd 2 of 2003, at 1.

[284] Ibid., at 22.

[285] Eugene Tan, "From Clampdown to Limited Empowerment: Soft Law in the Calibration and Regulation of Religious Conduct in Singapore" (2009) 31 Law and Policy 351.

in at least some engagement with what Clive Walker has described as the "neighbor terrorist"[286] who, in many Western democracies, is still seen as a demonized outsider.[287] These softer strategies are, however, backed up by harder strategies that, even after 9/11, would not be accepted in most Western democracies. For example, religious teachers and leaders can be heavily regulated under Singapore's Religious Harmony Act, which includes restriction or control orders reminiscent of those available under the ISA. In addition, speech is regulated, with the Danish cartoons depicting the Islamic prophet Mohammed simply being banned.[288]

In April 2003, the Internal Security Department, which administered the ISA, contacted the chairman of a local mosque and the president of an association of Muslim scholars and asked them to head a group to counter the JI's misunderstanding of Islam. The program involved volunteer Muslim scholars working with the detainees and their families.[289] Singapore's program was based in part on Yemen's theological dialogue model. The Yemen model had enjoyed some initial success with those trained in Afghanistan but was eventually abandoned when younger generations saw those administering the program as being coopted by the state.

Singapore's program engaged in more than 800 individual counseling sessions between 2003 and 2007. One study found that two-thirds of individuals detained under the ISA during this period were released after, on average, four years' detention. The apparent success of this program has been related both to the substantial resources devoted to it and to the average age of the detainees, which was 39 years, as well as the inclusion of their families in the program.[290] A recent RAND study stresses that Singapore's religious rehabilitation program is the best among the many programs the organization examined.

---

[286] Clive Walker, *The Anti-Terrorism Legislation*, 2nd ed. (Oxford: Oxford University Press, 2009), at 7.02–03.

[287] Roach, "National Security, Multiculturalism and Muslim Minorities" [2006] Singapore Journal of Legal Studies 405; Noor Aisha Abdul Raham, "The Dominant Perspective on Terrorism and Its Implication for Social Cohesion: The Case of Singapore" (2009) 27 Copenhagen Journal of Asian Studies 109; Norman Vasu, "(En)countering Terrorism: Multiculturalism and Singapore" (2008) 9 Asian Ethnicity 17.

[288] Tan, "From Clampdown to Limited Empowerment," at 360.

[289] Haniff Bin Hassan, Muhammad, and Kenneth George Pereire, "'An Ideological Response to Combating Terrorism – The Singapore Perspective" (2006) 17 Small Wars and Insurgencies 458, at 462. These researchers raise concerns that the work of the Religious Rehabilitation Group was, however, handicapped by a perception that it was promoting Sufism over the Salafi–Wahabi strand of Islam as well as by restrictions placed on the ability of some released detainees to speak after they were released. Ibid., at 472–4.

[290] Zachary Abuza, "The Rehabilitation of Jemaah Islamiyah Detainees in South East Asia," in *Leaving Terrorism Behind*, ed. Tore Bjorgo and John Horgan (London: Routledge, 2009), at 203.

It also stressed that an Aftercare Services Group provides care for the families of detainees in part to prevent the radicalization of children.[291] It reported that the program has resulted in the release of 40 of 60 JI detainees, with the subsequent rearrest of only one person.[292]

Singapore's rehabilitation program has attracted favorable attention in the West. In 2009, the *Washington Post* published an article titled "Best Guide for Gitmo: Look to Singapore" that described Singapore's religious rehabilitation program. It also reported that the United States was attempting to implement Singapore's approach in Iraq, but doing so would be difficult both because of the conditions in Iraq and because of the lack of an established religious infrastructure such as that found in Singapore.[293] The article failed to point out that some of the abuses at Guantánamo may have achieved the opposite result of rehabilitation and may have further radicalized and embittered detainees. It also did not deal with the difficulties that American constitutional traditions of separation of state and religion might create for a state-operated religious rehabilitation program. In any event, it is clear that Singapore's intensive program has worked better than the United States' release program from Guantánamo, after which significant numbers of those released are thought to have subsequently engaged in acts of terrorism.[294]

Summary

It is difficult to know what to make of Singapore's use of the ISA combined with its successful rehabilitation program. Most religious rehabilitation programs have been undertaken in Muslim majority countries. Singapore does not fall into this category, but it did rely on its sizeable Muslim minority in implementing its rehabilitation program. Israel has an even larger Arab minority among its citizens but unlike Singapore has not attempted to rehabilitate those who it subjects to administrative or military detention. At the same time, the Singaporean experience should not be romanticized. Rehabilitation in Singapore was done under the heavy shadow of potential indeterminate detention under the ISA and involved state involvement in religion that would not easily be accepted in most Western democracies.

[291] Angel Rabasa et al., *Deradicalizing Islamic Extremists* (Santa Monica, CA: RAND Corporation, 2010), at 100–2.

[292] Ibid., at 104.

[293] William Dobson, "The Best Guide for Gitmo? Look to Singapore," Washington Post, May 17, 2009.

[294] The U.S. government estimated that 81 of 600 detainees released from Guantánamo are known to have returned to terrorism and another 69 are suspected of being involved in terrorism. "Released from Guantánamo, They Took Up Arms," The New York Times, April 24, 2011.

Although the ISA was widely criticized before 9/11, it has been rehabilitated after 9/11 as an antiterrorism law and has also served as a vehicle that has resulted in the release of most detainees and less harsh treatment than they would have received if they had been convicted of criminal offenses either in the West or under Singapore's criminal laws or its post-9/11 offenses which carry punishments such as the death penalty and caning. Singapore has shown concern about the reintegration of terrorists and their families into society, in stark contrast to the punitive approach taken by Western democracies, which generally do not even attempt to rehabilitate terrorists. As much as the ISA offends due process, it appears to have been applied in Singapore in a truly preventive manner that focused on both future danger and rehabilitation.

vi. INDONESIA

The final country examined in this chapter does not fit into the general pattern observed with respect to Egypt, Syria, Israel, and Singapore. Unlike those countries, Indonesia did not rely on existing laws in the immediate aftermath of 9/11; rather it enacted a new terrorism law in 2002, but only after a democratic struggle with respect to an initial draft law and only after the Bali bombings in October 2002 killed 202 people. Indonesia's experience is relevant because it constitutes the world's most populous Muslim country and because of its struggle with issues of capacity, democracy, terrorism, and a repressive past. Indonesia resisted demands that it enact an ISA like its neighbors Singapore and Malaysia which faced a similar terrorist threat. The Indonesian experience also is relevant to possible directions in Egypt after Mubarak. Indonesia's experience suggests that a more restrained and democratic approach towards terrorism that renounces an authoritarian past is possible, but also that a country will face continued pressures if terrorism continues.

The Pre-9/11 Experience

Under a 1963 Anti-Subversion Law that was not repealed until 1999, Indonesia used security legislation to crush opposition to the Suharto regime. Article 1 defined subversive activities to include "distorting, stirring up trouble or digressing the state ideology" and "overthrowing, damaging, or undermining state power or the authority of the legal Government or the State Apparatus."[295] The vagueness of these terms "made it possible to prosecute persons merely

---

[295] Anti-Subversion Law, 1963, Articles 1(a) and 1(b), as quoted and translated in Amnesty International, *Indonesia: The Anti-Subversion Law: A Briefing*, AI Index 21/03/97, February 1997.

for peaceful expression of views contrary to those of the government."[296] The 1963 Anti-Subversion Law defined subversion as follows:

> spreading feelings of hostility or creating hostility, dissension, conflict, chaos, instability or restlessness among the population or society in general or between the Republic of Indonesia and a friendly State, or disturbing, hampering and stirring up trouble for industry, production, distribution, trade, cooperation and transportation run by the Government or based on Government's decision, or which has a wide influence on the life of the people.[297]

These provisions defined the state's security interests broadly to include speech that could spread "feelings of hostility" as well as interference with public or private services. Article 7 allowed the attorney general or the highest military prosecutor to authorize up to one year's investigative detention. As in Egypt and Syria, the accused could be tried in military as well as civilian courts. There were no provisions for counsel or in favor of ordinary criminal procedure. The 1963 law has been described as the "harshest of the repressive legislation available in the history of Indonesia to silence a government's alleged opponents."[298] The abuse of this law provides important contextual background that helps explain initial resistance to a post-9/11 antiterrorism law.

After widespread protests concerning the economy, corruption, and the influence of the military, Suharto fell in 1998, to be replaced by President Habibie. Many Indonesians remained concerned about the revival of authoritarianism, and widespread protests in 1999 led to President Habibie refusing to sign a new emergency law.[299] Indonesian democracy was both new and very volatile, buffeted by separatist movements within the vast country and by the advent of many Islamic political groups that had previously been repressed under Suharto. Many feared that the military would be repoliticalized. At the same time, as in post-Mubarak Egypt, the military also remained one of few effective institutions in a poor country with real capacity issues. There were also terrorist groups active in the region, led by the JI, who wanted a theoretic Islamic state spanning Indonesia, Malaysia, Brunei, and the Philippines. There was also much denial of the terrorist threat in Indonesia, most notoriously by Vice President Hamzah Haz, who asserted that there was no terrorism in Indonesia. In this context, there was also much suspicion that the Bush administration's emphasis on the war against terrorism was both hostile

---

[296] Nadirsyah Hosen, "Emergency Powers and the Rule of Law in Indonesia," in *Emergency Powers in Asia*, ed. Victor Ramraj and Arun Thiruvengadam (New York: Cambridge University Press, 2010), at 281–2.

[297] Anti-Subversion Law, Articles 1(c) and 1(d).   [298] Hosen, "Emergency Powers," at 270.

[299] Ibid., at 271.

to Islam and a potential vehicle for restoring military-led authoritarianism in Indonesia. This was especially so as the United States made it clear that it was much happier with the way Singapore and Malaysia used their ISAs to respond to terrorism, as opposed to Indonesia, which struggled to enact a terrorism law and which did not support the U.S.-led invasion of Afghanistan or, subsequently, of Iraq.

The Response to 9/11

Terrorism Financing and Money Laundering

Indonesia's initial response to 9/11 was to ratify the 1999 Convention on the Suppression of Terrorist Financing shortly after 9/11 and to enact a Money Laundering Law in April 2002. Like many post-9/11 laws, this law followed the emphasis on terrorism financing in Security Council Resolution 1373. Section 2 of the law defined the proceeds of crime as assets in the amount of five hundred million rupiah obtained from 15 crimes, including "terrorism," even though there was no such crime at the time and terrorism was not defined in the legislation. This haphazard approach underlined that the law was designed more to respond to Security Council and FATF demands than to provide a workable response to terrorism financing or money laundering.

Like many post 9/11 terrorism financing laws, the 2002 law merged the very different phenomena of money laundering and terrorism financing. The official elucidation of the law asserted that terrorism, like corruption, bribery, drugs, human smuggling, fraud, and "various white collar crimes," "involve or produce extremely large amounts of assets."[300] This elucidation wrongly conflated the large amounts of illegally obtained funds involved in money laundering with the smaller and often legitimate amounts involved in terrorism financing. Indonesia, like Egypt, has a special incentive to respond to both money laundering and terrorism financing because it had been identified by FATF as a noncooperative country.

The 2002 Indonesian law, like many post-9/11 antiterrorism laws, combined laws against terrorism financing with laws against money laundering, despite important differences between the two phenomena. The law required financial institutions to report "suspicious transactions" to a new reporting center, but suspicions were defined not in relation to terrorism but in relation to departures from a customer's usual transactions or attempts to avoid

---

[300] Elucidation of Law No. 15 Concerning Money Laundering, at https://www.unodc.org/tldb/pdf/Indonesia_Elucidation_of_Act_No.15–2002_on_Money_Laundering_Criminal_Act.pdf.

mandatory reporting of large amounts of money.[301] In countries with limited capacity and resources, such as Indonesia, it was unrealistic to think that the state could devise different strategies for tracing large amounts of money obtained through organized crime and corruption and the small amounts of money generally used for terrorism financing. Although Indonesia presented the laws as a means to comply with Resolution 1373 and the 1999 Financing Convention, the law was dominated by concerns about money laundering. Given the subsequent events of the 2002 Bali bombings, it is regrettable that money laundering and terrorism financing were Indonesia's first legislative priority after 9/11.

The Withdrawn Draft Terrorism Law

Indonesia was subject to continuing pressures to enact an antiterrorism law after 9/11. There were concerns that the Indonesian Penal Code was inadequate to deal with attempts and conspiracies to commit terrorist acts. The Indonesian Penal Code, derived from colonial Dutch law, had no general laws of conspiracy and defined attempted crimes narrowly so that a person would only be guilty "if the intention of the offender has revealed itself by a commencement of the performance and the performance is not completed only because of circumstances independent of his will."[302] There were also concerns about the activities of the JI and the return of many members of the JI to Indonesia after the fall of Suharto.

A draft antiterrorism law was developed after 9/11 and released by the government in early 2002. It defined terrorism as "an action using violence or the threat of violence having political background and/or motives" that created a broad range of harms, including "causing danger and the threat of danger to other person's lives; or destroying property or removing personal freedom or creating a sense of fear in society at large."[303] This broad definition of terrorism, like many post-9/11 antiterrorism laws, was influenced by the United Kingdom's Terrorism Act, 2000, which similarly defined terrorism

---

[301] Law Concerning Money Laundering, Law 15 of 2002, Articles 1 and 13, at https://www
.unodc.org/tldb/pdf/Indonesia_Act_No.15-2002_on_Money_Laundering_Criminal_Act.pdf.

[302] Indonesian Penal Code, Article 53, at https://www.unodc.org/tldb/showDocument.do?documentUid=6843&node=docs&cmd=add&country=INS.

[303] Draft Law Concerning the Eradication of Terrorism, Article 1, as quoted in Roach, "Militant Democracy and Terrorism: Some Eastern and Western Comparisons," in *Militant Democracy*, ed. Andras Sajo (Amsterdam, Netherlands: Eleven, 2004), at 195, and on file with the author. Various offenses were created under the draft law, and jurisdiction was asserted over violence or the threat of violence endangering lives, destroying property, or creating a sense of fear in society with respect to offenses outside as well as inside Indonesia.

to include all forms of politically (and religiously) motivated property damage and to include threats of actions. Although broad definitions of terrorism were accepted in many countries, they raised fears in Indonesia, which had so recently experienced the abuse of broadly defined subversion laws under Suharto.

There were other aspects of the withdrawn draft that raised alarm bells. Article 19 was particularly draconian because it provided that terrorist suspects during investigation "shall not have the right to be accompanied by the advocates; to remain silent, or refuse to answer the examiner's questions or to contact outsiders including family members."[304] Article 16 seemed to follow the Terrorism Act, 2000, by providing for a seven-day arrest on the basis of "adequate initial evidence," but then Article 17 departed from regular criminal procedure law by providing for a 90-day period of preventive detention that could be extended up to nine months. Other provisions authorized wiretapping on reasonable suspicion of terrorism and searches, including of homes, without judicial authorization. There were also procedures not only for the seizure but also for the destruction of material evidence, special detention facilities for terrorist suspects, and "special protections" for investigators and examiners that would shield their identities.[305] These latter provisions raised concerns that terrorism would not be dealt with as a matter for criminal trial but as one for extralegal force.

As with the 1999 Emergency Law, the government was forced to withdraw the draft law in the face of widespread opposition. The effective opposition to this bill should dispel any notion that the more authoritarian approach taken in Singapore or Malaysia was an expression of so-called Asian values. As Anthony Langlois has observed, those who invoke Asian values "all too often reduce culture to the state" and then allow state elites to impose Asian values on the populace and use them "as a device for delegitimizing internal or indigenous critics of the regimes in question, aided by the use of draconian legislation such as the Internal Security Acts of Malaysia and Singapore."[306]

---

[304] Ibid., at 203. Article 19 in full provided that "during the examination in investigation level, the suspect shall not have the right: (a) to be accompanied by the advocates; (b) to remain silent or refusing answer the examiner's questions; (c) to suspension of detention in lieu of personal or monetary guarantees; (d) to contact with outsiders including the family members."

[305] Ibid., Articles 19, 20, 21, 22, and 26. For a critique of the withdrawn draft, see Bivitri Susanti, "National Security, Terrorism, and Human Rights in Indonesia," paper presented at the International Workshop on National Security and Constitutional Rights in the Asia-Pacific Region, Australian National University, Canberra, October 8–9, 2002, at http://dspace.anu .edu.au/bitstream/1885/42063/1/Bivitri.pdf.

[306] Anthony Langlois, *The Politics of Justice and Human Rights: Southeast Asia and Universalist Theory* (Cambridge: Cambridge University Press, 2001), at 27–8.

The withdrawal of the draft terrorism law, however, meant that Indonesia was left without a terrorism law at a time when concerns were mounting about the terrorist threat and both Singapore and Malaysia were making use of their ISAs to arrest suspected JI terrorists. "Stressing its democratic credentials," the Indonesian government argued that "unlike Malaysia and Singapore, it was unable to use measures like preventive detention, wiretapping or investigation without warrant."[307] Andrew Tan observed that "tough action, such as the preventive detentions carried out by Malaysia and Singapore, would imperil the Megawati government [in Indonesia] given the probable strong domestic political repercussions of appearing to be responding to pressure from neighbors such as Singapore, and foreign powers such as the US."[308] Tom Friedman observed that Indonesia was "being orphaned because it is a messy, but real, democracy," while "some of its more authoritarian neighbors have ... become the new darlings of Washington."[309]

The Perpu in Response to the 2002 Bali Bombings

Work continued on drafting a new terrorism law after the official withdrawal of the draft terrorism law. Hadi Soesastro of the Jarkata-based Centre for Strategic and International Studies recognized the threat of repression in the withdrawn draft, which he termed "an ISA-type bill," but he also expressed doubts that "the government's 'soft' approach in dealing with this problem will not pose a threat to human security in the longer term."[310] A working group that included representatives from the police and military as well as lawyers and activists who had been imprisoned during the Suharto regime worked on a draft terrorism law. The group was especially concerned with how to distance a new draft from the withdrawn draft on issues relating to defining terrorism as associated with religious and political motives. It was also concerned with the relation between any new law and existing Indonesian criminal procedures and whether the military would play a role under the new law as it had under the Suharto era subversion law.[311]

[307] Leonard Sebastien, "The Indonesian Dilemma: How to Participate in the War on Terror without Becoming a National Security State," in *After Bali: The Threat of Terrorism in Southeast Asia*, ed. Kumar Ramakrishna and See Seng Tan (Singapore: Institute of Defence and Strategic Studies, 2003), at 361.

[308] Andrew Tan, "The 'New' Terrorism: How Southeast Asia Can Counter It," in *September 11 and Political Freedoms: Asian Perspectives*, ed. Uwe Johannen, Alan Smith, and James Gomez (Singapore: Select, 2003), at 107.

[309] Tom Friedman, "The War on What?" New York Times, June 8, 2002.

[310] Hadi Soesastro, "Global Terrorism: Implications for State and Human Security," in Johannen et al., *September 11 and Political Freedoms*, at 80.

[311] I disclose that with the assistance of a U.S.-based aid agency, I made two presentations to this working group in September 2002. In my first presentation, I discussed the Canadian experience

Work on a new antiterrorism law dramatically accelerated after the October 12, 2002, Bali bombings that killed 202 people. On October 18, 2002, President Megawati signed into law two perpus or presidential decrees in lieu of regulations. Such regulations had been used and abused during the Suharto era, but the legislature was in an extended recess and would not ratify the perpus until March 2003. One perpu provided an extensive 47-article Law on Combating Criminal Acts of Terrorism, while a second one purported to allow the first perpu retroactively to be applied to the Bali bombings committed a week earlier.

The first perpu departed from the withdrawn draft by not defining terrorism with respect to political motives or as being a political crime. Instead, Article 2 affirmed that acts of terrorism would be combated as "criminal acts . . . without discriminating in respect of ethnicity, religion, race or class," and Article 5 stated that the criminal acts set out in the law "are neither politically criminal acts nor criminal acts relating to political crimes nor criminal acts with political motives nor criminal acts with the political objective of obstructing an extradition process."[312] This approach rejected the emphasis in the United Kingdom's Terrorism Act, 2000, on religious and political motives and reflected some of the ambivalence about such motive requirements seen in the 2001 Canadian Anti-Terrorism Act, which qualified its inclusion of a religious or political motive requirement with a statement that religious and political expressions would not constitute acts of terrorism.[313]

At the same time, the law featured a broad definition of terrorism that raised concerns about vagueness and overbreadth. It defined terrorism as intentionally using "violence or the threat of violence to create a widespread atmosphere of terror or fear in the general population or to create mass casualties, by forcibly taking the freedom, life or property of others or causes damage or destruction to vital strategic installations or the environment or public facilities or international facilities."[314]

---

with terrorism, and in my second presentation, I offered advice about how Indonesia could either change its penal code or devise a new antiterrorism law that could be more restrained than the withdrawn draft.

[312] Government Regulation in Lieu of Legislation on Combating Criminal Acts of Terrorism, No. 1/2002, Articles 2 and 5, at https://www.unodc.org/tldb/showDocument.do?documentUid= 2927&node=docs&cmd=add&country=INS.

[313] Criminal Code of Canada, RSC 1985, c.C-34, Section 83.01 (1.1), discussed in Chapter 7. For commentary that stresses the Canadian influence on the law, see Sebastien, "Indonesian Dilemma," at 362.

[314] Government Regulation in Lieu of Legislation on Combating Criminal Acts of Terrorism, No. 1/2002, Articles 6 and 7, at https://www.unodc.org/tldb/showDocument.do?documentUid= 2927&node=docs&cmd=add&country=INS.

Following requests by the Security Council's CTC, the perpu empowered both judges and investigators to freeze terrorist assets. It also expanded terrorist financing laws by making it an offense intentionally to provide funds for terrorism or if there was "a reasonable likelihood" that the funds would be used in part or whole for terrorism.[315] This followed Singapore's approach but went beyond the offenses required by the 1999 Financing Convention. The CTC, however, remained concerned, as it was with Egypt, that terrorism financing provisions would not be applied to lawyers or charities or informal money transfer systems. Indonesia subsequently amended its money laundering law to provide that lawyers, real estate brokers, and luxury car salespersons were subject to the reporting requirements.[316] Indonesia was sensitive on these issues because of its noncooperative rating by FATF. Its approach remained firmly rooted in a money laundering model. Concerns about Indonesia's capacity to conduct complex terrorism financing investigations and prosecutions persist.[317]

The perpu also responded to the restrictive nature of the Indonesian Penal Code by enacting various new terrorism offenses, including intentional assistance, incitement, plotting or attempting to commit acts of terrorism, and also facilitating an act of terrorism outside Indonesia.[318] Like the withdrawn draft, the new law made the death penalty available for some terrorism offenses, but unlike the withdrawn draft, proof of intent was generally required.[319] The death penalty under the perpu was prohibited for crimes that were committed by a person under 18 years of age.[320] At the time, the death penalty was

---

[315] Ibid., Articles 29 and 11; also see Indonesia Country Report, S/2003/267, at para. 1.6.

[316] Indonesia Country Report, S/2006/311, at para. 1.4.

[317] Arabinda Acharya and Fatima Astuti, "Chinks in the Armour: Tightening Jakarta's Counter-Terrorism Financing Regime," RSIS Commentaries, July 27, 2010, at http://www.rsis.edu .sg/publications/Perspective/RSIS0822010.pdf.

[318] Government Regulation in Lieu of Legislation on Combating Criminal Acts of Terrorism, No. 1/2002, Articles 13–17, at https://www.unodc.org/tldb/showDocument.do?documentUid= 2927&node=docs&cmd=add&country=INS.

[319] Article 3 of the withdrawn draft provided that "any person using violence or the threat of violence having the political background and or motives by causing danger or the threat of danger on other persons' lives or destroying properties, thus rendering it unusable, shall be subject to capital or life imprisonment or the maximum prison penalty of 20 (twenty) years and minimum prison penalty of 5 (five) years." Article 6 of the perpu provided that "any person who intentionally uses violence or the threat of violence to create a widespread atmosphere of terror or fear in the general population or to create mass casualties, by forcibly taking the freedom, life or property of others or causes damage or destruction to vital strategic installations or the environment or public facilities or international facilities. Sentence: death penalty or life imprisonment or imprisonment for 20 (twenty) years at the maximum or 4 (four) years at the minimum." Ibid. The death penalty is also available under the perpu for importing firearms or explosives and for inciting or planning terrorism. Ibid., Articles 9 and 14.

[320] Ibid., at Article 19.

still available in the United States for crimes committed by juveniles, and Indonesia was able to claim that it was more respectful of human rights in its use of the death penalty than the United States. At the same time, the use of the death penalty in terrorism cases raised concerns about potential wrongful convictions.

The perpu also established that regular criminal and evidence procedures would apply to terrorism trials unless departures from them were specifically authorized. This approach suggested that Indonesia would not regress to the antisubversion paradigm of the Suharto era and that the police, as opposed to the military, would have the prime role in enforcing the new law. As Hikmanto Juwana, the dean of law at the University of Indonesia, has argued, fear of military involvement in antiterrorism efforts is "understandable in the context of Indonesia's recent history of the military interfering undesirably in civilian government."[321]

At the same time, however, the perpu also established some controversial new police powers and criminal procedures. The perpu followed British antiterrorism law at the time, and the withdrawn draft, by allowing seven days of preventive detention on suspicion.[322] An earlier draft provided a three-day maximum, following Canadian provisions, but this was expanded to seven days after the Bali bombing. The provision was opposed by a number of smaller Muslim parties.[323] This transplant was controversial, even though other provisions in the new antiterrorism law allowed six months for investigation and prosecution,[324] a period only slightly longer than would be allowed under normal Indonesian criminal procedure originally derived from Dutch law and only slightly less than the nine months available under the withdrawn draft. The controversy over this provision underlined the symbolic nature of the debate over maximum periods of preventive arrest. As will be seen in Chapter 5, the maximum period of preventive arrests has become a symbol in the United Kingdom about the government's approach to terrorism with Prime Ministers Blair and Brown failing to increase the maximum period to 90 or 42 days and Prime Minister Cameron reducing the 28 day maximum period to a 14 day maximum period. The Indonesian experience also demonstrates how local resistance to foreign transplants can be mobilized.

---

[321] Hikmanto Juwana, "Anti-Terrorism Efforts in Indonesia," in Ramraj, *Global Anti-Terrorism Law and Policy*. See also Sebastien, "Indonesian Dilemma," at 364.

[322] Government Regulation in Lieu of Legislation on Combating Criminal Acts of Terrorism, No. 1/2002, Article 28.

[323] Sebastien, "Indonesian Dilemma," at 367.

[324] Government Regulation in Lieu of Legislation on Combating Criminal Acts of Terrorism, No. 1/2002, Article 25.

Even more controversially, the perpu allowed the use of intelligence reports as preliminary evidence of a crime but subject to review in secret by judges.[325] This provision rejected the idea that a criminal conviction or prolonged detention should be based on secret evidence not disclosed to the accused. As such, it stopped well short of the use of secret evidence for long-term detention, as under Singapore's ISA, and also subjected the use of secret intelligence as preliminary evidence to judicial review. Although allowing intelligence to be used as preliminary evidence accommodated post-9/11 trends that stressed the importance of intelligence and, when necessary, the use of intelligence as evidence. At the same time, this provision was controversial because of Indonesia's particular history and experience of convicting people of subversion in military courts on the basis of secret evidence. The tension between new global antiterrorism mandates and local political and legal culture is a constant theme in this study.

Like the earlier money laundering bill, the success of the perpu would largely depend on the Indonesian capacity to enforce it. Both the United States and Australia, the latter of which had 88 of its citizens killed in the Bali bombings, increased aid to the Indonesian police after the attack. Many of the perpetrators of the Bali bombings were arrested and convicted, and some were executed. The perpu itself recognized some capacity issues by creating offenses involving attempts to intimidate witnesses, investigators, prosecutors, lawyers, and judge or providing false information to investigators.[326] The perpu also provided for compensation and rehabilitation of both victims of terrorism and those who were accused of terrorism but subsequently found not to be guilty.[327] This was a recognition absent in the withdrawn draft that the innocent could be victimized both by terrorism and excessive zeal in prosecuting terrorists. As in Singapore, those accused of terrorism were regarded as fellow citizens and not as demonized foreigners.

The perpu was not free from controversy. It was ratified by a vote of 220–46 in the Indonesian legislature in March 2003, but only after two parties abstained in protest.[328] Hikmanto Juwana explained in 2005 that the perpu was greeted by Indonesians "with ambivalence. Although they hoped terrorism would soon cease, they were also suspicious that the Law would give rise to authoritarian government and the revival of the military. In addition, people were afraid that Indonesia had joined an American-led war against Islam, not terrorism."[329] He

---

[325] Ibid., Article 26.   [326] Ibid., Articles 20-4, 33-4.
[327] Ibid., Articles 36-42.
[328] Sebastien, "Indonesian Dilemma," at 363-4.
[329] Hikmanto Juwana, "Indonesia's Anti-Terrorism Law," in Ramraj et al., *Global Anti-Terrorism Law and Policy*, at 299.

also argued that Western democracies, such as the United States and Australia, "have lost their persuasiveness and moral authority because their anti-terror efforts are perceived to be inconsistent with their prior human rights sermons to Indonesia."[330] Leonard Sebastien concluded that "from a legal perspective, the new laws were considered progressive and served as an important building block in strengthening the rule of law in Indonesia."[331]

The Administration of the Perpu

Unlike in Singapore, there have been public trials of suspected terrorists in Indonesia. The convictions of some of the Bali bombers and their executions were protested by thousands who saw them as heroes.[332] The Indonesian experience underlines that the concern that terrorism trials and convictions can create religious martyrs is a real one.[333] Nevertheless, there is little alternative but to run such risks in a system that does not have an ISA. It is also possible that Singapore, as well, might rely on the criminal law and the death penalty if it, like Indonesia, were to suffer multiple successful terrorist attacks.

The Indonesian Constitutional Court ruled in 2004 that the attempt to make the 2002 law retroactive to the Bali bombings was unconstitutional under a post-Suharto constitutional prohibition on retroactive laws. The retroactivity issue was complex, as reflected by the 5–4 decision in the Indonesian court and by the fact that human rights groups had opposed the constitutional provision because of fears that it would result in impunity for human rights abuses during the Suharto era. The dissenting judges on the court insisted that the right against retroactive laws could be subject to a general provision in the Indonesian Constitution allowing limits to be placed on rights "with the sole purpose of guaranteeing recognition and respect for the rights of others."[334] In any event, the court's decision seemed to have a minimal effect on antiterrorism enforcement, in part because it was only applied prospectively and because existing crimes, such as murder, could be used for the completed crime of the Bali bombings.

The main functional role of the 2002 terrorism law was to criminalize acts of preparation for terrorism, including financing and incitement, and the 2002 law could be applied in this respect to terrorist acts subsequent to the

---

[330] Ibid., at 300. [331] Sebastien, "Indonesian Dilemma," at 364.
[332] Juwana, "Anti-Terrorism Efforts in Indonesia."
[333] Hor, "Terrorism and the Criminal Law."
[334] Indonesian Constitution, Article 28(J). See also Ross Clarke, "Retrospectivity and the Constitutional Validity of the Bali Bombing and East Timor Trials" (2003) 5 Asian Law 128.

Bali bombings. At the same time, Indonesia's attempt to make the 2002 law retroactive can be seen as part of a general trend to enact antiterrorism laws to respond to traumatic terrorist acts. Established democracies also enacted reactive legislation, albeit without challenging notions of formal legality that prohibit retroactive offenses.[335]

There have been frequent and continuing demands for Indonesia to adopt tougher antiterrorism laws. In the aftermath of the 2003 bombing of the JW Marriott hotel in Jakarta, "a debate emerged in Indonesia . . . about the restoration of the old Anti-Subversion Law in order to target terrorist groups." The national intelligence chief called for military intelligence to be able to make terrorist arrests, and the defense minister advocated an ISA. Nevertheless, both measures were resisted in part because of memories of how the Anti-Subversion Law had, under Suharto, been used "to imprison political activists and radical Muslim leaders."[336] After another Bali bombing in 2005, Scott Atran argued in *The New York Times* that the event "augurs ill for American efforts to promote democracy as an antidote to terrorism elsewhere in the Muslim world" because Indonesia's "minority-led democratic government, whose very survival requires the support of Islamic parties that range from the militant to the mainstream, has spent the period between the two Bali attacks waffling in its response to terrorism for fear of alienating these Muslim parties and a largely anti-American populace."[337] This criticism of Indonesia, however, ignored Tom Friedman's earlier defense of Indonesia's democratic debate about terrorism laws and his warnings that Indonesians might conclude that they would be judged by the United States "not by the integrity of their elections or the justice of their courts, but by the vigor with which their army and police combat Al Qaeda."[338]

Concerns about terrorism in Indonesia continue.[339] In 2010, draft amendments to the terrorism law were released by the government. They included a proposal for British-style offenses of failing to report information about a

---

[335] The Supreme Court of Canada held that post-9/11 powers of investigative hearings could be used in the investigation of the 1985 Air India bombings because the provisions were procedural and did not create a new offense; Section 83.28 of the Criminal Code (2004) 2 S.C.R. 248. In Australia, terrorism laws were quickly expanded by the legislature shortly before the 2005 arrests in Sydney and Melbourne. See Chapter 6.

[336] Anthony Smith, "The Politics of Negotiating the Terrorist Problem in Indonesia" (2005) 28 Studies in Conflict and Terrorism 33, at 42.

[337] Scott Atran, "In Indonesia, Democracy Isn't Enough," New York Times, October 5, 2005.

[338] Friedman, "War on What?"

[339] "US worries that terrorism on the upswing in Indonesia" Jakarta Globe November 8, 2010.

potential terrorist attack and enhanced incitement offenses as well as a proposed expansion of the 7-day period of preventive arrest to 30 days.[340] These British-inspired imports, however, will, if enacted, play out quite differently in the distinct Indonesian context, and they may be resisted by Islamic political parties that have been gaining support in Indonesia. Even the new amendments, however, will not introduce proscription of terrorist groups. Although "there is intense international pressure on the Indonesia government to ban JI," this fails to recognize the reality that "no politician in the world's largest Muslim community has the political courage to ban an organization that simply translates as 'Islamic community.'"[341]

The treatment of the Muslim cleric Abu Bakar Basyir was a matter of controversy. Both the United States and Australia saw him as the spiritual leader of the JI and believed he was responsible for both the 2002 Bali bombing and the 2003 bombing of the Marriott Hotel in Jakarta. For many Indonesians, however, he was a leader of a legitimate Muslim organization, and they feared that the Indonesian government was bowing to pressure from the West to prosecute him. Basyir was first charged with both involvement in the Bali bombings and treason for advocating an Islamic state. He was acquitted of the terrorism charges but convicted of treason. This raised concerns because Basyir had been convicted of the same treason offense under Suharto.[342] The treason conviction was overturned on appeal, and he was only convicted on minor immigration offenses. On his release, Basyir was charged again and convicted of terrorism-related charges only to be released in 2006. In 2010, Basyir was again arrested on terrorism charges for which he faces the death penalty, and there was declining support for him in Indonesia.

There have been other irritants to Indonesia's attempt to deal with terrorism in a democratic manner. The American capture of Indonesian terrorist Hambli in Thailand and his subsequent detention at secret CIA prisons and Guantánamo have been a cause of concern. In 2010, Indonesia formally requested that the United States return Hambli to Indonesia for trial in relation to terrorism, but the United States refused.[343] The refusal of the United

---

[340] Juwana, "Anti-Terrorism Efforts in Indonesia." For arguments by security officials that the minimum sentence of 3 years should be increased to 10 years imprisonment and the preventive arrest period should be increased from 7 to 21 days see "Terrorists 'must get heavier sentences'" Jakarta Post June 19, 2010.

[341] Zachary Abuza, "The Social Organization of Terror in Southeast Asia," in *Countering the Financing of Terrorism*, ed. Thomas Biersteker and Sue Eckert (London: Routledge, 2008), at 84.

[342] Roach, "Militant Democracy and Terrorism," at 198.

[343] "US Rejects RI Request to Try Hambli in Indonesia," Jakarta Post, January 19, 2010.

States to hand over Hambli has, according to Indonesian expert Sidney Jones, fueled conspiracy theories and denial about terrorism that was only partially rebutted by the transparency of the Bali bombing trials.[344] In addition, there were concerns about extrajudicial execution of suspected terrorists, such as al-Ghozi, who was killed in the Philippines shortly before President Bush's visit to the country.[345] As will be seen, concerns about extrajudicial killings would also subsequently arise in Indonesia with respect to an American-funded and trained antiterrorism squad known as Detachment 88.

Detachment 88: Conflicting Claims of Religious Rehabilitation and Extrajudicial Killings

Several established religious organizations in Indonesia have issued fatwas against terrorism,[346] and organized Islamic groups can be an important resource in the ideological battle against terrorism. At the same time, Indonesia's rehabilitation program for terrorists is less structured and less successful than Singapore's program. Indonesia's program is centered around the specialized police force called Detachment 88, which has received both praise and criticism.

In June 2010, *Time* published an article titled "What Indonesia Can Teach the World about Counterterrorism" that painted a generally flattering portrait of the work of Detachment 88. The article stressed that through deradicalization programs, Detachment 88 "[took] on the role of spiritual counselors in working to convince militants of the error of their ways" and claimed that one-half of the 400 terrorist suspects in custody "have either co-operated with police or renounced violence."[347] These claims, however, are at odds with other studies that show, without the threat of indeterminate detention that is present in Singapore and Malaysia, there are very low rates of participation in Indonesia's rehabilitation programs.[348] There are, however, some high-profile cases of successful rehabilitation. Nasir bin Abas, a former member of JI, has written a book discrediting the terrorist tactics of the organization. He credits his turn away from violence in part to the fact that he was not beaten or tortured

---

[344] Rizal Suma, "The Quiet Achiever: Indonesia's Response to Terrorism," in *Proceedings of the Third Biannual Conference of the Counsel for Asian Terrorism Research*, ed. Caroline Ziemke et al. (Charlottesville VA: Institute for Defence Analysis, 2007), at 1–22.

[345] Juwana, "Indonesia's Anti-Terrorism Law," at 301.

[346] Suma, "Quiet Achiever: Indonesia's Response to Terrorism," at 25–6.

[347] Hannah Beech, "What Indonesia Can Teach the World about Counterterrorism," Time, June 7, 2010.

[348] Abuza, "Rehabilitation of Jemaah Islamiyah Detainees," at 200 (only 20 of 400 offenders took counseling).

when captured by Detachment 88 but treated in what he characterizes as a decent Islamic manner. At the same time, there have been failures of rehabilitation. For example, a convicted terrorist, Urwah, was released in 2007 but was involved in another bombing of Western hotels in Jakarta in 2009.[349] One report suggests that there have been 16 repeat offenders among 200 terrorism offenders convicted but released since 2002.[350]

The hard and coercive edge of Detachment 88 should not be underestimated. Although the *Time* article quoted a former and likely American trainer of Detachment 88 as saying that the unit "is one of the best I've ever seen,"[351] it has also been repeatedly accused of extrajudicial killings. From February to June 2010, the police killed at least 13 terrorist suspects in raids. Indonesia's National Commission on Human Rights raised concerns about extrajudicial killings by the police to avoid a legal system that the police perceive as too lenient.[352] Amnesty International has accused Detachment 88 of beating and torturing Malakan activists in 2007 after they displayed an independence flag. The case is also disturbing because the activists were convicted of conspiring to commit a rebellion under Suharto-era provisions of the penal code and sentenced to 7–20 years' imprisonment.[353] The torture and punishment of peaceful separatist groups in Indonesia underlines that the restrictions placed into the Indonesia antiterrorism law, including those that prevent discrimination on the basis of politics and religion, are no guarantee that authorities will not use other security measures to repress peaceful dissent. The use of Detachment 88 provides some legitimating cover for such events, given the praise that the detachment has received in some quarters for its antiterrorism activities.

Despite initial attempts to keep it out of antiterrorism activities, the military was deployed in 2010 to deal with terrorist attacks in northern Sumatra. A National Terrorism Agency was created in 2010 by presidential decree and includes parts of the military as well as the police. The head of that agency explained that the use of the military was designed "to send the terrorists the message that they are now the enemy of the state and not just the police."[354] Although Indonesia may have escaped old and repressive habits in the

---

[349] Juwana, "Anti-Terrorism Efforts in Indonesia."

[350] Agus Hadi Nahrowi and Laode Arham "Ordinary Prisons, Uncommon Prisoners" *Jakarta Globe* February 16, 2011.

[351] Beech, "What Indonesia Can Teach the World about Counterterrorism."

[352] Juwana "Anti-Terrorism Efforts in Indonesia."

[353] "Malukan Activists at Risk of Torture in Detention in Indonesia," at http://www.amnesty.org/en/news-and-updates/malukan-activists-risk-torture-detention-indonesia-2010-08-04.

[354] "Indonesian Military Joins a Local Terrorism Fight," New York Times, October 7, 2010.

immediate aftermath of 9/11, there are some signs that it may be slipping
back into them.

VII. CONCLUSION

Unlike the other countries examined in this chapter, Indonesia chose not to
rely on old, harsh laws in the aftermath of 9/11. It did, however, respond to 9/11
with a money laundering and terrorism financing law that was aimed more
at complying with Security Council and FATF mandates than at responding
to the real terrorist threat in the region. Similar legislation was enacted in
Egypt, Syria, Israel, and Singapore, but in all four countries, it remained very
peripheral to more forceful responses to terrorism. All these countries were
attentive to Security Council and FATF mandates with respect to terrorism
financing, but these mandates achieved little either in terms of preventing
terrorism or ensuring respect for human rights and the rule of law while
countering terrorism.

The Indonesian government attempted, after 9/11, to introduce a broadly
drafted antiterrorism law that vaguely defined terrorism as a political crime and
provided the state with similar authoritarian powers as used under Suharto.
Opposition to this law led to its withdrawal, but a perpu or government regulation in lieu of legislation was enacted less than a week after the 2002 Bali
bombings. This legislation has been criticized as both too harsh in its authorization of the use of intelligence as preliminary evidence and as too weak in
its failure to prevent a series of subsequent terrorist attacks in Indonesia. The
success of Indonesia's evolving counter-terrorism remains in doubt, and there
are disturbing signs of a more authoritarian turn, including involvement of
the military, concerns about extrajudicial killings, and draft amendments to
toughen the 2002 terrorism law. Nevertheless, Indonesia, as the world's largest
Muslim majority democracy, provides a valuable counterpoint to the way that
Egypt and Syria relied on harsh older laws and practices after 9/11. It may also
provide something of a model for Egypt after the overthrow of Mubarak.

Indonesia also provides a counterpoint to the reliance that both Singapore
and Malaysia placed on their old ISAs after 9/11. The ISA, like emergency
regulations in Israel's Occupied Territories, has its origins in British colonial
emergency rule. It features administrative detention based on secret evidence,
the use of control orders, and restrictive regulations on expression and associations based on terrorism. The 9/11 fallout has helped revive and relegitimate
such measures. In addition, elements of these measures are being extended
through new antiterrorism laws both in Israel and in Western democracies.
Israel's 2002 Internment of Unlawful Combatants Law extends administrative

detention based on colonial British emergency regulations but also borrows from post-9/11 American innovations that imposed military detention on noncitizens who were also classified as unlawful combatants. The Israeli Supreme Court has upheld the new law, but as in its targeted killing case, it has rejected the third category of unlawful combatant, even while recognizing the legitimacy of detaining and killing civilians directly involved in terrorism.

Although Singapore relied on and relegitimized the ISA as antiterrorism law, it also had significant success in rehabilitating and reintegrating those held and released under the act. Singapore, with its significant Muslim minority, also took steps to try to prevent terrorism from being socially divisive and this can be contrasted with the relative absence of attention to rehabilitation with respect to those subject to administrative and military detention in Israel as well as in the Western democracies. There is interest in rehabilitation in both Egypt and Indonesia, but the approaches used in all countries are very different and underline the importance of attempting to understand the particular contexts and capacities of different countries, even as they respond to common terrorism issues.

Both Egypt and Israel will likely be debating new and comprehensive antiterrorism laws in the near future, and Indonesia is also considering amendments of its 2002 law. There is a danger that laws featuring broad definitions of terrorism and extensive state powers can be justified on the basis that they are similar to antiterrorism laws enacted in other countries, most notably the United Kingdom. In Egypt, 2007 constitutional amendments would have protected any new terrorism law from constitutional challenge in much the same way as the ISA is entrenched and protected from rights review in Singapore and Malaysia. In addition, in an echo of American practice, the 2007 Egyptian amendments included an explicit constitutional power for the Egyptian president to transfer terrorism and other security cases to special security or military courts. Fortunately, these amendments will be repealed as a result of the overthow of President Mubarak and the approval of a referendum on constitutional change. Any new terrorism law in Egypt will as a result be subject to constitutional challenge and as a result of these constitutional proposals, there will be stricter limits on emergency powers in Egypt than in Israel.

This chapter provided a baseline with which to evaluate how 9/11 has altered the balance between state powers and liberty. The use of administrative detention on the basis of secret evidence once criticized in Singapore and Israel has been revived and expanded after 9/11 and, as will be seen in subsequent chapters, has become more accepted in Western democracies. The next chapter will examine how the United States has followed Mubarak-era Egypt's, Suharto-era Indonesia's, and Israel's practice of using military detention and military courts. It has also used targeted killings of suspected terrorists, but without the judicial review found in Israel in the post-9/11 era. Practices such as control orders and speech restrictions found in British colonial emergency rule in Malaya and Palestine have been revived in post-9/11 U.K. antiterrorism laws. From the United Kingdom, they have migrated to other countries, most notably Australia. A sense of history and an understanding of regimes that have traditionally experienced much terrorism, are necessary to have a full appreciation of the effect of 9/11 on Western democracies.

4 The United States Responds: Executive Power and Extra-Legalism

I. INTRODUCTION

The American response to 9/11 has been much criticized around the world but not always carefully understood in the context of the United States' unique legal and political culture. The American approach, especially in the three years after 9/11, was dominated by an aggressive assertion of executive power and by conduct that was supported by dubious claims of legality. The most infamous conduct was directed at non–American citizens outside the United States. It included detentions without trial at Guantánamo Bay and elsewhere, torture and abuse at Abu Ghraib and elsewhere, and increased use of extraordinary renditions to countries with poor human rights records. Some of the extralegal activity, such as the Presidential designation and military detention of Yaser Hamdi and Jose Padilla as enemy combatants and the illegal domestic spying of the National Security Agency (NSA), was directed at American citizens.

Less appreciated is that the American legislative response to terrorism in the years immediately after 9/11 was mild compared to the responses of other democracies. To be sure, the Uniting and Strengthening America by Providing Appropriate Tools Required to Intercept and Obstruct Terrorism Act (also known as the USA Patriot Act, or simply the Patriot Act) expanded surveillance and search powers and contemplated the use of immigration law as antiterrorism law; nevertheless, it did not attempt to derogate from rights by suspending habeas corpus, or enact new and controversial procedures such as the preventive arrests, investigative hearings, and questioning warrants that were introduced into Australian and Canadian law after 9/11. The Patriot Act stopped short of criminalizing membership in a terrorist group, and it defined terrorism more narrowly than many other post-9/11 laws. The Patriot Act was widely criticized, but the ferocity of this criticism from both the Left and the

Right demonstrated American exceptionalism. In comparative perspective, the Patriot Act was mild.

The most aggressive American responses to 9/11 were not authorized by the Patriot Act but done unilaterally by the executive. Immediately after 9/11, thousands of noncitizens were detained under pretextual uses of immigration laws that were followed by selective immigration registration programs that focused on those from Arab and Muslim countries before being abandoned as a strategic mistake. The Patriot Act expanded the ability to get warrants to spy on suspected members of foreign terrorist groups, but President Bush ordered the NSA to intercept communications involving Americans without judicial warrant or any legislative authorization. The Patriot Act did not attempt to authorize investigative or preventive arrests, but material witness warrants were used after 9/11 to achieve the same ends. Except for Congress's bare-bones Authorization of the Use of the Military Force (AUMF), the experiment at Guantánamo with military detention and harsh interrogation was conducted according to executive, not legislative, authorization. The real story of much of what the United States did to respond to 9/11 is found in executive action. That so many of the abuses committed by the executive in the wake of 9/11 have come to light is another sign of American exceptionalism, as manifested by the activity of a free press that is unrestrained by official secrets acts found in most other democracies.[1]

One of the reasons why the official American legislative response to 9/11 seems mild in comparative perspective is that the First Amendment has restrained the creation of criminal offenses against membership in terrorist groups or speech that advocates terrorism. To be sure, these prohibitions are not completely absolute, and the U.S. Supreme Court has upheld a broadly worded offense of material support of a foreign terrorist group that applies to otherwise lawful forms of support for such groups.[2] Nevertheless, the Court also stressed the continued freedom of Americans to say anything they wish about terrorism. American traditions of free press also help explain the disclosure of the torture memos, extraordinary rendition, Central Intelligence Agency (CIA) black sites, and NSA spying scandals. The aggressive and at times extralegal approach of the executive would have been far less visible in other countries, where freedom of the press is more severely restricted in the name of national security. At the same time, the American courts have shut down civil litigation that has attempted to hold officials accountable for extralegal actions through the use of a broad and blunt state-secrets doctrine.

---

[1] Richard Posner, *Not a Suicide Pact* (Oxford: Oxford University Press, 2006), at 108.
[2] *Holder v. Humanitarian Law Project*, 130 S.Ct. 2705 (2010).

Another reason for the relative mildness of the legislative and domestic American response to terrorism is the legal and political restrictions on what can be done in the United States and with respect to American citizens. Unlike the other democracies examined in this book, the United States does not have a domestic security intelligence agency. It relies on the Federal Bureau of Investigation (FBI) and other policing agencies to prevent domestic terrorism. The much criticized expansion of search powers in the Patriot Act was tied to the Foreign Intelligence Surveillance Act (FISA) that targets foreign power and international terrorists. The Guantánamo Bay detentions and now the Military Commissions Act apply only to non–American citizens. Although ultimately unsuccessful, the choice of Guantánamo was designed to escape the jurisdiction of American courts, which nevertheless remain reluctant to assert jurisdiction over other sites, including those in Afghanistan. To be sure, the United States is far from powerless in responding to domestic terrorists. It has made aggressive use of criminal prosecutions and in the immediate aftermath of 9/11 used material witness warrants as a de facto form of preventive and investigative detention. Nevertheless, the United States does not have explicit preventive arrest or detention regimes. It also does not have the control orders and membership and advocacy offenses used in the United Kingdom, which has much more experience with domestic terrorism. Even after 9/11, the United States has not moved toward a European-style militant democracy that is prepared to limit expressive and associational freedom in the name of protecting democracy.[3]

A willingness to use extralegal approaches also helps to explain the comparative mildness of the official American response to terrorism. Extralegal responses allow the executive to break the law in real or perceived emergencies while at the same time maintaining legal restraints without legislative amendments or emergency derogations.[4] It would be a mistake to think that American acceptance of extralegal approaches to emergencies was an invention of 9/11 or the Bush administration. The extralegal approach has deep roots in American history, and many prominent American commentators on both the Right and the Left celebrated President Lincoln's illegal suspension of habeas corpus during the Civil War.[5] The Bush administration's

---

[3] Mark Tushnet, "The United States of America," in *The "Militant Democracy" Principle in Modern Democracies*, ed. Marcus Thiele (London: Ashgate, 2009). But some forms of ideological and associational exclusions are imposed on noncitizens under immigration law. David Cole, *Enemy Aliens* (New York: New Press, 2003).

[4] Oren Gross and Fionnuala Ni Aolain, *Law in Times of Crisis* (New York: Cambridge University Press, 2006), chap. 3.

[5] Posner, *Not a Suicide Pact*, at 85; Mark Tushnet, "Defending Korematsu? Reflections on Civil Liberties in Wartime" (2003) Wisconsin Law Review 273.

favorite wartime precedent upholding the use of a military commission against nonuniformed Nazi saboteurs was decided against the backdrop of President Roosevelt's insistence that he would not hand the captives to any court purporting to use the writ of habeas corpus.[6] Jack Goldsmith, the official who withdrew the infamous 2002 torture memos in 2004, admits that many officials relied on them as "advance pardons"[7] for illegal practices such as waterboarding. Even the 2005 Detainee Treatment Act, which was designed to repudiate the shame of Abu Ghraib and torture, attempted to provide officials with defenses for relying on legal advice if they were sued or prosecuted for their abuses.

Unlike the extralegal model defended by Oren Gross,[8] American officials who broke the law after 9/11 generally did not admit to doing so and their conduct was only revealed by the free press. Much of the illegal conduct including torture but also warrantless spying by the NSA was supported by dubious claims of legality made by government lawyers such as John Yoo, the author of the infamous torture memos. Lawyers, including those employed by the Obama administration, have continued to provide legal protections by shutting down lawsuits about extraordinary renditions, military detention and the NSA programs through successful state secrecy claims and other legal devices. The American approach was based not so much on explicit extralegal conduct but extra-legalism in which illegal conduct was defended through claims of legality including arguments designed to deprive courts of jurisdiction to decide whether the governmental conduct was illegal. One of the themes in this chapter will be the symbiotic relationship between America's advanced sense of legalism and its post- 9/11 descent into illegal conduct. The term extra-legalism is meant to describe illegal conduct that was nevertheless supported by dubious claims of legality and the apparent paradox of the American response to 9/11 being dominated by lawyers[9] yet so often resulting in illegal acts such as rendition, torture and warrantless spying.[10]

The American approach to terrorism both before and after 9/11 has frequently been based on a war model in part because much of the American

---

[6] Jack Goldsmith, *The Terror Presidency* (New York: W. W. Norton, 2007), at 52 (describing the backdrop of *ex parte Quirin*, 317 U.S. 1, upholding the use of military commissions).

[7] Ibid., at 96.

[8] Oren Gross, "Chaos and Rules: Should Responses to Violent Crisis Always Be Constitutional?" (2003) 112 Yale Law Journal 1011.

[9] On the domination of lawyers in American antiterrorism policy including Guantanamo and torture see Goldsmith *The Terror Presidency* chapters 4 and 5.

[10] I am indebted to David Cole who in responding to an earlier draft helped me clarify my thinking about how the United States combined illegal conduct with claims of legality.

experience both before and after 9/11 has come from attacks launched from outside rather than inside the United States.[11] The Guantánamo detentions, extraordinary renditions and targeted killings are based on Congress's bare-bones AUMF, created in the immediate wake of 9/11. This authorization of military force plays a central role in American efforts in part because it imposes few, if any, restrictions on the state in its war against terrorism. The United States has also employed other paradigms to combat terrorism, including crime, immigration, preemption, and various hybrid models. The Military Commissions Act, enacted in 2006 and revised in 2009, represents a strange and incoherent mixture of the laws of war and crime. The United States has claimed the ability to prosecute people in military commissions for crimes, such as conspiracy and material support of terrorism, that are unknown to the law of war. It has ignored law of war restrictions on interrogations and not always treated those detained by the military with the dignity that should be accorded fellow soldiers. It has selectively used criminal law concepts in aid of Guantánamo but has not bound itself by the restrictions of criminal law, including the right to counsel of choice, an impartial jury, or the right to be released if found not guilty. American attempts to forge a third model different from the laws of war and crime have largely been unsuccessful. They have left the bitter impression of double standards that allow the state to cherry-pick those aspects of the law on war and crime that best facilitate its interests and powers. Such an approach is so casual when it comes to traditional legal categories that it smacks of extra-legalism.

The American approach also remains rooted in an executive model of counter-terrorism policy as opposed to a legislative one.[12] Congress enacted the AUMF, the Patriot Act, and massive laws on homeland security and intelligence and governmental reforms, but has only addressed detention and military trial issues when forced by the courts. As Philip Bobbitt has suggested, "rather than seeking legal reform, the United States has used the inadequacy of the currently prevailing law as a basis for avoiding legal restrictions on government entirely."[13] The Obama administration has attempted to change the

---

[11] David Cole has suggested that the external nature of the terrorist threat faced by the United States helps explain its "war on terrorism." He suggests that "when one is fighting an external foe" that "overreaction is almost inevitable . . . By contrast, when one is attacked from within, one searches for a cure, not a fight." He also relates the internal nature of the terrorist threat faced by the United Kingdom to its increased use of surveillance and criminal law responses. David Cole "English Lessons: A Comparative Analysis of UK and US Responses to Terrorism" (2009) 62 Current Legal Problems 136 at 165–167.

[12] Daphne Barak-Erez, "Terrorism Law between the Executive and Legislative Models" (2009) 57 American Journal of Comparative Law 877.

[13] Philip Bobbitt, *Terror and Consent* (New York: Anchor, 2009), at 456.

tone of American counter-terrorism, but its legislative legacy, so far, has been minimal. Many in the United States argue that the legislature should play a greater role in structuring counter-terrorism policy.[14] At the same time, the American legislative process can be quite populist and reactive. Legislation enacted in late 2010 has prevented the Obama Administration from transferring Guantánamo detainees to the United States for criminal prosecutions and led to criminal charges against Khalid Sheikh Mohammed and other alleged 9/11 conspirators being abandoned in favor of trial by military commissions at Guantánamo.

The role that courts have played in American counter-terrorism is complex. American free speech and free association doctrines as interpreted by the Supreme Court in the 1960s help explain why it is not a crime to be a member of a terrorist group in the United States and why calls for laws targeting speech associated with terrorism are likely to be resisted. The Court has also been active in rejecting first the Bush administration's and later Congress's attempts to preclude habeas corpus review at Guantánamo.[15] These decisions responded to growing international criticisms of Guantánamo as a legal black hole. At the same time, however, the Court warned that habeas review need not satisfy criminal law standards of disclosure and that courts should protect intelligence sources and methods.[16] Moreover, the Court, in *Hamdi*,[17] accepted that the detentions could be authorized simply on the basis of the bare-bones AUMF and that due process could be satisfied by military tribunals that departed from the rules of evidence and by a rebuttable presumption that the government's hearsay evidence was correct. In 2006, the Court ruled in *Hamdan*[18] that military trial rules designed on the basis of *Hamdi* were deficient and violated Common Article 3 of the Geneva Conventions because they allowed the use of secret evidence. These decisions created higher standards for military trials than military detention. The Court's 2008 decision in *Boumediene* allows Guantánamo detainees to challenge detention through habeas corpus, but also may have implicitly legitimated military detention without either military or civilian trial. The American courts have helped bring some due process to Guantánamo, but their decisions have not shut it down, and voluntary releases by the executive have dwarfed court-ordered releases and there have been few trials by military commissions. In addition, attempts to use the courts as a

---

[14] See Benjamin Wittes, *Legislating the War on Terror: An Agenda for Reform* (Washington, DC: Brookings Institution Press, 2009).

[15] *Rasul v. Bush*, 542 U.S. 466 (2004).

[16] *Boumediene v. Bush*, 128 S.Ct. 2229 (2008). The Court also refused to block a transfer of an American citizen in Iraq even to possible torture. *Munaf v. Geren*, 128 S.Ct. 2207 (2008).

[17] 542 U.S. 407 (2004). [18] 548 U.S. 557 (2006).

mechanism of accountability for extraordinary renditions, targeted killings, and warrantless spying have generally failed.

II. THE PRE-9/11 EXPERIENCE

Before 1996, much of the American response to terrorism focused on the protection of Americans abroad. The Reagan administration took a hard line on terrorism after the bombing of U.S. Marine barracks in Lebanon. It stressed actions against state sponsors of terrorism and assistance to states in terrorism prevention. Terrorism prevention was an extension of foreign policy and the threat of terrorism was seen as an external threat mainly to Americans outside of the United States.

The Reagan administration also initiated a criminal justice response under the 1984 Combat International Terrorism Act and 1986 Omnibus Anti-Terrorism Act. These acts allowed the FBI and the Department of Justice to investigate and prosecute terrorism committed abroad against U.S. citizens. American courts accepted that even the forcible abduction of the accused and rendering them to the United States would not deprive them of jurisdiction to try an accused.[19] In 1992, the U.S. Supreme Court affirmed that American courts could try a person who was rendered without legal process and essentially kidnapped from Mexico, despite the existence of an extradition treaty.[20] Although the decision was greeted with much domestic and especially international criticism, the Court after 9/11 would dismiss a civil action by the rendered fugitive in part on the basis that a claim could not be based on international law.[21] American exceptionalism with respect to a lack of concern with international law and a willingness to condone extralegal conduct predated 9/11. These cases also demonstrated extra-legalism in which the United States Supreme Court itself refused to concern itself with the underlying legality of an extraordinary rendition.

Extraordinary Renditions and the Extralegal Tradition

The focus of extraordinary renditions as in the Mexico cases discussed above was traditionally on bringing suspects to the United States for trial, and

---

[19] *Ker v. Illinois*, 119 U.S. 436 (1886); *Frisbie v. Collins*, 342 U.S. 519 (1952), followed in *United States v. Yunis*, 924 F.2d 1086 (D.C.Cir. 1991) (hijacker arrested and held on a naval ship); *United States v. Yousef*, 927 F. Supp. 673 (S.D.N.Y., 1996) (abduction and alleged torture in Pakistan does not deprive the court of jurisdiction in cases involving a plot to explode 12 airliners).

[20] *US v. Alvarez-Machain*, 504 U.S. 655 (1992).

[21] *Sosa v. Alvarez-Machain*, 542 U.S. 692 (2004).

President Reagan saw these efforts as a success witnessed by more than 40 terrorist arrests and convictions between 1986 and 1988.[22] The extraordinary rendition program was used during the Clinton administration to transfer several suspected terrorists to Egypt, where they were reported to have been tortured and executed.[23] The rendition program was carried on at the edges of legality. Assurances might have been received that the rendered person would not be tortured, but as Michael Scheuer, the head of the bin Laden unit at the CIA, admitted, such assurances "weren't worth a bucket of warm spit."[24] Extra-legalism-the deployment of dubious legal arguments in an attempt to legitimize illegal conduct-started before 9/11.

The extraordinary rendition program both before and after 9/11 tapped into a deep American tradition of resorting to extralegal measures in times of emergency. The United States is famous for the role that lawyers play, and it has a refined sense of legalism.[25] Despite this legalism, and perhaps because of it, it also has a deep extralegal tradition.[26] President Lincoln suspended habeas corpus at the start of the Civil War without congressional authorization, and the Supreme Court only intervened to protect habeas corpus after the war was over.[27] Judge Richard Posner has defended President Lincoln's actions as "an extralegal approach" that "places tighter constraints on the president than the legal approach of amending the Constitution to authorize suspending constitutional rights in emergencies."[28] President Roosevelt might have defied the Supreme Court during World War II if it had refused to ratify the military trial of German saboteurs in *ex parte Quirin*.[29] Jack Goldsmith, in his explanation of the Bush administration's "terror presidency," has recounted how President Roosevelt told his attorney general, "I won't give them up. . . . I won't hand them over to any U.S. marshal armed with a writ of habeas corpus." Chief Justice Stone learned of these comments and sought to avoid such a "dreadful"

---

[22] J. Brent Wilson, "The United States Response to Terrorism," in *The Deadly Sin of Terrorism*, ed. David Charters (Westport, CT: Greenwood Press, 1994), at 184–6, 197.

[23] Benjamin Wittes, *Law and the Long War* (New York: Penguin, 2008), at 26–8; Jane Mayer, *The Dark Side* (New York: Anchor Books, 2008), at 112–16; Human Rights Watch, *The Black Hole: The Fate of Islamists Rendered to Egypt* (2005).

[24] Mayer, *Dark Side*, at 113.

[25] Robert Kagan, *Adversarial Legalism: The American Way of Law* (Cambridge, MA: Harvard University Press, 2001).

[26] Oren Gross traces the extralegal tradition to Thomas Jefferson's arguments that "to lose our country by a scrupulous adherence to the written law, would be to lose the law itself, with life, liberty and property . . . thus absurdly sacrificing the end for the means"; as quoted in Gross, "Chaos and Rules," at 1106.

[27] *Ex parte Milligan*, 71 U.S. 2 (1866).   [28] Posner, *Not a Suicide Pact*, at 154.

[29] 317 U.S. 1 (1942).

prospect in his ruling.[30] Roosevelt's attorney general was later to write that "the Constitution has not greatly bothered any wartime President."[31]

The War Model

Military force was used against Libya in retaliation for the bombing of a German disco in 1986 that killed two U.S. soldiers and a civilian. It was also used to apprehend an Egyptian airliner carrying the hijackers of the *Achille Lauro*. Both actions were defended by the United States as acts of self-defense but were unpopular and condemned as violations of international law in much of the rest of the world, including by a General Assembly resolution that condemned the U.S. bombing of Libya.[32] The Clinton administration similarly responded with Tomahawk missile attacks in Afghanistan and Sudan in response to the 1998 African embassy bombings. It also considered but did not execute a targeted killing of bin Laden before 9/11,[33] something that Jack Goldsmith has blamed on a pre- 9/11 "paralyzing culture of risk-averse legalism in the military and, especially intelligence establishments."[34] The American approach to terrorism from Reagan to Clinton employed both law enforcement and military force.[35] It was prepared to engage in extra-legalism in which acts such as extraordinary renditions and targeted killings were undertaken, but only if supported by dubious claims of legality.

The Response to the 1993 World Trade Center and 1995 Oklahoma City Bombings

President Reagan first proposed legislation to make it an offense to provide support for terrorists, but this was rejected largely on the grounds that it would interfere with the First Amendment.[36] Momentum for such a law grew,

---

[30] Goldsmith, *Terror Presidency*, at 102.

[31] Francis Biddle, *In Brief Authority* (New York: Doubleday, 1962), at 219.

[32] A/Res/41/38, as discussed in Craig Forcese, *National Security Law* (Toronto, ON, Canada: Irwin Law, 2008), at 193.

[33] A cruise missile strike was contemplated against bin Laden in May 1999 but was abandoned when the director of the Central Intelligence Agency said that the chance of the intelligence being accurate was "50-50" during the same month that the United States had mistakenly bombed the Chinese Embassy in Belgrade during the war against Serbia. *9/11 Commission Report* (2004), at 4.5.

[34] Goldsmith *Terror Presidency* at 94-5.

[35] As Benjamin Wittes has observed, "the parallel use of criminal and military authorities in 1998 struck almost nobody as eccentric." Wittes, *Law and the Long War*, at 24.

[36] David Cole and James X. Dempsey, *Terrorism and the Constitution* (New York: New Press, 2002), at 34.

however, in the wake of the first World Trade Center bombing in 1993 that killed 6 people and injured over 1,000. The momentum accelerated after the 1995 Oklahoma City bombing killed 168 people, including 19 small children. In 1994, Congress first criminalized material support to terrorists, backed by executive measures listing and freezing the funds of terrorist groups.[37] The Edwards amendment, however, prohibited investigations of material support solely on activities protected by the First Amendment.[38] The Clinton administration proposed antiterrorism legislation in 1995, but this was not enacted until the passage of the 1996 Anti-Terrorism and Effective Death Penalty Act.[39] This act was pointedly enacted on the first anniversary of the Oklahoma City bombing and passed with a 91–8 vote in the Senate and a 293–133 vote in the House of Representatives.[40] This act repealed the prohibition on investigations based on First Amendment activities and contained offenses against material support for both acts of terrorism and designated terrorism organizations.

Although not related to terrorism at the time, the 1996 law also attempted to restrict but not remove federal habeas corpus review of state criminal convictions. This demonstrates the bipartisan political popularity of limiting habeas corpus, which was perceived by many as allowing criminals to get off on technicalities and as frustrating the administration of the death penalty. As will be seen, a somewhat similar but more drastic pattern is seen in post-9/11 attempts, first by President Bush but later by Congress, to preclude habeas corpus review of the Guantánamo detentions. Executive and legislative opposition to habeas corpus review at Guantánamo cannot be understood in isolation from larger criminal justice politics, in which many saw "the great writ" as a technicality used by lawyers to prevent the guilty from being punished and accepted mass and often harsh imprisonment.[41]

Two bills were proposed that would have criminalized membership in militias or paramilitary organizations such as the ones that the Oklahoma City bombers supported, but they were defeated on grounds that they would violate First Amendment protections of freedom of speech and association.[42] Citing concerns about the length of the trials arising from the 1993 World Trade Center bombings and the difficulty of applying the death penalty in

[37] Laura Donohue, "In the Name of National Security: US Counterterrorism Measures 1960–2000" (2001) 13 Terrorism and Political Violence 15, at 28–9.

[38] Cole and Dempsey, *Terrorism and the Constitution*, at 141.

[39] 110 Stat. 1214.

[40] Cole and Dempsey, *Terrorism and the Constitution*, at 133–4.

[41] Judith Resnik, "Detention, the War on Terror and the Federal Courts" (2010) 110 Columbia Law Review 579.

[42] Roberta Smith, "America Tries to Come to Grips with Terrorism" (1997) 5 Cardozo Journal of International and Comparative Law 249, at 276–8.

federal court, there were proposals to use military courts to try terrorists. The authors cited the World War II case of *ex parte Quirin*[43] as precedent for such military trials and argued that military commissions should depart from the Uniform Code of Military Justice because "enemy war criminals" were not "entitled to the same form of due process as our own soldiers."[44] They also argued that military commissions were necessary to allow for the increased use of hearsay in international terrorism cases involving foreign witnesses who may be difficult to find and produce. Moreover, military commissions were defended as a means to avoid exclusionary rules associated with *Miranda* and other rights in the domestic criminal justice system.[45] Such proposals seemed extreme before 9/11 and failed to account for convictions obtained in both the 1993 World Trade Center and Oklahoma City bombings. The advanced legalism of the American criminal justice with its *Miranda* rules and rights to confront all witnesses produced countervailing demands for less restrained alternatives involving military detention and trial. These demands received a much more receptive hearing and many were taken up by the Bush administration after 9/11.

Although the Oklahoma City bombings were acts of domestic terrorism, much of the 1996 law focused on international terrorism. The 1996 law also contained some immigration law reforms designed to combat terrorism. It removed a 1990 restriction that required that a noncitizen could only be removed if he or she participated in a terrorist organization and replaced it with a broader authorization based on membership in a terrorist organization. It created the Alien Terrorist Removal Court, to be composed of federal judges, who could order removal on terrorism grounds. Consistent with the lower standards of adjudicative fairness in immigration law, the court could consider evidence not disclosed to the noncitizen if the attorney general certified that its disclosure would harm national security or any person. At the same time, the court would be assisted by security-cleared counsel who could provide adversarial challenge to the secret evidence.[46] In a pattern that would be repeated under the Patriot Act, this novel immigration law procedure was never used because existing provisions were adequate enough to allow the removal of suspected alien terrorists.[47]

[43] 317 U.S. 1 (1942).
[44] Spencer Crona and Neal Richardson, "Justice for War Criminals of Invisible Armies: A New Legal and Military Approach to Terrorism" (1996) 21 Oklahoma City University Law Review 349, at 375–6.
[45] Ibid., at 384–5.
[46] 110 Stat, at 1262–3 (codified at 8 U.S.C.A. § 1534(e)(3)).
[47] David Martin, "Refining Immigration Law's Role in Counterterrorism," in Wittes, *Legislating the War on Terror*, at 206.

Although it received bipartisan support, the 1996 law was controversial. David Cole and James Dempsey argued that the felt need to respond to the 1993 World Trade Center bombing and the 1995 Oklahoma City bombing "overwhelmed all rational discussion, and the law was enacted as a response to these two crimes."[48] Concerns were expressed that the offense of material support for listed terrorist groups had been expanded to apply to contributions designed to assist even the lawful and peaceful activities of such groups. As will be seen, the U.S. Supreme Court would subsequently, in *Holder v. Humanitarian Law Project*,[49] affirm the breadth of the offense and justify it on the basis that support for the humanitarian activities of listed terrorist groups could free up other resources for their violent activities. Writing before 9/11, and citing the fears of terrorism at the millennium, Laura Donohue presciently expressed concerns that the United States would violate civil liberties and take military actions that might disenchant allies and make it easier to recruit terrorists.[50]

The United States, unlike the other Western democracies examined in this book, does not have a domestic security intelligence agency. The 9/11 Commission found that the FBI "did not have an effective intelligence collection effort"[51] and was handicapped by a lack of training, translation, and sharing of information both within itself and with intelligence agencies. It also found that the so-called wall between intelligence and law enforcement was more of an administrative than a legal matter, and even the administrative policy was misunderstood so that agents believed that no intelligence, especially intelligence obtained under the 1978 Foreign Intelligence Surveillance Act (FISA), could be shared with law enforcement.

FISA was created after the U.S. Supreme Court rejected claims that the president could engage in domestic security surveillance without a warrant.[52] Congress responded with FISA, which provided for court-ordered surveillance if there was probable cause not of a crime but that the person subject to surveillance was an agent of a foreign power defined to include those who knowingly prepare or engage in international terrorism. Consistent with the special regard for citizens and the First Amendment, FISA targeted foreigners, required that minimization procedures be used with respect to surveillance of citizens, and provided that a U.S. person should not be subject to surveillance solely because of expressive or associational activities protected by the First

---

[48] Cole and Dempsey, *Terrorism and the Constitution*, at 108.
[49] 130 S.Ct. 2705 (2010).
[50] Donohue, "In the Name of National Security," at 49.
[51] *9/11 Commission Report* (2004), at 3.2.
[52] *United States v. United States District Court*, 407 U.S. 297 (1972).

Amendment. In some other democracies, such as the United Kingdom and Australia, similar warrants to obtain security intelligence are granted by elected ministers and not by appointed judges. FISA came out of a Watergate inspired reform era in which the United States was particularly sensitive to invasions of the privacy of its citizens.

The administrative procedures, often called the "wall," that restricted the sharing of material obtained under FISA with law enforcement were designed to preserve FISA's original requirement that the primary purpose of such surveillance be the collection of foreign intelligence and as such minimize the domestic intrusions on privacy. At the same time, the impermeability of the wall between intelligence and evidence was often overstated. Before 9/11, judges upheld the constitutionality of FISA and ruled that a FISA investigation would not be tainted if it overlapped with a criminal investigation in a terrorism case.[53] Although the "wall" that impeded the sharing of intelligence with criminal investigators was overstated, it was also inspired by a deep bi-partisan American concern about privacy that even after 9/11 remained stronger than the privacy concerns and constituencies of the other democracies examined in this book.[54]

The American criminal justice system had worked reasonably well in complex terrorism cases before 9/11. Although enacted primarily to prevent alleged spies from graymailing the government in their trials by threatening to disclose classified information, the Classified Information Protection Act enabled judges to allow the government to redact or substitute classified material while satisfying its constitutional disclosure obligations to the accused. Although the trial in the first World Trade Center bombings took six months and heard from more than 200 witnesses, it resulted in convictions and a 240-year imprisonment sentence.[55] Seditious conspiracy convictions were also obtained in a second trial of a wider group involved in the plot to bring the twin towers down.[56] Timothy McVeigh was convicted of the Oklahoma City bombings and executed in June 2001. Americans had many reasons to be confident that their criminal justice system could effectively respond to terrorism, but that confidence would be severely shaken by the terrorist attacks of 9/11.

---

[53] *US v. Duggan*, 743 F.3d 59 (2d Cir. 1984); *United States v. Johnson*, 952 F.2d 565 (1st Cir. 1991).

[54] Foreign (and sometimes even domestic) intelligence can be collected on the basis of executive authorization in Australia, Canada and the United Kingdom whereas under FISA, judicial authorization is required. David Cole "English Lessons: A Comparative Analysis of UK and US Responses to Terrorism" (2009) 62 Current Legal Problems 136 at 148ff.

[55] *United States v. Salameh*, 152 F.3d 88 (2d Cir. 1998).

[56] *United States v. Rahman*, 189 F.3d 88 (2d Cir., 1999).

III. THE INITIAL RESPONSE TO 9/11

The coordinated hijacking of four planes on September 11, 2001, by 19 hijackers resulted in 2,752 deaths at the World Trade Center, 184 deaths at the Pentagon, and the deaths of all 246 passengers on the four planes. This was a truly shocking and horrific event. The United States' first response fit into a war model but departed from the executive dominance seen in the early years because it involved a congressional authorization of the use of military force. This was followed shortly after by the enactment of the Patriot Act by overwhelming majorities in both the Senate and the House of Representatives. Although the Patriot Act has been fiercely criticized, its comparative restraint is a testament to the hold of constitutionalism on Congress, even in the wake of 9/11. At the same time, many of the most forceful responses to 9/11 occurred through executive action and were much closer and often over the line of legality and constitutionalism.

The Authorization of the Use of Military Force

President Bush was clear in his response to 9/11 that "we're at war. There's been an act of war declared upon America by terrorists and we will respond accordingly. My message for everybody who wears a uniform is to get ready."[57] Bush's war model was shared by Congress. On September 14, the Senate passed, without debate but in a roll call vote, the AUMF, which provided that "the President is authorized to use all necessary and appropriate force against those nations, organizations, or persons he determines planned, authorized, committed or aided the terrorist attacks that occurred on September 11, 2001, or harbored such organizations or persons, in order to prevent future acts of international terrorism against the United States by such nations, organizations or persons."[58]

The AUMF was a broad grant of authority to use force against both nations and nonstate actors. It focused on the use of force against those responsible for the attacks and as a means to prevent future attacks. It was a curious mixture of criminal law concepts, such as its reference to the planning, aiding, or commission of terrorist acts, and war concepts, such as the use of all necessary and appropriate force. The focus of much of the AUMF and the United States'

---

[57] "After the Attacks: An Overview; Long Battle Seen," New York Times, September 16, 2001.

[58] PL 107–40; 115 Stat. 224. The House of Representatives did have a debate on the resolution before approving it by a vote of 420–1. David Abramowitz, "The President, the Congress and the Use of Force" (2002) 43 Harvard Journal of Legislation 71, at 71.

response to 9/11 was on responding to the grievous attack it had suffered and preventing future acts of international terrorism.

The AUMF has had a significance that may not have been anticipated when it was hastily passed by a virtually unanimous Senate and House of Representatives. It remains the authorizing force for the invasion and occupation of Afghanistan, the detentions of suspected terrorists at Guantánamo Bay until the end of hostilities, and the targeted killings of terrorists. Although the authorization is very broad, the Bush administration had originally proposed an even broader authorization that would have authorized the use of force not only against those who aided or harbored those responsible for 9/11 but also "to deter and pre-empt any future acts of terrorism or aggression against the United States."[59] The difference in wording between this proposal and that of the AUMF, however, did not mean that the Bush administration abandoned its broad preemptive ambitions. As will be seen, the Bush administration did not always rely on congressional authorization but instead invoked a controversial theory of inherent and broad presidential and executive power in times of war. The Obama administration has abandoned such claims but continues to rely heavily on the AUMF with respect to continued indeterminate detention at Guantánamo and targeted killing of terrorists.

iv. THE USA PATRIOT ACT

The Patriot Act is a very complex 342-page piece of legislation. It was signed into law on October 26, 2001, and enacted with little opposition. The Bush administration wanted the law enacted even sooner. On September 25, 2001, Attorney General John Ashcroft warned that "every day that passes with outdated statutes and the old rules of engagement is a day that terrorists have a competitive advantage."[60] The speed with which the act was passed, as well as its evocative and, for some, provocative title, meant that it became a lightning rod for much criticism of the initial American response to 9/11. The act became a symbol of the Bush administration's approach to 9/11, and civil libertarian critics of the act were understandably offended by Ashcroft's arguments that they were "scaring people with phantoms of lost liberty. . . . Your tactics only aid terrorists – for they erode national unity and diminish our resolve. They

---

[59] Abramowitz "The President," at 73; Curtis Bradley and Jack Goldsmith, "Congressional Authorization and the War on Terrorism" (2005) 118 Harvard Law Review 2048, at 2079.

[60] As quoted in Daniel Moeckli, *Human Rights and Non-Discrimination in the "War on Terror"* (Oxford: Oxford University Press, 2008), at 41.

give ammunition to America's enemies and pause to America's friends."[61] A closer and especially a comparative examination of the Patriot Act, however, suggests that it was not as repressive as many on both the Left and the Right in the U.S. thought. Much of the opposition to the Patriot Act was symbolic. The greatest abuses in the post-9/11 era were not authorized by the technical and complex legislation.

FISA Amendments

The Patriot Act amended the 1978 FISA to allow FISA warrants to be issued so long as a "significant purpose" remained the collection of foreign intelligence. Before the amendments, the "primary purpose" of a FISA search had to be the collection of foreign intelligence.[62] The change was less than the Bush administration had wanted because they proposed that FISA warrants should be granted so long as a purpose was the collection of foreign intelligence. The change from primary to significant purpose allowed foreign intelligence to be more easily shared with law enforcement officials and used in criminal prosecutions. Although one lower court found that the FISA amendments violated the Fourth Amendment prohibition of unreasonable search and seizures in the Brandon Mayfield case, in which an Oregon lawyer and Muslim convert was wrongly implicated in the Madrid bombing,[63] other courts have accepted that the FISA warrant requirements as amended by the Patriot Act are still constitutional, even in cases where evidence of a crime will be discovered.[64] The amendment recognizes the overlap of intelligence and criminal investigations in the terrorism field – an overlap that has only been enhanced throughout the world by the expansion of crimes targeting various forms of support and preparation for terrorism.

The FISA amendments in the Patriot Act are also significant because they are all directed at the collection of "foreign intelligence" and "foreign powers." Terrorism continued to be seen as an external matter. The foreign focus in American antiterrorism efforts reflects the paradox of domestic law enforcement being subject to robust restraints, while foreign-based enforcement is subject to few restrictions. The focus on foreign intelligence was

---

[61] As quoted in John Whitehead and Steven Aden, "Forfeiting 'Enduring Freedom' for Homeland Security" (2003) 51 American University Law Review 1081, at 1100.

[62] *United States v. Truong Dinh Hung*, 629 F.2d 908 (4th Cir., 1980); *United States v. Duggan*, 743 F.2d 59 (2d Cir., 1984); *United States v. Johnston*, 952 F.2d 565 (1st Cir., 1991).

[63] *Mayfield v. United States*, 504 F. Supp. 2d 1023 (D.Ore. 2007). An appeal was allowed on the basis that Mayfield did not have standing and the U.S. Supreme Court denied certiorari.

[64] *US v. Ning Wen*, 477 F3d 896 (7th Cir., 2007).

understandable in light of 9/11, but the fact remains that a decade after 9/11 and the prosecution of many homegrown terrorist plots, there has been little serious discussion or contemplation of new legislation that would limit the rights of American citizens in an attempt to prevent terrorism. The United States is significantly more restrained domestically than many other democracies, but has broad external powers that are only loosely restrained by law.

Other FISA amendments contained changes designed to modernize the 1978 act, including roving warrants, provisions of searches of e-mails, and delays on notifying a person that he or she had been the subject of a search.[65] Many of these changes "sensibly updated criminal law to reflect changing technologies." They also facilitated information sharing in recognition that "international terrorism is simultaneously a matter of foreign intelligence and criminal law enforcement."[66] Some of the Patriot Act amendments even enhanced protections for privacy.[67] The Patriot Act also included increased protection for First Amendment rights and contemplated an increase in judges who would grant the warrants.[68] In many other democracies, a judicial warrant would not even be required to collect foreign intelligence. Although FISA applications are reported to be 10 times pre-9/11 levels, it also takes about 200 hours of work to obtain each warrant.[69] As will be seen, restrictions inherent in FISA warrants and legislation played a role in the Bush administration's use of executive orders to allow the NSA to collect, without warrants or legislative authorization, conversations with foreign terrorist targets, where one end of the conversations take place in the United States.

The FISA amendments in the Patriot Act generated sustained criticism from civil liberties and privacy advocates. As Mark Sidel has shown, this resistance came from unlikely alliances of civil libertarians on the Right and Left of the American political spectrum.[70] The resistance to the amendments also came from the courts. The FISA court, in 2002, held that despite the Patriot Act's amendments of FISA, minimization procedures based on the so-called wall

---

[65] The latter power applied beyond terrorism investigations, and in a 2006 renewal of the Patriot Act, enhanced oversight was provided. Laura Donohue, *The Cost of Counterterrorism* (New York: Cambridge University Press, 2008), at 235.

[66] Cole, *Enemy Aliens*, at 57.

[67] Orin Ker, "Internet Surveillance under the Patriot Act: The Big Brother That Isn't" (2003) 97 Northwestern University Law Review 607.

[68] Reg Whitaker, "After 9/11: A Surveillance State?" in *Lost Liberties: Ashcroft and the Assault on Personal Freedom*, ed. Cynthia Brown (New York: New Press, 2003), at 60–1.

[69] David Kris, "Modernizing the Foreign Intelligence Surveillance Act," in Wittes, *Legislating the War on Terror*, at 220.

[70] Mark Sidel, *More Secure, Less Free?* (Ann Arbor: University of Michigan Press, 2004).

between intelligence gathering and criminal investigations were still required. It stressed the dangers to the FISA scheme if prosecutors could offer advice on FISA surveillance and concerns that FISA might be used in cases in which probable cause for ordinary criminal warrants was not present.[71]

The government successfully appealed this decision to the FISA Appeal Court. The Appeal Court expressed skepticism about the wall approach even before the Patriot Act, given that those subject to foreign intelligence gathering could also be guilty of crimes such as espionage. In a recognition of the overlap between intelligence and evidence collection, the Appeal Court stressed that in many cases, surveillance will have the dual goal of gathering both foreign intelligence and evidence for criminal prosecution.[72] In a veiled reference to the suicide hijackers of 9/11, however, the Appeal Court stated that "punishment of the terrorist or espionage agent is really a secondary objective; indeed, punishment of a terrorist is often a moot point."[73] The Appeal Court ruled that the Patriot Act amendments allowed greater sharing of information between intelligence and law enforcement. It also ruled that FISA, even as amended by the Patriot Act, still satisfied the Fourth Amendment right against unreasonable search and seizure because it required a judicial warrant on probable grounds standards, albeit standards relating to the target being an agent of a foreign power as opposed to probable cause of a crime. Although the overturned decision was celebrated by privacy advocates, it would have placed real burden on the use of intelligence in criminal prosecutions, and it ignored cleared congressional intent in the Patriot Act to allow dual intelligence and prosecution use of FISA materials.

National Security Letters

Another controversial part of the Patriot Act allowed national security letters or administrative subpoenas to be issued to third parties to turn over records sought in connection with a terrorism investigation. In an attempt to ensure that targets of the investigation were not alerted, section 215 imposed broad gag rules that prohibited third parties from communicating that they had received the national security letters. In 2004, a district court held that these gag orders violated both the First Amendment, by prohibiting speech, and the Fourth Amendment, by inhibiting unreasonable search and seizure challenges.[74] The case identified problems with the proportionality of the restrictions.

---

[71] *In Re all Matters Submitted to the FISA Court*, 218 F. Supp. 2d 611 (2002).
[72] *In Re Sealed Case*, 310 F.3d 717 (2002); leave to appeal denied, 123 S.Ct. 1615 (2003).
[73] Ibid., at 744–5.
[74] *Doe v. Ashcroft*, 334 F. Supp. 2d 471 (S.D.N.Y. 2004).

In the broader scheme of Guantánamo, illegal and warrantless electronic surveillance, however, the constitutional violations identified in this case, were relatively minimal. In any event, a similar result in a second case was reversed by the Second Circuit, and the Supreme Court refused to intervene.[75] The increase in the use of national security letters has been even more dramatic than the increase in FISA warrants, with reports that as many 30,000 have been issued to libraries, Internet service providers, and others who hold documents that may be relevant to national security investigations.[76] In 2006, Congress amended the provisions to ensure greater oversight, increased judicial review, and enhanced privacy protections for libraries. Concerns remain about increased retention and distribution of the information obtained through national security letters.[77] Nevertheless, counter-terrorism powers that were authorized by legislation could be subject to democratic debate, regulation and enhanced privacy and civil liberties oversight. As will be seen, at the same time as Americans litigated, debated and obtained reforms to national security letters, they were also subject to secret surveillance programs that were not authorized by the Patriot Act and had only been authorized by a presidential order of dubious legality.

Terrorism Financing

Other parts of the Patriot Act focused on terrorism financing, as required by United Nations (UN) Security Council Resolution 1373. The United States' first report to the Security Council's Counter-Terrorism Committee (CTC) underlined the centrality of legislative and executive measures aimed at terrorism financing to the act.[78] The Patriot Act, like other terrorism financing regimes, successfully encouraged the filing of suspicious activity reports by financial institutions but raised concerns that such institutions might err on the side of reporting transactions involving people with Muslim or Middle Eastern names. It imposed new customer identification standards and prohibited banks from disclosing to their customers that they had supplied information. As in other countries, much of the response to terrorism financing was based on a money laundering model, despite fundamental differences between the two phenomena.[79] For example, a number of sections focused on prohibiting

[75] *Doe v. Gonzales*, 126 S.Ct. 1, 2 (2005).

[76] Laura Donohue, "Anglo-America Privacy and Surveillance" (2006) 96 Journal of Criminal Law and Criminology 1059, at 1111.

[77] Ibid., at 1118; "Note National Security Letters and the Amended Patriot Act" (2007) 92 Cornell Law Review 1201.

[78] U.S. Country Report, S/2001/1220.

[79] Donohue, *Costs of Counterterrorism*, at 344–50.

the import of more than $10,000 and reporting the receipt of such amounts,[80] even though smaller amounts could often be used to finance deadly acts of terrorism.

Even before the Patriot Act was enacted, President Bush issued Executive Order 13224 two weeks after 9/11 to allow for terrorist organizations to be listed and their assets, including humanitarian donations, frozen. This fit a pattern seen in other democracies of the first implementation of Resolution 1373 coming from the domestic executive as opposed to the legislature. The Bush administration pursued a post-9/11 "Rose Garden Strategy" of regular announcement of the listing of terrorist groups and the freezing of assets without always carefully evaluating the evidence said to justify the listings. One participant recalled, "It was almost comical. We just listed out as many of the usual suspects as we could and said, Let's go freeze some of their assets."[81] Between October, 2001 and April, 2005, 743 people and 947 organizations had their assets frozen by executive order on the basis of secret evidence and without due process.[82]

The Patriot Act also allowed the freezing of the assets of organizations that were being investigated for terrorism. These powers were used against some Muslim charities on the basis of secret information not disclosed to them, even when challenged in court.[83] Freezing and forfeiture laws were not applied with the traditional standards of the criminal law, which prohibited the use of secret evidence. The emphasis on terrorism financing also meant that requirements for intent and knowledge were frequently removed and that the government was allowed to use secret evidence and lower standards of proof than required for criminal convictions. As Laura Donohue has argued, the emphasis on terrorism financing resulted in a move from a criminal law to an intelligence paradigm and one that focused on Muslim communities.[84]

Definitions of Terrorism

The Patriot Act defined terrorism in a manner that was more restrained than the definition of terrorism found in the United Kingdom's Terrorism Act,

---

[80] Patriot Act, Sections 362, 371.
[81] As quoted in Sue Eckert, "The US Regulatory Approach to Terrorist Financing," in *Countering the Financing of Terrorism*, ed. Thomas Biersteker and Sue Eckert (London: Routledge, 2008), at 215.
[82] Laura Donohue "The Perilous Dialogue" (2009) 97 California Law Review 357 at 364.
[83] David Cole, "The Course of Least Resistance: Repeating History in the War on Terrorism," in Brown, *Lost Liberties*, at 29; Donohue, *Cost of Counterterrorism*, at 160–4.
[84] Ibid., at 166, 172, 176.

2000, which inspired many other post-9/11 antiterrorism laws. Both international and domestic terrorism were defined under the Patriot Act as "violent acts or acts dangerous to a human life" that violate American laws and that "appear to be intended to intimidate or coerce a civilian population, or to influence the policy of a government by intimidation or coercion or to affect the conduct of a government by mass destruction, assassination or kidnapping."[85] Requirements that the terrorist act have a religious or political motive were not used as in the British law as a means of differentiating terrorism from other crimes; rather, consistent with the general definition of terrorism in the 1999 Financing Convention, the focus was on attempts to coerce governments or intimidate a population. This approach, as well as a refusal to criminalize threats of actions, as under the Terrorism Act, 2000, reflected a strong First Amendment culture that was not shaken by the horrors of 9/11. The United States' comparatively restrained approach to the definition of terrorism and the consistency of American definitions with the general definition in the 1999 Financing Convention underline the missed opportunity discussed in Chapter 2 when the American-crafted Security Council Resolution 1373 failed to encourage states to follow the general definition in the Financing Convention.

Even though it focused on violence and danger to human life, as opposed to the property damage, disruption of electronic systems, or politically or religiously motivated threats of such actions prohibited under the Terrorism Act, 2000, the Patriot Act's definition of terrorism was criticized. One commentator extravagantly argued that the definition of terrorism under the Patriot Act would apply to civil disobedience and "lump nonviolent civil disobedience in the tradition of Henry David Thoreau, Gandhi and Martin Luther King Jr. together with the Al Qaeda network's ruthless murder of innocent civilians under the single banner of terrorism."[86] Concerns about the definition of terrorism were expressed by prominent American commentators on both the Right and Left of the political spectrum,[87] without reference to the fact that terrorism as defined in the Patriot Act did not create any new crimes or Congress's comparative restraint in defining terrorism. Both the definition and the over-the-top criticisms of it underlined the exceptionalism of the American First Amendment tradition.

---

[85] Patriot Act, Section 801; amending 18 U.S.C. s2331 (international terrorism) and 18 U.S.C. 2.2331 (domestic terrorism).

[86] Nancy Chang, "How Democracy Dies: The War on Our Civil Liberties," in Brown, *Lost Liberties*, at 40.

[87] See, e.g., Whitehead and Aden, "Forfeiting 'Enduring Freedom,'" at 1093–4, and Erwin Chemerinsky, "Losing Liberties" (2003) 51 University of California at Los Angeles Law Review 1619, at 1623–4.

No Fundamental Changes to Criminal Justice

The Patriot Act did not attempt to change the criminal justice system to better prevent terrorism. Whereas Australia, Canada, and the United Kingdom introduced multiple new terrorist crimes in their post-9/11 legislation, the United States only introduced new crimes for terrorist attacks on mass transportation systems[88] and harboring or concealing terrorists,[89] with some minor changes to the existing offense of providing material support for terrorism.[90] The criminalization of membership in a terrorist group was not a real option because of First Amendment protections of freedom of association.[91] The Patriot Act did not provide for preventive arrests, as in the United Kingdom, or for new criminal justice procedures such as investigative hearings, as introduced in Canada after 9/11, or for intelligence questioning warrants, as introduced in Australia. It also did not attempt to curb due process procedural protections such as *Miranda* rights or the accused's right to disclosure from the state, and it did not amend the Classified Information Protection Act, which provided a mechanism to determine whether the state's unused and classified intelligence had to be disclosed to the accused.

The closest the Patriot Act came to fundamental criminal justice change were provisions designed to facilitate the sharing of grand jury information. These provisions contemplated a whole-of-government response to terrorism that would allow grand jury information to be disclosed to a wide range of federal officials, including those involved in immigration, protection, national defense, or national security.[92] These changes were criticized as infringing privacy and allowing dossier building, but they were subsequently extended to allow sharing with local, state, tribal, and foreign government officials.[93] Nevertheless, this was a relatively minor adjustment to criminal justice that responded to concerns that not enough information was shared before 9/11. The worst abuses of grand juries were not the information sharing provisions of the Patriot Act, but rather the use of material witness warrants to impose de facto preventive and investigative detention. This follows a pattern where the gravest abuses after 9/11 were achieved without formal legislative change or authorization.

---

[88] Patriot Act, Section 801.   [89] Ibid., Section 803.

[90] Ibid., Section 805.

[91] As will be seen, however, American immigration law would allow people to be removed on the basis of membership and ideological affiliation.

[92] Patriot Act, Section 203.

[93] Sara Sun Beale and James Felman, "The Consequences of Enlisting Federal Grand Juries in the War on Terrorism" (2002) 25 Harvard Journal of Law and Public Policy 699.

Immigration Law as Antiterrorism Law

Consistent with the Security Council's admonition in Resolution 1373 to ensure terrorists not abuse asylum, there was a temporary halt of refugee processing and a substantial decline in the number of refugees admitted to the United States.[94] The harshest parts of the Patriot Act also related to immigration law. Section 411 of the Patriot Act revived what David Cole has criticized as guilt by association and ideological exclusion by allowing the exclusion of representatives of groups that endorsed terrorist activities in a manner deemed to hinder American counter-terrorism activities.[95] Although the Patriot Act made no attempt to criminalize expression or association, it did burden such activities under immigration law. Many of the expanded grounds of exclusion under immigration could be applied retroactively, again something not done under criminal law.[96] As in other countries, the use of immigration law as antiterrorism law allowed limits to be placed on rights that would not be accepted for citizens.

An ominous provision that bore some resemblance to administrative detention schemes used in Singapore, Israel, Canada, and the United Kingdom was Section 412, which authorized the detention of aliens certified by the attorney general to be engaged in terrorism or other activities that endangered the national security of the United States. The Bush administration had sought to give the attorney general indefinite powers of detention, but these were limited by Congress to seven days' detention, after which the alien had to be released if removal proceedings were not commenced or criminal charges were not laid. Removal proceedings could be delayed as the state tried to respond to the problem identified by Security Council Resolution 1373 of deporting suspected terrorists to countries such as Egypt while also ensuring that they would not be deported to torture. In the meantime, section 412 authorized the attorney general to detain such persons for renewable six-month periods by certifying that their release would threaten national security or the safety of the community or of any person. It also contemplated that the noncitizen could be released on condition.

Section 412 was perhaps the most draconian provision in the Patriot Act. At the same time, it provided for habeas corpus review of the detentions it authorized, something that the Bush administration and, later, Congress

94 Margaret Stock, "The Role of Immigration in the Struggle against Terror," in *Legal Issues in the Struggle against Terror*, ed. John Moore and Robert Turner (Durham: Carolina Academic Press, 2010), at 443.

95 David Cole *Enemy Aliens* (New York: New Press, 2003) at 64-65.

96 Patriot Act, Section 411.

would attempt to deny to the Guantánamo detainees. In any event, Section 412 has never been used because existing immigration laws proved adequate to detain noncitizens who were suspected of involvement in terrorism. As seen earlier, a similar fate befell the Alien Terrorist Removal Court, created in 1996 in response to the first World Trade Center bombing and the Oklahoma City bombings.

When the Patriot Act is examined in a comparative perspective and in light of the national trauma caused by 9/11, the most pressing question becomes why the act was not tougher and more expansive than it was. Congress generally retained a sense of constitutional restraint, and it did not provide the Bush administration with all it requested either in the AUMF or in the Patriot Act. As will be seen, the more problematic actions came with respect to actions that the Bush administration took without asking for congressional approval.

v. WHAT THE PATRIOT ACT DID NOT AUTHORIZE

The NSA Warrantless Spying Controversy

Shortly after 9/11, President Bush issued an order that allowed the NSA to intercept phone calls and e-mails involving foreign terrorist suspects, even if one side of the conversation was in the United States. The executive order did not contemplate that warrants would be granted under FISA even as amended in the Patriot Act. Given this, as well as its impact on First Amendment freedoms and Fourth Amendment rights against unreasonable searches, the executive order was illegal. The only Office of Legal Counsel lawyer aware of this highly secretive program between 2001 and 2003 was John Yoo, one of the authors of the infamous 2002 torture memos. Yoo defended the program not as an illegal measure, but as one that was supported by the inherent powers of the President. Later officials would abandon this controversial claim and argue that the program was supported by the barebones AUMF. Yoo also asserted that the program did not violate the Fourth Amendment against unreasonable search and seizure even though it invaded the privacy of Americans and was inconsistent with FISA and conducted without judicial warrant.[97] These

---

[97] Offices of the Inspectors General of the Department of Defense, Department of Justice, Central Intelligence Agency, National Security Agency, and of the Director of National Intelligence *Unclassified Report on the President's Surveillance Program* 10 July, 2009 at 10ff. Although the memo he prepared for the Office of Legal Counsel remains almost completely classified, Professor Yoo after leaving government service wrote an academic article defending the legality of the warrantless spying program. See John Yoo, "The Terrorist Surveillance Program and

attempts to defend the program are examples of extra-legalism-the use of dubious but superficially learned and plausible claims of legality to support illegal measures.

The Bush administration's attempts to justify the legality of the NSA program were rebutted by joint letters written by eminent constitutional law scholars on both the Right and the Left who stressed that FISA, even after the Patriot Act, prohibited what the president purported to authorize.[98] One lower court did find that the surveillance program was unauthorized and violated the First and Fourth amendments, but this decision was overturned on the basis that the plaintiff, the American Civil Liberties Union, lacked standing and could not establish actual injury because of the state-secrets doctrine.[99] As will be seen, restrictive standing, case and controversy, state-secrets, and political questions rules have frequently shut down litigation against extralegal antiterrorism action. These restrictive and uniquely American doctrines[100] have served as agents of extra-legalism-namely the use of law to shelter illegal measures.

The NSA program only came to light when *The New York Times* broke the story late in 2005. Leading Democrats and the judge who headed the FISA court apparently knew about the program but had remained silent because it was highly classified.[101] President Bush argued that "it was a shameful thing for someone to disclose this very important program in a time of war,"[102] but there was nothing he could do to stop the story, given the absence of an Official Secrets Act in the United States and First Amendment rules restricting prior restraint. Consistent with the reference to preventing terrorist attacks in the AUMF, President Bush defended the program, stressing that "to save

the Constitution" (2007) 14 George Mason Law Review 565. Yoo argued in the article that the many critics of the program misunderstood the nature of the president's powers and asserted that the powers could be authorized by the president because the United States was at war with al Qaeda and the results of the surveillance would not be used in criminal prosecutions.

[98] The debate is set out in original documents contained in David Cole and Marty Lederman, "The NSA Surveillance Program" (2006) 81 Indiana Law Journal 1355. The scholars who rebutted the Department of Justice's approach included Ronald Dworkin, Richard Epstein, and Harold Koh.

[99] *ACLU v. National Security Agency* 493 F. 3d 644 (6th Cir., 2007); cert. denied U.S.S.C.

[100] Aharon Barak "Foreword: The Role of a Judge in a Democracy" (2002) 116 Harvard Law Review 16.

[101] James Risen and Eric Lichtblau, "Bush Lets US Spy on Callers without Courts," New York Times, December 16, 2005; "Terrorist Surveillance Program," New York Times, December 16, 2005.

[102] President Bush's New Conference, December 19, 2005, as quoted in Richard Pious, *The War on Terrorism and the Rule of Law* (Los Angeles, CA: Roxbury, 2006), at 53–4.

American lives we must be able to act fast and to detect those conversations so we can prevent new attacks."[103] Although Oren Gross's extralegal measures approach has some descriptive force in explaining the initial American response to 9/11, any normative bite that it might have depends on officials being transparent and seeking official ratification of their illegal conduct. Most illegal antiterrorism activities were, however, shielded by broad secrecy claims and dubious claims of legality that themselves were sheltered by secrecy and attorney-client privilege claims. Without illegal press leaks, the NSA program might still be conducted in secrecy and its dubious claims of legality may never have been exposed.

Having been exposed, the illegal surveillance was, consistent with Professor Gross's extralegal measures theory, quickly ratified and legalized by Congress. Congress enacted temporary legislation in the form of the Protect America Act[104] that allowed the director of national intelligence and the attorney general to authorize without judicial authorization FISA electronic surveillance directed at a foreign power such as al Qaeda, even if one side of the conversation involved an American citizen in the United States. In 2008, this temporary legislation was made permanent in complex reforms of FISA.[105] The 2008 reforms also provided more protections for American citizens, even when they are abroad, while also allowing foreign persons' communications to be intercepted more easily, even if their communications were routed through or stored in the United States.

The legislative ratification and regulation of NSA surveillance begs the question of why Congress did not authorize such surveillance in the first place. As will be seen in Chapter 7, Canada authorized its signals intelligence agency in its 2001 Anti-Terrorism Act to do much the same thing as the Bush order purported to authorize.[106] President Bush believed that he had the power to authorize an end run around FISA, even after it had been expanded in the Patriot Act. In no other democracy does the "executive have the authority to bypass the relevant statutory scheme, as President Bush claimed to have in the United States."[107] Unlike in Parliamentary democracies, the American President can claim and exercise democratic authority independent from the legislature and its authorization of executive action. The NSA controversy affirms the roles of both executive dominance and extra-legalism in the United States' initial response to 9/11.

---

[103] Ibid.   [104] Pub. L. No. 110–55, 121 Stat. 552.
[105] David Kris, "Modernizing the Foreign Intelligence Surveillance Act," at 231.
[106] S.C. (2001), c.41, Part 5.
[107] Mark Gittenstein, "Nine Democracies and the Problems of Detention, Surveillance and Interrogation," in Wittes, *Legislating the War on Terror*, at 34.

Preventive and Investigative Detention under Immigration Law

One of the first provisions in the Patriot Act was a nonenforceable sense of Congress that deplored violence against Arab and Muslim Americans in the wake of 9/11 and affirmed the need to protect "the civil liberties and rights of all Americans, including Arab Americans, Muslim Americans and Americans from South Asia" and affirmed "the concept of individual responsibility for wrongdoing" as "sacrosanct in American society."[108] These were noble and important values, but ones that, for the most part, were only extended to American citizens. The concept of "individual responsibility for wrongdoing" was unfortunately not always observed in the enforcement of immigration law.

Attorney General John Ashcroft announced that a preventive and pretextual approach would be taken, whereby suspected terrorists would be detained if they had overstayed their "visa by even one day."[109] Ashcroft's aggressive approach tapped into a deep bipartisan tradition that included the use of income tax laws against Al Capone and Bobby Kennedy's crusade against organized crime. It has been estimated that more than 5,000 foreign nationals were detained in the two years after 9/11 on a variety of grounds.[110] Many of the detainees were held for long periods before they were cleared by the FBI of involvement in terrorism. The clearance program avoided the specter of deporting a person who may have committed a terrorism crime, but it also allowed for prolonged de facto preventive and investigative detention. There was, however, some accountability for the abuse of the laws, as the inspector general of the Justice Department issued critical and lengthy reports that found that even in the immediate aftermath of 9/11, not enough care was taken in deciding who would be detained. In addition, some of the detainees were on lock-down for 23 hours a day and were allowed only one legal call a week and one social call a month. Some detainees were also subject to physical and verbal abuse.[111]

Many of the initial immigration hearings for the post-9/11 detainees were conducted in secret, following an order from the chief immigration judge. This policy was found to be invalid under the First Amendment by the Sixth Circuit[112] but was upheld 2–1 by the Third Circuit.[113] The U.S. Supreme Court declined to resolve the difference because the policy had lapsed. Although it

---

[108] Patriot Act, Section 102. [109] Cole and Lobel, *Less Safe, Less Free*, at 107.

[110] Ibid., at 107.

[111] Office of the Inspector General, "The September 11 Detainees," at http://www.justice.gov/oig/special/0306/index.htm.

[112] *Detroit Free Press v. Ashcroft*, 303 F.3d 681 (6th Cir., 2002).

[113] *North Jersey Media Group v. Ashcroft*, 308 F.3d 193 (3rd Cir., 2002); cert. denied 538 U.S. 1056 (2003).

was designed to prevent terrorists from being tipped off about arrests, the secrecy policy "compounded suspicions about the fairness of the removal proceedings" and "fueled charges that the government was improperly targeting defendants on the basis of their ethnicity and religion."[114] This also fit into a pattern of abuses of rights being potentially counter-productive by raising fears and suspicions among Muslims and others who feared being targeted by the state.

A special registration program required 80,000 male noncitizens from 25 countries to submit to detailed questioning and fingerprinting by the Immigration and Naturalization Service (INS). All the targeted countries were predominantly Muslim or Arab, with the exception of North Korea. In addition, 8,000 more young men of Arab and Muslim descent were sought for FBI interviews, with no reported terrorism-related arrests arising from any of these discriminatory policies. This caused David Cole and Jules Lobel to pronounce that the government's record on detentions was 0 for 93,000 – a most dismal batting average.[115] A former commissioner of the INS confirmed that the discriminatory policies were counter-productive when he admitted that this approach created "a lot of bad publicity, litigation and disruption in our relationships with immigrant communities and countries that we needed help from in the war on terror."[116] The immigration roundup also fit into patterns of executive policies being more important and draconian than legislative ones because there was nothing in the Patriot Act that authorized anything close to the post-9/11 immigration roundups and selective registrations.

Preventive and Investigative Detention under Grand Jury Material Witness Warrants

Immigration laws could not be used as pretext for preventive and investigative detention of citizens. To make up for this omission, a number of American prosecutors sought, and a number of judges issued, material witness warrants

---

[114] David Martin, "Refining Immigration Law's Role in Counterterrorism," in Wittes, *Legislating the War on Terror*, at 203.

[115] Cole and Lobel, *Less Safe, Less Free*, at 107. Professors Cole and Lobel were not alone in their criticism of the immigration roundup. Philip Heymann has observed that "there are about 20 million aliens in the United States at any given time, a high percentage of whom are at least technically in violation of one or another visa regulation. But that fact is now being used as a device for holding suspects – most only weakly linked to terrorism – for purposes of interrogation or incapacitation." Heymann, *Terrorism, Freedom and Security* (Boston: MIT Press, 2003), at 92. See also Edward Alden, *The Closing of the American Border: Terrorism, Immigration and Security after 9/11* (New York: HarperCollins, 2008).

[116] Cole and Lobel, *Less Safe, Less Free*, at 108.

that allowed persons suspected of involvement of terrorism to be detained without arresting them for terrorism crimes, but pending testimony before a grand jury. Attorney General Ashcroft condoned such an approach by arguing, in October 2001, that "aggressive detention of lawbreakers and material witnesses is vital to preventing, disrupting, or delaying new attacks. It is difficult for a person in jail or under detention to murder innocent people or to aid or abet in terrorism."[117] His statements revealed an appetite for preventive arrests and investigative detention such as found in the United Kingdom's Terrorism Act, 2000, or in Canada's response to 9/11, but not one that was satisfied in the Patriot Act. Viet Dinh, then assistant U.S. attorney general, explained that Ashcroft had instructed the Department of Justice to "think outside the box but never outside the Constitution." The Department of Justice concluded that it was not possible to legislate preventive detention in the United States because the Bill of Rights, unlike the European Convention on Human Rights, did not contemplate preventive detention.[118] Preventive arrests without criminal charges would have been controversial if they had been included in the Patriot Act and likely would have been challenged, perhaps successfully, as departing from probable cause standards under the Bill of Rights.[119] Nevertheless, Congress would have regulated them and provided some maximum period of detention as was done in the United Kingdom. None of this occurred because preventive arrests were conducted under the abuse of material witness warrants.

One material witness detention case involved Osama Awadallah, who appeared to have some associations with some of the 9/11 hijackers. He was detained on a material witness warrant for 83 days. He was kept in solitary confinement, shackled, strip searched, and interrogated at length. Awadallah's detention was eventually reviewed by the courts, but only because he was charged with perjury before a grand jury. Although these charges were dismissed at trial because of the abuse of the material witness warrant, they were reinstated on appeal, with the court refusing to exclude the statements that were the subject of the perjury charge.[120] Oregon lawyer Brandon Mayfield was detained for two weeks under a material witness warrant, not for the intended purpose of the statute – ensuring that witnesses provide information to the grand jury – but because he was falsely suspected of involvement in the 2004 Madrid bombing. Jose Padilla was arrested and held for a month

---

[117] Cole, *Enemy Aliens*, at 37.
[118] Viet Dinh, "Life after 9/11 Panel Discussion" (2003) 51 Kansas Law Review 219, at 224–5.
[119] David Cole, "Out of the Shadows: Preventive Detention, Suspected Terrorists and War" (2009) 97 California Law Review 693.
[120] *US v. Awadallah*, 349 F.2d 42 (2003).

under a material witness warrant before he was declared an enemy combatant and transferred to military custody just before a court was about to review his continued detention.

Because of the lack of legislative regulation, court-ordered closing of courts and files, and their decentralized nature, exact figures are not available on how many material witness warrants were used to detain terrorist suspects. This underlines the difference between the United Kingdom's or Canada's centralized, legislatively regulated approach to criminal justice and the United States' decentralized, judicially regulated approach.[121] Human Rights Watch and the American Civil Liberties Union reported in 2005, after a year of intensive research, that at least 70 men were detained in the aftermath of 9/11, with one-third being detained for two months. Of these men, only seven were charged with terrorism offenses, and two were designated as enemy combatants. In an affirmation of the global post-9/11 tendency to use immigration law as antiterrorism law, 24 of the men were deported, making them some other country's problem.[122] Many of the detainees were identified simply on the basis of associations with other terrorist suspects or attendance at the same mosque as one of the 9/11 hijackers. This suggests that an intelligence-based focus on suspect associations dominated in the immediate aftermath of 9/11.[123]

The conditions under which the men were detained and interrogated were not subject to any ex ante legislative regulation, unlike in the United Kingdom and Australia, which authorize but regulate preventive arrest and detention. In one American case, a detainee was subject to six interrogations and not taken before a court for 57 days or provided with a lawyer, despite his requests for one.[124] In another case, a detainee made a false statement about owning a radio transmitter found at a hotel near the World Trade Center after the investigators threatened that Egyptian authorities would "give your family hell if you don't co-operate." The government argued that the false confession could not be excluded because the detained witness faced no criminal charges and the court's contempt powers did not cover such interrogations. The judge reluctantly agreed, simply ordering that the matter be investigated.[125] As with extraordinary renditions, officials in Western democracies did not

---

[121] Kent Roach and M. L. Friedland, "Borderline Justice: Policing in the Two Niagaras" (1997) 23 American Journal of Criminal Law 241.

[122] Human Rights Watch, "Witness to Abuse," at http://www.aclu.org/FilesPDFs/material witnessreport.pdf, at 5.

[123] The government soon stated that this approach was overinclusive and produced many false positives. By 2005, it had apologized to 14 of the detainees. Ibid.

[124] Ibid., at 48.

[125] Ibid., at 59. See *Re Grand Jury Material Witness Detention*, 214 F. Supp. 2d 356; 271 F. Supp. 3d 1266 (2003).

hesitate to take advantage of the conduct of countries with poor human rights records.

Almost 30 of the material witness detainees never even testified before the grand jury, something that would have provided them with broad immunity under the U.S. Constitution if they had invoked their Fifth Amendment rights. The legal protections of the Bill of Rights provided an excuse in these cases to use material witness warrants illegally as an instrument for preventive detention. The U.S. Supreme Court has recently agreed to hear an appeal about whether Abdullah al-Kidd, a former star running back at the University of Idaho, can sue Ashcroft and other prosecutors in relation to his 14-day detention in 2003 under a material witness warrant.[126] The Obama administration has appealed a lower court ruling that would have allowed al-Kidd to proceed with his lawsuit alleging discriminatory and pretextual use of the material witness law and seeking compensation for his detention in high-security cells with 24-hour lighting.[127] The government may be successful in having the case dismissed by the Supreme Court in light of a 2009 decision in which the Court dismissed a claim of alleged discrimination against Ashcroft with respect to a post-9/11 detention under immigration law.[128] There has been a dearth of ex post accountability in American civil courts for pretextual and extralegal uses of powers in the aftermath of 9/11. This lack of accountability not only deprives victims of the immigration and material witness detentions of remedies but also breeds cynicism about future compliance with the spirit or even the letter of the law.

The al-Kidd case may fit into a larger pattern of civil litigation against the extralegal excesses of the Bush administration being brought but also dismissed. America's legalism allows the lawsuits to be commenced; its curious extra-legalism allows them to be dismissed on a broad range of technical legal grounds including state secrets, narrow standing rules, mootness, political questions doctrines and restrictions on the extra-territorial application of American laws. The use of the material witness law indicates how the executive was able to stretch existing laws to employ methods of investigative and preventive detention without criminal charge that were not authorized in the Patriot Act. The American tendency to abuse existing laws in this way resulted in less democratic debate than in many other democracies that provided for limited forms of preventive detention. For example, provisions to give the Australian Security Intelligence Organization (ASIO) investigative detention powers were the most controversial antiterrorism power claimed by

---

[126] "Justices to Hear Appeal over Liability for Detention," *The New York Times*, October 19, 2010.
[127] *Al-Kidd v. Ashcroft*, 580 F.3d 949 (9th Cir., 2009).
[128] *Ashcroft v. Iqbal*, 129 S.Ct. 1937 (2009).

the Howard government and were delayed after they were first introduced. Detention under that controversial legislative regime was finally capped at seven days.[129] Similarly, the United Kingdom fiercely debated the maximum period of preventive arrest and Prime Ministers Blair and Brown ultimately had to accept defeat in Parliament on proposals to extend this period to 42 or 90 days.[130] In contrast, individual prosecutors, on their own initiative but with support from Attorney General Ashcroft and individual judges, were able to use material witness warrants to detain people for equal or longer periods without any centralized legislative debate or constraint. The only constraint on such actions was the possibility of decentralized judicial review, which, at worse, could order that the suspect be released and perhaps might result in a civil lawsuit long after the detention.

Military Detention of Citizens as an Alternative to Criminal Prosecution

In the initial aftermath of 9/11, the Bush administration was prepared to use military detention of American citizens suspected of involvement with al Qaeda as a less restrained alternative to the criminal justice system. Given the preferred position of American citizens in much of the American response to 9/11, the willingness to subject American citizens to military detention underlines how much the Bush administration had lost confidence in the criminal law and was attracted to the model of a war against terrorism.

The most infamous case involves Jose Padilla, who was arrested at O'Hare International Airport in Chicago and initially detained on a material witness warrant. Just before his monthlong detention as a material witness was going to be subject to judicial review, President Bush issued an order in June 2002 that Padilla be detained as an enemy combatant in a military brig in South Carolina on the basis that he was closely associated with al Qaeda. Padilla was held incommunicado and was subject to extreme interrogation techniques. In 2004, the U.S. Supreme Court ducked his habeas corpus claim on the basis that he had litigated the issue in the wrong court because he had brought the case before a federal court in New York, where he was detained as a material witness, as opposed to South Carolina, where he was detained in a military brig.[131] The Court allowed the government to benefit from its forum shopping and displayed a legalistic approach that ignored the substance of Padilla's claims. This was another example of the extra-legalism of using legal forms to shelter illegal conduct. Justice Stevens and three others dissented and

---

[129] See Chapter 6.   [130] See Chapter 5.
[131] 542 U.S. 426 (2004).

warned that "incommunicado detention for months on end" was unlawful and "whether the information so procured is more or less reliable than that acquired by more extreme forms of torture is of no consequence. For if this Nation is to remain true to the ideals symbolized by its flag, it must not wield the tools of tyrants even to resist an assault by the forces of tyranny."[132]

Padilla continued to litigate and subsequently won a favorable decision, with the judge declaring that the allegations against him, including allegations of involvement in a dirty bomb plot, were "a law enforcement matter not a military matter. . . . The difference between invocation of the criminal process and the power claimed by the President . . . is one of accountability. The criminal justice system requires that defendants and witnesses be afforded access to counsel, imposes judicial supervision over governmental action, and places congressionally imposed limits on incarceration."[133] This ringing endorsement of the criminal justice system, however, did not last long, and the Fourth Circuit, on appeal, reversed and held that Padilla's detention was a military matter that was justified by the AUMF. Judge Michael Luttig, a conservative favored by many as a possible Supreme Court nominee, stressed that the criminal justice system was inadequate because it would not prevent Padilla's return to the battlefield and that its open processes might hinder effective intelligence gathering.[134] The use of military detention as an alternative to the criminal process suggested a profound lack of confidence in the American criminal justice system, despite its heavy use of imprisonment and pre-9/11 track record of obtaining convictions and long prison sentences, and even the death penalty in terrorism cases.

Just before the Supreme Court was about to hear Padilla's appeal and consider whether his detention was authorized by the AUMF, the Bush administration indicted him on criminal charges, not in relation to the alleged dirty bomb plot but for a broad conspiracy to engage in an unknown act of terrorism after he had returned from terrorist training in Afghanistan. Judge Luttig, who had previously sided with the government and stressed the inadequacy of the criminal justice system, appeared shocked and dismayed at the government's dramatic change of strategy. He warned that the government's actions were causing it to lose credibility before the courts.[135]

---

[132] Ibid., at 465.
[133] *Padilla v. Hanft*, 389 F. Supp. 2d 678, 691–2. (Dist.Ct. S.C., 2005)
[134] *Hanft v. Padilla*, 423 F.3d 388 (4th Cir., 2005); cert. denied 126 S.C.T. 1649.
[135] *Padilla v. Hanft*, 432 F.3d 582, 587 (4th Cir., 2005). In 2009, the Obama administration transferred the case of Ali al-Marri to the Federal Court after he had been detained in the United States as an enemy combatant since 2003. This avoided a Supreme Court decision on the government's authority to hold al-Marri under the AUMF. It also produced a guilty

One reason why Padilla might not have faced criminal charges on the original dirty bomb allegation was that much of the evidence, both from Padilla and other high-value detainees, may have been derived from torture.[136] Padilla was unsuccessful in having the charges dismissed on the basis that his mistreatment – including allegations of involuntary administration of drugs and use of stress positions and sleep deprivation – made him unfit to stand trial. He was subsequently convicted of the conspiracy charges and sentenced to 17 years' imprisonment.[137] The case underlines the initial willingness of the United States to depart from the crime model and employ a war model of indeterminate military detention of its own citizen, but combined with harsh interrogation that would be illegal if applied to enemy soliders. At the same time, the ultimate resolution of the case illustrates that the crime model remains accommodating in the United States, even in cases where specific terrorist plots are not alleged and the accused claims to have been severely mistreated in custody.

The minimal scrutiny that the criminal justice system provided in Jose Padilla's case was avoided entirely in the case of Yaser Hamdi. Hamdi was captured in Afghanistan and originally held in Guantánamo but was transferred to a military brig in Virginia when it was discovered that he was an American citizen. Lower courts expressed concerns that the government's evidence against Hamdi was based on hearsay and bald assertions, but the Fourth Circuit, as in Padilla, deferred to the government on matters of national security. In 2004, the Supreme Court, in a divided opinion, held that Hamdi's detention was authorized by the bare-bones AUMF, but two judges issued a strong dissent that a clear statement was required to justify the detention of an American citizen, and two others stressed that Hamdi, as an American citizen, either must be prosecuted in an ordinary court or Congress must suspend habeas corpus. A majority of the Court also found that Hamdi was entitled to some due process, such as notice of the charges and an opportunity to be heard, but four judges suggested that due process could be satisfied even if

plea including an admission that al-Marri entered the United States at the direction of Khalid Sheik Mohammed and had received terrorist training including in chemical weapons. Al-Marri received an 8 year sentence as opposed to the maximum of 15 years in recognition of his nearly 6 years detention in isolation in a military brig. "Judge credits time served in sentencing al Qaeda aide" *The Washington Post* October 30, 2009.

[136] Cole and Lobel, *Less Safe, Less Free*, at 95–6.

[137] Robert Chesney has suggested that "the Padilla prosecution provides a striking example of the preventive capacity of existing criminal law" while also expressing concerns about the spillover effects of broad conspiracy prosecutions that are based on general terrorist inclinations as opposed to agreements with respect to specific acts. Chesney, "Optimizing Criminal Prosecutions as a Counterterrorism Tool," in Wittes, *Legislating the War against Terror*, at 109.

hearsay was used and there was a presumption in favor of the government's evidence.[138]

As will be seen, this ruling was influential in shaping procedures at Guantá-namo, but it was not applied in Hamdi's case. The government agreed to release Hamdi to Saudi Arabia on the condition that he renounce his American citizenship; agree not return to the United States for 10 years; and agree not to travel to Afghanistan, Pakistan, Iraq, Syria, Israel, or the Occupied Territories. The agreement also meant that Hamdi relinquished any claims against the United States for his treatment. The banishment of Hamdi bears some resemblance to the use of banishment and deportation of insurgents by British colonial authorities in the Malaya emergency.[139] In this case, first military detention and then banishment and deportation were used as alternatives to the criminal process. These domestic enemy combatant cases are a testament to the Bush administration's initial lack of confidence in the criminal process even though both the Padilla and al-Marri cases eventually resulted in criminal convictions.

VI. SUBSEQUENT LEGISLATION AND THE DEMISE OF PATRIOT II

Although Congress was relatively silent on terrorism measures after the Patriot Act, it did engage in sweeping reforms of government and intelligence in an attempt to respond to some of the problems that had led to 9/11. The 2002 Homeland Security Act established a new and massive Department of Homeland Security that would contain 22 different agencies and 170,000 employees. In a trend seen in other countries, customs and immigration agencies were brought into a security-dominated department. Immigrations and Customs Enforcement was created as an enforcement agency with the first priority of preventing the entry of terrorists into the United States. It would constitute the second largest investigative agency, with 20,000 employees, second only to the FBI,[140] and would help create the notorious inconveniences and difficulties that many non-Americans have experienced when trying to enter the United States after 9/11.

In 2004, an even more massive law, the Intelligence Reform and Terrorism Prevention Act, was enacted following the recommendations of the 9/11 Commission. It created a new director of national intelligence with oversight, but not budgetary powers, over the United States' sprawling intelligence structure

---

[138] 542 U.S. 507 (2004).   [139] See Chapter 3.
[140] Norman Abrams, *Anti-Terrorism and Criminal Enforcement*, 3rd ed. (St. Paul, MN: Thomson West, 2008), at 40.

including 17 agencies spread throughout the armed forces and various governmental departments with budgets of over $50 billion (American). The law stopped short of creating a domestic security intelligence agency as found in the United Kingdom, Australia, and Canada. Richard Posner has been critical of attempts to centralize the intelligence function and of the decision not to create a separate domestic intelligence agency, which he argues could have the skills and incentives to focus on the collection of intelligence, as opposed to the FBI's incentives to make arrests.[141]

Although no domestic security intelligence agency has been created, there has been a massive expansion of intelligence capability since 9/11 with one estimate of 934 federal, state and local counter-terrorism organizations being created since 9/11.[142] Most intelligence programs reside in the Department of Defense and the Pentagon's Defense Intelligence Agency more than doubled from 7,500 employees in 2002 to 16,500 in 2010.[143] After 9/11, the newly established Northern Command of the Department of Defense established domestic intelligence-gathering centers with 290 intelligence officers.[144] Consistent with the war and executive-based model, military intelligence has increased dramatically since 9/11 with little legislative regulation and oversight.

The 2004 intelligence reform law also continued and expanded Patriot Act provisions that allowed the sharing of grand jury information to more state and local officials. It also amended the material support of terrorism offense and also created a new offense of terrorist hoaxes. Nevertheless, the focus of the massive 2002 and 2004 reforms has been on attempts to increase the centralization and coordination of security and especially intelligence functions in government. The rise of an intelligence paradigm, with its focus on prevention and suspect associations, is an important post-9/11 effect but one that may often sit uneasily with a crime model based on public evidence about criminal acts. This is especially the case given the dominance of the military in the American intelligence community. It is striking that even after 9/11, the United States did not seriously consider creating a domestic civilian security intelligence agency, even as the budgets and sizes of its other intelligence agencies increased dramatically. The lack of a domestic intelligence agency

---

[141] Richard Posner, *Uncertain Shield: The US Intelligence System in the Throes of Reform* (Lanham, MD: Rowman and Littlefield, 2006), at 79, 134–5.

[142] Dana Priest and William Arkin "Mointoring America" *The Washington Post* December 20, 2010.

[143] Dana Priest and William Arkin "A Hidden World Growing Out of Control" *The Washington Post* July 19, 2010.

[144] Laura Donohue *The Costs of Counterterrorism* at 247.

fits into a pattern of strict concerns about civil liberties at home, combined with almost unlimited powers directed at external terrorist threats.

The Rejection of Patriot II

In January 2003, a draft Domestic Security Enhancement Act, better known as Patriot II, was leaked and published. It proposed powers to take citizenship away from citizens associated with terrorist groups. As will be seen, powers to strip citizenship were expanded in the United Kingdom in relation to the David Hicks case.[145] Patriot II also proposed to eliminate the distinction between domestic and international terrorism in many of the expansions of state powers in the Patriot Act.[146] Provisions that would allow the formation of a DNA data bank of terrorists and terrorist suspects were particularly controversial among right-wing commentators, even though DNA is widely recognized as a powerful law enforcement tool that can assist the innocent as well as convict the guilty. Opposed by both the Gun Owners of America and the American Civil Liberties Union, Patriot II was "dead on arrival."[147] Similar bi-partisan concerns about privacy led Congress to bar expenditures of funds on the study of national identity cards, data mining under the Pentagon's Total Information Awareness program and the Justice Department's Operation TIPS programs to encourage the reporting of suspicions. Perhaps aware of past domestic spying abuses and responding to bi-partisan support on both the left and the right, the United States has been less willing to limit the privacy rights of citizens after 9/11 than other democracies.[148]

In retrospect, some parts of Patriot II would have restrained executive power that were at the time being exercised in a secret manner. Section 103 would have allowed the attorney general to engage in electronic surveillance on the basis of AUMF and without approval by the FISA court, but only for a 15-day period.[149] To be sure, this would have been a controversial expansion of search powers, but it would have, unlike the then secret Presidential orders for domestic spying by the NSA, been subject to legislative debate and regulation. Similarly, Section 322 of Patriot II would have allowed the attorney general to approve, on a case-by-case basis, extradition to countries, even if the United States did not have an extradition treaty with that country. This power could

---

[145] See Chapter 5.   [146] Cole, *Enemy Aliens*, at 71.

[147] Sidel, *More Secure, Less Free*, at 33.

[148] David Cole "English Lessons: A Comparative Analysis of UK and US Responses to Terrorism" (2009) 62 Current Legal Problems 136 at 165.

[149] Patriot Act II draft, confidential, not for distribution, January 9, 2003, at http://www.statewatch .org/news/2003/feb/patriot2draft.html.

have been dangerous but not as much as the enhanced extraordinary rendition program. Although some parts of Patriot II were implemented in other laws, most were not. The failure of Patriot II was a victory for civil liberties, but it may also have confirmed for the Bush administration the limits of a legislative approach to counter-terrorism.

VII. GUANTÁNAMO AND THE FAILED ATTEMPT TO PRECLUDE HABEAS CORPUS

Guantánamo has become a powerful symbol of America's response to 9/11. As will be seen, the Bush administration's initial attempt to declare Guantánamo a law-free zone failed in 2004, when the Supreme Court found that habeas corpus would apply. Congress then joined the battle and in 2005, and again in 2006, attempted to preclude habeas corpus review, only to finally be told by the Supreme Court in 2008 that habeas still applied and the strict constitutional conditions for a suspension of habeas corpus did not exist. President Obama has tried, but failed, to close Guantánamo. The Guantánamo saga is important because of what it illustrates about the respective roles of the executive, legislature, and judiciary. It also illustrates a willingness by both the Bush and Obama administrations as well as Congress to use indeterminate detention without trial and trial by military commission as alternatives to criminal prosecutions.

President Bush's November 2001 Military Order: The Attempt to Create a Law-Free Black Hole

On November 13, 2001, President Bush issued a military order under both the AUMF and his inherent presidential and commander in chief powers. It declared that a state of armed conflict with international terrorists existed as well as an extraordinary national defense emergency. The order authorized the detention and trial by military commission of individuals if there was reason to believe they were members of al Qaeda or have "engaged in, aided or abetted, or conspired to commit, acts of international terrorism, or acts in preparation therefore, that have caused, threaten to cause, or have as their aim to cause, injury to or adverse effects on the United States, its citizens, national security, foreign policy, or economy."[150] This order, like the September 2001 AUMF, blended war and crime concepts but leaned on the side of the war model. It targeted all past or present members of al Qaeda, even though membership

[150] Military Order of November 13, 2001; 66 Federal Register 57831–6, Section 2.

in al Qaeda was not a crime in the United States, including under the Patriot Act. Consistent with Resolution 1373, it focused on all international terrorists broadly defined to include those who prepare, conspire, aid, or abet acts of terrorism and those who harbor terrorists. Also consistent with most post-9/11 antiterrorism laws, (but not the Patriot Act with its narrower focus on danger to life), the Bush order defined the targeted harms broadly as including any injury or adverse effects to the United States, including its "national security, foreign policy or economy." The military order also provided that the detainees shall be "treated humanely" and "allowed the free exercise of religion consistent with the requirements of such detention."[151] The order stressed in a number of places that it did not authorize the disclosure of state secrets and allowed the use of secret evidence against the detainee.[152] Finally, it asserted that "military tribunals shall have exclusive jurisdiction with respect to offenses" and that detainees would not be able to seek remedies or have remedies sought on their behalf in "(i) any court of the United States, or any State thereof, (ii) any court of any foreign nation, or (iii) any international tribunal."[153] This last provision was a stunning and ultimately unsuccessful attempt to create a law-free black hole that would preclude any form of judicial review of military detention or trials.

The Bush administration relied on two World War II decisions upholding the use of military commissions against enemy forces, including an American citizen, as well as a cold war decision holding that U.S. courts had no jurisdiction over a prison administered by the United States in Germany.[154] The reliance on these precedents fit into the pattern of extra-legalism-reliance on legal arguments to shelter military detention and trial from legal challenge. The proposed use of military commissions that precluded the use of civilian juries and other safeguards generated much criticism in the United States[155] but also defenders, who stressed problems using criminal courts.[156]

---

[151] Ibid., Section 3. [152] Ibid., Sections 4 and 7(a).
[153] Ibid., Section 7(b).
[154] *Ex parte Quirin*, 317 U.S. 1 (1942); *Application of Yamashita*, 327 U.S. 1 (1946); *Johnson v. Eisenstrager*, 339 U.S. 763 (1950).
[155] Neal Katyal and Lawrence Tribe, "Waging War, Deciding Guilt: Trying the Military Tribunals" (2002) 111 Yale Law Journal 1259; Ronald Dworkin, "The Trouble with Tribunals," New York Review of Books, April 25, 2002; Harold Koh, "The Case against Military Commissions" (2002) 96 American Journal of International Law 337.
[156] Curtis Bradley and Jack Goldsmith, "The Constitutional Validity of Military Commissions" (2002) 118 Harvard Law Review 2047; Ruth Wedgwood, "Al Qaeda and Military Commissions" (2002) 96 American Journal of International Law 328. For an earlier defense, see Spencer Crona and Neil Richardson, "Justice for War Criminals and Invisible Armies: A New Legal and Military Approach to Terrorism" (2006) 21 Oklahoma City University Law Review 349.

Rasul v. Bush *and the First Judicial Affirmation of Habeas Jurisdiction*

In its 2004 decision in *Rasul v. Bush*,[157] the U.S. Supreme Court reversed lower courts that held they had no jurisdiction to review the detention of noncitizens held by the United States in a military camp in Cuba. Justice Stevens, for the majority, distinguished wartime precedents on the basis that the petitioners, nationals of Kuwait and Australia, were not from countries at war with the United States.[158] Justice Kennedy stressed that they were subject to indeterminate detention.[159] The Court emphasized American control over the prisoners and that the applicable habeas corpus statute did not differentiate between citizens and noncitizens. The decision "narrowly rested upon the territorial particularity of the Guantánamo Bay Naval Base and the Court's interpretation of the habeas statute."[160] As will be seen, this gave Congress an opening to affirm the Bush administration's decision to oust habeas jurisdiction. As discussed in the preceding chapter, the Israeli Supreme Court used a similar democracy-enhancing technique in its 1999 decision holding that extreme interrogation techniques must be authorized by specific legislation. Such an approach allows courts to assert themselves in matters of national security while not finally resolving them.

Justice Scalia, with two other judges, issued a vigorous dissent. He argued that the Court "springs a trap on the Executive, subjecting Guantánamo Bay to the oversight of the federal courts even though it has never before been thought to be within their jurisdiction – and this making it a foolish place to have housed alien wartime detainees."[161] As will be seen, *Rasul's* insistence on habeas review was affirmed in *Boumediene*, but only after four years of back-and-forth between Congress and the Court.

Habeas corpus may not, however, apply to other places where the United States detains suspected terrorists. In 2010, the D.C. Circuit held that it did not extend to those detained at the Bagram military base in Afghanistan on the basis that it would be more difficult to apply habeas in another country during a time of war, even in cases where the detainees were not originally captured in Afghanistan.[162] As Cass Sunstein has noted, American courts are attracted to limited case-by-case rulings or constitutional minimalism in order to leave the elected branches of government room to respond to their rulings. Professor

[157] 542 U.S. 466; 124 S.Ct. 2686 (2004).   [158] Ibid., at 475–9.
[159] Ibid., at 487–8.
[160] David Jenkins, "Habeas Corpus Jurisdiction and Extraterritorial Jurisdiction" (2009) 9 Human Rights Law Review 306, at 310.
[161] 542 U.S. 466, at 497–8.
[162] *Al Maqaleh v. Gates*, 605 F. 3d. 84 (DC Circuit, 2010).

Sunstein argues that courts may be especially attracted to such approaches in the sensitive area of national security.[163] Such a fact-specific approach means that American courts may not recognize the general principle that habeas corpus should apply to all those detained and in the control of American officials.[164] The fact specific legalism of the American courts promotes a certain cynicism toward the law that encourages and rewards legalistic hair splitting of the type also seen in the Court's companion decision to dismiss Jose Padilla's habeas application because he had commenced it in New York, while detained on a material witness warrant, and not in South Carolina, where he was subsequently detained in a military brig. It also encourages the government to attempt to duplicate the Guantánamo experiment of attempting to create a law free zone simply by selecting another location such as the Bagram base. The sheer volume of law in the United States and the penchant of its courts to make limited decisions on the facts create incentives for lawyers to evade the spirit of the law.

Hamdi *and Diluted Due Process*

Hamdi v. Rumsfeld[165] had important implications for Guantánamo. A plurality of the Court interpreted the AUMF as providing legal authorization for the detention of Hamdi in a military brig and presumably for the noncitizens detained at Guantánamo for so long as the war against the Taliban in Afghanistan lasted. In this way, Justice O'Connor avoided pronouncing on the broader war against terrorism that the government conceded could last for generations, beyond saying that "we agree that indefinite detention for the purpose of interrogation is not authorized." Justice Souter dissented on the basis that clear legislation was required to justify detention of American citizens under a law that had been enacted in 1971 to repudiate the detention of Japanese-Americans during World War II. Pointing to the fact that Section 412 of the Patriot Act had only authorized seven days' detention without criminal charges or removal proceedings for noncitizens suspected of terrorism, Justice Souter stressed that it would be difficult to accept that Congress had authorized indeterminate detention of American citizens.[166]

Justice O'Connor decided that Hamdi was entitled to a form of due process that would balance his liberty interests against the government's security interests. Due process did not require a full criminal trial but rather notice

[163] Cass Sunstein, "Minimalism at War" (2004) Supreme Court Law Review 47.
[164] This principle is defended in Jonathan Hafetz *Habeas Corpus After 9/11* (New York: New York University Press, 2011) ch 11.
[165] 542 U.S. 507 (2004).   [166] 542 U.S. 507, at 534.

of the factual basis for the government's decision and a fair opportunity to rebut those factual assertions before a neutral decision maker. She indicated that these standards could tolerate the use of hearsay, a rebuttable presumption in favor of the government's evidence and the use of military tribunals. These standards were quite vague and made generous allowances to the state's interests. They did not, however, address the critical issue of whether secret evidence would be permissible. Justice Scalia, in a dissent joined by Justice Stevens, criticized the "unheard-of system in which the citizen rather than the Government bears the burden of proof, testimony is by hearsay rather than live witnesses, and the presiding officer may well be a 'neutral' military officer rather than judge and jury."[167] This very system, which Justice Scalia ridiculed for American citizens, would quickly be used for noncitizens at Guantánamo.

The Government Responds to Hamdi

Within a week of *Hamdi* being released, the Bush administration established combatant status review tribunals for reviewing the Guantánamo detentions. Even though it was ideologically committed to exclusive and inherent presidential powers, the Bush administration leaped at the chance to implement a system at Guantánamo that had been blessed by the Supreme Court as constitutional.[168] As contemplated by Justice O'Connor in *Hamdi*, the detainees under the new rules would receive notice of the factual basis for their detention and some opportunity to respond, but the rules of evidence, including those against hearsay, would not apply; there would be a rebuttable presumption in favor of the government's evidence; and hearings would be before military officers. Moreover, secret evidence not disclosed to the detainee could be used to affirm detention. These rules demonstrate a tendency for governments to seek shelter in minimal standards of constitutionality when responding to post-9/11 dangers. They also suggest how court decisions can help legitimate questionable powers and procedures.

Courts conducting proportionality analysis can be influenced by starting points and baselines. Justice O'Connor provided detainees with substantially more process than they were entitled to under President Bush's November 13

---

[167] Ibid.

[168] Mark Tushnet suggests that the rules also demonstrate a sociological and political acceptance of the rule of law. Tushnet, "The Judicial Conception of Emergency Powers: Some Conceptual Issues," in *Emergencies and the Limits of Legality*, ed. Victor Ramraj (New York: Cambridge University Press, 2008), at 154–6. In my view, Professor Tushnet underestimates how much the rules with their use of secret evidence violate the rule of law. The timing of the adoption of the rules also suggests that the administration was eager to win support from the courts.

order, which attempted to preclude all judicial review and provided only for military commission trials and no detention reviews. The due process of *Hamdi* was an improvement, but it was still a diluted form of due process. The Guantánamo detention reviews based on *Hamdi* created unfair proceedings based on secret evidence. From July 2004 to February 2009, the tribunals found 539 detainees to be properly classified as enemy combatants and 39 not to be properly classified.[169] The process followed an intelligence paradigm that relied on unnamed sources and generalized allegations. As such, it created a significant risk of false positives, by which detainees would be determined to be enemy combatants associated with the Taliban or al Qaeda when, in fact, they were not. The government itself did not rely on this process and released many whose detentions had been upheld by the process. A lack of full process created false positives, but also false negatives. The U.S. government estimated that 150 of 600 detainees released from Guantánamo were suspected or known to have returned to terrorism.[170]

Legislative Attempts to Suspend Habeas Corpus and a Second Judicial Affirmation of Habeas Corpus

Congress responded to *Rasul* as well as to international outrage at abuse of prisoners at Guantánamo Bay and Abu Ghraib with the Detainee Treatment Act of 2005.[171] This act prohibited cruel, inhumane, and degrading treatment of detainees but also stripped federal courts of jurisdiction to consider the habeas corpus claims of detainees at Guantánamo in favor of review by the D.C. Circuit Appeal Court of the constitutionality of combatant status review tribunal decisions. Consistent with Professor Sunstein's theory of constitutional minimalism, the Supreme Court did not immediately confront the constitutionality of the habeas stripping provisions. In *Hamdan v. Rumsfeld*,[172] it held that the habeas stripping provisions of the 2005 act, as a matter of statutory interpretation, would not apply retroactively to Hamdan's habeas corpus petition, which was started before the legislation was enacted.

The Court ruled that the military commission convened to try Hamdan was without jurisdiction because it violated the Uniform Code of Military

---

[169] "Department of Defense Combatant Status Review Tribunal Summary," at http://www.defense.gov/news/csrtsummary.pdf.

[170] "Released from Guantánamo, They Took Up Arms," The New York Times, April 24, 2011. For arguments that a truncated process can increase both false negatives and false positives, see Kent Roach and Gary Trotter, "Miscarriages of Justice in the War against Terror" (2005) 109 Pennsylvania State Law Review 967, at 1014–32.

[171] 119 Stat. 2739.
[172] 548 U.S. 557; 126 S.Ct. 2749 (2006).

Justice and Common Article 3 of the Geneva Conventions, which requires that detainees be tried by "a regularly constituted court affording all the judicial guarantees which are recognized as indispensable by civilized people."[173] Justice Stevens stressed the unfairness of using secret evidence against the accused, stating that "an accused must, absent disruptive conduct or consent, be present for his trial and must be privy to the evidence against him." Although the government "has a compelling interest in denying Hamdan access to certain sensitive information . . . absent express statutory provision to the contrary, information used to convict a person of a crime must be disclosed to him." He also expressed doubts that some of the offenses with which Hamdan was charged, most notably conspiracy, were violations of the laws of war that could be tried by military commissions. Justice Scalia and two other judges again found themselves in dissent. They argued that the clear intent of Congress's 2005 act was to deprive federal courts of habeas corpus jurisdiction and that the military commissions were consistent with human rights.[174]

The Third and Final Judicial Affirmation of Habeas Corpus

In response to *Hamdan*, Congress enacted the Military Commissions Act of 2006 (MCA),[175] which clearly stripped the federal courts of habeas jurisdiction over the Guantánamo Bay detainees. In *Boumediene v. Bush*,[176] however, the Supreme Court held that the MCA did not satisfy the requirements of the Constitution, which only allows habeas corpus to be suspended "when in cases of Rebellion or Invasion the public Safety may require it."[177] The MCA did not provide an adequate substitute for habeas corpus, especially with respect to the ability of the detainee to present newly discovered evidence. Justice Kennedy rejected the government's argument that the process of the combatant status review tribunals was sufficient because they were based on the diluted due process of Justice O'Connor's judgment in *Hamdi*. He stressed that there was "a considerable risk of error" in the tribunals' findings of fact given that the proceedings were "closed and adversarial," and "the consequence of error may be detention of persons for the duration of hostilities that may last a generation or more, this is a risk too significant to ignore."[178]

Justice Scalia, in dissent, predicted grave consequences if there was increased judicial review of military detention. He stressed a war and an intelligence model and warned of "the dangers of disclosing information to attorneys

---

[173] Ibid., at 630.
[175] 28 U.S.C.A. s 2241(e).
[177] Ibid., at 2296.

[174] Ibid., at 665.
[176] 128 S.Ct. 2229.
[178] Ibid., at 2267–74.

representing our enemies" and made claims that disclosure in pre-9/11 criminal cases had already assisted al Qaeda.[179] Chief Justice Roberts argued, in dissent, that the MCA provided an adequate substitute for habeas corpus because it was based on *Hamdi*. He predicted that the new habeas regime would be no better for detainees and only add more delay to the process.

What explains the Court's resistance to attempts to preclude habeas review of the Guantánamo detentions? The Court reacted negatively to blatant attempts to preclude judicial review. Its decisions involved procedural issues well within the expertise of the judiciary. The Court may also have been active because of its awareness that it was engaged in a dialogue with the elected branches of government. For example, Justice Kennedy explained that the Court deliberately avoided the constitutional issue in its 2006 *Hamdan* decision to facilitate "a dialogue between Congress and the Court" so that Congress "could make an informed legislative choice either to amend the statute or to retain its existing text."[180] He recognized that Congress, in its legislative reply to *Hamdan*, had clearly affirmed its commitment to denial of habeas corpus. In light of that decision, the Court had to proceed "to its own independent judgment on the constitutional question."[181] The majority of the Court did not defer to Congress's judgment that the Constitution allowed it to deny habeas corpus, a practice of coordinate construction that has been defended by some prominent American constitutional scholars and is also consistent with extra-legalism because it allows the executive and the legislature to act on their own interpretation of the Constitution, even when that interpretation is inconsistent with judicial interpretations.[182] At the same time, the Court engaged in a form of constitutional minimalism by delegating to the lower courts the ultimate issue of whether there were valid legal grounds for detention. No one was released as a result of the Court's decision in *Boumediene*.

The Promised Land of Habeas?

The Court's judgment in *Boumediene* meant that the detainees could seek habeas corpus relief, but the court was vague about how such proceedings should be conducted The detainees should be able to introduce new exculpatory evidence, if it was available, but courts should also accommodate the government's interests in protecting intelligence sources and methods from

---

[179] *Boumediene v. Bush*, 128 S.Ct. 2229, at 2294.   [180] Ibid., at 2243.
[181] Ibid.
[182] Mark Tushnet, *Taking the Constitution away from the Court* (Princeton, NJ: Princeton University Press, 1999).

disclosure. On one level, the unelected Court was prepared to reject the combined forces of Congress and the Bush administration to defend the great writ of habeas corpus in a manner that may have surprised those who predicted that courts would defer to governments on security matters. At the same time, the Court remanded the complex task of making additional rules concerning the Guantánamo detentions to the judges in the D.C. Circuit who would hear the habeas corpus cases and warned those judges to accommodate the state's security interests to the greatest extent possible. The result was consistent with an American pattern of adversarial legalism that relies on the decentralized powers of courts to make rules that in other democracies would be made by the legislature and implemented by a bureaucracy.[183]

The judges of the D.C. Circuit followed the Supreme Court's admonition to focus on potentially exculpatory evidence, but they soon imposed slightly different disclosure standards on the government and discovery opportunities for habeas applicants.[184] The lead litigant in *Boumediene*, a man who was arrested in Bosnia shortly after 9/11 and who was rendered to Guantánamo and detained there from January 2002, was ordered released on habeas and was resettled in France after extensive hearings that were closed to the public, including 50 separate hearings in which the detainee attempted to obtain more discovery from the government. The government's case that he was an enemy combatant associated with al Qaeda was based on intelligence from one unnamed source that Boumediene planned to travel to Afghanistan to fight after 9/11. The judge who ordered Boumediene's release found that the government had not provided enough information about the source to evaluate the credibility or reliability of the information. He stressed that while the information "was undoubtedly sufficient for the intelligence purposes for which it was prepared, it is *not* sufficient for the purposes for which a habeas court must now evaluate it."[185] This case affirms the danger of using intelligence from unknown sources and unknown circumstances as evidence to justify long-term and potentially indeterminate detention. Similar evidentiary flaws and reliance on bare assertions and false confessions obtained by torture

---

[183] Robert Kagan, *Adversarial Legalism* (Cambridge, MA: Harvard University Press, 2001). For accounts of how American courts have been forced to run public schools and prisons in response to governmental defaults and to ensure constitutional standards, see Ross Sandler and David Schoenbrod, *Democracy by Decree: What Happens When Courts Run Government* (New Haven, CT: Yale University Press, 2003); Margo Schlanger, "Civil Rights Injunctions over Time: A Case Study of Jail and Prison Orders" (2006) 81 New York University Law Review 550.

[184] Note "A Dissentious 'Debate': Shaping Habeas Procedures Post-Boumediene" (2010) 88 Texas Law Review 1073.

[185] *Boumediene v. Bush*, 579 F. Supp. 2d 191.

have been found in other cases. As of February, 2011, habeas corpus has been granted in 37 of 57 cases decided.[186]

The D.C. Circuit stressed that habeas review need not match the standards of a criminal trial but could be tailored to the exigencies of military detention of noncitizens. It has rejected claims that the government must prove its case beyond a reasonable doubt or allow the detainee to confront all witnesses whose evidence is accepted. It has also not changed the substance of the liability rules for detention, which apply to those who have been members of al Qaeda, even if they have not committed a hostile act.[187] The court's disclosure rulings could also not deal with the fact that the government, especially in the early "legal black hole"[188] days of Guantánamo, had little incentive to collect or retain potentially exculpatory evidence. The habeas litigation has not, as some urged, moved the government towards greater use of the criminal law,[189] but rather may have added some legitimacy to military law of war detention without criminal trial at Guantánamo.

Some troubling limits to the habeas remedy have emerged, Thirteen detainees who have been granted habeas corpus are still detained as of February, 2011 primarily because of difficulties finding countries willing to accept them, concerns that they would be tortured if returned to their country of citizenship, concerns about security threats if they were returned to Yemen and appeals by the government.[190] The D.C. Circuit held that the courts lacked the power to order their release of Uighurs granted habeas corpus into the United States,[191] something that has been re-affirmed by legislation enacted by Congress at the end of 2010. The D.C. Circuit has also held that the Uighurs, a Muslim minority that faces persecution if returned to China, do not have the right to a hearing to second-guess the government's decision that their transfer to a third country would not result in torture, a decision that the U.S. Supreme Court has refused to hear.[192] It also held that former Guantánamo detainees could not bring civil suits in relation to their detention because of qualified

---

[186] Centre for Constitutional Rights "Guantanamo Habeas Scorecard" updated February 9, 2011 available at http://www.ccrjustice.org/files/2011-02-03%20Habeas%20SCORECARD%20Website%20Version.pdf.

[187] *Al-Bihani v. Obama*, 590 F.3d. 866 ((D.C.Cir., 2010).

[188] Lord Steyn, "Guantanamo Bay: The Legal Black Hole" (2004) 53 International and Comparative Law Quarterly 1.

[189] Jonathan Hafetz *Habeas Corpus After 9/11* (New York: New York University Press, 2011) ch 12.

[190] Centre for Constitutional Rights "Guantanamo Habeas Scorecard" updated February 9, 2011.

[191] *Kiyemba v. Obama*, 555 F.3d 1022. The decision was vacated by the Supreme Court but largely on the basis that the applicants had been resettled to third countries. *Kiyemba v. Obama*, 130 S.Ct. 1235 (2010).

[192] *Kiyemba v. Obama*, 561 F.3d 509 (D.C.Cir., 2009).

immunities enjoyed by governmental officials and restrictions on the extra-territorial application of constitutional rights to non-citizens.[193] Some of these results are forms of extra-legalism in which even successful legal wins such as the vindication of habeas in *Boumediene* do not always result in substantive victory.

Guantánamo and Continued Detention without Trial under President Obama

In January 2009, President Obama issued an executive order calling for the closure of Guantánamo within a year as a means to further "the national security and foreign policy interests of the United States and the interests of justice."[194] At the same time, the Obama administration continued the Bush administration's practice of relying on the AUMF to detain those associated with al Qaeda and the Taliban.[195] President Obama made it clear: "I am not going to release individuals who endanger the American people. Al Qaeda terrorists and their affiliates are at war with the United States, and those that we capture – like other prisoners of war – must be prevented from attacking us again."[196] This approach is not all that different than that advocated by the former Bush administration official who has argued that long-term detention of Guantánamo detainees is needed in part because either civil or military trials could result in acquittals or short sentences.[197] The common theme is again a lack of confidence in the criminal law.

---

[193] *Rasul v. Myers* 563 F 3d 527 (D.C. Cir. 2009) cert denied 130 S.Ct. 1013 (2009). A civil suit brought on behalf of two detainees who committed suicide at Guantanamo in 2006 and claimed damages for mistreatment and being force-fed before they took their lives was also dismissed on a similar basis *Talal Al-Zahrani v. Rumsfeld*. 684 F. Supp.2d 103 (D.D.C., 2010).

[194] "Closure of Guantanamo Detention Facilities" Executive Order President Obama January 22, 2009 available at http://www.whitehouse.gov/the_press_office/ClosureOfGuantanamo DetentionFacilities/.

[195] Mathew Waxman, "Administrative Detention: Integrating Strategy and Institutional Design," in Wittes, *Legislating the War on Terror*, at 45–6.

[196] Ibid., at 51.

[197] Professor Goldsmith writes, "A final problem with using any trial system, civilian or military, as the sole lawful basis for terrorist detention is that the trials can result in short sentences (as the first military commission trial did) or even acquittal of a dangerous terrorist. In criminal trials, defendants often go free because of legal technicalities, government inability to introduce probative evidence, and other factors beside the defendant's innocence. These factors are all exacerbated in terrorist trials by the difficulty of getting information from the place of capture, by restrictions on access to classified information, and by stale or tainted evidence." Jack Goldsmith, "Long-Term Detention and a National Security Court," in Wittes, *Legislating the War on Terror*, at 79.

The 2010 final report of the Guantánamo Review Task Force recommended that 126 detainees be transferred, 44 detainees be prosecuted either in military commissions or federal court, and 48 detainees continue to be held indefinitely under the AUMF because it was not feasible to prosecute them and they were too dangerous to release. The justifications for these latter detentions fit into an intelligence as opposed to a crime paradigm because they focused on the training and associations of the detainees and their expressed recidivist intent as opposed to definite criminal acts. The task force concluded that prosecution was not possible in these cases in large part because "the focus at the time of their capture was the gathering of intelligence and their removal from flight," and no criminal investigations designed to collect evidence were conducted.[198] In other words, criminal prosecutions were not possible because the detainees had been detained for intelligence reasons, and criminal investigations were not pursued. These reasons have some of the same circular and self-serving qualities as seen in the 2008 Israeli administrative detention case examined in Chapter 3, in which the Israeli Court accepted at face value assertions that evidence for criminal prosecution was not available, even though those collecting intelligence had no incentive to collect evidence because the lack of evidence justified preventive and indeterminate detention.

Other reasons for concluding that criminal prosecutions were not possible were rooted more in legal obstacles. The task force observed that the material support offenses were not extended to apply extraterritorially to non-U.S. persons until October 2001 and December 2004. It also expressed some concern that the maximum penalty of 15 years' imprisonment for material support might not be sufficient. This is also consistent with the Israeli practice of using administrative detention in cases in which the state concludes that criminal sanctions were inadequate.[199]

The task force also observed that 530 of the total 779 detainees at Guantánamo had already been transferred to third countries, including those with poor human rights records such as Egypt.[200] The Guantánamo detentions involved the same problems of deportation to possible torture as hinted at by Security Council Resolution 1373 and that bedeviled the counter-terrorism strategies of other countries such as the United Kingdom and Canada. That said, the American Guantánamo transfers, consistent with strong executive and extralegal strains in American antiterrorism policies, were achieved in secret without specific legislative authorization or judicial review. The Supreme

---

[198] Final Report, Guantánamo Review Task Force, January 22, 2010, at 22.
[199] Ibid., at 23. [200] Ibid., at iv.

Court even encouraged such an approach when, in a companion case to *Boumediene*, it unanimously held that it would not exercise its habeas jurisdiction and would defer to the government, even if an American citizen captured in Iraq might be tortured if transferred to Iraqi authorities.[201] There is a risk that some individuals released from Guantánamo would be tortured especially because the United States allows transfer so long as there is less than a 50% probability of torture.[202] The risk that adaptive behavior to the closing of Guantánamo or CIA prisons or the transfer of Iraq and Afghan detainees might even be worse for the detainees transferred to other countries should not be ignored.

In March, 2011, President Obama issued an executive order attempting to regularize detention without trial at Guantánamo. The executive order recognized that Guantánamo detainees would continue to have the right to seek habeas corpus in Federal Court, but also provided for periodic review of continued detention. The standards for such review were somewhat more generous than those allowed by the Bush administration. Reviews would be conducted by a board of senior officials not only from the military but other departments. The detainees could be assisted by privately retained counsel. At the same time, the review process could be based on secret evidence not disclosed to the detainee with "continued law of war detention" being authorized "if it is necessary to protect against a significant threat to the security of the United States."[203] This order requires oral periodic hearings every three years and file reviews every six months. It contemplates that detention without either a civilian or military trial will continue at Guantánamo for the forseeable future.

Trial under the Military Commissions Act

Congress enacted the Military Commissions Act of 2006 in response to the Supreme Court's ruling in *Hamdan* that trials by military commissions at Guantánamo did not accord with Common Article 3 of the Geneva Conventions or with the Uniform Code of Military Justice. The act improved military commission trials by prohibiting the use of secret evidence and by excluding the use of evidence obtained through torture. At the same time, it departed

---

[201] The Court stressed that "the Judiciary is not suited to second-guess such determinations – determinations that would require federal courts to pass judgment on foreign justice systems and undermine the Government's ability to speak with one voice in this area." *Munaf v. Geren*, 128 S.Ct. 2207 (2008), at 2226.

[202] "Guantanamo Detainee Naji Sent Back to Algeria against His Will," Washington Post, July 20, 2010; Gabriella Blum and Philip Heymann, *Laws, Outlaws and Terrorists* (Boston: MIT Press 2010) at 112.

[203] Executive Order 13567 of March 7. 2011 s.2.

from the speedy trial guarantees of the Uniform Military Code of Justice and expanded the range of crimes that could be tried under the laws of war to include terrorism, material support for terrorism, and conspiracy to commit any of the listed crimes. A number of commentators have argued that the inclusion of conspiracy may be unconstitutional.[204] The MCA is a lengthy and complex document that represents a further legalization of the process. At the same time, its attempts to blend the laws of war and the laws of crime are incoherent and troubling. By attempting to create a third model that avoids many of the restraints of either the laws of war or crime, the United States has sacrificed the legitimacy that could have come with either fair criminal convictions or a fair imposition of the laws of war.[205]

In 2009, Congress amended the MCA. The main change was that statements obtained through cruel, inhuman, or degrading treatment would be inadmissible, regardless of when they were made, whereas the 2006 act held open the possibility that statements obtained through such methods before the enactment of the 2005 Detainee Treatment Act might be admissible.[206] Reference is now made to the Classified Information Procedures Act that is used in criminal trials to determine whether classified information has to be disclosed to the accused. At the same time, there is a danger that the commissions, which are instructed to protect intelligence sources and methods, may substitute unclassified evidence for classified evidence without the accused being able to comment on the adequacy of the substitution.[207] The accused is provided with a military counsel. Any civilian counsel must be American citizens with security clearances, and their interactions with their clients have been subject to monitoring by the Department of Defense. Some of the changes in the MCA were cosmetic such as the replacement of the provisions for trials of alien unlawful combatants with trials of alien unprivileged enemy belligerents.[208] In both cases, the focus remains on members of the Taliban and al Qaeda who are not American citizens. Despite providing that no person should be subject to a retroactive criminal offense, the MCA continues to include offenses, such as conspiracy, terrorism, and material support for terrorism, that have not traditionally been treated as violations of the law of war. The 2009 act, like the 2006 act, exempts military commissions from provisions in the Uniform Military Code of Justice that

---

[204] George Fletcher, "Hamdan Confronts the Military Commission Act, 2006" (2007) 45 Columbia Journal of Transnational Law 427.
[205] David Glazier, "A Self-Inflicted Wound: A Half-Dozen Years of Turmoil over the Guantanamo Military Commissions" (2008) 12 Lewis and Clark Law Review 131.
[206] Military Commissions Act, P.L. 111-94 (2009), Section 948r.
[207] Ibid., Section 949(d)(f).　　　　　　　　[208] Ibid., Section 948(a)(7).

require a person to be informed of the right to silence and contemplate exclusion of statements obtained without such warnings or through other unlawful inducements.[209]

Very few cases have been resolved by trial by military commission though in early 2011, the Obama Administration announced that it would recommence new trials by military commission including those of Khalid Sheikh Mohammed and other alleged 9/11 conspirators. Australian David Hicks pled guilty to material support of terrorism, but only after he was promised that he could serve the remainder of his sentence in Australia. Hamdan was charged with conspiracy and material support of terrorism, and in 2008, he was found guilty of one count of providing material support for terrorism and sentenced to 66 months while being credited with five years for time served. In October 2010, Omar Khadr pled guilty to murder, attempted murder, spying, conspiracy, and material support of terrorism for acts he did as a 15-year-old in Afghanistan. Khadr received an eight-year sentence, with an understanding that he would serve the last seven years in Canada, where he was born. The result for Khadr is far better than the 40-year sentence that the jury of military officers would have imposed on him, even though the prosecutor had only asked for a 25-year sentence.[210] The military officers were obviously influenced by testimony from the widow of an American soldier that Khadr admitted killing and by inflammatory but contested expert witness testimony that suggested that Khadr had been "marinated in radical jihadism" and achieved "rock star" status at Guantánamo.[211] Concerns linger about the legitimacy of the guilty plea both in relation to the military commission's purported jurisdiction and a pretrial ruling by the military judge that Khadr's incriminatory statements were not tainted by threats that he would be raped in an American prison.[212] The guilty

---

[209] Ibid., Section 948(b)(d).

[210] "Child Soldier for al Qaeda Is Sentenced for War Crimes," New York Times, November 1, 2010.

[211] "Khadr Devoted to Jihad, Psychiatrist Says," Globe and Mail, October 27, 2010, A18. Dr. Michael Welner, the expert called by the government, consulted with and relied in part on the controversial work of a Danish psychologist, Nicolai Sennels, who has made claims about "massive inbreeding within Muslim culture" and called the Koran "a criminal book that forces people to do criminal things." "Emotional Testimony Evokes Speer's Legacy," Globe and Mail, October 28, 2010, A19.

[212] The military judge accepted that the threat was made but found that it did not amount to torture and was not connected to Khadr's confession. Colonel Parrish concluded that the statements were voluntary and not the product of torture or mistreatment, adding, "The videotape is not 'fruit of the poisonous tree' as there is no 'poisonous tree'"; *US v. Khadr* suppression motion, Ruling 17, August 2010, at para. 6; http://www.defense.gov/news/D94-D111.pdf.

plea agreements attempt, in a manner reminiscent of President Bush's November 2001 military order, to preclude all subsequent litigation arising out of the persons' capture, detention, and treatment at Guantánamo. In David Hick's case, it also included a provision preventing comments on his experience for a time. The time has lapsed, and Hicks has recently explained that he pled guilty, to "save my life and my remaining sanity" and because he did not believe that a military commission would ever acquit anyone at Guantánamo.[213]

The decision of the Obama administration in April 2011 to withdraw criminal charges against Khalid Sheikh Mohammed (KSM) and other alleged 9/11 conspirators and return them to face trial by military commission was attributed to Congress's decision to enact legislation placing a temporary ban on the transfer of KSM and other Guantánamo detainees to the United States. The alleged conspirators will face, as they had under the Bush administration, various charges under the Military Commission Act likely including conspiracy and material support of terrorism. Although he maintained that "military commissions can deliver fair trials and just verdicts," Attorney General Eric Holder also warned that a loss of faith in criminal prosecutions would impair "our heritage, our values, and our legacy to future generations."[214] Holder has previously defended criminal prosecutions as an ability to demonstrate to "mad men" that while the United States is "militarily strong, we are morally stronger" because "values matter in this fight."[215] The decision to transfer KSM and others back to military commissions responded to widespread public and bipartisan Congressional opposition to trials in New York City. Unfortunately, it also has the potential to hand the men a potential propaganda victory especially if they revive the decision in 2008 to plead guilty at the military commission alleging that they could not receive a fair trial in a case where the judge and jury were employed by the military and accepting the death penalty as a form of martyrdom.[216]

---

[213] David Hicks, "Pressure to Plea Guilty" (2010) 29(4) Human Rights Defender available at http://www.amnesty.org.au/hrs/comments/24281/.

[214] "Statement of the Attorney General on the Prosecution of the 9/11 Conspirators" April 4, 2011 available at http://www.justice.gov/iso/opa/ag/speeches/2011/ag-speech-110404.html.

[215] Jane Mayer "The Trial; Eric Holder and the battle over Khalid Sheikh Mohammed" *The New Yorker* February 15, 2010.

[216] "In a reversal military trials for 9/11 cases" *The New York Times* April 4, 2011. In 2008, KSM had indicated he would plead guilty before a military commission stating "we don't want to waste our time on motions . . . All of you are paid by the U.S. government. I'm not trusting any American." "5 charged in 9/11 attacks seek to plea guilty" *The New York Times* December 8, 2008.

VIII. CRIMINAL PROSECUTIONS

The least used alternative to detention without trial or trial by military commission of Guantánamo detainees has been criminal prosecutions in federal courts. The Obama administration initially announced a number of transfers for prosecution, including KSM and four other alleged 9/11 conspirators and defended the prosecutions as feasible and the best way to re-affirm traditional values in the fight againt terrorism. Nevertheless, only the case of Ahmed Ghailani, charged with the 1998 African embassy bombings, went forward. The Department of Justice backed down in early 2010 from its controversial plans to try Khalid Sheikh Mohammed (KSM) and others alleged to be responsible for 9/11 in federal court in New York City even though a New York grand jury issued an indictment on various conspiracy charges against the men. The plan to hold a trial faced widespread opposition including from Democratic Senators and the mayor of New York City. In early 2011, President Obama signed a law that prohibited the use of funds to transfer KSM and others held at Guantánamo to the United States for a year.[217] He later criticized this legislation as interfering with executive authority and for discounting the ability of the Federal Courts to conduct terrorism prosecutions.[218] Despite this strong rhetorical defense of criminal prosecutions, his actual executive order was more nuanced. It required the Attorney General and Secretary of Defense to assess whether prosecution "is feasible and in the national security interests of the United States."[219] Even in cases where a criminal prosecution was feasible, it might not be used if it would harm national security interests by, for example, risking the disclosure of sensitive information or perhaps in some cases risking an acquittal or an undesired sentence. The alternative to criminal prosecution would be detention with or without trial before a military commission at Guantánamo. As discussed above, a decision was subsequently made to transfer the case of KSM and other alleged 9/11 conspirators from Federal Court back to military commissions where they had also faced trial under the Bush administration.

Writing in 2008, Robert Chesney and Jack Goldsmith argued that there was a growing convergence between military and criminal models of detention.[220] The MCA 2006 moved away from the traditional focus on membership and

---

[217] H.R. 6525–215.

[218] Fact Sheet New Actions on Guantanamo and Detainee Policy March 7, 2011 available at   http://www.whitehouse.gov/sites/default/files/Fact_Sheet_-_Guantanamo_and_Detainee_Policy.pdf.

[219] Executive Order 13567 of March 7, 2011 s.6.

[220] Robert Chesney and Jack Goldsmith, "Terrorism and the Convergence of the Criminal and Military Detention Models" (2008) 60 Stanford Law Review 1079.

status in the military detention model toward one that focused on alleged war crimes and ensured basic procedural protections, for example, against the use of secret evidence. At the same time, the expansion of criminal offenses, including the broad crime of material support of terrorism, moved criminal law closer to punishing a person for associations and status. Professors Chesney and Goldsmith are correct to point out these convergences, but important differences between criminal trials and military commissions remain.

One difference is that civilian juries in Federal Court must unanimously decide guilt, whereas juries of military officers can render non-unanimous verdicts in cases not involving the death penalty. The accused in federal court would also have the benefit of the clear application of the Sixth Amendment right to confront witnesses. In addition, incriminating statements are allowed under the MCA without prior warning about the right to silence, whereas the accused could seek exclusion in federal court under *Miranda* and related doctrines. There would also be more choice of defense counsel in federal court as well as the possibility of speedy trial claims that are specifically precluded under the MCA.

The prosecutor in Ghailani's criminal trial did not even attempt to enter "confessions" made while Ghailani was detained by the CIA. Moreover, the trial judge excluded testimony from a key witness that he sold Ghailani explosives because it was tainted by "coercion of Ghailani."[221] The judge applied the fruit of the poisonous tree doctrine to evidence derived from torture and stressed that revulsion at terrorism should not overwhelm legal principle. In contrast, a military judge ruled that statements made by Omar Khadr were not "fruit of the poisonous tree" because there is no "poisonous tree"[222] despite Khadr being threatened with rape in an American prison by his interrogators when he was captured in Afghanistan at 15 years of age.

Despite the exclusion of Ghailani's confessions and other evidence tainted by his coercion and likely torture by the CIA, he was convicted on one charge in relation to the 1998 African embassy bombings while also being acquitted

---

[221] Judge Kaplan ruled, "If the government is going to coerce a detainee to provide information to our intelligence agencies, it may not use that evidence – or fruits of that evidence that are closely related to the coerced statements. . . . – to prosecute the detainee for a criminal offence. . . . [The court] is acutely aware of the perilous world in which we live. But we must adhere to the basic principles that govern our nation not only when it is convenient to do so, but when perceived expediency tempts to pursue some different course. The government may continue its prosecution of Ghailani without using this evidence. It probably may detain him as an enemy combatant as long as the present hostilities continue." Ruling of October 6, 2010, at 59–60, slip judgment (U.S. Dist. Ct., Southern District of New York).

[222] *US v. Khadr*, ruling of Military Commission on Suppression Motion August 17, 2010 available at http://www.defense.gov/news/D94-D111.pdf.

on 280 other charges. He subsequently was sentenced to life imprisonment without parole.[223] The Obama administration's subsequent decision, in light of a temporary Congressional prohibition on transfers of Guantánamo detainees to the United States, to try KSM and other alleged 9/11 conspirators in military commissions reaffirms a loss of confidence in the criminal law to respond to 9/11 even though American courts had frequently convicted terrorists and imposed long sentences on them.

Fears of Disclosure, and Miranda

Many fears were raised in the United States about the ability of the criminal justice system to respond to the challenges of terrorism, despite the robust pre-9/11 record of successful terrorism prosecutions. As seen earlier, a lack of confidence in the criminal justice system helps explain the initial designation of Jose Padilla as an enemy combatant. Many were also skeptical about the criminal prosecution of Zacarias Moussaoui. John Radsan, who served both as a federal prosecutor and as assistant general counsel of the CIA, expressed concerns that Moussaoui would get access to "the Bush Administration's crown jewels" of intelligence such as interrogations of Khalid Sheik Mohammed.[224] In the end, however, Moussaoui only received access to unclassified summaries of KSM's interrogation[225] before he was sentenced to life imprisonment without parole.

Concerns about the so-called technicalities of the American criminal process have continued and led to several bills being introduced in Congress after the failed airline bombing on Christmas 2009 to deprive suspected terrorists of their rights under *Miranda*. *Miranda* is a symbolic issue, not unlike the British debate about the maximum period of detention under preventive arrest provisions. Much of the debate ignored *Miranda*'s status as a constitutional rule that cannot be displaced by statute[226] or the fact that it includes a robust public safety exception that has been applied in terrorism cases.[227]

The U.S. government has had considerable success in post-9/11 terrorism prosecutions. One report has recorded 337 cases involving 804 individuals in the eight years after 9/11, with an overall conviction rate of 89 percent in

---

[223] "Ex-Detainee gets life sentence in embassy blasts" *The New York Times*, January 25, 2011.

[224] A. John Radsan, "The Moussaoui Case: The Mess from Minnesota" (2005) 31 William Mitchell Law Review 1417, at 1431.

[225] *United States v. Moussaoui*, 382 F.3d 453 (4th Cir., 2004). One judge in dissent argued that the witness should be called and the jury should be able to evaluate the testimony.

[226] *Dickerson v. The United States*, 530 U.S. 428 (2000).

[227] *New York v. Quarles*, 467 U.S. 649 (1984); *United States v. Khalil*, 214 F.3d 111 (2d Cir., 2000).

cases in which terrorism charges were laid. It concluded that in most cases, the government has been able to cope with the dangers of disclosing classified information.[228] A 2009 study that focused on the prosecution of al Qaeda terrorists found a 91 percent conviction rate, with some who were acquitted subsequently being charged with other crimes or being removed under immigration procedures.[229] Only 11 accused, however, received a life sentence, and the average sentence was under eight and a half years; the median sentence was under five years. These sentences may reflect that the government is intervening earlier in the plots or perhaps offering sentence reductions to induce guilty pleas, which are taken in the majority of the cases.[230] Another study found a high 91 percent conviction rate, with 82 percent of cases ending in guilty pleas.[231] Some have, however, criticized the methodology of these studies because they only look at prosecutions that went forward and do not examine cases that were declined for prosecution for various reasons.[232]

The American criminal trial has been able to adapt to the terrorism context. For example, in one case, video technology allowed evidence to be taken from Saudi security officials, who were subject to cross-examination.[233] In another case, Mossad agents were allowed to testify in disguise.[234] The Classified Information Procedures Act has worked reasonably well, despite not being significantly amended since 9/11. This statute is designed to provide a framework for deciding whether classified information has to be disclosed to the accused. It allows the government considerable room for proposing nonclassified substitutes for secret information. At the same, the American criminal trial process does not accept secret evidence, and the Sixth Amendment's confrontation clause admits of few exceptions to the rule against hearsay

---

[228] Center on Law and Security, *NYU School of Law Terrorist Trial Report Card*, at http://www.lawandsecurity.org/publications/TTRCFinalJan142.pdf.

[229] Richard Zabel and James Benjamin, *In Pursuit of Justice: Prosecuting Terrorism Cases in the Federal Courts* (New York: Human Rights First, 2009), at 9; http://www.humanrightsfirst.org/pdf/090723-LS-in-pursuit-justice-09-update.pdf.

[230] They may also reflect the Al Capone strategy of charging suspected terrorists with minor crimes. Robert Chesney, "Federal Prosecution of Terrorism Cases" (2007) 11 Lewis and Clark Law Review 851.

[231] Christopher Shields, Kelly Damphousse, and Brent Smith, "How 9.11 Changed Terrorism Prosecutions," in *The Impact of 9/11 and the New Legal Landscape*, ed. Matthew Morgan (New York: Palgrave, 2009), at 135.

[232] Robert Litt and Wells Bennett, "Better Rules for Terrorism Trials," in Wittes, *Legislating the War on Terror*, at 147.

[233] Stephen Vladeck, "Terrorism Trials and the Article III Courts after *Abu Ali*" (2010) 88 Texas Law Review 1501.

[234] *US v. Abu Marzook*, 412 F. Supp. 913 (2006).

evidence.[235] Perceptions, if not realities, of the difficulties of terrorism prose-cutions derived from fears about disclosure, *Miranda* and other due process restraints, light sentences, and acquittals have eroded confidence in the use of criminal prosecutions as a means to respond to terrorism. This is another example of how America's celebrated legalism in the form of its criminal trial system has encouraged resort to less restrained measures such as military detention without trial and trial by military commission.

ix. TORTURE

The attempt to legitimate torture of suspected terrorists is perhaps the most pernicious of all the 9/11 effects. Torture was always going to be an issue after 9/11, if only because of the dilemma of what Western democracies should do with noncitizens of countries like Egypt and Syria, who would likely be tortured if returned under suspicions of involvement with terrorism. Allegations of complicity of torture have and are being investigated in both the United Kingdom and Canada, but the American use of torture has been a particular focus of critical attention. Societal norms against torture were questioned through the American television show *24*, which was particularly popular among the American military.[236] Even after the 2002 torture memos that purported to define torture out of existence had been repudiated by both the executive in 2004 and Congress in 2005, torture continued at CIA black sites and through extraordinary renditions.

The Bush administration issued an executive order in February 2002 that decided that it would not apply the Geneva Conventions to detainees at Guantánamo, despite strong objections from Colin Powell that this would make allies more reluctant to cooperate with U.S. efforts. Alberto Gonzales stressed that the "new kind of war" being directed at terrorism "renders obsolete Geneva's strict limitations on the questioning of enemy prisoners" and that not applying Geneva would allow the United States to obtain information from detainees to prevent terrorist attacks and would minimize the chance that American officials would subsequently be charged with war crimes.[237]

---

[235] Chesney, "Optimizing Criminal Prosecutions," at 126.
[236] Jutta Brunee and Stephen Toope, *Legitimacy and Legality in International Law* (New York: Cambridge University Press, 2010), at 233.
[237] Gonzales to President, January 25, 2002, in Karen Greenberg and Joshua Dratel, *The Torture Papers* (New York: Cambridge University Press, 2005), at 119. There was some precedent for these actions, as the Reagan administration had not ratified Protocol 1 amendments to the Geneva Conventions on the basis that terrorists who targeted civilians should not enjoy the benefits of laws designed to protect soldiers. Goldsmith, *Terror Presidency*, at 111–13.

The Torture Memos

On March 13, 2002, Assistant Attorney General Jay Bybee, in the Office of Legal Counsel, issued a memo saying that captives could be transferred to third countries in part because the U.S. obligations under the Convention against Torture would not be applied outside the United States.[238] This allowed torture by proxy, something that may still be occurring. As will be seen, however, there was much more controversy when American officials became involved in torture, and much of it was related to concerns that American officials might be prosecuted for their actions.

On August 1, 2002, the most infamous torture memo, authored by John Yoo but signed by Bybee, was issued, concluding that the prohibitions on torture only prohibit the infliction of physical pain of the same intensity as "death or organ failure" or severe mental pain that causes "lasting psychological harm."[239] Even if torture so restrictively defined was committed, the memo concluded that necessity and self-defense could be used and that the torture statute "would be unconstitutional if it impermissibly encroached on the President's constitutional power to conduct a military campaign. As Commander-in-Chief, the President has the constitutional authority to order interrogations of enemy combatants to gain intelligence information concerning the military plans of the enemy."[240] Another memo written the same day, but not released until the Obama administration assumed power, held that waterboarding of Abu Zubayda would be legal because that waterboarding "does not, in our view, inflict 'pain or suffering.'"[241] The memo went on to say that while waterboarding constituted a threat of imminent death, it would not cause prolonged mental suffering and would not constitute torture.[242] Although written by lawyers who are now are a senior judge and a senior law professor respectively, these memos are an example of extra-legalism-dubious and flimsy legal arguments made to support illegal activities.

The extra-legalism of the torture memos served the purpose of helping to keep torturors out of jail. As Jack Goldsmith, who rescinded the torture memo in June 2004, explained, "The message of the August 1, 2002 OLC opinion was indeed clear: violent acts aren't necessarily torture; if you do

---

[238] Bybee to William Haynes, General Counsel, Department of Defense, March 13, 2002, at http://www.fas.org/irp/agency/doj/olc/transfer.pdf.

[239] Bybee to Alberto Gonzales, August 1, 2002, in Greenberg and Dratel, *Torture Papers*, at 214.

[240] Ibid., at 200.

[241] Jay Bybee to John Rizzo, Acting General Counsel for the CIA, August 1, 2002, at http://www.fas .org/irp/agency/doj/olc/zubaydah.pdf, at 11.

[242] Ibid., at 18.

torture, you probably have a defense; and even if you don't have a defense, the torture law doesn't apply if you act under color of presidential authority. CIA interrogators and their supervisors, under pressure to get information about the next attack, viewed the opinion as a 'golden shield,' as one CIA official later called it, that provided enormous comfort."[243] In a demonstration of the power of lengthy legal opinions written by the prestigious Office of Legal Counsel to legalize what should always be illegal, Abu Zubayda was waterboarded 80 times before the end of August 2002.[244] The torture memos distinguished American torture from Egyptian or Syrian torture because torture was justified through the convoluted mental gymnastics of extra-legalism-dubious claims of legality in an attempt to justify illegal and brutal acts.

Repudiation of Torture?

The enactment of the Detainee Treatment Act in 2005 can be seen as leg-islative repudiation of the torture memos produced by the executive and of the embarrassing excesses of Abu Ghraib where Iraqi detainees were tor-tured and humiliated. Section 1003 clearly provided that "no individual in the custody or under the physical control of the United States Government, regardless of nationality or physical location, shall be subject to cruel, inhu-man, or degrading treatment or punishment." This seemed to end argu-ments made within the Office of Legal Counsel that America's obligation not to torture could be evaded offshore. At the same time, the law was not exactly a ringing endorsement of international law obligations against tor-ture because it specified that cruel, inhuman, or degrading treatment would not be defined by international law but rather by the U.S. Constitution. As Mark Osiel has suggested, the approach is based more on military notions of honor and reciprocity, as personified by Senator John McCain, an advocate of the torture prohibition who had been tortured when detained as a prisoner of war in Vietnam, than on an adherence to an international human rights paradigm.[245]

Although Congress felt compelled to intervene, the law also delegated sig-nificant parts of interrogation policy back to the executive by providing that the Department of Defense would be bound by the U.S. *Army Field Manual*

[243] Goldsmith, *Terror Presidency*, at 144.
[244] Brunee and Toope, *Legitimacy and Legality*, at 239.
[245] Mark Osiel, *The End of Reciprocity: Terror, Torture and the Law of War* (New York: Cambridge University Press, 2009).

on Interrogation.[246] The 2005 act did not, however, subject the CIA to military standards of interrogation. It also tried to preserve at least some of the insulating get out of jail free effects of the torture memos by making "good faith reliance on advice of counsel . . . an important factor" when determining whether any official or agent charged or sued would have a defense.[247] This represented a partial ratification of past actions authorized under the torture memos. The threat of criminal punishment for torture may have motivated the negative reaction within the government to the withdrawal of the torture memos, but except for some low level military people at Abu Ghraib such threats have turned out to be largely illusory, thus negating some of the restraining effect that is suggested to accompany extralegal approaches.[248]

Behind the scenes of the Detainee Treatment Act and the withdrawal of the 2002 torture memos, the CIA continued to hold and torture people. In May 2005, Steven Bradbury of the Office of Legal Counsel issued a series of memos to the general counsel of the CIA condoning the use of waterboarding of CIA detainees.[249] In 2007, a presidential order permitted the CIA to hold detainees in secret sites and to subject them to coercive interrogation tactics.[250]

President Obama issued an executive order within his first 48 hours in office that shut down CIA prisons and bound the CIA by the *U.S. Army Field Manual on Interrogation*, something that President Bush refused to do. The Obama approach, however, was consistent with the executive domination of American counter-terrorism because it was achieved through executive orders and not legislative change. Moreover, the executive order allowed the attorney general to provide further guidance, including perhaps exemptions for the CIA from the *Army Manual*.[251]

---

[246] In 2006, the manual was amended to prohibit not only waterboarding, forced nakedness, and deprivation of food but also all coercion and threats. Stuart Taylor and Benjamin Wittes, "Refining US Interrogation Law," in Wittes, *Legislating the War on Terror*, at 306, 341.

[247] Detainee Treatment Act, Public Law 109-148, Section 1004.

[248] Gross, "Chaos and Rules."

[249] Bradbury to Rizzo, May 10, 2005, at http://www.fas.org/irp/agency/doj/olc/techniques.pdf, at 43. A second memo also concluded that waterboarding combined with other techniques, such as sleep deprivation, would not constitute torture. Another memo issued later that month concluded that the techniques did not violate the United States' obligations under the Convention against Torture.

[250] Executive Order 13340, 72 Fed. Reg. 40,707 (July 20, 2007) (interpreting Common Article 3 and the MCA to permit coercive interrogation so long as the purpose is to gain intelligence and not humiliate or degrade the detainee); see Taylor and Wittes, "Refining U.S. Interrogation Law."

[251] Ibid., at 309, 337.

Although the American executive and legislature both repudiated torture, there has not been individual accountability for the extralegal use of torture. Unlike in Canada or the United Kingdom, no inquiries have been appointed to examine complicity in torture.[252] Such inquiries would tend to stress organizational and societal accountability and would not have the power to impose civil or criminal sanctions on individuals. Much of the American discussion on accountability has focused on these latter forms of accountability. At the same time as he closed CIA prisons and released more torture memos, President Obama stressed that "it is our intention to assure those who carried out their duties relying in good faith upon legal advice from the Department of Justice that they will not be subject to prosecution. The men and women of our intelligence community serve courageously on the front lines of a dangerous world. Their accomplishments are unsung and their names unknown, but because of their sacrifices, every single American is safer. . . . This is a time for reflection, not retribution."[253] Some investigations were conducted, but it was announced in 2010 that the CIA official who took responsibility for the destruction of tapes of the interrogations of the high-value detainees would not be prosecuted for his actions.[254]

The lawyers have also escaped official sanction. The Department of Justice, in 2010, overruled findings of misconduct by its Office of Professional Responsibility and decided not to refer Jay Bybee, now a senior judge, or John Yoo, now a law professor to professional discipline on the basis that they did not knowingly, recklessly, or in bad faith provide misleading legal advice.[255] American investigations focused on whether officials were guilty of misconduct but found that criminal or disciplinary proceedings were not appropriate. In contrast, the British and Canadian inquiries into complicity with torture focus more on systemic responsibility and responses. Although they have been exposed, withdrawn, and denounced, the torture memos have been successful as a get out of jail free card for those who authorized and conducted torture. They stand as perhaps the prime example of extra-legalism: the deployment of legal arguments to justify extralegal conduct. Although the torture memos were exposed, withdrawn and repudiated, they did serve their purpose of

---

[252] For calls for such inquiries, see David Cole, "The Sacrificial Yoo: Accounting for Torture in the OPR Report" (2010) 4 Journal of National Security Law and Policy 455.

[253] "Statement of President Obama on Release of OLC Memos," April 16, 2009, at http://www.whitehouse.gov/the_press_office/Statement-of-President-Barack-Obama-on-Release-of-OLC-Memos.

[254] "No Charges in Destruction of CIA Tapes," New York Times, November 9, 2010.

[255] David Margolis, "Memorandum of Decision," January 5, 2010, at http://judiciary.house.gov/hearings/pdf/DAGMargolisMemo100105.pdf.

preventing individuals from being held to account for authorizing and conducting torture.

x. EXTRALEGAL CONDUCT AND OBSTACLES TO ACCOUNTABILITY

The Use of State Secrets to Shut Down Civil Litigation

One possible restraint on extralegal conduct is the threat of civil litigation. The United States is an especially litigious country, in part because of the high number of lawyers prepared to take cases on a pro bono or contingency basis and the general absence of cost-shifting rules that would require unsuccessful plaintiffs to pay the government's costs of litigation. Despite the relative accessibility of the American civil litigation system and numerous attempts to litigate issues arising out of extraordinary renditions and other extralegal actions, such litigation has been frequently shut down by successful invocations of the state-secrets doctrine. The state-secrets doctrine is founded on the 1876 decision in *Totten v. United States*,[256] involving a Civil War spy, allowing litigation to be judicially terminated, if necessary, to protect confidential information and on a 1953 decision in *United States v. Reynolds*[257] in which the Supreme Court warned that even the most compelling interests could not overcome the privilege if state "secrets are at stake."[258] These are more categorical and absolute rules compared to general balancing-of-interests tests used in other democracies.[259]

Khalid el-Masri's attempts to sue the CIA and private companies that assisted in his extraordinary rendition to Afghanistan, where he was tortured, were dismissed after the government invoked the state-secrets privilege and the lower courts agreed that privileged national security information would be central to the litigation. The courts took a very deferential approach and stressed that the state-secrets doctrine was supported by separation-of-powers concerns that suggested that the courts had a limited role in checking the executive's conduct in national security matters. The state-secrets doctrine applied even to details of the extraordinary rendition program that had become public.[260] Maher Arar's lawsuit with respect to his rendition from the United States and his subsequent torture in Syria was also dismissed on the basis of the state-secrets doctrine. The court held that separation of powers meant that Arar

---

[256] 92 U.S. 105 (1876).   [257] 345 U.S. 1 (1953).
[258] Ibid., at 11.   [259] *Conway v. Rimmer*, A.C. 910 (1968).
[260] *El-Masri v. United States*, 479 F.3d 296 (4th Cir., 2007).

could only claim damages if Congress specifically created a right of action in the extraordinary rendition context.[261] The Supreme Court refused to consider either case. Litigation arising from the NSA program has also been shut down on state-secrets grounds.[262]

The American state-secrets doctrine again demonstrates the curious relation between legalism and condonation of extralegal conduct that has been described in this work as extra-legalism. The American legal system has a strong form of constitutional review that has inspired many other nations, but constitutional review in the United States is restrained by doctrines that limit standing, avoid judicial review of political questions and allow litigation to be terminated on the basis of state secrets. All of these restrictive and distinctive American legal doctrines have been employed to protect illegal counter-terrorism activities since 9/11 that has been challenged with greater success in other democracies. Binyam Mohammed, for example, had his American lawsuit claiming torture stemming out of an extraordinary rendition dismissed on state-secrets grounds, even to the extent that it relied on information about the American extraordinary rendition program already in the public domain.[263] In contrast, his British lawsuit proceeded, even in the face of U.S. threats to cut off intelligence sharing with the United Kingdom if sensitive information was disclosed in the litigation. The British High Court was not influenced by these threats, stating that "we did not consider that a democracy governed by the rule of law would expect a court in another democracy to suppress a summary of the evidence . . . where the evidence was relevant to allegations of torture, cruel, inhuman or degrading treatment, politically embarrassing though it might be."[264] The Court of Appeal affirmed this approach and even expressed some skepticism about claims of secrecy made by the intelligence agencies.[265] To be sure, the U.K. government's subsequent settlement of this and other cases involving Guantánamo detentions was likely designed to prevent disclosure of additional information, but the different approaches of the American and British courts to state secrecy claims are striking and underline the difficulty of achieving accountability for extralegal and secret conduct by the American executive.[266]

---

[261] *Arar v. Ashcroft*, 585 F.3d 559 (2d Cir., 2009) (en banc).

[262] *A.C.L.U. v. N.S.A.* 493 F.3d, at 659–87; 507 F.3d 1190, 1205 (9th Cir., 2007).

[263] *Mohamed v. Jeppesen Dataplan*, No. 08-15693, 2010 WL 3489913 (9th Cir., 2010) (en banc).

[264] *Mohamed v. Secretary of State*, EWHC 152 (2009), at para. 69.

[265] *Mohamed v. Secretary of State*, EWCA 65 (2010), at para. 168. But see *Mohamed v. Secretary of State*, EWCA 158 (2010) for some changes that were made to para. 168 of the original judgment.

[266] Sudha Setty, "Litigating Secrets: Comparative Perspectives on State Secrets Privilege" (2009) 75 Brooklyn Law Review 201.

Congressional Oversight

The courts are not the only or, indeed, the main vehicle for review of the state's often secret national security activities. There is significant congressional oversight, but the fact that several legislators were briefed in on the problematic warrantless spying by the NSA long before it was exposed by *The New York Times* raises troubling issues. Legislators need access to secret information to conduct oversight, but they may be bound by government claims of secrecy. As will be discussed in Chapter 8, they need some way to challenge the government's secrecy claims.

The Patriot Act,[267] to its credit, recognized the need for review to increase with national security activities, and it gave the inspector general of the Department of Justice a specific mandate to hear complaints related to civil liberties. Subsequent laws also added Inspectors General to new departments such as the Department of Homeland Security and the Director of National Intelligence. One problem, however, is that inspectors general are attached to particular agencies at a time when government is promoting close cooperation between agencies in preventing terrorism.[268]

Another problem is that subsequent legislation has tended to hive out the civil liberties function by creating specific civil liberties officers for both the Department of Homeland Security[269] and the director of national intelligence.[270] The separation of civil liberties from efficacy review has risks if the body responsible for civil liberties does not have the same powers, prestige, and independence as the inspectors general or congressional committees. As Professors Heymann and Kayyem have argued, effective review of enhanced counter-terrorism activities should consider both the efficacy and the propriety of the activities being reviewed.[271] Reviewers should also be alive to the possibility that some measures may both harm human rights and be ineffective, or even counter-productive, in preventing terrorism.

Continued Extraordinary Renditions under Obama

A task force within the Department of Justice under President Obama examined extraordinary renditions, somewhat euphemistically called "transfers."

---

[267] H.R. S.1001.

[268] Philip Heymann and Julliette Kayyem, *Protecting Liberty in an Age of Terror* (Cambridge: MA: MIT Press, 2005), at 114–17.

[269] 6 U.S.C. Section 345 (2002).   [270] 50 U.S.C. Section 403-3d.

[271] Heymann and Kayyem, *Protecting Liberty in an Age of Terror*, at 110. In light of recent failures of review, I have rethought my earlier criticism of their advocacy of a combined focus on propriety and efficacy; Roach, "Review and Oversight of National Security Activities" (2007) 29 Cardozo Law Review 53.

The report has not been made public, but a press release indicates that "the Task Force made classified recommendations that are designed to ensure that, should the Intelligence Community participate in or otherwise support a transfer, any affected individuals are subjected to proper treatment."[272] The wording of this provision stops short of a prohibition on extraordinary rendition. Indeed, there is a danger that one adjustment to the closing of the CIA detention sites may be increased use of extraordinary renditions. One unnamed official was reported in 2009 to have said that extraordinary renditions were still being used under an executive order issued by President Obama, explaining, "Obviously you need to preserve some tools – you still have to go after the bad guys. The legal advisors working on this looked at rendition. It is controversial in some circles and kicked up a big storm in Europe. But if done within certain parameters, it is an acceptable practice."[273] Others drew distinctions between extraordinary renditions to torture for intelligence gathering under the Bush administration and the Obama administration's program of rendition which was said to be more consistent with Reagan and Clinton policies of rendering people to justice systems. [274] The exact nature of renditions under President Obama remains unclear.

Some of the legal advice that may have been provided to the Obama administration may be reflected in a recent and disturbing article published by an assistant general counsel for the CIA. The article concluded that "there are virtually no legal restrictions" on renditions and that "there does not appear to be a single case in which a U.S. court has deemed a rendition operation illegal."[275] The article features a narrow reading that precludes extraterritorial application of the Convention against Torture, including its prohibitions on refoulement to torture, combined with a judgment that individuals could neither be prosecuted nor sued civilly given the state-secrets precedents discussed earlier. It also stresses that the 2005 Detainee Treatment Act, including the famous McCain amendment prohibiting torture and cruel, inhuman, or degrading treatment, contains no enforcement clause. It concludes that international law does not prohibit renditions mainly on the basis of an absence of a specific prohibition of the practice and the U.S. Supreme Court's conclusion that a kidnapping of a fugitive in Mexico for return to trial in the United

[272] U.S. Department of Justice, Special Task Force on Interrogations and Transfers, August 24, 2009, at http://www.justice.gov/opa/pr/2009/August/09-ag-835.html.

[273] "Obama Preserves Renditions as Counter-Terrorism Tool," *The Los Angeles Times*, February 1, 2009. See also "US Says Rendition to Continue but with More Oversight," *The New York Times*, August 24, 2009.

[274] Scott Horton "Renditions Buffoonery" *Harpers* February 2, 2009

[275] Daniel L. Pines, "Rendition Operations: Does US Law Impose Any Restrictions?" (2011) 42 Loyola University Chicago Law Journal 523, at 533.

States violates "no norm of customary international law."[276] Like the torture memos, the article is an example of extra-legalism. It illustrates how a legalistic parsing of statutes can be used to place a superficial and ultimately unpersuasive veneer of legality on violent and illegal conduct. It also demonstrates the disturbing use in the United States of legalism to achieve extralegal and brutal ends.

XI. SPEECH ASSOCIATED WITH TERRORISM

The United States did not enact legislation responding to the Security Council's call in Resolution 1624 to ensure that incitement of terrorism was treated as a serious criminal offense. In its report to the CTC, the United States stressed its distinctive free speech tradition, noting that it had entered a reservation to the International Convention on Civil and Political Rights that none of the limits on free speech contemplated in that document would authorize or require the United States to enact laws prohibited by the First Amendment. The report stressed that the First Amendment, as interpreted in *Brandenburg v. Ohio*,[277] did not allow the criminalization of advocacy of force or lawless action unless that speech was likely to incite or produce imminent unlawful actions. As a result of these restrictions, "the majority of terrorist propaganda" cannot be prosecuted under U.S. criminal law because it lacks "the potential to produce imminent lawless action required under the *Brandenburg* exception."[278] American exceptionalism, in this case with respect to free speech, provided the United States with another reason to depart from an international mandate.

Although it is widely accepted that offenses against direct and indirect advocacy of terrorism of the type prohibited in the United Kingdom following Resolution 1624 would be unconstitutional under the First Amendment,[279] this does not mean that all speech in the United States is immune from prosecution. Ali Al Timimi was convicted of federal crimes of seditious conspiracy and inciting others to wage war against the United States for urging people at a secret meeting to fight against U.S. troops in Afghanistan and providing them with travel instructions. He was sentenced to life imprisonment in what strangely remains an unreported decision that is not available from the

---

[276] *Sosa v. Alvarez-Machain*, 542 U.S. 692, 738 (2005).

[277] 395 U.S. 444 (1969).

[278] U.S. Country Report, S/2006/397. See also Posner, *Not a Suicide Pact*, at 121 for similar conclusions.

[279] Michael Shaughnessy, "Praising the Enemy: Could the United States Criminalize the Glorification of Terror?" (2009) 113 Pennsylvania State Law Review 923.

court.[280] Before 9/11, Omar Abdel Rahman, the infamous blind sheik of New Jersey, was convicted of seditious conspiracy, with the courts rejecting his First Amendment challenge on the basis that he was punished for participating in an agreement to use force against the U.S. government and not for his speech.[281]

Some have questioned both the durability and wisdom of the United States' strong First Amendment tradition given increased concerns about radicalization and homegrown terrorism. Eric Posner and Adrian Vermeule have predicted that "if the United States ever develops problems similar to those in Britain, where radical Muslim preachers urge their followers to engage in terrorism with apparent success, we are likely to see efforts by the government to censor such preaching and other forms of advocacy."[282] They conclude that American judges could draw on pre-*Brandenburg* precedents that allowed more restrictions on political speech and assert that "the consequences of taking *Brandenburg* seriously during an emergency would be intolerable."[283] Professors Posner and Vermeule are correct to point out that pre-*Brandenburg* precedents would allow more speech regulation, but the fact remains that the United States has not seriously debated enacting criminal offenses that would apply to speech associated with terrorism.[284] This raises issues of how the United States would respond to a wave of homegrown terrorism such as that experienced by the United Kingdom in the 1970s with the Irish Republican Army (IRA). The restrictions on speech regulation, combined with the lack of a domestic intelligence agency and extensive domestic protections of privacy, suggest that the United States may not be legally well prepared to deal with dramatic increases in homegrown terrorism.

Congressional hearings into the radicalization of Muslims and the response of the Muslim community to radicalization were divisive with critics accusing

---

[280] S. Chehani Ekaratne, "Redundant Restriction: The UK's Glorification of Terrorism Offence" (2010) 23 Harvard Journal of Human Rights 205, at 220–1. For arguments that the case disregards *Brandenburg*'s imminence requirement, see Elisa Kantor, "New Threats, Old Problems: Adhering to Brandenburg's Imminence Requirement in Terrorism Prosecutions" (2008) 76 George Washington Law Review 752. For a contrary view that stresses the need to adapt the imminence requirement to the new War on Terror, see Robert Tanenbaum, "Preaching Terror: Free Speech or Wartime Incitement" (2005) 55 American University Law Review 785.

[281] *United States v. Rahman*, 189 F.3d 88, at 114 (2d Cir., 1999).

[282] Eric Posner and Adrian Vermeule, *Terror in the Balance* (Oxford: Oxford University Press, 2007), at 231–2.

[283] Ibid., at 234.

[284] Speech regulation is, however, accepted in American immigration law, and the U.S. Country Report on Resolution 1624 stressed actions that would make aliens inadmissible because they "endorse or espouse terrorist activity or persuade others to endorse or espouse terrorist activity." U.S. Country Report, S/2006/397, at 10.

the Chair of the committee, New York Congressman David King, of hypocrisy given his past sympathy for the IRA and of McCarthyism. Supporters of the hearings claimed that American Muslims were not doing enough to respond to radicalization within their communities, despite some evidence that Muslims had played a role in many successful prosecutions.[285] With extremist speech regulation apparently prohibited by the First Amendment and Congressional hearings being divisive, the United States remains ill equipped to respond to radicalization that may inspire home grown terrorism.

The American First Amendment tradition also helps to explain the important role of the press in revealing the torture memos; misdeeds in Guantánamo, Abu Ghraib, and CIA black sites; warrantless spying by the NSA; and the extraordinary rendition program. In the United Kingdom, in contrast, the legal advice provided with respect to possible complicity in torture remains a secret, and the forthcoming inquiry into the issue may face even stricter restrictions on what can be made public than the Canadian inquiries on similar subjects. As Richard Posner has noted, the United States is unique in having "no statute that punishes journalists or media for publishing illegally leaked classified material."[286] The ability of the free American press to reveal extralegal conduct can facilitate accountability by at least making people aware of the conduct. At the same time, however, it may also breed cynicism about the law, especially when officials are not prosecuted, disciplined, or successfully sued for the illegal activities and when they remain unrepentant about their conduct.

xii. TARGETED KILLINGS

The use of targeted killings has a long history in the United States.[287] The 9/11 Commission detailed how the United States considered the targeted killing of bin Laden before 9/11 but ultimately concluded that the danger of collateral damage was too high. Targeted killings were used after 9/11 as high-level al Qaeda leaders were killed in Yemen and Pakistan and one failed 2006 attempt to kill al-Zawahiri in Pakistan resulted in 18 other deaths and a diplomatic protest from Pakistan.[288] A missile fired from a drone killed a senior al Qaeda leader and five low-level operatives traveling by car in a remote part of the

---

[285] "Domestic terrorism hearings open with contrasting views on dangers" *The New York Times* March 10, 2011.

[286] Posner, *Not a Suicide Pact*, at 108.

[287] William C. Banks and Peter Raven-Hansen, "Targeted Killing and Assassination: The U.S. Legal Framework" (2003) 37 University of Richmond Law Review 667.

[288] Nils Melzer, *Target Killing in International Law* (Oxford: Oxford University Press, 2008), at 41–2.

Yemeni desert in November 2002. Justice Thomas cited this example in his dissent in *Hamdi*[289] and expressed fears that the Court's decision to require due process to justify military detentions at Guantánamo might be applied to such actions. Despite these fears, the American legal system seems procedurally unable to allow any application of due process norms to targeted killings. Targeted killings remain in the type of legal black hole that Justice Thomas celebrated in his lonely dissent in *Hamdi*.[290]

A May 2010 report by Philip Alston suggested that there have been 120 drone strikes, with accounts of collateral damage to nontargeted civilians ranging from 20 to many hundreds.[291] Professor Alston expressed concerns about the frequent use of "faulty intelligence"[292] and the development of a "'Playstation' mentality to killing" when the drones are operated by those not in the field.[293] He warned that claims of anticipatory self-defense, such as the ticking-bomb exception to torture, were "rare" and "can effectively institutionalize that exception."[294] He called for greater transparency, while recognizing that states will continue to shield the intelligence that is said to lie behind the targeted killings. The result is that "states are operating in an accountability vacuum."[295] The accountability vacuum in the United States is much greater than in Israel.[296]

Targeted killings have increased in number under the Obama administration.[297] This confirms Jack Goldsmith's prediction in 2007 that a future Democratic administration might "be even more anxious" than the Bush administration "to thwart the threat."[298] Four days after President Obama assumed office, five missiles were fired from drones in Pakistan, killing a reported 20 people.[299] The most famous targeted killing was the May 2011 killing of Osama bin Laden in Abbottabad by a team of U.S. Navy Seals.

---

[289] 542 U.S. 507 (2004).

[290] But for an attempt to apply due process standards to targeted killing that draws on the Israeli decision, see Richard Murphy and Afsheen John Radsan, "Due Process and Targeted Killing of Terrorists" (2009) 31 Cardozo Law Review 405.

[291] "Report of the Special Rapporteur on Extrajudicial, Summary or Arbitrary Executions," A/HRC/14/24/Add.6, May 28, 2010, at para. 19.

[292] Ibid., at para. 83.

[293] This latter allegation may be unfair given that technology allows those not in the field to see their targets with precision. Alan Dershowitz *Preemption* (New York: Norton, 2006) at 126-128 describing Israeli targeting practices.

[294] "Report of the Special Rapporteur on Extrajudicial, Summary or Arbitrary Executions," at paras. 94, 86.

[295] Ibid., at para. 92.   [296] See Chapter 3.

[297] Kenneth Anderson, "Targeted Killing in US Counterterrorism Strategy and Law," in Wittes, *Legislating the War on Terror*, at 346–7.

[298] Goldsmith, *Terror Presidency*, at 189–90.

[299] "2 US Airstrikes Offer a Concrete Sign of Obama's Pakistan Strategy," Washington Post, January 24, 2010.

President Obama defended the killing as an act of justice and there was much global celebration of bin Laden's death. Some commentators, however, raised questions about the legality of the killing, especially after it was learned that bin Laden was not armed when he was shot in the face and the chest. Pakistan also raised some concerns about the American operation, but they were muted in comparison to those it raised about earlier U.S. targeted killings in that country. As will be seen, the Obama administration would likely defend the killing as a proportionate act of self-defense authorized by the AUMF against an enemy that had not surrendered regardless of whether the killing in a city close to Pakistan's capital was committed during an armed conflict. It would also reject arguments that the killing violated domestic American bans on assassinations or Pakistan's sovereignty. Attorney General Eric Holder defended the killing as an "act of national self-defense" in vague terms that did not respond to growing international concerns about the legality of the killing.[300]

In a March 2010 speech, Harold Koh, the legal advisor to the State Department and a widely respected international law scholar, assured an audience of international lawyers that "US targeting practices, including lethal operations conducted with the use of unmanned aerial vehicles, comply with all applicable law, including the laws of war." He cited the 2001 AUMF as a justification under domestic law for targeted killings and stated that targeted killings do not infringe the domestic ban on assassinations because the United States was acting either in an armed conflict or in self-defense. This recognized that targeted killing will not be limited to situations of armed conflict. He appealed to "the inherent right to self-defense under international law," stressing that "al-Qaeda has not abandoned its intent to attack the United States, and indeed continues to attack us. Thus, in this ongoing armed conflict, the United States has the authority under international law, and the responsibility to its citizens, to use force, including lethal force, to defend itself, including by targeting persons such as high-level al-Qaeda leaders who are planning attacks."[301]

Koh stressed that careful decisions were made in each case and included consideration of "the imminence of the threat, the sovereignty of the other states involved, and the willingness and ability of those states to suppress the threat the target poses." He stressed that "civilians or civilian objects shall not be the object of the attack" suggesting that terrorists may, contrary to the

[300] Thomas Darnstadt, "Was bin Laden's killing legal?" Der Spiegel, May 3, 2011; "US responds to questions about killing's legality," The Guardian, May 3, 2011; "bin Laden killing prompts US-Pakistan War of Words," The Guardian, May 4, 2011; "bin Laden's killing in Pakistan lawful says US," BBC News, May 4, 2011.

[301] Harold Koh, "The Obama Administration and International Law," March 25, 2010, at http://www.state.gov/s/l/releases/remarks/139119.htm.

Israeli law examined in the last chapter, not be considered to be civilians. Koh stressed that American officials respected the "principle of *proportionality*, which prohibits attacks that may be expected to cause incidental loss of civilian life, injury to civilians, damage to civilian objects, or a combination thereof, that would be excessive in relation to the concrete and direct military advantage anticipated."[302] This appeal to proportionality draws from the Israeli court decision on targeted killing discussed in the preceding chapter, but without its requirements for judicial review and formalized ex ante and ex post reviews. Proportionality is a difficult concept to apply in the targeted killing context, especially when it asks the decision maker to balance domestic security and military advantages against foreign collateral damage. Unlike in Israel, American judgments about whether attacks would be proportional will only be reviewed by the executive and perhaps Congressional committees. The executive and the legislature, more than the judiciary, will have incentive to favor the benefits of domestic military and security advantages over the costs of foreign collateral damage.

The Obama Administration's resistance to attempts to judicially review its targeted killing practices was signaled by Koh's arguments that a "state that is engaged in an armed conflict or in legitimate self-defense is not required to provide targets with legal process before the state may use lethal force."[303] Koh's statement that the United States does not have to provide al Qaeda "with legal process" sounds quite similar to President's Bush famous arguments that it was not necessary to serve "legal papers" on al Qaeda.[304] The Obama administration successfully defended a lawsuit seeking to enjoin the targeting killing of U.S. citizen Anwar al-Aulaqi, who is believed to be hiding in Yemen and who communicated with Nidal Malik Hasan, the U.S. army major, shortly before he killed 13 people in the November 2009 shootings at Fort Hood. Without confirming or denying that there was a reported CIA kill list, the government argued that any decision to engage in targeted killing was a nonjusticiable political question precluded by state-secrets doctrine. The American Civil Liberties Union, which initiated the lawsuit, responded by arguing that "the idea that courts should have no role whatsoever in determining the criteria by which the executive branch can kill its own citizens is

---

[302] Ibid.

[303] Ibid. No mention in Professor Koh's speech was made of American constitutional restrictions on the use of lethal force. See *Tennessee v. Garner*, 471 U.S. 1 (1985).

[304] President Bush stated, "I know that some people question if America is really at war at all. They view terrorism more as a crime, a problem to be solved mainly with law enforcement and indictments. . . . After the chaos and carnage of September 11, it is not enough to serve our enemies with legal papers." State of the Union Address, January 20, 2004.

unacceptable in a democracy. . . . In matters of life and death, no executive should have a blank check."[305]

A federal district court dismissed the lawsuit, holding that al-Aulaqi's father lacked standing because his son could seek relief from Yemen but had shown no interest in the lawsuit. The court also suggested that the case raised questions relating to al-Aulaqi's connections with al Qaeda, alternatives to the use of lethal force, and risks to U.S. interests that are typically not decided by the courts under the political-questions doctrine. Without reference to the Israeli case, the court concluded that there were no judicially manageable standards that could be applied to interpretation of military intelligence or a decision whether and how to act on that intelligence. The court also hinted that litigation of the case would be barred by state-secrets doctrine, though it was not necessary to decide the case on such a basis.[306] This case confirms that targeted killings by the United States will remain resistant to judicial review and demonstrates extra-legalism in the sense that the government succeeded in using legal arguments to ensure that targeted killings were protected from merits-based legal challenge.

xiii. NATIONAL SECURITY POLICIES

In 2002, the Bush administration announced a national security policy that focused on the prevention of terrorist attacks. It stressed a war against terrorism by stating that "the enemy is not a single political regime or person or religion or ideology. The enemy is terrorism – premeditated, politically motivated violence perpetrated against innocents. In many regions, legitimate grievances prevent the emergence of a lasting peace. Such grievances deserve to be, and must be, addressed within a political process. But no cause justifies terror."[307] Terrorists were defined as a new-style enemy to be defeated, with an emphasis on military responses. At the same time, the United States accepted the need to use other measures, including criminal prosecutions, "vigorous efforts to cut off terrorist financing," and intelligence, even during the height of the global War on Terror.

The 2002 strategy was focused on terrorism, despite its references to the need to spread free democracies and free markets. It defined the possibility of terrorists acquiring weapons of mass destruction as "the gravest danger our nation

---

[305] "Obama Invokes 'State Secrets' Claim to Dismiss Suit against Targeting of US Citizen al-Aulaqi," Washington Post, September 25, 2010.

[306] *Al-Aulaqi v. Obama* 2010 U.S. Dist. Lexis 129601(U.S. Dist. Ct., D.C.), December 7, 2010, at https://ecf.dcd.uscourts.gov/cgi-bin/show_public_doc?2010cv1469–31.

[307] National Security Strategy of the United States (2002), at 5.

faces." It also stressed the need for preemptive force and to adapt the concept of imminent threat to terrorism in a way that had not yet been anticipated by "legal scholars and international jurists." The hostility to international law would become even more pronounced in a 2005 Pentagon document that grouped both terrorism and resort to the courts as a "strategy of the weak."[308] The 2002 strategy similarly proclaimed that the United States "will take the actions necessary to ensure that our efforts to meet our global security commitments and protect Americans are not impaired by the potential for investigations, inquiry, or prosecution by the International Criminal Court (ICC), whose jurisdiction does not extend to Americans and which we do not accept."[309]

A 2006 strategy demonstrated much the same focus, despite the intervening event of Hurricane Katrina, which took 1,836 lives and caused an estimated $81 billion in damage. It started with the familiar refrain that "America is at war. This is a wartime national security strategy required by the grave challenge we face – the rise of terrorism fueled by an aggressive ideology of hatred and murder, fully revealed to the American people on September 11, 2001." The only mention of Katrina came on page 47 of the document, where, in a discussion of the challenges of globalization, the strategy stated that the response to the hurricane "underscored the need for communications systems that remain operational and integrated during times of crisis."[310] As is seen in Chapter 7, Canada had articulated an all-risk national security policy in 2004 in part in response to a SARS crisis that caused 52 deaths in Toronto.

Philip Bobbitt has called for an all-risk approach to security, stressing that both natural catastrophes like Hurricane Katrina and terrorist attacks are inevitable. He argues that the legitimacy of the state will be challenged if it cannot effectively respond to a broad range of disasters and mitigate the damage they will cause.[311] He criticized the federal government for focusing on the demand side of terror, while delegating issues of vulnerability, preparedness, and recovery to the states and cities.[312] He recommended more federal involvement in disaster relief, including a federal quarantine statute and repeal of the 1878 Posse Comitatus Act to allow military assistance in a disaster.[313] Federal lawyers delayed assistance to New Orleans because of concerns about the Posse Comitatus Act, and some amendments were made in 2006, only to be repealed in 2008 because of concerns that they infringed the powers of the states and increased those of the

---

[308] As quoted in Bobbitt, *Terror and Consent*, at 503.
[309] National Security Strategy of the United States (2002), at 31.
[310] National Security Strategy of the United States of America (2006), at 47.
[311] Bobbitt, *Terror and Consent*, at 216–17.   [312] Ibid., at 236.
[313] Ibid., at 417–18. Others, however, stress that the act prohibits the military from assisting law enforcement and not with respect to either disaster relief or insurrections.

President.[314] This affirms the paradox of the unbridled military power of the American state abroad and the weakness of the American state at home.

Has U.S. national security policy changed under President Obama? The 2010 national security strategy has moved toward an all-risk security policy by stating that "at home, the United States is pursuing a strategy capable of meeting the full range of threats and hazards to our communities. These threats and hazards include terrorism, natural disasters, large-scale cyber attacks, and pandemics. As we do everything within our power to prevent these dangers, we also recognize that we will not be able to deter or prevent every single threat. That is why we must also enhance our resilience – the ability to adapt to changing conditions and prepare for, withstand, and rapidly recover from disruption."[315] This policy goal is more in line with current British and Canadian policies, though it is important in all cases to maintain a distinction between aspirational policy goals and their actual implementation. Spending on terrorism still dwarfs spending on other threats to human security such as climate change.[316]

The 2010 strategy also strikes a more conciliatory tone with respect to international law and institutions by stating that "we must focus American engagement on strengthening international institutions and galvanizing the collective action that can serve common interests such as combating violent extremism; stopping the spread of nuclear weapons and securing nuclear materials; achieving balanced and sustainable economic growth; and forging cooperative solutions to the threat of climate change, armed conflict, and pandemic disease."[317] The change in tone from presidents Bush to Obama is striking, but the Bush administration also made use of the UN in terms of the expansion of the 1267 sanctions against al Qaeda after 9/11 and Resolutions 1373 and 1540.[318] President Obama's policies on matters such as detention at Guantánamo, targeted killing, and extraordinary renditions are not as different from the policies of the Bush administration as the change in rhetoric might suggest.[319]

xiv. CONCLUSION

There is a danger of becoming lost in the sheer volume of what has happened in the United States since 9/11. Nevertheless, a few themes run through this

---

[314] Michael Greenberger, "Yes Virginia: The President Can Deploy Federal Troops to Prevent the Loss of a Major American City from a Devastating Natural Catastrophe" (2006) 26 Mississippi College Law Review 107; Jerad Sharum, "The Politics of Fear and the Outsourcing of Emergency Powers" (2010) 37 Lincoln Law Review 111.

[315] National Security Strategy (2010), at 17.

[316] Cass Sunstein, "On the Divergent American Reactions to Terrorism and Climate Change" (2007) 107 Columbia Law Review 503.

[317] National Security Strategy (2010), at 3. [318] See Chapter 2.

[319] Hafetz *Habeas Corpus after 9/11* ch 13.

chapter. The first is the relation between America's extensive legalism and its frequent resort to conduct that was extralegal or skirted very close to the edges of the law. The torture memos, for all their flaws, were not a naked assertion of lawless power; they were a highly legalistic and labored attempt to build a legal case for illegal activity. As Jack Goldsmith has suggested, the torture memos were a sign of an "excessively legalistic" War on Terror.[320] Extra-legalism uses legalistic and dubious claims of legality and/or lack of judicial jurisdiction to support illegal conduct. Although torture was repudiated by both the executive and Congress, there has been no individual or systemic accountability under either the Bush or Obama administration for the authorization or conduct of torture. The restraining effects attributed to the extralegal approach have failed: first by attempts to say that torture was legal and later by a failure to bring proceedings against those who authorized or conducted torture.

Another aspect of extra-legalism is a deep-seated ambivalence in the United States about law, especially international law, but also well-established laws such as *Miranda* rights. America's vast experience with law and lawyers has produced skepticism about legal processes. The Bush administration attempted in vain to create a law-free zone at Guantánamo, but even the Obama administration has been prepared to detain some suspected terrorists at Guantánamo indefinitely, without either a criminal or a military trial and with only the bare-bones AUMF as legislative authorization. In late 2010 Congress prohibited the transfer of KSM or other Guantánamo detainees to the United States for trial and the Obama administration reluctantly transferred their cases to be tried by military commission at Guantánamo. This episode underlines a loss of confidence in and patience with criminal prosecutions despite high conviction rates in American terrorism prosecutions and the life sentence received by Ghailani, the only Guantánamo detainee to stand trial in the United States. The use of military commissions not only results in less rights for the accused, but also risks giving those such as KSM a possible propaganda victory if they are seen as martyrs to an unfair process that goes beyond the laws of war and only applies to non-citizens.

The United States was impatient with civil litigation as well as criminal prosecutions. Sensing what might be unleashed, the courts have shut down civil litigation over various extralegal programs such as extraordinary rendition and warrantless spying on the basis of a state-secrets doctrine and have resisted attempts to impose judicial review on the United States' enhanced use of targeted killing. Habeas corpus was finally asserted at Guantánamo after sustained executive and legislative resistance and three trips to the Supreme Court, but courts have rejected other lawsuits brought by those who

---

[320] Goldsmith, *Terror Presidency*, at 102.

were detained at the military camp and held that habeas does not apply to American detention in Afghanistan. Although the American commitment to constitutionalism has inspired many countries and may even help explain a willingness of courts in Israel, Canada, and the United Kingdom to apply bills of rights to national security actions, it has long been tempered by a political-questions doctrine that assigns many national security activities to the unreviewable discretion of the executive.

A related theme is that national security issues in the United States are dominated by the executive in a manner that is striking in comparative perspective. The Patriot Act may have become a symbol of the United States' responses to 9/11, but it was a deeply misleading one. Americans on both the Right and the Left worried about how the Patriot Act would affect their privacy, while far more nasty things happened through executive action. These activities included the post-9/11 immigration roundup, de facto preventive and investigative detention under material witness warrants, illegal surveillance by the NSA, and executive authorization of harsh interrogation on the basis of the infamous torture memos. At the same time, the United States' robust commitment to a free press meant that these secret executive abuses were eventually exposed. The torture memos have only become infamous because they are in the public domain. Similar documents in the United Kingdom, Australia, and Canada would have likely remained secret. Even the ultrasecret activities of the United States' signals intelligence agency was revealed by *The New York Times*, which refused to back down, even when President Bush warned that it was putting lives at risk.

A lack of faith in criminal law as a prime response to terrorism runs through President Bush's arguments that it was not enough to treat terrorism as a crime or serve legal papers on the enemy to the Obama administration's defense of targeted killing without the need to provide targets with "legal process" before using lethal force and its acceptance of military detention without trial and military commissions including in the high profile case of KSM and other alleged 9/11 conspirators. This lack of faith in the criminal justice system persists, despite the high use of imprisonment in the United States and the high conviction rate of terrorism prosecutions. The Patriot Act did not dramatically expand the powers of the state to deal with domestic terrorism especially as compared with increased state powers under various terrorism laws enacted in the United Kindgom. With the possible exception of Israel, no other democracy has been as inclined as the United States – both before but especially after 9/11 – to see terrorism as a foreign policy issue demanding a military response. This approach can partially be explained by the external nature of the 9/11 attacks, but it makes the American approach somewhat exceptional and perhaps ill-suited should it face dramatic increases in home-grown terrorism.

5 The United Kingdom Responds: A Legislative War on Terrorism

I. INTRODUCTION

The experience with terrorism in Northern Ireland has been extensive, producing more deaths than 9/11, albeit over a much longer period. Although much attention has been focused on American antiterrorism efforts in the wake of 9/11, British antiterrorism laws have been much more influential in other parts of the world. The United Kingdom's Terrorism Act, 2000, and, in particular, its broad definition of terrorism, have been the starting point for definitions of terrorism in Australia, Canada, Israel, Singapore, South Africa, and elsewhere.[1] Australia has followed subsequent British developments with respect to the imposition of control orders and offenses that target speech associated with terrorism. The British influence not only projects forward from 9/11 but backward. As discussed in Chapter 3, British colonial emergency rule had a lasting impact on antiterrorism in Singapore, Malaysia, and Israel. Indeed, the roots of many practices, such as broad liability rules that attempt to prevent interference with essential services, indeterminate administrative detention, the use of secret evidence, administrative orders restricting the activities of terrorist suspects in the community, special courts, and the regulation of speech associated with terrorism, all have origins in the counter-insurgency practices of British colonial rule.

If an overriding theme of the American response to 9/11 is a frequent reliance on extra-legalism and executive measures, the overriding theme of the British response is a commitment to a legislative war on terrorism that is prepared to impose robust limits and derogations on rights normally enjoyed in the nonterrorist context. The British commitment to legalism helps explain why its antiterrorism laws have frequently been exported. It also explains why the

---

[1] Kent Roach, "The Post 9/11 Migration of the Terrorism Act, 2000," in *The Migration of Constitutional Ideas*, ed. Sujit Choudhry (New York: Cambridge University Press, 2006).

United Kingdom's use of administrative, preventive, and investigative detention is heavily regulated by law and does not have the ad hoc and extralegal
character of post-9/11 American experiments such as the initial Guantánamo
detentions, immigration roundups, and the abuse of material witness warrants.
This is not to say that the British approach has always been scrupulously legal
or proper; indeed, the British use and eventual repudiation of harsh interrogations and administrative detention or internment in Northern Ireland in the
early 1970s could have provided important lessons for American policy makers
in the immediate aftermath of 9/11.

The legislative nature of British approaches to terrorism also has meant that
the courts have played a prominent role in reviewing both laws and executive
actions taken to prevent terrorism. The result both before and after 9/11 has
been a number of high-stakes dialogues or interchanges between the courts
and legislation. Before 9/11, the European Court of Human Rights held that
officially endorsed British interrogation techniques constituted inhumane and
degrading treatment.[2] It also held that preventive arrest and detention without
judicial involvement violated the European Convention,[3] causing the United
Kingdom to respond with an official derogation from the convention that was
subsequently upheld by the court.[4]

Many expected that British courts would manifest the same deference to
post-9/11 actions as they did to emergency measures taken during the two
world wars.[5] This pessimistic view was confirmed when, a month after 9/11,
the House of Lords unanimously upheld the decision of the secretary of state
to deport a Pakistani-born imam because the Security Service alleged that he
was involved in terrorist activities. Lord Hoffmann invoked 9/11 as a reminder
that "in matters of national security, the cost of failure can be high." He argued
that 9/11 underlined "the need for the judicial arm of government to respect
the decisions of ministers of the Crown" because "the executive has access to
special information and expertise in these matters," and their decisions have
"a legitimacy" acquired "through the democratic process. If the people are
to accept the consequences of such decisions, they must be made by persons
whom the people have elected and whom they can remove."[6] In other words,
courts should defer to the legislature because it has a democratic legitimacy
that the judiciary does not, and it should defer to the executive because the

[2] *Ireland v. UK*, Series A, no. 25 (1978).

[3] *Brogan v. The United Kingdom*, Series A, no. 145-B (1988).

[4] *Brannigan v. The United Kingdom*, Series A, no. 258-B (1993).

[5] *R. v. Halliday*, A.C. 260 (1917); *Liversidge v. Anderson*, A.C. 206 (1942). See generally David
Dyzenhaus, *The Constitution of Law* (Cambridge: Cambridge University Press, 2006).

[6] *Secretary of State v. Rehman*, UKHL 47 (2001), at para. 62.

executive has access to secret intelligence that the courts do not. "The people" who would have to accept the consequences of security decisions were seen more as the majority who were potential victims of terrorism and not Muslim minorities who could be the victims of excessive counter-terrorism.

Although the *Rehman* vision of judicial deference has some defenders,[7] it has not been dominant since the immediate shock of 9/11. In 2004, the House of Lords in the Belmarsh case repudiated the idea that the courts were undemocratic and therefore should defer to the elected branches of government with respect to national security.[8] It declared the main plank of the United Kingdom's response to 9/11, the indeterminate detention of noncitizen terrorist suspects who could not be deported for fear of torture, to be disproportionate and discriminatory. The use of secret intelligence as evidence has forced judges to evaluate intelligence as it has been used to support proscription and control orders, and the result has not been the uniform judicial deference to executive expertise and secrecy that Lord Hoffmann advocated in the shadow of 9/11.[9] With a push from the European Court of Human Rights, the courts placed restrictions on the use of secret evidence to sustain control orders.[10] In the wake of the torture scandals in the United States, they affirmed that evidence derived from torture would not be admissible.[11] They also invalidated some terrorism financing schemes and random stop and search powers, albeit in a way that allowed for legislative replies.[12]

Another important theme running through the United Kingdom's response to terrorism and 9/11 is the overriding importance given to secrecy. Indeterminate immigration detention and control orders have featured the use of secret evidence. Although security-cleared special advocates can see and challenge the secret evidence, severe restrictions are placed on their ability to contact the affected person because of a fear of inadvertent disclosure of secrets. The U.K. government offered generous settlements to Britons detained at Guantánamo

---

[7] Eric Posner and Adrian Vermeule, *Terror in the Balance: Security, Liberty and the Courts* (Oxford: Oxford University Press, 2007); Richard Posner, *Not a Suicide Pact: The Constitution in a Time of National Emergency* (New York: Oxford University Press, 2006).

[8] *A. v. Secretary of State*, UKHL 56 (2004).

[9] Adam Tomkins, "National Security and the Role of the Court: A Changed Landscape?" (2010) 126 Law Quarterly Review 543.

[10] *Secretary of State v. AF (no. 3)*, UKHL 28 (2009).

[11] *A. v. Secretary of State*, UKHL 71 (2005).

[12] *Treasury v. Ahmed*, UKSC 2 (2010) (invalidating terrorist financing regulations); Terrorist Asset Freezing Act, 2010, c.38 (responding with legislative basis for terrorist financing sanctions) *Gillan v. The United Kingdom* (2010) 50 EHRR 45 c.38 (holding random stop and search powers to violate European Convention on Human Rights); Protection of Freedoms Bill (HC Bill 146) 2nd reading March 1, 2011 ss.58-60 (repealing s.44 of the Terrorism Act, 2000 and replacing it with more restricted search powers).

when it became apparent that the courts might order more disclosure of secret information even in the face of U.S. threats to cut off intelligence sharing. Unlike the United States, Canada, or Australia, the United Kingdom still does not use domestic electronic surveillance as evidence in terrorism prosecutions. This glaring omission underlines the government's unwillingness to risk interfering with the operations of security intelligence agencies and requiring them to retain or disclose intelligence.

The British approach to terrorism has also been much more prepared than the American approach to restrict associational and expressive freedoms in an attempt to prevent terrorism. Public displays of support for proscribed terrorist organizations have long been illegal in the United Kingdom. One of the main responses to the 2005 London bombings were attempts, both in the United Nations (UN) Security Council and Parliament, to place more restrictions on speech that might incite or inspire acts of terrorism. The British approach has also been supported by a European constitutional culture that is much more willing to accept limits on speech and association in the name of the ability of militant democracies to protect themselves than more libertarian North American constitutional cultures. The British emphasis on regulation of speech associated with terrorism has dangers, however, particularly with regard to how broadly terrorism is defined and the heavy export trade in U.K. terrorism laws to countries with less respect for democratic freedoms.

The United Kingdom's response to 9/11 is best understood in an historical context. Proscription, speech regulation, administrative detention based on secret evidence, emergency-based legislation, and derogations from rights, and even attempts to use immigration law as antiterrorism law, all had historical pre-9/11 roots in the United Kingdom's approach to Irish terrorism. The Terrorism Act, 2000, contemplated a more peaceful Northern Ireland and did not contain previous measures such as administrative detention or internment, the use of immigration measures such as exclusion orders, and the criminalization of failure to provide authorities with information relevant to terrorism investigations. At the same time, the Terrorism Act, 2000, was a much tougher and expansive terrorism law than the USA Patriot Act. It dramatically expanded existing definitions of terrorism from politically motivated violence to include politically and religiously motivated serious property damage and interference with electronic systems, with no exemptions for protests and strikes. It provided for a proscription regime based on secret intelligence, with offenses that made it a crime to be a member of or even identify with a proscribed organization. Other offenses pushed the boundaries of inchoate or precrime liability by criminalizing the possession of articles that give rise to a reasonable suspicion that they could be used for terrorism. It also provided broad police powers, including preventive arrests on suspicion and without charge and random stop and search powers for articles that could be used in connection with terrorism. The Terrorism Act, 2000, represented the state of the art and provided a heavy arsenal of legal tools to fight terrorism as many countries rushed to enact new antiterrorism laws to comply with Security Council Resolution 1373.

Although the Terrorism Act, 2000, was designed to provide a permanent and nonemergency basis for terrorism law, the U.K. Parliament enacted the massive Anti-Terrorism, Crime, and Security Act, 2001, in time to report to the Security Council's newly formed Counter-Terrorism Committee (CTC) at the end of 2001. The 2001 legislation reverted to pre-9/11 practices with a derogation from the European Convention on Human Rights, the use of immigration law as antiterrorism law, and the revival of offenses of failure to provide information to authorities. The derogation was used to authorize indeterminate administrative detention of noncitizens suspected of involvement with international terrorism who could not be deported because of torture concerns. This part of the 2001 act responded to the Security Council's call that countries ensure that refugee status not be abused by terrorists, but it also resulted in the only post-9/11 derogation from rights in Europe. Although much criticized, the derogation is also consistent with the United Kingdom's commitment to use legal and legislative means to combat terrorism. Whereas the Bush administration engaged in various extralegal measures and attempted to preclude all judicial review of the Guantánamo detentions, the United Kingdom entered a formal, legislated derogation from rights. As David Cole has commented "while the United States adopted and implemented its policy covertly and outside the law, the British transparently pursued a legal avenue...."[13]

The United Kingdom's commitment to fighting the battle against terrorism through legislation meant that Parliament and the courts have engaged in a critical and robust dialogue over counter-terrorism policy. The House of Lords ruled, in the famous 2004 Belmarsh case, that the post-9/11 derogation was both disproportionate and discriminatory in focusing on noncitizens as the only terrorist threat.[14] This decision has been justly celebrated as the most important judicial decision of the post-9/11 era. Nevertheless, it was hardly the last word on how suspected international terrorists would be treated. In early 2005, Parliament enacted control orders that, while applying formally to both citizens and noncitizens, were used against those previously subject to

---

[13] David Cole "English Lessons: A Comparative Analysis of UK and US Responses to Terrorism" (2009) 62 Current Legal Problems 136 at 146.
[14] *A. v. Secretary of State*, UKHL 56 (2004).

indeterminate administrative detention under the 2001 act. Precedents for control orders can be found in the far past of British colonial emergency rule[15] and the near past of criminal justice innovations such as antisocial behavior orders that attempted to diminish the risk of crime in the future.[16] Parliament contemplated that if necessary, the government could impose control orders that derogated from the European Convention, and in a pattern seen in previous British antiterrorism laws, the legislation has been renewed each year since 2005.[17] The House of Lords was initially cautious about control orders holding that one that imposed 18 hours of house arrest violated the right to liberty but another that imposed 14 hours did not.[18] The courts, however, imposed restrictions on the use of secret evidence, and control orders are now winding down. Control orders were not, however, the only response to the Belmarsh decision: the government responded with security-based immigration laws.[19] It unsuccessfully attempted to persuade the European Court of Human Rights to follow a post-9/11 Canadian case that contemplated exceptions to the right not to be deported to torture[20] but enjoyed more success in convincing the courts to accept that suspected terrorists could be deported to Algeria and Jordan on the basis of assurances that they would not be tortured.[21]

The July 2005 London bombings produced another wave of reactive legislation and activity. The government originally proposed to create a new offense of glorification of terrorism. Prime Minister Blair embraced the theme of militant democracy by stressing the need to criminalize the ideas that encouraged and motivated terrorists. His proposals were quickly accepted by the U.N. Security Council in Resolution 1624 discussed in Chapter 2 and influenced Australian legislation in 2005, but they were controversial and eventually watered down at home so that the Terrorism Act, 2006,[22] prohibited indirect encouragement of terrorism by statements that glorify terrorism when the public could reasonably infer that the terrorism should be emulated in existing circumstances. Prime Minister Blair's proposal to extend

---

[15] See Chapter 3 for discussion of antecedents of control orders found in emergency regulations in Malaya and Palestine.

[16] Lucia Zedner, "Preventive Justice or Pre-Punishment? The Case of Control Orders" (2007) 60 Current Legal Problems 174.

[17] Prevention of Terrorism Act, 2005, c.11.

[18] *Secretary of State v. AF*, UKHL 45 (2007); *Secretary of State v. MB*, UKHL 46 (2007); *Secretary of State v. E*, UKHL 47 (2007).

[19] Immigration, Asylum and Nationality Act, 2006, c.13; Criminal Justice and Immigration Act, 2008, Part 10.

[20] *Saadi v. Italy*, [2008] ECHR 179, rejecting the exceptional circumstances approach in *Suresh v. Canada*, 1 S.C.R. 3 (2002), to be discussed in Chapter 7.

[21] *RB (Algeria) v. Secretary of State*, UKHL 10 (2009).

[22] Terrorism Act, 2006, Section 1.

the maximum period of preventive arrest on reasonable suspicion to 90 days was defeated in the House of Commons, which accepted a 28 day period despite the Prime Minister's dire warnings that it was inadequate. Another response to the London bombings was the Countering International Terrorism (CONTEST) strategy based on preventing extremism, pursuing terrorists, protecting areas vulnerable to terrorism, and preparing to respond to further terrorist attacks.[23] This strategy survived the change of government in 2010, but is also being complemented by broader, all-risk security strategies.

In early 2011, the new Conservative Liberal Democratic Coalition government announced that it would reduce the maximum period of detention after a preventive arrest to 14 days while also preparing legislation that could be enacted to return to the 28 day period for a three month period in response to an emergency. The government also announced that it would, following an adverse European Court of Human Rights decision, restrict random stop and search powers. Control orders would be repealed to be replaced by a less restrictive regime that would not amount to house arrest or forced re-location.[24] In both the ramping up of counter-terrorism powers in response to 9/11 and the 2005 London bombings and the "correction in favor of liberty" a decade after 9/11, the British approach remains committed to legislation.

II. PRE-9/11 EXPERIENCE

It has been estimated that more than 3,300 people died and 40,000 were injured in terrorism relating to Northern Ireland.[25] At various junctures, the United Kingdom enacted reactive and emergency measures both in Northern Ireland and England. Some of these laws featured formal derogations from the European Convention on Human Rights. Other responses to Irish terrorism included administrative detention or internment on the basis of secret evidence, extreme interrogation, immigration measures, the use of special procedures and courts, and restrictions on expressive and associational freedoms.

Administrative Detention or Internment

Between 1971 and 1972, almost 2,500 people were interned in Northern Ireland under emergency regulations. These regulations were strikingly similar

---

[23] Countering International Terrorism: The United Kingdom's Strategy, Cmnd. 6888, July 2006.
[24] *Review of Counter-Terrorism and Security Powers Review Findings and Recommendations* January 2011 Cm 8004
[25] Laura Donohue, *Counter-Terrorist Laws and Emergency Powers in the United Kingdom 1922–2000* (Dublin: Irish Academic Press, 2001), at 263; Clive Walker, *The Anti-Terrorism Legislation*, 2nd ed. (Oxford: Oxford University Press, 2009), at 276.

to emergency regulations used in the former British colonies of Singapore, Malaysia, and Palestine discussed in Chapter 3. The Northern Ireland regulations allowed indefinite detention of those suspected of acting in a manner prejudicial to the preservation of peace or the maintenance of order. Review committees could only offer advice to the executive about whether a detainee could be released, and the committees frequently relied on secret evidence.[26] In 1972, Lord Diplock recognized that many had been interned on the basis of "inadequate and inaccurate information." At the same time, he accepted that "the current atmosphere of terror"[27] would make it impossible to call witnesses to testify in regular criminal trials.

In response to criticisms of internment, the advisory committees (still found under Singapore's Internal Security Act) were replaced by direct review by commissioners, with further review by a detention appeal tribunal. Detention had to be justified on the basis that the detainee was "suspected of terrorism,"[28] as opposed to being a threat to peace and order. Even under the improved procedures, however, the commissioners and detention appeal tribunal relied on secret evidence and hearsay testimony. The hearsay was often provided by testimony from Special Branch officers about allegations from unnamed and perhaps unreliable informers or statements extracted from the detainee. Because so much secret evidence was considered, detainees often did not know the details of the allegations against them.[29]

Lord Diplock recognized in 1972 that even improved administrative procedures "can never appear to be as complete safeguard that none but the guilty will be deprived of their liberty, as in the safeguard which is provided by a public trial in a court of law, in which the actual witnesses can be produced in person and their evidence tested by cross-examination on behalf of the accused."[30] In 1975, the Gardiner report similarly concluded that though administrative detention "produces justice in the vast majority of cases, it is not perceived as being just by members of the general public. Delays, the admission of hearsay evidence, the inability to cross-examine witnesses and the lower standard of proof provided much material for propaganda on the

---

[26] Internment in Northern Ireland was initially authorized under regulations enacted by the Civil Authorities (Special Powers) Act, 1922, which were subsequently replaced by a system that allowed a commissioner to decide whether detention was justified on the basis of secret evidence and also provided a detention appeal tribunal. See Donohue, *Counter-Terrorist Law and Emergency Powers*, at 134; Laura Donohue, *The Costs of Counterterrorism* (Cambridge: Cambridge University Press, 2008), at 42.

[27] Lord Diplock, *Report of the Commission to Consider Legal Procedures to Deal with Terrorist Activities in Northern Ireland*, Cmnd. 5185, 1972, at paras. 32 and 33.

[28] Northern Ireland (Emergency Provisions) Act, 1973, Section 11.

[29] David Lowry, "Internment: Detention without Trial" (1976) 5 Human Rights 261, at 297–305.

[30] Diplock, *Report of the Commission*, at para. 33.

grounds that this is not British justice."[31] Although administrative detention might effectively contain violence in the short term, it "cannot remain as a long-term policy" because it created "a widespread sense of grievance and injustice and obstructed those elements in Northern Ireland society that could lead to reconciliation."[32]

Internment was a counter-productive mistake. Inside internment camps, those detained often only for republican sympathies were mistreated, radicalized and sometimes coerced into false confessions. Outside the camps, protest marches against internment and the number of terrorist explosions increased.[33] The Bush administration should have learned much from the sorry history of administrative detention in the United Kingdom.[34] Even if it had considered such lessons, it might have distinguished al Qaeda from Irish terrorism on the basis that the latter could be negotiated with, whereas the former could not.[35] Such an approach, however, ignores the apparently successful experience in Singapore and elsewhere with rehabilitation based on religious counseling.[36]

Interrogation in Depth

The increased use of internment in the early 1970s was also accompanied by the use of harsh interrogation techniques: wall standing; hooding; and noise, sleep, and food deprivation. These techniques "had been developed post World War II as part of British counter-insurgency operations"[37] in places such as Malaya and Palestine. They were authorized in military directives "in internal security operations overseas,"[38] which stressed the need to gather intelligence in colonial emergencies through sustained interrogations facilitated by internal security laws.

In 1971, the Compton Committee, in language reminiscent of the discredited Yoo-Bybee torture memos, found that no "brutality" had occurred, but

---

[31] *Report of a Committee to Consider in the Context of Civil Liberties and Human Rights Measures to Deal with Terrorism in Northern Ireland*, Cmnd. 5847, 1975, at para. 145.

[32] Ibid., at Recommendation 37.

[33] Donohue, *Counter-Terrorist Law and Emergency Powers*, at 62.

[34] The first jet into Washington after 9/11 contained high British security officials, one of whom warned the CIA not to "turn the terrorist attacks back on them" because although it might work for a time, "it's dangerous. It makes you the bad guys. And when it gets to court – and in your society, just like ours, it will – every one of these guys will get off." Jane Mayer, *The Dark Side* (New York: Anchor Books, 2008), at 30.

[35] Michael Ignatieff, *The Lesser Evil* (Toronto, ON, Canada: Penguin, 2004), at 99–101.

[36] See Chapter 3.

[37] Donohue, *Counter-Terrorist Laws and Emergency Powers*, at 120.

[38] Donohue, *Costs of Counter-Terrorism*, at 50.

only because it was narrowly defined as "an inhuman or savage form of cruelty" with a "disposition to inflict suffering combined with an indifference to, or pleasure in, the victim's pain."[39] The majority of the Parker Commission in 1972, like the Israeli Landau Commission years later, concluded that the five techniques of harsh interrogation could save innocent lives and recommended that they continue to be used, subject to better executive and administrative control.

Lord Gardiner dissented on the ground that the five techniques were illegal and immoral. He concluded that "the blame for this sorry story, if blame there be, must lie with those who, many years ago, decided that in emergency conditions in Colonial-type situations we should abandon our legal, well-tried and highly successful wartime interrogation methods and replace them by procedures which were secret, illegal, not morally justifiable and alien to the traditions of what I believe still to be the greatest democracy in the world."[40] Even though they had been approved by two committees, the U.K. government announced in March 1972 that the five techniques would cease to be used and that legislation would be required should they ever be used in the future.[41] Contrary to the Bush administration, the British government was not prepared to use the five techniques simply because they had received legal advice that the techniques were legal.

Harsh interrogation leaves a lasting stain. The use of the techniques was subsequently found to constitute torture and degrading treatment by the European Commission on Human Rights. In a decision relied on in the American torture memos, however, the European Court of Human Rights would only find that the techniques constituted cruel and degrading treatment.[42] A number of internment detainees were subsequently able to obtain damages for the abuse they suffered and applications are still being heard alleging that miscarriages of justice occurred because of harsh interrogation.[43] The use of the techniques created a stain on British justice. Nevertheless, the stain was mitigated by open discussion of the techniques and the government's decision in 1972 to renounce them.

---

[39] *Report of the Inquiry into Allegations of Brutality against the Security Forces*, Cmnd. 4823, 1971, at para. 66. See Ian Brownlie, "Interrogation in Depth: The Compton and Parker Reports" (1972) 35 Modern Law Review 501.

[40] *Report of the Committee of Privy Councillors Appointed to Consider Authorized Interrogation Techniques for Suspected Terrorists*, Cmnd. 4901, 1971, at para. 21.

[41] Prime Minister Edward Heath told the House of Commons that the techniques would not be used in the future and if the government did decide they should be used it "would probably have to come to the House and ask for the powers to do it." As quoted in Donohue *The Costs of Counter-Terrorism* at 54.

[42] *Ireland v. The United Kingdom*, 2 EHRR 25 (1976).

[43] Lowry, "Internment," at 281–3.

Diplock Courts and Criminalization

In 1972, the Diplock Commission recommended increased use of criminal law to respond to terrorism. To achieve this objective, he recommended the abolition of trial by jury in what became known as one-judge Diplock courts. Diplock argued that abolition of juries was required because of jury intimidation. The need to dispense with juries remains disputed, with even his own lightly researched report stressing that witness intimidation was a greater problem.[44]

Although Lord Diplock was prepared to sacrifice the jury to criminalize terrorism, he was not prepared to accept the use of secret evidence or anonymous witnesses. He concluded that both practices would be inconsistent with basic fairness toward the accused.[45] The Diplock courts continue to this day in a somewhat modified form and have not been held to be inconsistent with the European Convention on Human Rights.[46] Indeed, the European courts accept some uses of anonymous witnesses, even though any use of them would not be allowed in the United States because of the Sixth Amendment right to confront witnesses. Since 9/11, there has been increased interest in special courts not so much in relation to fears of jury or witness intimidation but more with respect to attempts to use secret intelligence as evidence and to impose indeterminate detention.[47] Lord Diplock, for his part, unequivocally rejected secret evidence in criminal courts but was prepared to accept it as a basis for administrative detention.

The Diplock Commission recommended other innovations to facilitate the use of criminal law against suspected terrorists. They included the imposition of reverse onuses in cases of accused found with explosives or firearms. Diplock also stressed the importance of interrogations in terrorism cases. He recommended that the state be relieved of the burden of proving beyond a reasonable doubt that confessions were voluntary. Instead, and following the minimum standards in the European Convention on Human Rights, confessions would only be excluded if the accused established on a balance of probabilities that they were obtained by torture or by inhumane and degrading treatment. As

---

[44] William Twining, "Emergency Powers and the Criminal Process: The Diplock Report" (1973) Criminal Law Review 406.

[45] Diplock, *Report of the Commission*, at paras. 21–6.

[46] Stefan Sottiaux, *Terrorism and the Limitation of Rights: The ECHR and the US Constitution* (Oxford: Hart, 2008), at 337–8.

[47] Jack Goldsmith, "Long-Term Detention and a National Security Court," in *Legislating the War against Terror*, ed. Benjamin Wittes (Washington, DC: Brookings Institution Press, 2009), at 79.

Conor Gearty has argued, "in the hands of Lord Diplock, the Convention was turned from a charter of rights to a yardstick of repression."[48]

It was difficult for the suspected terrorist to establish that torture or degrading treatment occurred in police custody, and many convictions in the Diplock courts were based on uncorroborated confessions. One retired detective has commented, "Do repeated slaps around the face amount to torture? What about an occasional kick in the balls?"[49] The result of such tactics has been miscarriages of justice, with 24 terrorist convictions from Northern Ireland having been overturned on grounds that the convictions were not safe. The legacy of the brutality is not over, as the Criminal Cases Review Commission, which investigates claims of wrongful convictions in the United Kingdom, is still considering "hundreds"[50] of applications largely stemming from allegations of false confessions made under duress. Harsh techniques that caused false and unreliable confessions were not limited to Northern Ireland. A number of wrongful convictions occurred in Irish Republican Army (IRA) terrorism cases in the 1970s, including those of the Birmingham Six, the Guildford Four, and Judith Ward.[51]

Most of the Diplock recommendations were enacted in the 1973 Northern Ireland (Emergencies Provisions) Act.[52] The 1973 law empowered the police to prohibit public assemblies on the basis of concerns of breach of peace, public disorder, or undue demands on the police.[53] The law also provided for the proscription of terrorist groups, including the IRA and Sinn Fein, and made it an offense to be a member of or raise or solicit funds for such illegal terrorist organizations.[54] It also made it an offense to dress or behave in public "in such a way as to arouse reasonable apprehension" that a person belonged to a proscribed organization.[55] This followed a long and largely unsuccessful history of attempting to ban republican symbols in Ireland.

The 1973 act only applied in Northern Ireland, but similar provisions were enacted in the Prevention of Terrorism (Temporary Provisions) Act 1974[56] in response to the Birmingham bombings that killed 21 people and injured 184. Paul Wilkinson noted that in the 18 months before the act, nearly

---

[48] Conor Gearty, "The Cost of Human Rights: The English Judges and the Northern Irish Troubles" (1994) 37 *Current Legal Problems* 19.

[49] Ian Cobain, "Hundreds of Northern Ireland 'Terrorists' Allege Police Torture," *The Guardian*, October 11, 2010.

[50] Ibid.

[51] These cases are described in Kent Roach and Gary Trotter, "Miscarriages of Justice in the War against Terror" (2005) 109 *Penn State Law Review* 967.

[52] C.53. [53] Ibid., Section 21.

[54] Ibid., Section 19. [55] Ibid., Section 23A.

[56] C.56.

700 people had been injured by IRA bombs directed at such targets as the Old Bailey, Scotland Yard, and the Tower of London.[57] As one member of Parliament noted, the 1974 law was "introduced in a mood of panic,"[58] as seen by widespread calls for revival of the death penalty, something that was thankfully not done, given the wrongful convictions arising from the bombings.

Use of Immigration Law as Antiterrorism Law

The 1974 law also featured the use of immigration law as antiterrorism law through provisions that thickened the border by providing for up to 12 hours' detention at ports between England and Northern Ireland. Exclusion orders were also enacted to prohibit those suspected of involvement with terrorism from entering England from Northern Ireland or the Republic of Ireland. One such order was applied in 1982 to Gerry Adams but was revoked when Adams was elected to Parliament in 1983.[59] Adams attempted to challenge his exclusion in court but was rebuffed by concerns that the case might require disclosure of secret intelligence.[60] A 1978 report by Lord Shackleton warned that much intelligence was based on a person's associations and views and "has no evidential quality in the judicial sense. . . . It may reveal a good deal about a person, but any conclusions drawn from it have to be carefully judged."[61] As Clive Walker has observed, the lifting of the ban on Adams puts in doubt the propriety of its initial issuance.[62]

Forcing suspected terrorists to remain in Northern Ireland was a dubious strategy to prevent terrorism.[63] As Fionnuala Ni Aolain has argued, "exclusion orders challenge any rational understanding of purpose. They challenge the basic principles of due process by creating a punishment without proof of wrongdoing. Further, the notion that persons are considered dangerous in one part of the territory, but not in another, defies common sense."[64] Nevertheless,

---

[57] Paul Wilkinson, "Report," in *Lord Lloyd Inquiry into Legislation against Terrorism*, Cmnd. 3420, 2006, vol. 2, at 67.

[58] Donohue, *Counter-Terrorist Laws and Emergency Powers*, at 217.

[59] Clive Walker, *The Prevention of Terrorism in British Law* (Manchester, UK: Manchester University Press, 1986), at 71.

[60] *R v. Secretary of State ex parte Adams*, All ER (EC) 177 (1995).

[61] *Review into the Operation of the Prevention of Terrorism (Temporary Measures) Acts 1974 and 1976*, Cmnd. 7324, at 41. Shackleton did not recommend ending exclusion orders, and he accepted that ambiguous acts such as a person's associations and his or her silence in the face of questioning could provide a basis for an exclusion order. Donohue, *Counter-Terrorist Laws and Emergency Powers*, at 237.

[62] Walker, *Prevention of Terrorism in British Law*, at 71.

[63] Donohue, *Counter-Terrorist Laws and Emergency Powers*, at 237.

[64] Fionnuala Ni Aolain, "The Fortification of an Emergency Regime" (1996) 59 Albany Law Review 1353, at 1385.

as will be seen, the United Kingdom reverted to irrational uses of immigration law as antiterrorism law in the wake of 9/11.

Warrantless Arrest on Suspicion and Derogation from Rights

Section 7 of the 1974 law provided for arrest on suspicion of involvement in terrorist activities and detention for up to 7 days on executive authorization. These powers were used mainly to gather intelligence and resulted in relatively few charges.[65] They were held by the European Court of Human Rights in *Brogan v. The United Kingdom*[66] to violate rights to be brought promptly before a judicial official. Rather than increasing judicial involvement, the United Kingdom responded by issuing a formal derogation under both the European Convention on Human Rights and the International Covenant on Civil and Political Rights. The government justified the derogation on the basis of concerns that judicial involvement would either result in the disclosure of sensitive intelligence or entail the use of closed proceedings and secret evidence contrary to judicial traditions. The derogation was enacted as a response to an adverse court decision as opposed to an emergency threatening the life of the nation, as seemingly required under the European Convention.[67] Nevertheless, it was upheld by the European Court of Human Rights, which stressed judicial deference to states on matters of national security.[68] As will be seen, derogation and judicial review of derogations would play an important role in the post-9/11 British response to terrorism, as would issues about the disclosure of intelligence and secret evidence.

Restrictions on Freedom of Expression

There was a long tradition of banning many forms of expression associated with the IRA and republicanism in Northern Ireland. The British courts deferred to executive action in Northern Ireland, including the banning of so-called republican clubs.[69] A Public Order Act, 1986,[70] prohibited threatening, abusive, or insulting words not only if they would cause violence but also if they resulted in harassment, alarm, or distress. This offense was applied to a poster titled "Ireland: 20 Years of Resistance" that showed boys throwing

---

[65] Donohue, *Counter-Terrorist Laws and Emergency Powers*, at 231.

[66] 11 EHRR 117 (1989).

[67] Ni Aolain, "Fortification of an Emergency Regime," at 1366.

[68] *Branigan and McBride v. The UK*, Series A no 145-B, at paras. 59 and 60.

[69] *McEldowney v. Forde*, A.C. 632 (1971). See Stephen Livingston, "The House of Lords and the Northern Ireland Conflict" (1994) 57 Modern Law Review 333.

[70] C.64, Section 5.

stones.[71] In 1988, a broadcast ban on direct statements by members of pro-scribed groups was imposed. Like proscription in general, this ban was justi-fied on the symbolic basis that allowing representatives of terrorist groups to speak in the media would give offense. In 1991, the media ban was upheld by the House of Lords and, three years later, by the European Court of Human Rights.[72] The European Court of Human Rights found that the limit on speech was prescribed by law, proportionate, and justified for reasons relating to national security. The broadcasting ban was eventually lifted in 1994 because it was not effective. This is consistent with a pattern seen with respect to other harsh antiterrorism measures such as house demolitions in Israel and intern-ment in Northern Ireland. Harsh measures can be counter-productive even if upheld by the courts. As will be seen, however, the United Kingdom would return to prohibiting speech associated with terrorism after the 2005 London bombings.

Terrorism and the Permanent Emergency

The enactment of emergency laws first in Northern Ireland in 1973 and then throughout the United Kingdom in 1974 coincided with increases in arrests and detentions and drops in deaths and injuries from terrorism.[73] Quickly enacted in response to the Birmingham bombings, the 1974 law was renewed on multiple occasions. Proscription was retained to respond to the public offense caused by open displays of support for the IRA. At the same time, loyalist terrorist groups were not proscribed under the act, and this lack of parity undermined some of the symbolic message of proscription. There were also concerns that proscription might only drive support underground and make it more difficult to detect.[74] The 1974 law allowed proscription to be used as a political means to denounce terrorism, and it allowed immigration law to be used by the executive on the basis of secret evidence as a means to displace terrorists, even if the result was only that suspected terrorists would not be able to enter England from Northern Ireland.

In subsequent years, offenses of soliciting funds for terrorism and withhold-ing information from terrorist investigators were added to the laws of Northern Ireland.[75] With respect to the financing provisions, Clive Walker observed

---

[71] Donohue, *Costs of Counterterrorism*, at 289.
[72] *R v. Secretary of State ex parte Brind*, AC 696 (1991); *Brind v. the United Kingdom*, 17 EHHR 76 (1994). See Stefan Sottiaux, *Terrorism and the Limitation of Rights: The ECHR and the US Constitution* (Oxford: Hart, 2008), at 136–7.
[73] Donohue, *Counter-Terrorist Laws and Emergency Powers*, at 322.
[74] Walker, *Prevention of Terrorism in British Law*, at 44.
[75] Ibid., at 233.

that fund-raisers "are likely to be on the fringes of terrorism, so their removal will inflict limited damage on the terrorists but may sever one of the few leads which could identify important organizers and activists."[76] Broad search powers, including the power to search for items associated with terrorism, even in the absence of a reasonable suspicion, were also introduced in response to a series of pre-9/11 bombings in London.[77] They would find their way into Section 44 of the Terrorism Act, 2000, only to be found incompatible with the European Convention in 2010.[78] A new terrorism law was enacted with blinding speed in response to the 1998 Omaagh bombings that killed 29 people. As he would in response to the London bombings, Prime Minister Blair stressed that terrorism was an "appalling act of savagery and evil" and that "these people will not win."[79]

The British experience with terrorism also made some inroads into traditional criminal justice processes. The juryless Diplock courts first introduced in 1973 have been extended to some nonterrorism cases, including complex fraud cases. In 1988, the criminal law was amended in Northern Ireland to allow silence to be used against a suspect in a terrorist investigation.[80] In 1994, the ability to draw adverse inference from silence was extended to all criminal law and throughout the United Kingdom.[81] The British experience with the right to silence provides an important example of how innovations made in the terrorism context can spread to other parts of criminal law. These concerns remain alive post-9/11.[82] At the same time, however, post-9/11 criminal law developments were influenced by increased use of civil and criminal processes that attempt to prevent crime long before it occurs[83] and immigration and intelligence concepts that focus on the status, character, and associations of individuals and accept the use of secret evidence.[84] Before 9/11,

---

[76] Ibid., at 97.

[77] Lord Lloyd recommended that these stop-and-search powers should be continued in permanent legislation stressing the bombings and the deterrent effect of such stops and searches. Lloyd, *Inquiry into Legislation against Terrorism*, at paras. 10.21 and 10.24.

[78] *Gillan v. U.K.*, (2010) 50 EHRR 45.

[79] "Omagh Bombing Kills 28," at http://news.bbc.co.uk/2/hi/events/northern_ireland/latest_news/152156.stm.

[80] Criminal Evidence (Northern Ireland) Act, 1988.

[81] Criminal Justice and Public Order Act, 1994.

[82] Oren Gross, "Cutting Down Trees: Law-Making under the Shadow of Great Calamities," in *The Security of Freedom: Essays on Canada's Anti-Terrorism Bill*, ed. Ronald Daniels, Patrick Macklem, and Kent Roach (Toronto, ON, Canada: University of Toronto Press, 2001).

[83] Lucia Zedner, "Preventive Justice or Pre-Punishment? The Case of Control Orders" (2007) 60 Current Legal Problems 174.

[84] Kent Roach, "The Eroding Distinction between Intelligence and Evidence in Terrorism Investigations," in *Counter-Terrorism and Beyond*, ed. Nicola McGarrity, Andrew Lynch, and George Williams (London: Routledge, 2010).

terrorism-based innovations tended to migrate into the rest of the criminal law whereas after 9/11, less restrained administrative and intelligence based concepts have tended to migrate into criminal laws used to respond to terrorism.

Peace Talks and Mainstreaming Counter-Terrorism

Peace talks in Northern Ireland affected approaches toward counter-terrorism. The Northern Ireland (Sentences) Act, 1998, provided for the accelerated release of prisoners who renounced violence and support for specified terrorist organizations. This represented a rare incorporation among Western democracies of rehabilitation within antiterrorist discourse. A commission was appointed to determine who should be released and included a person who had served in a similar capacity in South Africa.[85] The Belfast Agreement included provisions for the release of those imprisoned for terrorism conditional on a renunciation of violence and can be seen as a transitional justice process that responded to many grievances in Northern Irish society.[86]

There was also interest in regularizing the United Kingdom's antiterrorism laws and bringing them in line with human rights norms so that the United Kingdom would not have to continue to derogate from various rights instruments. Lord Lloyd issued an important 1996 report calling for the terrorism laws to be consolidated in one statute that would operate without derogation from human rights or a declaration of an emergency. He was sensitive to the criticism that the United Kingdom had received from the European Court of Human Rights, the UN Human Rights Committee, and the Committee against Torture regarding the conduct of antiterrorism campaigns.[87] He recommended repealing administrative detention or internment, exclusion orders, and the offense of failing to provide authorities with information in a terrorism investigation, all reforms implemented with the Terrorism Act, 2000. At the same time, he also recommended creating new offenses relating to terrorism financing and preparation for terrorism and an increased focus on international terrorism. Although the Terrorism Act, 2000, implemented many of Lord Lloyd's recommendations,[88] it was, in some respects, even

---

[85] Kieren McEvoy, "Prisoners, the Agreement and the Political Character of the Northern Ireland Conflict" (1999) 22 Fordham International Law Journal 1539, at 1559n83.

[86] Ibid.; Colm Campbell, Fionnuala Ni Aolain, and Colin Harvey, "The Frontiers of Legal Analysis: Reframing the Transition in Northern Ireland" (2003) 66 Modern Law Review 317; Victor Ramraj, "Counter-Terrorism and Minority Alienation: Some Lessons from Northern Ireland" (2006) Singapore Journal of Legal Studies 385.

[87] Lloyd, *Inquiry into Legislation against Terrorism*, at para. 3.7.

[88] The notable exceptions were that the 2000 law did not follow Lloyd's recommendations that Diplock courts be abolished or that electronic surveillance be used as evidence in terrorism

broader than previous laws. This is a lesson for countries such as Egypt and Israel that are presently looking to consolidate their emergency antiterrorism laws into comprehensive nonemergency regimes.

III. THE TERRORISM ACT, 2000

The Terrorism Act, 2000, was a significant change in the United Kingdom's antiterrorism policy because it was enacted as permanent legislation that would apply throughout the United Kingdom and was designed to allow the government to withdraw the derogation that it entered to allow for up to 7 days of preventive detention without judicial review. It also reflected the growing concern with international terrorism and the lessening of Irish terrorism in the wake of the 1998 Belfast Agreement. The timing of the 2000 law also meant that it became very influential as many countries enacted new antiterrorism laws in the wake of 9/11.

A Broad and Influential Definition of Terrorism

One of the most influential features of the Terrorism Act, 2000, is its broad definition of terrorism. This definition is the lynchpin of the act being effectively read into a wide variety of offenses, powers of proscription, and police powers both in the 2000 legislation and in much post-9/11 legislation. Although there is some understandable frustration about the difficulties of defining terrorism, it remains hard to overestimate the importance or influence of the 2000 act's definition.

Before the 2000 act, terrorism had been defined in the Prevention of Terrorism Act, 1989,[89] as the "use of violence for political ends," including "for the purpose of putting the public or any section of the public in fear," as well as through scheduled preexisting offenses in Northern Irish legislation. Section 1 of the Terrorism Act, 2000, departed from this approach by defining terrorism as the use or threat of action that involves (1) serious violence against

prosecutions. With respect to the latter, Lord Lloyd stressed that "the UK stands alone in excluding such material" after reviewing its extensive use in the United States, Canada, and Australia. He responded to concerns that the use of intercept would harm the secret operation of the intelligence services by arguing that "the prosecution will not be obliged to disclose the existence of any intercept material, and the defense will not be permitted to ask whether such material exists." Ibid., at para. 7.19. As will be seen, those who have examined the issue since 9/11 have found the retention and disclosure issues to be somewhat more difficult to resolve than Lord Lloyd, and the United Kingdom still stands alone in not allowing the use of such material in criminal trials.

[89] Prevention of Terrorism Act, 1989 c.4 s.20(1).

a person, (2) serious damage to property, (3) endangerment of a person's life, (4) serious risk to public health or safety, or (5) serious interference with or disruption to an electronic system. Activity that caused or threatened such a broad range of harms would have to be designed "to influence the government or to intimidate" the public and be done "for the purpose of advancing a political, religious or ideological cause." Influence on any government or intimidation of any public in the world would satisfy this new globalized definition of terrorism.[90] This definition of terrorism responded to international terrorism and to the broad range of vulnerabilities of modern society, but also went well beyond the best efforts to develop international definitions of terrorism examined in Chapter 2.

The definition of terrorism in the 2000 law has been very influential in many other countries. It was affirmed in the United Kingdom after a thorough review by Lord Carlile, the Liberal Democrat peer who served as the independent reviewer of antiterrorism legislation. Carlile rejected the idea that property damage should not be included by making reference to bombs in the subway system and the targeting of water or electricity supplies.[91] He also dismissed opposition to singling out religious motives as "just foolish,"[92] even though a Canadian court had found that Canada's political and religious motive requirement was discriminatory and unnecessary to distinguish terrorism from other crimes[93] and international and American definitions did not require proof of political and religious motives.[94] Carlile rejected proposals that exemptions to the extraterritorial reach of the definition should be made with respect to violence against repressive regimes largely because of the difficulties of distinguishing repressive from nonrepressive regimes and the "zero-tolerance" approach to terrorism required by international mandates.[95] Finally, he rejected arguments that the definition should include state terrorism on the basis of diplomatic immunity.[96]

The U.K. government accepted Lord Carlile's report, and the only changes to the broad 2000 definition have been minor expansions in 2006 to include actions designed to influence international organizations and in 2008 to include actions designed to advance "racial" as well as political, religious, or ideological causes. Carlile's one recommendation for restricting the

---

[90] There were also specific provisions asserting extraterritorial jurisdiction over terrorist bombing and financing offenses. Terrorism Act, 2000, Sections 62–3.

[91] Lord Carlile, *The Definition of Terrorism*, Cmnd. 7052, March 2007, at para. 50.

[92] Ibid., at para. 53.

[93] See Chapter 5. The Canadian decision has now been overruled on appeal. *R. v. Khawaja*, ONCA 862 (2010).

[94] See Chapters 1 and 4.

[95] Carlile, *Definition of Terrorism*, at para. 78.   [96] Ibid., para. 85.

definition, namely, his suggestion that there be a requirement of an attempt to intimidate as opposed to influence the government, has not been followed, though it was based on Australian and Canadian definitions of terrorism. The United Kingdom's experience is consistent with the thesis that laws against terrorism will often expand but are not easily restricted. Although fears that the broad definition of terrorism will be used against animal rights, environmental, and antiglobalization protesters have largely not been realized in the United Kingdom, there are concerns that a similar definition could be used against non-violent dissent including protests, strikes and political and religious minorities in other countries given the influence of the British definition. In a manner probably not contemplated when it was enacted, the Terrorism Act, 2000 has set something of a global standard on the definition of terrorism in light of the failure of the U.N. to agree or promote a workable definition of terrorism after 9/11.

Proscription

The 2000 act included an elaborate system of executive proscription of terrorist groups and extended the system from Northern Irish groups to potentially any terrorist group in the world. Proscription was linked to a membership offense subject to 10 years' imprisonment,[97] offenses against inviting support or arranging meetings of proscribed organizations,[98] and offenses against wearing items of clothing or articles that "arouse reasonable suspicion" that the person is a member of a proscribed organization.[99] These offenses have deep roots in an antisubversion and anti-insurgency paradigm in colonial British emergency regulations.

The easy acceptance of proscription and related membership and speech offenses in the United Kingdom in conjunction with a new emphasis on human rights under the Human Rights Act, 1998, can be explained in part by a European constitutional culture that accepts the concept of militant democracy,[100] compared to a more libertarian concept of freedom of expression and association in North America, where such offenses were not introduced even after 9/11. Section 17 of the European Convention on Human Rights

---

[97] Terrorism Act, 2000, c.11, Section 10.   [98] Ibid., Section 12.

[99] Ibid., Section 13. This offense is only subject to a maximum of six months' imprisonment.

[100] The idea of militant democracy has its roots in the writings of Karl Lowenstein, who argued that Germany slipped into Nazism in part because of the abuse of democratic rights. On militant democracy, see Andras Sajo, ed., *Militant Democracy* (Amsterdam, Netherlands: Eleventh, 2004); Makus Thiele, ed., *The "Militant Democracy" Principle in Modern Societies* (Farnham, UK: Ashgate, 2009).

embraces some militant democracy concepts by providing that "nothing in this Convention may be interpreted as implying for any State, group or person any right to engage in any activity or perform any act aimed at the destruction of any of the rights and freedoms set forth herein." In 2004, the House of Lords determined that the restrictions on freedom of expression and association inherent in proscription offenses are reasonable limits on rights simply by asserting that "the necessity of attacking terrorist organizations is clear" and without conducting any serious or sustained analysis of the proportionality or necessity of these restrictions on rights.[101] As Clive Walker has suggested, "those who espouse totalitarian views will find themselves disfavoured,"[102] either under Article 17 of the convention or under the limitation provisions that apply to freedom of expression and association.

Proscription under the Terrorism Act, 2000, remained an executive-dominated process but one that could be appealed to a Proscribed Organizations Appeal Commission. Appeals are not, however, full merit-based reviews and may involve the commission considering intelligence that is not disclosed to the applicants, including even electronic surveillance, which remains inadmissible in British criminal trials.[103] As seen in relation to the discussion of Security Council Resolution 1267 in Chapter 2, blacklisting or watchlisting is an intelligence-based concept often based on secret material that will not be disclosed even if this makes due process difficult to achieve. The Proscribed Organizations Appeal Commission is, however, able to appoint a security-cleared special advocate who can challenge secret evidence claimed to support the listing. Section 10 provides a partial response to the difficulties that those representing proscribed organizations may have in challenging the proscription by providing that material submitted to challenge the listing cannot be used in some subsequent prosecutions. Nevertheless, very few challenges to proscription have been mounted, even as the list of proscribed organizations and the grounds for proscription have grown since 9/11.[104]

---

[101] *Sheldrake v. DPP*, UKHL 43 (2004), at para. 54. The freedom of expression of argument and association argument were dismissed so casually by Lord Bingham that they occupied one paragraph of a 54-paragraph judgment, with the vast bulk of the analysis devoted to reading down reverse onuses in the Terrorism Act, 2000, to evidential burdens. Lord Rodger also stressed that proscription offenses were "no innovation in the law" and had deep roots in the Northern Ireland legislation. Ibid., at para. 60.

[102] Walker, *Anti-Terrorism Legislation*, at 54.   [103] Ibid., at 45.

[104] But see *Lord Alton of Liverpool and Others (In the matter of the People's Mojahdeen Organization of Iran) v. Secretary of State*, EWCA (Civ) 443 (2008), where a group of parliamentarians successfully challenged the listing of an Iranian group that had renounced violence.

Terrorism Financing

Another feature of the Terrorism Act, 2000, was a focus on terrorism financing that would become even more influential after 9/11. The new act extended prior offenses that had applied first to the funding of proscribed groups in Northern Ireland and later to international terrorist groups. The new offenses applied if the accused had "reasonable cause to suspect" that funds would be used for terrorism.[105] These serious offenses had low fault levels and went beyond what was required to comply with the 1999 Convention for the Suppression of Terrorism Financing, which focused on intentional and knowing financing of terrorism. Another provision in relation to terrorist property imposed a reverse onus on the accused to establish that he or she did not know or have reasonable cause to suspect that an arrangement related to terrorist property.[106]

Terrorist financing schemes relied on enforcement by third parties and as such followed modern security strategies that often deputized private actors into law enforcement. Section 19 made it an offense for a person not to report beliefs or suspicions in relation to these terrorism financing offenses that came to his or her attention through employment. Reports increased dramatically after 9/11 but, in some cases, were likely based on stereotypes that associated Muslims and Arabs with terrorism. The offense of not reporting suspicions was, however, much more limited than the general offense of withholding information relevant to terrorist investigations that applied to all individuals under prior emergency-based acts. As will be seen, however, the general withholding information offense abolished in 2000 was quickly revived after 9/11.

Preventive Arrest and Investigative Detention

A prime feature of the Terrorism Act, 2000, was the withdrawal of the derogation from the European Convention that had been previously entered to allow a maximum of seven days' preventive arrest detention without judicial review. The 2000 law did not abandon preventive arrest on suspicion, but provided for judicial review after the first 48 hours of detention. Although the detainee was able to make representations, the judge could consider information not disclosed to the detainee[107] and was only asked to decide whether there were reasonable grounds to conclude that further detention was necessary to obtain relevant evidence and that the investigation was conducted diligently.[108] The

---

[105] Terrorism Act, 2000, Sections 16 and 17.
[107] Terrorism Act, 2000, Sch. 8, para. 34.
[106] Ibid., Section 18(2).
[108] Ibid., Sch. 8, para. 32.

judicial role in the process was critical to the withdrawal of the derogation, but it was limited by the legislation and did not contemplate a merit-based review of the possibility of criminal charges. This raises a recurring issue regarding the degree to which judicial involvement restrains or legitimates antiterrorism measures.

Preventive warrantless arrests have been defended as a means to disrupt possible terrorists and to gather intelligence. They have resulted in charges in only about one-third of the cases in which they have been used.[109] Prolonged periods of detention under these provisions may produce conditions conducive to the type of abusive interrogations that generated false confessions and wrongful convictions in a series of Irish terrorism cases in the 1970s.[110] In subsequent years, the focus of debate over preventive arrest would be on the symbolic issue of how long the seven-day maximum period of detention should be extended. Some concerns were, however, rightly raised about the limited judicial role in the preventive arrest process, and some Crown counsel and courts read in an evidential test to the limited statutory test that only asked whether extension of preventive arrest periods was needed to facilitate a diligent investigation.[111]

Stop-and-Search Powers

The Terrorism Act, 2000, also contained powers to conduct warrantless stops and searches. They included powers to move and prohibit people and vehicles from cordoned areas[112] as well as powers to stop and search a person for evidence of terrorism when a police officer reasonably suspects the person to be a terrorist.[113] In addition to these powers, Section 44 allowed stops and searches without even reasonable suspicion in areas designated by the police. As will be seen, this very broad police power was challenged in the courts in part because of concerns about its disproportionate use against those of Asian and Muslim appearance. Although the domestic courts upheld this broad power, the European Court of Human Rights ruled that it was overbroad. In 2011, new legislation was proposed that would tighten the search powers.[114] The point here is that even when it authorized overbroad and objectionable police powers, the United Kingdom did so through legislation. The legislation even

---

[109] Walker, *Anti-Terrorism Legislation*, at 157.

[110] Clive Walker, "Briefing on the Terrorism Act, 2000" (2000) 12 Terrorism and Political Violence 1, at 20–4.

[111] Joint Committee on Human Rights, *Counter-Terrorism and Human Rights: Bringing Rights Back In* (2010), at paras. 69–80.

[112] Terrorism Act, 2000, Section 36.   [113] Ibid., Section 43.

[114] Protection of Freedoms Bill (HC Bill 146) 2nd reading March 1, 2011 ss.58-60 (repealing s.44 of the Terrorism Act, 2000 and replacing it with new legislated search powers).

required the police to collect statistics about who they stopped and searched, facilitating determination of the discriminatory effects of the search powers. In contrast, much North American legislation is silent on police powers, and police powers are often only subject to ex post judicial regulation,[115] without the benefit of legislative guidance or requirements for the collection of statistics. The United Kingdom's legislative approach allowed issues of discriminatory profiling to be challenged, whereas the less regulated North American approach produced only sporadic and episodic information or complaints.

Terrorism Offenses

The Terrorism Act, 2000, contained many broad terrorism offenses. Consistent with the United Kingdom's obligations under the 1997 Terrorist Bombing Convention and the 1999 Terrorist Financing Convention, extraterritorial jurisdiction was asserted over many offenses. Section 59 made it an offense for a person to incite various acts of terrorism overseas. Subsequent attempts by accused to have British courts read in freedom fighter exemptions for acts against repressive governments were unsuccessful. The courts have deferred to Parliament's ability to define terrorism and have accepted the government's zero-tolerance approach to terrorism regardless of the political context. They have also stressed that the U.K. government has "decided, in the national interest, to make common cause with the governments of countries whose representative credentials were open to profound reservations. It would be unrealistic to approach the terrorist legislation on the basis that Parliament envisaged that it should not apply to countries allied to us or to other members of the United Nations."[116] As will be seen later, this is not the only time that a "the UN made us do it" defense was considered by the British courts.

Section 56 of the Terrorism Act, 2000, created an offense punishable by life imprisonment of directing, at any level, the activities of an organization that is concerned with the commission of acts of terrorism as broadly defined in the act. This offense, which was developed in the 1990s to apply in Northern Ireland, could apply to directions even of an otherwise lawful nature, including directions not to commit terrorist acts.[117] The 2000 act included broader and more frequently applied offenses against possession of articles that could give rise to a reasonable suspicion that they are connected with terrorism and the possession of information likely to be useful for terrorism. Possession-based

[115] Craig Bradley, *The Failure of the Criminal Procedure Revolution* (Philadelphia: University of Pennsylvania Press, 1993).
[116] *R. v. F*, EWCA Crim. 243 (2007), at para. 31.
[117] Walker, *Anti-Terrorism Legislation*, at 6.22–3.

offenses such as these impose fewer restraints on the police than those that require the proof of some definite act toward an illegal end.[118] Both offenses allow the accused to demonstrate that his or her purposes were not connected with terrorism or a reasonable excuse for the possession of the material.[119] The House of Lords has embraced a broad reading of these offenses that can make a person guilty even in the absence of proof that the person had an intent to commit a terrorist act.[120] Although courts have opportunities to interpret both the definition of terrorism and offenses in the Terrorism Act, 2000, they have frequently accepted Parliament's intent to make these provisions very broad. Although the Terrorism Act, 2000, contained many broad terrorism offenses, more would be created after 9/11.

IV. THE INITIAL RESPONSE TO 9/11

Terrorism Financing Regulations and the need for Legislative Authorization

The United Kingdom's efforts to comply with Resolution 1373 started with the enactment of the Terrorism (United Nations Measures) Order[121] on October 10, 2001. The regulation was proclaimed by executive order without Parliament's involvement and made it an offense to provide funds for or facilitate terrorism. It also provided for freezing of assets and disclosure of financial information. As in other countries, the immediate response to Security Council Resolution 1373 was a regulation proclaimed in force without parliamentary debate. The rationale for the regulations and, indeed, for many post-9/11 laws was that they were necessary to prevent further acts of terrorism and to comply with international mandates. In subsequent years, however, courts have recognized that preventive actions by the state often have punitive and extreme effects on individuals and that the secret evidence said to justify such actions can be flawed.

In 2010, the new U.K. Supreme Court found various regulations implementing UN terrorism financing obligations to be ultra vires the United Kingdom's

---

[118] Markus Dubber, "Policing Possession" (2002) 91 Journal of Criminal Law and Criminology 829.

[119] Terrorism Act, 2000, Sections 57 and 58. The reverse onus was, following an early court case under the Human Rights Act, 1998, read down to only place an evidential burden requiring the accused to adduce evidence capable of raising a reasonable doubt. Ibid., Section 118.

[120] *R. v. G*, UKHL 13 (2009). For criticisms of this approach, see Jacqueline Hodgson and Victor Tadros, "How to Make a Terrorist out of Nothing" (2009) 72 Modern Law Review 984.

[121] SI 2001, no. 3365.

United Nations Act, even though required by Chapter VII obligations. The court stressed the severity of the permanent individual sanctions and concluded that sanctions against individuals without access to a judicial remedy were not contemplated by Parliament when it enacted the United Nations Act after World War II. The court criticized the 1267 regime as one that was made by a "political" as opposed to a "judicial" body, who acted on information that might never be disclosed to the listed person or even to an ombudsperson appointed by the Security Council in 2009 to assist persons in applications for delisting. The court did not accept the government's "the UN made us do it" defense. It held that at the very least, specific legislation was required to displace the "basic common law rights" of those adversely affected by the terrorist financing listing process.[122] Parliament responded by enacting first temporary and then permanent legislation to allow it to implement various UN terrorism financing obligations.[123]

The Supreme Court's approach was more cautious than that taken by the European Court of Justice and Court of General Instance in the *Kadi* case[124] because it only required explicit legislative authorization for the implementation of the UN's sanctions. It remains to be seen whether British courts will insist on more robust due process standards that will allow those subject to asset freeze and other financing sanctions to know and challenge the case against them. As suggested in Chapter 2, such a fair trial approach may be impossible because of an unwillingness of the countries represented on the Security Council to disclose the intelligence that is said to justify terrorist listings.

The Antiterrorism, Crime, and Security Act, 2001

Despite having in place a modern and very broad law in the form of the Terrorism Act, 2000, the U.K. government, like so many others, felt compelled to respond to 9/11 and Resolution 1373. The massive, 14-part Anti-Terrorism,

---

[122] Lord Rodger observed that "the individuals who are wrongly designated will find their funds and assets frozen and their lives disrupted, without their having any realistic prospect of putting matters right. On one view, they are simply the incidental but inevitable casualties of the measures which the Security Council has judged it proper to adopt in order to counter the threat posed by terrorism to the peace and security of the world. The Council adopts those measures in order to prevent even worse casualties – those who would be killed or wounded in terrorist attacks." *Treasury v. Ahmed*, UKSC 2 (2010), at paras. 182–3.

[123] Terrorist Asset Freezing (Temporary Provisions) Act, 2010, c.2; Terrorist Asset Freezing Act, 2010, c.38.

[124] As discussed infra chapter 2.

Crime, and Security Act, 2001,[125] was introduced into Parliament in November 2001 and was law less than a month later, with only 16 hours of debate in the House of Commons and eight days of debate in the House of Lords.[126] The law was denounced by Adam Tomkins as "the most draconian legislation that Parliament has passed in peacetime in over a century."[127] Home Secretary David Blunkett, however, dismissed the concerns of "airy fairy" civil libertarians and defended the law for ensuring that terrorists "don't threaten those civil liberties."[128] Blunkett argued that various antiterrorism measures were designed to "protect our human rights" and he "deeply resent[ed]" those who suggested that "taking decisive measures to protect the country against terrorism- and the measures have protected us- is somehow to deny those very rights."[129] Blunkett, like some politicians in Australia and Canada, was prepared after 9/11 to invoke the language of rights including the right to life of potential victims to defend antiterrorism measures without much consideration of the rights that could be adversely affected by counter-terrorism.[130]

The 2001 law reverted to many of the traditions of the pre-9/11 experience: it was enacted quickly as a response to an act of terrorism; it derogated from the European Convention on Human Rights to provide for administrative detention; and it reintroduced the offense of refusing to supply authorities with information that would be relevant to terrorist investigations. At the same time, the 2001 act also responded to the particularities of 9/11 and Resolution 1373 by providing enhanced measures to target terrorism financing, measures to target potential refugees who might also be terrorists, and various aviation security and other target-hardening measures designed to restrict access to sites and substances that could be used for terrorism.

---

[125] Ant-Terrorism, Crime, and Security Act, 2001, c.24.

[126] Daniel Moeckli, *Human Rights and Non-Discrimination in the "War on Terror"* (Oxford: Oxford University Press, 2008), at 42. The Home Affairs Committee concluded, "A bill of this length – 125 clauses and eight schedules covering 114 pages – with major implications for civil liberties should not be passed by the House in such a short period and with so little time for detailed examination in committee." House of Commons Home Affairs Committee First Report, November 15, 2001, at para. 11.

[127] Adam Tomkins, "Legislating against Terror," Public Law 205 (2002).

[128] "Draconian Measures Target Foreigners," The Times (London), July 31, 2002.

[129] David Blunkett "Freedom from terrorist attack is also a human right" *The Independent* August 12, 2004.

[130] For criticisms of this approach see Kent Roach "Did September 11 Really Change Everything?" (2002) 47 McGill Law Journal 893 at 907–911; Greg Carne "Reconstituting 'Human Security' in a New Security Environment: One Australian. Two Canadians and Article 3 of the Universal Declaration of Human Rights" (2006) 25 Australian Year Book of International Law 1.

Terrorism Financing

The United Kingdom had already invested in a regime against terrorism financing in the Terrorism Act, 2000. Like the U.N, it did not re-evaluate this regime in light of the failure to prevent 9/11, the most expensive act of terrorism in history, but re-invested and created more measures aimed at terrorism financing. The 2001 act thus followed Security Council Resolution 1373 by stressing terrorism financing in its first three parts, without any apparent concern about the efficacy of applying a proceeds of crime or money laundering model to the often small and legitimate funds used for terrorism.

With respect to forfeiture, the 2001 act accelerated the shift away from the criminal law model by allowing terrorist cash and property to be forfeited in civil proceedings on a balance of probabilities. Such an approach was consistent with the European Convention on Human Rights because the courts had held in several cases that the safeguards of the criminal process were not necessary because forfeiture laws were intended as preventive measures.[131] Although the seizure of property is much less drastic than the deprivation of liberty, the state's preventive purposes were deemed by both the legislature and the courts to be more important than the effects of state actions on individuals. Similarly instrumental reasoning was used in Israel and Singapore to justify administrative detention. The civil model used for forfeiture also demonstrated the attraction of less restrained alternatives to criminal law.[132] One of the main effects of 9/11 in many countries was to generate greater use of less restrained instruments than criminal law, with its emphasis on the proof beyond a reasonable doubt of individual guilt on the basis of public evidence.

The focus on terrorism financing promoted by Security Council Resolution 1373 also facilitated the expansion of executive power. Part II of the 2001 act allowed the Treasury to make freezing orders on foreign assets without judicial review. Freezing orders did not even have to be connected to terrorism and included desires to protect "the United Kingdom's property (or part of it)."[133]

---

[131] *Welch v. the UK*, 20 EHRR 247 (1995).

[132] "As the antiterrorist finance regime in the United Kingdom has moved from criminal law to civil law standards, the forfeiture of one's property ultimately has become divorced from one's conviction for any underlying criminal offence." Donohue, *Costs of Counterterrorism*, at 145. See also Lucia Zedner, "Seeking Security by Eroding Rights: The Side-Stepping of Due Process," in *Security and Human Rights*, ed. Benjamin Goold and Liora Lazarus (Oxford: Hart, 2007), at 268.

[133] Anti-Terrorism, Crime, and Security Act, 2001, c.24, Section 4.

The Proceeds of Crime Act, 2002,[134] extended much of the same civil model of forfeiture in the 2001 terrorism act to an even wider range of crimes. As had occurred with regard to restrictions on the right to silence, innovations made and defended on the basis of countering terrorism were extended to other crimes and used for other purposes.

Disclosure of Information

Part III of the 2001 act recognized the call in Resolution 1373 for an acceleration of the exchange of information about terrorism but opportunistically expanded such information exchanges to all criminal investigations within or outside the United Kingdom. Attempts in the upper legislative chamber to restrict disclosure of information to terrorism investigations were defeated on the basis that terrorists might commit other crimes and that abuses could be remedied under the Human Rights Act, 1998.[135] As examined in Chapter 7, increased sharing of information between the Canadian government and others contributed to the torture of Maher Arar and three other Canadian citizens in Syria. Section 18 of the United Kingdom's 2001 act appropriately recognized that the United Kingdom might have some legitimate reasons to prohibit the disclosure of information for overseas purposes but provided only vague criteria that were not tied to human rights concerns and obligations.

The domestic implications of Part III for both privacy and information sharing were staggering. As the advocacy group Liberty stressed, Part III allowed the police to have access to a vast number of files in the absence of either reasonable suspicion or judicial authorization.[136] Similar powers had been proposed in an earlier bill in 2001 but were dropped after severe criticism.[137] The new powers underlined the whole-of-government approach that would be taken after 9/11 by reinterpreting 66 statutory provisions ranging from the Agriculture Act to the Transport Act and by authorizing disclosure of information for the purposes of criminal investigations in the United Kingdom or abroad. Section 19 provided both police and intelligence agencies with access

---

[134] Chapter 29.

[135] Helen Fenwick, "The Anti-Terrorism, Crime and Security Act, 2001: A Proportionate Response to September 11?" (2002) 65 *Modern Law Review* 724, at 760–1.

[136] Liberty raised concerns that "the police will not need reasonable suspicion that the file contains evidence of a crime merely that it is useful in an investigation. The police will not need to go to a magistrate or court for authorization and they will be able to access files without subsequent checks or audits. The subject of these investigations is unlikely ever to be told that the police have rifled through their files and there will be no real remedy if the police are mistaken, overzealous or plain malicious." As quoted in Walker, *Anti-Terrorism Legislation*, at 107.

[137] Tomkins, "Legislating against Terror," at 209.

to otherwise secret tax information. These powers went well beyond the provisions of the Patriot Act for increasing sharing of grand jury information among various government agencies. As such, they support the idea that with some exceptions, there are less privacy protections in the United Kingdom than in the United States.[138]

The British response to 9/11 was often to expand state powers generally and beyond the context of terrorist investigations. For example, from January 2002 to September 2003, almost 20,000 requests were made to the British revenue authorities for otherwise secret tax information, but only 4 percent of those requests were even related to terrorism offenses.[139] The Newton Committee, in its 2003 review of the act, found that the protections offered by the Human Rights Act, 1998, and the Data Protection Act, 1998, were "illusory" because potential complainants would not generally know when their information had been accessed. It suggested that external oversight should be enhanced.[140] A recurring theme in this book is that accountability for whole-of-government responses to terrorism lags well behind the increased intensity and integration of governmental actions to prevent terrorism.

Data Retention

Another part of the 2001 law that adversely affected privacy involved the retention of data. Like terrorism financing, the data retention provisions required the state effectively to deputize the private sector. The state's approach to data retention by the private sector was less heavy-handed than its approach to terrorism financing, which relied on broad criminal offenses for not reporting objectively suspicious transactions. Instead, the data retention provisions simply empowered the secretary of state to issue advisory codes of practices and enter into agreements with providers of communication data.[141] If these voluntary measures did not work, however, the law empowered the secretary of state to issue directions through regulations to require the retention of data deemed necessary for national security.[142] Both terrorism financing and data retention represented neoliberal forms of governance that conscripted the power of the private sector in state security strategies. The data retention provision

[138] David Cole "English Lessons: A Comparative Analysis of UK and US Responses to Terrorism" (2009) 62 Current Legal Problems 136 at 148–153.

[139] Privy Counsellor Review (Newton) Committee, *Anti-Terrorism, Crime and Security Act, 2001 Review Report*, HC 100 (2003), at para. 157.

[140] Ibid., at paras. 164, 166, 171.

[141] Anti-Terrorism, Crime, and Security Act, 2001, Chapter 24, Section 102.

[142] Ibid., Sections 104, 106.

demonstrated more concern about the costs that the state was imposing on the private sector than the terrorism financing provisions. At the same time, it is striking that the costs imposed on the private sector were a more important factor than the dangers to privacy through increased data retention and increased transfer of information from the private sector to government.

The Offense of Withholding Information

If data retention represented a new and relatively consensual way of gaining access to information from corporate third parties that might be valuable in terrorism investigations, Parliament also was prepared to revert to old and coercive means to ensure that individuals cooperated in terrorism investigations. The 2001 act revived and expanded the old offense of withholding information by providing that it was an offense for a person not to provide information that he or she knows would be of material assistance in either preventing or prosecuting a terrorism offense.[143] The offense follows an old style of security that demands loyalty to the state by criminalizing misprision of treason. The U.K. government had only repealed the old offense in 2000 after extensive and long-standing criticism. In the wake of 9/11 and a new emphasis on the prevention of terrorism, however, Parliament quickly restored the old offense and extended it to all forms of terrorism. The revival of the old-style offense also failed to address more modern concerns about possibly mandating persons to incriminate themselves or chilling press freedoms.[144]

Use of the withholding information offense has increased in the post-9/11 era. Professor Walker has reported that whereas only 15 charges were brought under the previous offense from 1984 to 2001 in Great Britain, 27 charges were brought between 2003 and 2007. The prosecutions have resulted in maximum five-year sentences against the wife of Omar Sharif, who committed a suicide bombing in 2003; the wife of one of the July 21, 2005, bombers; and the brother of one of the Glasgow Airport bombers.[145]

Perhaps because it revived and extended an old offense that previously existed, the British offense of withholding information did not generate extensive controversy.[146] In contrast, attempts to provide questioning warrants in

---

[143] Ibid., Section 117, adding Section 38B to the Terrorism Act, 2000.
[144] Walker, *Anti-Terrorism Legislation*, at 126–30.   [145] Ibid.
[146] The revival of the offense does not merit a comment in Professor Tomkins's otherwise blistering and important critique of the 2001 act. Tomkins, "Legislating against Terror." But see Clive Walker, "Conscripting the Public in Terrorism Policing: Towards Safer Communities or a Police State?" (2010) Criminal Law Review 441 noting that there was some discussion of the new offense, but the discussion was influenced by the experience with the offense in Northern Ireland.

Australia were the most controversial part of that country's response to 9/11, and because of widespread opposition in civil society and parliament, the legislation was not enacted until 2003.[147] In Canada, the enactment of investigative hearings to require people to provide information to judges that was relevant to terrorism investigations was also very controversial, and this novel procedure was allowed to expire under a statutory sunset in 2007.[148] In both Australia and Canada, there were debates about the effects of such innovations on the right to silence, rights against self-incrimination, the right to counsel, and freedom of expression and of the press. Such debates, however, were not nearly as prominent in the United Kingdom because the offense delegated much discretion to police and prosecutors whether to charge an uncooperative witness. The calm acceptance in the United Kingdom of the revived and expanded offense of withholding information supports the thesis that countries with more experience with terrorism are often more prepared than those with less experience to accept limits on rights.

Expanded Police Powers

There were some relatively minor expansions of police powers in the 2001 act relating to fingerprinting and photographing those subject to preventive arrests under the Terrorism Act, 2000 and the removal of disguises. As with the provisions relating to the disclosure of information by governmental authorities, the expansion of these powers was generally not limited to terrorism investigations. In the American context, such an approach might have been justified by the Al Capone approach of using any means to target suspected terrorists. In the United Kingdom, however, it was more related to the Blair government's general tough-on-crime approach. The government took the opportunity offered by 9/11 to expand various state powers including those relating the disclosure of information within government for general crime-control purposes.

Racial and Religious Hatred

The 2001 act as originally introduced in Parliament proposed to extend existing offenses of racial hatred to religious hatred in a response to threats and violence against Britain's Muslim communities. As will be seen, the Canadian response to 9/11 also featured expansion of existing hate laws and can be contrasted with the absence of such general legislation in the United States. This proposal was,

---

[147] See Chapter 6.   [148] See Chapter 7.

however, dropped by the government because of concerns that it might inhibit freedom of expression. One of the few successful human rights objections to the 2001 law came with respect to a proposal that the government proposed in large part to protect Muslim minorities from hatred. At the same time, some Muslim groups themselves had problems with the proposal, and others predicted that religious hatred prosecutions might be brought against Muslims. The 2001 law did increase the maximum penalty for racial hatred from two to seven years' imprisonment and allowed religious hatred to be considered as an aggravating factor at sentencing.[149] Anti-Semitic comments by some Muslim extremists were subsequently prosecuted, and offenses against religious hatred were created in 2006.[150] These provisions provided some recognition that community relations with racial and religious groups could be relevant to preventing terrorism. At the same time, they also underlined the limited instruments that many Western democracies had to deal with such complex and potentially divisive issues.

Weapons of Mass Destruction and Aviation Security

The 2001 act addressed some of the dangers of nuclear, chemical, and biological materials falling into the hands of terrorists long before the Security Council would issue Resolution 1540 on this issue in 2004. Access to biological and chemical weapons was limited, and new offenses were created with respect to the transfer of toxins and nuclear weapons. Although access was restricted, the creation of a Pathogens Access Appeal Commission recognized the dangers of preventing legitimate uses of such materials. In principle, an administrative and regulatory focus on substances that might be used for particularly deadly forms of terrorism is well justified. Like Resolution 1540, those parts of the 2001 act relating to weapons of mass destruction had the potential to decrease risks of nuclear, chemical, or biological terrorism while imposing minimal restrictions on liberty. Unfortunately, the limited consultation undertaken before the 2001 act was enacted led to some important materials being left off the list of regulated pathogens.[151] Lack of deliberation when quickly enacting antiterrorism laws typically restricts liberty, but like other shortcuts, it could also adversely affect security.

Not surprisingly given the nature of the 9/11 attacks, the 2001 law addressed aviation security. It provided for increased powers to remove intruders from

[149] Anti-Terrorism, Crime, and Security Act, Sections 39–41.
[150] Racial and Religious Hatred Act, 2006, c.1.
[151] Privy Counsellor Review (Newton) Committee, *Anti-Terrorism, Crime and Security Act*, at para 294.

restricted zones of airports, the making of lists for approved private-sector providers of security and cargo, and allowance for the Department of Transport Inspectors to detain aircraft for security reasons. The Newton Committee concluded that the new provisions provided "useful powers for tightening security at airports" but also noted that the post-9/11 focus on passengers left the cargo end of aviation security vulnerable.[152] In providing tighter regulation of sites and substances that could be used for terrorism, the 2001 act provided a constructive response to 9/11 that did not rely on the ability of intelligence and police agencies to identify all potential terrorists. These administrative parts of the law also placed fewer limits on human rights, including values of privacy, liberty, and equality, than many other parts of the act. At the same time, target hardening in some areas could lead terrorists to focus on less protected areas.

The Use of Immigration Law as Antiterrorism Law and the Part IV Derogation

The most controversial feature of the 2001 act by far was Part IV, which provided for the indeterminate detention of noncitizens suspected of involvement in terrorism who could not be deported because of the United Kingdom's international agreements or "a practical consideration."[153] This part was accompanied by a renewable 15-month derogation from Article 5(1)(f) of the European Convention on Human Rights that provided that noncitizens could only be detained "with a view to deportation." Derogations under Article 15 of the European Convention can only be made in times of war or other public emergencies affecting the life of the nation and only to the extent strictly required by the exigencies of the situation. Part IV reverted to administrative detention and derogations even though the 2000 law has specifically rejected both harsh measures in an attempt to normalize antiterrorism law. The difference this time was that only noncitizens suspected of involvement with terrorism and who would be tortured if returned to countries such as Egypt and Syria were affected by this derogation. This was a return to internment, but internment of a much more limited scope than used in Northern Ireland.

Part IV was responsive to the mandate in Security Council Resolution 1373 that states ensure that terrorists not abuse refugee status but do so in a manner that accords with international human rights law. Indeed, the United Kingdom reported its derogation in its first country report to the CTC as if it were nothing remarkable. The CTC also apparently agreed and only inquired whether the

---

[152] Ibid., at paras. 314, 330.
[153] Anti-Terrorism, Crime, and Security Act, Section 23(1).

noncitizens detained indefinitely would be detained in prison.[154] The CTC took a nonconfrontational approach with the United Kingdom, as it did with other countries. Nevertheless, the United Kingdom's approach attracted much more criticism at home in large part because the United Kingdom was the only European state to employ a derogation.

The United Kingdom's use of the derogation was controversial, but it affirmed its commitment to legality, in stark contrast to the United States' extra-legal approach of rendering suspected terrorists to countries where they would be tortured. Australia and Canada similarly imposed indeterminate detention on noncitizens suspected of involvement with terrorism, but without any clear legislative authorization or any derogation from international or national rights-protection instruments. The Supreme Court of Canada even contemplated that deporting a terrorist suspect to torture might be consistent with the Canadian Charter of Rights, even though it would breach the absolute right against torture in international law.[155] In contrast, the United Kingdom respected the absolute and nonderogable right not to be deported to torture but, while doing so, consciously derogated from the right not to be detained indefinitely with no trial or real prospect of being deported. The United Kingdom may have acted irrationally, hastily, and in a manner that was discriminatory toward noncitizens in restoring indeterminate detention without trial in the months after 9/11, but it acted legally in a way that respected both the right against torture and the European Convention, which allows derogations.

Part IV went beyond Security Council Resolution 1373 because it applied not only to asylum seekers who "planned, facilitated or participated in the commission of terrorist acts"[156] but to those that the secretary of state reasonably suspected were members of international terrorist groups or had links with such groups. The concept of "links" with a terrorist group was more of an intelligence than a legal concept. Concerns about such a broad and vague standard were raised in Parliament, and the concept was partially narrowed by a definition that links required a person to assist or support an international terrorist group. Even with the definition, a noncitizen who offered financial or perhaps only ideological support to an international terrorist group could still be included in the indeterminate detention regime. The definition of a terrorist in Part IV was broader than even the broad definition of terrorism in the Terrorism Act, 2000. One of the attractions of using immigration law as

---

[154] U.K. Country Report, S/2001/1232, at 9; U.K. Country Report, S/2002/787, at 6.
[155] *Suresh v. Canada*, 1 S.C.R. 3 (2002), as discussed in Chapter 7.
[156] Resolution 1373 (2001), para. 3(3).

antiterrorism law was that it allowed broad liability rules that would generally not be accepted if applied to citizens.

Another reason why the use of immigration law as antiterrorism law was attractive was that it allowed secret evidence to be used in a manner that would not be acceptable in criminal courts. Part IV would be administered by the Special Immigration Appeal Commission (SIAC), which was created in the wake of the European Court of Human Rights's 1996 decision in *Chahal v. The United Kingdom*[157] that held that the United Kingdom could not deport a suspected Sikh terrorist to India because of a torture risk. The *Chahal* decision also raised concerns about the use of secret evidence that prevented noncitizens from knowing and challenging the case against them. SIAC was created in response and it provided an innovative response to the dilemma of secret evidence. It was a specialized tribunal composed of a judge, an expert on immigration, and an expert on national security. In addition, security-cleared special advocates could challenge secret evidence not disclosed to the affected noncitizen when it was presented to SIAC. Special advocates were, however, generally prohibited from consulting with the affected person after they had seen the secret evidence for fear of inadvertent disclosures. Secret evidence in immigration cases would frequently come from foreign states that did not consent to the public disclosure of the information. The Joint Committee on Human Rights supported the use of SIAC, noting that it provided "reasonable protection for the appellant's rights."[158] At the same time, SIAC was only required to review the basis for detention every six months after its first review, and the secretary of state could issue a new certificate should SIAC cancel one.[159] These provisions resembled the provisions for indeterminate administrative detention under the Internal Security Acts examined in Chapter 3, though of course they would, like American measures at Guantanamo, only be applied against non-citizens. As will be seen, the singling out of non-citizens would be much more legally controversial in the United Kingdom than in the United States.

Part IV allowed the secretary of state to short-circuit a person's application for refugee status by certifying that the person was not entitled to refugee status on security grounds, as recognized in the refugee convention. The focus then shifted to whether the applicant was or had been a terrorist as opposed to whether the applicant would face political persecution if returned to his or her home country. Although this approach followed exclusions in the refugee

---

[157] 23 EHRR 413 (1997).
[158] *Joint Committee on Human Rights Second Report*, November 12, 2001, at para. 47.
[159] Anti-Terrorism, Crime, and Security Act, 2001, Sections 26 and 27(9).

convention, it also meant that issues of security and terrorism dominated and displaced those of political or religious persecution and repression that may have contributed to the person being involved in either terrorism or terrorist groups. In this way, the determination of national security exemptions from refugee law contributed to a narrow and even a contextual focus on security and crime.

Part IV powers were used rather sparingly and were limited to noncitizens believed to be associated with al Qaeda. In December 2001, eight persons were detained, and by November 2003, 14 persons were in detention, with two voluntarily leaving for France and Morocco.[160] In 2003, the Newton Committee, composed of life peers, judges, and elected members of Parliament from all major parties, recommended that Part IV be repealed as soon as possible and replaced with provisions that would apply to all terrorist suspects and would not require derogation. It stressed that the United Kingdom was the only country to derogate from the European Convention after 9/11 and that a noncitizen could be subject to indefinite detention on the basis of reasonable belief and suspicion and on secret evidence. It also emphasized that the terrorist threat to the United Kingdom was not limited to noncitizens and that almost "30% of Terrorism Act, 2000 suspects in the past year have been British," including British citizen Richard Reid, who attempted to ignite a shoe bomb on a transatlantic flight.[161] The Newton Committtee also warned about the danger of "exporting terrorism"[162] by deporting suspected terrorists or allowing them to leave the United Kingdom. Its influential and powerful analysis demonstrates how concerns about human rights and discrimination can be blended with concerns about the lack of effectiveness of some harsh antiterrorism measures.

Although the Newton Committee was unequivocal in its critique of Part IV, it was less certain about what should replace it. It predicted that more criminal prosecutions might be possible if the United Kingdom's self-imposed ban on the use of electronic surveillance was lifted. At the same time, it recognized that the disclosure of intelligence could create problems for the intelligence services and recommended that the use of a security-cleared investigative judge, as used in Continental Europe, be investigated.[163] The Home Office investigated the French system of investigating magistrates working closely with intelligence agencies but ultimately concluded that it was not compatible with adversarial traditions and the historical unwillingness to use secret

---

[160] Privy Counsellor Review (Newton) Committee, *Anti-Terrorism, Crime and Security Act*, at para 138.

[161] Ibid., at para. 193.   [162] Ibid., at para. 195.

[163] Ibid., at para. 224.

evidence in criminal trials. The Newton Committee also proposed other less rights-invasive alternatives. They included control orders restricting a suspect's freedom of movement and associations and access to communications and deportations with assurances of no mistreatment. The Newton Committee warned, however, that such "measures are less attractive than conventional prosecution and surveillance but in our view they are preferable to Part 4 as it stands."[164]

The Newton Committee's report affirms the importance of review of emergency measures. It also demonstrates both the strengths and weaknesses of proportionality analysis. On one hand, proportionality analysis allowed the Newton Committee to argue that there were many less rights-invasive means for the government to pursue its important objective of preventing terrorism. On the other hand, the committee threw open a broad array of alternative approaches without carefully evaluating the adverse effects that those alternatives might have. Proportionality analysis, with its focus on less drastic alternatives, is very influenced by starting points. Almost everything looked better than the indeterminate detention without trial authorized by Part IV. As will be seen, the United Kingdom eventually opted for the alternatives of control orders and deportation with assurances. At the same time, it refused to budge on the use of electronic surveillance evidence to increase the viability of criminal prosecutions even though the Newton Committee indicated that criminal investigations and prosecutions were preferable to the other alternatives it identified.

Home Secretary David Blunkett responded negatively to the Newton Committee by asserting that Part IV remained necessary. He stressed that the detainees were free to leave the United Kingdom and that they could challenge the basis for their detention in SIAC with the assistance of special advocates. The government defended the focus on noncitizens as proportionate and suggested that extending "draconian powers" of internment to citizens "would be difficult to justify. Experience has demonstrated the dangers of such an approach and the damage it can do to community cohesion and thus to the support from all parts of the public that is so essential to countering the terrorist threat."[165] The rejection of internment for citizens represented important learning from past mistakes in Northern Ireland, but it also underlined how Part IV could be adopted and defended with little concern for the noncitizens whom it affected. Although some argue that fears of the tyranny of the majority are overblown,[166] legislators remain willing to impose measures

[164] Ibid., at para. 250.
[165] Counter-Terrorism Power; a Discussion Paper, CM 6147, February 2004, at para. 36.
[166] Joo-Cheong Tham, "Parliamentary Deliberation and the National Security Executive: The Case of Control Orders" (2010) Public Law 79.

on noncitizens that they would not be willing to impose on the citizens who elect them.

The government quickly concluded that the Newton recommendations on the criminal trial "[do] not offer a solution to the need to protect sensitive information whilst enabling the defendant to know the full case that has been put against him."[167] Although the use of electronic surveillance in criminal trials was recommended by both Lord Lloyd in his 1996 report and by the Newton Committee, the government continues stubbornly to remain committed to the security services' desire to avoid having intelligence collected through electronic surveillance disclosed. Interestingly, the government also rejected the Newton Committee's proposal for control orders as a less restrictive alternative to indeterminate detention on the basis that they would not provide "sufficient security to address the threat posed by international terrorists."[168] The Newton Committee made a persuasive case that there were other less rights-invasive ways to respond to noncitizens suspected of involvement with al Qaeda than indeterminate administrative detention, but the government was not willing to take the risks involved until faced by a surprising and important judicial decision.

v. THE BELMARSH LITIGATION

With the government rejecting the Newton Committee's recommendations, the issue shifted to the courts. This shift from majoritarian politics is understandable given that Part IV only targeted a small number of noncitizens who were imprisoned at Belmarsh Prison in London. The detainees included Abu Qatada, a radical Islamic preacher who made tapes that were watched by some of the 9/11 terrorists as well as men from Algeria, Egypt, Jordan, Palestine and Tunisia. These men were very unpopular because they were suspected of involvement with al Qaeda. Although the Newton Committee included elected representatives who had expressed concern about their treatment, the government itself was not prepared to risk alternatives to their imprisonment.

As contemplated in the 2001 act, the derogation was first challenged in SIAC, which, unlike the courts, reviewed secret material offered by the state to justify the derogation. SIAC determined that there was an emergency threatening the life of the nation because the United Kingdom was a prime target for al Qaeda terrorism "second only to the United States."[169] SIAC, however, found that Part IV was discriminatory under Article 14 of the European Convention

---

[167] *Counter-Terrorism Power*, at para. 38.   [168] Ibid., at para. 45.
[169] SIAC judgment quoted in *A v. Secretary of State*, EWCA 1502 (2002), at para. 33.

because its provisions only applied to noncitizens. It stressed that many terrorist suspects were British nationals. The focus on equality rights was particularly important because, as Ronald Dworkin had noted, much of the rebalancing of rights and security after 9/11 exchanged rights of Muslim minorities for the security interests of the non-Muslim majority.[170]

Following the example of *Rehman*,[171] where the courts had overturned a SIAC decision that had also taken a critical approach to the state's security efforts, the Court of Appeal overturned SIAC and upheld Part IV from challenge, stressing that there was no discrimination because noncitizens had no right to remain in the United Kingdom.[172] The Australian High Court and the Supreme Court of Canada used similar reasoning to reject an equality challenge to the use of immigration law as antiterrorism law, but the reasoning in both cases is flawed because it avoids evaluating the necessity for the differential treatment of noncitizens.[173] Lord Woolf cited Security Council Resolution 1373 as a sign of the emergency and concluded that "the unfortunate fact is that the emergency which the government believes to exist justifies the taking of action which would not otherwise be acceptable."[174] This ignored that the SIAC had also accepted that there was an emergency but had stressed that the state was responding to it in an irrational and discriminatory manner.

SIAC's more critical approach was vindicated by the House of Lords, which decided, in December 2004, that though an emergency existed, Part IV was both discriminatory and disproportionate. The House of Lords decision made headlines claiming that it had provoked a "constitutional crisis" and contributed to Home Secretary David Blunkett's resignation. The initial reaction from the government suggested that it would, as it could under the Human Rights Act, 1998, which does not give the courts power to strike down legislation, ignore the court's declaration of incompatibility. It would also continue to detain the 12 noncitizens detained at Belmarsh Prison under the legislation. Hazel Blears, the police minister, stressed that the House of Lords had not seen intelligence that had authorized the detention of the noncitizens under the legislation,[175] even though the majority of the Lords had accepted that there was an emergency threatening the life of the nation.[176]

---

[170] Ronald Dworkin, "The Threat to Patriotism," New York Review of Books, February, 28, 2003.
[171] UKHL 46 (2001), at para. 62.
[172] A v. *Secretary of State*, EWCA 1502 (2002), at para. 47.
[173] Dyzenhaus, *Constitution of Law*, at 165.
[174] A. v. *Secretary of State* UKHL 56 (2004), at para. 64.
[175] "Judges Verdict on Terror Law Provokes Constitutional Crisis," The Guardian, December 17, 2004.
[176] The majority of the House of Lords was deferring to SIAC, which had examined the secret intelligence, albeit in 2002. Its decision also reflected the deferential standard under the

In an complete shift from his post-9/11 judgment in *Rehman*, Lord Hoffmann went farther than the other judges and decided there was no emergency and that "the real threat to the life of the nation is not from terrorism but from laws such as these."[177] He took note of "the widespread skepticism which has attached to intelligence assessments since the fiasco over Iraqi weapons of mass destruction."[178] This bold approach received much praise, but Hoffmann's assumptions that some terrorists plots existed begged the question of just how many were being investigated, something that the Court would not know because it did not receive secret information about the threat level. Two years later, the head of MI5, the United Kingdom's domestic security intelligence agency, announced that her service and the police were investigating 200 "groups or networks" involving 1,600 individuals who "are actively engaged in plotting, or facilitating, terrorist acts here and overseas."[179] My point is not to suggest that Lord Hoffmann was wrong to hold that there was no emergency or that the majority was right. In the absence of review of the government's secret material, any judicial decision about the existence of an emergency would be suspect because it lacked full information. The refusal to examine secret information left courts vulnerable to criticisms of the "if you knew what I knew" kind made by Minister Blears. As late as 2009, the Joint Committee on Human Rights raised concerns that the government was maintaining "a permanent state of emergency" on the basis of information not publicly disclosed.[180]

Lord Hoffmann's approach to security issues was erratic. The government had relied on his *Rehman* postscript to urge the court to defer to the legislation, only to earn criticism from Lord Bingham for stigmatizing judicial decisions "as in some way undemocratic,"[181] even though that was precisely what Lord Hoffmann had done in *Rehman*. As will be seen, Lord Hoffmann frequently sided with the state in cases dealing with control orders that replaced the Part IV scheme and severely criticized the decision of the European Court of Human Rights to place limits on the use of secret evidence. His approach was a binary one that veered between a business-as-usual approach that discounted

---

European Convention with respect to the declaration of emergencies that was affirmed by the European Court of Human Rights on appeal in *United Kingdom v. A*, 49 EHRR (2009).

[177] UKHL 56 (2004), at para. 97.   [178] Ibid., at para. 94.

[179] The speech was ambiguous because it also suggested that there was "nearer thirty" plots "to kill people and damage our economy." Dame Manningham-Buller, "The International Terrorist Threat to the UK," speech at Queen Mary's College, November 9, 2006, at https://www.mi5.gov.uk/output/the-international-terrorist-threat-to-the-uk-1.html.

[180] Joint Committee on Human Rights, *Counter-Terrorism Policy and Human Rights (17th Report): Bringing Human Rights Back In* (2010), at paras. 9–24.

[181] *A v. Secretary of State*, UKHL 56 (2004), at para. 42.

the terrorist threat and one that deferred to what the state determined was necessary in an emergency. Most other judges took a more nuanced approach that, like the Newton Committee, focused on whether the state's objectives could be achieved in a less rights-invasive manner.

Although the majority of the House of Lords accepted that there was an emergency threatening the life of the nation, it concluded that Part IV and the use of immigration law as antiterrorism law was not a rational response to the emergency. Lord Bingham stressed "that the choice of an immigration measure to address a security problem had the inevitable result of failing adequately to address that problem (by allowing non-UK suspected terrorists to leave the country with impunity and leaving British suspected terrorists at large) while imposing the severe penalty of indefinite detention on persons who, even if reasonably suspected of having links with Al-Qaeda, may harbour no hostile intentions towards the United Kingdom."[182] The House of Lords cast doubts on the American practice of making frequent distinctions between the rights of citizens and noncitizens by suggesting that doing so might violate the American Convention on Human Rights and that, in any event, "US authority does not provide evidence of general international practice."[183] As will be seen, however, the government remained attracted to attempting to use immigration law as antiterrorism and amended immigration laws for security reasons in both 2006 and 2008.

The Belmarsh case was affirmed five years later by the European Court of Human Rights which also awarded nominal damages to the Belmarsh detainees.[184] It is likely the most important case of the post-9/11 era and resulted in the repeal of a major plank of the United Kingdom's response to 9/11; it rejected the idea that judicial review in the security context was undemocratic and undesirable, and it found the widespread practice of relying on immigration law to be irrational, disproportionate, and discriminatory because the terrorist threat was not limited to citizens. At the same time, the Belmarsh case must be viewed as somewhat exceptional. Much of the basis for the court's conclusions had been laid by the Newton Committee. The Human Rights Act, 1998, allowed the court to make a bold declaration of incompatibility without striking the legislation down or releasing any of the detainees. The decision left the government with the wide range of alternatives outlined by the Newton Committee, including even the possibility of preserving the Part IV regime of indeterminate detention or extending it to citizens.

---

[182] Ibid., at para. 43.   [183] Ibid., at para. 69.
[184] *A v. United Kingdom* 49 EHRR 29 (2009) (Grand Chamber).

VI. THE RESPONSE TO THE BELMARSH CASE

Control Orders

The government decided in January 2005 that it would repeal Part IV of the 2001 act, and by March 2005, Parliament had enacted the Prevention of Terrorism Act, 2005.[185] The debate in the House of Commons was limited to two days, even though there was no urgency, as Part IV remained in place even after the House of Lords had declared it incompatible with the Human Rights Act, 1998. The government stressed that the threat from al Qaeda was great, that the security services and the police wanted control orders, and that criminal prosecutions could not be used as an alternative, despite the creation of many new terrorism offenses that apply long before any acts of terrorism. The government refused to follow Lord Lloyd's and the Newton Committee's recommendations that electronic surveillance be used as evidence to facilitate criminal prosecutions. The new act facilitated the use of secret information, whereas the use of electronic surveillance in criminal prosecutions would have forced the security service to retain and disclose more intelligence. Although Professor Tham has defended the parliamentary debates as deliberative and not reflecting a tyranny of the majority,[186] the fact remains that the judges who subsequently saw the secret evidence and considered the sometimes devastating effects of control orders on individuals have imposed more restraints on control orders than parliamentarians who were willing to allow control orders that would derogate from the right to liberty in the European Convention.

Control orders echoed back to restriction orders found in many "colonial emergency codes."[187] They also drew on the precedents of more modern anti-social behavior orders[188] and community sanctions by providing for house arrest, curfews and electronic tagging.[189] In 2007, some of the concepts found in control orders were expanded to other crimes by the creation of serious crime prevention orders.[190] All these instruments involve what Lucia

---

[185] Chapter 2.

[186] Although suggesting that some degree of trust of the security services is inevitable, Professor Tham rightly criticizes parliamentarians for deferring to the national security executive on matters relating to the degree of the threat. Tham, "Parliamentary Deliberation."

[187] Clive Walker, "Keeping Control of Terrorists without Losing Control of Constitutionalism" (2007) 59 Stanford Law Review 1395, at 1403–4, and as discussed in Chapter 3.

[188] Crime and Disorder Act, 1998, c.37; Sexual Offences Act, 2003.

[189] Julian Roberts, *The Virtual Prison* (Cambridge: Cambridge University Press, 2004).

[190] Serious Crime Act, 2007, c.27, Sections 1, 19. Like control orders, serious crime prevention orders are characterized as a civil process. As such, they require something much less than proof of guilt beyond a reasonable doubt, and they can be renewed without the protections against

Zedner has called "preventive justice," "future law," and "pre-punishment."[191] As Professor Zedner suggests, the expansion of the law toward prepunishment is troubling. Courts should not blindly accept the state's characterization of such interventions as civil and preventive when they have punishing effects on controlled individuals and their families. In addition, the state's tools for predicting future behavior – including the use of intelligence – are imprecise and have not typically been used for imposing legal consequences. The British attraction to control orders suggests impatience with the use of criminal law and a willingness to restrict liberty in an attempt to manage even ambiguous and uncertain risks of crime.

The 2005 act allowed a control order to be made on the basis of reasonable suspicion of involvement in terrorism-related activities. Terrorism was defined in accordance with the broad definition in the 2000 act, with terrorism-related activities defined even more broadly to include conduct that facilitates or gives encouragement to the commission, preparation, and instigation of acts of terrorism.[192] Courts could review control orders, but as with Part IV, Parliament attempted to establish a deferential standard of judicial review that only allowed courts to quash a control order or a condition of a control order if it was "obviously flawed."[193] Attempts to legislate such deferential standards of review presented a risk that courts could be used to legitimate control orders. Indeed, Sullivan J., in one of the first control order cases, declared the procedure incompatible with fair trial rights because the limited judicial review available applied only a "thin veneer of legality" to an executive decision based on "one-sided information."[194] This decision was overturned on appeal in a judgment which emphasized that judges should quash control orders if they were obviously flawed at the time of review.[195] Judges have been able, in some cases, to quash control orders and terms of control orders on the basis that though the intelligence may have initially revealed that the person was

---

double jeopardy applying. Like control orders, they can impose wide-ranging restrictions on a person's liberty, including his or her movement within and outside the United Kingdom, possession and use of items, and employment, with breach of their provisions being a criminal offense that can be punished by up to five years' imprisonment. An important difference, however, is that serious crime prevention orders unlike control orders, require a conviction of a serious crime and have been enacted as permanent legislation.

[191] Zedner, "Preventive Justice or Pre-Punishment?"

[192] Prevention of Terrorism Act, 2005, c.2, Section 1(9).

[193] Prevention of Terrorism Act, 2005, c.2, Section 3. There are stronger judicial review requirements relating to the necessity for conditions and a risk associated with a public emergency, but these are only imposed for control orders that explicitly derogate from the right to liberty. Ibid., Section 4(7).

[194] *Re MB*, EWCA (Admin) 1000 (2006), at paras. 103–4.

[195] *Re MB*, EWCA (Civ) 1140 (2006), at para. 46.

a security threat, the passage of time had diminished the threat.[196] Although preventive justice practiced in control orders departs from criminal justice in its focus on risks and prevention, as opposed to past acts and punishment, preventive justice has its own logic and standards, and judges are capable of deciding that some intelligence is flawed, dated, insufficient, or unreliable.

The 2005 act also borrowed from the 2001 act by providing for the use of secret evidence not disclosed to the controlee but disclosed to special advocates. Judges were precluded from ordering disclosure if disclosure would "be contrary to the public interest,"[197] even if it was essential to ensure fairness to the controlee. This is a broad authorization of secrecy more in common with the secrecy provisions used in Singapore's Internal Security Act or Israel's administrative detention law examined in Chapter 3 than with public interest immunity principles used in criminal law that allow judges to balance the harms of disclosure to the state against the unfairness of non-disclosure to the directly affected person. The use of secret evidence and special advocates in control orders reveals a danger that such innovations may spread from immigration law to terrorism measures with at least quasi-criminal effects.[198]

Control orders represented a curious mixture of an intelligence-based approach, with its focus on risks, training, association, and travel of those subject to surveillance, combined with punitive house arrest conditions that are usually imposed as punishment short of actual imprisonment. The criminal law lurks in the background of control orders because the violation of a condition is an offense subject to up to five years' imprisonment.[199] There is also a requirement that the possibility of prosecution be considered as an alternative to the use of a control order.[200] Control orders can be used as a less onerous administrative backstop to criminal prosecutions. As in Australia,[201] control orders have been issued in the United Kingdom in the wake of decisions that criminal convictions were not warranted or could not be sustained.[202]

---

[196] R. (on the application of Secretary of State for the Home Department) v. Bullivant, EWHC 337 (Admin) (2008); Secretary of State for the Home Department v. NN sub nom. Secretary of State for the Home Department v. GG; Secretary of State for the Home Department v. Al Saadi, EWHC 3390 (Admin.) (2009). See generally Tomkins, "National Security and the Role of the Court."

[197] Prevention of Terrorism Act, 2005, Section 4(3)(d).

[198] This criticism is stressed in Secret Evidence (London: Justice, 2009).

[199] Prevention of Terrorism Act, 2005, c.2, Section 9.

[200] Ibid., Section 8. The courts have stated that the obligation to inquire into the possibility of prosecution should be "taken seriously" but have also not overturned a control order on such a basis. Re E, UKHL 47 (2007), at para. 15.

[201] Chapter 6.

[202] In 2006, a control order was issued against Rauf Abdullah Mohammed after he was acquitted of possession of an item for terrorist purposes. Walker, Anti-Terrorism Legislation, at 229.

One U.K. control order was issued after a person was convicted of a terrorist conspiracy but sentenced to time served and released on bail.[203] Another was ordered against a man acquitted of involvement in the 2006 transatlantic bombing plot, with the judge stating that "the fact that AY was acquitted at his trial, has little relevance to these issues.... The jury was not sure of AY's guilt, on the basis of the evidence placed before them, but the evidence placed before me is different."[204] Such uses of control orders in both the United Kingdom and Australia resemble the use of administrative detention in Israel in security cases even after the accused has served a set sentence for criminal behavior.

Control orders, like Part IV powers before them, have been used against only small numbers of terrorist suspects. Initially, only noncitizens who have previously been subject to Part IV detention were subject to control orders. These noncitizens were all asylum seekers who had been detained under Part IV, but in subsequent years, some have been deported with assurances that they will not be tortured. One study found that 45 individuals have been subject to control orders with 26 of them known to be asylum seekers and 9 of them known to be British citizens.[205] A subsequent government report revealed that 28 of 48 people subject to control orders were foreign nationals and 10 of the 28 were on control orders pending deportation proceedings.[206] This raises the issue of whether the House of Lords decision was more a victory for formal equality as noncitizens still composed the majority of those subject to control orders. In a further irony, given that Part IV was originally designed to respond to the difficulties of deporting terrorist suspects, a number of control orders have been ordered to prevent the controlees from traveling to places like Syria and Iraq. Control orders in these cases are being used to keep people in the United Kingdom because of fears that they may commit acts of terrorism abroad. In other cases, however, the United Kingdom has persisted with its deportation efforts and has obtained questionable assurances against torture to deport some of the original detainees under Part IV of the 2001 act to Algeria and Libya.[207]

---

[203] *Secretary of State v. AT*, EWCA (Civ) 512 (2009), at para. 2.

[204] *Secretary of State v. AY*, EWCA 3053 (Admin) (2009), at para. 196.

[205] Robin Wilcox, *Control Orders: Strengthening National Security* (London: Centre for Social Cohesion, 2010), at 8.

[206] *Review of Counter-Terrorism and Security Powers Review Findings and Recommendations* January 2011 Cm 8004 at 36.

[207] One of the persons approved for deportation to Jordan to face a military trial in *RB (Algeria) v. Secretary of State*, UKHL 10 (2009), was one of the original detainees in Belmarsh under Part IV of the 2001 act. His case is presently being appealed to the European Court of Human Rights.

Although the total numbers are small, control orders have generated much litigation. Between 2006 and 2009, about 13 million pounds was spent on control orders, most on legal costs.[208] A similar pattern will be observed with respect to the use of immigration law security certificates in Canada, which also uses secret evidence not disclosed to the detainee as a means to impose administrative detention and control order–type restrictions in the community. The endless number of judgments produced in a few cases reveals legal pathologies produced by departures from established procedures, most notably the use of secret evidence. The government eventually abandoned most of the troublesome proceedings, especially as increasing limits were imposed by the courts on the ability to rely on secret evidence. At the same time, the state and its security services clung to the need for a diminishing number of these controversial measures.

Control orders were challenged substantively for violating the right to liberty and procedurally for violating the right to a fair trial by their use of secret evidence. In a series of decisions in 2007, the House of Lords decided that whereas an 18-hour curfew was excessive, a 14-hour curfew did not infringe the right to liberty.[209] These decisions were criticized as judicial legitimation of control orders,[210] an argument supported by the fact that the government responded to the 2007 decisions with statements that the courts had upheld control orders and, in some cases, even increased lower curfews to the apparent 16 hour curfew ceiling. As seen in the preceding chapter, Justice O'Connor's decision in *Hamdi* served as a blueprint for a combatant status review process at Guantánamo that used secret evidence and departures from the rules of evidence. In Canada, the government quickly adopted a special advocate system once the Canadian Supreme Court had mentioned it as a less restrictive alternative to the use of secret evidence without any adversarial challenge, even though the court also mentioned other systems that might have provided more robust challenges to secret evidence.[211] The critique of judicial legitimation of minimal standards is, however, somewhat diminished by the fact that both the lower courts and the House of Lords have reserved the right to judge the necessity of control order conditions in individual cases and subsequently invalidated 16-hour control orders in particular circumstances.[212]

---

[208] Joint Committee on Human Rights, *Annual Renewal of Control Orders*, 2010 (16th report), at para. 102.

[209] *JJ*, UKHL 45 (2007); *E*, UKHL 47 (2007); *MB and AF*, UKHL 46 (2007).

[210] K. D. Ewing and Joo-Cheong Tham, "The Continuing Futility of the Human Rights Act" (2008) Public Law 668.

[211] See Chapter 7.

[212] *Secretary of State for the Home Dept v. AP*, UKSC 24 (2010), holding that a control order with a 16-hour curfew violated the right to liberty in part because it also required the subject to locate

There were also numerous challenges to the use of secret evidence to support control orders. After much hesitation and confusion,[213] the House of Lords, following the lead of the European Court of Human Rights,[214] held that there must be enough disclosure of specific allegations to those subject to control orders to allow them to instruct counsel.[215] These rulings attempt to respond to criticisms that special advocates are unable to challenge secret evidence effectively if the affected person cannot provide instructions and information that may be needed to challenge the secret information. Restrictions on how much evidence could be used but kept secret diminished the allure of control orders and by December, 2010, only eight control orders remained in effect.[216]

As discussed earlier, the government originally rejected control orders as not sufficiently restrictive enough to deal with international terrorists when they were proposed by the Newton Committee. One man subject to a control order observed, "I go everywhere now – on the underground, the buses, the mosque. But I must be home by 7.00 pm. . . . The government is playing games, why are they letting me out to be with people?"[217] Concerns have been raised that 7 people subject to control orders have absconded.[218] This raises the possibility of arguing that control orders are both ineffective and infringe rights. Professor Zedner warns against an efficacy-based critique on the basis that it may only invite more drastic responses. She suggests that "perhaps efficacy should not count in our arguments because it is not a justification in its own right."[219] Although I agree with Professor Zedner that there is a danger of harsher responses if control orders are rejected as inefficacious, efficacy in my view should count in arguments about the proportionality of control orders. If those

---

150 miles away from his primary residence. The appeal was somewhat moot as the control order has been rescinded in favor of an attempt to deport the person to Ethiopia. On the role of the lower court review, see Tomkins, "National Security and the Role of the Court."

[213] For strong criticisms of the House of Lords approach in these earlier cases and their deference with respect to control orders, see Helen Fenwick and Gavin Phillipson, "UK Counter-Terrorism Law Post 9/11," in Ramraj, *Global Anti-Terrorism Law and Policy*, 2nd ed. (Cambridge: Cambridge University Press, forthcoming 2011).

[214] *A. v. United Kingdom*, 49 E.H.R.R. (2009).

[215] *Secretary of State v. AF (no 3)*, UKHL 28 (2009).

[216] *Review of Counter-Terrorism and Security Powers Review Findings and Recommendations* January 2011 Cm 8004 at 36

[217] As quoted in Zedner, "Preventive Justice or Pre-Punishment?" at 191.

[218] Wilcox, *Control Orders*, at 8.

[219] Zedner, "Preventive Justice or Pre-Punishment?" at 191. At the same time, the adverse effects of control orders on controlees and their families should not be discounted. The Joint Committee on Human Rights heard evidence from solicitor Gareth Piece that once she had three clients who were in the health section of Belmarsh Prison after having breached their control orders, attempting to take their lives after their wives had left them. Joint Committee on Human Rights, *Annual Renewal of Control Orders*, at para. 40.

subject to control orders are really involved in terrorism, then they should be prosecuted, even if that qualifies as a harsher response. The harsher response of prosecution would also be a fairer one because it would not rely on secret evidence and it would require proof of guilt beyond a reasonable doubt.

Lord Carlile, the long-time independent reviewer of terrorism legislation, defended the use of control orders in the remaining cases, warning that their repeal would make the United Kingdom "more vulnerable to a terrorist attack." He also concluded prosecutions would not be viable in the remaining cases.[220] In contrast, Lord Macdonald, the former Director of Public Prosecutions, recommended that control orders should not be continued because they were "an impediment to prosecution" because they imposed such tight restrictions that they prevented the gathering of evidence of crimes based on preparations for terrorism. He argued that had those who plotted to explode multiple aircraft over the Atlantic been subject to restrictive control orders "they would be living amongst us still, instead of sitting for very long years in the jail cells where they belong."[221] Both of these reviewers had access to the secret information said to justify the use of control orders and their differing conclusions reflected different views about tolerable risk levels and different assumptions about the ability to prosecute terrorist suspects.

The Cameron–Clegg government accepted in early 2011 that control orders should be replaced by less restrictive Terrorism Prevention and Investigation Measures that would retain some of the travel, association, and monitored use of the computer or phone provisions found in control orders, but would not allow the imposition of house arrest or relocation orders. Consistent with Lord Macdonald's approach, the government stressed that "successful prosecution will always be the objective."[222] At the same time, consistent with Lord Carlile's warnings, which were also echoed by former Ministers, the government decided to continue control orders until the end of 2011. The Joint Committee on Human Rights approved of the former decision to end control orders, but expressed concerns about the decision to renew the existing orders till the end of 2011. It also expressed concerns that the new measures could be applied to individuals for more than two years and that the new

[220] Lord Carlile *Sixth Report of the Independent Reviewer Pursuant to Section 14(3) of the Prevention of Terrorism Act, 2005* February 3, 2011 at para 94. Without reference to the wide rights of the accused to disclosure in both the United States and Canada, Lord Carlile stressed the difficulty of using electronic surveillance because disclosure standards in the United Kingdom "are far more demanding and revealing than in the jurisdiction of any comparable country." Ibid at para 69.

[221] Lord Macdonald *Review of Counter-Terrorism and Security Powers* January, 2011 cm 8003 at 9.

[222] *Review of Counter-Terrorism and Security Powers Review Findings and Recommendations* January, 2011 Cm 8004 at 41–42.

regime, unlike the control order regime, may be a permanent one not subject to annual Parliamentary renewals.[223] Finally, it is not clear whether secret evidence will continue to be used under the new regime despite the concerns raised by special advocates about their inability to consult a detainee after they have seen the secret evidence. The repeal of control orders demonstrates a renewed confidence in the criminal process and a fading sense of emergency. Nevertheless, the proposed introduction of less restrictive control measures also underlines a more permanent merging of counter-terrorism powers with other preventive powers such as anti-social behavior orders.

Control orders, like the Guantánamo detentions in the United States and security certificates in Canada, fit into a pattern of post-9/11 attempts to forge methods of justice that avoid the restraints of criminal law. In all three cases, however, these efforts have resulted in numerous and often successful legal challenges and much political controversy. Although shortcuts around criminal law will be attractive to governments, especially when they allow intelligence to be used as secret evidence, they will not generate the same public confidence or acceptance as criminal convictions under even an expanded criminal law. Control orders were an unstable and incoherent blend of intelligence and legal concepts. They risked being too strong for those who may only arouse suspicion and should perhaps be subject to surveillance, while being too weak with respect to those who could be prosecuted for acts of preparation or support for terrorism. The gap between what must be disclosed to sustain a control order and what must be disclosed in a criminal prosecution was narrowed by the courts. As such, criminal prosecutions should be both more attractive for the state and also fairer for the accused. The British government recognized the failure of control orders and how they acted as an impediment to prosecutions whereas the American government has persisted with military detention and trial at Guantánamo and the Canadian government has persisted with the use of security certificates as alternatives to criminal prosecutions.

Immigration Law Responses to the Belmarsh Case

It would be a mistake to conclude that the U.K. government, in the wake of the House of Lords decision in the Belmarsh case, abandoned all uses of immigration law as antiterrorism law. Even though the House of Lords strongly concluded that immigration law was an irrational and discriminatory response

---

[223] Joint Committee on Human Rights *Renewal of Control Order Legislation*, 2011 March 2, 2011 HL paper 106; HC paper 838.

to a threat of terrorism that was not limited to non-citizens, the government responded with a variety of immigration law initiatives.

In recognition that the prohibition against torture was at the heart of the problem of what to do with suspected terrorists previously held at Belmarsh, the U.K. government attempted to persuade the European Court of Human Rights to follow the approach taken in 2002 by the Supreme Court of Canada in *Suresh*, which contemplated that deportation to torture could be accepted in "exceptional circumstances."[224] The Canadian approach was misguided from the start, with even the Supreme Court of Canada recognizing that any exception to the right against torture would violate clear international law. Fortunately, the European Court of Human Rights, in *Saadi v. Italy*,[225] affirmed the absolute nature of the prohibition against torture.

The U.K. government had more success in pursuing another strategy that allowed it to deport suspected terrorists. It has developed assurances with a number of countries including Algeria, Jordan and Libya that a suspected terrorist would not be tortured if returned. In 2009, the House of Lords upheld a decision made by SIAC that accepted that suspected terrorists could be returned to Algeria and Jordan without a substantial risk of torture. It relied on the deferential standard articulated by the Supreme Court of Canada in *Suresh*, itself influenced by Lord Hoffmann in *Rehman*, to stress that courts did not have expertise in determining the risk of torture in foreign countries.[226] Deportation with assurances has been controversial because of real concerns about whether countries that have mistreated terrorist suspects in the past can be trusted to change their ways and about the use of evidence derived from torture in Jordanian and Algerian terrorism prosecutions.[227] Abu Qatada, one of the original Belmarsh detainees, has appealed the House of Lords ruling to the European Court of Human Rights alleging that he will be tortured if deported to Jordan. His case is supported by Amnesty International, Justice and Human Rights Watch who have all warned about the dangers of relying on "paper promises from torturers."[228] Nevertheless, the U.K. government has continued to be attracted to deportations of terrorist suspects and confirmed

---

[224] *Suresh v. Canada*, 1 S.C.R. 3 (2002), as discussed in Chapter 7.
[225] [2008] ECHR 179.
[226] *RB (Algeria) v. Secretary of State*, UKHL 10 (2009), at paras. 116–17.
[227] Lord Hoffmann stressed that British courts should not impose higher standards with respect to the use of evidence derived by torture in Jordanian courts than were imposed in British courts. Ibid., at para. 202. In both British and Jordanian courts, an applicant has to establish on a balance of probabilities that evidence was obtained under torture, despite the manifest difficulties of doing so.
[228] "Abu Qatada takes deportation fight to European court after law lords ruling" *The Guardian* February 18, 2009.

their importance in 2011,[229] despite the risk recognized both by the Newton Committee and the House of Lords in the Belmarsh case that deportation may simply export international terrorism.

Immigration law has been used as antiterrorism law in other contexts. In August 2005, new guidelines were issued to encourage the deportation of noncitizens on grounds that they fomented, justified, or glorified terrorism.[230] Such immigration law measures were much easier to implement than the government's original proposals to create a criminal offense for the glorification of terror that would apply to citizens. As in the United States, immigration law avoided the requirements for criminal prosecutions for speech that incited or indirectly advocated terrorism.

In 2006, a new Immigration, Asylum, and Nationality Act[231] provided enhanced powers to deprive people of British citizenship "in the public good" in response to a decision that refused to strip Guantánamo detainee David Hicks of British citizenship on the basis of his training with al Qaeda.[232] The vagueness of the public good standard harkened back to colonial emergency rule in Singapore, where officials boasted that the laws had been written so well that they allowed them to achieve all their wishes.[233] The 2006 act also clarified that a person could be denied refugee status for committing, preparing, instigating, encouraging, or inducing others to commit acts of terrorism, regardless of whether those acts constituted an actual or inchoate offense in criminal law.[234]

In 2008, Parliament enacted new legislation so that "foreign criminals" who cannot be deported because of torture concerns can be subject to a designation scheme that functions as a form of control order. Controls could include electronic monitoring and other restrictions on the person's movements and employment within the United Kingdom. These provisions were not terribly controversial even though somewhat at odds with the House of Lords' concerns in the Belmarsh case about the irrational and discriminatory nature of singling out non-citizens for security measures.[235] The 2008 immigration provisions, as well as the government's 2011 proposals to replace control orders with

---

[229] *Review of Counter-Terrorism and Security Powers Review Findings and Recommendations* January, 2011 Cm 8004 at 33–35.

[230] Clive Walker, "The Treatment of Foreign Terror Suspects" (2007) 70 Modern Law Review 427, at 434.

[231] C.13, Section 56.

[232] *Secretary of States v. Hicks*, EWCA (Civ) 400 (2006), at para. 37.

[233] See Chapter 3.

[234] Immigration, Asylum and Nationality Act, c.13, Section 54.

[235] Criminal Justice and Immigration Act, 2008, c.4, Part 10.

Terrorism Prevention and Investigation Measures demonstrates a normalization of control orders.

Although it was an important case that led to the end of indeterminate detention, the British government responded aggressively to the Belmarsh case. These responses included 1) 2005 legislation for control orders that was renewed to the end of 2011 2) the proposed creation of Terrorism Prevention and Investigation Measures to replace control orders 3) unsuccessful attempts to persuade the European Court of Human Rights to allow deportation to torture 4) successful attempts to persuade the courts to allow deportation with assurances of no torture, 5) enhanced controls on immigration and 6) a form of control orders that applies only to non-citizens convicted of crimes. For some, such developments confirm "the continued futility"[236] of the Human Rights Act. At the same time, however, these responses to the Belmarsh decision are all less drastic than indeterminate detention that had been previously authorized by Part IV of the 2001 law. Although the sheer number of responses gives one pause, all of the responses were subject to Parliamentary debate and control orders and attempts to deport to torture or with assurances were subject to continued judicial review that was frequently successful. There was no easy answer to the dilemma of what to do with non-citizens suspected of terrorism who would be tortured if returned to their country of citizenship. The prolonged British engagement with this intractable problem at least demonstrates a commitment to a legislative response to terrorism and one that respects the ability of courts to enforce human rights including an absolute right against torture that unfortunately was not fully respected in either the United States or Canada.

VII. TORTURE

The United Kingdom's post-9/11 derogation was motivated in part by an acceptance that some terrorist suspects could not be deported without offending the absolute right against torture. As will be seen, the United Kingdom has struggled with a variety of torture-related issues and is currently conducting an inquiry into whether British officials have been complicit with torture abroad.

Secret Evidence and Torture

Torture is conducted in secret, and there is a danger that secret evidence may have been obtained through torture. The House of Lords confronted this issue in 2005 in a follow-up case brought by the Belmarsh detainees when they claimed that the secret evidence used against them had been obtained through

---

[236] Ewing and Tham, "Continuing Futility of the Human Rights Act."

torture in unnamed foreign countries but presumably including Algeria and Jordan. After a review of domestic and international law on the topic, the judges in the House of Lords agreed that the admission of evidence derived from torture would be improper. They disagreed, however, about the appropriate standard to be applied in determining whether evidence was actually derived from torture. The majority held that the detainees would have to establish that the secret evidence was obtained by torture. Lord Hope, for the majority, argued that excluding evidence simply because of doubts it was obtained by torture would not strike the appropriate "balance" between "our revulsion against torture" and the right to life of "innocent victims" of "terrorist outrages."[237] He also cited in support the conclusion of a German court in a 2005 trial of an alleged 9/11 attacker that "generalized allegations of torture" in relation to Khalid Sheikh Mohammed were not sufficient.[238] This example has proven unfortunate, given that it has subsequently come to light that the Central Intelligence Agency did indeed torture Khalid Sheikh Mohammed.[239] The majority were unwilling to exclude secret evidence because of a doubt that it may be obtained from torture, even though under criminal law, such a rule has traditionally been used to exclude involuntary confessions obtained through lesser forms of mistreatment than torture.[240]

Lord Bingham issued an eloquent dissent that warned that the majority's standard "can never be satisfied. The foreign torturer does not boast of his trade. The security services, as the Secretary of State has made clear, do not wish to imperil their relations with regimes where torture is practised. The special advocates have no means or resources to investigate. The detainee is in the dark." He predicted that under the majority's approach, "despite the universal abhorrence expressed for torture and its fruits, evidence procured by torture" would be used because of a failure to establish that the material was obtained through torture.[241] He suggested that the Belmarsh detainees should only be required to demonstrate a plausible case that the evidence came from torture by showing that it came "from one of those countries widely known or believed to practice torture (although they may well be parties to the Torture Convention and will, no doubt, disavow the practice publicly)."[242] Once that was done, it would fall to the specialized expertise of SIAC to exclude evidence if there was a "real risk that the evidence has been obtained by torture."[243] As seen in Chapter 7, Canadian courts have effectively imposed a standard similar to that proposed by Lord Bingham in his dissent.

[237] *Secretary of State v. A*, UKHL 71 (2005), at para. 119.
[238] Ibid., at para. 124.   [239] Mayer, *Dark Side*, at 273–9.
[240] *R. v. Ibrahim*, A.C. 599 (1914); Police and Criminal Evidence, 1984, Section 76.
[241] *Secretary of State v. A*, UKHL 71 (2005), at para. 59.
[242] Ibid., at para. 56.   [243] Ibid.

Although the U.K. court condemned torture, the majority's decision departed from more demanding criminal law standards and did not recognize the difficulties in proving that transnational partners in terrorism investigations obtained evidence and intelligence through torture.

VIII. FOREIGN COUNTER-TERRORISM ACTIVITIES

Britons Held at Guantánamo

An important 9/11 effect is the increased interconnection of many nations in their terrorism investigations. This means that one state cannot turn a blind eye to the activities of other states. In such a globalized environment, Guantánamo became a problem for governments and courts throughout the world.

In 2002, the mother of Feroz Abbasi, a British citizen captured in Afghanistan and detained in Guantánamo, brought a case in British courts in an attempt to require the United Kingdom to make a request to the United States for her son's release. The Court of Appeal did not order this remedy, but it did characterize Guantánamo as a "legal black hole," in which Abbasi was subject to "indefinite detention in territory over which the United States has exclusive control with no opportunity to challenge the legitimacy of his detention before any court or tribunal."[244] The litigation helped direct attention to Abbasi's plight, and by 2003, the government had secured assurances from the Americans that the death penalty would not be applied to British citizens detained at Guantánamo; by January 2005, it had secured the release of British citizens held at Guantánamo, including Abbasi. Although the detainees were questioned and in some cases arrested when they arrived back in the United Kingdom, none of the nine were charged.[245] In 2006, the Divisional Court rejected similar claims made by three British residents, including two granted refugee status, who were detained at Guantánamo. At the same time, the court documented some of the techniques used at Guantánamo such as stress positions, hooding, and the use of phobias to induce stress.[246] Diplomatic efforts proceeded, and these applicants were released from Guantánamo in 2007. The British courts in these cases used a form of moral suasion or soft power to draw attention to the plight of the detainees and their efforts contributed to growing condemnation of Guantánamo. As will be seen in the next two chapters, Australian and Canadian courts also stopped short of ordering their governments

---

[244] *Abbasi v. Secretary of State*, EWCA (Civ) 1598 (2002), at paras. 62, 66.

[245] C. R. G. Murray, "The Ripple Effect: Guantanamo Bay in the UK Courts" (2010) 1 Pace International Law Review Online Companion 9, at 18, 25.

[246] *Al Rawi v. Secretary of State*, EWHC 972 (2006), at para. 29 (Admin).

to make what would be difficult diplomatic representations to the Americans. From a traditionalist perspective, these cases seemed to recognize rights without real remedies or hard judicial power. At the same time, the courts in these cases grappled with the complexities of overlapping sovereignties that are implicated in transnational terrorism investigations. They also avoided the danger that court-order diplomatic representations might be rebuffed by the Bush administration.

British citizens and residents, on their return from Guantánamo, brought civil claims against the British government and its security agencies. The British courts were less willing to shut down such litigation on the basis of concerns about disclosing state secrets than the American courts. For example, the Court of Appeal refused to order nondisclosure of some information in the face of U.S. threats to cut down on intelligence cooperation. It recognized that there were important state interests in nondisclosure but also stated that "democratic accountability, freedom of expression, and the rule of law"[247] all supported disclosure. In another case involving torture claims by former Guantánamo detainees, the Court of Appeal concluded that civil litigation should be conducted in open court.[248] Although the diplomatic representation cases reveal the dangers of concrete remedies getting lost in transnational complexities, in these cases the transnational context provided the former detainees with multiple forums in which to bring their claims. Although the United States was most directly responsible for the harms they suffered, the former detainees forum shopped and took advantage of the British court system that was more willing to balance the state's secrecy claims against the detainee's interests in seeking compensation and vindication.

Concerns about further disclosures in Guantánamo-related litigation prompted newly elected prime minister David Cameron to appoint a public inquiry to investigate claims of British complicity in torture. He argued in July 2010 that "these allegations are not proven but today we do face a totally unacceptable situation. Our services are paralysed by paperwork as they try to defend themselves in lengthy court cases with uncertain rules."[249] In November 2010, his government went a step further and settled civil claims with the detainees for an undisclosed amount. At the same time, the government revealed that the litigation that was settled involved more than 500,000 secret documents and 60 government officials and lawyers. The government estimated that the litigation would cost 30–50 million pounds and argued that the

---

[247] *Binyam Mohamed v. Secretary of State*, EWCA 65 (2010), at para. 39.
[248] *Al Rawi v. Secretary of State*, EWCA (Civ) 482 (2010).
[249] "Torture Claims: David Cameron Announces an Inquiry," at http://www.bbc.co.uk/news/10521326.

litigation could compromise national security (and intelligence sharing with the United States) by resulting in the disclosure of sensitive information. Not surprisingly, the settlement was welcomed by the head of the United Kingdom's foreign and domestic intelligence services.[250] The settlement reveals the complexity of the constitutional framework even within one domestic system. The executive always retains the option of settling cases and withdrawing prosecutions as a way to pre-empt judicial disclosure of secret information. It is difficult to believe that the British courts were not aware that such executive safety valves existed. The presence of such executive options makes the decisions of American courts to shut down similar litigation on state secrets grounds even more striking and disturbing.

The fate of the inquiry into complicity in torture remains to be seen. In 2008, the Joint Committee on Human Rights called for an inquiry stressing that state responsibility for turning a blind eye to the use of torture should be distinguished from more exacting standards of criminal liability that required knowledge of and direct contribution to torture. It indicated that sending questions to a foreign intelligence service known for torture could constitute complicity in torture. As seen in Chapter 7, two Canadian inquiries have found that such practices indirectly contributed to the torture of Canadians held in Egypt and Syria. The Canadian inquiries had to struggle with the government with respect to how much information they could make public. The Joint Committee stressed that an inquiry was necessary because of an "accountability gap."[251] This gap was created because of secrecy claims that surround transnational terrorism cooperation, the refusal of ministers to answer questions in Parliament about the conduct of the security services, the complaint-driven nature of other accountability bodies, and the government's refusal to release legal guidance provided to the security services on these matters. The Joint Committee urged the government to follow the American example with respect to the torture memos, waive legal privilege, and release its legal advice on such matters.[252] The government has, however, refused to follow this recommendation.

The appointment of the complicity in torture inquiry is an important but discretionary and temporary attempt to fill the accountability gap. Inquiries are only appointed at the discretion of the government and they are a slow, expensive, and extraordinary method of accountability. Particular concerns have been expressed about whether the United Kingdom inquiry into complicity

---

[250] "Compensation to Guantanamo Detainees 'Was Necessary,'" at http://www.bbc.co.uk/news/uk-11769509.

[251] Joint Committee on Human Rights, *Allegations of UK Complicity in Torture*, 23rd Report of Session 2008–2009, HC 230 (2009), chapter 4.

[252] Ibid., at para. 96.

in torture has a broad enough mandate to examine all aspects of possible complicity. In addition, concerns have been raised about the government's selection of the intelligence services commissioner, who may already have reviewed some matters, to head the inquiry. As seen in the next chapter, Australia has used existing watchdogs to good effect in committees that have reviewed antiterrorism legislation,[253] but the use of an existing commissioner in the British inquiry is dangerous because he may already be implicated in the events being reviewed. A recent inquiry in Canada into the investigation of the 1985 Air India bombing also found that previous reviewers of the investigation had been misled by security officials and police forces and denied full information.[254] Regardless of the composition of the United Kingdom's inquiry, the fundamental point about the dangers of filling a structural accountability gap with a discretionary and temporary appointment of a public inquiry remains.

British Use of Force and Internment in Iraq

The United Kingdom has also faced litigation arising from its participation in the invasion of Iraq. In one case, the House of Lords applied the European Convention to the case of Baha Mousa, a man detained and beaten to death by British soldiers in Iraq, while holding that the convention did not apply to five others who were killed by British soldiers when on patrol but not detained.[255] In another case, the court held that the United Kingdom was responsible for the three years of military detention without trial of al-Jedda, a British citizen suspected of involvement in terrorism.[256] This seemed to be a clear violation of the right to liberty in the European Convention. Nevertheless, the House of Lords held that the right was displaced by Security Council Resolution 1546, which authorized the multinational forces to use "all necessary measures to contribute to the maintenance of security and stability in Iraq." The resolution also annexed a letter from U.S. secretary of state Colin Powell that contemplated "internment when this is necessary for imperative reasons of security."[257] As discussed in Chapter 2, the Security Council provided no restraints on or procedures for internment, and none were specifically required

---

[253] See Chapter 6.
[254] Commission of Inquiry into the Investigation of the Bombing of Air India Flight 182, *Air India Flight 182: A Canadian Tragedy* (Ottawa: Public Works, 2010), vol. 2, chapter 5.
[255] *R (Al Skeini) v. Secretary of State*, UKHL 26 (2007).
[256] *R (Al Jedda) v. Secretary of State*, UKHL 58 (2007). Lord Brown acknowledged that the appellant's internment without trial would have violated Article 5 of the European Convention if it had not been authorized by the UN Security Council. Ibid., at para. 138.
[257] Security Council Resolution 1546 (2004), at para. 10, 11, annexing letter for Colin Powell to president of the Security Council.

by the House of Lords.[258] The House of Lords decided that the Chapter VII status of the Security Council resolution displaced human rights obligations in the European convention even though domestically and without Security Council authorization such internment without judicial review or trial would be unacceptable. In short, the House of Lords accepted the government's "the UN made us do it" defense.

Al-Jedda, like the *Kadi* case discussed in Chapter 2, raises a potential conflict between a Chapter VII Security Council resolution and constitutional and human rights protections, in this case in the European Convention of Human Rights. The case has been appealed to the European Court of Human Rights. Although that court might be tempted to try to reconcile Security Council authorizations and human rights, it will be difficult to reconcile these two sources of laws given the facts of the case in which al Jedda was subject to military internment in Iraq for three years without trial and with only periodic reviews by the military commander. If the Court favors rights under the Convention, the result will undermine the Security Council's resolution which unfortunately as examined in Chapter 2, did not give adequate consideration to human rights. On the other hand, if the Court follows the approach of the House of Lords, then the Security Council will be able to trump and displace human rights at least when it acts under Chapter VII of the United Nations Charter.

IX. STOP-AND-SEARCH POWERS AND DISCRIMINATORY PROFILING

As discussed earlier, the Terrorism Act, 2000, enhanced many police powers. One of the most controversial was the power in Section 44 to engage in random stops and searches without even reasonable suspicion to discover items associated with terrorism within areas declared by the police to be at risk for a terrorist incident. These powers were available whenever senior police officers deemed them to be "expedient."[259] They were used extensively, especially in

---

[258] Baroness Hale recognized that Geneva Conventions which were recognized in Colin Powell's letter but not the resolution proper might not apply to the applicant because he was a British citizen and suggested that he be repatriated to the United Kingdom, where his rights would be respected. *R (Al Jedda) v. Secretary of State*, UKHL 58 (2007), at paras. 126–8. Lord Rodger suggested that compliance with the Geneva Conventions was a matter for the Security Council. Ibid., at para. 113, while Lord Bingham suggested that the Security Council resolution should be reconciled with the right to liberty. Ibid., at para. 39. Al-Jedda was released at the end of 2007 and is presently suing the U.K. government.

[259] Terrorism Act, 2000, c.11, Section 44(3).

London, where much of the city was declared to be a stop-and-search zone for prolonged periods.

In the *Gillan* case, section 44 was challenged by a protester against arms sales and a journalist covering the protest after they were both stopped and searched. All levels of British courts rejected the challenges. The House of Lords was particularly dismissive of concerns that the law was being used for discriminatory racial and religious profiling. Unlike in the Belmarsh case, Lord Bingham sidestepped the discrimination issue by stating that given that there were no allegations of discrimination in the particular stops and searches, "I prefer to say nothing on the subject of discrimination."[260] Lord Hope ignored that the burdens of random stops were not distributed equally when he argued that the public would be "reassured by what they see the police doing at the barriers. They are in the front lines of those who would be at risk if there was another terrorist outrage."[261] Lord Brown also made reference to the 2005 London bombings and stressed the value of "intuitive stops" and the impossibility of stopping everyone in the subway. He then seemed to condone racial profiling by stating that "it seems to me inevitable . . . that so long as the principal terrorist risk . . . is from al Qaeda, a disproportionate number of those stopped and searched will be of Asian appearance."[262] No mention was made of the wrongful police killing of Brazilian Charles de Menezes in July 2005, in the wake of the London bombings, or of the dangers to community relations of intuitive stops that focused on those who appeared to be Muslim. It is very disturbing that the independent judiciary, which should protect the rights of unpopular minorities, was so insensitive to discriminatory profiling. Lord Brown's approach, however, unfortunately represented a common attitude that echoed Home Office Minister Hazel Blears's statement a year earlier that the nature of terrorism "inevitably means that some of our counter-terrorism powers will be disproportionately experienced by people in the Muslim community."[263]

In 2010, the European Court of Human Rights reversed the British courts and found that the random stop-and-search powers were an unreasonable and arbitrary invasion of privacy. The European Court found that the statutory standard of expediency was too vague even to qualify as a legal limit on privacy rights. Whereas Lord Brown had praised "intuitive stops," the European Court concluded that "there is a clear risk of arbitrariness" in stops based on intuition or hunches.[264] Whereas the House of Lords assumed that the police would not

---

[260] *Gillan v. Commissioner of Police*, UKHL 12 (2006).

[261] Ibid., at para. 48.   [262] Ibid., at para. 80.

[263] As quoted in Clive Walker, "Neighbor Terrorism and the All-Risks Policing of Terrorism" (2009) 3 Journal of National Security Law and Policing 121, at 152.

[264] *Gillan v. UK*, [2009] ECHR 28 at para. 85.

discriminate, the European Court concluded that "while the present cases do not concern black applicants or those of Asian origin, the risks of discriminatory use of the powers is a very real concern"[265] given the statistics on who was stopped. The European Court also did not ignore efficacy concerns and they stressed the very few terrorist arrests produced by the random procedures. The government has accepted this decision and proposed the repeal of s.44 of the Terrorism Act, 2000 in a new *Protection of Freedoms Bill*. The power of random stop and seizure is to be replaced by a more tightly circumscribed power that only allows police officers to engage in more limited random stops and searches when it is necessary to respond to a reasonable suspicion of terrorist activities.[266] As with the Belmarsh case, there was much support for repeal of this controversial antiterrorism law in various reports, but it took a court decision to force the government to take action.

x. RESPONDING TO THE LONDON BOMBINGS: TERRORISM ACT, 2006

Control orders had been enacted in response to the Belmarsh case and were in place before the London bombings in July 2005 that killed 52 people. A subsequent inquiry found that two of the London bombers were known to MI5 before the bombing but were not a priority because they were among the 4,000 contacts made by those involved in an active plot that ended in successful criminal prosecutions in both the United Kingdom and Canada.[267] A second attempt at a bombing was thwarted a few weeks later, and threat levels and fear remained elevated for some time. Prime Minister Blair stressed the need to respond to the extremism that motivated British citizens to engage in such horrific violence. As discussed in Chapter 2, the United Kingdom spearheaded Security Council Resolution 1624, calling on all states to enact laws against the incitement of terrorism, and that resolution was enacted in September 2005. Even though Blair's Labor Party had a majority in Parliament, it took

[265] Ibid., at para. 85.
[266] Protection of Freedoms Bill, HC Bill 146 Second Reading March 1, 2011 ss.58-60 (requiring a senior police officer who authorizes search powers to have reasonable suspicions that an act of terrorism will take place and that the search powers are necessary in the place and time where the search will take place. Searches will also be more narrowly restricted, but still can be undertaken without reasonable suspicion that they will discover evidence of terrorism).
[267] Intelligence and Security Committee, *Could 7/7 Have Been Prevented?* May 2009 Cm 7617, at para. 31. The committee found that MI5 did not have the resources to conduct even adequate surveillance of its known targets, ibid., at para. 146, and that to provide comprehensive coverage of all known associates would require an "unacceptable and unachievable" number of several hundred thousand officers as opposed to 3,500 officers. Ibid., at para. 150.

longer for his domestic extremism agenda to be implemented. Initial proposals to criminalize speech that glorified terrorism and to extend the powers of investigative detention for preventive arrests under the Terrorism Act, 2000, from 14 to 90 days encountered significant opposition both in Parliament and society. Prime Minister Blair did not accept the 323 to 290 vote against the 90 day proposal graciously arguing that the police and security services supported 90 days and that it was "very odd" that Parliament would come up with a 28 day proposal on its own and "I just hope in a longer time we don't rue it."[268] The amendment of the 90 day proposal as well as the amendments to the government's glorification proposals demonstrated the ability of Parliament to resist the most extreme of the government's proposals. Such resistance, however, took time, with the bill being first introduced on October 12, 2005, and not being enacted until February 15, 2006.

The speech-related provisions of the Terrorism Act, 2006, follow a British tradition extending from colonial emergency rule of attempting to regulate speech in an effort to prevent terrorism. As enacted, the new offense applies to speech that directly or indirectly encourages terrorism, provided that the speaker either intends or is reckless with respect to that result. Indirect advocacy of terrorism is then broadly defined to include "every statement which glorifies the commission or preparation (whether in the past, in the future or generally)" of acts of terrorism and that "is a statement from which those members of the public could reasonably be expected to infer that what is being glorified is being glorified as conduct that should be emulated by them in such circumstances."[269] Unlike in the United States, there is no requirement that the incitement actually produce any imminent risk of actual terrorism. There is not even, as in Israel, a requirement that the speech produce a real possibility of violence.

The Blair government's persistence with respect to the new speech offense is striking given that existing offenses of soliciting murder and racial hatred had already been applied to the speech of extremists who had called on people to kill in the name of Islam. El-Faisal had been convicted in 2003 of such offenses for calling for suicide bombing,[270] and Abu Hamza[271] was convicted in February 2006 of similar offenses and sentenced to seven years' imprisonment just as the Terrorism Act, 2006, was being enacted. The 2006 offense is perhaps best seen as a symbolic statement of repudiation of speech that comes close to advocating violence. The government can point to ample authority from

---

[268] "Blair defeated over terror laws" November 9, 2005 British Broadcast News.
[269] Terrorism Act, 2006, c.11, Section 1.   [270] R. v. El Faisal, EWCA (Crim 624) (2004).
[271] R. v. Abu Hamza, EWCA (Crim) 2918 (2006).

the European Court of Human Rights that supports the criminalization of speech associated with terrorism, including one 2008 decision that upheld a French conviction for a cartoon drawn in praise of the 9/11 attacks.[272] Despite all the struggle to enact the offense, there has been minimal use of it. Although provisions that require emulation in present circumstances may protect those who celebrate past acts of terrorism associated with successful revolutionary movements, they may not assist Muslim groups who base their advocacy on contemporary grievances throughout the world. The possibility that speech prosecutions under the new law could be counter-productive and persuade some radicals that the U.K. state does not understand or care about Muslim grievances cannot be discounted.

Practically more important than the controversial new offenses are provisions that empower police to request Internet providers to remove material that the police conclude is "unlawfully terrorism-related."[273] In addition, the grounds for proscription of terrorist groups were expanded in the 2006 act to include groups that glorify terrorism in circumstances suggesting that the terrorism should be emulated.[274] This provision is wider than the criminal offense, and both the proscription and notice to Internet providers provisions can be exercised without any judicial involvement. The Terrorism Act, 2006, contained a minor expansion of the definition of terrorism to include attempts to influence international organizations as well as governments. It also included a new offense punishable by life imprisonment of any intentional conduct to prepare for acts of terrorism or assisting others to engage in acts of terrorism.[275] This offense was designed to apply to even remote acts of preparation. It was also supplemented by new offenses relating to terrorism training.[276] The terrorist training offense has been applied to fitness training, if it is known that the training will be put to terrorist purposes.[277] The attendance at a training site offense can apply to one who "could not reasonably have failed to understand that instruction or training was being provided"[278] either wholly or partially for terrorism purposes. The expansion of the prohibited act to apply to remote and ambiguous acts of preparation for terrorism is standard fare in modern antiterrorism law but is usually counter-balanced by a requirement to establish some form of subjective intent, albeit not in relation to particular acts. The attendance at a training site offense creates the possibility of convicting someone of a terrorism offense essentially for negligence. Police

---

[272] *Leroy v. France*, 36109/03, October 2, 2008 (5th section).
[273] Terrorism Act, 2006, c.11, Section 3(3).   [274] Ibid., Section 3(5B).
[275] Ibid., Section 5.   [276] Ibid., Sections 6 and 8.
[277] *R v. DeCosta*, EWCA (Crim) 482 (2009).   [278] Terrorism Act, 2006, Section 8(2)(b).

and prosecutorial discretion can always mitigate overbroad offenses, but such offenses can still be used as a threat to recruit informers.

The 2006 act also expanded police powers by extending powers to compel a person to answer questions and produce documents that would be valuable to an investigation into organized crime, revenue, and terrorism financing offenses to all terrorism investigations.[279] As with the 2001 revival of the offense of withholding information, this new power did not create great controversy, even though compelled questioning could be conducted without judicial authorization and on the basis of a reasonable suspicion that a listed offense had occurred. In contrast, compelled questioning in Australia and investigative hearings in Canada both require judicial authorization and as will be seen in the next two chapters even then caused great controversy. The British approach suggests that a crime-based approach to terrorism may both spread into the investigation of other crimes and be influenced by a country's general approach to crime. The Blair government was willing to expand state powers to punish and prevent crime, and its aggressive approach to terrorism was consistent with its approach to other crimes.

XI. COUNTER-TERRORISM ACT, 2008

The 2008 act continued the trend in the 2006 act toward facilitating criminal prosecutions and criminal investigations. The government's proposal to expand the maximum 28-day period following a preventive arrest to 42 days was again controversial. It was passed in the House of Commons by an 8 vote margin, but defeated in the unelected upper house by a vote of 309 to 118. The maximum period of detention had become a symbolic issue, largely disengaged from the actual use of the existing powers. Nevertheless, it is significant that first Prime Minister Blair and then Prime Minister Brown were defeated on their respective requests for a maximum 90- and 42-day period of preventive arrest. Party discipline was less of a restraint in the United Kingdom than in Australia and Canada, and backbenchers rebelled at both proposals as well as the unelected peers in the House of Lords. The elected upper houses in the United States and Australia might have offered less resistance to similar antiterrorism measures.

In 2008, the definition of terrorism was expanded to include the commission of acts of terrorism for "racial" as well as religious and political motives. This change perhaps reflected anxiety over the possible loss of terrorism prosecutions because of an inability to prove religious or political motive beyond a

---

[279] Ibid., Section 33, amending Serious Organized Crime and Police Act, 2005.

reasonable doubt, as has occurred in Australia.[280] It also recognized that some Islamic extremists had been convicted under racial hatred laws. The broad concept that terrorism could be designed to influence rather than intimidate government was, however, retained, despite the use of the stricter standard of intimidation in other countries, including Australia and Canada and recommendations by Lord Carlile, the independent reviewer, that the broad notion of influence be replaced by the stricter requirement of coercion.[281]

The 2008 act recognized the frequent need in terrorism prosecutions to attempt to convert intelligence into evidence by authorizing all three intelligence agencies, including the foreign intelligence service and the signal intelligence agency, to disclose information for the purposes of criminal proceedings.[282] Legal changes are at most a necessary condition, and much will depend on how the cultures of intelligence agencies react to the prospect of evidentiary and court-based discipline regarding the way they collect and retain intelligence. The continued resistance to the use of electronic surveillance evidence in terrorism prosecutions is a potent demonstration of the ability of the intelligence agencies successfully to resist demands that their secret intelligence sometimes be used as public evidence.

The 2008 act also included provisions for imposing requirements on those convicted of terrorism offenses that they notify authorities of their location and travel.[283] At one level, notification can be seen as an attempt to extend the sentences of those convicted of terrorism offenses and put them under light but long-term control orders. On the other hand, notification can be seen as a healthy recognition that those convicted of terrorism offenses will eventually be released. At the same time, notification orders seem to presume the need for further surveillance of convicted terrorists even after they have served long periods of imprisonment. In 2010, the head of the domestic security intelligence agency MI5 expressed concerns about the release of those convicted of terrorism offenses from prison. He argued, "It is very rarely the case that anyone who has been closely involved with terrorist-related activity can be safely taken off our list of potentially dangerous individuals; the tail of intelligence 'aftercare' gets increasingly lengthy."[284] None of the Western democracies examined in this book have devoted much effort to the question of rehabilitating terrorists, in part because they have assumed that terrorists cannot be rehabilitated.

---

[280] See Chapter 6.
[281] Lord Carlile *The Definition of Terrorism* March, 2007 Cm 7052 at para 59.
[282] Terrorism Act, 2006, Section 19.						[283] Ibid., Part IV.
[284] Jonathan Evans, "The Threat to National Security," at para. 19; https://www.mi5.gov.uk/output/the-threat-to-national-security.html.

XII. NATIONAL SECURITY POLICIES

In 2006, the United Kingdom released a countering international terrorism strategy named CONTEST. It is built around four pillars: preventing people from becoming terrorists, pursuing them to stop terrorist acts, protecting society and infrastructure against terrorist acts, and preparing to mitigate the effects of terrorist attacks. Although the strategy focused on international terrorism, it also responded to the risk of homegrown or what Clive Walker has called "neighbor terrorism,"[285] which led to the London bombings.

The Prevent strand of CONTEST included not only deterrence but responses to the causes of terrorism, including "inequalities and discrimination" both in the United Kingdom and overseas. This recognition of the need to respond to the causes of terrorism was balanced against the use of criminal and other sanctions to deter terrorism and the Blairite idea that the state must engage "in the battle of ideas"[286] with respect to extremism. This latter idea was connected with the 2006 criminalization of direct and indirect incitement of terrorism, as supplemented by an earlier list of "unacceptable behaviors" of engaging in such speech that would be used to exclude noncitizens.[287] Although the Prevent strand made some reference to the causes of terrorism and the need for outreach to Muslim communities both in the United Kingdom and abroad, it was dominated by a more aggressive approach based on militant democracy concepts that asserted the right of democracies not only to engage in a battle of ideas but to criminalize and otherwise render unacceptable some ideas that were seen as antithetical to democracy. Concerns have been raised that Prevent is not sufficiently differentiated from policing and intelligence gathering strategies,[288] and a 2010 report recognized that some aggressive policing and questioning practices had themselves caused grievances.[289]

The Pursue arm of CONTEST stressed the wide array of legal instruments available to respond to international terrorism, including criminal prosecutions, financial controls, proscription, control orders, and immigration

---

[285] Clive Walker, "Keeping Control of Terrorists without Losing Control of Constitutionalism" (2007) 59 Stanford Law Review 1395, at 1397.

[286] Home Office Countering International Terrorism (Cmnd. 6888) (2006), at para. 6.

[287] Ibid., at para. 50. The strategy featured a statement from a speech by Prime Minister Blair stating that "this terrorism will not be defeated until its ideas, the poison that warps the minds of its adherents, are confronted, head-on, in their essence, at their core." Ibid., at para. 53.

[288] Clive Walker and Javaid Rehman, "'Prevent' Responses to Jihadi Extremism," in Ramraj, *Global Anti-Terrorism and Law*, 2nd ed.

[289] Contest Annual Report 2010, Cm 7883 (2010), at 3.12.

measures. It also featured a British version of the Al Capone approach used in the United States by stating that "many disruptions of terrorist networks lead to prosecutions for other, non-terrorist offences – sometimes major offences such as crimes of violence, and sometimes lesser offences such as fraud – or to actions for deportation, or to impose control orders."[290] The strategy also warned that the details of such disruptions must often be kept secret. There were limits to Pursue, as the 2010 annual report confirmed that intercept evidence still was not used in criminal prosecutions and that nine suspected terrorists had been deported with assurances that they not be tortured, suggesting a desire to expel rather than to pursue and punish.[291] Pursue also reaffirmed a commitment to trying to stop terrorism financing, including the passing of legislation in response to the U.K. Supreme Court's decision in *Ahmed*[292] striking down regulations implementing the UN's terrorist financing asset freezing regime and the issuance of guidance by the Charities Commission to ensure that charities did not fund terrorists.[293] These elements of Pursue may rely on an unfair listing process and have a disproportionate effect on Muslim charities.

The Protect strand featured border controls and protection of critical infrastructure, while the Prepare strand featured recovery, including the new Civil Contingency Act, 2004.[294] Although that act took an all-risks approach that did not focus solely on terrorism, CONTEST focused on terrorism and bore the marks of the trauma of the 2005 London bombings in its single minded focus on terrorism and the fact that even within that terrorism strategy, the Pursue strand overshadows the Prevent, Protect, and Prepare strands.[295]

In 2008, the Brown government published a national security strategy that identified a number of different threats in addition to terrorism including civil emergencies, climate change, nuclear weapons, failed states and organized crime.[296] The new Cameron–Clegg coalition government continued the trend to an all-risk policy by publishing a new national security policy that identifies terrorism as one of four priority areas along with cyberattacks, the need to respond to natural hazards such as floods, and international military crises. This new strategy continues the whole-of-government approach taken to terrorism but expands it to a broader range of risks and also supplements it with a

---

[290] Ibid., at para. 70.
[291] Contest Annual Report 2010, Cm 7883 (2010), at 2.09.
[292] UKSC 2 (2010).
[293] Contest Annual Report 2010, Cm 7883 (2010), at paras. 2.11–12.
[294] C.36.					[295] Contest Strategy, Cm 7547 (2009), at 62.
[296] *The National Security Strategy of the United Kingdom* Cm 7291 (2008).

new multiministry National Security Council and a new position of national security advisor.[297]

With respect to CONTEST, the new government has indicated that Prevent activities with respect to violent extremism and terrorism will go back to the Home Office and be separated from work on social integration done by other ministries. This seems wise but also recognizes that aggressive security measures may themselves become an obstacle in better integrating Muslim minorities into British society. In addition, the new government indicated that it would "review our most sensitive and controversial counter-terrorism and security powers and, where possible and consistent with protecting the public, provide a correction in favour of liberty."[298] The government's subsequent decision to repeal random stop-and-search powers and control orders may take away some of the grievances of Muslim communities. At the same time other developments such as Prime Minister Cameron's criticism of multiculturalism and his suggestion that Islamic extremism may grow out of a lack of a common British identity may hinder progress on community relations.[299]

The UK's "correction in favour of liberty" follows its commitment to a legislative approach against terror. The Cameron/Clegg government has in a shorter time produced more tangible outcomes than achieved by the Obama administration which has relied upon executive orders on issues like detention and failed to close Guantánamo. At the same time, the British correction should not be overestimated given that the reduction from 28 days to 14 days will still allow 28 days to be re-introduced in an emergency and control orders will be replaced by similar measures.

---

[297] *A Strong Britain in an Age of Uncertainty: The National Security Strategy*, Cm 7953 (2010), at 0.8.

[298] *Securing Britain in an Uncertain Age: The Strategic Defence and Security Review*, Cm 7948 (2010), at 4A.5.

[299] Prime Minister Cameron in a manner quite similar to Prime Minister Blair appealed to militant democracy when he argued that Islamic extremists must be combated "whether they are violent in their means or not...We must ban preachers of hate from coming to our countries. We must also proscribe organisations that incite terrorism against people at home and abroad... we must stop these groups from reaching people in publicly-funded institutions like universities or even, in the British case, prisons. Now, some say, this is not compatible with free speech and intellectual inquiry. Well, I say, would you take the same view if these were right-wing extremists recruiting on our campuses? Would you advocate inaction if Christian fundamentalists who believed that Muslims are the enemy were leading prayer groups in our prisons? And to those who say these non-violent extremists are actually helping to keep young, vulnerable men away from violence, I say nonsense." David Cameron "Speech at Munich Security Conference" February 5, 2011 available at http://www.number10.gov.uk/news/speeches-and-transcripts/2011/02/pms-speech-at-munich-security-conference-60293.

The British experience along with the American, Australian and Canadian experience all suggest that radical corrections in favor of liberty after the post-9/11 ramping up of counter-terrorism laws and powers may be quite difficult to achieve.

XIII. CONCLUSION

The British response to 9/11 has been rooted in both frequent legislation and increasing reliance on criminal law. Although it dispensed with emergency derogations from rights, the Terrorism Act, 2000, was a forceful legal response to terrorism that provided a very broad definition of terrorism that was influential in many post-9/11 antiterrorism laws. It provided no exemptions for protests or strikes or acts of terrorism committed against repressive governments. The United Kingdom has not wavered from this definition since 9/11, expanding it slightly. The 2000 act also provided for proscription and a variety of proscription-related offenses as well as other crimes that targeted activities well in advance of acts of terrorism and even when there was some ambiguity about whether there would be an act of terrorism and what it would be.

The 2000 act sought to regularize preventive arrest by requiring judicial approvals of a maximum of seven days' imprisonment, but after 9/11, the length of the maximum figure became a symbol of the government's toughness on terrorism, with both prime ministers Blair and Brown having to settle for 28 days, well below their preferences for 90 and 42 days, respectively. The symbolic nature of the maximum period continues under Prime Minister Cameron, with proposed legislation to reduce the maximum 28-day period to 14 days as a sign of the government's commitment to a correction in favor of liberty.

The 2001 antiterrorism law is best understood in historical context. Faced with the trauma of 9/11 and the reporting deadline set by Security Council Resolution 1373, the United Kingdom reverted to form with quickly enacted emergency legislation that derogated from the European Convention. Although the derogation was eventually found by the courts to be disproportionate and discriminatory in authorizing the indeterminate detention of noncitizens suspected of terrorism, it had some virtues. One virtue was respect for the absolute nature of the right not to be deported to torture, a right that the United States violated in extralegal renditions and that the Canadian Supreme Court but not the European Court of Human Rights considered might be violated in undefined exceptional circumstances. Another virtue was that the derogation was accomplished by formal and legal means. It was also accompanied by various review mechanisms, which, in due course, commented negatively on the need for the derogation. A final virtue was that even though the derogation brought back administrative detention, it did so in a more focused and fairer fashion than the previous use of internment in Northern Ireland. Fewer than 20 persons were subject to the derogating provisions, and while secret evidence was used against them, it was subject to challenge by security-cleared special advocates. The U.K. government, to its credit, rejected broad use of internment as a strategy. Ironically, however, it successfully defended long-term military internment in Iraq on the basis that it was authorized by a UN Security Council resolution that displaced the human rights obligations of the European Convention on Human Rights. This case like the 1267 listing regime raises another potential conflict between Chapter VII Security Council powers and human rights.

The House of Lords's 2004 Belmarsh decision accepted that a state of emergency relating to terrorism existed but nonetheless declared that the administrative detention of noncitizens suspected of terrorism was disproportionate and discriminatory. This decision is the most significant of all post-9/11 judicial decisions. It announced that courts did not necessarily have to defer to the state in security matters and had some institutional advantages in determining the rationality of the state's response to perceived crisis and its treatment of vulnerable minorities such as noncitizens. The Belmarsh case is not, however, without its critics. Some point to its acceptance of government's declared state of emergency as a sign of weakness. Others attempt to diminish its impact by arguing that it only resulted in some of the detainees being subject to controversial control orders and some being deported on the basis of risky assurances that they would not be tortured. To be sure, the government responded vigorously to the Belmarsh decision, but these alternatives remain less drastic than indeterminate detention, and they themselves were subject to continued judicial review and challenge both in court and in Parliament.

Although criminal prosecutions have been the main response to terrorism in the United Kingdom, other instruments, such as administrative control orders and immigration law measures, are still used. Control orders were ripe for reconsideration given legal decisions that imposed limits on the use of secret evidence and thus narrowed the gap between them and criminal prosecution under many broad new terrorism offenses. The Cameron/Clegg government has indicated that it will repeal control orders, but replace them with more limited restrictions on liberty that are somewhat consistent with other orders used to prevent crime.

Despite the widespread use of criminal prosecutions, British concerns about secrecy remain strong, and the intelligence agencies have been able to resist the use of electronic surveillance as evidence. The government has settled with Guantánamo detainees rather than risk disclosure of more information that might harm British intelligence agencies and their sharing of intelligence with the United States. An inquiry into possible British complicity in torture has been appointed but it remains unclear how much information it will be able to make public. The legal advice given to British officials in their dealings with foreign officials, unlike the American torture memos, still remains secret. Moreover the discretionary appointment of an extraordinary and temporary inquiry into complicity in torture, like similar Canadian inquiries, cannot plug a structural accountability gap with respect to intensified and transnational counter-terrorism investigations.

6   Australia Responds: Hyper-Legislation

I. INTRODUCTION

Australia provides an interesting case study of how a country with little direct experience with terrorism can get caught up in the 9/11 effect of dramatically increased counter-terrorism. Australia borrowed heavily from the British response to terrorism, even though there are significant differences in the threats of terrorism faced by the two countries. Australia's definition of terrorism and its many new terrorism offenses are largely derived from the United Kingdom's Terrorism Act, 2000. After the 2005 London bombings, Australia adopted British innovations such as control orders, preventive arrests, and laws against the advocacy of terrorism. Since the defeat of the Howard government, Australia has also borrowed some British review models by creating an independent and security-cleared monitor.

Although Australia comes closer to direct transplants of terrorism laws than other countries examined in this book, the transplants from the United Kingdom are nevertheless affected by important environmental differences. For example, far fewer control orders have been ordered in Australia than in the United Kingdom, and there are no special security-cleared advocates in Australia as there are in the United Kingdom. Australia also lacks the European tradition of militant democracy, and its regulation of speech associated with terrorism has struck out on its own in an attempt to modernize treason and sedition offenses so that support for terrorist groups can be prosecuted as a form of disloyalty to the state. Finally, Australian terrorism laws and activities are not supervised by a court such as the European Court of Human Rights that enforces a bill of rights.

Despite lacking a bill of rights, the Australian Constitution has shaped the nation's counter-terrorism laws. Unlike the United Kingdom, Australia provides exemptions for protests and strikes from terrorism and requires that a terrorist act coerce or intimidate a government rather than simply influence it. This definition follows Canadian definitions, but it also reflects Australia's constitutional protection for political speech. Care has been taken in drafting Australia's laws to ensure that sitting judges do not exercise executive functions, albeit through the fiction of sitting or retired judges acting as prescribed authorities who preside at Australian Security Intelligence Organization (ASIO) questioning hearings or who issue preventive detention orders. The Commonwealth government has obtained from the states and also successfully asserted its powers to legislate with respect to terrorism, but some state criminal legislation supplements Commonwealth terrorism legislation. The absence of a national bill of rights may also explain why parliamentary and watchdog accountability in Australia has kept better pace with the increased integration and intensity of antiterrorism activities than in other democracies with a bill of rights. Australia thus provides a good case study in the advantages and disadvantages of parliamentary and executive-based review of antiterrorism laws and policies compared to systems that rely more on judicial review under a bill of rights.

Australia has exceeded the United Kingdom, the United States, and Canada in the sheer number of new antiterrorism laws that it has enacted since 9/11: from 9/11 to the fall of the Howard government in 2007, Australia enacted 44 different pieces of terrorism legislation.[1] Although some of these numbers can be attributed to styles of legislative drafting, this degree of legislative activism is striking compared even to the United Kingdom's active agenda and much greater than the pace of legislation in the United States or Canada. Australia's hyper-legislation strained the ability of the parliamentary opposition and civil society to keep up, let alone provide effective opposition to, the relentless legislative output. The pace of the legislation increased and the limits on parliamentary opposition decreased after the Howard government obtained a double majority in both houses of the Commonwealth Parliament in 2004. The pace of legislation under Howard also reveals the danger of terrorism law being used for political advantage and as a wedge issue in an attempt to divide political parties. Terrorism was a winning political issue for the Howard government when it was re-elected in both 2001 and 2004.[2]

The most controversial Australian law was legislation first announced after 9/11 but not enacted until 2003 that gave Australia's domestic security

---

[1] George Williams, "Anti-Terror Legislation in Australia and New Zealand," in *Global Anti-Terrorism Law and Policy*, 2nd ed., ed. Victor Ramraj et al. (Cambridge: Cambridge University Press, forthcoming).

[2] Michael Tolley "Australia's Commonwealth Model and Terrorism" in *Courts and Terrorism* Mary Volcansek and John Stack (New York: Cambridge University Press, 2011) at 148.

intelligence agency, the Australian Security Intelligence Organization (ASIO), new powers to detain and question those with information relevant to terrorism investigations. The legislation as originally introduced was fiercely resisted because of concerns that it would allow indeterminate and incommunicado detention of anyone, including children. Some additional protections were provided before the legislation was enacted in 2003, but it remains exceptional among Western democracies in giving an intelligence agency explicit and coercive powers to collect intelligence from human sources. This legislation was subject to a three-year sunset but was subsequently renewed by the Howard government until 2016. New governments elected in 2007 and 2010 have not repealed ASIO's extraordinary powers, even though they have amended other terrorism laws, and ASIO has not used the powers in recent years. This suggests that 9/11 effects are often enduring and that new governments may sometimes be unable or unwilling to repeal or drastically change laws and practices that had been presented to a scared public as essential for their safety.

Like the United Kingdom, Australia has developed a broad array of different instruments that can be used for counter-terrorism purposes. They include immigration law, criminal law, and administrative measures such as control orders. The state can pick and choose among these powers and use less restrained ones when another fails to obtain the desired results. As in the United Kingdom, administrative control orders have been issued to supplement the criminal process with its higher standards of proof of guilt beyond a reasonable doubt. A control order was issued against "Jihad Jack" Thomas 10 days after his criminal conviction was overturned on the basis that it had been obtained through the use of involuntary statements taken from him in Pakistan. Thomas unsuccessfully challenged the constitutionality of the control order,[3] and control orders remain available in Australia even though they will soon be subject to legislative reform in the United Kingdom. Immigration law has also been used as a backstop for the criminal process. Dr. Mohamed Haneef was charged with a criminal offense of supporting terrorism but had his visa canceled immediately after he was granted bail on the criminal charges. The Haneef case also demonstrates how aggressive counter-terrorism measures can stretch the limits of the law. He was subject to 12 days' detention through a strategic use of "dead time" provisions that exempted unused hours from provisions that allowed detention for questioning. Dr. Haneef has now received a settlement and an apology from the government for his treatment. An inquiry was also appointed to examine how he was treated by various parts

---

[3] Andrew Lynch, "Control Orders in Australia: A Further Case Study of the Migration of British Counter-Terrorism Law" (2008) 8 Oxford University Commonwealth Law Journal 159.

of government, including the police, ASIO, and immigration officials. As in Canada and elsewhere, inquiries have played an important but discretionary role in scrutinizing whole-of-government responses to terrorism. The Australian inquiry into the Haneef affair had difficulty accessing all the relevant information, but it did make recommendations that have recently resulted in a seven-day limit on detention for questioning.[4]

Australia under Prime Minister Howard was a particularly enthusiastic ally of the United States in the invasions of both Afghanistan and Iraq.[5] There is a faint echo of an American-style war on terror in some Australian antiterrorism laws. Key components of Australia's counter-terrorism measures, including control orders, have been upheld by the courts under the federal government's defense power. Treason was expanded in 2002 to include support for terrorist groups as well as countries that were in armed conflict with Australia. Sedition was similarly expanded to include support for organizations engaged in armed hostilities or a declared or undeclared war against Australia. As seen in Chapter 4, however, the American War on Terror did not lead to restrictions on speech associated with terrorism because of the United States' strong First Amendment tradition. Although Australia under the Howard government was attracted to the concept of a war on terror, it followed more the British legislative model than the American executive model[6] or the American tendency to engage in what was described in Chapter 4 as extra-legalism.

Australia, like Canada, also has a somewhat troubled history of terrorism prosecutions. A number of terrorism prosecutions, including Australia's first post-9/11 prosecution, floundered over an inability to prove that the accused had a political or religious motive. Other prosecutions have encountered difficulties as statements taken from suspects in Australia and Pakistan have been excluded as involuntarily obtained. Even without a bill of rights, Australian courts have enforced some traditional criminal justice values and have not used secret evidence, as is done under immigration law. At the same time, however, Australian courts have accepted a particularly aggressive post-9/11 law that instructs them to give greater weight to the dangers of the disclosure of secret information than to the dangers that the accused may suffer from nondisclosure. This law, like the more controversial ASIO questioning powers, affirms the importance given to secret intelligence in the post-9/11

---

[4] National Security Legislation Amendment Act, 2010, no. 132, Schedule 3.

[5] Jack Holland and Matt McDonald, "Australian Identity, Interventionalism and the War on Terror," in *International Terrorism Post 9/11: Comparative Dynamics and Responses*, ed. Asaf Siniver (London: Routledge, 2010).

[6] Daphne Barak-Erez, "Terrorism Law between the Executive and Legislative Models" (2009) 57 American Journal of Comparative Law 878.

era. Attempts to ensure that secret intelligence is not disclosed also present in Australia as elsewhere a significant challenge to the conduct of efficient, public, and fair criminal trials. Defense lawyers in Australia may be excluded from critical aspects of the criminal trial if they do not obtain a security clearance and agree not to share information with their clients. They may also be threatened with prosecution if they do not inform the government before attempting to call evidence that may be classified.

Australia provides an interesting contrast to the otherwise similar country of Canada, which will be examined in the next chapter. Although both Australia and Canada borrowed heavily from the United Kingdom's Terrorism Act, 2000, in their original responses to 9/11, the Australian approach to terrorism has, unlike the Canadian approach, accelerated and intensified. Australia has extended controversial ASIO questioning warrants until 2016, whereas Canada allowed less severe but equally as controversial investigative hearings to expire in 2007. Australia has followed the United Kingdom by enacting control orders and laws against terrorist speech, but Canada has not. In both countries, governments defended post-9/11 antiterrorism laws on the basis that they were necessary to protect a right to "human security" derived in part from international mandates. In Canada, however, this discourse was balanced with concerns about the rights of suspected terrorists whereas in Australia, there was less concern about such rights.[7] Australia followed the United States and the United Kingdom in developing a terrorist-specific national security plan, whereas Canada, in 2004, adopted an all-risks national security plan that includes terrorism but also stresses other risks to security.

A number of hypotheses may explain the striking differences between the Australian and Canadian responses to 9/11. Canadian law is subject to a constitutional bill of rights, the Canadian Charter of Rights and Freedoms (the Charter), which is not present in Australia. As will be seen in the next chapter, the Canadian government stressed that its initial response to 9/11 was

---

[7] In Canada, the leading proponent of the human security approach balanced the idea that terrorism laws were necessary to protect human security with concerns about traditional rights of those suspected or accused of terrorism. See Irwin Cotler "Thinking Outside the Box: Foundational Principles for a Counter-Terrorism Law and Policy" in Ronald Daniels, Patrick Macklem and Kent Roach eds. *The Security of Freedom: Essays on Canada's Anti-Terrorism Bill* (Toronto: University of Toronto Press, 2001). In Australia, Attorney General Philip Ruddock invoked Cotler's human security approach but without the same concern about the rights of those suspected or accused of terrorism. See Philip Ruddock "Australia's Legislative Response to the Ongoing Threat of Terrorism" (2004) 27 University of New South Wales Law Journal 254. See Greg Carne "Reconstituting 'Human Security' in a New Security Environment: One Australian. Two Canadians and Article 3 of the Universal Declaration of Human Rights" (2006) 25 Australian Year Book of International Law 1 at 27–30.

consistent with the Charter. Another hypothesis is that Australians have been more emotionally affected by terrorism than Canadians. John Howard was in Washington on 9/11, the 2002 Bali bombings killed 88 Australians, and subsequent terrorist acts targeted the Australian embassy in Jakarta. Although 24 Canadians died in the 9/11 attacks, and 331 people died in the 1985 bombings of two Air India planes originating in Canada, Canada has internalized the trauma of international terrorism less than Australia. Another possible difference is Canada's particular sensitivity toward multiculturalism, which is constitutionally recognized in the Charter. Although Australia is also a multicultural country with an even higher level of foreign-born residents than Canada, the Howard government pursued restrictive immigration policies and did not hesitate to give the Muslim Advisory Council an explicit mandate to control radicalization within its Muslim communities. Another factor in explaining Australia's greater legislative activism may be that Canada has had minority governments since 2004 whereas the Howard government in Australia was particularly active in legislating in terrorism issues after 2004 when it gained a majority in both houses of Parliament. Even subsequent Labor minority governments in Australia, however, have continued to enact laws, albeit softer laws with an increased emphasis on review of counterterrorism activities.

II. PRE-9/11 EXPERIENCE

Although Australia has less experience with terrorism than the United Kingdom, the United States, and even Canada, it has had some experience. In an early echo of a warlike response to terrorism, nearly 2,000 soldiers were deployed in response to a 1978 bombing that killed three people outside the Sydney Hilton during a Commonwealth meeting and may have been intended for the prime minister of India.[8] The Commonwealth government asserted that it could exercise these powers without a request from the states as part of its "responsibility to protect people against possible acts of terrorism."[9] Professor Jenny Hocking has observed that "the massive security developments in the name of countering terrorism found no real opposition from any quarters. To appear 'soft on terrorism' was simply 'politically impossible.'"[10] In the wake of the bombing, a number of inquiries were launched by the Commonwealth government, including one by Sir Robert Mark, a former London police commissioner, who maintained that violence to "achieve political or

[8] Jenny Hocking, *Terror Laws* (Sydney, NSW, Australia: New South Wales Press, 2004), at 86.
[9] Ibid., at 91.   [10] Ibid., at 103.

industrial ends" was "worse than murder."[11] These inquiries warned about rising amounts of both domestic and international terrorism in Australia and demonstrated the great influence that British approaches to counter-terrorism would have on Australia.

Criminal charges were laid but subsequently dropped against members of the Ananda Marga, a Hindu group. The members were, however, charged with conspiracy to murder the leader of the Australian National Front, in what many believed was a plot related to the Hilton bombings. They were convicted, but the high court subsequently found that ASIO should have disclosed files that related to the reliability of a key informer. ASIO, and as will be seen in the next chapter, Canada's domestic security intelligence agency, had difficulties during the cold war living up to the disclosure standards of criminal law. The majority of the court stressed that without examination of the ASIO material, the accused "would not be able to test the evidence of the witness by comparing it with the report, and it would be likely to give rise to the reproach that justice had not been seen to be done."[12] After examining the ASIO material, however, the court concluded that it was not necessary to disclose it to the accused. Justice Lionel Murphy, who, in his former life as a minister, had conducted a raid on ASIO to assert ministerial control, issued a strong dissent and would have allowed the accused access to the material and warned about a miscarriage of justice. A subsequent judicial inquiry into the convictions found that the informer was not reliable and that doubt existed about the conviction. The accused were eventually pardoned and released in 1985.[13] One person eventually confessed and was convicted of the Hilton bombing in 1989, but doubts as to his credibility and his confession were raised when a second person was acquitted on appeal in 1991. As in the United Kingdom, the terrorist context provided a fertile ground for miscarriages of justice.

Controversy has continued about ASIO's role in the Sydney bombings. The degree and nature of ASIO's infiltration of the Ananda Marga before the bombing is not known. The Commonwealth government refused to follow two requests by the state of New South Wales to appoint an inquiry into the matter.[14] Inquiries can be a powerful instrument of accountability over the secret activities of intelligence agencies, but governments retain discretion to appoint them.

---

[11] Ibid., at 108.
[12] *Alister v. The Queen*, 154 C.L.R. 404 (1984), at 415.
[13] Tom Molomby, *Spies, Bombs and the Path of Bliss* (Sydney, NSW, Australia: Potoroo Press, 1986), at 385.
[14] Hocking, *Terror Laws*, at 117–18.

In 1979, the ASIO Act was amended to include the collection of intelligence about terrorism as a specific part of the intelligence agency's mandate. Terrorism was defined as including "acts of violence for the purpose of achieving a political objective in Australia or in a foreign country."[15] Hocking suggests that the emphasis placed on political motive allowed officials to selectively define security threats, often focusing more on foreign groups than on domestic violence. She also suggests that it provided a link between terrorism and counter-insurgency, where the focus is on a military response to security threats, including concerns about disruptions of essential services and propaganda. This approach drew on the militarized British model, "despite the clear differences in the nature and extent of political violence."[16]

The 1979 act also gave ASIO power to conduct searches and engage in electronic surveillance on the basis of warrants issued by the minister. The Australian minister can grant warrants on the basis of a reasonable suspicion that a person was engaged in activities that could threaten national security. This followed the British model of executive authorization of electronic surveillance but can be contrasted with the use of judicial warrants under Canada's 1984 Canadian Security Intelligence Service Act and the United States' 1978 Foreign Intelligence Surveillance Act. The breadth of ASIO's powers to collect intelligence about a wide range of people was confirmed in a 1982 high court decision.[17] Even before 9/11, Australia was closer to the British model of counter-terrorism, as opposed to more libertarian North American models.

There was also a history of politicalization of intelligence in Australia that had led Lionel Murphy in part to conduct his ministerial raid on ASIO in the early 1970s, to discover what information the agency had about terrorism committed by Croatian extremists in Australia. The intelligence agency was mired in cold war politics and was slow to take the threat of diaspora terrorism seriously, a pattern that, as will be seen, was repeated in Canada in the 1980s with respect to Sikh terrorism. Murphy wanted to assert ministerial control over an agency with a history of investigating radicals and even the Labor Party as subversives, but a subsequent inquiry stressed the dangers of political interference in its operations.[18] The 1979 ASIO Act addressed these concerns by restricting the Minister from directing ASIO about the nature of the advice

---

[15] ASIO Act, 1979, Section 4.

[16] Hocking, *Terror Laws*, at 193–4 and chapter 4.

[17] *Church of Scientology v. Woodward*, 154 CLR 25 (1982).

[18] Jenny Hocking, *Beyond Terrorism: The Development of the Australian Security State* (St. Leonards Australia: Allen and Unwin, 1993), chapter 4.

it offered to other departments or about individual investigations.[19] This was an attempt to avoid the politicalization of security intelligence, but it also created dangers that ASIO would avoid ministerial accountability, a very important issue especially because the watchdog inspector general was not created until 1986. As will be seen, intelligence became politicalized again after 9/11, as the government made claims that intelligence required rapid legislative amendments.

III. THE INITIAL RESPONSE TO 9/11

In October 2001, a number of counter-terrorism initiatives were announced by the Howard government, but a November 2001 election prevented the bills from being introduced into Parliament until March 2002. Some immediate changes were, however, made by listing groups and individuals as terrorists under the United Nations Act. As in the United States, the United Kingdom, and Canada, the Australian executive was able to respond more quickly to the terrorism financing mandate from the United Nations Security Council than the legislature.[20] Australia also joined the many countries that ratified the 1999 Terrorism Financing Convention.

Although the electoral cycle slowed down Australia's response to 9/11, the response itself demonstrated many of the same features of the rushed responses to Security Council Resolution 1373 in other countries. Five bills were introduced into Parliament in March 2002 and quickly enacted. Plans by the Labor opposition to delay the bills were denounced by those on the government side as "not patriotic, not committed, not anti-terrorist."[21] Borrowing heavily from the Terrorism Act, 2000, the bills provided a broad definition of terrorism, the enactment of broad new terrorism offenses, and executive proscription of terrorist groups. There was relatively little journalistic coverage and criticism of the original security proposals[22] in contrast to the situation in Canada.

The initial measures were defended by the Howard government as necessary to comply with Australia's international obligations and to respond to the threat of international terrorism, even though the government maintained that there was "no known specific threat of terrorism to Australia."[23] Governments in

---

[19] ASIO Act, no. 113 of 1979, Section 8.

[20] Charter of the United Nations (Sanctions – Afghanistan), Regulations SR 2001, no. 298; Charter of the United Nations (Anti-Terrorism Measures), Regulations SR 2001, no. 297.

[21] As quoted in Andrew Lynch, "Legislating with Urgency" (2006) 30 Melbourne University Law Review 747, at 777.

[22] Hocking, *Terror Laws*, at 193–4 at 11.   [23] Ibid., at 197.

Australia were selective in their use of international law.[24] It was invoked as a support for crime control measures such as the new antiterrorism laws but resisted when used to impose human rights obligations on the state. The attorney general and senior justice officials also defended the need for the new laws by falsely claiming that the regular criminal law would only apply after an act of terrorism.[25] This approach demonstrated a lack of confidence in criminal law seen in other countries. It also ignored that Jack Roche was charged and eventually convicted of the pre-existing criminal offense of conspiracy for pre-9/11 plans to bomb the Israeli embassy in Canberra.[26]

The five bills were quickly passed in the government-dominated House of Commons but then referred to a Senate committee, which received 431 submissions, despite the length and complexity of the bills and the fact that individuals and groups only had eight days to respond during a period that involved several holidays.[27] The Howard government did not have a majority in Australia's elected Senate, and this would lead to some important amendments before the new antiterrorism package became law.

Defining Terrorism

Australia, like many other countries, was confronted with the difficult task of defining terrorism. The Australian definition of terrorism is quite similar to the broad definition found in Section 1 of Britain's Terrorism Act, 2000,[28] and discussed in the previous chapter. It includes politically or religiously motivated threats to life, health, safety, and property and interference with electronic systems. The inclusion of religious and political motives was much less controversial in Australia than in Canada, even though the requirement

---

[24] Greg Carne, "Neither Principled nor Pragmatic? International Law, International Terrorism and the Howard Government" (2008) 27 Australian Yearbook of International Law 11.

[25] Attorney General Philip Ruddock argued to an academic audience that "if Australia did not have such preparatory offences and a terrorist attack were to occur, the best we could expect from our criminal justice system would be convictions for murder. It would be too late, however, for the innocent victims claimed by the attack. That is too high a price for our society to pay when we are capable of acting sooner." Ruddock, "Law as a Preventive Weapon against Terrorism," in *Law and Liberty in the War on Terror*, ed. Andrew Lynch, Edwina MacDonald, and George Williams (Sydney, NSW, Australia: Foundation Press, 2007), at 5. Such arguments were made not only by politicians but also by senior civil servants. Robert Cornall argued that existing criminal offenses "largely depend on the completion of an act – such as murder – before the offense is committed." Cornall, "The Effectiveness of Criminal Laws on Terrorism," in Lynch et al., *Law and Liberty in the War on Terror*, at 52.

[26] *R. v. Roche*, 188 F.L.R. 336 (2005).   [27] Hocking, *Terror Laws*, at 197.

[28] C.11. On the influence of the broad British definition, see Kent Roach, "The Post 9/11 Migration of Britain's Terrorism Act, 2000," in *The Migration of Constitutional Ideas*, ed. Sujit Choudhry (Cambridge: Cambridge University Press, 2006), at 377–9, 382–9.

to prove "motive as well as intention is venturing into unchartered territory"[29] and would subsequently frustrate some terrorism prosecutions.

The Australian definition followed the British definition in its references to action or threat of action and to political or religious motive but eventually departed from it by requiring that actions be intended to coerce governments or influence them by intimidation, as opposed to the broader British law that applies to actions "designed to influence the government." The coercion or influence by intimidation requirements in Australia were only introduced "after an outcry from legal and community groups" who expressed concerns about the breadth of the broader British concept of influencing governments.[30] Perhaps because of its constitutional protection of political expression,[31] Australia had more sensitivity toward freedom of expression issues than did the United Kingdom. This sensitivity was also manifested in a specific exemption for "advocacy, protest, dissent or industrial action." As in Canada, this exemption was originally limited to lawful protests, but the requirement of lawfulness was dropped after concerns were expressed about illegal protests and strikes being caught by the definition. As examined in the preceding chapter, the British definition contains no exemption for protests and strikes, suggesting that it fits into a counter-insurgency model prepared to use the law against protests and strikes. Although the lack of a bill of rights affected Australian antiterrorism law,[32] it did not affect this particular aspect of the definition of terrorism, perhaps because Australia had constitutional protections for freedom of speech.

Australia followed the Terrorism Act, 2000, in defining the harms of terrorism broadly and in a way that far exceeded the intentional killing and murder of civilians. Australia followed the British inclusion of serious interference and disruption of an electronic system but then defined an electronic system to include, but not be limited to, "i) an information system; or ii) a telecommunication system; or iii) a financial system; or iv) a system used for the delivery of essential government services; or v) a system used for, or by, an essential public utility; or vi) a system used for, or by, a transport system."[33] This definition

---

[29] Bernadette McSherry, "Terrorism Offences in the Criminal Code: Broadening the Boundaries of Australian Criminal Laws" (2004) 27 University of New South Wales Law Journal 354, at 363.

[30] Andrew Lynch and George Williams, *What Price Security? Taking Stock of Australia's Anti-Terror Laws* (Sydney, NSW, Australia: University of New South Wales Press, 2006), at 15.

[31] *Lange v. Australian Broadcasting Corporation*, 189 CLR 520 (1997); *Australian Capital Television Pty Ltd v. Commonwealth*, 177 CLR 106 (H.C.) (1992).

[32] George Williams, "Anti-Terror Legislation in Australia and New Zealand," in Ramraj et al., *Global Anti-Terrorism Law and Policy.*

[33] Criminal Code of Australia, Section 101.1(2).

amounted to the same broadening of the British reference to electronic systems to all essential public or private services, facilities, or systems as found in Canada's post-9/11 legislation.[34] The broad definition of terrorism was intended to respond to the vulnerabilities of modern societies and as such employed a precautionary principle. The style of the legislative drafting also demonstrated a precautionary principle directed not against terrorists but against the threat that judges might give the legislative definition of terrorism a narrow reading.

The Simplified World of Terrorism Financing

To comply with Security Council Resolution 1373 and the 1999 International Convention on the Suppression of Terrorism Financing, broad new crimes relating to the financing of terrorism were created. Although necessary to comply with international obligations, the financing offenses have not been extensively used. In 2006, "Jihad Jack" Thomas was acquitted by a jury of providing funds to al Qaeda even while convicted of receiving funds from the terrorist group.[35] The latter conviction was, however, overturned on the basis that statements made by Thomas in Pakistan were not voluntary.[36] Mr. Thomas was charged again with receiving funds from a terrorist group as a result of remarks he made in the Australian media about his attendance at an al Qaeda training camp but again was acquitted by a jury in October 2008.[37] The Thomas case raises questions about whether successive Australian juries saw terrorism financing as the same grave threat that the UN Security Council and Australian government envisaged.

Prosecutions of alleged supporters of the Tamil Tigers in Australia have caused controversy. Three Melbourne men were originally charged with terrorism financing and being members of a terrorist organization. The men were granted bail, and the charges were eventually dropped because the Tamil Tigers were not one of the 19 groups listed as terrorist organizations in Australia.[38] This led to demands from the Sri Lankan government that the Tamil Tigers be listed as a terrorist group, but the Australian government

---

[34] Criminal Code of Canada, Section 83.01 See generally Kent Roach, "A Comparison of Australian and Canadian Anti-Terrorism Laws" (2007) 30 University of New South Wales Law Review 53.

[35] Nicola McGarrity, "'Testing' Our Counter-Terrorism Laws" (2010) 34 Criminal Law Journal 92, at 101.

[36] See Andrew Lynch, "Maximising the Drama: 'Jihad Jack,' the Court of Appeal and the Australian Media" (2006) 27 Adelaide Law Review 311.

[37] McGarrity, "'Testing' Our Counter-Terrorism Laws," at 102.

[38] The judge stressed the length of the investigation, the ties of the men to Australia, and the importance of the presumption of innocence. *Vinayagmoorthy v. DPP*, VSC 265 (2007), at paras. 19–20.

did not list the Tamil Tigers and maintained its focus on Islamic terrorist groups. The charges were, however, revived under the United Nations Act under which the Tamil Tigers were listed.The three men pled guilty to providing over a million dollars to the Tamil Tigers. They were sentenced to either two or one years of imprisonment, but all three were released on a good behavior bond, with the judge stressing that the Tamil Tigers were acting as a de facto government in the north of Sri Lanka at the time and that the funds were intended to assist the Tamil community and not terrorism. One of the men, Arumugen Rajeevan, stated outside of the court that "Tamils in Sri Lanka cannot expect justice from the Sri Lankan government but today we have received justice from the Australian justice system."[39] As will be seen in the next chapter, the Tamil Tigers have been a listed group in Canada since 2006, but a person who pled guilty to providing them with $3,000 received a six-month sentence and argued out of court that the Sri Lankan government was guilty of state terrorism.[40] The light sentences received in both Australia and Canada have been controversial, but they reveal the complexity of criminalizing financial support for the Tamil Tigers: a complexity that is obscured by the listing and the process of criminalization of all financial support for a terrorist group.

As discussed in Chapter 2, the UN Security Council promoted terrorism financing laws without apparent recognition of the complexities that they presented in criminalizing diaspora politics in multicultural countries such as Australia and Canada. Listing of terrorist groups or other forms of criminalization simplified evolving and difficult political situations. Terrorism financing is based on a technocratic and zero-tolerance approach that is exemplified by what is known about the manner in which the Security Council's Counter-Terrorism Committee (CTC) interacted with countries. For example, in its first country report to the CTC, Sri Lanka reported that its 1979 Prevention of Terrorism (Temporary Provisions) Act "provided the necessary substantive and procedural infrastructure to effectively investigate and prosecute offences of terrorism, including financing of terrorism committed within the territory of Sri Lanka."[41] Unmentioned, however, is that the act, dating back to British colonial rule, provides powers similar to those found in Singapore's Internal Security Act as examined in Chapter 3.[42] These powers have provided a template for emergency regulations in Sri Lanka that have been used to detain

---

[39] "No Jail for Trio Who Funded Tamil Tigers," at http://www.abc.net.au/news/stories/2010/03/31/2861834.htm.
[40] See Chapter 7.   [41] Sri Lanka Country Report, S/2001/1282, at 5.
[42] Prevention of Terrorism (Temporary Provisions) Act, no. 48 of 1979, Parts III–V, at https://www.unodc.org/tldb/showDocument.do?documentUid=3306&node=docs&cmd=add&country=SRL.

almost 11,000 people as affiliated with the Tamil Tigers, with plans only to subject about 200 to criminal trials. Grave concerns have also been raised about disappearances and conditions of detention in Sri Lanka.[43] None of these complexities, however, will be relevant once the Tamil Tigers have been listed or come to satisfy the legal definition of a terrorist group, though they have been reflected in lenient sentences in both Australia and Canada.

Broad New Terrorism Offenses

Australia enacted a broad array of terrorism offenses heavily borrowed from the Terrorism Act, 2000. The most serious offense, subject to life imprisonment, was the doing of a terrorist act.[44] This offense has not yet been charged in Australia.[45] Within a preventive framework, this could be seen as a sign of success in responding to risks before they happen. As Christopher Michaelsen has argued, however, it might also be seen as evidence that the threat of terrorism in Australia has been exaggerated by the government.[46]

Australia created multiple new offenses relating to preparation for terrorism and participation and association with terrorist organizations. These offenses include the provision of training, the receiving of training,[47] and the possession or collection of a thing or the making of a document connected with preparation or assistance in a terrorist act.[48] The offenses also distinguished between intentional and reckless commission of such acts, providing higher penalties for the higher fault level. The Australian offenses appropriately paid attention to varying fault levels and refrained from criminalizing negligent conduct, as was sometimes done in the United Kingdom. At the same time, they contained the lower fault level of recklessness specifically rejected in Canadian offenses because of constitutional concerns.[49]

The broad Australian offenses represented acceptance of an intelligence mind-set that focused on a person's status as someone who had received training and the person's associations with others. The new offenses expanded

---

[43] The emergency regulations provide for military detention of those acting "in any manner prejudicial to the national security or to the maintenance of public order, or to the maintenance of essential services." Human Rights Watch, *Legal Limbo: The Uncertain Fate of Detained LTTE Suspected in Sri Lanka* (New York: Human Rights Watch, 2010), at 17.

[44] Criminal Code, Section 101.1.

[45] Lynch and Williams, *What Price Security?* at 17; McGarrity, "'Testing' Our Counter-Terrorism Laws," at 125.

[46] Christopher Michaelsen, "Australia and the Threat of Terrorism in the Decade after 9/11" (2010) 18 Asian Journal of Political Science 248.

[47] Criminal Code, Section 101.2.   [48] Ibid., Sections 101.4, 101.5.

[49] Roach, "A Comparison of Australian and Canadian Anti-Terrorism Laws," at 62–3.

inchoate offenses into what has been called the "precrime" and even the "pre-precrime" stage.[50] The focus was more on the risk that a person might, some time in the future, engage in terrorism and the person's capabilities of doing so than on specific acts that might lead to definite harms. The new crimes allowed charges to be laid on the basis of ambiguous actions that might otherwise only have been of interest to intelligence agencies mandated to report on possible security risks.

The preventive and precautionary approach to criminal law increased the overlap between the law enforcement and crime prevention mandate of the police and the intelligence gathering role of ASIO. This forced Australian police forces, often without success, to struggle with the ambiguities of intelligence. In the Haneef case, for example, police and immigration authorities misread the available intelligence to wrongly conclude that Dr. Haneef was involved in terrorism when ASIO, the intelligence professionals, took a more cautious approach. Conversely, it required ASIO, again often without success, to struggle with evidentiary implications and legal rules that accompany attempts to use intelligence as evidence. In the Izhar ul-Haque case, ASIO gathered intelligence in a manner that resulted in statements being excluded in court for violating the evidentiary rule that confessions be established to be voluntary. The blurring of the lines between intelligence and evidence also meant that trials of new terrorism offenses would often be slowed down by attempts by the state to prevent unused but relevant intelligence from being disclosed to the accused.[51]

The The/A Amendments, the Precautionary Ideal, and the Politicalization of Intelligence

Even though the 2002 crimes were very broad, there was still anxiety that they were not broad enough. Shortly before arrests were made in Melbourne and Sydney in 2005, the Australian Parliament rushed through amendments to make clear that a person could be guilty of the new terrorism offenses even if the training, thing, or document was not connected to specific terrorist activity. These amendments were justified by Prime Minister Howard on the basis

---

[50] Jude McCulloch and Sharon Pickering, "Counter-Terrorism: The Law and Policing of Pre-emption," in *Counter-Terrorism and Beyond*, ed. Nicola McGarrity, Andrew Lynch, and George Williams (London: Routledge, 2010), at 17–22, citing Lucia Zedner, "The Pursuit of Security," in *Crime, Risk and Insecurity*, ed. Tim Hope and Richard Sparks (London: Routledge, 2000), at 183, for the precrime concept.

[51] Kent Roach, "The Eroding Distinction between Intelligence and Evidence in Terrorism Investigations," in McGarrity et al., *Counter-Terrorism and Beyond*, at 54–60.

of "specific intelligence and police information this week which give cause for concern about a potential terrorist threat" in Australia that "could well occur."[52] Howard added that he had briefed the leader of the opposition about the intelligence. The legislation was particularly rushed, even by Australian standards, and demonstrates the politicalization of intelligence assessments even at the risk of alerting potential terrorists to the state's awareness of their plans.[53] As discussed above, there are cold war precedents for the political-ization of intelligence. In this case, the government used ASIO and police intelligence to justify its last-minute amendment of terrorism laws in a man-ner that had previously been requested by the police.

The amendments, which involved the switching of a reference to the com-mission of "the" terrorist act to the broader concept of "a" terrorist act, were designed to ensure that judges would not accept a narrow reading of the offense. As such, they applied the precautionary principle as much to judicial conduct as to terrorist conduct. In any event, the concern about the risk of possible judicial reading down of the offense turned out to be unwarranted as the courts adopted a broad reading of the offenses even before they were amended.[54] As Andrew Lynch has argued, the government's claims that the amendments were necessary were somewhat at odds with Prime Minister Howard's claims of the existence of "specific" intelligence and police infor-mation about the plots.[55] This disjuncture again hints at a certain politicaliza-tion and manipulation of intelligence. The rushed amendments were enacted before the Melbourne and Sydney arrests in December 2005 and, as such, were applied to those trials. In this way, Australia avoided Indonesia's unsuccessful attempt to make its terrorism law retroactive.[56] Nevertheless, these amend-ments came close to the line and demonstrated a willingness to politicalize intelligence and amend the law shortly before major arrests were made.

Treason and the War on Terrorism

Australia, like some other jurisdictions such as Hong Kong,[57] was quite capable of combining new security concepts that focused on risk and preemption with

---

[52] As quoted in Andrew Lynch, "Legislating with Urgency" (2006) 30 Melbourne University Law Review 747, at 750.

[53] Ibid., at 751–2.

[54] *R. v. Lodhi*, 199 F.L.R. 303 (N.S.W.C.A.) (2006).

[55] Andrew Lynch, "Legislating with Urgency" (2006) 30 Melbourne University Law Review 747, at 769–70.

[56] See Chapter 3.

[57] Kent Roach, "Old and New Visions of Security: Article 23 Compared to Post-September 11 Security Laws," in *National Security and Fundamental Freedoms: Hong Kong's Article 23*

older security concepts based on the notion of betrayal of the state through treason and sedition. The Security Legislation Amendment (Terrorism) Act, 2002, expanded the offense of treason to include acts that "assist by any means whatsoever" not only countries but "an organisation" that is engaged in armed hostilities against the Australian Defence Forces. The organization could be a terrorist group, such as al Qaeda, that was engaged in armed hostilities against Australian Defence Forces in Afghanistan and, later, in Iraq. This expansion of treason blurred the distinction between war and crime models and adapted older visions of security to the post-9/11 terrorist threat. In response to initial concerns about the broadly defined act of assisting organizations, aid and humanitarian measures were exempted. As will be seen, Australia returned to older versions of security when it expanded its sedition offenses in the wake of the 2005 London bombings.

Proscription of Terrorist Groups

Second only to the ASIO questioning powers, new powers of the executive to proscribe terrorist groups generated much critical comment in Australia. A number of commentators argued that proscription was at odds with the high court's famous cold war decision that held that the Communist Party could not be outlawed and with the subsequent defeat of a national referendum to achieve that objective. In response to these criticisms, the government narrowed its original proposal to allow only the proscription of organizations also listed by the UN Security Council. This amendment demonstrated the potential of the Security Council's actions to be used to legitimate domestic crime control measures. As discussed in Chapter 2, listing by the Security Council was accomplished through an intergovernmental process involving secret intelligence. Nevertheless, the idea that proscription would be tied to UN Security Council decisions provided a temporary response to the many Australian critics of proscription.

The Security Council proved too slow for Australia's hyperactive approach to terrorism. In 2003, legislation was enacted to allow Hamas and Lashkar e Tayibba to be listed, even though these groups had not been listed by the UN Security Council. The law was enacted in only two days, with the government claiming that intelligence had been received from abroad indicating that the latter group had operations in Australia.[58] As with the the/a amendments, the

---

under Scrutiny, ed. Fu Hualing, Carole Petersen, and Simon Young (Hong Kong: Hong Kong University Press, 2005).

[58] Joo-Cheong Tham, "Casualties of the Domestic War on Terror: A Review of Recent Counter-Terrorism Laws" (2004) 28 Melbourne University Law Review 512, at 521.

Howard government did not hesitate to make political use of intelligence. The quick listing of these groups also underlined how proscription decisions can be made on the basis of undisclosed and unchallenged intelligence of unknown reliability. The specificity of the listing legislation also underlined how listings act as a bill of attainder that fuses executive, legislative, and judicial power by effectively outlawing a specific group or person.

In 2004, a general law was enacted so that proscribed terrorist groups no longer had to be listed by the UN Security Council. One factor that was said to justify this expansion of proscription was that Jemaah Islamiyah, widely believed to be responsible for the 2002 Bali bombings, had not at the time been listed by the Security Council, though the group was quickly added to the UN list. These amendments demonstrate ambivalence and even at times hostility in Australia to international mechanisms and a sense that listing decisions should be made in the national interest.[59] The grounds for proscription were again expanded in 2005 to include groups that advocate terrorist acts.[60]

Australia did not follow the United Kingdom in creating a specialized administrative tribunal to consider delisting requests. It also did not follow the Canadian model of explicitly providing for judicial review (albeit with secret evidence) of listings. There were, however, requirements that the leader of the opposition be briefed on some listing decisions and that the Joint Parliamentary Committee be able to review some listings. That committee, however, has had difficulties obtaining all relevant intelligence from ASIO to review listing decisions, and it has not disallowed any listing.[61] The record is no better in Canada, where no group has attempted to judicially review listings. In the United Kingdom, one group has succeeded in obtaining a delisting on the basis that it had renounced violence.[62]

In 2006, the Security Legislative Review Committee noted that almost all of the 19 listed groups were Muslim and that listing decisions had been controversial within Muslim communities. It proposed that listing be subject either to judicial review or to review by an expert advisory group. These reforms have not been made, even though 2010 legislation extended the period before listings had to be renewed from two to three years. Listing in Australia remains

---

[59] Parliamentary Joint Committee on Intelligence and Security, *Inquiry into the Proscription of "Terrorist Organizations" under the Australian Criminal Code*, September 2007, at 4.29.

[60] Criminal Code, Section 101.1(2).

[61] Russell Hogg, "Executive Proscription of Terrorist Organisations in Australia: Exploring the Shifting Border between Crime and Politics," in *Fresh Perspectives on the "War on Terror*," ed. Miriam Gani and Penelope Mathew (ANU Press, 2008).

[62] *Lord Alton of Liverpool (In the Matter of the People's Mojahadeen Organization of Iran) v. Secretary of State*, EWCA (Civ) 443 (2008).

subject to less independent review than in either the United Kingdom or Canada. Australia continues to list only 19 groups, almost all of them Muslim whereas the United Kingdom and Canada have larger and more diverse lists of over 40 proscribed groups. In all these countries, however, proscription is failing to keep pace with the growth of homegrown terrorism inspired but not linked to al Qaeda. Indeed, only the prosecution of Jack Thomas has been able to rely on proscription of al Qaeda and major terrorism prosecutions in Sydney and Melbourne relied on the creation of ad hoc terrorism groups that had not been listed.[63] Proscription is a common feature in post-9/11 antiterrorism law and in the UN Security Council, but it has failed to keep pace with the development of al Qaeda morphs into an ideology as well as an organizing group.[64]

Membership and Association Offenses

Section 102.3 of the Australian Criminal Code makes it a crime subject to 10 years' imprisonment for a person intentionally and knowingly to be a member of a terrorist organization defined either as a listed group or as a group that satisfies the broad general definition of a terrorist group. This offense follows the British offense of membership, but does not extend the offense to those who profess their membership. It departs, however, from both American and Canadian reluctance to criminalize membership in a terrorist organization because of concerns about freedom of association and freedom of speech.

In addition to the membership offense, it is an offense to direct the activities of a terrorist organization; recruit a person to join or participate in the activities of a terrorist organization; provide or receive training from a terrorist organization; or provide funds, support, or resources to a terrorist organization or receive funds from one. These offenses have been relatively uncontroversial, but they expand the criminal law by criminalizing various forms of participation and association with a terrorist organization without the need to demonstrate any nexus to a particular terrorist plot. The emphasis is on prevention and disruption, as opposed to punishment of specific plots.

The most controversial offense related to terrorist organizations is the offense of association with a formal or informal member of a terrorist group. This offense has no parallel in the United Kingdom, let alone the United States or

---

[63] McGarrity, "'Testing' our Counter-Terrorism Laws" (2010) 34 Criminal Law Journal 92, at 126. See also Hogg, "Executive Proscription of Terrorist Organisations in Australia."

[64] Andrew Lynch, Nicola McGarrity, and George Williams, "The Proscription of Terrorist Organizations in Australia" (2009) 37 Federal Law Review 1.

Canada. This offense is subject to imprisonment for three years and requires a person on two or more occasions intentionally to associate with another person who is a member of or who promotes or directs an organization that the accused knows is a terrorist organization with the intention to support the organization. This offense represents an extreme example of an intelligence mind-set in which all associates of a suspected terrorist themselves become suspect. In Canada, Maher Arar came to the attention of Canadian authorities when he had lunch and went for a walk with the target of a terrorist investigation.[65] In the United Kingdom, MI5 and the police had known contacts with two of the London bombers when they came into contact with the targets of an active terrorism investigation. Nevertheless, the Intelligence Committee concluded that it was both unrealistic and dangerous to liberty to expect authorities to investigate all associates of a terrorist target.[66] In Australia, however, all the associates of terrorists are potentially subject to prosecution and conviction under Australia's association offense.

The breadth of the association offense forced the Australian legislature to impose some specific exemptions for associations between family members, for public religious worship, for humanitarian aid, and for the provision of legal assistance. The exemption also provides protection for the constitutional doctrine of implied freedom of political communication.[67] The 2006 *Report of the Security Legislation Review Committee* recommended the repeal of the association offense because it was imprecise and could adversely affect Muslim communities. Nevertheless, the offense remains in place in early 2011, more than three years after the defeat of the Howard government. The association offense has not been used extensively, suggesting that it may be a deliberatively symbolic and provocative measure. It might also be used as a means to induce those who may associate with suspected terrorists to cooperate with the police or intelligence agencies. That the problematic offense remains on the books underlines the difficulties that even new governments may have in repealing overbroad antiterrorism laws.

iv. ASIO QUESTIONING WARRANTS

The most controversial parts of Australia's initial response to 9/11 involved attempts to give ASIO new powers to question people about terrorism. On March 22, 2002, Attorney General Daryl Williams defended the proposed new

---

[65] See Chapter 7.   [66] See Chapter 5.
[67] Criminal Code, Section 102.8.

powers on both a criminal law and a precautionary basis. To ensure that the perpetrators of the new terrorism offenses are "discovered and prosecuted, preferably before they perpetuate their crimes," Williams argued that "it is necessary to enhance the powers of ASIO to investigate terrorism offences."[68] This approach envisaged the domestic security intelligence agency taking a lead role in terrorism investigations and differs from the approach taken in the United States, the United Kingdom, and Canada, where the police would take the lead. That said, the idea of compelling people to assist in terrorism investigations was not exclusive to Australia. American grand juries and Canadian investigative hearings could be used to compel a person to provide such information, but in both cases, compelled statements and evidence derived from them could not be used against the person compelled to answer questions. In the United Kingdom, the offense of refusing to provide information relevant to a terrorism investigation was reinstated after 2001.

The ASIO questioning law as proposed was draconian because it provided for renewable periods of 48 hours' detention and denied those questioned the right to legal representation, the right to silence, and even the right to contact others. In this way, the law had more in common with the Indonesian draft law that was withdrawn after complaints that it could result in a return to Suharto-era repression than the post-9/11 Canadian innovation of investigative hearings.[69] As originally introduced, there was no protection against self-incrimination because anything said by a detained person could be used in a prosecution for any of the new terrorism offenses.[70] There was no requirement of reasonable grounds or even reasonable suspicion that a crime had been or will be committed, but only that the information would substantially assist in the collection of important intelligence in relation to a terrorist attack. Intelligence collection was an important end in its own right, with only an attenuated connection to criminal investigations and prosecutions. The government also defended the original proposal on the basis that nonjudicial officials would authorize detention for questioning as a preventive measure and not as a punitive measure reserved for the judiciary.[71] As seen in Chapter 3, long-term administrative detention in Israel and Singapore was similarly justified on the basis of the state's preventive motives. Such reasoning ignored the effects of detention on the individual.

---

[68] As quoted in Hocking, *Terror Laws*, at 213.
[69] See Chapter 3 for a discussion of the withdrawn Indonesian draft terrorism law.
[70] Hocking, *Terror Laws*, at 218.   [71] Ibid., at 215.

The original proposal was severely criticized in the press and in parliamentary committees. One of the most popular criticisms was that the bill could allow children to be detained for questioning. The government was unrepentant and argued that teenagers had been known to engage in suicide bombings. Another popular critique was that police officers with the permission of the prescribed authority could strip search the person being questioned. Another objection was that the proposals authorized incommunicado detention. Again, the government was not apologetic and argued that such legislated restrictions were necessary to prevent a person detained for questioning from alerting others who might flee and/or destroy evidence.[72] The government spelled out the powers to be given to the state in frightening and precise detail and did not rely on extralegal uses of existing powers as the United States did when it abused grand jury material witness warrants in the aftermath of 9/11.[73] This government's legislative precision, combined with the easily understood harms that could follow – detention of teenagers, strip searches, and incommunicado detention – meant that the proposals caught the public imagination in a way that the other post-9/11 provisions did not. The government probably expected some of this negative reaction and introduced the ASIO questioning bill a week after the five original bills, which were quickly enacted into legislation. This raises the possibility that tough antiterrorism legislation can be used as a form of political theater. A deluge of civil libertarian criticisms of proposed legislation could help the government make clear to its supporters and allies that Australia was prepared to be tough on terrorism.

The ASIO questioning bill lapsed in December 2002, but only after a continuous 27-hour debate in which both the government and the Labor opposition "contended their opponents would have to wear the blame for any Australian blood that might be spilt by terrorists because of the deadlock."[74] In the wake of the Bali bombings a few months earlier, each party was afraid of looking soft on terrorism. The focus on coercive forms of intelligence gathering, however, ignored questions about whether ASIO had adequate sources and how those sources could be used, if necessary, in terrorism prosecutions. There is a danger that reactive and symbolic legislation can fail to address more important and functional security issues.[75] This is particularly true given the challenges faced by intelligence agencies such as ASIO in converting intelligence into usable evidence and in dealing with unfamiliar Muslim communities.

---

[72] Ibid., at 217–19.   [73] See Chapter 4.
[74] Lynch and Williams, *What Price Security?* at 33.
[75] Lynch, "Legislating with Urgency," at 775ff.

An amended bill was introduced in June 2003 and enacted that month as the Labor opposition supported it under the threat of the government calling an election on the issue.[76] The government backed down considerably, despite its robust defense of its original proposals. This underlines the continued relevance of civil society and parliamentary opposition to antiterrorism initiatives. At the same time, it also suggests that the original proposals may have had the government's desired effect of underlining its symbolic commitment to be tough on terrorism. The new bill placed a one-week limit on detention and a 24-hour limit on questioning, but the latter limit was soon extended to 48 hours in cases where translators were required. The perceived foreignness of the target thus became a justification for longer interrogations. Only those aged 16 years and over could be detained, and there were provisions for contact with lawyers and others, but the contact could be monitored and denied if it would alert others or lead to the destruction of evidence. There were also provisions that allow both the subject's lawyer and the inspector general, who has a watchdog role over ASIO, to attend the questioning. The answers provided under a questioning warrant could not be used against the person forced to answer in a subsequent trial, but the legislation did not prohibit the subsequent use of evidence that could not have been discovered without the questioning, something prohibited with respect to American grand juries and Canada's now lapsed investigative hearings.

ASIO questioning or detention warrants are granted by judges on the grounds that other methods of collecting intelligence would be ineffective and that there are reasonable grounds to believe that the warrant will "substantially assist the collection of intelligence that is important in relation to a terrorism offence."[77] This standard blurs the traditional distinction between the collection of intelligence about threats to security and law enforcement in its reference to the collection of intelligence in relation to terrorism offenses. The questioning warrants thus reflect a blurring of the lines between crime and intelligence seen in many recent developments that stress the need to prevent horrendous crimes such as 9/11.

The ASIO questioning procedure is coercive because a refusal to answer questions or the giving of either false or misleading answers is an offense punishable by up to five years' imprisonment.[78] The actual questioning under

[76] Hocking, *Terror Laws*, at 226.
[77] Australian Security Intelligence Organisation Act 1979, Section 34G (as amended).
[78] Ibid., Section 34L.

ASIO warrants is not carried out before a judge but before a prescribed authority appointed by the attorney general. This provision is designed to prevent a
challenge based on the limits of the judicial function if a federal judge were
involved.[79] It is an offense to disclose operational information obtained during
the questioning process or even to reveal that someone has been detained or
questioned while the warrant is in effect, generally for 28 days, except for the
purposes of obtaining legal advice.[80] Such provisions can limit public awareness and criticism of the operation of the controversial scheme,[81] but they also
accord with the traditional emphasis that intelligence agencies give to secrecy
about their operations and methods of investigation. These very restrictive
conditions have justly been subject to strong criticism.[82]

Despite all the controversy about ASIO questioning warrants, they have
been used quite rarely. From 2003 to 2005, 14 questioning warrants were
issued for 13 people,[83] but ASIO's annual reports for 2006 through 2010 report
that no questioning or detention warrants have been sought or granted in the
intervening years. This should not be seen as a sign of inactivity or complacency
because the voluntary recruitment of human sources is in many respects
to be preferred to their coercive detention and questioning. ASIO's budget
has increased dramatically in the post-9/11 environment from $65 million
Australian in 1999–2000[84] to almost $410 million in 2009–2010.[85] ASIO has also
made more frequent use of its enhanced search powers and powers to conduct
security clearances. ASIO warrants, however, will not be up for legislative
renewal until 2016, and the new Australian government has not repealed
them. They remain as a symbolic statement about the state's commitment to
intelligence gathering in terrorism investigations but also one that likely causes
fear and resentment in Australia's Muslim communities.

---

[79] Two judges in dissent in Canada would have struck down investigative hearings on a similar
basis that they violated judicial independence by requiring judges to preside at essentially what
are police investigations. The majority of the court held, however, that investigative hearings
did not necessarily compromise judicial independence, especially if they were carried out in
an adversarial fashion with defense counsel present, subject to the presumption of open courts
and application of the rules of evidence. *Re Section 83.28 of the Criminal Code*, 2 S.C.R. 248
(2004).

[80] ASIO Act, Section 34ZS.

[81] Tham, "Casualties of the Domestic War on Terror."

[82] Jude McCulloch and Joo-Cheong Tham, "Secret State, Transparent Subject: The Australian
Security Intelligence Organization in the Age of Terror" (2005) 38 Australian and New Zealand
Journal of Criminology 400.

[83] Lynch and Williams, *What Price Security?* at 39.

[84] ASIO Report to Parliament, 1999–2000, at 56.

[85] ASIO Report to Parliament, 2009–10, at 134.

v. IMMIGRATION LAW AS ANTITERRORISM LAW

In both the United Kingdom and Canada, the use of immigration law as antiterrorism law played an important role in the initial response to 9/11, but that does not seem to be the case in Australia. Although a Border Security Legislation Amendment Bill[86] provided for increased border controls in response to 9/11, there were no other explicit uses of immigration law as antiterrorism law. This omission may, however, simply reflect the breadth and severity of existing Australian immigration laws. For example, the ASIO Act already allowed noncitizens to be removed on national security grounds on the basis of secret evidence, and courts continued to defer to ASIO's intelligence assessments after 9/11.[87] Unlike in the United Kingdom or Canada, there are no provisions for special advocates who can see and challenge the secret evidence and no requirement that non-citizens receive a minimum of disclosure to ensure that they can respond to the government's secret allegations.[88] One comparative study of procedures for excluding refugees on security grounds found that the Australian system maximized secrecy to the extent of even denying adjudicators access to ASIO's negative security assessments and requiring claimants to make collateral attacks on ASIO security assessments.[89]

The lack of an immigration-specific response to 9/11 can best be understood in the context of Australia's generally harsh immigration laws, including, until 2008, mandatory detention of unlawful noncitizens. A somewhat similar pattern is seen in the United States where as discussed in Chapter 4, terrorism specific measures in 1996 laws and the Patriot Act were not used only because of the breadth of existing immigration law powers relating to detention and removal. 9/11 affected the treatment of all non-citizens in Australia as it did elsewhere. Shortly before 9/11, a Norwegian cargo ship the *Tampa* picked up 438 asylum seekers from Indonesia who were eventually subject to detention by the Australia military. Australian civil liberties groups challenged the military actions and obtained a judgment issued on 9/11 that the detention of the asylum seekers was illegal. This judgment, however, was reversed in a

---

[86] No. 64 of 2002.

[87] *Leghaei v. Director General of Security*, FCA 1576 (2005), at para. 84, affd. FCAFC 37 (2007).

[88] Ben Saul, "The Kafka-esque Case of Sheikh Mansour Leghaei," (2010) 33 University of New South Wales Law Journal 629.

[89] Won Kadane, "The Terrorism Bar to Asylum in Australia, Canada, the UK and the US" (2010) 33 Fordham International Law Journal 300, at 368; Savitra Taylor, "Guarding the Enemy from Oppression: Asylum Seekers Rights Post September 11" (2002) 26 Melbourne University Law Review 396, at 411–13.

2–1 decision of the federal court on September 18, 2001.[90] A UN commission criticized Australia in 2002 for its detention of all illegal migrants, including asylum seekers.[91] Nevertheless, the Howard government saw its political fortunes increase for the actions it took to make it more difficult for asylum seekers to enter Australia.

Professor Hocking has observed that in the aftermath of 9/11, "an easy elision between 'terrorists' and 'asylum seekers' was constructed by both government and the media."[92] In such an environment, there was little need for specific new legislation linking security and terrorism. This demonstrates the need to take into account starting points and existing measures when evaluating the effects of 9/11 on any particular jurisdiction. In immigration law, Australia, like the countries examined in Chapter 3, did not need to respond to 9/11 because it already had tough laws and practices. As in those countries, however, it would be a mistake to conclude that 9/11 had no effect. Despite earlier decisions suggesting that noncitizens should not be held if there was no realistic possibility of deportation,[93] the Australian High Court decided in 2004 that non-citizens could be held indefinitely.[94] The majority of the court stressed that the state did not have punitive purposes, a common but unconvincing defense of many of the administrative detention regimes discussed in Chapter 3. As will be seen in the next chapter, Canadian courts have also allowed de facto indeterminate detention of noncitizens judged to be security risks could not be deported because of concerns that they would be tortured.[95]

VI. RESPONDING TO THE LONDON BOMBINGS

The transnational nature of antiterrorism policy making is underlined by the fact that at the end of 2005, Australia enacted a raft of new provisions providing for preventive arrests, control orders, and the regulation of speech. These laws were not enacted in response to domestic terrorism in Australia or even attacks on Australian citizens abroad but in response to the London bombings of July 2005 and the subsequent UN Security Council Resolution

---

[90] *Ruddock v. Vadarlis*, FCA 1329 (2001).

[91] *Report of the Working Group on Arbitrary Detention Visit to Australia*, October 24, 2002.

[92] Hocking, *Terror Laws*, at 9.

[93] *Minister for Immigration v. Al Masri*, 126 FCR 54 (Fed. Ct.) (2003).

[94] *Al-Kateb v. Godwin*, 219 CLR 562 (2004).

[95] For criticisms of both the Australian and Canadian positions, see Rayner Thwaites, "Discriminating against Non-Citizens" (2009) 34 Queens Law Journal 669.

1624 call for laws against the incitement of terrorism. In some respects, the London bombings had a more direct influence on Australian policy than the October 2002 Bali bombings that killed 88 Australians. To be sure, the Bali bombings were invoked in the debates about ASIO questioning warrants, and they played a role in the expansion of proscription powers and new offenses of murder and harm to Australians outside of Australia.[96] Nevertheless, the main pieces of Australia's initial response to 9/11 were in place before the 2002 Bali bombings. As will be seen, the 2005 London bombings provided an opportunity for the Howard government dramatically to increase Australia's antiterrorism legislation.

Speech Associated with Terrorism

Consistent with the focus on speech in Security Council Resolution 1624 and the Blair government's response to the London bombings, much of the Australian response focused on speech associated with terrorism. This allowed European concepts of militant democracy to migrate to the very different constitutional culture of Australia where they would become something quite different.[97] The grounds for proscribing terrorist groups were expanded to include groups that "advocate the doing of a terrorist act (whether or not a terrorist act has occurred or will occur)."[98] Advocate was broadly defined to include not only direct or indirect counseling or providing instructions but also praising "the doing of a terrorist act in circumstances where there is a risk that such praise might have the effect of leading a person (regardless of his or her age or any mental impairment) . . . to engage in a terrorist act."[99] This formulation went even beyond Prime Minister Blair's original glorification of terrorism proposals in its focus on any risk that anyone, including a young or mentally impaired person, might be inspired by speech to commit an act of terrorism. In any event, Blair's original terrorism proposals were watered down before being enacted in the United Kingdom's Terrorism Act, 2006. Ironically Blair had more influence with the UN Security Council and the Australian Parliament than in his own Parliament.

---

[96] Criminal Code Amendment (Offences against Australians), Act 106 of 2002; Criminal Code Amendment Regulations, SR 2002, no. 250.

[97] Helen Irving, "Australia," in *The "Militant Democracy" Principle in Modern Democracies*, ed. Markus Thiele (London: Ashgate, 2009).

[98] Criminal Code (as amended), Section 102.1(2).

[99] Ibid., Section 102.1(1A).

Andrew Lynch and George Williams have effectively criticized the 2005 provision as far too broad in allowing whole groups to be banned and membership and association with them to be made criminal on the basis of speech acts by one of the members of the group.[100] In 2006, the Sheller Committee recommended that praising terrorism be removed as a ground for proscribing a terrorist organization. In the alternative, the committee recommended that the law be amended to require "a substantial risk" that the praise might lead someone to engage in a terrorist act.[101] In 2010, the latter proposal was enacted.[102] This responds to the worst excesses of the 2005 law, but it also leaves in place the basic structure that groups that advocate terrorism can be proscribed even if they are not necessarily involved in terrorist activities. Governments that address the excesses of antiterrorism laws enacted in response to either 9/11 or subsequent terrorist acts run the risk of nibbling at the margins of new repressive and seemingly permanent security structures such as proscription regimes.

Sedition and the War on Terrorism

The 2005 amendments contained controversial changes to sedition laws that were designed to respond to extremism that could motivate terrorism. As in many democracies, sedition offenses had not been used in Australia since the 1950s, when a newspaper editor was convicted for opposing the war against Communists in Malaya and Korea.[103] Subsequently, however, both the courts and the people of Australia rejected attempts to ban the Communist Party. In the post-9/11 environment, however, the banning of organizations was accepted as a necessary part of an international battle against terrorism, and old treason and sedition offenses were dusted off and modernized.

Under the new law, a person could be convicted of sedition for urging a person to engage in conduct that would intentionally assist either another country or an organization engaged in armed hostilities against the Australian Defence Forces.[104] The new sedition offense built on the 2002 expansion of treason potentially to apply to terrorist groups who might be engaged in hostilities against Australian Defence Forces in Afghanistan, Iraq, and elsewhere.

[100] Lynch and Williams, *What Price Security?* at 62–4.
[101] *Report of the Security Legislative Review Committee*, June 2006, at 8.10, 8.11.
[102] National Security Legislation Amendment Act 2010, no. 127 of 2010, Schedule 2.
[103] Simon Bronitt and James Stelios, "Sedition, Security and Human Rights" (2006) 30 Melbourne University Law Review 923, at 926–7.
[104] Criminal Code, Section 80.2(7)(8).

The new treason and sedition laws demonstrated how terrorist groups as non-state actors now were conceived as enemies of the state on a par with foreign and warring governments. In this way, Australia more than the United Kingdom and Canada embraced the idea of a war against terrorism, albeit a more legislatively based war than conducted by the United States under President Bush. British-inspired restrictions on speech were reshaped in an Australian context that was more comfortable with the notions of a war on terrorism[105] than the United Kingdom and less comfortable or familiar with European notions of militant democracy and abuse of rights. The Australian approach was influenced both by the American war on terrorism and the British defense of militant democracy, but it produced something different from both and distinctly Australian. The revised sedition offense like the 2002 treason reforms affirmed Australia's ability to revise old security laws based on betrayal of the state to incorporate a new emphasis on preventing terrorism.

Sedition and Hate Speech

The new sedition offense did not apply just to those who would assist terrorists engaged in a war against Australia but also to those who would engage in extremist speech that urged a group distinguished by race, religion, nationality, or political opinion to use force and violence against other such groups in a manner that disrupts peace, order, and good government.[106] This provision was based not so much on concerns about betrayal of the state in its armed conflicts against other states or terrorist groups but the support of equality values and peaceful multiculturalism. As in the United Kingdom and Canada, hate laws were included in antiterrorism laws. The hate speech element of sedition distinguished the Australian approach from the United States where hate speech laws were still seen as unconstitutional content regulation of speech. The hate speech approach in Australia's federal structure, however, raised specific concerns in Australia about whether the federal government had jurisdiction to enact such laws given the states' primary jurisdiction over criminal law.

The combination of antihate and antiterror rationales has supporters, such as Irwin Cotler, who have argued that they respond to the realities of

---

[105] Jack Holland and Matt McDonald, "Australian Identity, Interventionalism and the War on Terror," in *International Terrorism Post 9/11*, ed. Asaf Silver (London: Routledge, 2010).

[106] Criminal Code of Australia, Section 80.2. The phrase "peace order and good government" is found in Canada's Constitution Act, 1867, and was often associated with a Canadian preference for order compared to an American preference for liberty. As is seen in Chapter 7, however, Canada did not enact new speech offenses in response to Security Council Resolution 1624.

terrorism, in particular, al Qaeda–inspired terrorism that is frequently based on the dehumanization of victims of terrorism including anti-Semitism.[107] Nevertheless the combination of rationales allowed the state to argue that even if sedition prosecutions were not justified on antiterror grounds, they were justified on antihate grounds, and vice versa.[108] In such a context, it is difficult to evaluate the effectiveness of speech prosecutions, and there is a danger that governments may engage in divisive prosecutions to respond to hateful speech that might be rebutted through less coercive means. Australia followed Security Council Resolution 1624 and the United Kingdom's example in investing in the regulation of speech as an antiterrorism instrument, but the efficacy of such laws in preventing terrorism are perhaps even more suspect than the Security Council's previous focus on terrorism financing. Although terrorism might be prevented by prohibiting speech that provides concrete instructions about acts of terrorism,[109] it is less clear that punishing speech that praises terrorism, especially in other countries, or even speech that urges intergroup violence will prevent terrorism. Indeed, speech prosecutions could be counter-productive by contributing to a sense that the state's antiterrorism efforts are directed at certain political and religious views as opposed to violence.

The new sedition offenses were controversial, and critics of them were not mollified by the existence of good faith defenses or the requirement that the attorney general approve prosecutions. In a bizarre move that underlined the priority it gave to quick enactment of the law, the government asked the Australian Law Reform Commission to review the newly enacted law. The commission issued a very critical report, and a new government in 2010 enacted a new law that followed some of the commission's recommendations, including the removal of the term *sedition* in favor of the phrase *urging violence* and some changes to the treason offense to require that assistance of an enemy be material and not include just rhetorical support or dissent.[110] These amendments may have increased free speech, but they also confirm Australia's revival, modernization, and repackaging of old treason and sedition offenses in the post-9/11 environment.

[107] Irwin Cotler, "Terrorism, Security and Rights: The Dilemmas of Democracies" (2002) 14 National Journal of Constitutional Law 13.
[108] Katharine Gelber, "The False Analogy between Vilification and Sedition" (2009) 33 Melbourne University Law Review 270.
[109] Laura Donohue, "Terrorist Speech and the Future of Freedom of Expression" (2005) 27 Cardozo Law Review 233.
[110] *National Security Legislation Amendment Act 2010*, no. 127 of 2010, Schedule 1.

Preventive Detention

Australian federal law did not authorize either preventive detention or control orders for terrorist suspects until the passage of the Anti-Terrorism Bill (No. 2) in late 2005. These amendments were a response to the London bombings of July 2005. They were rushed through Parliament with only six hours and 24 minutes of parliamentary debate.[111] The Australian provisions for preventive detention allow detention on a broad range of grounds relating to concerns that a person will commit a terrorist act and on the basis that a person has done an act of preparation or possesses things in connection with terrorism. Most of these grounds are already crimes for which a person can be arrested, though preventive detention can also be used after a terrorist act in order to preserve evidence. This suggests that preventive detention can often only be distinguished from the criminal law by the fact that the state can use preventive detention on the lower basis of suspicion than required for arrest or prosecution under the criminal law.

The duration of federal preventive detention appeared comparatively mild because it only authorized a maximum of 72 hours' detention. Nevertheless, at the Commonwealth's urging, Australian states have enacted complementary legislation that allows the period of preventive detention to be extended for considerably longer periods including an additional 14 days of preventive detention.[112] More generally, the states in Australia have supplemented federal antiterrorism laws and borrowed concepts such as proscription, wide offenses, and control orders and have applied them to other crimes, most notably organized crime.[113] This demonstrates the recurring danger that innovations made to prevent and prosecute terrorism may spread to other serious crimes.

In an attempt to avoid the controversies that accompanied ASIO questioning warrants, restrictions were placed on interrogating those subject to preventive detention. For the first 24 hours, the detention can be authorized by a senior member of the Australian Federal Police Force.[114] An extension of the initial

[111] Greg Carne, "Prevent, Detain, Control and Order? Legislative Process and Executive Outcomes in Enacting the Anti-Terrorism Act (No 2) 2005 (Cth)" (2005) 10 Flinders Journal of Law Reform 17, at 50. For a much more optimistic account of the legislative process that does, however, concede that much trust was placed in the security risk estimates made by the intelligence community, see Joo-Cheong Tham, "Parliamentary Deliberation and the National Security Executive: The Case of Control Orders" (2010) Public Law 79.

[112] Lynch and Williams, *What Price Security?* at 47.

[113] Gabrielle Appleby and John Williams, "The Anti-Terror Creep," in McGarrity et al., *Counter-Terrorism and Beyond.*

[114] Criminal Code of Australia, Sections 105.8, 105.10.

period of preventive detention for up to another 48 hours is authorized by a prescribed authority who is not a sitting federal judge.[115] These arrangements reflect Australian constitutional concerns about the separation of powers and the limits of the judicial function, but as suggested earlier, they are a fiction that also raises problems with respect to self-selection and judicial independence. Preventive detention as well as control orders also can be seen as intelligence-based instruments that run parallel to a regular and more demanding criminal process.[116]

Control Orders

The 2005 legislation included control orders that could restrict a suspect's liberty for a renewable 12-month period on the basis that the control order "would substantially assist in preventing a terrorist act" or on the alternative basis that a person had provided or received training from a listed terrorist organization.[117] This alternative focus on the status of the person underlines the blurring of intelligence with law enforcement and crime prevention. A person who has received terrorist training is a legitimate target for investigation and surveillance by a security intelligence agency, but the person's status as a person who once received training tells us nothing about whether he or she is likely to commit a terrorist act. The status-based alternative also means that a person who has received training but who has renounced violence or is not at all likely to engage in it can still be subject to a control order. Status based crimes are strongly resisted in the criminal law because they avoid the need to establish a definite harmful act and intent and because they maximize law enforcement discretion. The status based training ground for granting an Australian control order makes a person who has received or given training from al Qaeda or another listed terrorist organization a permanent target for a control order. In addition, the precautionary mindset that is applied against those who have received terrorist training is also applied against judges because the alternative ground would require judges to approve control orders even if they concluded that the controllee was not a risk to commit a terrorist act or engage in any preparatory activity to commit or assist in the commission of a terrorist act.

Control orders require the consent of both the attorney general and a sitting judge. The grounds for ordering a control order only have to be established on a

[115] Ibid., Section 105.13.
[116] Claire Macken "The Counter-Terrorism Purposes of an Australian Preventive Detention Order" in McGarrity et al., *Counter-Terrorism and Beyond.*
[117] Criminal Code (Australia), Section 104.4.

balance of probabilities as opposed to the criminal law standard of proof beyond a reasonable doubt.[118] Control orders are part of an increased willingness to use alternatives to criminal prosecutions that place less of a burden on the state and avoid the need to prove guilt beyond a reasonable doubt. Governmental officials defended control orders by stressing that preventive detention and control orders "are not to do with guilt or innocence."[119] Such governmental defenses are similar to those given for administrative detention in some of the countries examined in Chapter three. They focused on the state's preventive and intelligence based objectives and discounted the stigmatizing and punitive effects that the issuance of a control or preventive detention order could have on a person who will be publically associated with terrorism.

As in the United Kingdom, the Australian legislation specifically lists possible conditions, including wearing a tracking device and not associating with persons. The Australian conditions also contemplate that a person receive specified counseling or education, a condition not listed in the 2005 U.K. legislation, even though that legislation lists 16 possible restrictions that can be placed on a person subject to a control order.[120] The Australian approach may recognize the use of rehabilitation of terrorists in the Asia-Pacific region, most notably Singapore,[121] but it differs from those approaches with a specific legislative requirement that the controllee must consent to any counseling or education.

Andrew Lynch has argued that though Australian control orders are clearly modeled on U.K. control orders, they have migrated into a different context. Australian control orders were not a response to a judicial decision that ruled that indeterminate detention of noncitizens suspected of terrorism was disproportionate and discriminatory, as they were in the United Kingdom. On the contrary, the Australian High Court in 2004 confirmed the constitutionality of indeterminate detention of noncitizens. Australian control orders will also not be supervised by the European Court of Human Rights which as seen in the last chapter imposed minimum disclosure requirements that restricted the use of secret evidence to support control orders and would also impose limits on how much control orders would restrict liberty. In addition, Australian control orders, unlike British ones, can be imposed without regard to whether a criminal prosecution is possible and even though terrorism prosecutions should be more viable in Australia because of its use of electronic surveillance

[118] Lynch and Williams, *What Price Security?* at 55–6.
[119] Geoff McDonald, "Control Orders and Preventive Detention – Why Alarm Is Misguided," in Lynch et al., *Law and Liberty in the War on Terror*, at 106.
[120] Prevention of Terrorism Act, 2005 (U.K.), Section 1(4).
[121] Chapter 3.

as evidence.[122] Australian officials, however, defended both control orders and preventive detention as less intrusive than criminal prosecutions, which often involve extensive periods of pretrial detention.[123] In addition, the Australian legislation has a longer sunset clause and was not subject to the same reporting or review provisions as control orders in the United Kingdom.[124] As examined in the last chapter, the coalition government in the United Kingdom announced at the start of 2011 its plans to repeal control orders and replace them with a less restrictive regime, but no similar plans have been announced in Australia. Control orders may persist in Australia even though they are subject to less judicial supervision than in the United Kingdom and even though criminal prosecutions should be a more viable option in Australia.

The "Jihad Jack" Thomas Case

Control orders have been used even less than ASIO questioning warrants raising the possibility that they may exist more as a symbol of the government's get tough approach to terrorism than an instrument to control terrorist suspects. The first control order in Australia was granted against "Jihad Jack" Thomas just days after a court of appeal reversed his conviction for receiving support from al Qaeda on the basis that the trial judge had erred by allowing the jury to consider an involuntary statement extracted from Thomas while he was in custody in Pakistan. The media reaction to this decision was hostile, in large part because Thomas had admitted in a television interview to attending a training camp and having contact with al Qaeda. The decision was unfairly dismissed in the press as a "legal technicality" and related to the fact that one of the judges had been associated with a civil liberties group.[125]

The control order against Thomas was improbably made on the basis that despite his notoriety, he might be a sleeper agent who could engage in terrorism. If Thomas was indeed a sleeper agent, it was far from clear that the control order imposed on him would restrain him because it was relatively light compared to those used in the United Kingdom where a number of controlees escaped. Thomas's control order imposed a curfew between midnight and 5:00 A.M. and prohibited communication with individuals listed as terrorists, travel outside of Australia, and possession of explosives and some communications technology. The control order was also justified on the alternative basis that Thomas received training from al Qaeda. This alternative training ground

---

[122] Lynch, "Control Orders in Australia."
[123] McDonald, "Control Orders and Preventive Detention," at 114–15.
[124] Carne, "Prevent, Detain, Control and Order?" at 58–9.
[125] Lynch, "Maximizing the Drama," at 324–30.

was more certain than the idea that Thomas might engage in terrorism in the future. Nevertheless, the status based training ground underlined that Thomas would be vulnerable to having a control order placed on him for so long as control orders (or he) continue to exist.

The magistrate who granted the control order against Thomas relied on the involuntary statements taken in Pakistan. As Andrew Lynch has argued, this case is a dramatic example of jurisdictional and jurisprudential forum shopping that allowed the state to avoid the restraints of criminal law.[126] As seen in the previous chapter, similar jurisdiction shopping has occurred in the United Kingdom, with control orders being used, for example, against a person acquitted in the 2006 transatlantic liquid bomb plot.[127] Control orders, like administrative detention schemes, reveal a lack of confidence in the criminal law and state impatience and circumvention of the criminal process when it does not convict terrorist suspects.

The High Court of Australia affirmed the constitutionality of Thomas's control order in 2007. The court accepted that control orders to prevent acts of terrorism could be justified under the defense power. Consistent with the new laws that expanded treason and sedition to support of terrorists and not only hostile states, Chief Justice Gleeson concluded that the defense power "is not limited to aggression from a foreign nation; it is not limited to external threats; it is not confined to waging war in a conventional sense of combat between forces of nations. . . ."[128] Justice Kirby dissented and stressed the breadth of the new crimes of terrorism and traditions of keeping the military out of civil peacekeeping.[129] The high court's acceptance of a large federal presence in counter-terrorism favored a war model over a crime model, at least for the purposes of administering the constitutional division of powers.

The high court rejected the argument that control orders violated the separation of powers by stressing the similarity between control orders and peace bonds, denials of bail, and dangerous offender designations, all of which are made by sitting judges.[130] Although these analogies can be disputed on the basis that they, unlike control orders, are generally tied to criminal trials or convictions,[131] they do underline how innovations in the antiterrorism field can take inspiration from preventive aspects of criminal law and the melding

---

[126] Lynch, "Control Orders in Australia," at 168.
[127] *Secretary of State v. AY*, EWCA (Civ) 3053 (2009); discussed in Chapter 5.
[128] *Thomas v. Mowbry*, HCA 33 (2007), at para. 7.
[129] Ibid., at paras. 266–7. He also concluded that the provisions were not required to implement Security Council Resolution 1373. Ibid., at para. 290.
[130] Ibid., at para. 28.
[131] Andrew Lynch, "Australia's 'War on Terror' Reaches the High Court" (2008) 32 Melbourne University Law Journal 1182, at 1203.

of less restrained civil models into criminal law. The majority of the court concluded that it was within judicial powers to make predictive judgments about future threats when deciding whether to impose a control order, whereas two dissenters argued that such predictive judgments were beyond judicial powers, especially when made on the basis of secret intelligence.[132]

The majority judgment allows judges to evaluate risk assessments made by the state in an adversarial context. Given the increased post-9/11 use of intelligence as evidence, there are dangers in a purist position where judges declare that intelligence and risk assessments are beyond their ability to supervise.[133] Judges in both the United Kingdom and Canada have been able in some cases to reject intelligence assessments of risks when they have been subject to adversarial challenge. In some respects, this should be easier to do in Australia because its control order legislation does not authorize the use of secret evidence, as does British legislation. Another factor may be whether the judges have some experience and confidence in evaluating intelligence. The magistrates who have granted the two control orders issued in Australia unfortunately accepted the state's risk assessment at face value, whereas some British and Canadian judges have found that intelligence used by the state was stale, contradicted by other evidence, obtained from unreliable sources, or obtained through mistreatment.[134]

The David Hicks Case

Australia's second control order was issued against David Hicks after his return from Guantánamo. The Australian government under Prime Minister Howard refused to request that the United States return Hicks to Australia. Hicks commenced legal action to force Australia to do so, and the government lost an application to have the litigation dismissed as a matter that should be left to politics.[135] As in the United Kingdom and Canada, the courts refused to hold

[132] Hayne J., in dissent, stated that "intelligence material will often require evaluative judgments to be made about the weight to be given to diffuse, fragmentary and even conflicting pieces of intelligence. Those are judgments of a kind very different from those ordinarily made by courts." Ibid., at *Thomas v. Mowbry*, HCA 33 (2007), at para. 510. For similar concerns, see Denise Meyerson, "Using Judges to Manage Risk: The Case of *Thomas v. Mowbry*" (2008) 36 Federal Law Review 209, at 223.

[133] See David Dyzenhaus and Rayner Thwaites, "Legality and Emergency – The Judiciary in a Time of Terror," in Lynch et al., *Law and Liberty in the War on Terror*, at 17–22, for similar criticisms.

[134] Adam Tomkins "National Security and the Role of the Court: A Changed Landscape?" "(2010) 126 Law Quarterly Review 543; Kent Roach "When Secret Intelligence Becomes Evidence" (2009) 47 Supreme Court Law Review 147.

[135] *Hicks v. Rudd*, FCA 299 (2007).

that diplomatic representations to the United States over Guantánamo were nonjusticiable. At the same time, however, no court in any of these countries required their executive to make diplomatic representations, and they could not, in the transnational context, ensure any concrete remedy for those held at Guantánamo. In a subsequent case brought by another Australian citizen detained at Guantánamo, the Australian courts have refused to hold that the Australian state was immune from damage claims.[136] Courts in Australia, the United Kingdom, and Canada have all been more receptive to civil claims arising from Guantánamo and other arguably extralegal activities than the American courts.

Hicks pleaded guilty to material support of terrorism at Guantánamo. The plea agreement included as a condition that Hicks would not bring litigation anywhere over his detention at Guantánamo and that he would not speak to the media for a year about his illegal activities or detention.[137] Although President Bush's attempt to declare Guantánamo a law-free zone had failed, similar attempts live on in Guantánamo plea agreements that attempt to preclude the released person from bringing any litigation with respect to years of confinement and mistreatment. The gag order on Hicks has expired, and he has stated that he only pled guilty because he feared for his sanity and because he was convinced that military commissions would never acquit anyone at Guantánamo.[138] An observer for the Law Council of Australia similarly concluded, after visiting Guantánamo, that the process was "not impartial or independent" because "the US military is captor, jailer, prosecutor, defender, judge of fact, judge of law, and sentence."[139] Sir Anthony Mason, the former chief justice of Australia, expressed concerns about the jurisdiction of military commissions over material support charges, the retroactive nature of charges not supported by the traditional laws of war, and the mistreatment of Hicks while in Guantánamo. Indeed, he has criticized the Australian government for not requesting Hicks's repatriation.[140] The Howard government deferred to the United States on Guantánamo; other Australians did not.

Despite these concerns about the legitimacy of the guilty plea, a control order was issued against Hicks after he had served a short prison sentence

---

[136] *Habib v. Australia*, FCA 12 (2010).

[137] Plea agreement, at http://www.defense.gov/news/Mar2007/US%20v%20David%20Hicks%20ROT%20(Redacted).pdf.

[138] David Hicks, "Pressure to Plea Guilty" (2010) 29(4) Human Rights Defender.

[139] Lex Lasry, "Military Justice: David Hicks and Guantanamo Bay," in *Counter-Terrorism and the Post Democratic State*, ed. Jenny Hocking and Colleen Lewis (Cheltenham, UK: Edward Elgar, 2007), at 55.

[140] Anthony Mason and Geoffrey Lindell, "Book Review" (2008) 9 Melbourne Journal of International Law 515.

in Adelaide. The magistrate granted the control order both on the basis that Hicks had received training from al Qaeda and that it would substantially assist in preventing a terrorist act. This latter decision was based on old letters that Hicks had written home indicating a willingness to defend Muslims in conflicts abroad. The magistrate's decision demonstrates the dangers that judges might accept speculative intelligence assessments as a basis for issuing control orders.[141] In any event, Hicks's control order was subsequently loosened and allowed to expire without incident.[142] Both David Hicks and Jack Thomas, however, are permanently vulnerable to having subsequent control orders placed upon them because of their common and permanent status as persons who have received training from al Qaeda. The focus on both men's status as those who have received terrorist training has codified an intelligence mindset into the law in a seemingly permanent manner that would allow control orders to be imposed even long after intelligence agencies might conclude that they are no longer a security threat. The migration and codification of intelligence concepts into post-9/11 counter-terrorism laws have resulted in blunter, more coercive and more permanent restraints on liberty than would have been achieved had the concepts only been used by intelligence agencies in making discretionary decisions about surveillance and the collection of intelligence.

VII. CRIMINAL PROSECUTIONS

The alternative to less restrained instruments such as control orders and preventive or immigration detention is a terrorist trial. A particular challenge for countries such as the United Kingdom, Australia, and Canada, which have domestic security intelligence agencies and often rely on evidence from foreign agencies about international terrorism, is ensuring that the use of criminal trials does not result in disclosure of secrets. At the same time, accused have broad rights to disclosure of not only the evidence that is presented by the state but other relevant information in the state's possession. As discussed earlier in relation to cases stemming from the bombing of the Sydney Hilton, a denial of disclosure from an intelligence agency can result in miscarriages of justice.[143]

---

[141] The magistrate concluded, "When the expressed views of the Respondent are coupled with the capacity to engage in such activities, I am satisfied on the balance of probabilities that there is a risk of the Respondent either participating in a terrorist act or training others for that purpose. It then follows, having regard to the control order sought, that such order in the terms contemplated would substantially assist in preventing such an act." *Jabbour v. Hicks*, FMCA 2139 (2007), at para. 31.

[142] Lynch, "Control Orders in Australia."

[143] *Alister v. The Queen*, 154 CLR 404 (1984); discussed earlier.

The National Security Information Act

The Australian Law Reform Commission examined the treatment of secret information in the criminal process after a 2001 espionage prosecution nearly collapsed after the government refused to disclose a relevant document. The commission contemplated that secret information that would otherwise be disclosed to the accused could be denied to the accused so long as it was not central to the case or could reasonably assist the accused. It drew a firm line, however, at the use of secret evidence in a criminal trial because such a process would violate basic principles of a fair trial.[144] In 2004, Australia enacted the National Security Information Act. It requires participants to notify the attorney general in advance with respect to the disclosure of information that may harm national security.[145] The judge is required to adjourn the proceedings until the Commonwealth attorney general decides whether to allow the evidence to be disclosed, perhaps in a redacted or summarized manner. These procedures increase Commonwealth involvement in criminal proceedings and detract from both the efficiency and the public nature of the proceedings. Parties that disclose information that the attorney general has not authorized risk being found guilty of an offense punishable by two years' imprisonment. One defense lawyer with extensive experience has commented on how terrorism trials can be "very intimidating" because of the presence of lawyers for the Commonwealth who "are there to maintain national security" and can do so by threatening punishment or motions to exclude the lawyer from the case because of a "loosely framed question or a decision to call a witness about a matter that will disclose information touching on national security."[146]

The attorney general's certificate setting out the terms of disclosure is subject to judicial review by the trial judge, but the court may exclude not only the media but the accused and any defense lawyer who does not have security clearance from the review proceedings. Concerns have been raised that requirements for security clearances may adversely affect the person's choice of a lawyer, the independence of the bar and the traditional lawyer-client relationship.[147] At the same time, the accused's own lawyer may have a better understanding of the case than special advocates who might be used in similar proceedings in the United Kingdom or Canada.

---

[144] Australian Law Reform Commission, *Keeping Secrets: The Protection of Classified and Security Sensitive Information*, 2004, at 11.203.
[145] National Security Information Act, Section 24.
[146] Phillip Boulten, "Preserving National Security in the Courtroom: The New Battleground," in Lynch et al., *Law and Liberty in the War on Terror*, at 100.
[147] Lynch and Williams, *What Price Security?* at 8.

The judge who reviews the attorney general's decision about disclosure must balance the adverse effects of nondisclosure on the accused's fair hearing with the adverse effects of disclosure on the state's interests. The law defines the latter broadly to include national security, national defense, international relations, and law enforcement interests, including the protection of informants, not discouraging foreign agencies from disclosing intelligence to Australian agencies, the protection of methods used to obtain intelligence, and not disrupting national and international investigations. The legislature was very precise in its attempts to educate judges about the dangers of disclosing secrets. Moreover, Section 31(8) of the National Security Information Act overtly tilted the balance in favor of the state and secrecy by instructing the court to give greatest weight to the risk of prejudice to national security. Such an approach represented a conscious decision to increase the risk of wrongful convictions by erring on the side of not disclosing intelligence to the accused that may assist his or her defense. As a retired judge of the Australian High Court has written, such legislation "does not direct the court to make the order the Attorney-General wants. But it goes as close to it as it thinks it can."[148]

Despite its dangers, Section 31(8) has been upheld against constitutional challenges, with judges stressing that it does not deprive a judge of judicial powers, including the power to stay proceedings if an unfair trial will occur as a result of the court upholding the attorney general's nondisclosure certificate.[149] In 2010, some reforms to the National Security Information Act were enacted, such as abolishing mandatory adjournment requirements in an attempt to increase the efficiency of terrorism trials, but the new government did not change Section 31(8), with its problematic assertion of the primacy of the state's interests in protecting secrets over the accused's interest in a fair trial and a full defense.[150] The danger here is that 9/11 may have permanently tilted the balance towards secrecy and away from fair trials.

Terrorism Prosecutions

There have been a number of terrorist trials in Australia, and they have encountered their share of difficulties. The first person charged under the new terrorism offenses, Zeky Mallah, was acquitted by a jury of doing acts in preparation for a terrorist act, even though he was discovered with weapons and a video threatening to kill ASIO officers after he was denied a passport on the basis of ASIO's adverse security assessment. He argued that he acted for personal and

---

[148] Hon Michael McHugh, "Terrorism Legislation and the Constitution" (2006) 28 Australian Bar Review 117.

[149] *Lodhi v. The Queen*, 179 A. Crim. R. 470 (2007).

[150] National Security Legislation Amendment Act, no. 127 of 2010, Schedule 8.

not political or religious reasons, but the prosecution responded with a video in which Mallah read versions of the Koran and emphasized his possession of a document titled "How Can I Prepare for Jihad?" Such evidence demonstrates how the religious and political motive requirement forces the accused's religion and politics to become an important factor in terrorism trials. Given the breadth of the offense of doing acts for preparation of a terrorist act, it is likely that the jury had doubts about whether Mallah was acting for political or religious reasons. In any event, he was eventually released and granted an Australian passport.[151] The Commonwealth DPP responded to the acquittal by asking that the requirement to establish political or religious motive be dropped from the law,[152] but this change has not been made. In another case, terrorism charges were dropped in favor of explosive charges against a man who apparently acted out of personal motives but with a staggering amount of explosives.[153] Although the political and religious motive requirement was challenged for a time in Canada on the basis of its effects on religious and political freedoms, it has emerged as a partial restraint on terrorism prosecutions in Australia, albeit one that places the accused's religious and political beliefs at the heart of terrorism trials.

Terrorism prosecutions have encountered difficulties other than those presented by the political and religious motive requirement. Jack Thomas was convicted in February 2006 of receiving funds from al Qaeda but was acquitted by the jury of supplying funds to al Qaeda. Attorney General Philip Ruddock stressed that Thomas was convicted of one terrorist offense and committed by a magistrate for trial on others and suggested that the jury's reasonable doubt about guilt "ought not to be seen as some form of victory. This isn't a victory issue. This is an issue of protecting the Australian community and terrorist offences are very serious offences."[154] In any event, Hick's conviction was overturned when the Victorian Court of Appeal found that statements taken from him in Pakistan by a joint team of the Australian Federal Police and ASIO were involuntary in large part because he had been mistreated and threatened with torture by Pakistani and American officials while held in solitary confinement in Pakistan.[155] This judgment underlines the transnational complexity of

---

[151] McGarrity, "'Testing' Our Counter-Terrorism Laws," at 96. Mallah did plea guilty to a non-terrorism offense of threatening Commonwealth officers and received a two and a half year sentence.
[152] Lynch and Williams, *What Price Security?* at 73.
[153] McGarrity, "'Testing' Our Counter-Terrorism Laws," at 104.
[154] "Ruddock says Thomas trial acts a warning" AM Transcript February 27, 2006 available at http://www.abc.net.au/am/content/2006/s1578987.htm.
[155] The court of appeal concluded, "Put bluntly, there can be little doubt that it was apparent to the applicant, at the time of the AFP interview, as it would have been to any reasonable person so circumstanced, that, if he was to change his current situation of detention in Pakistan and

terrorism investigation and how mistreatment in foreign countries can frustrate terrorism prosecutions. A Canadian court has recently refused to extradite a Canadian to the United States to face terrorism charges because of similar concerns that he was mistreated by Pakistani and American officials when he was originally captured in Pakistan.[156] The Australian and Canadian courts are correct to maintain standards even when evidence is collected abroad, but their actions may also encourage extralegal practices such as rendition to countries with poor human rights records or lying about the conditions under which evidence was obtained abroad. Other domestic courts may be inclined to wash their hands of abuses committed abroad by holding that domestic rules do not apply outside of their country.

As discussed earlier, a control order was quickly imposed on Thomas in response to his victory in the criminal courts. He also faced a second criminal trial on the basis of new evidence of his interviews with the media where he admitted to attending a terrorist training camp and shaking hands with Osama bin Laden and receiving money to allow him to return to Australia after 9/11. Despite these revelations, the jury after two days of deliberations acquitted him of receiving funds from a terrorist organization while convicting him of more minor passport offenses. He was subsequently sentenced to time served with the judge recognizing that he suffered severe post traumatic stress and depression as a result of his prior imprisonment in both Pakistan and Australia.[157] As with the Tamil Tiger decision, the decisions of sentencing judges often revealed a more complex and ambiguous story than presented by the enactment of many new terrorism offenses.

Australian juries have been reluctant to convict some people charged with terrorism offenses. Some commentators suggest that jury nullification might be involved.[158] Another possibility is that the juries are baffled by the complexity of the broadly and vaguely worded offenses. The juries may also be fashioning justice on their perceptions of the intent and danger of the accused and the equities of the case as opposed to being overly bound by the broad, prolix, and confusingly drafted new offenses. For example, a Sydney jury convicted a man of knowingly making a document in relation to a terrorist act when he wrote and posted a book on "rules for the jihad" that included terrorist targets

---

reduce the risk of indeterminate detention there or in some unidentified location, co-operation was far more important than reliance on his rights under the law. Indeed, it is apparent that he believed – and, we would add, on objectively reasonable grounds – that insistence upon his rights might well antagonise those in control of his fate." *R. v. Thomas*, VSCA 165 (2006), at para. 85.

[156] *USA v. Khadr*, ONSC 4338 (2010).

[157] McGarrity, "'Testing' Our Counter-Terrorism Laws," at 102.

[158] Miriam Gani, "How Does It End? Reflections on Completed Terrorism Prosecutions under Australia's Anti-Terrorism Legislation," in Gani and Mathew, *Fresh Perspectives*, at 290.

and techniques. At the same time, the jury acquitted him of intentionally inciting acts of terrorism.[159] The unpredictability of juries may, however, be another reason why the state might use less restrained and more judge-centered instruments such as control orders and immigration proceedings. Some of the main virtues of the criminal justice system – the presumption of innocence, the requirement for proof of fault, the ability to have a trial by jury, the ability to confront witnesses, the ability to obtain disclosure from the state – may encourage states to avoid its rigors. At the same time, however, alternatives to the criminal law, such as control orders and preventive detention, will only provide temporary measures and will not denounce and punish actual attempts to commit terrorism in the same way as criminal law.

A number of complex and lengthy terrorism prosecutions have resulted in convictions. Faheem Lodhi was charged with four terrorism offenses in connection with an alleged terrorist bombing plot in Sydney. He was convicted after a seven-week trial in June 2006 and received a 20-year sentence. Both the trial judge and the court of appeal accepted that a person could be guilty under the new terrorism offenses even though no precise terrorist act was intended and even though the case was decided before the rushed the/a amendments discussed earlier. Witnesses in the trial were allowed to give evidence anonymously and from remote locations. There were also long pretrial proceedings over matters of disclosure of secret information and extensive publication bans. The trial judge was frustrated by the many attempts to preserve secrecy and subsequently observed that ASIO, "for all its skill in intelligence gathering, is perhaps not well equipped to gather evidence for a criminal trial; and its individual agents are not well tutored in the intricacies of the criminal law relating to procedure and evidence."[160] These comments reflect many of the tensions caused by the increased use of intelligence as evidence.

Thirteen men in Melbourne were arrested in November 2005 and charged with various terrorism offenses. One of the men pled guilty and received a more lenient five and a half year sentence in exchange for his testimony in the trials of the others. After a six-month trial featuring many witnesses and much evidence derived from electronic surveillance, most of the men were found guilty, but four were acquitted outright. Because of the allegations of homegrown terrorism, the prosecution had to prove the existence of a terrorist group.[161] As suggested earlier, proscription may be a dated counter-terrorism instrument given the increase in al Qaeda–inspired terrorism. On appeal some

---

[159] *R v. Khazaal*, NSWSC 1061 (2006), as discussed in McGarrity, "'Testing' Our Counter-Terrorism Laws," at 106.

[160] Justice A. G. Whealy, "Difficulty in Obtaining a Fair Trial in Terrorism Cases" (2007) 81 Australian Law Journal 743, at 757.

[161] McGarrity, "'Testing' Our Counter-Terrorism Laws," at 108–9.

of the convictions were overturned and some of the sentences were reduced in recognition of the overlapping nature of the terrorism offenses and the dangers of double punishment. The Court of Appeal also stressed that the legislative definition of terrorist acts and organizations was "extraordinarily broad" and there was a need in sentencing to distinguish between "a rag-tag collection of malcontents" and sophisticated and deadly groups such as al Qaeda. Many of the membership offenses were reduced to four years imprisonment.[162]

Convictions of conspiring to commit acts of preparation for terrorism were also obtained after a year long trial involving five men in Sydney. Four men arrested at that time had earlier pled guilty and received much shorter sentences than the men who were convicted after trial and sentenced to from 23 to 28 years' imprisonment. In both the Melbourne and Sydney cases, those who testified against their colleagues received significant sentence reductions. Such an approach recognizes that the state may need insider testimony to make its case, but it also creates a risk that witnesses may lie to be able to give evidence for the state and obtain a lighter sentence.

The Izhar ul-Haque and Dr. Mohamed Haneef Cases

The changing relationship between intelligence and evidence means that in many cases, intelligence investigations will overlap with criminal investigations. Police forces will have to deal with the ambiguities of intelligence, and intelligence agencies will have to deal with the evidential demands of criminal law. A terrorism prosecution that illustrates the latter problem involved Izhar ul-Haque, a medical student charged in 2004 with receiving training from a terrorist organization in Pakistan. He successfully challenged the admissibility of several statements he made to the police after ASIO officers picked him up and transported him to his home, where they executed an ASIO search warrant. The trial judge was very critical of ASIO's conduct, concluding that it amounted to false imprisonment and kidnapping.[163] The inspector general (IG) who reviewed ASIO's work disagreed with these conclusions but found that ASIO should be more aware of the effects of its interview practices on the admissibility of statements and other evidence in court. The IG rightly stressed that ASIO's "'intelligence collection' work can no longer be separated neatly from the 'evidence collection' work of the police services" and that ASIO was being more exposed "to the requirements of the judicial system and participation in court processes."[164] The IG recommended that ASIO should

---

[162] *Benbrika and Others v. The Queen* [2010] VSCA 281 at para 555.

[163] *R. v. Ul-Haque*, NSWSC 1251 (2007).

[164] Inspector General of Intelligence and Security, *Report of Inquiry into the Actions Taken by ASIO in 2003 in Respect of Mr. Izhar Ul-Haque and Related Matters*, 2008, at para. 182.

receive training on evidential standards in the collection of intelligence, while at the same time admitting that there is a "significant... potential for the work of the Australian Federal Police and ASIO to overlap and clash."[165] As examined in the next chapter, there is similar evidence of a judicialization of intelligence in Canada as well as concerns about the need to resolve potential disputes between intelligence agencies who want to keep their intelligence and sources and methods secret and police and prosecutorial agencies who want intelligence to be used as evidence to obtain convictions.

A case that illustrates the problems that police and prosecutors have in evaluating intelligence involved Dr. Mohamed Haneef, who was arrested on July 2, 2007, and held for 12 days without charge in connection with the Glasgow airport bombings because he had given a SIM card to the brother of one of the Glasgow bombers, who was also Dr. Haneef's second cousin. The long detention without charge period was possible because of complex provisions that allowed "dead time" not used to interview the accused not to be included in the detention period after an arrest. Haneef was charged with recklessly providing support to a terrorist organization, but this charge was dropped on July 27, 2007. He was granted bail on July 16, 2007, but within hours, the minister for immigration and citizenship canceled his visa and required his detention on character grounds largely related to his family connections.[166] This decision was later overturned on the basis that the minister had misinterpreted the character provisions of immigration law and not disclosed enough information to Haneef, but the issue was moot because Dr. Haneef, had voluntarily left the country.

A subsequent inquiry was appointed by the new Labor government, and it revealed that both the police and the immigration officials ignored ASIO's advice that Haneef was not a security threat throughout the whole episode.[167] Just as intelligence agencies are, as in the ul-Haque case, having difficulties adjusting to new evidentiary responsibilities, so, too, may police, immigration, foreign affairs, and the private sector all have difficulties interpreting intelligence. They will be less expert and perhaps more risk adverse than intelligence professionals who are used to dealing with the fragmentary nature of intelligence and have more experience with the context of security threats at home and abroad. As will be seen in the next chapter, police forces in Canada have badly handled intelligence in a way that has indirectly contributed to

---

[165] Ibid., at para. 191.
[166] Mark Riz, "The Show Must Go On: The Drama of Dr. Mohamed Haneef and the Theatre of Counter-Terrorism," in McGarrity et al., *Counter-Terrorism and Beyond*, at 200–1.
[167] *Report of the Clarke Inquiry into the Case of Dr. Mohamed Haneef*, 2008.

the torture of Canadians held abroad and the use of unreliable intelligence as evidence at home.

The Haneef affair also demonstrates how a whole-of-government approach to terrorism can allow the government to use less restrained alternatives, such as immigration detention, in cases in which criminal law cannot be used. As in Canada and the United Kingdom, it is also noteworthy that a discretionary public inquiry had to be called to study a case that involved multiple juris-dictions and multiple agencies. Much review still takes place in traditional silos that are confined to single agencies, even though governments have, since 9/11, taken a whole-of-government approach to terrorism and frequently interact with other governments in counter-terrorism activities.

VIII. REVIEW OF NATIONAL SECURITY ACTIVITIES

The inquiry into the Haneef affair was hampered by an inability to com-pel the production of all relevant evidence, including an inability to access secret evidence.[168] At the same time, however, the IG does have the power to access secret information. Unlike in Canada, where a similar watchdog only has jurisdiction over the domestic security intelligence agency, the ASIO watchdog has jurisdiction over all of Australia's intelligence agen-cies. Moreover, as a result of 2010 legislation, the IG now can be tasked by the Prime Minister to inquire into any intelligence or security matter relating to any federal department or agency.[169] This approach recognizes that under a whole-of-government approach to terrorism, intelligence will likely play an important role in many parts of government, including for-eign affairs and the provision of consular services, financial matters, customs, and immigration. The Australian approach of empowering one watchdog to have access to and review all intelligence matters within government is much to be preferred to the segmented approach used in both Canada and the United States, where various review agencies remain in agency-based silos even while governments break down such silos in an attempt to prevent ter-rorism. The Australian approach also seems less fragmented than the U.K. approach, which involves two separate intelligence commissioners, one who focuses on interception of communications and one who examines other matters. Although each commissioner has jurisdiction over the three foreign, domestic, and signal intelligence services in the United Kingdom,[170] it is not

---

[168] In contrast, the Canadian public inquiries discussed in the next chapter all had access to secret information, though they did clash with governments about what secret information could be made public.

[169] National Security Legislation Amendment Act, no. 127 of 2010, Schedule 9.

[170] Regulation of Investigatory Powers, 2000, c.23, Part IV.

clear that these commissioners have adequate power to deal with the manner in which intelligence is used in other parts of government or that they have exercised their functions in a particularly vigorous manner.[171]

In 2010, legislation providing for an independent national security monitor was enacted in Australia, though no appointment to this position had been made a year later.[172] The independent monitor position follows the practice in the United Kingdom, where Lord Carlile served as a security-cleared independent reviewer of terrorism laws and practices. The Australian independent monitor has a mandate to evaluate both the effectiveness of antiterrorism efforts and their compliance with human rights.[173] This legislation rejected the idea that propriety- and efficacy-based review should be conducted separately and as such recognized that determining the proportionality of the state's response to terrorism requires attention to both the effectiveness and necessity of counter-terrorism actions and alternative policies. It will be suggested in Chapter 8 that the most sustainable form of review will combine review for both effectiveness and propriety.

In addition to review within the executive by the IG and the independent monitor, Australia also has parliamentary review. Legislation enacted in 2010 established a Parliamentary Joint Committee on Law Enforcement that can review the Australian Federal Police and also can be briefed by the Ombudsman on specific complaints.[174] In addition, the Parliamentary Joint Committee on Intelligence and Security reviews terrorist listings, though concerns have been expressed about its difficulties gaining access to all relevant secret intelligence. The committee has engaged in two studies of its proper role in the listing process as well as counter-terrorism legislation in general.[175] The size of this committee was expanded in 2011 legislation that also expanded the ability of ASIO to share intelligence with law enforcement and other intelligence agencies. This approach demonstrates some commitment to increase the powers of review bodies in tandem with increased powers to collect and share intelligence.[176] It will be suggested in Chapter 8 that Australia has done

---

[171] See Simon Chesterman, *One Nation under Surveillance* (Oxford: Oxford University Press, 2011), chapter 7.

[172] "One year on, no terror watchdog" *Sydney Morning Herald* March 24, 2011.

[173] Independent National Security Legislation Monitor, 2010, no. 32, Section 3.

[174] National Security Legislation Amendment Act, no. 127 of 2010. Schedule 10; Parliamentary Joint Committee on Law Enforcement Act, no. 128 of 2010.

[175] Parliamentary Joint Committee on Intelligence and Security, *Review of Security and Counter-Terrorism Legislation*, December 2006; Parliamentary Joint Committee on Intelligence and Security, *Inquiry into the Proscription of "Terrorist Organisations" under the Australian Criminal Code*, September 2007.

[176] Telecommunications Interception and Intelligence Services Legislation Amendment Act no. 4 of 2011 Schedule 8.

better than some other democracies in attempting to make sure that review powers expand and keep pace with increased security powers.

Parliamentary review in Australia is more advanced than in Canada, where parliamentarians still do not have regular access to secret information.[177] This raises the possibility that the absence of a bill of rights in Australia may have inspired greater attention to various forms of parliamentary and watchdog-based review within the executive. Although much will depend on the resourcing and energies of the review bodies, and difficulties may still emerge, especially with respect to review of joint operations between the state and the Commonwealth, the Australian approach to review has significant potential. In some respects, it has greater potential than reliance on judicial review, given that most national security activities will be conducted in secret and not result in acts that will readily be subject to judicial review.

Another virtue of the Australian approach to review can be seen in the 2006 Sheller Committee that conducted a wholesale review of Australia's antiterrorism laws. The review committee was headed by a retired judge but included the IG, the privacy commissioner, the human rights commissioner, and the ombudsman. The composition of the committee recognizes that many watchdog agencies within the executive have overlapping jurisdictions over national security matters and need to develop expertise in the area. Although many of the recommendations by the 2006 committee have still not been implemented,[178] they were crafted by those with knowledge of the adverse effects of excessive counter-terrorism and they helped develop national security expertise as the watchdogs continued their work. Although similar watchdog agencies exist in the other democracies examined in this book, they have generally not acted in concert or provided forward-looking law reform advice that might decrease the number of individual grievances that they will be asked to resolve.

IX. NATIONAL SECURITY POLICIES

The Howard government stressed its close relationship with the United States and participated in the invasions of both Afghanistan and Iraq.[179] In 2004,

---

[177] For recent conclusions that Canada lags behind other Parliamentary democracies in this respect see Interim Report of the Special Senate Committee on Anti-Terrorism *Security, Freedom and the Complex Terrorist Threat: Positive Steps Ahead* March, 2011 at 42–46.

[178] For a critique of the government's response, see Greg Carne, "Remedying the Past or Losing International Human Rights in the Translation" (2009) 13 University of Western Sydney Law Review 37.

[179] Jack Holland and Matt McDonald, "Australian Identity, Interventionism and the War on Terror," in Siniver, *International Terrorism Post 9/11*, at 184–206.

the Howard government released a white paper titled "Transnational Terrorism: The Threat to Australia," that presented terrorism as the main threat to national security. It identified Muslim terrorism and, in particular, al Qaeda and Jemaah Islamiyah as threats to Australia and noted that bin Laden had mentioned Australia as a target. In an echo of the "enduring freedom" campaign in Afghanistan, the white paper proposed an "enduring campaign" against what was portrayed as a new and intractable form of terrorism. The policy declared that "Australia's alliance with the United States is a key plank of our international counter-terrorism strategy"[180] and stressed the military support that Australia had provided to the United States in both Afghanistan and Iraq and its close intelligence and law enforcement connections. As will be seen in the next chapter, this policy differed from the one taken by Canada in its first national security policy, also released in 2004. That policy took an all-risks approach to the threats to national security and did not mention the United States.

This white paper was also accompanied by a national counter-terrorism plan that focused on the prevention of terrorism, including the use of alert systems, intelligence, critical infrastructure protection, consequence management, and coordinated responses. As with the 2006 British CONTEST strategy, this plan focused on terrorism.[181] The Howard government formed a Muslim Advisory Council in the aftermath of the London bombings but also stressed a focus on national unity, including assimilation. There were concerns that the group was unrepresentative and too focused on security issues, and it was replaced by a Multicultural Advisory Council under the Rudd government.[182] As in the United Kingdom, the issue of terrorism has perhaps unhelpfully grafted on to discussions of national identity and integration. In any event, Australia like the other Western democracies examined in this book have struggled with community relations and the treatment of its Muslim minorities in the post-9/11 era.

In December 2008, Prime Minister Rudd delivered a national security statement to Parliament. It continued to recognize the importance of the alliance with the United States and the threat of terrorism but placed this in a broader context that included middle-power diplomacy, climate change, e-security, organized crime, and energy security. It rejected proposals to create an Australian Homeland Security Department. Following a report that highlighted the "agenda beyond terrorism" and the need to respond to other

---

[180] Australia, *Transnational Terrorism: The Threat to Australia*, 2004, at 78.
[181] Australia National Counter-Terrorism Plan, 2nd ed., 2005.
[182] For a description of the council, see http://www.immi.gov.au/about/stakeholder-engagement/national/advisory/amac/.

threats and hazards, the Rudd government proposed the creation of an all-risks Crisis Co-ordination Centre.[183] A 2009 defense white paper stressed that Australian forces have been deployed not only in Afghanistan and Iraq but in Indonesia to respond to a tsunami and in Papua New Guinea for humanitarian purposes.[184] It devoted only four paragraphs to the threat of terrorism.[185] Recent announcements under Prime Minister Gillard have moved in the direction of an all-risks approach, with the attorney general stressing that disaster funds should be available "in the event of a terrorist attack, just as they would be for a flood or bushfire."[186] To be sure, terrorist-specific programs are still in place, but the Australian government has shown increased interest in situating terrorism within the larger context of other security threats and this trend will likely increase in light of the billions in damage caused by floods in Australia in 2010–11.

x. CONCLUSION

Australia provides an interesting case study of how a country with minimal experience with terrorism can be caught up in the 9/11 effect of enacting many new antiterrorism laws and measures. The pace of terrorism legislation under Prime Minister Howard was staggering and revealed the dangers of politicalization of the terror issue by governments. The Howard government was prepared to make political use of intelligence reports both to justify the listing of terrorist groups in 2003 and to justify amendments that were rushed through the legislature just before major terrorist arrests in Sydney and Melbourne at the end of 2005. The legislative process was able to resist some of the government's proposals, such as the truly draconian original ASIO questioning warrants, and to ensure an exemption for most protests and strikes from the definition of terrorism. Nevertheless, the legislature provided less resistance as time progressed and especially after the Howard government secured a majority in both houses.

Australia provides a good example of post-9/11 pressures to facilitate both intelligence gathering and the changing relation between intelligence and

---

[183] Prime Minister Rudd, "First National Security Statement to the Parliament," December 4, 2008.

[184] Australia, "Defence White Paper," 2009, at para. 1.7. In contrast, much of a defense update issued in 2003 focused on terrorism and weapons of mass destruction. Australia, *Australia's National Security Defence Update 2003*, 2003, at 8–17.

[185] Ibid., at paras. 4.47–50.

[186] "All-Hazards Approach to Disaster Funding," news release, at http://www.ag.gov.au/www/ministers/mcclelland.nsf/Page/MediaReleases_2010_ThirdQuarter_2July2010-All-hazards approachtodisasterfunding.

evidence. ASIO questioning warrants are an extreme example of the priority that many states placed on intelligence gathering in their attempts to prevent another 9/11. The intelligence mindset is also codified and indeed hardened in provisions that allow control orders to be applied to whoever has received or provided terrorist training, thus exposing those such as Jack Thomas and David Hicks to the possibility of perpetual status based control orders. Australia's many broad terrorism offenses, with their focus on associations, membership, training, and political and religious motives, can be seen as a migration of a preemptive intelligence mind-set into the law. This development, however, meant that intelligence and criminal investigations would often overlap in terrorism cases, and there have been some growing pains in dealing with the changed relationship between intelligence and evidence, as represented by the ul-Haque case, in which ASIO officers produced intelligence that could not be used as evidence, and the Thomas case, in which AFP officers secured involuntary statements in Pakistan that were eventually rejected as evidence. The 2004 National Security Information Act constituted an attempt to keep intelligence secret, including a statement that judges should give greater weight to the interests of the state than the individual when reviewing the attorney general's decision about what can be disclosed in trials. Recent amendments have been made to the act not to provide a correction for greater disclosure but mainly in response to concerns that its use may compromise the efficiency of criminal trials.

Australia also provides an intriguing case study of the migration of post-9/11 terrorism laws while also affirming the important differences between various constitutional and political cultures. Australia has borrowed heavily from the United Kingdom, first in its original post-9/11 laws, which featured a broad definition of terrorism and broad terrorism offenses, and later in Australia's curiously robust response to the 2005 London bombings in the form of increased regulation of speech associated with terrorism, preventive detention, and control orders. Even though the Australian–U.K. nexus is the closest one seen in this book, it would be a mistake to think of Australian imports of British antiterrorism laws as simple carbon copies or even transplants. Australia, in part in recognition of its constitutional protections for freedom of expression, departed from the British example by exempting most protests and strikes from its definition of terrorism. In contrast, Australia's use of British-inspired speech and control orders failed to recognize some of the safeguards present in the United Kingdom such as recourse to the European Convention. Indeed, the Australia approach is singular in its interest in extending old treason and sedition offenses to apply to assistance to terrorist groups as well as in its use of sedition offenses to respond to hate speech. In this way,

Australia placed its own war on terror and hate speech glosses on British-inspired offenses against speech associated with terrorism. The Australian control order legislation does not require that criminal prosecutions not be possible, but it also does not authorize the use of secret evidence against the controllee, as the British legislation does. In any event, control orders in Australia have been much more infrequent and mild than in the United Kingdom, even though the high court has affirmed their constitutionality.

The Australia case study also lends itself to comparisons with Canada. As will be seen in the next chapter, the existence of a constitutional bill of rights in Canada explains some differences between Australian and Canadian laws, most notably Canada's omission of an offense of membership and perhaps its lack of speech regulation. In these areas, Canada has more in common with the United States. The Charter may also explain why proscription decisions in Canada are subject to judicial review, whereas Australian decisions are subject to legislative review. Widespread pessimism in Australia about the ability of courts to protect human rights may also help explain why Australia's legislative and executive review mechanisms have kept better pace than Canada's with the increased intensity and co-ordination of national security activities. In particular, Australia has expanded the jurisdiction of its intelligence watchdog to allow it to inquire into intelligence and security matters throughout the Commonwealth government. Australia has created an independent monitor tasked to review both the propriety and effectiveness of the government's counter-terrorism measures. At the same time, Australia like Canada has been forced to appoint an ad hoc commission of inquiry to inquire into the responsibility of multiple agencies for counter-terrorism excesses, namely the detention of Dr. Haneef, wrongly suspected of involvement in terrorism.

The different political cultures of the two similar countries should not be ignored. Australia extended its controversial ASIO questioning warrants until 2016 and did not repeal them even after the defeat of the Howard government whereas Canada allowed its investigative hearings and preventive arrests to expire in 2007 and has not enacted new speech based offenses. The lack of a constitutional bill of rights cannot explain why Australia felt compelled to respond to the London bombings with its own barrage of new legislation. Even when counter-terrorism laws migrate, they will be adapted to the particular legal, constitutional, political and social cultures of the receiving country.

7 Canada Responds: Border and Human Security

I. INTRODUCTION

Canada's response to terrorism reflects many of the same 9/11 effects seen in other countries. Canada quickly responded to both 9/11 and United Nations (UN) Security Council Resolution 1373 with a new law that featured a broad definition of terrorism, new terrorism and terrorism financing offenses, and new state powers to investigate terrorism. Canada also responded to the danger of suspected terrorists abusing refugee status by imposing administrative detention on secret evidence and placing new restrictions on the admission of all refugees. What was unique about Canada's response was the border it shares with the United States. Canada was singled out in the Patriot Act,[1] which contained a section titled "Protecting the Northern Border" which responding to American security fears about Canada provided for increased numbers of border guards and scrutiny of those entering the United States.

Canada's response to 9/11 was aimed in part at compliance with UN Security Council Resolution 1373, but also at an American audience skeptical of Canada's commitment to security. Canada drafted a new antiterrorism law with an eye to American fears that it might provide a safe haven for terrorists. A 2001 border agreement focused on security and included a safe third-country agreement that prohibits refugees from applying for asylum in Canada's more liberal immigration system if they have reached American soil first. Among business especially, there was much interest in a common security perimeter with the United States,[2] but Canada stopped short of full visa

---

[1] *Uniting and Strengthening America by Providing Appropriate Tools to Intercept and Obstruct Terrorism (USA Patriot Act), Act of 2001*, H.R. 3162, Title 4, Subsection A, "Protecting the Northern Border."

[2] Reg Whitaker, "How Canada Confronts Terrorism," in *Understanding Terror: Perspectives for Canadians*, ed. Karim-Ally Kassam (Calgary, AB, Canada: University of Calgary Press, 2010), at 51.

convergence.[3] Concerns about the thickened American border continued and
Canada entered into a framework agreement with the United States in early
2011 for perimeter security and economic competitiveness.[4] It also enacted a
new law that required airlines to comply with American laws regarding passenger information for flights that fly over American territory. This law potentially
exposed air passengers in Canada to the large American no-fly list even if their
flights did not land in the United States.[5] The need for Canada to keep goods
and people flowing over the border it shares with the United States remains a
driving force in post-9/11 Canadian security policy.

In the immediate aftermath of 9/11, Canadian officials cooperated with
American officials in secret and problematic ways. The Royal Canadian
Mounted Police (RCMP) passed on inaccurate information about Maher
Arar that played a role in his detention in the United States and his subsequent rendition to Syria, where he was tortured and held for almost a year
before being released and allowed to return to Canada. Arar was exonerated
by a Canadian inquiry and became something of a hero in Canada. The
Canadian government settled his civil claim for $10.5 million Canadian. At
the same time, he remains on the U.S. no fly list, and his civil action against
the United States was stopped by the state-secrets doctrine.

The Canadian government did not spend its limited capital on security
issues with the United States by asking for Omar Khadr's return to Canada,
despite two rulings by the Supreme Court of Canada that Canadian officials
had violated his rights when they questioned the then teenager at Guantánamo
Bay. The supreme court reversed a lower court ruling that required Canada
to ask for Khadr's repatriation because of concerns that such a remedy would
interfere with Canada's delicate diplomacy with the United States.[6] The Canadian government only agreed to his return to Canada when the United States
asked it to do so as part of a plea agreement that avoided a military commission
trial of Khadr, who admitted that at 15 years of age, he had thrown a grenade
that killed an American soldier during a battle in Afghanistan. As of the start of

---

[3] Kent Roach, *September 11: Consequences for Canada* (Montreal, QC, Canada: McGill Queens
  Press, 2003), at 133–51.
[4] *Beyond the Border: A Shared Vision for Perimeter Security and Economic Competitiveness: A
  Declaration by the Prime Minister of Canada and the President of the United States* 4 February,
  2011 available at http://www.pm.gc.ca/eng/media.asp?id=3938.
[5] Even before the enactment of the law, a British convert to Islam who had previously applied
  for a teaching job in Yemen was temporarily not allowed to fly from Toronto to the United
  Kingdom because he had been flagged by the American no-fly list. "Brit going home after
  'no-fly' list had him trapped in Toronto" Toronto Star February 16, 2011. See now *An Act to
  amend the Aeronautics Act* S.C. 2011 c.9.
[6] *Khadr v. Canada*, SCC 3 (2010). See also *Khadr v. Canada*, 2 S.C.R. 125 (2008).

2011, Khadr remains the only citizen of a Western democracy still imprisoned at Guantánamo, but he is expected soon to return to Canada to serve the remainder of his eight-year sentence.

Although a desire to keep the United States happy and the border open can explain many of Canada's post-9/11 security policies, there are other factors that have restrained Canadian security policy compared to the policies of Australia and the United Kingdom. Canadian responses have been shaped in part by its constitutional bill of rights, the 1982 Canadian Charter of Rights and Freedoms (the Charter), and by concerns about preserving multicultural community relations including with Canada's growing Muslim communities.[7] Canada's 2001 Anti-Terrorism Act (ATA) stopped short of making membership in a terrorist organization a crime in part because of concerns that such an offense would be inconsistent with the Charter. Canada has not enacted new offenses in response to UN Security Council Resolution 1624, calling for laws against the incitement of terrorism. Although its original response to 9/11 allowed the state to have hate speech removed from the Internet, Canada has not embraced the criminalization of speech or association as a response to terrorism. In this respect, Canada's constitutional culture is more similar to that of the United States than that of the United Kingdom or Australia.

Although it was quickly enacted by the end of 2001, in time for Canada's first report to the new UN Counter-Terrorism Committee (CTC), the ATA was subject to a much more vigorous debate in civil society than the Patriot Act or even the United Kingdom's and Australia's initial responses to 9/11. One particular area of concern was the effect that the law might have on Canada's multicultural population, including the one-fifth of citizens born outside Canada. The government amended the ATA after it was introduced to provide that the expression of political and religious views would not in itself constitute terrorist activity. It also provided five-year sunsets for new police powers of preventive arrests and investigative hearings, and these powers were allowed to expire in 2007. Canada's minority Conservative government has been unable to restore them, even though the powers are more restrained than comparable ones in the United Kingdom and Australia and were held to be consistent with the Charter in 2004.

Another theme in Canada's response to 9/11 has been the use of immigration law as antiterrorism law. Despite the enactment of the ATA, the first charges under the new criminal law were not laid until 2006, and the first conviction

---

[7] Muslims in Canada still constitute only 2% of Canada's population, but are the largest of its non-Christian population. Kent Roach "Canadian National Security Policy and Canadian Muslim Communities" in Abdulkader Sinno *Muslims in Western Politics* (Bloomington: Indiana University Press, 2009) at 220.

was not registered until 2008. In the immediate aftermath of 9/11, Canada used immigration law as a means to detain suspected international terrorists. Both the United States and the United Kingdom used immigration law in this manner, but the Canadian reliance on immigration law was even more pronounced. Canada's Immigration and Refugee Protection Act[8] (IRPA) allows the removal of noncitizens on the basis of secret evidence not disclosed to the deportee. Such procedures have been both legally and politically controversial. Successful Charter challenges to the use of secret evidence[9] have resulted in the introduction of a British-style system of security-cleared special advocates who can challenge secret evidence and increased retention and disclosure of raw intelligence by the Canadian Security Intelligence Service (CSIS).[10]

Like other countries, Canada faced the dilemma exposed but not resolved by Security Council Resolution 1373 of what to do with noncitizens suspected of terrorism who might be tortured if deported. In early 2002, in the immediate aftermath of 9/11, the Supreme Court of Canada deliberately and provocatively refused to rule out the possibility that noncitizens could constitutionally be deported to torture in undefined "exceptional circumstances," even while recognizing that such an approach would violate international law.[11] This approach has rightly been criticized by UN human rights committees and not followed by the European Court of Human Rights, but it facilitated the continued immigration detention of suspected terrorists from Egypt, Syria, Morocco and Algeria. The Canadian approach was more candid than the U.S. approach to torture, based on absurdly narrow executive interpretations of torture as opposed to judicial approvals of torture, but more extreme than the United Kingdom or Australia, which were prepared to indeterminately detain noncitizens who would be tortured if returned to their countries of citizenship. Fortunately, no Canadian court has yet found that there are exceptional circumstances that justify deportation to torture. The more likely danger is that Canadian courts, relying on a deferential review standard inspired by Lord Hoffmann's approach in *Rehman*,[12] will defer to executive judgment that people can be deported without a substantial risk of torture.[13] Canada has gone beyond other democracies in using immigration law as antiterrorism law.

---

[8] S.C. (2001), c.27.   [9] *Charkaoui v. Canada*, 1 S.C.R. 350 (2007).
[10] *Charkaoui v. Canada*, 2 S.C.R. 326 (2008).
[11] *Suresh v. Canada*, 1 S.C.R. 3 (2002), at para. 78.
[12] [2001]UKHL 47, at para. 62, cited with approval in *Suresh v. Canada*, 1 S.C.R. 3 (2002), at paras. 32–3.
[13] *Ahani v. Canada*, 1 S.C.R. 72 (2002) (judicial deference to executive claim that deportation to Iran would not result in torture).

Although the supreme court was willing to contemplate deportation of noncitizens to torture, the Canadian government was forced to respond to public concerns about the torture of its own citizens detained in Syria. It appointed public inquiries to examine the conduct of all Canadian officials in relation to Maher Arar and three other Canadians detained and tortured in that country. These expensive multiyear public inquiries were run by judges and examined the activities of the RCMP, CSIS, customs, and foreign affairs departments. Like the ongoing U.K. inquiry into complicity in torture, they provided extraordinary accountability for whole-of-government approaches to terrorism. At the same time, however, they were unable to review the involvement of foreign governments, including Egypt, Syria and the United States. The inquiries were appointed at the discretion of the government, and the government has refused subsequent calls to appoint inquiries to determine if Canada's transfer of its Afghan detainees resulted in torture. Both the Arar Commission and a commission subsequently appointed to examine failures that led to the 1985 Air India bombing made recommendations to improve review of both the propriety and efficacy of counter-terrorism activities, but the Canadian government has resisted such proposals for intensified review.

In 2004, Canada proclaimed its first official national security policy. In response not only to 9/11 but also to a 2003 SARS episode that killed 52 people in Toronto, this policy took a broad all-risks approach. It was accompanied by the creation of an enhanced Department of Public Safety that included emergency preparedness and the enactment of a Public Safety Act[14] that featured administrative regulations designed to secure sites and substances vulnerable to terrorism and enhance the ability of the federal government to respond to a range of emergencies. The Canadian emphasis on human security and emergency preparedness can be contrasted with the American and Australian focus on terrorism as the prime threat to national security. In subsequent years, however, the United States, the United Kingdom, and Australia have shown more interest in an all-risks approach.

II. PRE-9/11 EXPERIENCE

Before 9/11, Canada was affected by both domestic and international terrorism.[15] It had less experience than the United Kingdom but more than

---

[14] S.C. (2004), c.15.
[15] David Charters, "The (Un)peaceable Kingdom? Terrorism and Canada before 9/11" (2008) 9(4) IRPP Policy Matters 19, at http://www.irpp.org/pm/archive/pmvol9no4.pdf.

Australia or the pre-9/11 United States. Canada's reactions demonstrated the dangers of both overreacting and underreacting to terrorism.

The October Crisis

In October 1970, two cells of the Front de Liberation du Quebec (FLQ) kidnapped James Cross, a British diplomat, and Pierre Laporte, a Quebec cabinet minister. The FLQ was responsible for hundreds of bombings in the 1960s, and large public meetings in Montreal were held in support of its demand for the release of prisoners. The government reacted by declaring a state of emergency under the War Measures Act[16] and sending 6,000 troops into Montreal. Following patterns of British colonial emergency rule discussed in Chapter 3, the War Measures Act provided for broad powers of detention, deportation, forfeiture, and censorship in response not only to wars but to real or apprehended insurrections. It had been used to intern Japanese Canadians during World War II and to detain and force those suspected of spying for Russia to incriminate themselves without warning or counsel immediately after the War. It provided that the cabinet's proclamation was conclusive proof that an emergency existed.[17] Like the Internal Security Act in Singapore, the operation of the War Measures Act was exempted from protections for free speech, due process, and habeas corpus under the Canadian Bill of Rights,[18] enacted in 1960.

Regulations proclaimed in force by the executive under the War Measures Act declared that the FLQ and any other group that advocated the use of force or the commission of a crime as a means of accomplishing government change were unlawful associations. This approach was somewhat similar to the post-9/11 use of regulations to implement the UN's terrorist financing list. Section 4 of the regulations created an incredibly broad offense, making it a crime, subject to five years' imprisonment, to be a member, profess membership, contribute to, or fund-raise for an unlawful association or to advocate for the use of force or crime to accomplish a governmental change in Canada.[19] The specific listing of the FLQ as an unlawful association was unsuccessfully

---

[16] R.S.C. (1970), c.W-2.

[17] Whitaker, "How Canada Confronts Terrorism"; Alan Manson, "Canada after Gouzenko," in *Free Speech in Fearful Times*, ed. James Turk and Alan Manson (Toronto, ON, Canada: Lorimer, 1997).

[18] S.C. (1960), c.44.

[19] Public Orders Regulation 1970, SOR/70-444, Section 4 4. Section 8 made attendance at a meeting of an unlawful association or speaking on its behalf proof of membership in the unlawful association in the absence of evidence to the contrary.

challenged as an incursion on judicial power and the creation of a retroactive crime.[20] Although more limited than the United Kingdom, Canada had a pre-9/11 history of proscription.

The regulations proclaimed under the War Measures Act allowed the police to arrest without judicial warrant those they suspected to be members and supporters of unlawful organizations or advocates of illegal governmental change. Following the Northern Ireland model of the time, such persons could be detained without access to a judge for seven days, but the attorney general could extend this period to 21 days.[21] Almost 500 people were arrested and detained during the October Crisis, with only 62 people being charged and 18 convicted.[22] As in Northern Ireland, the intelligence that identified the persons to be detained often did not make distinctions between support for political causes, such as sovereignty, and involvement in politically inspired violence. The police could also search on suspicion and without a judicial warrant, and more than 3,000 searches were conducted under these powers.[23] The regulations were replaced by a similar law enacted by Parliament notwithstanding the Canadian Bill of Rights in December 1970. In this manner, emergency action by the executive was ratified by the legislature. The emergency was not a permanent one and the law was allowed to sunset in April 1971.[24]

Canada's eventual use of criminal law after the October Crisis was not particularly harsh. Those involved with the kidnapping and murder of Pierre Laporte were convicted of serious criminal offenses, including murder, but were all paroled by 1982. Cross's kidnappers were allowed to go to Cuba in exchange for the diplomat's release and received sentences of no more than three years imprisonment when they voluntarily returned to Canada.[25] Kenneth McNaught suggested that the treatment of the terrorists reflected a Canadian tradition of using criminal law but tempering punishment with

[20] *Gagnon v. Vallieres*, 14 C.R.N.S. 132 (1971). But for persuasive arguments that the proscription of the FLQ meant that "the judiciary was reduced to the role of a time keeper, keeping track of who attended what meetings." See Noel Lyon, "Constitutional Validity of Sections 3 and 4 of the Public Order Regulations, 1970" (1971) 18 McGill Law Journal 136, at 140.

[21] Public Orders Regulation 9170, SOR/70-444, Section 9.

[22] Dominique Clement, "The October Crisis: Human Rights Abuses under the War Measures Act" (2008) 42 Journal of Canadian Studies 160, at 167.

[23] Ibid.

[24] *Public Order (Temporary Measures) Act*, 1970, S.C. (1970–71–72), c.2. This legislation expired on April 30, 1971. See generally John Saywell, *Quebec 70* (Toronto, ON, Canada: University of Toronto Press, 1971); Thomas Berger, *Fragile Freedoms* (Toronto, ON, Canada: Clarke Irwin, 1981), chapter 7; Walter Tarnopolsky, *The Canadian Bill of Rights*, 2nd ed. (Ottawa: Carlton Library, 1975), chapter 9.

[25] Clement "The October Crisis," at 179–80.

responses to underlying grievances.[26] As will be seen, Canadian sentences for terrorism would become much longer after 9/11.

There was widespread revulsion at the murder of Laporte and an almost complete end to violence associated with separatism. In 1976, the people of Quebec elected a Parti Quebecois (PQ) provincial government committed to the separation of Quebec from Canada. PQ governments held referenda on Quebec sovereignty in 1980 and 1995. Both referenda were defeated. After the 1995 referenda, the Supreme Court of Canada decided that Quebec did not have a unilateral right to separate under either Canadian or international law but also that the rest of Canada could not ignore a clear vote in favor of Quebec's separation from the rest of Canada.[27] The Canadian example, like that of Northern Ireland, provides some support for the thesis that political terrorism may be combated by open and robust democratic debate and dialogue, including democratic consideration of secession.

Most Canadians soon accepted that the government had overreacted to the October Crisis. Although Prime Minister Pierre Trudeau never admitted doubts about his use of the War Measures Act, he campaigned hard to enact Canada's constitutional bill of rights, the Charter, in 1982. The Charter included rights to habeas corpus and other rights designed to restrict police powers. Unlike Section 6(5) of the statutory Canadian Bill of Rights, the Charter did not provide that acts and regulations made under the War Measures Act would not violate its terms, though it did allow governments to enact laws notwithstanding fundamental freedoms and legal and equality rights for a renewable five-year period.

The War Measures Act was replaced in 1988 by an Emergencies Act.[28] This act provides some precommitment against detention on grounds of race, religion, or ethnic origin as well as for different regimes to govern public order as opposed to natural disaster emergencies. The Emergencies Act also ensures that there can be parliamentary review of any secret regulations, that small numbers in Parliament can initiate debates about whether to end the emergency, and that compensation will be paid for damage inflicted under the act.[29] The act also foreshadowed the important role that judicial inquiries

---

[26] Kenneth McNaught, "Political Trials and the Canadian Political Tradition," in *Courts and Trials*, ed. M. L. Friedland (Toronto, ON, Canada: University Toronto Press, 1974).

[27] *Reference Re Quebec Secession*, 2 S.C.R. 217 (1998).

[28] S.C. (1988), c.29, Section 4(b).

[29] For praise of the Canadian act, see Kim Lane Scheppele, "North American Emergencies: The Use of the Emergency Power in Canada and the United States" (2006) 4 International Journal of Constitutional Law 213; Bruce Ackerman, *Before the Next Attack* (New Haven, CT: Yale University Press, 2005), at 93.

would play after 9/11 by requiring the appointment of an inquiry to examine the government's conduct during any declared emergency.

In the aftermath of the October Crisis, the Security Service of the RCMP engaged in illegalities including the theft of membership lists of the PQ. Concerns about these illegalities led to the appointment of both federal and provincial public inquiries. The federal inquiry recommended that security intelligence functions be transferred from the RCMP to a civilian security intelligence agency in 1984. This agency, the CSIS, is subject to extensive review by the Security Intelligence Review Committee (SIRC), which has access to all of CSIS's secret information and can audit CSIS activities as well as hear complaints about it.

The October Crisis, like the use of internment in the early 1970s in Northern Ireland or the internment of Japanese Americans or Japanese Canadians in World War II, seems to have served as an effective negative example in the post-9/11 era. In none of the democracies examined in this chapter has there been a declaration of martial law or internment on the basis of group membership or political or religious views. This is an important point that can sometimes be lost in the discussion of the increased global security agenda launched by 9/11.

The 1985 Air India Bombings

In 1985, two bombs were placed on planes departing from Vancouver's airport. One bomb, destined for an Air India plane, prematurely exploded in Narita International Airport, killing two baggage handlers, while another exploded on an Air India plane that had left Canada. All 329 people on board were killed, literally blown out of the sky, in what was, before 9/11, the most deadly single act of aviation terrorism. The bomb was placed on Air India flight 182, despite increased security precautions and after an x-ray machine for luggage broke down and an unreliable explosive sniffer was used by employees of a private security firm who had not been properly trained. Had sniffer dogs or passenger baggage reconciliation been used, the bombing might have been prevented. It might also have been prevented had CSIS agents who had been conducting surveillance of the mastermind of the bombing realized that what they thought was a gunshot in a remote area shortly before the bombing was actually a test explosion or if other important intelligence from various sources had been shared in a timely manner.[30]

---

[30] Commission of Inquiry into the Investigation of the Bombing of Air India Flight 182, *Air India Flight 182: A Canadian Tragedy* (Ottawa: Public Works, 2010), at 1:23–8; vol. 2, part 1, at 109–12.

The newly formed civilian security agency, CSIS, had conducted electronic and physical surveillance on some of the main suspects but had experienced difficulties both with translating the wiretaps and with maintaining surveillance. CSIS destroyed wiretaps on the suspected mastermind of the plot after they were translated and summarized as well as notes of interviews with potential witnesses. CSIS justified these actions on the basis that it was an intelligence agency that did not collect evidence. There was poor exchange of intelligence about the threats of bombs being placed on an Air India airplane by Sikh extremists in response to India's actions against the Golden Temple.[31] The Air India bombing was a horrible precursor of 9/11 in its use of technology and multiple terrorist attacks to inflict mass casualties. Canada overreacted to the 1970 October Crisis, but it underreacted both before and after the Air India bombings.

Failed Terrorism Prosecutions

The investigation of the bombing was delayed by conflicts between CSIS and the RCMP over access to sources and concerns about intelligence being used and disclosed as evidence. These problems reflected the very different mandates of an agency designed to collect secret intelligence and one designed to prosecute individuals on the basis of public evidence. One person, a Canadian Sikh, pled guilty to manslaughter in relation to both bombings, but two others were acquitted in 2005 after one of the longest trials in Canadian history. The trial judge stressed that the Crown must prove guilt beyond a reasonable doubt, even in cases of horrific violence. He had problems accepting the credibility of key state witnesses, some of whom were in witness protection programs after another key witness in the case was murdered in 1998.[32] The trial judge found that CSIS's destruction of wiretaps and notes of interviews with witnesses was an abuse of process. He did not have to devise a remedy for these abuses – a remedy that might have resulted in the prosecution being permanently stopped – because of the acquittals.

The prosecutor in the case agreed to allow the defense counsel to inspect secret material held by CSIS and others on an understanding that the defense counsel would not disclose the information to anyone, including their client. Such an agreement avoided the difficulties of having to litigate whether the government could validly claim national security confidentiality or public

---

[31] Ibid., vol. 2. "Critical information remained siloed within each agency's holdings, robbing CSIS of the opportunity to effectively carry out its mandate to assemble the puzzle for the benefit of national security." Ibid., at 437.

[32] *R. v. Malik and Bagri*, BCSC 350 (2005).

interest immunity over such intelligence in a separate administrative court, the federal court, which has exclusive statutory jurisdiction over such matters.[33] Until 1982, no Canadian court was allowed to review state secrecy claims in reaction to cold war concerns that Canada might reveal secrets that the United States and the United Kingdom had shared with it.[34] The 1982 Canadian legislation contemplated that only specially designated judges in Ottawa would have access to information that the government claimed was secret. This legislation maximized secrecy, but Canada's unique two court system would make terrorism prosecutions difficult. The two court approach was avoided in the Air India trial. It was also avoided in post-9/11 Toronto terrorism prosecutions after a trial judge rule that the exclusive jurisdiction of the Federal Court over state secrecy claims violated the Charter rights of the accused and the inherent powers of the trial court. In 2011, however, the Supreme Court of Canada overruled that decision, emphasizing that concerns about the wisdom of the two court approach did make it unconstitutional and that the trial judge could protect fair trial rights by staying proceedings if it was not clear whether a fair trial was possible because of a non-disclosure order by the Federal Court.[35] The two court system for terrorism prosecutions remains in place in Canada as an attempt to maximize secrecy, but it may also unnecessarily place terrorism prosecutions in jeopardy.

The alleged mastermind of the Air India plot, Talwinder Singh Parmar, a Canadian citizen, was prosecuted in Canada not in relation to the bombing but for a conspiracy to commit acts of terrorism in India. The prosecution

---

[33] As the Air India Commission noted, the "undertaking avoided the need for litigation under s.38 of the Canada Evidence Act.... The defence and prosecution teams were never required to undergo the logistically difficult and lengthy process of bringing section 38 issues before the Federal Court." Commission of Inquiry into the Investigation of the Bombing of Air India Flight 182, *Air India Flight 182*, at 3:273.

[34] These concerns started right after World War II when Igor Gouzenko, a clerk at the Soviet embassy in Ottawa, defected and revealed an espionage ring in Canada. In response, Canada appointed an inquiry chaired by two Supreme Court judges which detained and interrogated people in secret and without counsel with subsequent prosecutions under the Official Secrets Act. The judges attempted to justify their actions as necessary to prevent the alleged spies from warning each other about the information obtained by authorities and the commission. Hon. Robert Taschereau and Hon. R.I. Kellock *The Report of the Royal Commission* (Ottawa: Kings Press, 1946) at 661-662. The Commission also concluded that "much vital technical information which should still be secret to the authorities of Canada, Great Britain and the United States, has been made known to the Russians by reason of the espionage activities reported on herein." Ibid at 618.

[35] *R. v. Ahmad* 2011 SCC 6. The Court also cast doubt on the appropriateness of the undertaking to counsel used to avoid having to litigate secrecy issues in the Federal Court in the Air India prosecution despite the fact that such undertakings are used in both Australia and the United Kingdom.

collapsed when the state refused to disclose the identity of a key informant.[36] Canada refused to extradite Parmar to India because of concerns that he would be tortured, and Parmar was eventually tortured and killed by police when he returned to India. A prosecution of another plot to bomb another Air India plane in 1986 was eventually stayed after persistent refusal by the police to disclose the identity of another key informer.[37] A prosecution of a conspiracy to kill an Indian cabinet minister visiting Canada was dropped after inaccuracies in the information used to obtain a CSIS electronic surveillance warrant were revealed.[38] Before 9/11, terrorism prosecutions in Canada often floundered on the unwillingness or inability of the state to make full disclosure to the accused and troubles in converting intelligence into evidence.

The unwillingness to make disclosure can be related to a preference for secrecy that characterized the cold war era. Canada, which imports most of its intelligence from foreign partners, has particular concerns about preserving (other nation's) secrets. In 1982, the Supreme Court of Canada upheld state claims of secrecy as absolute, even though courts in the United Kingdom and Australia at the time took a more flexible approach that balanced the competing interests in disclosure and nondisclosure.[39] Although specially designated Federal Court judges after 1982 were given the power to review secret information to determine whether it should be disclosed, old habits of absolute secrecy died hard. In a 1984 case involving the shooting of a Turkish diplomat in Ottawa, the federal court rejected claims that CSIS surveillance should be disclosed to the accused. The trial judge at the subsequent trial expressed unease that neither he nor the federal court judge had even examined the CSIS material to determine if it contained exculpatory material.[40] An unwillingness to disclose relevant intelligence in criminal prosecutions can jeopardize both convictions and fair trials.

Summary

The October Crisis demonstrated the dangers of overreacting to crimes committed by two terrorist cells through the declaration of martial law and arrests

---

[36] *R. v. Parmar*, 31 C.R.R. 256 (Ont.H.C.) (1987). See Kent Roach, *The Unique Challenges of Terrorism Prosecutions* (Ottawa: Public Works, 2010), at 105–13, for a full discussion of this case.

[37] *R. v. Khela*, 126 C.C.C.(3d) 341 (Que.C.A.) (1998). See Roach, *Unique Challenges of Terrorism Prosecutions*, at 160–9, for a full discussion of this case.

[38] *R. v. Atwal*, 36 C.C.C.(3d) 161 (Fed.C.A.) (1987). See Roach, *Unique Challenges of Terrorism Prosecutions*, at 97–102, for a full discussion of this case.

[39] Compare *Commission des droits de la personne v. A.G. Canada*, 1 S.C.R. 215 (1982) and *Conway v. Rimmer*, A.C. 910 (1968) and *Alister v. The Queen*, 154 C.L.R. 404 (1984).

[40] *Re Kevork*, 17 C.C.C.(3d) 426 (F.C.T.D.) (1984), at 431; *R. v. Kevork*, 27 C.C.C.(3d) 523 (Ont.H.C.) (1985).

of 500 people, the vast majority of whom were only associated with the political cause of Quebec separatism as opposed to political violence. Canada, however, learned from this overreaction and responded with measures such as the creation of CSIS, a civilian security intelligence agency without law enforcement powers that would be subject to careful review. The 1982 enactment of the Charter as a constitutional bill of rights and the 1988 Emergencies Act to restrain emergency powers were other valuable lessons learned from the overreaction to the October Crisis.

Canada's flawed response to the 1985 Air India bombings demonstrates the dangers of underreacting to terrorism. Many Canadians refused to recognize that the bombings, which were motivated by Sikh grievances against the government of India, were murders by Canadians against Canadians. A public inquiry into the bombing was not appointed until 2006, after the trial of two accused had resulted in acquittals. The inquiry documented how the investigation both before and after the bombings was adversely affected by turf wars between intelligence agencies and the police. Terrorism trials before 9/11 were delayed and beset by problems involving destruction and nondisclosure of intelligence and by problems with source handling and witness protection.

The 2010 report of the Air India Commission found that problems in translating intelligence to evidence, conducting terrorism prosecutions, providing witness protection, ensuring aviation security, and distributing intelligence persisted in the post-9/11 era. The government has responded with a vague plan to better distribute intelligence, improve aviation security and witness protection, and make terrorism prosecutions more efficient.[41] At the same time, it remained silent on two of the commission's most important recommendations: (1) enhancing the role of the prime minister's national security advisor in resolving conflicts between agencies and ensuring the coordination and effectiveness of whole-of-government approaches to terrorism and (2) giving trial judges the jurisdiction to decide whether intelligence not used in terrorism prosecutions must be disclosed to the accused to ensure a fair trial. As will be seen, the government has also resisted recommendations by the Arar Commission for enhanced review of the propriety of whole-of-government responses to terrorism. The security agencies in Ottawa have successfully been able to oppose increased review of their work in a way that has not occurred in Australia, which, as examined in the preceding chapter, has increased the review powers of both the inspector general of intelligence and of parliamentary committees. The Canadian government's reluctance to allow criminal

---

[41] Canada, *Action Plan: The Government of Canada Response to the Commission of Inquiry into the Investigation of the Bombing of Air India Flight 182 December, 2010* (Ottawa: Her Majesty the Queen in Right of Canada, 2010).

trial judges to have access to information over which it claims secrecy can also be seen as an example of a similar emphasis on secrecy that, in the United Kingdom, has prevented the use of electronic surveillance in criminal terrorism prosecutions.

III. THE INITIAL RESPONSE TO 9/11

Canada felt immediate repercussions from 9/11 as it accepted 224 airplanes destined for the United States (including one suspected of being hijacked) when the United States closed its airspace. The border remained closed for several days, causing huge economic worries in Canada, given its reliance on export with its southern neighbor. There were also erroneous claims made in reputable American media that some of the terrorists had entered the United States through Canada. The false reports were not incredible because Ahmed Ressam, a failed refugee applicant in Canada traveling on a fake Canadian passport, had been apprehended and detained by an alert American border official in 1999. He was subsequently convicted of planning to bomb the Los Angeles airport. Canada knew that the United States was worried about the security of its northern border, and it went out of its way to cooperate by committing troops to the invasion of Afghanistan.[42]

Panicked Responses

In the immediate aftermath of 9/11, Canadian officials cooperated with American security officials in secret and problematic ways. An inadequately trained unit of the RCMP disclosed to the Americans complete investigative files on terrorist suspects and persons of interest without vetting the files for relevance, accuracy, and reliability or attaching the usual restrictions or caveats on the subsequent use of the Canadian information. Included in these files was inaccurate information that labeled Canadian citizen Maher Arar and his wife as Islamic extremists linked to al Qaeda. This information likely played a role in the U.S. decision to detain Maher Arar in New York City and subsequently render him to Syria, where he was tortured.[43]

Other problematic forms of cooperation were the actions of CSIS in facilitating the transfer of a Canadian citizen, Mohammed Jabarah, suspected of involvement in the Jemaah Islamiyah terrorist plot in Singapore, into

---

[42] See generally Roach, *September 11*.
[43] Commission of Inquiry into the Actions of Canadian Officials in Relation to Maher Arar, *Report of the Events Relating to Maher Arar* (2006).

American custody in 2002.[44] Although CSIS was created as a civilian security intelligence agency with no law enforcement powers, it detained Jabarah, denied him access to counsel, and transferred him to U.S. custody, where he subsequently pled guilty to terrorism charges.[45] The day after 9/11, Canadian officials also summarily transferred Algerian Benamar Benatta, a refugee applicant suspected of involvement with terrorism, to the United States without an extradition hearing. After five years' detention in the United States, he was released from U.S. custody and now has claimed refugee status in Canada and is suing Canadian officials for $35 million.[46] These cases suggest that Canadian as well as American officials were prepared in the immediate aftermath of 9/11 to act in a manner that was extralegal or at least very close to the line of legality.

Listing Regulations

Canada's first official response to 9/11 was the cabinet's quick passage, under the United Nations Act, of regulations extending terrorism financing listings and sanctions.[47] In Canada, as in other democracies, the domestic executive was the first to implement the mandate of the Security Council. Any concerns that using regulations to outlaw specific groups followed the pattern of the October Crisis were assuaged by the fact that they were enacted under the benignly titled United Nations Act and not the repealed War Measures Act. As discussed in Chapter 2, however, Security Council resolutions now sanctioned individuals and not just states. The Canadian regulations followed the UN in providing sweeping sanctions on listed individuals and criminalizing with up to 10 years' imprisonment any financial dealings with listed persons. The Canadian regulations that implement the 1267 sanction regime are currently being challenged, as they were successfully in the United Kingdom, as ultra vires the United Nations Act on the basis that Parliament never intended for the act to be used to implement individual sanctions without judicial remedies.[48]

---

44 Stewart Bell *The Martyr's Oath* (Toronto: Wiley, 2005).
45 Security Intelligence Review Committee Annual Report 2006–2007 (2008), at 12ff.
46 Initial concerns have been raised about the Crown's disclosure of relevant documents. *Benatta v. A.G. Canada*, Can LII 70999 (Ont.S.C.) (2009).
47 See United Nations Suppression of Terrorism Regulations, SOR 2001-360. Before 9/11, Canada already had regulations implementing the 1267 listing process, including its extension to al Qaeda. United Nations al-Qaeda and Taliban Regulations, SOR 99-444. Under the regulations, it was an offense punishable by up to 10 years' imprisonment to have financial dealings with a listed person.
48 R.S.C. (1985), c.U-2. See Carmen Cheung, *The UN Security Council 1267 Regime and the Rule of Law in Canada* (Vancouver, BC, Canada: British Columbia Civil Liberties Association,

The Anti-Terrorism Act

Canada responded to 9/11 and Security Council Resolution 1373 by enacting a massive new law that, for the first time, created and defined crimes of terrorism under the Canadian Criminal Code. The bill also provided for various mechanisms to implement Canada's obligations concerning terrorism financing, including amendments to its money laundering laws and provisions to allow charitable status to be withdrawn for charities that associated with terrorists. It provided for enhanced protections for secrecy, including provisions requiring parties including the accused to notify the attorney general of Canada if they proposed to disclose or call classified evidence during trial. Canada's 2001 ATA[49] also provided, for the first time, a statutory framework for Canada's signals intelligence agency. The law authorized the type of surveillance involving foreign conversations with a domestic side that President Bush would authorize the National Security Agency to conduct.[50] In this way, the bill provided a legislative basis for what in the United States was only authorized by an executive order of dubious legality.

The bill containing what was to become the ATA was first introduced into Parliament on October 15, 2001. It was defended by the Liberal government as consistent with the Charter and required to meet Canada's international obligations under Resolution 1373. The government relied on arguments made by backbencher Professor Irwin Cotler that the legislation was designed to protect rights to human security. Cotler argued both before and after 9/11 that "the domestic criminal law due process model, standing alone, is insufficient" to deal with terrorism as an international crime against humanity.[51] At the same time, Cotler, as well as many others, raised some due process concerns about the bill. Although the bill was enacted quickly and in time for Canada's first report to the Security Council's CTC at the end of 2001, there was a robust debate that led the government to amend some of its original proposals.[52]

2010), chapter 4. In the United Kingdom, a similar challenge in *Treasury v. Ahmed*, UKSC 2 (2010), resulted in legislation providing a statutory basis for implementation of the 1267 regime.

[49] S.C. (2001), c.41.   [50] See infra chapter 4.

[51] Irwin Cotler, "Terrorism, Security and Rights: The Dilemmas of Democracies" (2002) 14 National Journal of Constitutional Law 13, at 18–19. See also Cotler, "Towards a Counter-Terrorism Law and Policy" (1998) 10 Terrorism and Political Violence 1.

[52] For an account of how a large coalition, including unions, civil liberties organizations, Muslim groups, and rights watchdogs, within government opposed various parts of the Bill, see Roach, *September 11*, chapters 3 and 4.

Defining Terrorism

One of the weaknesses of Irwin Cotler's arguments that terrorism should be treated as a crime of humanity under an international as opposed to a domestic criminal justice model was that the definition of terrorism continued to escape international agreement even after 9/11. Cotler argued that violence against civilians could never be justified and that the mantra that "one person's terrorist is another person's freedom fighter" should be rejected as based on "moral relativism, or false moral equivalence."[53] The fact remained, however, that the UN Security Council provided no guidance as Canada and other countries struggled to define terrorism.[54] Canada, like Australia, looked to the broad definition of terrorism in the United Kingdom's Terrorism Act, 2000, as the starting point for its own definition. This meant that terrorism in Canada would cover not only violence but property damage and interference with essential services.

The Canadian approach was not, however, a carbon copy of the British approach. Canada took a more restrained approach and did not include all serious property damage but only property damage that endangered life, health, and safety. This minimized the chance of protesters being investigated or charged with terrorism. In addition, the ATA as originally introduced contained a specific exemption for lawful protests and strikes. A broad range of civil society groups expressed concerns that not all illegal protests and strikes should be seen as terrorism, and the government agreed to drop the requirement that protests and strikes must be lawful to be exempted from the definition of terrorism. At the same time, protests and strikes that endangered life, health, or safety could still fall within the definition of terrorism. As seen in the preceding chapter, Australia's approach to exempting protests and strikes followed a similar trajectory.

Canada's definition of terrorism remained much broader than the definition used in the October Crisis, which had focused on the "use of force or the commission of crime as a means of or as an aid in accomplishing governmental change within Canada."[55] Post-9/11 definitions defined terrorism more broadly

---

[53] Irwin Cotler, "Thinking outside the Box: Foundational Principles for a Counter-Terrorism Law and Policy," in *The Security of Freedom: Essays on Canada's Anti-Terrorism Bill*, ed. Ronald Daniels, Patrick Macklem, and Kent Roach (Toronto, ON, Canada: University of Toronto, 2001), at 113.

[54] The Security Council finally provided some guidance in 2004, too late for Canada and most other states. See Chapter 2.

[55] Public Order Regulations 1970, SOR/70-444, Section 3.

to recognize that citizens and even corporations, and not only the state, could be victims of terrorism. The neoliberal expansion of Canada's definition of terrorism can be seen by the inclusion of serious interference with "an essential service, facility or system, whether public or private"[56] as one of the prohibited harms. This provision was even broader than the comparable British reference to serious interferences with electronic systems. The concern with protecting essential public and private services related to modern phenomena, such as cyberterrorism, that could attack banking and transportation systems that were in private hands. At the same time, there were also some historical precedents in British colonial emergency regulations and Internal Security Acts for the state's concern that essential services should be protected from sabotage.[57]

The neoliberal orientation of Canada's definition of terrorism was confirmed by its references to actions designed to intimidate the public or a segment "with regard to its security, including its economic security" as well as actions designed to compel "a person" as well as a government or a "domestic or an international organization" to act.[58] This definition meant that acts targeting corporations could be acts of terrorism. Canada's broad definition of terrorism recognized the vulnerabilities of modern societies, but it also increased the risk that antiglobalization and aboriginal protesters who targeted corporations could be treated as terrorists. The reference in the Canadian legislation to threats to "economic security" also recognized that a shutting or thickening of the border with the United States would have disastrous economic consequences for Canada.

The Canadian definition of terrorism also stressed the international pedigree of Canada's commitments against terrorism more than similar legislation in the United States, the United Kingdom, or Australia. Thus Canada's new law incorporated parts of various international conventions against terrorism in the new terrorism offenses.[59] The result was extremely complex legislation, but legislation that underlined Canada's commitment to be an international good citizen in combating terrorism.

Controversy over Political and Religious Motives

The ordinary criminal law functioned under the traditional principle that a political or religious motive could not excuse the commission of the crime. In contrast, the ATA, following the United Kingdom's Terrorism Act, 2000, required proof that terrorist crimes were committed for religious or political

---

[56] Criminal Code, Section 83.01(1)(b)(ii)(E).   [57] See Chapter 2.
[58] Criminal Code, Section 83.01(1)(b)(i)(B).   [59] Ibid., Section 83.01(1)(a).

motives. This was defended by the government as a means to restrict the ambit of crimes of terrorism, and the Australian experience demonstrates how some terrorism prosecutions have floundered on the state's inability to establish that the accused acted for a political or religious reason.

The religious and political motive requirement was much more controversial in Canada than in the United Kingdom or Australia. A number of critics, including Irwin Cotler, expressed concerns that its inclusion could lead to discriminatory targeting of those who shared the politics or religion of terrorists but not necessarily their violent tendencies.[60] The criticism echoed back to the arrests of peaceful separatists during the October Crisis as well as contemporary concerns about racial and religious profiling. Although the government refused to include a nondiscrimination clause in the ATA, as recommended by Cotler, it added a curious interpretative clause providing "for greater certainty" that the "expression of a political religious or ideological thought, belief or opinion" would not fall under the definition of terrorist activity unless it satisfied the definition of terrorist activity.[61] The provision had little legal effect, but it was a symbol that attempted to respond to concerns that the ATA might be used against protesters or to target Muslim speakers. It also revealed Canada as halfway between a British constitutional culture that saw no problem with the motive requirement and more robust restrictions on expressive and associational freedoms in the name of militant democracy and a more libertarian American First Amendment culture that refused to define terrorism in reference to political or religious motive or to criminalize membership in terrorist organizations. As will be seen, both Canada and the United States would be a less fertile field for new laws targeting the incitement or glorification of terrorism than either the United Kingdom or Australia.

New and Broad Terrorism Offenses

The ATA was defended as a necessary means to prevent terrorism, with minister of justice Anne McLellan falsely suggesting that the existing criminal law could "only convict terrorists who actually engage in acts of violence."[62] The ATA criminalized a broad array of activities in advance of the actual commission of a terrorist act, including providing finances, property, and other forms of

---

[60] Cotler, "Terrorism, Security and Rights," at 34; Kent Roach, "The New Terrorism Offences and the Criminal Law," in Daniels et al., *Security of Freedom*, at 156; Don Stuart, "The Dangers of Quick Fix Legislation," in ibid., at 208–12.

[61] Criminal Code, Section 83.01.

[62] As quoted in Roach, *September 11*, at 22. The minister, like other officials, ignored wide Canadian laws criminalizing conspiracies, attempts, and incitement of crimes.

assistance to terrorist groups; participating in the activities of a terrorist group; and instructing the carrying out of activities for a terrorist group. There were no requirements of a proximate nexus to any planned act of terrorism, and many of the offenses contained interpretative clauses designed to ensure that the courts opted for the broadest possible reading of the new offenses.[63] The drafters of the Canadian law employed a precautionary principle against both terrorists and judges. The precautionary principle was used against terrorists to criminalize their activities well in advance of any act or specific plan to engage in terrorism. The precautionary principle was used against judges through interpretative clauses that displaced traditional principles that legislative ambiguities should be resolved in favor of the liberty of the accused. The ATA's approach was heavy-handed but consistent with other pre-9/11 expansions of the criminal law in Canada in the name of protecting victims and potential victims of crime.[64]

In part because of concerns about compliance with the right to freedom of association protected under the Charter, the ATA stopped short of making membership in a terrorist group or association with terrorists a crime. Instead, an offense of knowingly participating in a terrorist group for the purpose of enhancing its ability to carry out or facilitate a terrorist activity was created.[65] This participation offense deemed that certain conduct, such as the use of a name, word, or symbol associated with a terrorist group, would be admissible evidence.[66] In effect, this meant that conduct that before 9/11 would only have been of interest to an intelligence agency could now be used as evidence in the prosecution of broad new terrorism offenses. The Canadian approach was more subtle than the British and Australian approaches in not directly criminalizing the display of names of terrorist groups or association with terrorists, but Parliament made clear that such acts could be evidence of guilt.

The new act also followed the United Kingdom in providing for the executive proscription of terrorist groups. It provided that such proscription was conclusive proof in a criminal trial that the group was a terrorist group. There are strong arguments that the substitution of an executive proscription decision based on secret evidence for proof beyond a reasonable doubt in a criminal trial violates the presumption of innocence.[67] As in Australia, however, this issue has yet to be litigated, in large part because most criminal prosecutions

---

[63] A specific clause was included to ensure that a passive member of a sleeper cell could be guilty of the participation offense. Ibid., Section 83.18(3).

[64] Kent Roach, *Due Process and Victims' Rights* (Toronto, ON, Canada: University of Toronto Press, 1999).

[65] Criminal Code, Section 83.18.   [66] Ibid., Section 83.18(4).

[67] David Paciocco, "Constitutional Casualties of September 11" (2002) 16 Supreme Court Law Review (2d) 199.

have not been able to rely on the cabinet's designation of 42 groups as terrorist organizations. In other words, proscription lags behind the diffusion of al Qaeda into an ideology and the creation of small, homegrown terrorist groups.

The government's desire to stress that the ATA was consistent with the Charter meant that the new terrorism offenses did not contain any reverse onuses and generally required high levels of subjective fault such as knowledge or purpose. Unlike in the United Kingdom, negligence liability was not used, and unlike in Australia, recklessness liability was not used. The Canadian approach reflected the possibility that courts would add terrorism to the small list of high-stigma crimes that would, under the Charter, require proof that the accused knowingly and intentionally intended the prohibited act.[68] At the same time, the Canadian government was concerned that those operating in a terrorist cell might not know the specifics of a terrorist plot until the last minute, if at all.[69] The 2001 law anticipated what in Australia became the the/a issue, requiring emergency amendments in 2005 that made clear that the accused could be guilty even if he or she did not know the specific nature of the terrorist activity.[70]

The new offenses apply to a broad range of acts committed inside or outside Canada. This was done to make clear that Canada was implementing various international conventions concerning specific forms of terrorism. There is an exemption for armed conflict conducted according to customary or conventional international law or the official activities of a state military force "to the extent that those activities are governed by other rules of international law."[71] Canadian courts have rejected the idea that support for al Qaeda or Taliban actions in Afghanistan qualifies under this exemption.[72] The legal issue may have been resolved, but political disputes remain. The Tamil Tigers were not listed as a terrorist group in Canada until 2006, when a new Conservative government was elected. Prapaharan Thambaithurai pled guilty in 2010 to providing $3,000 to the Tamil Tigers and argued out of court that the Sri Lankan government "were the real terrorists."[73] He received a controversially light six month sentence, but the government's appeal of the sentence was dismissed with the court of appeal noting that a "civil war" existed between the Sri Lankan government and the Tamil Tigers and that the offender, whose

[68] *R. v. Martineau*, 2 S.C.R. 633 (1990) (murder); *R. v. Logan*, 2 S.C.R. 731 (1990) (attempted murder); *R v. Finta*, 1 S.C.R. 701 (1994) (war crimes).

[69] Richard Mosley, "Preventing Terrorism," in *Terrorism, Law and Democracy*, ed. David Daubney et al. (Montreal, QC, Canada: Les Editions Themis, 2002).

[70] Criminal Code, Sections 83.18(2), 83.19 (2).   [71] ATA, 83.01(1)(b).

[72] *R. v. Khawaja*, ONCA 862 (2010). See also Craig Forcese, *National Security Law* (Toronto, ON, Canada: Irwin Law, 2008), at 273, as updated at http://www.cforcese.typepad.com/ns/.

[73] "Man Pleads Guilty in Landmark Terrorism Financing Case," Globe and Mail, May 11, 2010.

father and brother had been killed in the war, had no prior criminal record. It added that "Mr. Thambaithurai's lack of remorse was perhaps not surprising, given his Tamil heritage, the impact of the war on his family, and his continuing concern for the dire circumstances of the Tamil population in Sri Lanka." Nevertheless, the Court of Appeal was satisfied that he did not present an ongoing threat especially in light of the military defeat of the Tamil Tigers.[74] Like similarly light sentences in Australia, the six month sentence in this case demonstrates how proscription of terrorist groups simplifies a complex situation where both governments and organizations such as the Tamil Tigers have abused human rights.

Terrorism Financing

As required by Security Council Resolution 1373, a significant part of the ATA featured terrorism financing regulations. New offenses were created under the criminal code of knowingly providing funds to carry out a terrorist activity. Terrorist activity was defined to include both Canada's British-inspired broad definition, which included some forms of politically motivated property damage and disruptions of essential services, and the narrower general definition of terrorism in the 1999 International Convention on the Suppression of Terrorism Financing which was limited to causing death or serious bodily injury to civilians.[75] This offense underlines the conscious choice that Canada made to adopt a broader definition of terrorist activities than used in the 1999 Convention and subsequently used by the Supreme Court of Canada in 2002 to provide a limiting definition to an undefined reference to terrorism in Canadian immigration law.[76] As discussed in Chapter 2, the Security Council also missed an opportunity after 9/11 to promote the use of the restrained general definition of terrorism in the 1999 Financing Convention.

Another offense made it a crime to provide property or financial or other services knowing that they would be used to benefit a terrorist group either as defined in the act or as listed by the cabinet.[77] This provision demonstrates how the problematic process of executive listing was built into terrorism financing legislation. The listing procedure in the ATA, unlike the Australian proscription provision, specifically provided for judicial review. At the same time, the judge could base a decision on secret intelligence not disclosed to the applicant challenging the listing because its disclosure would injure national

---

[74] *R. v. Thambaithurai* 2011 BCCA 137 at paras 3, 22.
[75] Criminal Code, Section 83.02.
[76] *Suresh v. Canada*, 1 S.C.R. 3 at para 98 (2002).
[77] Criminal Code, Section 83.03.

security or endanger a person.[78] The law even provided a procedure whereby the government could show the judge information obtained in confidence from a foreign government or international organization but then withdraw the information if the judge determined that the information could be disclosed to the applicant.[79] Canada relies heavily on foreign intelligence and did not want to take any risk that intelligence might be disclosed in Canadian legal proceedings. Both internationally and domestically, listing is an intelligence-led process and one often based on secret evidence that will not be disclosed to anyone who challenges the listing.

As in many other parts of the world, efforts against terrorism financing in Canada were built on a money laundering model. Canada's money laundering law was amended to include terrorism financing, with various financial institutions having duties to report suspicious and large transactions to the Financial Transactions and Report Analysis Centre of Canada (FINTRAC).[80] FINTRAC receives 25 million transaction reports from various financial institutions each year. The detection of terrorism financing, however, often requires more discriminate intelligence. Although FINTRAC has improved its performance on terrorism financing, it still reports far more cases of suspected money laundering than terrorism financing to authorities.[81] A recurring problem is that money laundering is designed to detect large amounts of illicit money, whereas terrorism financing often involves smaller amounts of funds that can come from legitimate or illegitimate sources.

There has only been one pure terrorism financing conviction in Canada and as noted above it resulted in a six-month sentence for a man who provided $3,000 to the Tamil Tigers.[82] At the same time, authorities enjoyed more success when in early 2011 they obtained orders of forfeiture of property worth millions of dollars controlled by the Tamil Tigers in Montreal and Toronto. As in the United States and the United Kingdom, Canada's use of forfeiture laws allowed the state to escape the demands of criminal prosecutions which require proof of facts beyond a reasonable doubt and may require confidential informants to testify and be cross-examined. The forfeiture orders were the result of a nine year investigation that did not result in criminal charges. They were not contested by the Tamil groups who had disbanded after the military defeat of the Tamils Tigers in Sri Lanka. Under the Canadian forfeiture

[78] Ibid., Section 83.05. [79] Ibid., Section 83.06.

[80] In 2006, the law was expanded in anticipation of a 2008 evaluation of Canada by the Financial Action Task Force (FATF). S.C. (2006), c.12.

[81] FINTRAC 2010 Annual Report (Ottawa: FINTRAC, 2010), at 8, 15.

[82] "Six Months in Jail Too Lax," Globe and Mail, May 14, 2010. The sentence was upheld in *R. v. Thambaithurai* 2011 BCCA 137 discussed above.

provisions created in 2001, the state only had to establish that the property was owned or controlled on behalf of a terrorist group and could use affidavit and hearsay evidence and evidence from informants not produced for cross-examination that in some cases would not have been accepted in a criminal prosecution.[83]

Canada has been questioned by the UN's CTC on its lack of terrorism financing prosecutions and, in 2008, received 11 non-compliant ratings from the Financial Action Task Force (FATF).[84] Both entities took an acontextual and bureaucratic approach that ignored the complexities of providing funds for groups such as the Tamil Tigers and Hamas. The Air India Commission recently suggested that given the paucity of concrete results from Canada's terrorism financing regulations and the small amounts used to fund deadly acts of terrorism, there was merit to decoupling terrorism financing from money laundering. Contrary to criticisms that Canada received from FATF, the Air India Commission stressed that FINTRAC should rely more, not less, on intelligence when tracking the small amounts that may be used for terrorism financing. The government has demonstrated some support for this approach, stating that it will ensure that FINTRAC is better implemented into the intelligence cycle and that it will develop a new forum for terrorism financing.[85]

Charities and Terrorism Financing

Another part of the ATA that responded to concerns about terrorism financing was the Charities Registration (Security Information) Act,[86] which provided an elaborate scheme to allow the ministers of public safety and national revenue to certify that a charity should be stripped of charitable status on the basis of information, perhaps not disclosed to the applicant, that the charity has directly or indirectly made or will make resources available to a terrorist organization. This act was a recognition that the Babbar Khalsa, a Sikh separatist group

---

[83] Criminal Code, Section 83.14. See Re World Tamil Movement of Quebec and Her Majesty the Queen Forfeiture Order December 30, 2010 (F.C.T.D.) available at http://decisions.fct-cf.gc.ca/en/2010/t-307-09_33697/t-307-09.pdf; Re World Tamil Movement of Ontario and Her Majesty the Queen April 7, 2011 (F.C.T.D.) available at http://decisions.fct-cf.gc.ca/en/2011/t-308-09_33696/t-308-09.pdf. See also Stewart Bell "Tamil group ordered to forfeit cash" National Post January 22, 2011. These decisions were ratified by the Federal Court on the basis of extensive affidavits submitted by the RCMP involving information from unnamed informants with information being redacted when the affidavit was released with the forfeiture order.

[84] Commission of Inquiry into the Investigation of the Bombing of Air India Flight 182, *Air India Flight 182*, at 181–4.

[85] Canada, *Action Plan*, at 6.   [86] S.C. (2001), c.41, Section 113.

founded by Talwinder Singh Parmar, widely believed to be the mastermind of the Air India bombings, had received charitable status in Canada for a time in the 1990s.[87]

The new legislation responded to Canada's past underreaction to the use of charities to fund terrorism, but it also raised concerns that the activities of legitimate charities would be chilled. Irwin Cotler and others expressed concerns that the new law should allow charities a due diligence defense that they had taken reasonable efforts not to be associated with or fund terrorists. He also raised concerns that attention might be focused on Muslim charities.[88] The law remains in effect, but no charity has been stripped of charitable status under its terms. The Air India Commission warned that a charity deprived of status under the new law could simply continue as a nonregistered nonprofit organization that would still not have to pay taxes, even though it could no longer issue tax receipts. More generally, the Air India Commission, like the American 9/11 Commission,[89] expressed skepticism about the utility of terrorism financing regulation to prevent acts of terrorism while also accepting that Canada, like other countries, must maintain its terrorism financing regime if only to comply with Security Council and FATF mandates.[90]

Canadians Caught in Listing Processes

Two Canadian cases reveal the real costs imposed on individuals who are listed under various international and domestic terrorism financing regimes. Liban Hussein was listed under the Canadian UN terrorism financing regulations on November 7, 2001, the same day he was listed under U.S. Executive Order 13244. Two days later, Hussein was added to the UN's 1267 list, most likely at the request of the United States. The United States also started extradition proceedings against Hussein in Canada for running a money transfer operation without a license. In June and July 2002, however, Hussein's name was removed first from the Canadian lists and subsequently from the American and UN lists, and extradition proceedings against him were abandoned. Hussein's

---

[87] Commission of Inquiry into the Investigation of the Bombing of Air India Flight 182, *Air India Flight 182*, at 186, 195.

[88] Cotler, "Terrorism, Security and Rights," at 48.

[89] National Commission on Terrorist Attacks upon the United States, *The 9/11 Report* (New York: St. Martin's Press, 2004), at 12.3.

[90] The Air India Commission warned that the money laundering model "is not well-suited to terrorist financing" and that "discovering terrorist financing activity amidst the millions of reports about financial transactions or thousands of applications for charitable status is like finding the proverbial needle in a haystack." Commission of Inquiry into the Investigation of the Bombing of Air India Flight 182, *Air India Flight 182*, at 185–6.

lawyers were prepared to challenge the listing approach on the basis that it violated the presumption of innocence and freedom of association under the Charter. They were also prepared to argue that Hussein should not be made an outlaw through the enactment of a regulation and without any opportunity to know or challenge the reasons for the listing.[91] Hussein would not be the last Canadian to be caught up in the listing process, but his case sent an early warning about the dangers of an intelligence-based and secret listing process.

The Canadian willingness to delist Liban Hussein put Canada temporarily in breach of its Chapter VII obligations to comply with Security Council Resolution 1267 until the UN delisted Hussein. As discussed in Chapter 2, the UN Security Council process would have given the United States a veto over delisting, and it would not have required that Hussein be made aware of the reasons for his listing or refusal to delist. Today, a person in Hussein's position could appeal to a new ombudsperson for assistance with delisting, but the ultimate decision would still be made by the 1267 committee. The United States or any other member of the Security Council could still veto a delisting request on the basis of secret evidence never disclosed to the listed person or subject to adversarial challenge.

Controversy in Canada over the 1267 list of those associated with al Qaeda and the Taliban continued in the Abousfian Abdelrazik case. Abdelrazik was listed by the United States and then subsequently by the 1267 committee in 2006, because of his associations with fellow Montrealers Ahmed Ressam, who was convicted of plotting to bomb the Los Angeles airport, and Adil Charkaoui, who was the subject of a now abandoned security certificate. He commenced litigation in Canada when he was unable to return to Canada from Sudan, where he had been visiting his ill mother. The trial judge concluded that CSIS had been complicit in his detention in Sudan where Abdelrazik alleges he was tortured. Abdelrazik was eventually in 2008 allowed by a Canadian government chastened by criticisms of its complicity in the torture of Maher Arar and other Canadians in Syria, to live in the Canadian embassy in Khartoum. The trial judge rejected the Canadian government's arguments that the 1267 regime prohibited Abdelrazik's return to Canada on the basis that the regime allowed a person to travel to return to a country of citizenship. At the same time, the judge made clear that he had grave concerns about the 1267 process, noting that its use of secret evidence placed Abdelrazik in a position similar to Josef K. in Kafka's *The Trial*.[92]

91 E. Alexandra Dosman, "For the Record: Designating 'Listed Entities' for the Purposes of Terrorist Financing Offences at Canadian Law" (2004) 62 University of Toronto Faculty of Law Review 1.

92 *Abdelrazik v. Canada*, F.C. 580 (2009), at para. 53.

Shortly after the critical Canadian decision, the 1267 committee released a narrative listing that attempted to explain why Abdelrazik remained on the 1267 list, despite Canada's request that he be delisted. Following usual practice, however, the narrative summary was based on unsourced and uncircumstanced allegations, including those involving Abu Zabadayah, who was repeatedly waterboarded while in U.S. custody.[93] Despite requests by Canada for his removal, Abdelrazik remains on the 1267 list with a petition pending before the 1267 Ombudsperson. He is also challenging Canada's domestic implementation of the 1267 listing obligations that prohibit people from various financial dealings with him. Liban Hussein and Abousfian Abdelrazik provide two examples of what happens to individuals who get caught in the listing processes of various UN and domestic terrorism financing regimes.

Secrecy Provisions

Canada, as a net importer of intelligence, has always been very concerned about protecting secrets. As part of its 2001 antiterrorism legislation, section 38 of the Canada Evidence Act was amended to require all participants to notify the attorney general of Canada if they anticipated the use of information that, if disclosed, could injure national security, international relations, or national defense or any information that was being safeguarded by the government of Canada. As in Australia, the attorney general could authorize the disclosure of such information, including imposing conditions on its disclosure, or such issues could be litigated in the Federal Court. The new Canadian law did not, like the Australian law, attempt to tilt the balance toward the state's interests in secrecy; rather it allowed specially designated judges of the federal court to balance the competing interests in disclosure and secrecy in the individual cases. The Canadian law did, however, allow the state to play a trump card in the form of an attorney general's certificate that would reverse any court order that material be disclosed.[94] There were also mandatory statutory publication bans on national security confidentiality proceedings including that such proceedings were even taking place. These statutory restrictions were struck down under the Charter because they constituted inflexible restrictions

---

[93] Kent Roach, "The Eroding Distinction between Intelligence and Evidence in Terrorism Investigations," in *Counter-Terrorism and Beyond*, ed. Nicola McGarrity, Andrew Lynch, and George Williams (London: Routledge, 2010), at 63–4.

[94] As the ATA was initially introduced, the trump card was permanent and nonreviewable, but the government amended the bill in November 2001 to provide a very limited form of judicial review to ensure that the certificate was only used in relation to national security, in relation to national defense, or with respect to information obtained in confidence from a foreign entity. Canada Evidence Act, Section 38.131.

on the open court principle.[95] Although the Canadian government sold the ATA as consistent with the Charter, litigants continued to enjoy some success in challenging Canada's security legislation under the Charter.

The other provision designed to maximize secrecy was that the litigation of secrecy issues would only occur in the Federal Court of Canada, an administrative law court. Canadian law only allowed judges to order the disclosure of secrets since 1982, and the only people with such powers were specially designated judges of the federal court, even if these issues arise in a criminal trial. If the federal court orders nondisclosure, then the criminal trial judge must follow that order but can make any order, including staying proceedings, that is necessary to protect the accused's right to a fair trial.[96] As previously discussed, this awkward and time-consuming procedure was avoided in the Air India trial and in recent Toronto terrorism prosecutions. It will now have to be used in subsequent terrorism prosecutions given the Supreme Court's 2011 ruling that the two court procedure was constitutional because trial judges had full powers and should not hesistate to stay terrorism prosecutions if they concluded that a fair trial was not possible because of a non-disclosure order by the Federal Court.[97] So far, the Canadian government has refused to follow the Air India Commission's recommendations that trial judges must be able to see and decide whether secret information must be disclosed to the accused if terrorism prosecutions are to be conducted efficiently and fairly in Canada.[98] Trial judges in the United States, the United Kingdom, and Australia all have such powers. The resistance of the Canadian government can only be explained on the basis of exaggerated fears that the secrecy of intelligence would be compromised if trial judges were given access to the intelligence.

The ATA also modernized Canada's Official Secrets Act to prohibit the disclosure of protected sensitive information for the benefit of terrorist groups as well as foreign powers. These changes signaled a post-9/11 change that would see terrorism committed by nonstate actors as a prime threat to national security, as opposed to the espionage of the cold war era. As seen in the preceding chapter, Australia extended this approach by extending its treason and sedition offenses to apply to support of terrorist groups. Canada's new secrecy law followed a similar approach by criminalizing both the sharing of secrets with terrorist groups and the sharing of secrets with foreign powers. At the same time, the new law failed to provide an objective definition of what should

---

[95] *Ottawa Citizen Group Ltd v. Canada (Attorney General)*, 255 F.T.R. 173 (F.C.T.D.) (2004), at paras. 34–45.

[96] Canada Evidence Act, Section 38.14.   [97] *R. v. Ahmad* 2011 SCC 6.

[98] Commission of Inquiry into the Investigation of the Bombing of Air India Flight 182, *Air India Flight 182*, vol. 3, chapter 7; Canada, *Action Plan*.

be secret and extended its protections to all information that the government was taking measures to safeguard.[99] It also failed to reform an old offense of possessing secrets and in a case involving secret information that was leaked in an attempt to discredit Maher Arar, the courts struck the offense down as unconstitutional.[100] This ironically left Canada without an offense that could be used to prosecute those who possessed leaked information and no one has been charged with the leaks in the Arar case.

If the government has been lax about official secrets prosecutions, it has not hesitated to make secrecy claims in public inquiries, civil lawsuits and in criminal trials. Unlike in the United States, these state-secrets claims have frequently failed. Courts and inquiries have found that the government has frequently overclaimed secrecy sometimes in an attempt to prevent embarrassment.[101] The overclaiming of secrecy has frustrated and delayed the work of both public inquiries and trials.

Newly Recognized Intelligence Powers

The ATA recognized the role of the Communications Security Establishment (CSEC), Canada's signals intelligence agency. The ATA amendments to the National Defence Act allowed the minister of defense to authorize the interception of communications either originating or intended to be received in Canada, but only on the condition that the intercept was directed at foreign entities outside Canada; measures were in place to protect the privacy of Canadians; and private communications would only be used or retained if essential to security, defense, or international relations.[102] Such intercepts would be authorized by a minister as opposed to a judge who authorizes both the police and CSIS to conduct domestic electronic surveillance. The use of a minister has been defended in part on the basis of similar international practices with signals intelligence.[103] This approach, however, would make it difficult to use such intelligence as evidence in terrorism prosecutions.

The ATA amendments allow the CSEC to engage in electronic surveillance that would include Canadian private conversations in a manner similar to

---

[99] Stanley Cohen, *Privacy, Crime and Terror* (Toronto, ON, Canada: Butterworths, 2005), at 311.

[100] *O'Neill v. Canada*, 272 D.L.R.(4th) 193 (Ont.S.C.J.) (2006).

[101] *Canada (Attorney General) v. Commission of Inquiry into the Actions of Canadian Officials in Relation to Maher Arar* 2007 FC 766.

[102] National Defence Act, Section 273.68.

[103] Cohen, *Privacy, Crime and Terror*, at 230. CSIS obtains warrants from the federal court on reasonable grounds relating to threats to national security. This search power was upheld from a Charter challenge in *R. v. Atwal*, 36 C.C.C.(3d) 161 (Fed.C.A.) (1987). For arguments that the CSEC powers violate the Charter, see Steven Penney, "National Security Surveillance Powers in an Age of Terror" (2010) 48 Osgoode Hall Law Journal 247.

the controversial powers that the U.S. National Security Agency used in the aftermath of 9/11. An important difference, however, is that the Canadian approach was legalized in the 2001 ATA, whereas the American approach was initially only authorized by an arguably illegal presidential order and remained secret until it was disclosed by *The New York Times*. The Canadian amendments also provided for continued review of the activities of the CSEC by a retired judge who has access to all the secret information and could report to both the minister of defense and the attorney general about any illegal activity.[104] This review body has expressed concerns that the ministerial authorizations have been broadly written to apply to methods of collecting foreign intelligence rather than to individuals.[105]

New and Now Expired Police Powers: Preventive Arrests and Investigative Hearings

The ATA expanded police powers by providing for preventive arrests when there were reasonable grounds to believe that a terrorist activity would be carried out and reasonable suspicion to believe that the detention or imposition of conditions was necessary to prevent the carrying out of the terrorist activity. Both the attorney general and, except in exigent circumstances, a judge had to authorize such arrests. This was a significantly stricter standard than the comparable British provision that applied whenever a constable reasonably suspected that a person was a terrorist, with no judicial authorization required until 48 hours after the preventive arrest.[106]

The maximum period of preventive arrest was limited to 72 hours (compared to the U.K. powers, which, at the time, were 7 days and would subsequently be expanded to 28 days before being reduced to 14 days in 2011), but the arrestee could be required by a judge to enter into a recognizance or peace bond for up to a year, with breach of the bond being punishable by up to two years' imprisonment and a refusal to agree to a peace bond punishable by one year's imprisonment.[107] This latter provision built on increased interest in Canada in interventions designed to respond to even small risks of a growing list of serious crimes including organized crime, domestic violence and sexual

---

[104] National Defence Act, Section 273.63.

[105] Communications Security Establishment Commissioner, *Annual Report 2009–2010* (Ottawa: Public Works, 2010), at 4–6. The reviewer has also made 129 recommendations to CSEC since 1997, and 121 have been implemented. Ibid., at 8.

[106] Terrorism Act, 2000, Section 41. See David Jenkins, "In Support of Canada's Anti-Terrorism Act: A Comparison of Canadian, British and American Anti-Terrorism Law" (2003) 66 Saskatchewan Law Review 421, at 450.

[107] Criminal Code, Section 83.3.

offenses. It relied on a decision upholding the constitutionality of similar peace bonds to respond to "reasonable fears" that a person would commit a sexual offense.[108] As with U.K. control orders, Canadian preventive arrests built on precrime precedents in other parts of the justice system. In any event, no preventive arrests were made under the ATA, and they were allowed to expire in 2007.

There has been some support for the reinstatement of preventive arrests, which, at a maximum of 72 hours, are mild compared to the U.K. provisions. Australia also has a 72-hour period, but this can be extended for up to 14 days by state legislation.[109] At the same time, even with the repeal of the formal preventive arrest provisions in Canada, there is still the possibility of requiring a suspect to enter into a potentially restrictive peace bond on the basis that there is a "reasonable fear" that he or she will commit a terrorist act.[110] No conviction or criminal charge would be required, and "peace bonds for terrorists"[111] are part of a growing number of peace bond provisions in the Canadian Criminal Code that are designed to respond to risks (or reasonable fears) of a variety of serious crimes.

The Canadian approach to both preventive arrests and peace bonds, like British control orders, was built on a model of legislative authorization and regulation that can be contrasted to the U.S. experience, where there is no authorization of preventive arrests but where grand jury material witness warrants were abused and used as a preventive arrest device in the wake of 9/11.[112] The Canadian and British laws at least imposed maximum periods of detention. At present, Canada, like the United States, does not have explicit powers of preventive arrest or detention. This suggests that Canada may share a more libertarian culture with the United States. At the same time, the American experience suggests that the absence of formal preventive detention powers may encourage extralegal conduct. The British example, however, also

---

[108] Criminal Code, Section 810.1; *R v. Budreo*, 142 C.C.C.(3d) 225 (Ont.C.A.) (2000). On precrime generally, see Lucia Zedner, "Preventive Justice or Pre-Punishment? The Case of Control Orders" (2007) 60 Current Legal Problems 174.

[109] Craig Forcese, "Catch and Release: A Role for Preventive Detention without Charge in Canadian Anti-Terrorism Law" Institute for Research on Public Policy study no. 7, July 2010.

[110] Criminal Code, Section 810.01. Similar provisions also apply to sexual offenses, organized crime, spousal and child abuse, and intimidation of a justice system participant and serious personal injury offenses.

[111] Gary Trotter, "The Anti-Terrorism Bill and Preventative Restraints on Liberty," in Daniels et al., *Security of Freedom*, at 241, who observed that "as absurd as it is to think that a recognizance could be efficacious in the circumstances, beyond adding to the clutter, this amendment is unobjectionable."

[112] See Chapter 4.

suggests that there is a danger that the maximum period of preventive detention can become a symbol that will be increased in an attempt to underline
the state's willingness to be tough in its battle against terrorism.

The ATA also included provisions making it easier to obtain wiretap warrants in terrorism investigations. These provisions removed requirements for
findings that other investigative methods would not be sufficient, increased
the duration of the wiretap warrant to a maximum of a year, and allowed three
years before targets had to be notified that they were the subject of electronic
surveillance by the police. These changes were not subject to a sunset and
were in fact based on prior loosening of warrant requirements in organized
crime investigations.[113] They have been upheld from Charter challenge in a
Toronto case in which wiretaps of more than 80,000 phone conversations were
obtained.[114]

A more controversial new power was the ability to hold investigative hearings to compel a person to answer questions relating to terrorist activities
either in the past or the future. Investigative hearings would be authorized
and conducted by judges on the basis that there were reasonable grounds
to believe that a terrorism offense had or would be committed and reasonable attempts had been made to obtain the information by other means.[115]
The subject cannot refuse to answer on the grounds of self-incrimination, but
the compelled statements and evidence derived from the statements cannot
be used in subsequent criminal proceedings against the person compelled. In
2004, the Supreme Court of Canada upheld the constitutionality of investigative hearings, stressing that compelled evidence should not be used against the
person in any subsequent proceedings, including immigration and extradition
proceedings.[116] Three judges dissented on the basis that investigative hearings
violated the institutional independence of the judiciary by requiring judges to
preside over police investigations[117] and that the use of an investigative hearing
without notice to the accused in the middle of the Air India trial constituted
an abuse of process. The court also held that the presumption in favor of open
courts applied to the conduct of investigative hearings, but two judges dissented
on the basis that such a presumption "would normally defeat the purpose of
the proceedings by rendering them ineffective as an investigative tool."[118] The
result was that investigative hearings in Canada would be much more open

[113] M. L. Friedland, "Police Powers under Bill C-36," in Daniels et al., *Security of Freedom*,
at 274–5.
[114] *R. v. N.Y.*, CanLII 15908 (ON S.C.) (2008).   [115] Criminal Code, Section 83.28.
[116] *Re Section 83.28 of the Criminal Code*, 2 S.C.R. 248 (2004).
[117] Ibid., at para. 180.
[118] *Re Vancouver Sun*, 2 S.C.R. 332 (2004), at para. 60.

than either grand jury proceedings in the United States or Australian Security Intelligence Organization questioning proceedings in Australia.[119]

Even though upheld as constitutional and more restrained than comparable proceedings, investigative hearings were a questionable innovation. The law assumed that an uncooperative person would suddenly cooperate and tell the truth when threatened with contempt of court at an investigative hearing. The only attempt to use an investigative hearing was made during the Air India trial, which culminated in acquittals in 2005 in large part because of concerns about the credibility of Crown witnesses including one who was in witness protection and another who was subsequently convicted of perjury for his testimony.[120] The Air India investigation was plagued by problems of poor source handling and serious problems of witness protection, including the murder of at least one potential witness.[121] An investigative hearing could be a coercive substitute for adequate source development and witness protection and no guarantee that reluctant witnesses would tell the truth either at the hearing or at any subsequent trial. It could also result in broad use and derivative use immunity requirements that could make it impossible to prosecute a compelled witness should that witness turn out to be involved in terrorism.[122] The Air India inquiry did not recommend that investigative hearings be revived but rather focused on improvements to witness protection. Attempts by the minority Conservative government to reintroduce investigative hearings, however, continue,[123] and the RCMP has expressed a desire to use investigative hearings in the ongoing Air India investigations.

Hate Speech and Community Relations

The ATA recognized an increase in hate crimes after 9/11 by providing for a new offense of hate-motivated mischief to religious property and enhanced

[119] Kent Roach, "A Comparison of Australian and Canadian Anti-Terrorism Legislation" (2007) 30 University of New South Wales Law Journal 53.

[120] "Air India Bomber Gets 9 Years for Perjury," 7 at http://www.cbc.ca/canada/british-columbia/story/2011/01/07/air-india-reyat-sentencing-perjury.html.

[121] Commission of Inquiry into the Investigation of the Bombing of Air India Flight 182, *Air India Flight 182*, vol. 2, part 11, chapter 1; vol. 3, chapter 8.

[122] The statutory use and derivative use immunity provisions in Canadian investigative hearings are even broader than those provided when American grand juries compel a witness to reveal information. See Kent Roach, "A Comparison of American Grand Juries and Canadian Investigative Hearings" (2008) 30 Cardozo Law Review 1089.

[123] Over the government's opposition, the House of Commons' public safety and national security committee voted to revive the hearings and preventive arrest procedures, but subject to a two year sunset and review provision. "Committee votes to revive anti-terror measures for two years" *Globe and Mail* March 1, 2011. The bill died on the order paper when Parliament was dissolved for the May 2, 2011 election.

provisions allowing hate literature to be removed from the Internet.[124] These provisions were popular with the public and prescient given post-9/11 increases in hateful al Qaeda–inspired literature on the Internet. At the same time, they allowed the government to argue that the whole bill was supportive of human rights. The Liberal government relied on Irwin Cotler's arguments that terrorism was an assault on human rights to distinguish the bill from "a law and order agenda."[125] Cotler argued that the many civil libertarians who opposed the bill needed to alter their traditional paradigms and also see terrorism as an assault on international human rights. Cotler, then a backbencher, combined these arguments with his own civil libertarian criticisms of the bill, but others in government that used his ideas did not. The minister of justice who invoked Cotler's ideas soon grew frustrated with civil libertarian criticisms of the bill and, a week after the bill was introduced in Parliament, told reporters that she wished critics were in her shoes "for 24 hours" and "knew what I know, in terms of how hard it is to detect these guys and stop their fundraising or whatever."[126] Philip Ruddock, the Australian minister of justice, also invoked Cotler's idea that terrorism was an assault on human rights to defend his country's much more heavy-handed legislation.[127]

The Canadian government's use of human rights to support the ATA was an example of using the rights of victims and potential victims of crime to support traditional crime control legislation. As such, it was consistent with the use of victims' rights to defend criminal laws throughout the 1990s.[128] The government's commitment to both equality and victims was, however, partial. Although it was prepared to create a new crime of hate-motivated mischief to religious property, it rejected Irwin Cotler's proposal that the ATA, like the 1988 Emergencies Act, contain a nondiscrimination clause designed to protect the same religious and ethnic minorities from discriminatory forms of profiling,[129] and the ATA, unlike the Patriot Act, did not contain even a symbolic affirmation of individual responsibility.[130] The Canadian government invoked the victims of 9/11 but was far less generous in its treatment of the

---

[124] Criminal Code, Sections 431.2, 320.1.   [125] As quoted in Roach, *September 11*, at 80.

[126] "Anne McLellan's New Ideals," Globe and Mail, October 22, 2001.

[127] Philip Ruddock, "Australia's Legislative Response to the Ongoing Threat of Terrorism" (2004) 27 University of New South Wales Law Journal 254, at 254. For a critique of the Ruddock approach see Greg Carne "Reconstituting 'Human Security' in a New Security Environment: One Australian. Two Canadians and Article 3 of the Universal Declaration of Human Rights" (2006) 25 Australian Year Book of International Law 1.

[128] Roach, *Due Process and Victims' Rights*.   [129] Cotler, "Thinking outside the Box," at 128.

[130] An antiprofiling amendment based on pre-9/11 American legislation was proposed but rejected. Sujit Choudhry and Kent Roach, "Racial and Ethnic Profiling" (2003) 41 Osgoode Hall Law Journal 1.

Canadian victims than the U.S. government. Concerns also remain over the adequacy of compensation paid to the Air India victims.[131]

As in the United Kingdom and Australia, Canada seemed only able to offer hate crimes as a response to concerns about maintaining relations with its Arab and Muslim communities in the wake of 9/11. In 2004, however, the government created a Cross-Cultural Roundtable on National Security Issues as part of its first national security policy. The roundtable is designed to work closely with the Department of Public Safety to "ensure that there is zero tolerance for terrorism or crimes of hate in Canada."[132] The roundtable has had 15 meetings, mainly consisting of governmental briefings and 6 outreach meetings, but none since 2006.[133] It has, unfortunately, not emerged as an active presence in security or community relations debates. One factor may be the difficulty of representing the variety of minorities and regions in Canada, including the diversity of Canada's Muslim population, which comes from many different nations and sects.[134] Another factor may be that the roundtable is perceived not to be independent from the Department of Public Safety.[135] An institution like the roundtable could play a valuable role if it was the focus for genuine dialogue between communities and the government on security issues.

The importance of maintaining good relations with multicultural communities is underlined by the fact that informers within the Muslim community, including so-called extremists who had previously and unsuccessfully advocated for the use of Sharia law in some divorce proceedings, played an important role in the prosecution of a Toronto terrorism plot. Post-9/11 events have put Canadian Muslims into the spotlight. Some, like the Khadr family who admits to being an al Qaeda family, are extremely unpopular, whereas others, especially Maher Arar, have been recognized as victims of government excess after they were exonerated by a commission of inquiry.

IV. IMMIGRATION LAW AS ANTITERRORISM LAW

Consistent with the United States' initial reliance on immigration and military detention and the United Kingdom's use of indeterminate immigration

---

[131] Roach, *September 11*, at 80–3.
[132] Canada, *Securing an Open Society*, April 2004, at 2.
[133] The activities of the roundtable are described on the Ministry of Public Safety's Web site at http://www.publicsafety.gc.ca/prg/ns/ccrs/index-eng.aspx.
[134] Kent Roach, "Canadian National Security Policy and Canadian Muslim Communities," in *Muslims in Western Politics*, ed. Abdulkader Sinno (Bloomington: Indiana University Press, 2009).
[135] Kent Roach, "Multiculturalism, Muslim Minorities and Security Policy" (2006) Singapore Journal of Legal Studies 405.

detention without trial, Canada relied on immigration law as antiterrorism law in the immediate aftermath of 9/11. While civil society focused on debating the ATA, a revised immigration law affirming administrative detention of noncitizens suspected of being a security threat was enacted in November 2001, with comparatively little controversy. As my colleague Audrey Macklin argued at the time, "laws that arouse deep concern about civil liberties when applied to citizens are standard fare in the immigration context."[136] The use of immigration law allowed Canadian officials to use investigative detention,[137] secret evidence obtained by Canada and from its allies, a lower standard of proof, and wider liability rules than were available even under the ATA. At the same time, these alternatives to criminal law have proven to be both legally and politically controversial and to lack the moral and denunciatory force of criminal prosecutions.

Security Certificates: Administrative Detention

Security certificates were introduced in Canadian immigration law in 1978. They enable the ministers of immigration and public safety to declare a permanent resident or foreign national to be inadmissible on security grounds, which include "engaging in terrorism" or "being a member of an organization that there are reasonable grounds to believe engages, has engaged or will engage" in acts of terrorism.[138] These liability rules are much broader than the new criminal offenses of the ATA, which stopped short of making membership in a terrorist group a crime because of concerns that a membership offense would attract Charter challenge. In addition, membership in a terrorist organization can be proven on standards less onerous than the criminal law standard of proof beyond a reasonable doubt. In the immediate aftermath of 9/11, security certificates became Canada's prime counter-terrorism instrument.

---

[136] Audrey Macklin, "Borderline Security," in Daniels et al., *Security of Freedom*, at 393, 397.

[137] In August 2003, 21 noncitizens from Pakistan were detained under immigration law powers of investigative detention. A media release made sensational claims that the men had associations with a group associated with al Qaeda and that one of them took flying lessons that took him over a nuclear plant outside Toronto. The case made headlines, but the terrorism allegations were not pursued, and the men were eventually released as not being a security threat, with most being deported. A number of them, however, made refugee applications on the basis that the highly publicized but false allegations made against them would lead to torture if they were deported to Pakistan. The powers of preventive detention used under immigration law were much broader than the preventive arrest provisions of the ATA enacted immediately after 9/11, which allowed for a maximum of 72 hours' preventive arrest. On the moral panic created by the operation, see Felix Odartley-Wellington, "Racial Profiling and Moral Panic: Operation Thread and the al Qaeda Sleeper Cell That Never Was" (2009) 2(2) Global Media Journal, Canadian Edition 25.

[138] Immigration and Refugee Protection Act, S.C. (2001), c.27, Section 34.

Security certificates are subject to judicial review in the federal court to determine their reasonableness. Judicial review of security certificates preempts other proceedings, including applications for refugee status. This approach is common in many countries but also took an approach that ignored the broader context in which a person might have joined or participated in a terrorist group. Security certificate cases are reviewed by the same specially designated judges who have exclusive power to make public interest immunity determinations in criminal trials and to grant CSIS warrants to conduct electronic surveillance. Such a centralized approach is designed to maximize the security of secret information and expertise and was borrowed from American practice with respect to the Foreign Intelligence Surveillance Act Court.[139]

Secret Evidence

The procedure for reviewing security certificates was extraordinary because it involved the judge being required to hear evidence in the absence of the person named in the certificate and their counsel if, in the judge's opinion, the disclosure of information would be injurious to national security or the safety of any person.[140] The Supreme Court of Canada upheld the constitutionality of this use of secret evidence in a nonterrorist case in 1992.[141] Although the ATA included enhanced provisions for obtaining nondisclosure orders of sensitive information, it did not allow the use of secret evidence in criminal trials and contemplated that criminal trial judges could permanently stop a trial if a nondisclosure would deprive the accused of a fair trial.[142] A toleration of secret evidence is the defining difference between administrative detention and criminal prosecutions.

In 2002, Justice James Hugessen of the federal court made a speech in which he commented that the judges of his court "do not like this process of having to sit alone hearing only one party and looking at the materials produced by only one party and having to try to figure out for ourselves what is wrong with the case that is being presented before us . . . "[143] Justice Hugessen, who had been a judge since 1972, ended his speech with an extraordinary confession: "I sometimes feel a little bit like a fig leaf."[144] This speech, as well as civil society campaigns against security certificates as "secret trials,"

---

[139] Ian Leigh, "Secret Proceedings in Canada" (1996) Osgoode Hall Law Journal, at 136–7.
[140] IRPA, Section 83.   [141] *Chiarelli v. Canada*, 1 S.C.R. 711 (1992).
[142] CEA, Section 38.14.
[143] James Hugessen, "Watching the Watchers: Democratic Oversight," in Daubney et al., *Terrorism, Law and Democracy*, at 384.
[144] Ibid., at 386.

mobilized much support for the five men suspected of involvement in al Qaeda held in Canada on security certificates.

Richard Fadden, the head of CSIS, which is the lead agency in the security certificate cases, bitterly complained in 2009 that " suspected terrorists are given tender-hearted profiles, and more or less taken at their word when they accuse CSIS or other government agencies of abusing them. It sometimes seems that to be accused of having terrorist connections in Canada has become a status symbol, a badge of courage in the struggle against the real enemy, which would appear to be, at least sometimes, the government. To some members of civil society, there is a certain romance to this. This loose partnership of single-issue NGOs, advocacy journalists and lawyers has succeeded, to a certain extent, in forging a positive public image for anyone accused of terrorist links or charges."[145] Fadden, however, ignored that the support that Canada's security certificate detainees received was related to the government's insistence that it could use secret evidence against them and its position that, if necessary, the detainees could be deported to face torture in Egypt, Syria, Morocco, and Algeria.

It took five years, but Justice Hugessen's concerns about the problems associated with the use of secret evidence in security certificate proceedings were finally recognized when the supreme court, in 2007, in *Charkaoui I*, held that the absence of any adversarial challenge to the secret evidence submitted to the judge violated the Charter. The court stressed that fairness of the proceedings "rests entirely on the shoulders of the designated judge. Those shoulders cannot by themselves bear the heavy burden of assuring, in fact and appearance, that the decision on the reasonableness of the certificate is impartial, is based on a full view of the facts and law, and reflects the named person's knowledge of the case to meet." In a passage reminiscent of Judge Hugessen's speech, the Court stressed that "the judge sees only what the ministers put before him or her. The judge, knowing nothing else about the case, is not in a position to identify errors, find omissions or assess the credibility and truthfulness of the information in the way the named person would be."[146] The court held that the right to a fair hearing could only be satisfied by an adequate substitute for disclosure to the detainee.[147]

In holding that the use of secret evidence was contrary to the Charter, the court identified a number of less rights-invasive alternatives. One alternative was to borrow from prior practices and have the certificates reviewed by SIRC,

[145] Richard Fadden, "Remarks," at http://www.csis-scrs.gc.ca/nwsrm/spchs/spch29102009-eng.asp.
[146] *Charkaoui v. Canada*, 1 S.C.R. 350 (2007), at para. 63.
[147] Ibid., at para. 61.

CSIS's watchdog agency, and to allow counsel for SIRC to test the intelligence, including, when necessary, consulting with the affected person.[148] A similar approach was used in the Arar Commission, where security-cleared commission counsel as well as a security-cleared amicus tested secret information that was not disclosed to Mr. Arar or his counsel. These counsel were also allowed to consult with Mr. Arar and his counsel even after having seen the secret material. Another possibility used in the Air India trial was to have counsel for the affected person enter into an undertaking that would allow them to examine secret information but not disclose it to their client.

The final alternative articulated by the court was a British-style special advocate, though the court noted that "U.K.'s special advocate system has also been criticized for not going far enough" because of "three important disadvantages faced by special advocates: (1) once they have seen the confidential material, they cannot, subject to narrow exceptions, take instructions from the appellant or the appellant's counsel; (2) they lack the resources of an ordinary legal team, for the purpose of conducting in secret a full defence; and (3) they have no power to call witnesses."[149] Proportionality analysis can be influenced by starting points and can legitimate a range of less rights-invasive alternatives. From the starting point of no adversarial review of secret evidence, there was a range of less drastic alternatives.

The court suspended its declaration of invalidity for a year to give the government time to devise a new scheme. As in the U.K. Belmarsh case and the American Guantánamo cases, the court had invalidated a major plank of the government's antiterrorism effort. As in those other cases, however, the court did not order the release of any suspected terrorists, and it was convinced that the government had a range of less rights-invasive alternatives to pursue its important aim of attempting to prevent terrorism.

Special Advocates

Parliament responded to the decision and enacted a special advocate scheme just as the one-year suspension of the delayed declaration of invalidity was about to end. The new scheme maximized the government's interest in

---

[148] Murray Rankin, "The Security Intelligence Review Committee: Reconciling National Security with Procedural Fairness" (1990) 3 Canadian Journal of Administrative Law 173. This was the practice used when the European Court of Human Rights, in *Chahal v. The UK*, 23 EHRR 413 (1996), wrongly assumed that a special advocate system was already in place in Canada.

[149] *Charkaoui v. Canada*, 1 S.C.R. 350 (2007), at para. 83.

secrecy[150] while at the same time providing for the new constitutional minimum of adversarial challenge to secret evidence.[151] Once the special advocate
has seen the secret evidence under Canada's new law, he or she cannot com-
municate with anyone else without judicial authorization. Canadian judges
have been more willing than British judges to authorize special advocates to
contact various people, including the detainee, after they have seen the secret
information. Another factor that has made the Canadian special advocate
system more successful than the British system is the higher level of public
disclosure available to the detainee. Since their creation, special advocates in
Canada have had some success in demonstrating concerns about the reliability of human sources[152] and in demonstrating that some secret evidence may
have been obtained through torture in Egypt.

The Canadian courts have also taken a stricter approach than the British
courts to the use of evidence obtained through torture. Following the new
legislation, Canadian courts have required the government to bear the onus of
establishing that the secret evidence was reliable.[153] This approach has placed
a greater onus on the state than contemplated by the majority of the House
of Lords which required applicants to establish that evidence was obtained
through torture.[154] The Canadian standard seems more realistic given the
nature of secret evidence, but the head of CSIS apparently complained to
American officials that Canadian courts were placing his organization in a
"reverse onus" of having to "'prove' the innocence of partner nations."[155]

The Limited Reform of Security Certificates

Although the supreme court, in *Charkaoui*, confronted the problem of secret
evidence, it did not squarely confront the limits and unfairness of relying

---

[150] For further arguments, see Kent Roach, "Charkaoui and Bill C-3" (2008) 42 Supreme Court
Law. Review 281, and Craig Forcese and Lorne Waldman, "A Bismarkian Moment: *Charkaoui*
and Bill C-3" (2008) 42 Supreme Court Law Review 355. For a defense of the new legislation
that stresses the ability of the judge to give the special advocates additional powers on a case-by-
case basis, see David Dunbar and Scott Nesbitt, "Parliament's Response to *Charkaoui*" (2008)
42 Supreme Court Law Review 415.

[151] The new scheme has subsequently been upheld from Charter challenge. *Re Harkat*, FC 1242
(2010).

[152] *Almrei v. Canada*, F.C. 1263 (2009), at para. 163–4, noting that cross-examination by special
advocates reveals accounts by human sources as inconsistent with CSIS's own surveillance
records.

[153] *Re Mahjoub*, FC 787 (2010), at para. 48.

[154] *A v. Secretary of State*, UKHL 71 (2005), discussed in Chapter 5.

[155] Wiki leak document from the U.S. embassy, at http://www.nytimes.com/interactive/2010/11/
28/world/20101128-cables-viewer.html#report/gitmo-08OTTAWA918.

on immigration law as antiterrorism law in the same way as the House of Lords did in the Belmarsh case.[156] The court quickly rejected an equality rights challenge to security certificates on the basis that noncitizens, unlike citizens, do not have an independent Charter right to remain in Canada. The court's summary conclusion that equality rights were not violated precluded it from addressing whether there were more proportionate means to address the terrorist threat, an issue that was central in the Belmarsh case. The court also stressed that long-term detention under the security certificate regime has yet to "become unhinged from the state's purpose of deportation."[157] The court's justification for this conclusion is presumably that none of the three applicants had reached the point where it had been determined that they were in need of protection from a substantial risk of torture if deported to Syria, Algeria, and Morocco and that no exceptional circumstance justified their deportation to torture.[158]

Security Certificates and Deportation to Torture

The risk of deportation to torture in security certificate cases was not abstract or remote. Many of the detainees had sought refugee status on the basis of political or racial persecution, and if the allegations that they were terrorists were accepted in their countries of citizenship, there was a substantial risk that they would be tortured. This threat was also underlined by the recognition that Canadian citizens such as Maher Arar had been tortured in Syria.

The Supreme Court of Canada dealt with the deportation to torture issue in the *Suresh* decision, released in January 2002, when the initial shock of 9/11 was still quite severe. The unanimous court indicated that it would deferentially review the minister's decision of whether deportation of an alleged member of the Tamil Tigers to Sri Lanka would present a substantial risk of torture. In reaching this conclusion, the court approved of Lord Hoffmann's approach in *Rehman*, where he declared that the 9/11 attacks underlined the need for judges to respect executive security decisions in part because "the executive has access to special information and expertise in these matters" and in part because such decisions "require a legitimacy which can be conferred only by entrusting them to persons responsible to the community through the democratic process. If the people are to accept the consequences of such decisions, they must be made by persons whom the people have elected

---

[156] *A v. Secretary of State*, HL 56 (2004).   [157] *Charkaoui*, 1 S.C.R. 350 (2007), at para. 131.
[158] Ibid., at para. 15.

and whom they can remove."[159] This deferential approach discounted the incentives faced by the executive to deport a suspected terrorist, even if there was a risk of torture. As discussed earlier, Canada was well aware that many in the United States believed that Canada's immigration policies had created risks to American security. In a companion case to *Suresh*, the court deferred to the minister's decision that an Iranian citizen previously granted refugee status could be deported to Iran without a substantial risk of torture, despite the poor human rights record of the regime.[160] This decision to deport Ahani to Iran even while his application before the UN Human Rights Committee was later criticized by that committee.[161]

The supreme court's approach in *Suresh* suggested that courts would generally defer to ministerial decisions that a detainee would not be tortured, but it also went beyond that determination to assess the constitutionality of deportation to torture. Even though the court recognized that Canada's international obligations not to participate in torture were absolute, the court defined the issue as one that "requires us to balance Canada's interest in combating terrorism and the Convention refugee's interest in not being deported to torture."[162] The court ruled that the Charter, will, in most cases, prohibit the deportation of a person to a country where there is a substantial risk of torture.[163] Regrettably, the court suggested that deportation to a substantial risk of torture might be justified under the Charter in undefined "exceptional circumstances,"[164] even while recognizing that such a result would violate Canada's international obligations. This ruling was not necessary to make in the case, and it caused various UN rights-protection bodies to remind Canada about its obligations with respect to torture. The UK government subsequently asked the European

---

[159] *Suresh v. Canada*, 1 S.C.R. 3 (2002), at para. 33, quoting *Rehman v. Secretary of State*, UKHL 47 (2001), at para. 62.

[160] *Canada v. Ahani*, 1 S.C.R. 72 (2002).

[161] This episode including unsuccessful attempts in Canada to delay Ahani's deportation pending decisions on his UN petition is set out in Kent Roach, "Constitutional, Remedial and International Dialogues about Rights" (2005) 40 Texas International Law Journal 537.

[162] *Suresh v. Canada*, 1 S.C.R. 3 (2002), at paras. 47 and 58.

[163] Although a refugee applicant facing the risk of torture is entitled to heightened due process in terms of written reasons from the minister for the deportation, the minister's decisions as to whether a person faces a substantial risk of torture or is a threat to the security of Canada will only be overturned by the courts if they are patently unreasonable.

[164] The Court reasoned "that insofar as the *Immigration Act* leaves open the possibility of deportation to torture, the Minister should generally decline to deport refugees where on the evidence there is a substantial risk of torture. We do not exclude the possibility that in exceptional circumstances, deportation to face torture might be justified.... We may predict that it will rarely be struck in favour of expulsion where there is a serious risk of torture. However, as the matter is one of balance, precise prediction is elusive. The ambit of an exceptional discretion to deport to torture, if any, must await future cases." Ibid., at paras. 77–8.

Court of Human Rights to follow the *Suresh* approach, but the European Court declined to do so.[165] Fortunately, the exceptional circumstances exception created by the Canadian court has not been used. In *Suresh*, the court accepted that the suspect had made a prima facie case that he would be tortured if returned to Sri Lanka and even warned about the dangers of relying on assurances from countries with poor human rights records that a person would not be tortured. Suresh has subsequently been released and allowed to stay in Canada.[166] In another case, a court refused to find that exceptional circumstances justified the deportation of a suspected terrorist to Egypt.[167] Nevertheless, the government has relied on this *Suresh* exception as part of its justification for the continued immigration law detention of suspected terrorists from countries including Syria, where the use of torture against terrorist suspects is notorious. The court's willingness to define the issue of torture in balancing terms and to contemplate exceptional circumstances contributed to a process whereby support for the norm against torture was undermined at least as a matter of domestic law.

The Judicialization of Intelligence

Problems with the use of secret evidence in security certificates continued. In 2008, the supreme court released its decision in *Charkaoui II*[168] that rejected a long-standing CSIS policy that raw intelligence should generally be destroyed after it has been used as the basis for analytical reports. This policy had, for example, led to the destruction of wiretaps and interview notes that harmed the Air India investigation and trial. The court rejected the idea that CSIS should never collect evidence, noting that "the activities of the RCMP and those of CSIS have in some respects been converging as they, and the country, have become increasingly concerned about domestic and international terrorism."[169] The court stressed that the "consequences of security certificates are often more severe than those of many criminal charges" and that the "original operational notes" or "raw intelligence" would be a better and more accurate source of evidence and should be retained when CSIS conducts investigations focused on individuals.[170] *Charkaoui II* is consistent with a theme seen throughout this book of increased use of intelligence as evidence.

---

[165] David Jenkins, "Rethinking *Suresh*" (2009) 47 Alberta Law Review 125.
[166] *Suresh v. Canada*, 1 S.C.R. 3 (2002), at para. 124.
[167] *Jaballah v. Canada*, F.C. 1230 (2006), at para. 83.
[168] SCC 38 (2008).   [169] Ibid., at para. 26.
[170] Ibid., at para. 54.

It responds to this phenomenon by attaching safeguards such as the retention of original notes and materials that are associated with evidentiary practices.[171]

Charkaoui II contributed to a process that Jim Judd, the former director of CSIS, had astutely identified as "the judicialization of intelligence," in which intelligence agencies had to grapple with difficult issues arising from the disclosure and use of intelligence as evidence.[172] The current head of CSIS, Richard Fadden, has less thoughtfully commented that *Charkaoui II* "turned one of our founding principles on its head. Our *Act* instructed us to collect/retain information that was 'strictly necessary' in order to determine if a person was a threat. This was seen as *protecting* civil liberties. Now the highest court in the land has told us to do just the opposite. Retaining everything is now seen as the best defence of civil liberties." Fadden then warned, "I am not sure if Canadians or even our national security community can foresee the full effects of this decision. . . . I do predict, however, and I would be happy to talk about this in a few years, that within several years, someone will accuse us of acting like the Stasi because of the information we are now compelled to keep."[173] These comments reveal resistance to the idea that intelligence may sometimes have to be disclosed as evidence. They also ignore that Section 12 of the CSIS Act,[174] even after *Charkaoui II*, only allows the collection of intelligence when "strictly necessary" to investigate activities "that may on reasonable grounds be suspected of constituting threats to the security of Canada," as defined in that act. The primary protection for privacy should be restrictions on the ability of CSIS to collect intelligence, not on its destruction of evidence. Given Fadden's warnings, however, review bodies should pay close attention to CSIS's collection and retention policies.

The Failure of Security Certificates as Sustainable Antiterrorism Instruments

After two trips to the Supreme Court, the Charkaoui case wound down when the government withdrew the certificate rather than disclose more information as required by a reviewing court.[175] In 2009, another security certificate was quashed, with the judge holding that while the certificate was reasonable when

---

[171] For a fuller discussion of the costs and benefits of this process, see Kent Roach, "When Secret Intelligence Becomes Evidence" (2009) 47 Supreme Court Law Review 247.

[172] Remarks by Jim Judd, Director of CSIS, at the Global Futures Forum Conference in Vancouver, April 15, 2008, at http://www.csis-scrs.gc.ca/nwsrm/spchs/spch15042008-eng.asp.

[173] Remarks by Richard Fadden, Director of CSIS, November 29, 2009, at http://www.csis-scrs .gc.ca/nwsrm/spchs/spch29102009-eng.asp.

[174] R.S. (1985), c.C-23.   [175] *Charkaoui v. Canada*, FC 1030 (2009).

it was first issued immediately after 9/11, there was no evidence that Hasan Almeri, originally from Syria, had engaged in terrorism, was a member of a terrorist group, or was a threat to the security of Canada.[176] Three more security certificates remain, but in each case, judges have released the detainees on a form of control order, a practice approved by the supreme court when it stressed that the state's onus to justify detention will increase with the duration of the administrative detention.[177] In one case in which a security certificate was upheld as reasonable, Canadian courts may have to confront the same issue as British courts in determining whether the person can be deported to Algeria on the basis of assurances that he will not be tortured.[178]

The prolonged legal proceedings in all these cases[179] demonstrate difficulties that result from attempts to impose indeterminate detention, use of secret intelligence as evidence, use of ambiguous and often old intelligence to determine security risks, and attempts to deport terrorist suspects to countries where they may be tortured. Security certificates in Canada have failed as antiterrorism policy: they have resulted in many successful legal challenges, they have morphed into a de facto and controversial control order regime, they have eventually required secret intelligence to be disclosed and subject to adversarial challenge, and they have been much more politically controversial than criminal prosecutions. The type of long-term detention allowed under security certificates may incapacitate suspected terrorists, but without a clear finding of guilt. Some of the public cannot help but have some sympathy for detainees who face secret evidence and have the threat of deportation to torture hanging over them. The detainees cannot be deported to countries such as Egypt and Syria without Canadian complicity in torture. Even if they could be deported to a safe country, it is not clear that deportation of suspected international terrorists to other countries will actually increase security; rather it may simply displace the problem of global terrorism. Finally, immigration law cannot be used against terrorist suspects who are Canadian citizens and may have contributed to Canada's inexperience in the difficult task of terrorism prosecutions.

---

[176] *Almrei v. Canada*, FC 1263 (2009).

[177] *Charkaoui v. Canada*, 1 S.C.R. 350 (2007), at para. 101.

[178] *Harkat v. Canada*, FC 1241 (2010). See *RB (Algeria) v. Secretary of State*, UKHL 10 (2009), discussed in Chapter 5.

[179] The *Charkaoui* case resulted in 38 decisions in the federal court and two separate decisions in the supreme court before the security certificate was abandoned. The Almrei case resulted in 14 judgments before the security certificate was quashed. Of the remaining cases, the Harkat case has so far resulted in 34 decisions, the Jaballah case in 32 decisions, and the Mahjoub case in 24 decisions; many more decisions may result if the government continues its attempts to deport these men to Egypt and Algeria.

Changes in Refugee Policy

In addition to the use of immigration law as antiterrorism law against individuals, Canada and the United States agreed to a safe third-country agreement as part of a smart border agreement signed in December 2001 to increase security and ease the flow of goods and people at the border. The agreement responded to American perceptions that Canada's refugee policy was too liberal and generous as well as false media reports that some of the 9/11 hijackers entered the United States through Canada. It contributed to dramatic decreases in the number of refugee applicants entering Canada. Although there have been some increases, the numbers have not returned to pre-9/11 levels.[180]

The safe third-country agreement was subsequently challenged by advocacy groups on the basis that Canadian actions in deflecting refugee applicants to the United States violated the Charter. A trial judge decided that the act violated both the Charter and Canada's international obligations toward refugees because of the more restrictive standards and greater use of incarceration in the American immigration system, but this decision was overturned on appeal.[181] The use of immigration law and antiterrorism law remains problematic. It is dramatically overinclusive in targeting innocent noncitizens, including refugees, and underinclusive in responding to terrorist threats from citizens.

v. CRIMINAL PROSECUTIONS

The use of immigration law and administrative detention as antiterrorism law in Canada and elsewhere demonstrated a lack of confidence in the criminal law. For most of the security certificates issued in 2000 and 2001, it was not possible to charge the men under the ATA's new terrorism offenses, which did not apply retroactively and even then extends universal jurisdiction over its new crimes unevenly. Even after the ATA was passed, however, the government opted to use a security certificate as opposed to a criminal charge in the *Charkaoui* case. The lack of confidence in criminal law in Canada had some justification given the failed terrorism prosecutions in the 1980s arising from alleged Sikh terrorism.[182]

---

[180] In 2001, more than 44,457 refugee applicants entered Canada, but that figure declined to 19,691 in 2005 and rose to 36,851 in 2008. See "Total Entry of Refugee Claimants 2008," at http://www.cic.gc.ca/english/resources/statistics/facts2008/temporary/21.asp.

[181] *Canada v. Canadian Council of Refugees*, FCA 229 (2008).

[182] For an account of these failed prosecutions see Kent Roach, *The Unique Challenges of Terrorism Prosecutions* (Ottawa: Public Works, 2010).

The first charges under the ATA were laid against Mohammad Momin Khawaja in 2004. He was eventually convicted in 2008 of having participated in the activities of a terrorist group and of facilitating terrorist activity in Canada, England, and Pakistan. The Crown has originally stressed Khawaja's role in a London-based cell, but the trial judge found that he could be convicted of other terrorist activities even if there was a reasonable doubt about whether he was aware of the London fertilizer bomb plot.[183] The courts also decided that even if Khawaja was supporting insurgency in Afghanistan, such actions were not conducted in accordance with international law, as required under the armed conflict exception of the ATA.[184]

Khawaja's trial was delayed by his challenge to the constitutionality of the new ATA offenses under the Charter and by two trips to the federal court to determine whether secret intelligence not used in his trial had to be disclosed to him. As noted earlier, the litigation of such public interest immunity applications in a court separate from the trial court can be explained by Canada's concerns about keeping other people's secrets. Nevertheless, it makes terrorism prosecutions both inefficient and potentially unfair if the federal court judge and the trial judge do not recognize the significance of the undisclosed intelligence.

Khawaja failed in most of his challenges to the ATA, but the trial judge struck down the religious and political motive requirement on the basis that it would "chill freedom protected speech, religion, thought, belief, expression and association, and therefore, democratic life; and will promote fear and suspicion of targeted political or religious groups, and will result in racial or ethnic profiling by governmental authorities at many levels."[185] He also found that the motive requirement was not necessary given that other definitions of terrorism, most notably American and UN definitions, did not distinguish terrorism from other crimes on the basis of religious and political motives. This decision responded to concerns at the time that the ATA was enacted about the adverse effects of the motive requirement on Muslim minorities. At the same time, the judge's approach actually expanded the definition of terrorism, did not prevent the use of religious motive evidence in Khawaja's trial, and was not followed by other courts.[186]

---

[183] *R. v. Khawaja*, 238 C.C.C.(3d) 114 (Ont.Sup.Ct.) (2008). The accused's appeal that the Crown has impermissibly shifted the theory of the case was rejected on the basis of the breadth of the offense charges. *R v. Khawaja*, ONCA 862 (2010), at paras. 139–51. The companion British case is *Khyam v. The Queen*, EWCA 1612 (C.A.) (2008) and involved an investigation known as Operation Crevice.

[184] *R. v. Khawaja*, ONCA 862 (2010), at paras. 152–69.

[185] *R. v. Khawaja*, 214 C.C.C.(3d) 399 (2006), at para. 73 (Ont.Sup.Ct.), rev'd ONCA 862 (2010).

[186] Kent Roach, "Terrorism Offences and the Charter: A Comment on *R. v. Khawaja*" (2007) 11 Canadian Criminal Law Review 371.

In 2010, an appeal court overturned the striking down of the political or religious motive requirement concluding that violent activity would not be protected under the Charter and that any nonviolent activity caught by the broad definition of terrorism would not be protected because the activity would be "destructive of the principles underlying freedom of expression." This decision embraced some militant democracy principles to the extent that it suggested that speech that is destructive of the principles underlying freedom of expression would not be protected. The appeal court also argued that it was terrorist attacks "perpetrated by radical Islamic groups fueled by a potent mix of religious and political fanaticism" that were responsible for a "racial and cultural stereotype of a radical Islamist"[187] as opposed to the law's motive requirement. The decision has ended the controversy about political and religious motive and brings Canada in line with the United Kingdom and Australia, where the motive requirement is accepted. The same appeal court underlined its tough approach to terrorism by raising Khawaja's sentence from 10.5 years to life imprisonment, noting that Khawaja's British associates had been sentenced to life imprisonment.[188]

In 2006, 18 people, including 4 youths, were arrested in Toronto on the grounds that they were involved in separate plots to storm Parliament and behead politicians until Canada withdrew from Afghanistan and to explode three truck bombs in Toronto. Most of the accused were born abroad but had grown up in Canada. The case was based on extensive wiretaps, two infor- mers within the Muslim community, and controlled deliveries of 25 bags of a substance held out to be ammonium nitrate. In the end, 7 of the 18 pled guilty, 7 had charges dropped by the prosecutor, 2 were convicted of various terrorism offenses in a judge-alone trial, and 2 were convicted of participating in a terrorist group after a trial by jury. Zakaria Amara pled guilty to participating in the activities of a terrorist group in relation to a terrorist training camp north of Toronto and offenses committed for terrorist purposes in relation to plans to explode three truck bombs in Toronto. In sentencing him to life imprisonment, the judge stressed the "catastrophic" effects that the bombs would have had, concluding that it "would have changed the lives of many, if not all Canadians forever,"[189] and Amara's role as the "directing mind" of the plot. The life sentence was upheld on appeal, with the appeal court not being swayed by Amara's remorse, his guilty plea, his young age at the time of the offense (20 years), his lack of a prior record, and his good prospects for rehabilitation.

---

[187] *R v. Khawaja*, ONCA 862 (2010), at paras. 117, 125–6.
[188] *R v. Khawaja*, ONCA 862 (2010), at paras. 232, 240–3, 248–250.
[189] *R. v. Amara*, ONSC 441 (2010), at para. 102, affd. ONCA 858 (2010).

Others who pled guilty received lesser sentences, but these sentences were increased to 20 and 18 years on appeal.[190] The court of appeal took note of high sentences for terrorism in both the United Kingdom and Australia, but as discussed in Chapter 6, some much lower sentences were given in Australia for accused who pled guilty and provided needed evidence in subsequent trials and the Australian courts were also aware of the overlapping nature of many new terrorism offenses.[191] Although many applauded the tougher sentences awarded on appeal, they could, in new cases, have the effect of taking away the accused's incentive to plead guilty and, by doing so, save the state the time and cost of a lengthy trial that may require the disclosure of intelligence. The sentences also demonstrate a major ratcheting up of punishment compared to some of the lenient sentences received by those who kidnapped a British diplomat during the October Crisis. Even when the accused is young, has renounced violence, and has pled guilty, Western democracies have placed little emphasis on the rehabilitation of terrorists in contrast to jurisdictions such as Singapore.

The Toronto terrorism case represented a major challenge both to post-9/11 terrorism laws and to cooperation between the RCMP and CSIS. Unlike in the Air India case, two human sources were successfully transferred from CSIS to the RCMP, with one of them being paid $4 million Canadian and being placed in witness protection.[192] The prosecutions were handled sensitively, with briefings being provided to Muslim groups shortly after the arrests. There has been little political or legal controversy about the Toronto terrorism prosecutions as opposed to the continued legal and political controversy over the use of administrative detention and secret evidence in the security certificate cases.

The convictions obtained in the Khawaja, Toronto 18, and other post-9/11 cases can be contrasted with the 2005 acquittals of two men charged in relation to the 1985 Air India bombings as well as other prosecutions of Sikh terrorism that collapsed because of disclosure and other problems. These prosecutions suggest that Canada is slowly gaining experience with terrorism

---

[190] The court of appeal stressed that the trial judge had given too much emphasis to youth, lack of a criminal record, and prospects for rehabilitation and stressed that "the sad truth is that young home-grown terrorists with no criminal antecedents have become a reality." *R. v. Khalid*, ONCA 861 (2010), at para. 47. Similarly, an 18-year-old who pled guilty to the same offense had his sentence increased from 12 to 18 years in *R v. Gaya*, ONCA 860 (2010).

[191] The court of appeal did, however, note that sentences below a 15- to 20-year range may be justified in terrorism cases where those "lower down in the chain" provide invaluable information about the secret activities of other terrorists. *R v. Khawaja*, ONCA 862 (2010), at para. 220.

[192] See generally "The Toronto 18," at http://www3.thestar.com/static/toronto18/index.html.

prosecutions.[193] The Toronto 18 case suggests that the RCMP and CSIS have learned from past mistakes with respect to the handling of sources and witness protection. At the same time, the success of the Toronto prosecutions also depended on a bold decision by the trial judge effectively to strike down Canada's unique two-court approach to determining state secrecy claims, a decision subsequently overturned by the Supreme Court.[194] The sentences imposed in the Toronto terrorism prosecution also require an increase in punishment of terrorism, even where the accused are young and have pled guilty and renounced violence by the time of sentencing.

VI. FOREIGN COUNTER-TERRORISM ACTIVITIES

Counter-terrorism activities since 9/11 frequently extend beyond borders. The transnational nature of these activities raises concerns about dealing with countries with poor human rights records and about ensuring accountability for extraterritorial state activities.

Canada's Afghan Detainees

Canada participated in the invasion of Afghanistan but not Iraq. In the immediate aftermath of 9/11, Canadian forces transferred some of their detainees to American forces with little apparent concern about whether they would end up in Guantánamo.[195] In subsequent years, Canada transferred some of their detainees to Afghan security intelligence, raising concerns that the detainees might be tortured.

In 2007, Amnesty International and the British Columbia Civil Liberties Association brought an action to restrain Canadian transfers to Afghan intelligence agencies. The government argued that the groups did not have standing and that the issues were not justiciable. Although these arguments would have worked in the United States and influenced the U.S. Supreme Court not to second-guess the transfer of American citizens to possible torture in Iraq,[196] they did not work given Canada's rejection of a political question doctrine. In this respect, Canada's expansive approach to judicial review is more like Israel's than the restrictive American approach.[197] The public

---

[193] There has been less success with so-called Al Capone strategies, with a judge excluding pornography that CSIS found on a computer of a terrorist suspect because of an unconstitutional search. *R. v. Mejid*, ONSC 5532 (2010).

[194] *R. v. Ahmad* 2011 SCC 6.

[195] Roach, *September 11*, at 159–61.   [196] See *Munaf v. Geren*, 128 S.Ct. 2207 (2008).

[197] *Operation Dismantle*, 1 S.C.R. 236 (1985). For further discussion of the post-9/11 importance of this case, see Kent Roach, "National Security and the Charter," in *Contested Constitutionalism*,

interest litigants were allowed to proceed on the assumption that the transfer to Afghan authorities would result in a substantial risk of torture. Nevertheless, the federal court held that the Charter would not apply because of concerns about applying the Charter outside Canada and because the detainees were not Canadian citizens and had no connection to Canada.[198] These decisions, however, ignored that the relevant Charter right applied to noncitizens and that the Supreme Court of Canada had recognized that the Charter should be applied outside Canada to Canadian actors who acted in violation of Canada's international human rights obligations. Unfortunately, the Supreme Court of Canada declined to hear an appeal in this case. A ruling by the Supreme Court on this issue would have clarified the Court's own position on torture and hopefully would have made clear that Canadian troops should not be complicit in torture.[199]

Despite the judicial ruling that the Charter did not apply, controversy continued over the Afghan detainee issue. The government refused to appoint a public inquiry into the matter, and an existing review body for the military police had limits imposed on its ability to investigate the matter. Parliamentary committees were also hindered by the government's secrecy claims. A panel of retired judges, however, has been enlisted to help determine what material parliamentarians can see in the matter. Unfortunately, the prolonged process has detracted from public attention to the issue. The Afghan detainee issue has revealed the lack of effective review, including the inability of parliamentary committees to have access to secret information, as well as the difficulties in dealing with countries with poor human rights records.

The Torture of Maher Arar and Other Canadian Citizens in Syria

Two public inquiries were appointed to examine the actions of Canadian officials in relation to Canadian citizens who were detained and tortured in Syria because they were suspected of involvement in terrorism. The inquiry into Maher Arar concluded that Canadian officials had passed on inaccurate intelligence about Arar to American officials without restrictions

---

ed. James Kelly and Christopher Manfredi (Vancouver, BC, Canada: University of British Columbia Press, 2009).

[198] *Amnesty International v. Canada*, FC 336 (2008), affd. FCA 401 (2008); leave denied S.C.C.

[199] The supreme court does not give reasons for not hearing a case. For my consideration of possible reasons that the court may have had for not hearing the case, including its possible reluctance to affirm an absolute obligation on Canadian troops not to be complicit with torture in the wake of the exception in *Suresh v. Canada*, 1 S.C.R. 3 (2002), at para. 78, for deportation to torture, see Kent Roach, "'The Supreme Court at the Bar of Politics': The Afghan Detainee and Omar Khadr Cases" (2011) 28 National Journal of Constitutional Law 115.

on its subsequent use and were not sufficiently aware of his mistreatment in Syria. The commission revealed that CSIS visited Syria while Arar was detained and that the RCMP sent questions for Syrian intelligence to ask about another Canadian, Abdullah Almalki, who was also detained in an infamous prison run by Syrian military intelligence. The RCMP had also used a false confession obtained by Syrian officials about a plot to blow up Parliament in obtaining a search warrant without noting any concerns about its reliability.

The Arar Commission found that Canadian agencies had sent mixed signals about whether they wanted Arar returned to Canada.[200] The mixed signals underline some of the tensions in a whole-of-government approach to national security as CSIS, the RCMP, and the Department of Foreign Affairs all had their own interests before the prime minister of Canada broke the logjam and successfully requested that Mr. Arar be allowed to return to Canada. The commission also expressed misgivings about comments made by the Canadian foreign minister that Arar could receive a fair trial in Syria shortly before Arar's release in October 2003, especially given the possibility that Arar might be tried in a Syrian military court.[201] The commission recommended that Canada register a formal objection to both the United States and Syria about Arar's treatment. It also recommended that CSIS and the RCMP be supplied with better information about the human rights records of the countries with which they dealt in terrorism investigations and take care not to be complicit with torture and to assess the reliability of intelligence received from countries with poor human rights records.[202] In the wake of the Arar affair, Canada and the United States signed a protocol that each would consult with the other before transferring a citizen to a third country, but Canada was unable to negotiate a veto over the deportation of its citizens to third countries.[203]

A subsequent inquiry found that Canadian officials indirectly contributed to the torture of Abdullah Almalki, Ahmad Abou-Elmaati, and Muayyed Nureddin, three other Canadian citizens held abroad, by sending questions to Syrian and Egyptian officials for the Canadian detainees to answer.[204] One of those tortured in Syria has reported that one of his interrogators told him, "We were

---

[200] Commission of Inquiry into the Actions of Canadian Officials in Relation to Maher Arar, *Report of the Events Relating to Maher Arar: Analysis and Recommendations* (Ottawa: Public Works, 2006).

[201] Ibid., at 246.

[202] Ibid., chapter 9.   [203] Ibid., 2:527.

[204] *Internal Inquiry into the Actions of Canadian Officials in Relation to Abdullah Almalki, Ahmad Abou-Elmaati and Muayyed Nureddin* (Ottawa: Public Works, 2008).

the first people who faced terrorism in the 80's. We fought it with iron and fire, and everyone in the West criticized us. But now when they are faced with terrorism, they come to us for help."[205] In a supplement to that report, it was revealed that CSIS traveled to Egypt in June 2002 and that its actions indirectly contributed to Ahmad Elmaati's mistreatment and torture in Egypt. During this time period, Mr. Elmaati was handcuffed 24 hours a day, was kept in a small cell where rats and cockroaches ate his food, was hooded with a rotten blanket, and was kicked and punched during interrogations.[206] Justice Iacobucci determined that testimony by both CSIS and the RCMP that it was only the Department of Foreign Affairs's job to be concerned about the human rights of Canadians detained abroad was not satisfactory.[207] This inquiry had a more limited mandate than the Arar Commission, held more limited public hearings, and did not address the guilt or innocence of the three men. All three men are now bringing civil suits against the Canadian government. As in comparable U.K. cases alleging complicity in torture, but not similar U.S. cases, they have enjoyed some success in defeating secrecy claims by the government.[208]

These two Canadian inquiries reveal the dangers of torture, mistreatment, false confessions, and inaccurate intelligence when Canada cooperates with countries with poor human rights records. Canada, consistent with Security Council Resolution 1373, intensified the sharing of information with a variety of countries after 9/11. Nevertheless, Canadian officials did not pay enough attention to the accuracy of the information they exchanged, the use that other countries would make of that information, or the dangers of dealing with countries with poor human rights records. The Arar Commission did not recommend that Canada not deal with such countries but rather that more care be taken in such dealings. As will be discussed subsequently, the inquiries were an extraordinary exercise in accountability for secret national security activities, but they were appointed at the discretion of the government, and fundamental accountability gaps remain with respect to the review of both whole-of-government and transnational counter-terrorism activities.

---

[205] Kerry Pither, *Dark Days* (Toronto, ON, Canada: Viking, 2008), at 222.
[206] *Internal Inquiry into the Actions of Canadian Officials*, at 282–4.
[207] Ibid., supplement.
[208] *Canada v. Almalki*, FC 1106 (2010). Decisions about state secrets in civil litigation will be made in the Federal Court and not in the provincial superior court. The Ontario Court of Appeal upheld the exclusive jurisdiction of the Federal Court from constitutional challenge by stressing that the Federal Court regime is a liberalization of a regime that before 1982 was absolute in preventing disclosure or even judicial inspection of state secrets relating to national security. *Abou-Elmaati v. Canada* 2011 ONCA 95.

Omar Khadr

Canada's treatment of the one Canadian citizen detained at Guantánamo since 2002 has also been the subject of much political and legal controversy.[209] In 2005, a judge issued a temporary injunction that prevented Canadian intelligence officials from continuing to go to Guantánamo Bay to question Omar Khadr, a Canadian citizen who was captured in a battle in Afghanistan when he was 15 years old.[210] The supreme court twice held that Canadian interrogations of Khadr at Guantánamo in 2003 and 2004 violated both the Charter and international law. In 2008, the court ordered disclosure of the results of the Canadian interviews as a remedy subject to the government making a case for state secrets.[211] In 2010, the court held that the effects of the violation continued even after the disclosure but reversed a lower court order that required Canada to request that the United States repatriate Khadr to Canada as a remedy on the grounds that it interfered with the Canadian government's foreign affairs prerogatives. The government initially appeared as if it would do nothing in response to the supreme court's decision but eventually responded with a diplomatic note requesting that the United States not use evidence obtained by Canadian officials.

The United States did not provide a favorable response to the diplomatic note, and Khadr's lawyers commenced a third round of Canadian litigation on his behalf. They secured a ruling that Khadr still had not received an effective remedy. The trial judge also indicated that courts could order Canada to request Khadr's repatriation if that was the only way he could receive an effective remedy.[212] This went beyond the reluctance of U.K. courts to order the government to make diplomatic representations on behalf of their Guantánamo detainees.[213] The Canadian government, like the Howard government in Australia, remained firmly opposed to asking the United States for repatriation of its citizen. It promptly obtained a stay of the lower court judgment, with the appellate judge expressing skepticism that a court could order Canada to request Khadr's repatriation in light of the supreme court's 2010 decision that had overturned such an order as insufficiently respectful of executive prerogatives over the conduct of foreign affairs.[214] The scope of judicial remedial powers with respect to Canada's diplomatic representations about Guantánamo detainees remains unclear and the appeal may be declared moot in light of Khadr's subsequent guilty plea before an American military commission. Faced with cases arising from the detention of their citizens

[209] Michelle Shephard, *Guantanamo's Child* (Toronto, ON, Canada: John Wiley, 2008).
[210] *Khadr v. Canada*, FC 1076 (2005). [211] *Khadr v. Canada*, 2 S.C.R. 125 (2008).
[212] *Khadr v. Canada*, FC 715 (2010). [213] See Chapter 6.
[214] *Khadr v. Canada*, FCA 199 (2010).

in Guantánamo, courts in Canada, the United Kingdom, and Australia all refused to declare diplomatic representations to be nonjusticiable, whereas in the United States, they would likely be seen as political questions assigned to the unreviewable power of the executive. At the same time, the Canadian courts, like the British and Australian courts, hesitated to order the government to make diplomatic representations in an attempt to get their citizens released from Guantánamo, even though the transnational nature of terrorism investigations may require governments to more frequently intervene with other governments to protect their own nationals.

Omar Khadr pled guilty to five offenses, murder, attempted murder, conspiracy, spying, and material support of terrorism, under the U.S. Military Commissions Act in October 2010.[215] As discussed in Chapter 4, his guilty plea was influenced by a prior ruling by a military judge that threats made to Khadr while he was in Bagram that he would be raped in an American prison did not affect the voluntariness and reliability of his confessions. Khadr's guilty plea was also influenced by the U.S. decision to ask Canada to support Khadr's transfer back to Canada, where he could seek parole. Canada replied that given the U.S. request, it would look favorably on Khadr's transfer request.[216] The Canadian government was only willing to accept Khadr back when the Americans asked Canada to do so. The Canadian government's reluctance in this matter reflects widespread public resentment about Khadr's self-professed al Qaeda family[217] and an unwillingness to expend diplomatic capital with the U.S. on sensitive security matters by requesting Khadr's repatriation. Khadr's plea agreement attempts to prevent him from bringing litigation in any court in the world relating to his detention and the agreement, but it remains to be seen whether Khadr will attempt to challenge his sentence on his return to Canada and/or will be released on parole.

---

[215] "Pre Trial Agreement," October 13, 2010, at http://www.defense.gov/news/Khadr%20Con
vening%20Authority%20Pretrial%20Agreement%20AE%20341%2013%20Oct%202010%
20(redacted).pdf.

[216] "Exchange of Diplomatic Notes between US and Canada," October 23, 2010, at http://
www.defense.gov/news/Khadr%20Convening%20Authority%20Diplomatic%20Papers%
20AE%20342%2013%20Oct%202010%20(redacted).pdf.

[217] Omar Khadr's father was an associate of Osama bin Laden, and Canada's prime minister helped
secure his release from Pakistan in 1996, where he was detained on terrorism suspicions. This
led to a so-called Khadr effect, whereby Canadian politicians were reluctant to intervene with
respect to other Canadians suspected of terrorism in other lands. The father was killed fighting
in Afghanistan in 2001. See Stewart Bell, *Cold Terror* (Toronto, ON, Canada: John Wiley,
2004), chapter 6. Khadr's brothers have also been suspected of involvement in terrorism but
have won some legal victories in Canada. One brother had a decision to deny a Canadian
passport quashed, but the passport was subsequently denied after authorizing regulations were
enacted. *Khadr v. Canada*, FC 727 (2006); Forcese, *National Security Law*, at 517–18.

The Supreme Court of Canada was quite cautious in opining on Guantánamo in Omar Khadr's case and relied on a finding of the U.S. Supreme Court in *Hamdan*[218] for the proposition that detention at Guantánamo violated international human rights in 2003 and 2004 when Canadian officials interviewed Khadr at the military camp. One effect of the increased transnational linkages in terrorism investigations is that domestic courts more frequently have to evaluate the counter-terrorism efforts of other states and other legal orders. For example, in 2010, a Canadian judge stayed an American attempt to extradite one of Omar Khadr's brothers to face material support of terrorism charges in the United States. The judge based this ruling on both American and Pakistani misconduct in capturing and detaining Abdullah Khadr in Pakistan.[219] In the Abdelrazik case previously examined, Canadian courts were asked indirectly to the rule on the Security Council's 1267 terrorist listing process. Transnational counter-terrorism activities require different legal orders to be reconciled. In these and other cases, Canada has recognized that its counter-terrorism activities are affected by what happens abroad.

VII. REVIEW OF NATIONAL SECURITY ACTIVITIES

The ATA as criminal law is administered by police officers throughout Canada. The McDonald Commission concluded in 1981 that the RCMP had engaged in illegalities and had trouble distinguishing radical dissent from terrorism in the wake of the 1970 October Crisis.[220] In 2006, the Arar Commission found that RCMP officers without adequate national security training had exchanged inaccurate information about Maher Arar with the Americans in a manner that likely played a role in his rendition by the United States to Syria and his subsequent torture. It also found that the RCMP had used information obtained from Syria to obtain a search warrant without noting any concerns that the information may have been obtained through torture.[221] The Arar Commission recommended that the body that hears complaints against the RCMP be given broad powers to audit national security investigations and examine secret information.[222] It also recommended that the mandate of the SIRC, which has full access to secret information held by CSIS, be expanded

---

[218] 458 U.S. 557 (2006).

[219] *USA v. Khadr*, ONSC 4338 (2010), aff. ONCA 358 (2011).

[220] Commission of Inquiry Concerning Certain Activities of the Royal Canadian Mounted Police, *Second and Third Reports* (Ottawa: Queens Printer, 1981).

[221] Commission of Inquiry into the Actions of Canadian Officials in Relation to Maher Arar, *Report of the Events Relating to Maher Arar*.

[222] Commission of Inquiry into the Activities of Canadian Officials in Relation to Maher Arar, *A New Review Mechanism for the RCMP's National Security Activities* (Ottawa: Public Works, 2006).

to cover the national security activities of the Canada Border Services Agency, Citizenship and Immigration Canada, Transport Canada, the Financial Transactions and Reports Analysis Centre, and the Department of Foreign Affairs. Finally review bodies should have the ability to share information and conduct coordinated investigations in order to match increased co-ordination among agencies in counter-terrorism investigations. These recommendations were based on the principle that review activities should mirror the increasing intensity and coordination of the government's national security activities.[223] The focus of the Arar Commission's recommendations was on review of the propriety of national security activities as opposed to their efficacy.[224]

The Canadian government did not respond to these recommendations until it introduced a bill in June 2010 that unfortunately allows the RCMP to continue to deny its review body access to privileged information. In cases of dispute, the bill contemplates a complex process whereby a retired judge appointed by the minister will provide a confidential report on disputes about access to secret intelligence that arise between the commissioner of the RCMP and the head of the review body. The retired judge does not have the power to decide the question of access to secret intelligence, let alone what material may be made public, and there is a possibility of litigation on both matters.[225] The bill is in direct contradiction to the Arar Commission's warning that disputes between reviewers and the reviewed about access to secret information can defeat a review system. In addition, the bill is silent on the expansion of SIRC's mandate to include other agencies with important national security powers and the absence of any dedicated review of the national security activities of border, immigration, transport, and foreign affairs officials.

Although the Canadian government has taken a whole-of-government approach to national security, the review mechanisms to determine the propriety of the government's coordinated and transnational national security activities have not kept pace with those activities. Unlike in Australia, there has been little interest in appointing a security-cleared independent reviewer of antiterrorism laws and activities[226] or of expanding the jurisdiction of existing watchdogs to allow them to review whole-of-government approaches to terrorism. As

[223] Kent Roach, "Review and Oversight of National Security Activities" (2007) 29 Cardozo Law Review 53.

[224] For criticisms of the focus of review on propriety as too narrow, see Reg Whitaker and Stuart Farson, "Accountability in and for National Security" (2009) 15(9) Institute for Research on Public Policy Choices 1, at 35, 38.

[225] Ensuring the Effective Review of RCMP Civilian Complaints Act, Bill C-38, 40th Parliament, 3rd Session, First Reading, June 14, 2010.

[226] Craig Forcese, "Fixing the Deficiencies in Parliamentary Review of Anti-Terrorism Law" (2008) 14(6) Institute for Research on Public Policy Choices 1, at 14–15.

discussed in Chapter 6, the jurisdiction of the Australian inspector general has recently been expanded to allow investigation of all intelligence activities within government.[227]

Canada also lags behind other democracies in terms of legislative review. Various parliamentary committees examine aspects of national security policies but are hampered by not having access to secret information. As discussed earlier, parliamentary hearings into possible transfer by Canadian forces of Afghan detainees to torture have been bogged down in disputes over access to classified information. In 2005, a bill was introduced to allow a committee of parliamentarians to have access to classified information, but this committee would not have had parliamentary privileges.[228] This bill was not enacted before the 2006 election and has not been revived by the new Conservative government. Canada's unwillingness to give its legislators access to secret material can be related to Canada's anxiety as a net importer of intelligence about leaking the secrets of others, but can be contrasted with the ability of legislators in the United Kingdom, Australia, and the United States to have access to secret information.[229]

Other problems with parliamentary review in Canada are the lack of research support for the committees, their changing membership, their need to work quickly to comply with various timetables, and the fact that committees may make conflicting recommendations on some matters. Unlike in the UK, there is no dedicated committee that examines human rights. There is also some evidence that Canada's unelected upper house, like the House of Lords in the United Kingdom, has been more responsive than the Commons to concerns raised by Muslim minorities.[230]

The Air India inquiry dealt with some of the difficulties of a whole-of-government approach to national security after finding that turf wars between various agencies hindered cooperation both before and after the 1985 bombing. The inquiry was particularly critical about the discretion CSIS has to decide whether to disclose intelligence to the RCMP. It recommended that in cases where CSIS did not disclose relevant information to the RCMP that it should have to disclose the information to the prime minister's national security advisor, who could then decide, from a whole-of-government perspective,

---

[227] See Chapter 6.   [228] Forcese, *National Security Law*, at 110–12.

[229] Interim Report of the Special Senate Committee on Anti-Terrorism *Security, Freedom and the Complex Terrorist Threat: Positive Steps Ahead* March, 2011 at 42–46 recommending that a joint committee of Parliament have access to all secret material except Cabinet confidences in order to provide Parliamentary oversight of national security activities.

[230] Kent Roach, "The Role and Capacities of Courts and Legislatures in Reviewing Canada's Anti-Terrorism Laws" (2008) 24 Windsor Review of Legal and Social Issues 5.

whether it was in the public interest to risk subsequent public disclosure of the intelligence by disclosing it to the police. It also stressed that the national security advisor should provide oversight of the effectiveness of national security activities and resolve disputes between the agencies. These recommendations for enhanced review appear to have been rejected by the government because the government's 2010 response to the Air India recommendations did not include any enhancement of the national security advisor's role.[231] A subsequent Senate Committee report, however, has called on the government to enact legislation to expand the national security advisor's role as recommended by the Air India commission.[232]

The Canadian government has now rejected both the Arar and Air India commissions' recommendations for enhanced review of government's intensified whole-of-government antiterrorism activities. The Arar Commission had stressed the need for propriety-based review, whereas the Air India Commission stressed the need for efficiency- and effectiveness-based review. The commissions were, however, united in their belief that a whole-of-government and increasingly transnational approach was required to deal with the challenges of international terrorism. The government has also not revisited the idea of giving a committee of parliamentarians access to secret information. Canada continues to lag well behind the United States, the United Kingdom, and Australia in its review of the propriety and especially the efficacy of national security activities. The important issue of review of both the effectiveness and the propriety of antiterrorism activities will be revisited in Chapter 8.

All three post-9/11 inquiries into national security matters reported that their work was made more difficult by the overclaiming of secrecy by the Canadian government. The Arar Commission engaged in largely successful litigation against the government over the release of some disputed parts of its reports.[233] It documented how the government, at first, claimed secrecy with respect to the perhaps two most damning events eventually revealed by the inquiry: the inaccurate reference to Maher Arar and his wife as Islamic extremists associated with al Qaeda and the RCMP's sending of questions to Syrian military intelligence to ask Abdullah Almalki, another Canadian held

[231] Commission of Inquiry into the Investigation of the Bombing of Air India Flight 182, *Air India Flight 182*, vol. 3; "Air India Action Plan," at http://www.publicsafety.gc.ca/prg/ns/ai182/index-eng.aspx.

[232] Interim Report of the Special Senate Committee on Anti-Terrorism *Security, Freedom and the Complex Terrorist Threat: Positive Steps Ahead* March, 2011 at 39–41.

[233] *Canada v. Commission of Inquiry*, FC 766 (2007).

and tortured in Syria.[234] Justice O'Connor also documented how unknown security officials selectively leaked information about Mr. Arar in an unfair attempt to justify their actions and to smear his reputation. He warned that overclaiming of secrecy will promote "public suspicion and cynicism about legitimate claims by the Government of national security confidentiality."[235]

Despite these findings, overclaiming continued in the two subsequent inquiries as well as in relation to some immigration and criminal law proceedings. The inquiries were unpopular among the security agencies. A former high CSIS official whose conduct was examined by all three inquiries criticized them as a "legal jihad," and a former RCMP official who headed an integrated national security enforcement team in Toronto called the Arar commission "judicial terrorism."[236] Notwithstanding these disrespectful but telling remarks, the Canadian inquiries demonstrate the need for new institutions to ensure effective review of whole-of-government approaches to terrorism to help prevent systemic failures, such as those that resulted in the 1985 Air India bombings, or abuses such as Canada's complicity in the torture of four of its citizens in Syria and Egypt.

VIII. NATIONAL SECURITY POLICIES

The first use of the human security concept in counter-terrorism policy came when the Liberal government and, in particular, Irwin Cotler defended the ATA as legislation designed to respect the rights of Canadians to human security.[237] This use of human security was designed to stave off civil libertarian criticisms of the act and to argue that the security of innocent civilians from lethal acts of terrorism should itself be seen as a human right. The deployment of the human security concept to legitimate the ATA was only partially successful. As discussed earlier, a broad coalition of civil society groups continued to oppose the ATA on the basis that it gave the state excessive power.

The human security concept was subsequently used by the government in 2004 to justify a subtle shift in direction in its domestic security policy from the criminal law reforms of the ATA to a broader approach that sought to limit harms to all Canadians from a broad range of risks, including floods and pandemics as well as terrorism. This all-risks approach was adopted in a national security policy released in April 2004 that included commitments to better emergency preparedness, better public health, better transport security,

---

[234] Commission of Inquiry into the Actions of Canadian Officials in Relation to Maher Arar, *Report of the Events Relating to Maher Arar*, at 303.

[235] Ibid., at 302.   [236] Pither, *Dark Days*, at 400.

[237] Cotler, "Thinking outside the Box."

and better peacekeeping as well as the more traditional terrorism-specific proposals relating to better intelligence and better border security.[238] This national security policy can be contrasted with post-9/11 U.S. policies that focused on terrorism. Nevertheless, the U.S. policies have, subsequent to Hurricane Katrina, evolved in a more all-risks direction. Although introduced by a Liberal government, Canada's all-risks national security policy has been retained by the Conservative government and supplemented by measures such as a modernized Quarantine Act[239] and a new Emergency Management Act[240] giving the minister of public safety a lead role in coordinating responses to emergencies. The 2011 border declaration between Canada and the United States also contemplates a common all-risk approach to security by recognizing common interests not only in preventing terrorism, but also in responding to a wide range of natural and man-made emergencies and protecting "health security."[241]

Another component of the all-risks approach was the creation of a new Ministry of Public Safety in late 2003. The minister has responsibility for a new Canada Border Services Agency and the Office of Critical Infrastructure and Emergency Preparedness. The new ministry was designed in part to allow for better integration with the new U.S. Department of Homeland Security. It was created in response not only to 9/11 but also to a SARS crisis that killed 52 people in Toronto in 2003 as well as concerns about the contamination of food and water and electricity blackouts. The Public Safety Ministry has the potential to develop a more comprehensive and rational approach to the various risks that Canadians face to their well-being, but it also faces challenges because of the federal division of powers which assigns much emergency response to provincial and local governments.

Although it was originally introduced in 2001, just after the enactment of the ATA, Canada did not enact the Public Safety Act[242] until 2004. The delay was caused in large part because of controversy over an abandoned proposal to allow the minister of defense to declare military security zones from which the military could exclude the public.[243] Perhaps because of the experience of

---

[238] "This system is capable of responding to both intentional and unintentional threats. It is as relevant in securing Canadians against the next SARS-like outbreak as it is in addressing the risk of a terrorist attack." Canada, *Securing an Open Society*, at 10. For arguments for an all-risks national security policy, see Roach, *September 11*, chapter 3. See also Forcese, *National Security Law*, chapter 9.

[239] S.C. (2005), c.20.   [240] S.C. (2007), c.15.

[241] *Beyond the Border: A Shared Vision for Perimeter Security and Economic Competitiveness: A Declaration by the Prime Minister of Canada and the President of the United States* 4 February, 2011 available at http://www.pm.gc.ca/eng/media.asp?id=3938.

[242] S.C. (2004), c.15.   [243] Forcese, *National Security Law*, at 177–8.

martial law in October 1970 as well as forceful responses to anti-globalization protests, many Canadians resisted an increased domestic role for the military in security matters and feared that it might be used against legitimate dissent and protest.

The Public Safety Act included increased control over dangerous materials, such as explosives and toxins, and aviation security measures similar to those included in the United Kingdom's Anti-Terrorism, Crime, and Security Act, 2001. Like that law, it also facilitated the collection and sharing of information within governments and between governments.[244] Administrative and environmental controls that help secure sites and substances that can be used to commit acts of terrorism are promising antiterrorism measures that present less of a threat to due process and equality values than reliance on immigration or even criminal law.[245] It is unfortunate that defining new crimes of terrorism was a priority for the Canadian government, while administrative measures to reduce the damage that could be caused by terrorists were not. At the same time, the criminal law approach taken in the ATA, as well as the immigration law approach that was subsequently relied on, was partially encouraged by UN Security Council Resolution 1373 (2001), which called for criminalization of financing and participation in terrorism and better border controls.[246] The public safety approach responded in part to Security Council Resolution 1540 (2004) which required states to ensure that chemical, biological, and nuclear material not fall into the hands of terrorists.

As discussed in Chapter 2 in relation to Resolution 1540, an administrative and environmental approach designed to prevent terrorists from gaining access to substances such as explosives, chemical or nuclear materials, or sites vulnerable to terrorism, such as airplanes and nuclear plants, has a number of benefits. Such strategies do not rely on punishment and detention to the same extent as criminal and immigration law. They also work as a fail safe should it prove impossible to deter, incapacitate, or identify all the terrorists. Measures such as more effective screening of all passengers, baggage, and

---

[244] E.g., Part 5 of the act amends the Department of Citizenship and Immigration Act to permit the sharing of information with other governments and foreign organizations, and Part 11 allows the collection and disclosure of information for national security purposes under IRPA. Part 17 extends the government databases and agencies that can be consulted in relation to terrorist financing. These information-sharing provisions raised concerns about privacy, transparency, and review, as well as practical concerns about decision makers being swamped by too much information. Vast databases can undermine privacy while producing information about potential terrorists that may not be accurate or helpful.

[245] Canadian police monitor the sale of large quantities of fertilizer that can be used in bombs. "How a Terror Plot Turned into a 'Gardening Incident,'" *Globe and Mail*, June 10, 2010.

[246] See Chapter 2.

cargo[247] on aircraft through technology may also limit or at least equalize the damage done to liberty, privacy, and equality. Technology can be used to screen all passengers and not just those who fit into a perhaps faulty profile of a terrorist. To be sure, technology, such as the use of biometrics, could have a negative impact on privacy. When applied to large-scale populations, it will also produce a considerable number of false positives and false negatives. Terrorists can also adjust to target-hardening measures. It will not be possible to screen all passengers of mass transit, but it should be possible to provide better controls on explosives and other materials that can be used for bombs.

Some environmental measures, such as better monitoring of public health and the safety of food and water, have the important additional benefit of providing protections against disease and accidental contamination of food and water as well as terrorism. Better security for computer systems would protect them not only from a cyberterrorism attack but also from random attacks by hackers. Better emergency preparedness also serves a similar all-risks function as it better prepares society to deal with a wide range of natural and man-made disasters such as earthquakes and blackouts. The Public Safety Act[248] contained provisions that allow ministers of transport, the environment, health, and defense to take temporary measures in a wide range of emergencies, not just with respect to terrorism. The American National Research Council has concluded, in a post-9/11 report, that we should invest in strategies that will make us safer not only from terrorist attacks but from disaster, disease, and accidents.[249] Such strategies also present less of a risk, both for the targets and for society, of targeting the wrong people.

IX. CONCLUSION

Canada is an interesting case study of how a democracy can respond to terrorism. In response to 9/11, Canada did not declare a state of emergency, as it did in response to the terrorism in October 1970, but rather enacted a broad

---

[247] The Air India Commission stressed the threat to aviation security caused by cargo carried on passenger planes that is not screened. Commission of Inquiry into the Investigation of the Bombing of Air India Flight 182, *Air India Flight 182*, vol. 4.

[248] Part 1 allows emergency directions, when necessary, to deal with immediate risks to safety, security, health, and the environment in relation to aeronautics, Part 3 in relation to environmental protection, Part 6 in relation to health, Part 9 in relation to food and drugs, Part 10 in relation to hazardous products, Part 15 in relation to navigable waters, Part 18 in relation to pest control products, Part 20 in relation to quarantines, Part 21 in relation to radiation-emitting devices, and Part 22 in relation to shipping.

[249] National Research Council, *Making the Nation Safer: The Role of Science and Technology in Countering Terrorism* (Washington, DC: National Academy Press, 2002).

new ATA. This law followed Security Council Resolution 1373 in its emphasis on terrorism financing and used the U.K. Terrorism Act, 2000, as a starting point for its broad definition of terrorism. There was a fairly robust civil society debate about the effect of this permanent legislation on civil liberties and preventive arrests and investigative hearings were allowed to expire in 2007. Like the United States, Canada has not responded to Security Council 1624 (2005) with new legislation criminalizing speech associated with terrorism. Canada's caution about criminalizing extremist speech and its interests in cross-cultural dialogue on security issues may have long-term dividends with respect to both human rights and security.

Border security and immigration laws dominated the Canadian response in the immediate aftermath of 9/11. In the initial years after 9/11, Canada relied on immigration law as antiterrorism law as opposed to criminal prosecutions. The use of security certificates was both legally and politically controversial. The supreme court held that secret evidence had to be subject to some adversarial challenge and has required CSIS to retain and disclose raw intelligence used in these proceedings. Security certificates have been abandoned in some cases, and there may be difficulty deporting suspects to countries in the three remaining cases. Immigration law remains both overinclusive and underinclusive. The safe third-country agreement has led to reductions in the number of refugees Canada has accepted. Immigration law shortcuts can also not be used against those citizens who participated in recent homegrown plots and the 1985 Air India bombing.

Since 2004, more emphasis has been placed on criminal prosecutions. The convictions in the Toronto and other cases suggest that Canada is moving away from its legacy of failed prosecutions with respect to the 1985 Air India bombings and related acts of Sikh terrorist activity in Canada. The courts have also indicated that they will take a more punitive approach in sentencing terrorists that will make little allowance for rehabilitation. Like other Western democracies, Canada seems at a loss of what to do to rehabilitate terrorists other than to impose long prison terms.

Canada's foreign antiterrorism activities have been controversial and have resulted in two public inquiries that have found that Canadian officials have contributed to the torture of Canadians held abroad on suspicion of terrorism and eventually released and allowed to return to Canada. These inquiries provide important reminders of the challenges of transnational terrorism investigations involving countries with poor human rights records. They also reveal accountability gaps in reviewing whole-of-government and transnational counter-terrorism activities that cannot reliably be plugged by the discretionary appointment of public inquiries. Litigation designed to stop the possible transfer of Canada's Afghan detainees to torture failed, the government has refused to appoint a public inquiry, and Canada's legislative committees do not have ready access to the classified information concerning Canada's activities in Afghanistan.

Although Canada lags behind other democracies in its review of both the propriety and efficacy of counter-terrorism activities, it was something of a leader when in 2004 it adopted an all-risks national security policy and reorganized its Public Safety Ministry around emergency preparedness. The United States, the United Kingdom, and Australia all subsequently moved in an all-risks direction. Canada's all-risks approach to national security also has the potential to stress the common interest shared by all Canadians in responding to a wide range of threats to human security, but its implementation remains largely untested.

8   Conclusions

After examining the responses to terrorism of six countries, David Charters concluded in 1994 that countries were more likely to threaten their democratic character when responding to domestic as opposed to international terrorism.[1] As Martha Crenshaw has observed, "since the American declaration of a war on terror, however, that argument that internal terrorism is most provocative can certainly no longer be sustained."[2] As seen in Chapter 2, the globalization of terrorism has meant that the United Nations (UN), and particularly its Security Council, has assumed a much greater role in counter-terrorism policy. Although this process started before 9/11, it has accelerated greatly since that time. The Security Council has acted as a global legislator in Resolutions 1267, 1373, and 1540 and as a global executive in compiling secret lists of those associated with the Taliban and al Qaeda. It has, however, failed to provide basics for legislative combat of terrorism such as a clear definition of terrorism or processes that afford a right to fair hearings and a judicial remedy.

The focus on international terrorism has allowed some democracies to move closer toward a war as opposed to a crime model in combating terrorism. As the Guantánamo detentions reveal, however, the war model fits awkwardly when applied to terrorists as nonstate actors. The result has often been the creation of an unstable hybrid in which terrorists do not fully enjoy the rights of either soldiers or civilians and states can opportunistically alternate between both models. Such opportunism was perhaps most obvious during the Bush administration but continues under the Obama administration, by which targeted killings, extraordinary renditions, indeterminate detention without trial, and military commissions are all used to respond to terrorism, while terrorism

---

[1] David Charters, *The Deadly Sin of Terrorism: Its Effects on Democracy and Civil Liberties in Six Countries* (Westport, CT: Greenwood Press, 2004).
[2] Martha Crenshaw, introduction to *The Consequences of Counterterrorism*, ed. Martha Crenshaw (New York: Russell Sage Foundation, 2010), at 3.

is also, in some circumstances, treated as a crime subject to prosecution. The categories of war and crime have become unstable since 9/11.

There has been a good deal of convergence in counter-terrorism and these convergences constitute a strong 9/11 effect in counter-terrorism that has placed increased emphasis on the state's interests in security over individual interests in liberty. Many countries have responded to UN Security Council mandates to ensure that terrorism and terrorism financing are treated as serious crimes and that those listed as associated with al Qaeda are subject to asset freezes, to exchange intelligence among and between governments, to prevent terrorists from gaining refugee status, to prevent them from gaining access to weapons of mass destruction, and to criminalize incitement to terrorism. At the same time, the UN has failed to produce agreement on an international definition of terrorism, and most domestic definitions of terrorism are much broader than the best efforts to secure international agreement. In the absence of such guidance, many countries have looked not to the United States but to the United Kingdom for guidance. The result has often been the enactment of very broad terrorism offenses that target not only the murder and maiming of civilians but property damage and disruptions of essential services. The British influence on antiterrorism moves both forward and backward. States such as Israel, Singapore, and Sri Lanka have inheritances of British colonial emergency laws designed to detain and target speech and support for insurgents. Many other states have looked to British laws enacted throughout the 2000's as the starting point for crafting their own terrorism laws including control orders and laws against speech associated with terrorism. British transplants or migrations have been adapted to very different and often less democratic local cultures.

The 9/11 effect constitutes a fundamental shift in the respective importance given to liberty and security. In the immediate aftermath of 9/11, the Security Council and many states prioritized security efforts to prevent terrorism over liberty and respect for human rights. The United States has infamously been associated with practices such as torture, extraordinary rendition, and indeterminate military detention at Guantánamo without trial. The United States, however, was not alone as the United Kingdom derogated from the European Convention on Human Rights to impose indeterminate detention under immigration law. Australia and Canada followed similar practices, and the Canadian courts regrettably refused to rule out the possibility of deporting a terrorist suspect to face torture in a country such as Mubarak's Egypt or Syria. Examples of bad behavior by the United States coupled with the Security Council's and its Counter-Terrorism Committee's (CTC's) apparent indifference to human rights provided other countries with plenty of excuses for not reforming their own practices of torture and indeterminate military or administrative detention. Indeed, things got worse after 9/11: Egypt entrenched emergency powers and military courts, Israel expanded administrative detention and targeted killing, and Singapore revived the use of its Internal Security Act (ISA) and re-legitimized that old law as an antiterrorism law. The baselines have changed since 9/11 and in a manner that has harmed human rights without necessarily increasing security from terrorism or other threats to human security.

At the same time, the 9/11 effect has not been consistent or all negative. There has been some learning from past mistakes, and countries did not intern whole populations with the same ethnic origins or religion as the 9/11 hijackers. Both the U.S. executive and legislature, to their credit, repudiated their post-9/11 descent into torture, and Canada and the United Kingdom inquired into their own complicity with torture and refused to accept evidence obtained through torture. Torture of suspected terrorists has been widely documented and increased post-9/11 awareness and repudiation of torture may help to strengthen an absolute prohibition on torture that, though strong in law, was unfortunately never absolute in practice.[3]

Developments at the start of 2011 in Egypt suggest that the citizens of some countries that were at the forefront of often brutal attempts to repress both terrorism and Islamic movements have not been content with the balance between state security powers and liberty and democracy in their countries. Egyptians have voted by a large majority to repeal the 2007 constitutional amendments that would have sheltered terrorism laws from constitutional challenge and entrenched the President's right to transfer security cases to special courts. They also have voted to place new democratic restraints on the declaration of states of emergency. The Egyptian story is ongoing and imperfect, but it is also consistent with a post-9/11 rejection by Indonesians of a harsh draft counter-terrorism law that many feared would return to the abuses of the Suharto era. Both Egypt and Indonesia face many challenges, including those of conducting counter-terrorism in a manner consistent with the rule of law and democracy, but their experiences belie the idea that the 9/11 effect of increased security powers is a monolith or that countries with Muslim majorities can only take repressive measures against Islamic movements and terrorism. It is also striking that some of the most dramatic post-9/11 rejections of security laws come from countries such as Egypt and Indonesia that are

---

[3] Jutta Brunee and Stephen Toope, *Legitimacy and Legality in International Law* (New York: Cambridge University Press, 2010), chapter 5.

struggling to become democracies and not from the established democracies that have perhaps been too confident that they can increase state security powers without sacrificing democratic freedoms.[4] Reforms in Indonesia and Egypt may also be consistent with the convergence thesis because even after reform these countries are likely to devote much emphasis on responding to terrorism and failures to do so will affect their international standing.

One surprising development given the past judicial record in emergencies has been the role of courts. Courts have forced the United States, the United Kingdom, and Canada to reform the practices of military and administrative detention on the basis of secret evidence not disclosed to the detainee or subject to adversarial challenge. The Bush administration's attempts to create a law-free black hole at Guantánamo failed. The House of Lords's 2004 Belmarsh decision was an important statement about the discriminatory and irrational nature of relying on immigration law as antiterrorism law. To be sure, the judicial record has not been even and in Canada and the United Kingdom post-9/11 innovations such as investigative hearings and control orders have been ended by political and not judicial decisions. The American courts also did not close Guantánamo, but neither has the Obama administration. Nevertheless, the courts have emerged as more active players in counter-terrorism law and policy than many had predicted. Courts have also entered transnational debates about Guantánamo and provided a domestic pushback to the human rights and judicial deficit in the UN Security Council. Although the Security Council continues to exercise its strong Chapter VII powers to enforce measures such as sanctions against those listed as associated with al Qaeda and the Taliban, even it has been forced to pay greater respect to human rights as domestic resistance and adverse domestic judicial decisions have increased. Media exposés, judicial cases, investigations by transnational civil society groups, and public inquiries have made antiterrorism practices more transparent than they were before 9/11.

Although all countries examined in this book have experienced a 9/11 effect, there are some important divergences. The U.S. approach has frequently been an executive one as opposed to the legislative approach taken in the Parliamentary democracies examined in this book. The U.S. approach has also been exceptional in other ways. It has resisted the regulation of speech and has not attempted to restructure the domestic criminal justice system to better deal with terrorism. The American approach has also often been

---

4 Kent Roach "Anti-Terrorism and Militant Democracy: Some Western and Eastern Responses" in *Militant Democracy* ed. Andras Sajo (Amsterdam: Eleven Publishing, 2004).

based on what has been described as extra-legalism in which dubious claims of legality and lack of judicial jurisdiction have been used to support illegal practices such as torture, extraordinary rendition, detention without trial and warrantless spying. American extra-legalism uses resources within the legal system including the political questions doctrine, narrow standing rulings and a comparatively broad and blunt state secrets doctrine to shelter illegal practices from legal challenge. Large parts of American antiterrorism efforts, even under President Obama, fit into an executive- and war-based model, with targeted killings not being subject to judicial review and only being authorized by Congress's post-9/11 authorization of the use of military force. In contrast, the United Kingdom and Australia waged a legislative war against terrorism that has resulted in multiple new laws designed to give the state a great variety of legal tools that can be used to prevent terrorism. Many of these legal tools, such as control orders and questioning warrants, however, are less restrained alternatives to criminal prosecutions and others involve the regulation of expressive and associational freedoms that would not be accepted in the United States.

Neither the United States nor Canada has followed the trend toward increased regulation of speech associated with terrorism or formal regimes of preventive detention used in the United Kingdom or Australia. This raises the question of whether a more libertarian North American constitutional culture would survive dramatic increases in homegrown terrorism. In particular, one wonders what the United States would do if it were to suffer a string of terrorist bombings of the type seen in the United Kingdom in the 1970s. For all its foreign might and power, the United States is domestically weak when it comes to responding to terrorism. Although much criticized, the Patriot Act is comparatively mild, and the most drastic American domestic responses to 9/11 occurred outside its framework and through executive actions of dubious legality. Finally, it is striking that two of the countries that have pursued the harshest policies toward terrorists – Egypt and Singapore – have also explored and had some success in the rehabilitation of terrorists, an issue that Western democracies have failed to confront.

In what follows, I outline some responses to 9/11 that seem already to have failed as effective and sustainable approaches to combating terrorism. These failures include the Security Council's initial rights-free approach, the United States' approach of extra-legalism, and the reliance that many countries place on less restrained alternatives to criminal law. Having identified these failures, however, the path forward is not certain, and the next section identifies some complexities that have become clearer since 9/11, including increased acceptance of older and more repressive counter-terrorism laws and practices refined in countries with extensive experience in terrorism and poor human rights records, transnational migration of both terrorism laws and investigations, and an increased focus on using intelligence to prevent terrorism. The last part of this chapter identifies a range of challenges going forward. The preventive turn raises the question of whether criminal law, with its traditional focus on public trials about guilt and innocence concerning specific acts and intent, can survive. The relation between secret intelligence and public evidence has changed but continues to present challenges in many countries. Another challenge is whether Western democracies will be able to respond to the related challenges of rehabilitating terrorists and maintaining community relations with their Muslim minorities. The challenges of sustainable counter-terrorism policies are examined, including the need to close accountability gaps that have emerged for whole-of-government and transnational counter-terrorism efforts. I will argue that better review of both the efficacy and propriety of counter-terrorism is required and that the real threats of terrorism can be placed in better perspective by adopting all risk security policies that include the many different threats to human security.

I. SOME POST-9/11 MISTAKES

Looking back on the few clear failures in global responses to 9/11 can help us better understand the criteria for success. A common theme in the failures identified in this chapter is that they all harm human rights while not having clear success in preventing terrorism.[5] It is often easier to be confident that various measures have infringed on human rights than to know whether they have been effective in preventing terrorism. The often secret nature of national security means that many successes in preventing terrorism remain secret.[6] Nevertheless, educated estimates can and must be made about the efficacy of counter-terrorism measures if they are to remain a subject of legal and political debate. As citizens, we cannot transfer our self-governance to security professionals. Judges who evaluate the proportionality of counter-terrorism measures also must concern themselves with the efficacy of impugned measures as well as the effectiveness of alternative measures that may infringe on human rights to a lesser extent. Although we may always know less about the successes than the failures of counter-terrorism, we must be concerned with both the efficacy and propriety of what is done in our name to prevent terrorism.

---

[5] Kent Roach, "Must We Trade Rights for Security?" (2006) 27 Cardozo Law Review 2151.
[6] Laura Donohue, *The Costs of Counter-Terrorism* (New York: Cambridge University Press, 2008), at 3.

The Failure of the United Nations

If anything should have revealed to the world the essence of unacceptable terrorism, it was 9/11. Unfortunately, a decade later, we seem no closer to reaching agreement on a definition of terrorism that cannot be justified in any circumstances. In the wake of 9/11 and the widespread solidarity with its many victims, it was possible to imagine that the member states of the UN would finally agree on a definition of terrorism that would focus on the murder and maiming of people not engaged in armed conflict to coerce populations and governments and that it would be widely accepted that no motive or cause could justify such actions. Agreement on such a definition could have led to a new comprehensive convention on terrorism and inclusion of terrorism within the jurisdiction of the International Criminal Court. The Security Council in Resolution 1373 successfully promoted the 1999 International Convention on Terrorism Financing, but unfortunately failed to promote a promising general definition of terrorism in that convention that defined terrorism as the intentional causing of death or serious bodily injury to those not taking an active part in hostilities in order to intimidate a population or compel a government to act. This definition would have covered 9/11 including the attack on the Pentagon and it was consistent with the definitions of terrorism used by the United States in the Patriot Act. Even though the United States drafted Resolution 1373, the Security Council provided no guidance on how member states should define terrorism until 2004 when for many states it was too late because they had already enacted broad new terrorism law to respond to Security Council mandates and reporting deadlines.[7] International agreement on a definition of terrorism would, of course, not have ended terrorism or even abuses in the name of counter-terrorism. Nevertheless, it would have provided a much sounder framework for transnational counter-terrorism.

Although the Security Council engaged in global legislation after 9/11, it has largely failed to provide a principled foundation for global counter-terrorism. It avoided the controversial issue of the definition of terrorism, even though there was a sound general definition of terrorism in the 1999 Financing Convention that the Security Council otherwise promoted. The General Assembly has still not reached agreement on terrorism – and may never do so – unless it can offload contentious issues of state terrorism and freedom fighting to the evolving laws of war. Many countries inspired by the United Kingdom's Terrorism Act, 2000, enacted new terrorism laws featuring broad definitions of terrorism. Although these laws recognize the vulnerabilities of modern societies, they

---

[7] Security Council Resolution 1566 (2004); Ben Saul *Defining Terrorism in International Law* (Oxford: Oxford University Press, 2006) at 248.

also increase the risk that terrorism investigations and laws could be turned against dissenters, especially in regimes that do not have democratic traditions. These concerns have only increased when, in response to the strong desires of Prime Minister Blair in the wake of the London bombings, the Security Council called on all states to ensure that the incitement of terrorism was a serious crime without attempting to define either term. The Security Council's new focus on speech was another untested trend in counter-terrorism, one that might be even more dangerous than its previous emphasis on the financing of terrorism.[8]

The Security Council stubbornly focused on terrorism financing, despite the failure of the 1267 listing process to prevent al Qaeda from committing the 9/11 attacks, likely the most expensive act of terrorism in history. Under the influence of the Financial Action Task Force (FATF), terrorism financing has often been unhelpfully merged with money laundering, despite that terrorism can be committed with small amounts of clean money. The low costs of subsequent acts of terrorism in Bali, Madrid, London, Mumbai, and elsewhere underline the folly of the UN's continued investment in attempts to stop terrorism by focusing on its finances. As seen in Chapter 3, Egypt, Syria and Indonesia at the urgings of FATF and the CTC dutifully enacted off the shelf money laundering/terrorism financing laws after 9/11 that had little regard for and likely little effect on local circumstances. Counter-terrorism efforts at the Security Council and in FATF have been dominated by developed countries and "some governments in the global South . . . consider the current UN emphasis on counter-terrorism a U.S., or Western imposition that diverts attention from other international needs, such as overcoming poverty or resolving conflict in Africa."[9] These observations are particularly true of the emphasis on terrorism financing documented in Chapter 2 because terrorism financing laws often presume sophisticated banking systems and are not easily applied to less formal money transfer systems. The listing of terrorists by the 1267 committee and its many domestic analogues have not caught up and probably never can with the evolution of al Qaeda from a central organizing group to one also that inspires local and self-financed groups.[10]

---

[8] Kent Roach, "Sources and Trends in Post 9/11 Anti-Terrorism Laws," in *Security and Human Rights*, ed. Benjamin Goold and Liora Lazarus (Oxford: Hart, 2007).

[9] David Cortright et al "Global Cooperation Against Terrorism: Evaluating the United Nations Counter-Terrorism Committee" in *Uniting Against Terrorism* eds. David Cortright and George Lopez (Cambridge: MA: MIT Press, 2007) at 28.

[10] Richard Barrett, the head of the 1267 monitoring group, has recognized that with the evolution of al Qaeda "financing may become decreasingly relevant to efforts to contain the threat." Richard Barrett "Time to Reexamine Regulation Designed to Counter the Financing of Terrorism" (2009) 41 Case Western Reserve Journal of International Law 7 at 17.

Terrorism financing laws are not only often ineffective in preventing acts of terrorism but they have human rights costs. Because terrorism financing laws are enforced by financial institutions, they depend on lists of terrorists. Thus proscription not only of terrorist groups but of individuals associated with them is an integral feature of international and domestic terrorism financing regimes. In recent years, there has been domestic pushback against the unfairness of listing on the basis of secret intelligence and without judicial review, but the Security Council remains unprepared either to provide those listed with a judicial remedy within the UN system or to reevaluate the costs and benefits of the listing process and related terrorism financing regulations. Cases such as *Kadi*[11] on terrorist listing on the basis of secret evidence and *al-Jedda*[12] on military internment without judicial review in Iraq threaten to result in a conflict between domestic and supra-national constitutional norms and Security Council powers. The competing norms and legal regimes implicated in these cases might have been more easily reconciled had the Security Council been more attentive to human rights in its counter-terrorism work.

Resolution 1373 also failed in its promotion of the use of immigration law as antiterrorism law. In addition to its human rights costs and frequent use of secret evidence, the use of immigration law as antiterrorism law is the antithesis of a global strategy against terrorism and its traditional principle of prosecute or extradite. Immigration law attempts to deflect and deport terrorists to weaker and failed states, where they may be able to thrive and strike again. Although it is perhaps understandable why nations, especially the United States, would rely on immigration law in the aftermath of 9/11, it is difficult to understand why the UN would do so. The Security Council's admonition to states to deny asylum to terrorists while respecting human rights simply revealed the intractable complexity of al Qaeda terrorism. The United Kingdom first opted for indeterminate detention without trial but is now attempting to deport suspected terrorists to Algeria and Jordan on risky assurances that they will not be tortured. The United States and Canada either rendered or contemplated rendering terrorist suspects to Egypt and Syria, where they would be tortured.

---

[11] *Kadi and Al Barakaat International Foundation v. Council of the EU and Commission of the EC* Joined Cases C-402/05 P and C-415/05 P, *Yassin Abdullah Kadi and Al Barakaat International Foundation v. Council of the EU and Commission of the EC* (ECJ Judgment), September 3, 2008.; *Kadi v. European Commission (Judgment of the General Court, Seventh Chamber)*, September 30, 2010; http://eur-lex.europa.eu/LexUriServ/LexUriServ.do?uri= CELEX:62009A0085:EN:HTML. These cases are discussed in Chapter 2 of this book.

[12] *R (Al Jedda) v. Secretary of State*, UKHL 58 (2007). This case is discussed in Chapter 5 of this book.

The use of immigration law as antiterrorism law produced no satisfactory solutions. It harmed human rights while exporting terrorism.

Some of the Security Council's post-9/11 work was more sensible that its focus on terrorism financing, immigration, and speech associated with terrorism. It was understandable why the council encouraged states to exchange intelligence. At the same time, not enough attention was paid to the reliability of the intelligence or the danger that intelligence would lean in the direction of falsely identifying security risks as opposed to not providing warnings. The UN uses secret intelligence in its 1267 listing regime, and it has encouraged the exchange of intelligence between states, but it has not confronted the challenges of the increased post-9/11 emphasis on intelligence to human rights or the rule of law based on public evidence that can be seen and challenged.[13]

The Security Council's emphasis in Resolution 1540 on ensuring that terrorists do not gain access to weapons of mass destruction is sensible. It recognizes that administrative measures designed to regulate substances and sites that can be used for terrorism are an important fail-safe strategy that does not depend on the ability to identify all potential terrorists. In addition, such environmental controls can be effective, while providing a minimal threat to human rights and imposing equal inconveniences on us all.[14] Unfortunately, by the time the Security Council issued Resolution 1540 in 2004, states were starting to rebel at the Security Council's new role as a global counter-terrorism legislator. In addition, the issue of weapons of mass destruction reminded many of false intelligence claims about the presence of such weapons in Iraq. Resolution 1540 also ducked the question of the proliferation of weapons of mass destruction by states, some of whom may sponsor or facilitate terrorism. The Security Council, like domestic legislators, has been attracted to "governing through crime."[15] The focus has been on the evil of the crime of terrorism and not on the state's role with respect to conditions conducive to terrorism.

Although the Security Council bears the bulk of the blame for the UN's failure to guide global responses to 9/11 in a more constructive manner, other parts of the UN are also implicated. The rights-protection bodies of the UN have been active, but their critiques have been fragmented among the work of numerous bodies and rapporteurs. They have also failed to convince the Security Council and many nation-states that human rights are not a soft

---

[13] Simon Chesterman, *One Nation under Surveillance* (Oxford: Oxford University Press, 2011).

[14] National Research Council, *Making the Nation Safer: The Role of Science and Technology in Countering Terrorism* (Washington, DC: National Academy Press, 2002); Kent Roach, *September 11: Consequences for Canada* (Montreal, QC, Canada: McGill Queens Press, 2003), chapter 7.

[15] Jonathan Simon, *Governing through Crime* (Oxford: Oxford University Press, 2007).

luxury that can be abandoned in times of perceived emergency but rather a hard-headed factor that can accommodate various threat levels and discipline both the propriety and effectiveness of the state's antiterrorism efforts.

The General Assembly was largely missing in action until it produced a sound and balanced global strategy against terrorism in 2006. This strategy, with its concerns about human rights, state capacity, causes of terrorism, and measures to prevent terrorism, should now provide an organizing framework for a more coordinated and principled UN approach to terrorism. Unfortunately, much damage has already been done. The Security Council, like the United States, must struggle to make up for its initial post-9/11 neglect of human rights. Its committees and especially the CTC must become more transparent in its work to respond to its initial post-9/11 neglect of human rights. The UN, like many countries, also faces challenges in coordinating a whole-of-government approach to terrorism that will combine the Security Council's focus on security with the emphasis placed on human rights and state capacities in other parts of the UN. There is a need for the UN to better evaluate both the effectiveness and the propriety of its own counter-terrorism work.

The Failure of American Extra-Legalism

In the wake of 9/11, the United States infamously explored the "dark side" through various extralegal measures such as increases in extraordinary renditions; attempts to preclude all judicial review of the detention of suspected terrorists at Guantánamo; waterboarding and other forms of torture and humiliation, and electronic surveillance authorized by presidential order but not by legislation. The Patriot Act was comparatively mild, but the post-9/11 pretextual immigration detentions and abuse of material witness warrants were not. All these extralegal measures have, however, failed to produce a sustainable platform for principled counter-terrorism. In subsequent years, secret programs came to light; some, such as torture programs, were repudiated, whereas others, such as increased electronic surveillance and the use of military commissions, were ratified and regulated by the legislature. Attempts by affected individuals to hold the state accountable for extralegal practices have largely been thwarted by the United States' uniquely expansive state-secrets doctrine. Part of the logic of the extralegal approach is that the threat of sanctions will restrain officials,[16] but this will not work if the actions remain secret or if there is no real threat of sanctions.

---

[16] Oren Gross, "Chaos and Rules" (2003) 112 Yale Law Journal 1011.

The American approach was not crudely extralegal. Befitting its status as a nation with a developed sense of legalism, many of its extralegal measures were supported by elaborate claims of legality, most notably the infamous torture memos which purported to render torture legal and have provided a shield from accountability for those who wrote them and those who acted upon them. Nevertheless the world has not been particularly impressed with American extra-legalism that allowed the United States even during the Bush administration to claim that it respected the right against torture and acted legally. The legal resources of American extra-legalism-restrictive standing rulings, political questions doctrine, broad states secret doctrine, case- by- case adjudication that eventually holds that habeas corpus is available to detainees held by the United States at Guantánamo but not Bagram airbase, are increasingly unpersuasive to those not schooled in the intricacies of American law but who take the basic concepts of legality and constitutionalism seriously.[17] The United States has unfortunately gained a global reputation as a country that cynically bends and breaks the rules when it is in its interests to do so even though much of the world expects much more from it.[18]

The reliance on extralegal shortcuts has also contributed to a process in which the United States lags behind other democracies in providing domestic legal tools and restraints with which to counter terrorism.[19] The extralegal approach harmed rights but has also left the United States unprepared to deal firmly but legally with terrorism. The United States' reliance on extralegal, executive, and war measures leaves it strangely powerless to cope with a series of successful homegrown terrorist attacks. The United States can vigorously conduct international wars against terrorists, but it may not have the tools for a legislative war at home. The necessary domestic tools include both powers

[17] See for example Aharon Barak "Foreword: The Role of a Supreme Court in a Democracy" (2002) 116 Harvard Law Revew 16 for a critique of American avoidance of adjudication of many national security issues.

[18] Eric Posner and Adrian Vermeule, in their critique of extralegal approaches, rightly stress that the public will understandably focus on outcomes and not on the legal rules that were violated. Posner and Vermeule, *Terror in the Balance* (Oxford: Oxford University Press, 2007), chapter 5. At the same time, they also argue that coercive interrogation is not likely to harm the United States' international reputation because it "increasingly has a reputation as a conservative, religious, punitive, and even militaristic country." Ibid., at 206. In contrast, the United Nations' special rapporteur on protecting human rights while countering terrorism has argued that the U.S. leadership in counter-terrorism post-9/11 "carries with it a special responsibility to also take leadership in the protection of human rights while countering terrorism. The example of the US will have its followers, in good and in bad." U.S. Country Report, A/HRC/6.17/Add. 3, at para. 3.

[19] Benjamin Wittes, ed., *Legislating the War on Terror* (Washington, DC: Brookings Institution Press, 2009).

to deal with terrorism and restraints that will inspire public confidence in the state's response.

The attempt first by the Bush administration, and later by Congress, to create a law- and habeas-free black hole at Guantánamo failed. At the same time, the United States' approach to detention without trial seems ad hoc and even amateur compared to the more developed regimes of administrative detention used in Israel or Singapore. In another demonstration of how propriety and efficacy are often intertwined, many innocent people were detained at Guantánamo, but the same procedural improvisation that contributed to their detention also led to the release of people who have subsequently engaged in terrorism. This is not to say that administrative detention on the basis of secret evidence and rehabilitation based on the Singapore model could or should be accepted in the United States but rather that the American approach even when augmented by habeas corpus review seems chaotic and incoherent compared to countries that waged an aggressive legislative war against terror. As suggested in Chapter 4, the comparative mildness of the often criticized Patriot Act may have actually contributed to extralegal measures such as warrantless surveillance and the use of material witness warrants as a form of preventive detention. Although the United States abandoned some of its initial extralegal practices, such as torture, and now legislatively regulates some of them, concerns still remain under the Obama administration about the use of extraordinary renditions and targeted killing. Without effective legislative or judicial review, these practices may result in conduct that is both improper and not effective in combating terrorism. Indeed, the possibility that some extralegal American practices have been counter-productive in terms of preventing terrorism cannot be discounted.

The Failure of Less Restrained Alternatives to Criminal Law

In the wake of the horrors of 9/11, many countries seemed to lose faith in the ability of criminal law to prevent and punish terrorism. Many leaders from Australia to Singapore dangerously dismissed criminal law as something that could only apply after a bomb exploded. Such misinformed comments made criminal law look manifestly inadequate in the wake of what the suicide terrorists did on 9/11. The United States attempted, at Guantánamo, to create a new system that does not follow the traditional laws of either crime or war. The result, however, has not been satisfying as many detainees have been released, habeas litigation drags on, and few convictions and even fewer trials have been completed under a Military Commissions Act that blurs the established laws of war and crime. Although it has increasingly bipartisan support, the American model of military detention is a fundamental mismatch when it comes to terrorists. U.S. withdrawal from Iraq and Afghanistan will not result in release of suspected terrorists. The War on Terror, like terrorism, will last forever. The decision by both Congress and subsequently the Obama administration to abandon criminal prosecutions against Khalid Sheikh Mohammed and other alleged 9/11 conspirators in favor of military commission trials at Guantánamo will result in less rights for the accused. It also has the potential to hand al Qaeda a propaganda victory if the accused are seen by some as martyrs to an unfair system that goes beyond the laws of war and that the United States would not use against its own citizens.

It was not only the United States that attempted to avoid criminal law with its demands for proof of guilt beyond a reasonable doubt on the basis of public evidence. The United Kingdom derogated from the European Convention to impose indeterminate administrative detention on noncitizen terrorist suspects who could not be deported because of torture concerns. This was declared to be a disproportionate, discriminatory, and irrational response to a terrorist threat that was not limited to noncitizens. Control orders were enacted as an alternative, but they, too, have been controversial and successfully challenged in court and soon will be repealed. A similar story can be told about Canada's post-9/11 reliance on immigration law. Courts have, to their credit, reacted negatively to detention without trial and the use of secret evidence so that the differences between alternatives to criminal law and use of criminal law have diminished.

Immigration detention, like military detention, is a fundamental mismatch for terrorism. The ultimate remedy of immigration law – deportation – will only export terrorism. Prolonged administrative detention will incapacitate suspected terrorists but will not justly punish or denounce them. It will also give intelligence agencies an excuse not to reform their practices so that they can satisfy more demanding evidentiary standards. Intelligence agencies will protest that criminal law will require them to disclose all their sources and methods, but this radically discounts the ability of criminal trial judges to protect unused intelligence from disclosure, while also being vigilant in ensuring that criminal trials are fair and do not result in miscarriages of justice.[20]

Judicial resistance to secret evidence and administrative detention, combined with post-9/11 expansions of criminal law, has narrowed the wide gap that many detected after 9/11 between administrative or military detention and

---

[20] Kent Roach, *The Unique Challenges of Terrorism Prosecutions: Towards a Workable Relation between Intelligence and Evidence* (Ottawa: Public Works, 2010).

criminal law.[21] As Conor Gearty has argued, "the alternative that dare not speak its name" is "charge or release."[22] This is an old slogan but one that would mean something different after 9/11. The state can now charge people with a broad array of new terrorist crimes that respond to even remote and generalized acts of preparation for terrorism. States should recognize that criminal prosecutions can obtain more satisfactory results in terms of legitimate and public denunciation and punishment of terrorism and better press than detention without trial on the basis of secret evidence. The United Kingdom learned this lesson in Northern Ireland in the early 1970s and abandoned internment as a counter-productive strategy. A similar lesson now needs to be learned globally.

States will, however, be reluctant to give up the multiple counter-terrorism instruments that they now enjoy. In Israel, the United Kingdom, and Australia, the state has been prepared to use administrative detention and control orders, in cases in which criminal prosecutions failed to obtain the desired result. Control orders may be reformulated in the United Kingdom, but they will remain attractive to the state, especially if they allow the use of secret evidence to protect informers, ongoing investigations, and foreign intelligence. But the use of secret evidence will often produce controversy and make those detained secret trial martyrs. If the battle against terrorism is becoming a battle of ideas, the ability of criminal law to expose and discredit terror and manifest the virtues of due process should be better appreciated. Shortcuts around criminal law may both harm human rights and be ineffective, even counter-productive, in countering terrorism.

II. THE COMPLEXITIES OF THE POST-9/11 WORLD

Even if it is accepted that the Security Council's global legislation and listing of terrorists, the United States' extra-legalism, and the flight away from criminal law were moral and strategic mistakes, the way forward is far from clear. The post-9/11 world is a complex one in which what happens in one part of the world can have immediate repercussions in other parts. The comparative study of counter-terrorism law and policy is important because it helps reveal the deep interconnectedness of the world.

---

[21] Although he still maintains the need for military detention, Benjamin Wittes now admits that in his earlier work, he discounted the role of criminal law in responding to terrorism. Wittes, *Detention and Denial* (Washington, DC: Brookings Institution Press, 2011), at vii.

[22] Conor Gearty, "Human Rights in an Age of Counter-Terrorism: Injurious, Irrelevant or Indispensable?" (2005) 58 Current Legal Problems 25.

The Old Becomes New Again

It was fashionable for a time after 9/11 to say that the world had forever changed. Such an approach was, however, deeply misleading because there were many historical precedents for the way that various states responded to 9/11. Writing in 1996, the late A. W. B. Simpson described British colonial emergency practices used in Malaya, Palestine, and elsewhere that relied on administrative detention, the suspension of habeas corpus, deportations, and prohibitions on the speech and associations of insurgents. In a prescient statement that captured much of the 9/11 effect, Professor Simpson warned that those targeted by such colonial emergency regulations "were treated worse than combatants in regular wars or than criminals under normal conditions."[23] As discussed in Chapter 3, the legacy of such colonial emergency practices on contemporary antiterrorism law is direct in Israel's Occupied Territories, where British emergency regulations still operate, and in Singapore and Malaysia, where ISAs derived from British colonial rule provide an old and steely backbone to contemporary counter-terrorism efforts.

Some colonial emergency practices have been repatriated, as the United Kingdom has used detention without trial, deportation, control orders, and speech regulations to respond to the terrorist threat since 9/11. As discussed in Chapter 5, 9/11 was not the first time the United Kingdom had repatriated its own colonial anti-insurgency tactics. In the early 1970s, administrative detention on the basis of secret evidence and harsh interrogation techniques were repatriated to Northern Ireland for a time. As Kim Lane Scheppele has suggested, 9/11, instead of making everything different, made a number of countries "even more like themselves."[24] At the same time, it would be unfair to say that nothing was learned from the past. Even before the Belmarsh case, the United Kingdom rejected the option of internment of citizens based on its counter-productive effects when used in Northern Ireland in the early 1970s.[25] The United States also reverted to the use of war powers used before by Presidents Reagan and Clinton to respond to terrorist attacks, but with the exception of the immigration round-up immediately after 9/11, it did not use

---

[23] A. W. B Simpson, "Round Up the Usual Suspects: The Legacy of British Colonialism and the European Convention of Human Rights" (1996) 41 Loyola Law Review 629, at 631.

[24] Kim Lane Scheppele, "Other People's Patriot Act" (2004) 50 Loyola Law Review 49, at 148.

[25] The U.K. government rejected the idea of extending administrative detention to citizens on the basis that "experience has demonstrated the dangers of such an approach and the damage it can do to community cohesion and thus to the support from all parts of the public that is so essential to countering the terrorist threat." *Counter-Terrorism Power: A Discussion Paper*, CM 6147, February 2004, at para. 36.

wholesale internment of the type used against "enemy aliens" in the world wars.

The Migration of Terrorism Law

Although there were fears in many countries after 9/11 that attempts would be made to import the USA Patriot Act,[26] a more realistic fear was the migration of the United Kingdom's Terrorism Act, 2000. The Terrorism Act, 2000, was a formidable law that bore the mark of the United Kingdom's long experience with terrorism in Northern Ireland. It has many strong powers not found in the USA Patriot Act. It defined terrorism as a crime based on political and religious motive and provided for executive proscription of terrorist groups and related offenses, preventive arrests, and investigative detention and searches without suspicion. In subsequent years, control orders and the regulation of speech were added to the British arsenal of legislative tools. In part because of the broad ties of the Commonwealth and in part because it was fresh, state-of-the-art legislation, the Terrorism Act, 2000, was very influential as many countries drafted new terrorism laws to comply with Security Council Resolution 1373.[27]

British terrorism laws were never simply transplanted in any other country. Each country made its own adaptations. Australia and Canada modified the U.K. definition of terrorism to provide exemptions for even unlawful protests and strikes. Canada softened the reliance on political and religious motives while Singapore rejected it entirely. Singapore also used the British definition of terrorism as a starting point but also expanded it with concepts taken from its ISA. Israel borrowed from the British definition of terrorism to expand the definition of terrorism in its new terrorism financing law and this definition, much broader than that in Israeli's 1948 law, is also used in a proposed new comprehensive antiterrorism law.[28] British laws changed as they migrated, but even the transplantation of an identical law would function differently in a different political, social, and legal environment.

The emphasis on laws against the advocacy of terrorism found in Security Council Resolution 1624 and the United Kingdom's Terrorism Act, 2006, was

---

[26] Scheppele, "Other People's Patriot Act."

[27] Other post-9/11 terrorism laws influenced by the Terrorism Act, 2000, include Uganda's Terrorism Act, 2002; Tanzania's Prevention of Terrorism Act, 2002; Zimbabwe's Public Order and Security Act, 2002; Barbados's Anti-Terrorism Act, 2002; the Bahamas' Anti-Terrorism Act, 2004; South Africa's Protection of Constitutional Democracy Act, 2004; and Zambia's Anti-Terrorism Act, 2007.

[28] Kent Roach, "The Post 9/11 Migration of Britain's Terrorism Act, 2000," in *The Migration of Constitutional Ideas*, ed. Sujit Choudhry (New York: Cambridge University Press, 2006).

formulated in a particular British social and legal context, one influenced by European understandings of militant democracy. This concept plays out very differently when it is injected into a more libertarian North American context or used by nations that have just become or are not yet democracies. Indonesia rejected a draft terrorism law that borrowed from U.K. law in its definition of terrorism as a political crime because of its concern about returning to Suharto-era repression. At the same time, it is faced today with British-inspired amendments such as the proposed creation of a new offense of failing to provide information about a terrorist act and extension of periods of preventive arrests.[29] The post-9/11 environment, including the need to comply with various international mandates and imperatives, promoted and accelerated the migration of terrorism law among nations. Many developing countries, such as Indonesia and Egypt, quickly adopted terrorism financing and merged them into money laundering laws to comply with the Security Council and FATF. That said, terrorism laws were adapted for their new surroundings and functioned in very different contexts. Both before and after 9/11, a law that worked in London may have had a very different impact in another country.

It would be wrong to conclude that the United Kingdom completely overshadowed the United States as a post-9/11 exporter of counter-terrorism. Consistent with the executive and extralegal character of U.S. counter-terrorism, however, American policies and practices rather than laws had the most influence. In 2002, the Israeli Knesset followed the Bush administration's attempt to forge unlawful combatant status as a distinct category from civilian or prisoner of war status. Israel like the United States was willing to detain noncitizen enemy combatants indefinitely without trial in its 2002 Internment of Unlawful Combatants Law. The Israeli Supreme Court upheld this law in 2008 but avoided using the controversial category of unlawful combatant in both that case and its 2006 targeted killing case. Egypt was also prepared to follow the American example. President Mubarak boasted that the United States' extraordinary rendition program confirmed the wisdom of Egypt's tough approach to terrorism, and Egypt amended its constitution in 2007 to make clear that its president had a power to refer terrorism cases to special security or military courts. These amendments will, however, be repealed as a result of the overthrow of Mubarak and a referendum in Egypt on constitutional change. Egypt, Israel, and Singapore all took comfort that American practices post-9/11 provided support for their traditional measures, but the United States failed

---

[29] See Chapter 3.

to learn important lessons from those countries on issues such as rehabilitation, the difficulties created by torture, and the benefits of judicial review in legitimizing practices such as detention without trial and targeted killing.

Terrorism laws not only migrate between countries but within them. Many countries found in immigration law a legal form that would allow them to employ broader liability rules, lower standards of proof, and secret evidence that would not be acceptable under criminal law. In the United States, the law of war has assumed a central place in any discussion of counter-terrorism law and policy. Even within criminal law, there was a move to less restrained civil and administrative proceedings with respect to both terrorism financing and control orders. Traditional concerns about the seepage of counter-terrorism innovations into regular criminal law remain and can be seen in the United Kingdom's serious crime control orders and Australia's terrorism-inspired organized crime legislation. Nevertheless, the most immediate danger has been that antiterrorism law has been shaped by less restrained concepts taken from immigration law, the law of war and the practices of intelligence agencies.

The Transnational Reality of Counter-Terrorism

Just as the 9/11 attacks were transnational, having been plotted in Afghanistan, Malaysia, and Germany, the responses to them were transnational. Many countries had to grapple with the difficulty that deporting terrorist suspects to countries such as Egypt and Syria would violate their obligations not to deport people to torture. The United Kingdom responded by derogating from rights and creating a new regime that allowed noncitizens suspected of involvement with terrorism to be detained indefinitely if they could not be deported because of torture concerns. Canada contemplated that it would allow deportation to torture in undefined exceptional circumstances. In a recurring pattern, especially in the immediate aftermath of 9/11, the United States relied more on measures that were extralegal or of questionable legality such as the extraordinary rendition program, by which flimsy and false assurances were obtained from Egypt and Syria, that rendered persons would not be tortured as they were interrogated, not so much for prosecution but to obtain intelligence. The closing of CIA prisons and some transfers from Guantánamo raise risks that American reforms might have a substitute effect in which suspects are transferred to countries with poor human rights records. A common thread is that torture in the prisons of Cairo and Damascus affected what was done in London, Ottawa and Washington.

The complexities of transnational terrorism investigations were not limited to deportations to torture. As examined in the last chapter, two Canadian inquiries examined whether Canadian officials were complicit in the torture of Canadian citizens detained in Syria and Egypt. The United Kingdom appointed a similar inquiry to examine the numerous dealings between British officials and those in Pakistan and elsewhere in order to determine whether there was complicity in torture. The reality of torture and other forms of mistreatment also means that the reliability of intelligence from countries with poor human rights records is often suspect, and there may be legal impediments to its use. Courts in both the United Kingdom and Canada have stated that they will not accept evidence obtained through torture. If 9/11 was a dramatic demonstration of the globalization of terrorist organizations and terrorism, the response to 9/11 has been no less transnational. Just as grievances in one part of the world can inspire terrorism in another part of the world, brutal investigative processes in one part of the world can affect and often infect terrorism investigations in another part of the world.

More frequent assertion of extraterritorial jurisdiction was another manifestation of the increased transnational complexity of antiterrorism law. Many post-9/11 antiterrorism laws asserted jurisdiction over terrorism crimes committed abroad. This assertion of extraterritorial jurisdiction was, however, often symbolic and a sign of cooperation in an international battle against terrorism. Many courts also confronted the issue of whether they would apply domestic rights-protection laws extraterritorially to restrain offshore counter-terrorism activities. The American courts took a categorical approach in asserting habeas corpus jurisdiction over Guantánamo but not Afghanistan,[30] while the British courts applied more of a balancing test so that the European Convention on Human Rights would apply to their treatment of prisoners of Iraq but not to civilian deaths outside their control.[31] The House of Lords also held that a Security Council resolution could displace the European Convention in its authorization of long-term military internment in Iraq.[32] This again underlined the failure of the Security Council to incorporate human rights into its work. The Canadian courts only applied the Charter abroad to the extent that Canadian officials participated in international human rights violations and even then would not apply the Charter to the transfer of Canada's Afghan

[30] The court also held that while it may have habeas jurisdiction, it would not interfere in the transfer of an American citizen detained in Iraq, even if the result was transfer to torture. *Munaf v. Geren* 128 S.Ct. 2207 (2008).

[31] *Al Skeini v. Secretary of State*, UKHL 26 (2007).

[32] *Al Jedda v. Secretary of State*, UKHL 58 (2007).

detainees to the Afghan intelligence agency, even on the assumption that the detainees would be tortured.[33] The failure to restrain the state even as it is empowered to act abroad to prevent terrorism contributed to accountability gaps for transnational counterterrorism.

The transnational nature of counter-terrorism also means that courts are increasingly placed in a position of having directly or indirectly to judge the counter-terrorism activities of other countries and of the UN. Courts must determine whether deportation of suspected citizens with or without assurances will result in torture[34] and whether evidence or intelligence used in domestic proceedings was obtained by torture abroad.[35] A number of courts have indirectly been asked to rule on Guantánamo and on American extraordinary renditions even in cases for which American courts have shut down parallel litigation to protect state secrets.[36] Australian courts have excluded involuntary statements taken from suspects in Pakistan, and Canadian courts have refused to extradite a Canadian terrorist suspect to the United States because of concerns about how that person was treated by Pakistani and American officials when originally captured in Pakistan.[37] A number of domestic courts have commented adversely on the fairness of the Security Council's 1267 listing process, affirming the ability of domestic courts applying their own standards to resist anticonstitutional practices of the Security Council.[38] This approach, however, can create conflict between various legal regimes. Both terrorism and human rights transcend domestic boundaries. The need for better global cooperation in the struggle against terrorism and the need to protect human rights should go hand in hand. Democracies will find it easier to cooperate with countries that take steps to improve the protection of human rights and, in particular, the absolute right against torture. The Security Council will also find its various counter-terrorism mandates more easily observed and respected if they better incorporate human rights. A lack of respect for human

---

[33] *Amnesty International v. Canada*, FC 336 (Fed.C.A) (2008).

[34] *RB (Algeria) v. Secretary of State*, UKHL 10 (2009).

[35] *Secretary of State v. A*, UKHL 71 (2005).

[36] *Abbasi v. Secretary of State*, EWCA (Civ) 1598 (2002); *Canada v. Khadr*, 1 S.C.R. 44 (2010). Compare *Mohamed v. Jeppesen Dataplan*, no. 08-15693, 2010 WL 3489913 (9th Cir. 2010) (en banc), with *Mohamed v. Secretary of State*, EWCA 65 (2010).

[37] *DPP v. Thomas*, 163 A Crim R 567 (2006) (excluding statements obtained in Pakistan as involuntary); *United States of America v. Khadr*, ONSC 4338 (2010) (staying proceedings in U.S. extradition request).

[38] Kim Lane Scheppele, "The Migration of Anti-Constitutional Ideas," in Choudhry, *Migration of Constitutional Ideas*.

rights has a way of catching up with those who seek transnational cooperation in combating terrorism.

Increased Emphasis on Prevention and Intelligence

A constant theme in responses to 9/11 was an increased emphasis on the prevention of terrorism. There was much interest in preventive detention regimes in countries like Singapore, Israel, and the United Kingdom. Prevention is the traditional preserve of intelligence agencies, and the budgets of many intelligence agencies dramatically expanded after 9/11. In addition, the focus of intelligence agencies on a person's security risk, associations, training, and ambiguous conduct migrated into criminal law. In response to 9/11 and the call by the UN Security Council in Resolution 1373 to ensure that terrorism was treated as a serious crime, countries all around the world enacted broad new antiterrorism laws. Many new offenses were created that targeted the financing of terrorism and many forms of preparation for terrorism. The new crimes included the receiving of training, the creation of documents, or the instructing of persons to perform otherwise lawful acts – all quite remote from any particular act of terrorism. In addition to the criminalization of a very broad range of acts of preparation, the new criminal laws also criminalized various forms of association with terrorist groups and terrorism. These new laws, with their focus on remote risks, ambiguous acts of preparation, and suspect associations, have helped bring the preventive paradigm of intelligence into antiterrorism law. They have endowed intelligence about risks and capacities with new evidential significance.

Intelligence and criminal investigations of terrorist suspects frequently overlap, and the same piece of information could be used both as secret intelligence to inform government(s) of security risks and as evidence of a crime. Intelligence agencies struggled with new evidentiary and disclosure requirements while police forces grappled with the difficulties of interpreting ambiguous fragments of intelligence. As described in Chapters 6 and 7, police forces in Australia and Canada dealt with intelligence poorly in the Mohammed Haneef and Maher Arar cases involving innocent people wrongly suspected of terrorism. Intelligence agencies in those countries in turn sometimes failed to ensure that intelligence was properly collected and retained so that it was available for use as evidence in legal proceedings. British intelligence agencies as outlined in Chapter 5 have so far been successful in resisting numerous calls that electronic surveillance be available as evidence in terrorism trials in large part because of concerns that evidential standards would adversely affect secrecy and retention policies. In short, there have been many growing pains in adjusting to the changed relation of intelligence and evidence, with intelligence agencies failing to satisfy evidentiary standards and police misinterpreting and mishandling intelligence.[39]

Although the distinctions between intelligence and evidence and between the roles of intelligence agencies and police forces may continue to fade, there is a danger in ignoring the very different values of evidence and intelligence. Intelligence is about prediction of security risks. It often focuses on a person's associations, beliefs, character, and past. The sources and methods used to obtain intelligence must generally remain secret. Intelligence favors false positives that identify a person as a security risk when he or she is not, as opposed to false negatives that fail to connect the dots and provide warnings. In contrast, evidence is about determining whether specific factual allegations can be proven. Rules restricting hearsay evidence and prohibiting involuntary confessions require that the sources and methods used to obtain evidence be publicly disclosed. The conflicting values of publicity and secrecy will clash both in joint terrorism investigations and when attempts are made to use intelligence as evidence or to prevent the disclosure of intelligence to the accused or other directly affected person. Governments, judges, and ultimately citizens will have to choose between intelligence approaches that err on the side of falsely identifying people as security risks and evidence-based approaches that require higher standards of proof and allow adversarial challenge.

III. SOME CHALLENGES GOING FORWARD

The complexities of post-9/11 transnational terrorism and counter-terrorism and the increased emphasis on prevention and intelligence help define many of the challenges that lie ahead. They raise serious questions of whether criminal law can endure as a just and public vehicle for punishing terrorism and whether governments and the UN can be held to account for the propriety and efficacy of their counter-terrorism actions. They also raise questions of whether we have lost perspective and devoted too much of our limited resources to preventing terrorism when there are many other threats to human security.

---

[39] Kent Roach, "The Eroding Distinction between Intelligence and Evidence in Terrorism Investigations," in *Counter-Terrorism and Beyond*, ed. Nicola McGarrity, Andrew Lynch, and George Williams (London: Routledge, 2010).

Criminal Law under Strain

Criminal law has not remained static since 9/11. Although politicians were wrong after 9/11 to claim that criminal law was powerless to respond to terrorism until it was too late, there are limits on how far in advance of violence criminal law can apply. Many new terrorism offenses enacted after 9/11 pushed the envelope of inchoate liability and came dangerously close to creating status offenses, thought crimes, and guilt by association. For example, the frequently used British offense of possessing items that may be of use in terrorism, an offense also found in Australia, creates a high risk of unjust conviction.[40] Drafters of post-9/11 antiterrorism laws employed a precautionary principle that went well beyond criminalizing violence and often spelled out that a person could be guilty even if he or she did not know the specifics of any particular terrorist activity. In some cases, the new laws trenched on the traditional domain of the judiciary by deeming certain evidence to be admissible and by trying to preclude any attempt by the courts to adopt anything but the broadest reading of the offense. Such an expansion of criminal law runs the risk of distorting criminal law.

To be sure, the drafting of many post-9/11 antiterrorism laws reflected the reality that those within a terrorist cell might not know the specifics of an attack.[41] Nevertheless, the end result was to create a mass of overlapping crimes targeting preparation and association in a way that strained criminal law's traditional insistence on proof of harm and fault. As Lucia Zedner has demonstrated, the challenges of moving to a precrime model started before 9/11, with moves toward risk management and a blurring of distinctions between criminal law and less restrained civil processes.[42] Nevertheless, 9/11 accelerated the trend in a manner that raises questions about whether criminal law will remain a just method for punishing harmful acts and not just harmful thoughts and suspect associations. The expansion of post-9/11 terrorism offenses also creates a risk of sentences that the public consider too lenient given the emotive terrorist label or, alternatively, sentences that are disproportionate to the actual severity of what the accused did and intended.[43]

---

[40] Victor Tadros, "Crimes and Security" (2008) 71 Modern Law Review 969.

[41] Richard Mosley, "Preventing Terrorism," in *Terrorism, Law and Democracy*, ed. David Daubney et al. (Montreal, QC, Canada: Yvon Blais, 2002), at 147.

[42] Lucia Zedner, "Preventive Justice or Pre-Punishment? The Case of Control Orders" (2007) 60 Current Legal Problems 174.

[43] For example, sentences for sending funds to the Tamil Tigers have, as examined in Chapters 6 and 7, been criticized as excessively lenient given the terrorist label. On the other hand, some sentences given for speech associated with terrorism, preliminary terrorist offenses and failing to provide information to authorities about terrorism can be criticized as too severe given what

The criminal trial is also under strain. A new type of terrorism trial is emerging that features multiple accused, multiple offenses, and evidence about the accuseds' politics or religion. The new terrorism trial also features frequent applications to close courts and not to disclose secret but perhaps relevant intelligence to the accused. Witnesses in terrorism trials have given evidence anonymously and from remote locations. Defense lawyers who stray into matters affecting broadly defined security interests may find themselves excluded and threatened with punishment for disclosing information that the government claims should be secret. Judges who have presided in terrorism trials have expressed frustration about how secrecy claims may adversely affect both the fairness and the efficiency of the criminal trial.[44] Although there is increased support for terrorism prosecutions as a just means to denounce, incapacitate, and punish terrorists, the challenges of these prosecutions are considerable.

The risk of wrongful conviction may be greater in terrorism cases than other criminal cases. In the United Kingdom, a series of wrongful convictions occurred with respect to Irish Republican Army bombings and the harsh treatment of suspects in Northern Ireland. Suspects were identified in part because of their nationality and political sympathies. They were mistreated in custody and did not have adequate disclosure, which may have cast doubt on their false and coerced confessions and the faulty forensic evidence used against them.[45] Ronald Dworkin has eloquently warned of the dangers of concluding that "the requirements of fairness are fully satisfied, in the case of suspected terrorists, by laxer standards of criminal justice which run an increased risk of convicting innocent people."[46] There is a risk of wrongful conviction in post-9/11 terrorism trials. Criminal law, at least, still prides itself on not punishing the innocent and providing a fair trial. The same cannot be said of less restrained alternatives such as administrative detention and targeted killing.

It is important that criminal law not lose sight of its foundational principles. Criminal law should still provide meaningful act and fault requirements. The punishment for the crime should not be disproportionate to what the accused actually did. Listing decisions made by the executive in secret should not

the accused actually did and intended. See Ali Naseem Bajwa "Sentencing Terror Offences" *Criminal Law and Justice Weekly* August 14, 2010; Michael Crowley "Tough on Terrorists: Challenging Traditional Sentencing Principles in Australia?" (2010) 22 Federal Sentencing Reporter 279; Kent Roach "Sentencing Terrorists" (2011) 57 Criminal Law Quarterly 1.

[44] A. G. Whealy, "Difficulty in Obtaining a Fair Trial in Terrorism Cases" (2007) 81 Australian Law Journal 743.

[45] Kent Roach and Gary Trotter, "Miscarriages of Justice in the War against Terror" (2005) 109 Penn State Law Review 976.

[46] Ronald Dworkin, "The Threat to Patriotism," New York Review of Books, February 28, 2002.

be substituted for proof that the accused actually assisted or participated in a terrorist group. Evidence about the accused's religious and political views should be excluded if it will prejudice the trial. The accused should receive enough disclosure, especially of exculpatory material, to ensure a fair and accurate trial. The accused should be able to confront most witnesses and determine the reliability of any hearsay evidence. Fair and public criminal trials can be an important part of a heart-and-minds approach that exposes and denounces terrorism. Terrorists should be treated as criminals intent on murder and not as "enemy combatants" who require special procedures and courts. At the same time, the unique legitimacy of criminal law can be diminished if it is distorted and becomes unjust.

Rehabilitation, Multiculturalism, and Community Relations

Another challenge, especially for Western democracies, are the related questions of rehabilitation of terrorists and maintaining good community relations with their Muslim minorities. These minorities may be radicalized by both the treatment of Muslims around the world and by their own treatment in Western societies. The United Kingdom has attempted to deal with some of these issues through the Prevent strand of its CONTEST strategy, and Canada created a Cross-Cultural Roundtable as part of its 2004 National Security Plan. Nevertheless, it is fair to say that Western democracies have struggled with such issues, especially compared to Singapore, which, in response to its homegrown terrorism arrests in late 2001 and 2002, created elaborate community relations programs and apparently successful rehabilitation programs for detainees and their families.[47] Singapore's candid use of religious reeducation and its placing of direct responsibility on its sizeable Muslim minority to police extremism would not be acceptable in many Western democracies. Many of these countries see religion as a private matter that should be respected unless, as in the United Kingdom and Australia, it results in speech that crosses the line and can be prosecuted as advocacy of terrorism or hate speech. In the United States, speech-based prosecutions are generally not an option.

Another instrument that has been used in the West indirectly to deal with community relations is immigration policy. Following the warnings in Resolution 1373 about terrorists abusing asylum, many democracies dramatically decreased the number of refugees they accepted. Like other uses of immigration law as antiterrorism law, this blunt approach is radically overinclusive in harming many innocent people and radically underinclusive in not responding

---

[47] See Chapter 3.

to terrorism from citizens. Denial of refugee status may, like other immigration law responses, simply displace terrorism. One of the lessons of 9/11 should be that the displacement of terrorism to other countries does not provide reliable protection even for Western democracies.

Western democracies must develop more nuanced responses than immigration exclusion, speech prosecutions, and tough terrorism sentences. Recent developments such as the start of divisive Congressional hearings on Muslim radicalization in the United States or Prime Minister Cameron's speech denouncing Islamic extremism and linking it with a lack of a common British identity suggest that Western democracies are not particularly close to finding solutions to difficult and delicate issues of community relations. [48] A looming problem is what will happen when terrorist offenders or suspects are released and whether counter-terrorism policies and other world events are significantly adding to the pool of people who are prepared to engage in terrorism. Definite answers to these questions are not possible, but their importance underlines the need to consider both the propriety and efficacy of counter-terrorism activities both at home and abroad. The possibility that some counter-terrorism measures may not only violate human rights but also be counter-productive should not be ignored.

The Role of Courts

The role of the courts in providing accountability for abuse of human rights in counter-terrorism activities is controversial. On one side are those who argue that courts do not have the experience, expertise, or legitimacy to review national security activities,[49] and on the other are those who argue that the courts have a special responsibility to uphold the rule of law and protect vulnerable minorities.[50] This debate about judicial review is a familiar one. What is new, however, are the challenges faced by courts in reviewing secret and transnational counter-terrorism activities that are sometimes mandated by the UN Security Council. Courts in the United States, the United Kingdom, Canada, and Indonesia have played a more active role since 9/11 than most

---

[48] See infra Chapters 4 and 5 for further discussion of these events.

[49] Lord Hoffmann in *Secretary of State v. Rehman*, UKHL 47 (2001), at para. 62; Posner and Vermeule, *Terror in the Balance*; K. D. Ewing and Joo-Cheong Tham, "The Continuing Futility of the Human Rights Act" (2008) Public Law 668, at 691.

[50] David Dyzenhaus, *The Constitution of Law* (Cambridge: Cambridge University Press, 2006); Aileen Kavanaugh, "Judging the Judges under the Human Rights Act: Deference, Disillusionment and the 'War on Terror'" (2009) Public Law 287; Kent Roach, "Judicial Review of the State's Anti-Terrorism Activities: The Post 9/11 Experience and Normative Justifications for Judicial Review" (2009) 3 Indian Journal of Constitutional Law 138.

would have predicted given their previous deference to the state in times of emergency. One factor may have been that, rightly or wrongly, many judges do not believe that 9/11 produced a global emergency comparable to world wars. Another factor is that courts have recognized that the application of proportionality standards enables them to invalidate state actions while allowing the state to select among an array of alternative policy instruments.

Much judicial supervision of antiterrorism activity has been driven by the requirement that states justify the proportionality of measures that restrict rights. Such ideas are implicit in most bills of rights that provide for justification of reasonable limits on rights. Courts readily accept that state objectives, such as the prevention of terrorism and the protection of secret intelligence from disclosure, are important enough to justify limits on rights. They then focus on whether the law is a rational and necessary way to achieve the objective. This analysis is generally designed to weed out irrational laws, including those blinded by prejudice or stereotyping of unpopular minorities. The House of Lords, in *A v. Secretary of State*,[51] concluded that an immigration law response was not rationally connected to the objective of preventing terrorism because the terrorist threat was not limited to noncitizens. The Supreme Court of Canada, in *Charkaoui*,[52] stressed that the state's legitimate objective in protecting intelligence from disclosure could be achieved with a less drastic infringement of the detainees' rights by allowing some adversarial challenge to secret evidence. The court was essentially saying that the state could achieve its objective just as well while infringing rights less.

The idea that judicial review does not necessarily result in judicial supremacy and that it allows the legislature to engage in a dialogue with the judiciary by enacting reply legislation is closely connected to proportionality analysis.[53] In many cases, a court that decides that a law is disproportionate can safely contemplate that the legislature can formulate a better-tailored law to advance the same objective. In both the United Kingdom and Canada, there is the possibility that the state can implement this alternative law before the unconstitutional law is allowed to lapse. The idea that courts can engage in a dialogue with the legislature is also useful when courts review executive action. If executive action that infringes rights is not specifically authorized by the legislature,

[51] UKHL 56 (2004).   [52] 1 S.C.R. 350 (2007).

[53] For judicial references to the concept of dialogue, see *A v. Secretary of State*, UKHL 56 (2004), at para. 42; *Boumediene v. Bush*, 128 S.Ct. 2229, at 2243. See also Baroness Hale, "Human Rights in the Age of Terrorism: The Democratic Dialogue in Action" (2008) 39 Georgetown Journal of International Law 383. For my own discussion of dialogue, see Kent Roach, *The Supreme Court on Trial: Judicial Activism or Democratic Dialogue* (Toronto, ON, Canada: Irwin Law, 2001), and Roach, "Dialogic Judicial Review and Its Critics" (2004) 23 Supreme Court Law Review 49.

the court can declare the action invalid. Such judicial activism affirms both the rule of law and democracy. It provides the legislature with an opportunity to assume responsibility for the executive action by explicitly authorizing it. Although most debates about the appropriate judicial role pit the unelected judiciary against the elected legislature, in the national security context, the most frequent contest is between judges and the executive.

It can be argued that the idea that courts interact with legislatures and society proves too much. The House of Lords's decision in A led to the creation of problematic control orders, raising concerns that the judges were mere "irritants" rather than "obstacles" to counter-terrorism.[54] Such criticisms, however, only underline that courts have not assumed a position of judicial supremacy in the post-9/11 environment and under modern bills of rights that provide for legislative limitations and derogations from rights. They have left room for elected governments to continue to make choices about antiterrorism policy. This will require democratic engagement and supervision of counter-terrorism. Nevertheless, judicial decisions have helped publicize the often secret security activities of the state, and they provide resources to challenge and restrain even second-generation counter-terrorism measures created in the wake of judicial invalidation.

The type of judicial deference that traditionally motivated courts in national security cases was driven by the idea that the elected branches of government had a greater democratic legitimacy and expertise concerning matters of national security than the courts. Legislatures, however, often enact antiterrorism laws very quickly, without full information or time for proper deliberation. The immediate aim of much legislation is to reassure the public.[55] Elected bodies may have an incentive to overestimate risk and overreact to it.[56] As examined in Chapter 2, the Security Council acted as a kind of global counter-terrorism legislator after 9/11 and the authority it claims to enact mandatory measures to protect international peace and security presents challenges for courts. One approach as seen in *Kadi* is to impose domestic or European constitutionalism on the Council's work. Another approach as represented by the House of Lords decision on internment in Iraq is to allow Security Council mandates to trump constitutionalism. It would be better if courts could reconcile the competing legal orders but this will require the Security Council better to incorporate human rights in its work. Even then, courts should

---

[54] Ewing and Tham, "Continuing Futility of the Human Rights Act," at 691.

[55] Bruce Ackerman, *Before the Next Attack* (New Haven, CT: Yale University Press, 2006).

[56] David Feldman, "Human Rights, Terrorism and Risk: The Roles of Politicians" (2005) Public Law 364, at 379.

not assume that the Security Council like domestic legislators, cannot make mistakes when enacting terrorism legislation.

Another rationale for judicial deference defended by Lord Hoffmann in the *Rehman* case decided immediately after 9/11 is the idea that the executive has greater knowledge and expertise than the judges. One of the fallouts of a range of well-publicized intelligence failures from 9/11 and the Iraq weapons of mass destruction debacle has been a growing lack of confidence in the ability of intelligence agencies to make and act on accurate determinations of danger. Cases like the Maher Arar case in Canada and extraordinary renditions and targeted killings that have harmed the wrong people have demonstrated the frailties of intelligence. Judges have also gained more experience with evaluating intelligence since 9/11. They have discovered that intelligence agencies sometimes overclaim secrecy to hide their mistakes and abuses of human rights. Although judges have been criticized as amateurs in intelligence matters,[57] they can and have developed some expertise.[58] They must do so if the increased use of intelligence as evidence is to be subject to adversarial challenge and the rule of law both domestically and in the Security Council. Courts should not assume that the national security executive does not make mistakes.

Accountability Gaps

Even if courts are prepared to be more active than they have traditionally been with respect to the review of national security activities, they cannot review most of a government's secret counter-terrorism efforts. David Dyzenhaus, a vigorous proponent of judges enforcing the rule of law on the security state, nevertheless recognizes the need for the rule of law and human rights to have allies in the legislature and the executive.[59] There is a need for creative institutional hybrids that combine the judiciary's commitment to legality and openness with the executive's ability to initiate review and audit performance and the legislature's ability to encourage public deliberation and consultation.

One of the most disturbing fallouts from 9/11 is the yawning accountability gap that has been created as governments have intensified and integrated counter-terrorism activities, while various review agencies in the legislature and the executive have failed to keep pace. Review of national security activities should match and mirror the national security activities that are subject to review. Increased national security activities require increased resources and

---

[57] Posner and Vermeule, *Terror in the Balance.*
[58] Adam Tomkins, "National Security and the Role of the Court: A Changed Landscape?" (2010) 126 Law Quarterly Review 543.
[59] Dyzenhaus, *Constitution of Law*, at 230.

powers for the reviewers. More specifically, it means that reviewers in the legislative and executive branches should share information and engage in more coordinated review to mirror and match the increased coordination and information sharing that is occurring within the executive branch.

Domestically, most review mechanisms remain confined to specific agencies or silos, with little ability to conduct coordinated reviews that will follow greater integration in government.[60] In both Canada and the United Kingdom, special inquiries with jurisdiction to examine all officials have had to be appointed to investigate whether police, intelligence agents, and foreign affairs officials have been complicit in torture. Perhaps in part because of the minimal role of judicial review in that nation, Australia has made the most headway on non-judicial forms of accountability. In 2010, Australia gave its inspector general the ability to examine all intelligence and security matters within the Commonwealth government, albeit only at the request of the Prime Minister. It also created a parliamentary committee on law enforcement and a new special security-cleared monitor to evaluate both the propriety and effectiveness of whole-of-government approaches to terrorism.[61] Various review bodies, including the inspector general, the ombudsperson, the human rights commissioner, and the privacy commissioner, have combined to review all Australian security legislation.[62] The existence of quasi-judicial watchdogs within the executive as well as the important work of the Joint Committee on Human Rights in the United Kingdom[63] demonstrate how the executive and the legislature, as well as the judiciary, can be enlisted to better protect human rights while countering terrorism. Even optimal domestic accountability devices, however, will not easily extend to coordinated activities of national governments with other states and governments. Canadian inquiries into complicity in torture were frustrated by the refusal of American, Egyptian and Syrian governments to cooperate.

In the international arena, the UN has provided some much-needed review of transnational counter-terrorism activities. Special rapporteurs and other rights-protection bodies of the UN have reviewed a range of issues since 9/11,

---

[60] Philip B. Heymann and Juliette N. Kayyem, *Protecting Liberty in an Age of Terror* (Cambridge MA: MIT Press, 2005), at 111.

[61] National Security Legislative Amendment Act, 2010, no. 127, Schedule 10; Independent National Security Legislation Monitor Act, 2010, no. 32; Parliamentary Joint Committee on Law Enforcement Act, 2010, no. 128.

[62] Simon Sheller, *Report of the Security Legislation Review Committee*, 2006.

[63] For a summary of the committee's many reports on counter-terrorism since 9/11, see Joint Committee on Human Rights, *Counter-Terrorism and Human Rights: Bringing Human Rights Back In*, 2010.

including disappearances and secret detention, the role of intelligence agencies, and attacks on human rights defenders.[64] The special rapporteur on the promotion and protection of human rights while countering terrorism has also conducted country-specific missions to a number of countries, including Egypt, the United States, and Israel and the Occupied Territories. One problem with the UN approach, however, is that the rights-protection bodies remain isolated from the work of the Security Council and its CTC, which also conduct country visits.

Although a bifurcated approach that separates review for propriety and compliance with human rights from review for efficacy can, in theory, maximize both forms of review,[65] it also risks marginalizing review for propriety on the basis that the reviewer does not appreciate the need for robust efforts to prevent terrorism. Although such criticisms are often unfair if reviewers take the mandate of determining the proportionality of the state's activities seriously, they are a reality. The separation of rights and efficacy review in the UN has allowed the Security Council and its committees to marginalize human rights concerns in their work. Although it is true that both the 1267 committee and the CTC pay more attention to human rights today than just after 9/11, the fact remains that these committees have few human rights experts. Moreover, they have not worked together with the rights-protection bodies of the UN to produce country reviews that examine both the efficacy and the propriety of counter-terrorism actions. Combined reviews by both security and human rights experts will carry more weight and have more credibility in different constituencies than the isolated security or human rights review that has been the norm.

Modern proportionality principles blend propriety- and efficacy-based review, and some of the most abject counter-terrorism failures since 9/11 have arguably harmed both human rights and the effort to prevent terrorism. There is much to be said for combining efficacy- and propriety-based review wherever possible, especially if efficacy-based review does not involve real-time operational oversight whereby the reviewer is part of the decision-making process or otherwise becomes heavily implicated in questionable activities that must remain secret. In this respect, congressional oversight of U.S. programs, such as National Security Agency warrantless spying and extraordinary renditions, has

---

[64] One positive development includes a joint study by the special rapporteur on the promotion of human rights and fundamental freedoms while countering terrorism, the special rapporteur on torture, and the Working Group on Arbitrary Detention on global practices involving secret detentions while countering terrorism that examined the practices of 66 different states. A/HRC/13/42.

[65] Kent Roach, "Review and Oversight of National Security Activities" (2007) 29 Cardozo Law Review 53.

failed to provide real accountability and has arguably coopted the legislators who have been "briefed in." Review bodies, including legislative committees and courts, face a dilemma in dealing with secret information. Being privy to secrets comes at the price of silence about those secrets. Not having access to secrets, however, leaves one vulnerable to the criticism that a number of ministers have used in the post-9/11 era, namely: "if you knew what I know."

Civil society groups and the media are also very important in providing publicity and accountability for transnational counter-terrorism. The extralegal activities of various American counter-terrorism officials would have been considerably more dangerous were it not for the work of investigative reporters who exposed the torture memos, extraordinary rendition, targeted killing, CIA black sites and warrantless spying by the National Security Agency. In many other democracies, not to mention states that are not democratic, such investigative reporting might have been blocked by official-secrets legislation or by extralegal actions. One of the positive effects of the post -9/11 fall out is that there is much more information in the public domain about national security activities.

Transnational civil society groups also play an important role in providing accountability. The International Commission of Jurists had a panel of eight distinguished jurists hold 16 hearings around the globe about counter-terrorism. These hearings combined concerns about the propriety and efficacy of counter-terrorism by allowing both human rights defenders and governmental officials to testify. The result was an important report, published in 2009, that rejected the idea that human rights and security were incompatible and outlined a range of historical, human rights and efficacy concerns about reliance on a war model of terrorism led by the military; the increased power of intelligence agencies; and less restrained alternatives to criminal law such as control orders, listing, and administrative and immigration detention.[66] Other civil society groups, such as Amnesty International[67] and Human Rights Watch,[68]

---

[66] Eminent Jurists Panel of the International Commission of Jurists, *Assessing Damage, Urging Action* (Geneva, Switzerland: International Commission of Jurists, 2009).

[67] Amnesty International, *In Whose Best Interests? Omar Khadr, "Child Enemy Combatant" Facing Military Commission* (London: Amnesty International, 2008); Amnesty International, *A Case to Answer: From Abu Grahib to CIA Secret Custody: Khaled al-Maqtari* (London: Amnesty International, 2008).

[68] See, e.g., Human Rights Watch, *No Questions Asked: Intelligence Co-operation with Countries That Torture* (New York: Human Rights Watch, 2010); *Cruel Britannia: British Complicity in the Torture and Ill-Treatment of Terrorist Suspects in Pakistan* (New York: Human Rights Watch, 2009); *No Direction Home: Returns from Guantanamo to Yemen* (New York: Human Rights Watch, 2009); *Ghost Prisoner: Two Years in Secret CIA Detention* (New York: Human Rights Watch, 2007).

have issued many important reports. They have the global expertise to scrutinize transnational counter-terrorism activities, including those that involve rendition and intelligence sharing with countries with poor human rights records.

Toward Sustainable Security Policies

A final issue is whether the approach taken by countries to the prevention of terrorism since 9/11 is a sustainable and constructive one. The Security Council and many countries neglected human rights in the immediate aftermath of the horrors of 9/11. There has, however, been an increasing recognition that such neglect was a mistake that undermined the legitimacy of counter-terrorism efforts. There is a growing consensus that any sustainable approach to counter-terrorism will require attention to human rights not only in democracies but in countries with poor human rights records. There is also a danger that human rights abuses may be counter-productive. President Obama recognized this reality when he determined that it was in American interests to close Guantánamo, but unfortunately he has been unable to do so and international focus on Guantánamo may be revived by the proposed trial of alleged 9/11 mastermind Khalid Sheikh Mohammed before a military commission.

As suggested earlier, sustainable security policies will have to be reviewed continuously to evaluate both their effectiveness and their propriety. Terrorism quickly evolves so that strategies that may have once made sense, such as the proscription of known terrorist groups and a focus on their financing, may become outdated as al Qaeda evolves. The prosecution of speech associated with terrorism and efforts to deal with radicalization and extremism should be closely monitored to determine if they have constructive or counter-productive effects.

In the immediate aftermath of 9/11, many countries displayed a striking lack of confidence in the ability of criminal law to respond to terrorism, even as they created many broad new terrorism offenses. In recent years, however, there has been increasing, albeit not universal, recognition that criminal prosecutions are the most sustainable method to deal with terrorists. Shortcuts around criminal law, such as attempts to deport, administrative or military detention, and control orders, often result in legal and political controversy, without providing sustainable solutions to terrorism.

The attraction of criminal prosecutions as a fair and transparent means to denounce and punish terrorists does not mean that states should rely exclusively on criminal law. It is unfortunate that Security Council Resolution 1540 encountered more resistance than Resolutions 1267 or 1373 because the

1540 process of securing chemical, biological, and nuclear material is a more promising means to minimize the most deadly forms of terrorism than reliance on terrorism financing prohibitions. An administrative approach that focuses on sites and substances that can be used for terrorism recognizes that it will be impossible for intelligence and police agencies to identify and apprehend all potential terrorists. It also allows for regulation that has a minimal effect on human rights.

The inevitability of intelligence failures and of terrorism also speaks to the need to develop emergency response plans that will mitigate the harm caused by acts of terrorism. Before such an approach is dismissed as defeatist damage control, it is important to recall that the 9/11 Commission found that between 14,000 and 16,000 people were successfully evacuated from the World Trade Center after the first plane hit in part because of better preparedness in light of the four hours it took to evacuate the World Trade Center after it was the subject of a terrorist bombing in 1993.[69] As Philip Bobbitt, an analyst who cannot be accused of underestimating the threat of terrorism, has argued, more harm can be caused by a failure of government effectively to govern and recover than by terrorism.[70]

Searches for sustainable counter-terrorism policies also lead to considerations of whether nations are wise, even after the horrors of 9/11, to focus on terrorism as the prime threat to national security. Writing in 2003, I argued that the best approach to national security was an all-risks one that recognized terrorism as a risk but also included other natural and man-made disasters.[71] Subsequent events such as the failure of the U.S. government effectively to respond to the devastation and almost 2,000 deaths from Hurricane Katrina and the 2011 Japanese earthquake, tsunami and nuclear disasters, have confirmed the importance of an all-risks approach.

After having focused on terrorism as the prime risk to national security, the United States and other countries are increasingly embracing an all-risks approach. The UN has not yet followed this important trend, but the General Assembly's counter-terrorism strategy at least takes a more holistic approach to terrorism that focuses on conditions that contribute to terrorism, state capacities, and human rights. An all-risks approach does not mean that terrorism and the threat of another 9/11 is ignored: it means that the threat of terrorism is integrated with other threats and that multiple purpose interventions that address the causes of terrorism including failed states, emergency preparedness

---

[69] *The 9/11 Report*, 2004, at 9.4.

[70] Philip Bobbitt, *Terror and Consent: The Wars for the Twenty-first Century* (New York: Anchor, 2009), at 223–36, 541.

[71] Roach, *September 11*, chapter 7.

and the protection of lethal material receive more attention and funding to balance off the increased efforts that have been made to identify terrorists and prevent terrorism.

IV. CONCLUSION

Much has happened since the terrible events of 9/11. Although there have been acts of terrorism since 9/11, we have been fortunate that another act of the same magnitude has not occurred. There have been abuses and mistakes in the global response to 9/11. The practices of Western democracies have regrettably moved closer to those of more repressive regimes and countries with more experience with terrorism. Nevertheless, there is some hope that learning from the past and from others and continuous review will lead to more sustainable security strategies in the future.

Index

A v. Secretary of State, 17, 240, 242, 453. *See also* Belmarsh case
Abbasi, Feroz, 292
Abdel Rahman, Omar, 228
Abdelrazik, Abousfian, 386–387
Abou-Elmaati, Ahmad, 97–98, 412–413
Abu Ghraib, 164, 203, 220
accountability
  accountability gaps, 19–20, 294, 424–425, 455–459
  civil liability, 191–192
  extralegal conduct and, 223–227
  individual, 222–223
  review for efficacy, 419, 457–458
  review for propriety, 419, 457–458
  transnational cooperation, 12, 424–425
  whole of government, 11–12, 18, 19–20, 365, 424–425
Achille Lauro hijackers, 169
Ackerman, Bruce, 33
Adams, Gerry, 250
administrative detention, 439. *See also* immigration detention
  Australia, 3–4
  Canada, 3–4, 395–397
  Egypt, 82–84
  Israel, 3–4, 11, 79, 112–113, 117–123, 124
  Singapore, 3–4, 130
  United Kingdom, 3–4, 244–246
Afghan detainees, Canada, 410–411
Afghanistan War, Security Council Resolution 1368 and, 29–31
African embassy bombings 1998, 169
Agiza, Ahmed, 81
Air India bombings 1985, 369–370
  Canada's flawed response, 373–374

failed terrorism prosecutions, 370–372
inquiries, 418–420
investigative hearings, 393
al Jedda 295–296, 434–445
al Qaeda
  bin Laden, Osama 26–28, 73, 229, 231
  proscription and, 327
  prosecution, in U.S., 217
  Security Council Resolution 1267, 27–28
Algeria, speech, terrorism and, 58
al-Ghozi, 156
Alien Terrorist Removal Court, U.S., 171
Almalki, Abdullah, 97–98, 412–413
Alston, Philip, 230
Al-Skeini, 295–296, 434, 435
Alzery, Mohamed, 81
Amara, Zakaria, 408–409
American Civil Liberties Union, 190, 197, 232–233
Amnesty International, 12, 72, 157, 458
Annan, Kofi, 67
Ananda Marga, 315
Anti-Subversion Law 1963, Indonesia, 143–144
Anti-Terrorism Act (ATA) 2001, Canada, 363, 376
Anti-Terrorism and Effective Death Penalty Act 1996, U.S., 169–170
Anti-Terrorism Crime and Security Act, 2001, U.K., 17, 242, 263–265
  data retention, 267–268
  disclosure of information, 266–267
  expanded police powers, 269
  immigration law, as antiterrorism law, 271–276
  offense of withholding information, 268–269

Anti-Terrorism Crime and Security Act (*cont.*)
  Part IV derogation, 271–276
  racial and religious hatred, 269–270
  terrorism financing, 265–266
  WMD and aviation security, 270–271
Arab Convention for the Suppression of
    Terrorism 1999, 93, 94
Arar Commission, Canada, 398–399, 412,
    416–417, 419–420
Arar, Maher
  associations, 328
  inaccurate intelligence, 43, 362, 374
  lawsuit, states-secret doctrine and, 223–224
  torture of, 97–98, 411–413
Ashcroft, John, 175, 187, 189
ASIO. *See* Australian Security Intelligence
    Organization
ATA. *See* Anti-Terrorism Act
Atran, Scott, 154
Aulaqi, Anwar al, 232–233
AUMF. *See* Authorization of the Use of
    Military Force 2001
Australia
  Canadian response to 9/11, *vs.*, 313–314, 360
  control orders, 311, 340–342
  criminal prosecutions, 346–347
  definition of terrorism, 318–320
  Haneef, Mohamed, 311–312, 353–354
  ul-Haque, Izhar, 352–353
  Hicks, David, 344–346
  hyper-legislation, response to 9/11, 310
  immigration law as anti-terrorism law,
    333–334
  initial response to 9/11, 317–318
  "Jihad Jack" Thomas case, 311, 320, 342–344
  London bombings, 2005, response to,
    334–335, 339
  membership, association offenses, 327–328
  national security activities review, 354–356
  National Security Information Act, 347–348
  national security policies, 356–358
  pre-9/11 experience, 314–317
  preventive detention, 339–340
  proscription, of terrorist groups, 325–327
  response to 9/11, 17–18
  sedition, hate speech and, 337–339
  sedition, war on terrorism and, 336–337
  speech, terrorism and, 319, 335–336
  Sydney Hilton bombings 1978, 314–316
  terrorism financing, 320–322
  terrorism offenses, 322–323

  terrorism prosecutions, 312–313, 348–352
  the/a amendments, 323–324
  treason, war on terrorism and, 324–325
Australian Law Reform Commission
  secret information, in criminal process, 347
  sedition and hate speech, 338–339
Australian National Front, 315
Australian Security Intelligence Organization
    (ASIO)
  investigative detention powers, 191
  questioning warrants, 310–311, 328–332
  Sydney bombings, role in, 310–311, 315–316
Australian Security Intelligence Organization
    (ASIO) Act 1979, 316
Authorization of the Use of Military Force
    (AUMF) 2001, 4–5, 162, 174–175
aviation security, Anti-Terrorism Crime and
    Security Act 2001, U.K., 270–271
Awadallah, Osama, 189

Baathist coup 1963, 93
Babbar Khalsa, 384
Bagram military base, Afghanistan, 200
Bali bombings, 2002
  cost of, 35
  Indonesia's response to, 10, 148–153
  proscription and, 326
Bali bombings 2005, 154
Barak, Aharon, 101, 105
  on administrative detention, 118–119
  on harsh interrogation practices, 115
Barghouti, Marwan, 110–111
Barrett, Richard, 35–36
Basic Law on Human Dignity and Liberty
    1992, Israel, 108, 115
Basyir, Abu Bakar, 155
Beinisch, Dorit, 120, 122
Belfast Agreement 1998, U.K., 254
Belgium, Human Rights Committee
    (Council) review and, 71–72
Belmarsh case, 17, 240, 242, 453. *See also* A v.
    Secretary of State
  control orders, as response to, 280–287,
    289–290
  immigration law responses to, 243, 287–290
  litigation of, 276–280
bin Abas, Nasir, 156–157
bin Laden, Osama
  Security Council Resolution 1267, 26–28
  U.S., targeted killings and, 229
  U.S. killing of, 73, 231

Blair, Tony
London bombings, legislation and, 243–244
Security Council Resolution 1373, 64
Security Council Resolution 1624 and,
55–56
speech, terrorism and, 57
terrorism, causes of, 68
Blears, Hazel, 277–278
Blunkett, David, 264, 275, 277
Bobbitt, Philip, 234, 460
border control
Canada and, 39–40, 361–362, 374, 421
Security Council Resolution 1373 and,
39–40
Border Security Legislation Amendment Bill,
Australia, 333
Boumediene v. Bush, 166, 204, 205–207
Bradbury, Steven, 221
Brandenburg v. Ohio, 58, 227
British colonial emergency rule, 441
Israel and, 101–103
Malaysia and, 130–133
Singapore and, 130–133
Brogan v. The United Kingdom, 251
Bush administration
authorization of military force, 174–175
executive order, terrorism and, 34
extralegalism, 186, 192–193, 199–200
Geneva Conventions, Guantánamo and,
218–219
military courts, terrorism cases and, 90
military detention, *vs.* criminal prosecution,
192–195
November 2001 military order, 198–200
NSA warrantless spying controversy,
184–187
Patriot Act, 175–176
presidential powers, 186
Security Council resolutions and, 28
terrorist assets, freezing of, 180
unlawful combatants, Guantánamo and, 34
Bybee, Jay, 219, 222

Cameron, David, 293–294
Canada, 399–403
accountability, 18
Afghan detainees, 410–411
Air India bombings 1985, 369–370,
373–374
Anti-Terrorism Act, 376
Australian response to 9/11, *vs.*, 313–314, 360

charities, terrorism financing and, 382–384
commissions of inquiry, 6
criminal prosecutions, 406–410
definition of terrorism, 377–378
hate speech, community relations and,
393–395
immigration law as antiterrorism law, 18,
363–364, 424
initial response to 9/11, 374–375
intelligence, 389–390, 403–404
investigative hearings, 392–393
listing, 375, 385–387
national security activities review, 416–420
national security policies, 365, 420–423
October Crisis, 366–369, 372–373
political, religious motive controversy,
378–379
pre-9/11 experience, 365–374
preventive arrests, 390–392
refugee policy, 406
response to 9/11, 18, 423–425
secrecy provisions, 387–389
secret evidence, 397–399
security certificates, 242–243, 396–397,
400–403, 404–405, 424
special advocates, 399–400
Suresh, "exceptional circumstances" and,
288, 401–403
terrorism, definition of, 51
terrorism financing, 382–384
terrorism offenses, 379–382
terrorism prosecutions, 370–372
torture, 272, 365, 411–413
Canada Border Services Agency, 421
Canada Evidence Act, 387
Canadian Charter of Rights and Freedoms
(the Charter) 1982, 363
Canadian Security Intelligence Service
(CSIS), 364
Canadian Security Intelligence Service Act
1984, 316
Canadian Supreme Court, 11
capacity building
1540 committee, 54–55
UN Global Counter-Terrorism Strategy, 69
Central Intelligence Agency (CIA)
rendition program, Egypt and, 3, 80
torture and, 221–222
Centre for Strategic and International Studies,
Jarkata, 148
Chahal v. The United Kingdom, 273

Charities Registration (Security Information)
    Act, Canada, 384–385
charities, terrorism financing and, 384–385
Charkaoui, Adil, 386
Charkaoui v. Canada, 398, 403–404, 453
Charter, Canadian, 368
Charters, David, 77, 426
Chechen terrorists, Beslan, Russia 2004,
    52
Cheshin, Mishael, 105
Chesney, Robert, 214–215
CIA. *See* Central Intelligence Agency
Classified Information Procedures Act, U.S.,
    217
Clinton administration
    African embassy bombings 1998, 169
    antiterrorism legislation, 169–170
Cole, David, 188, 242
collective punishment, Israel, 104–108
Combat International Terrorism Act 1984,
    U.S., 167
Committee against Torture, 24, 219
Communications Security Establishment
    (CSEC), 389–390
community relations
    Canada and, 363, 393–395
    racial and religious hatred, U.K., 269–270
    rehabilitation, multiculturism and, 451–452
    Singapore and, 140–141
Compton Committee, U.K., 246–247
consensual treaty making, Security Council
    and, 65–66
CONTEST. *See* Countering International
    Terrorism
control orders
    Australia, 311, 340–342
    Historical precedents, 102, 133
    United Kingdom, 244, 280–287, 289–290,
        333–334
Convention against Torture, U.S., 226
Cooper-Blum, Stephanie, 124
Cotler, Irwin, 337–338, 376–377, 394
Countering International Terrorism
    (CONTEST), 244, 303–306
Counter-Terrorism Act 2008, U.K., 301–303
Counter-Terrorism Committee (CTC), 3
    creation of, 45–51
    Egypt, torture and, 81–82
    human rights and, 21, 69–70
counter-terrorism law
    post-9/11 convergence and, 8–9
    post-9/11 divergences and, 9–11

courts, role of
    national security activities review, 452–455
    post-9/11 terrorism and, 11, 429
Crenshaw, Martha, 426
Criminal Cases Review Commission, U.K.,
    249
criminal law, 18–19
    changes to, 19, 449
    Diplock courts, 248–250
    existing, adequacy of, 450, 459–460
    fault requirement, 450–451
    Israel, 110–113
    Security Council Resolution 1267 and,
        27–28
    Security Council Resolution 1373 and,
        44–45
    strains on, 449–451
    United Kingdom, 253–254
criminal prosecutions, 14
    Australia, 346–347
    Canada, 406–410
    United States, 214–218
Cross, James, 366, 367
Cross-Cultural Roundtable on National
    Security Issues, Canada, 395
CSEC. *See* Communications Security
    Establishment
CSIS. *See* Canadian Security Intelligence
    Service
CTC. *See* Counter-Terrorism Committee

Darul Islam, 138
Data Protection Act 1998, U.K., 267
data retention, Anti-Terrorism Crime and
    Security Act 2001, U.K., 267–268
death penalty, terrorism offenses
    Indonesia, 150–151
    United States, 169–170
Defence Regulations (State of Emergency)
    1945, Israel, 101–102, 109
Dempsey, James, 172
Detachment 88, 156–158
Detainee Treatment Act 2005, U.S., 164,
    203–204, 226
Dinh, Viet, 189
Diplock Commission, U.K., 248–250
disclosure of information, Anti-Terrorism
    Crime and Security Act 2001, U.K.,
    266–267
discriminatory profiling, U.K., 296–298
Dworkin, Ronald, 127–128, 450
Dyzenhaus, David, 455

Egypt
  constitutional amendments 2007,
    89–90
  counter-terrorism, *vs.* U.S., 78
  definition of terrorism, law and, 84–87
  emergency law, administrative detention
    and, 82–84
  extraordinary renditions, 78, 80–82
  initial response to 9/11, 3
  money laundering law, 88–89
  Mubarak, after fall of, 90–91
  old laws, reliance on, 84–87
  speech, terrorism, laws and, 87–88
  terrorism and, 79–80
  violence, deradicalization and renunciation
    of, 91–92
Egyptian Islamic Jihad group, 92
Egyptian Penal Code, Section 86, 84–85
el-Baradei, Mohamed, 80
Emergencies Act 1988, Canada, 368–369
Emergency Management Act, Canada,
    421
Emergency Powers (Detention) Law 1979,
    Israel, 117–118
European Convention on Human Rights
  detention, noncitizens, 271
  militant democracy, 57
  Security Council Resolution 1368, 31
European Court of Human Rights, 11
  1267 listing process, 61–62
  Security Council Resolution 1368,
    31
  United Kingdom and, 239
European Union, 61, 72
evidence, intelligence and, 447–448
  Australia and, 358–359
  Boumediene v. Bush, 206–207
  Canada and, 370–373, 403–404, 407
  Indonesia and, 152
  Israel and, 123, 152
  United Kingdom and, 240
ex parte Quirin, 171
Executive Order 13224, U.S., 180
executive power, extralegalism and, U.S.,
    161–167, 235–237
extralegal conduct, U.S. and
  congressional oversight, 225
  extraordinary renditions, Obama and,
    225–227
  state secrets doctrine, 223–224
extralegalism, 14
  American history of, 163–164

  definition, 10, 164
  extraordinary rendition, 167–169
  failure of, in U.S., 235–237, 436–438
  harsh interrogation, 117
  material witness warrants, 188–192
  NSA, warrantless spying and, 184–187
  state secrets doctrine, 16–17
  torture, 218–223
extraordinary renditions
  Egypt and, 78, 80–82
  Obama and, 225–227
  United States and, 4, 167–169
extra-territorial application of law, 110,
    445–446
extra-territorial counter-terrorism activities,
    446–447
  Canada, 381, 410–416, 424–425
  United Kingdom, 295–296
  United States, 200–201

Fadden, Richard, 398
Far Falestin detention centre, 97–98
Fassbender, Bardo, 29–30
Federal Bureau of Investigation (FBI), 163,
    172
Financial Action Task Force (FATF), 35, 88,
    433
Financial Transactions and Report Analysis
    Centre of Canada (FINTRAC), 383
First Amendment. U.S., 58–59, 162–163,
    227–229
FISA. *See* Foreign Intelligence Surveillance
    Act
FLQ. *See* Front de Liberation du Quebec
food deprivation, interrogation and, 246–248
Foreign Intelligence Surveillance Act (FISA),
    U.S., 163, 172–173, 176–178, 316
Fourth Geneva Convention, 106
France, Syrian nationalist movements and,
    92–93
Friedman, Tom, 154
Front de Liberation du Quebec (FLQ), 366

Garland, David, 5
Gearty, Conor, 248–249, 440
Geneva Conventions, 31, 218–219
Ghailani, Ahmed, 215–216
Goldsmith, Jack, 164, 214–215, 219–220, 230
Gonzales, Alberto, 218–219
Graham, Bill, 96
Greenstock, Jeremy, 29, 45–46
Gross, Oren, 50–51, 70, 164

GSS. *See* Israeli General Security Service
Guantánamo
Australian citizens held, 344–345
black hole, 198–200
British citizens held, 292–295
Canadian citizen held, 212–213, 414–416
Geneva Conventions, 218–219
habeas corpus, 198, 200–201, 203–208
Hamdi, 202–203
military commissions, 210–214
Obama and, 208–210
Guantánamo Review Task Force, 209–210
Gurney, Sir Henry, 130

Habibie, Bacharuddin Jusuf, 144
Hadi Soesastro, 148
Hamas, proscription, Australia, 325
Hamazah Haz, 144
Hambli, 155–156
Hamdan v. Rumsfeld, 166, 203–204, 212
Hamdi v. Rumsfeld, 166, 201–203
Hamdi, Yaser, 194–195
Haneef, Mohamed, 311–312, 353–354
ul-Haque, Izhar, 352–353
harsh interrogation
Israel, 113–115, 117
special rapporteur, 116
United Kingdom, 246–248
United Nations Committee against
Torture, 116
hate speech, 134, 337–339, 393–395
Hezbollah, 83
Hicks, David, 212, 213, 344–346, 349–350
high commissioner for human rights, 24
Hikmanto Juwana, 151, 152–153
Hocking, Jenny, 314
Holder, Eric, 213
Holder v. Humanitarian Law Project, 112,
172
Homeland Security Act 2002, 195
hooding, 246–248
Hor, Michael, 129, 133
Hugessen, James, 397–398
human rights
CTC and, 46–51, 69–70
records, initial response to 9/11, countries
and, 3–5
Security Council and, 67, 69–70
terrorism financing, terrorist lists and, 36–38
UN Global Counter-Terrorism Strategy,
26–28
Human Rights Act 1998, U.K., 267

Human Rights Committee (Council), 24, 50,
71–72
Human Rights Watch, 72, 458
accountability gap, 12
Syria and, 96, 97
human security
Australia, 313
Canada, 420–423
Cotler, Irwin and, 420
Hussein, Liban, 385–386

ICC. *See* International Criminal Court
Immigration and Naturalization Service
(INS), 188
Immigration and Refugee Protection Act
(IRPA), Canada, 364
Immigration, Asylum, and Nationality Act
2006, U.K., 289
immigration detention, 395–396, 439. *See also*
administrative detention
immigration law
liability rules, 41
preventive and investigative detention,
187–188
secret evidence, 41
United Kingdom, response to Belmarsh
case, 287–290
immigration law, as antiterrorism law, 39–41,
42, 64, 75
Anti-Terrorism Crime and Security Act
2001, U.K., 271–276
Australia, 333–334
Canada, 18–19, 288, 363–364, 395–406, 424
Security Council and, 67, 434–435
United Kingdom, 18–19, 250–251
USA Patriot Act, 182–183
Immigrations and Customs Enforcement,
U.S., 195
indeterminate detention
Canada, 3–4
initial response to 9/11, 3–5
Israel, 101–102
Malaysia, 101–102
Northern Ireland, 101–102
Singapore, 78, 101–102
United Kingdom, 107
United States, Guantanamo, 202–203,
208–210
Indonesia, 153–156, 158–159
antiterrorism law, post 9/11, 10–11
Constitutional Court, 10
Detachment 88, 156–158

perpu 2002, administration of, 214–218
perpu, in response to Bali bombings,
  148–153
pre-9/11 experience, 143–145
response to 9/11, 78, 145–153
terrorism financing, money laundering and,
  145–146
withdrawn draft terrorism law, 146–148
Indonesian Penal Code, 146
information
  disclosure of, 266–267
  withholding of, 268–269
inquiries
  Air India, 418–420
  Arar, 411–413, 416–417, 419–420
  Australia, 314–315
  Canada, 6, 11, 365, 412–413
  complicity in torture, 293–294
  United Kingdom, 11
  United States, 11–12
INS. *See* Immigration and Naturalization
    Service
intelligence
  Australia, 323–324
  Canada, 389–390, 403–404
  as evidence, 123, 152, 206–207, 240,
    447–448
  General Assembly, 43
  Security Council Resolution 1373 and,
    42–44
  Syria and, 98
  1267 Taliban and al Qaeda Sanctions
    Committee, 28
  United Nations and, 435
  United States, 196–197
Intelligence Reform and Terrorism
    Prevention Act 2004, 195–196
Internal Security Act, Singapore
  British colonial emergency rule and,
    130–133
  overview of, 133–134
  use of, 134–136
International Commission of Jurists, 72, 458
International Convention for the Suppression
    of Acts of Nuclear Terrorism, 55
International Convention for the Suppression
    of the Financing of Terrorism 1999, 28,
    33, 34
  definition of terrorism, 26
  Singapore and, 136
International Covenant of Civil and Political
    Rights, 71, 118, 227

International Criminal Court (ICC), 234
Internet material, terrorism and, U.K.,
    314–317
Internment of Unlawful Combatants law
    2002, Israel, 119–124, 158–159
internment, U.K. and, 244–246, 295–296
interrogation. *See* harsh interrogation
investigative detention
  Canada, 396
  grand jury material witness warrants, U.S.,
    188–192
  immigration law, U.S., 187–188
  United Kingdom, 259–260
investigative hearings, Canada, 392–393
Iraq War, Security Council Resolution 1368
    and, 29–31
Irish Republican Army (IRA), 228, 249
IRPA, Canada. *See* Immigration and Refugee
    Protection Act, Canada
Israel, 100–101, 128–129
  administrative detention, 117–124
  criminal law model, 110–113
  Defence Regulations 1945, 101–102
  definition of terrorism, new laws and,
    103–104
  forfeiture of terrorist property, 104–105
  harsh interrogation, torture, 113–117
  house demolitions, 104–108
  initial response to 9/11, 3
  old laws, reliance on, 101–103
  Prevention of Terrorism Ordinance 1948,
    102–103
  Prohibition on Terrorist Financing Law
    2004, 103
  response to 9/11, 78–79
  speech, terrorism, laws and, 108–110
  targeted killings, 124–128
Israeli Defence Force, 107
Israeli General Security Service (GSS),
    113–117
Israeli Landau Commission, U.K., 247
Israeli Supreme Court
  administrative detention, 11, 118–123
  harsh interrogation, 114–115
  house demolition, 105–108
  targeted killings, 105–108, 125–128

Jabarah, Mohammed, 374–375
Jemaah Islamiyah (JI)
  arrests, 138–139
  proscription, 326
  rehabilitation, 140–142

"Jihad Jack" Thomas case, 342–344, 349, 350
  control order, 311
  proscription, 327
  terrorism financing, 320
JW Marriott hotel bombing 2003, Jakarta, 154

*Kadi and Al Barakaat International
  Foundation v. Council of the EU and
  Commission of the EC*, 61–62
Khadr, Omar, 212–213, 362–363, 414–416
Khawaja, Mohammad Momin, 407–408
al-Kidd, Abdullah, 191
King, David, 228–229
Koh, Harold, 231–232
Krieken, Peter van, 28–29
Krisch, Nico, 46
KSM. *See* Mohammed, Khalid Sheik
Kurdish Workers Party, 96
Kurds, Syria, 96

Landau Commission, 113–114
Langlois, Anthony, 147–148
Laporte, Pierre, 366, 367
Lashkar e Tayibba, 325
legalism, 9
Libya
  German disco bombing 1986, 169
  Pam Am bombing, 26
Lincoln, Abraham, extralegalism, 168
listing. *See* terrorist lists
Liversidge v. Anderson, 135
Lobel, Jules, 188
Lodhi, Faheem, 351
London bombings 2005
  association offense, 328
  Australia's response to, 334–335, 339
  legislation, response to, 13, 64, 243–244,
    298–301
  speech regulation and, 241
long-term administrative detention, 67
Lowenstein, Karl, 56
Luttig, Michael, 193
Luxor attack, 79
Lynch, Andrew, 324, 336

Macklin, Audrey, 396
Madrid bombings, 35
Malaysia
  British colonial emergency rule, 130–133
  initial response to 9/11, 3
  insurgency, 132

Malik Hasan, Nidal, 232
Margulies, Peter, 38
Mark, Sir Robert, 314–315
Mason, Anthony, 345
el-Masri, Khalid, 223
Mayfield, Brandon, 176, 189
MCA. *See* Military Commissions Act
McCain, John, 220
McDonald Commission, Canada, 416
McLellan, Anne, 379
McNaught, Kenneth, 367–368
McVeigh, Timothy, 173
Megawati Sukarnoputri, 149
Mehsud, Baitallah, 230
Menezes, Charles de
MI5. *See* Military Intelligence, Section 5
Michelson, Christopher, 322
migration of terrorism laws, 19
  Australia, 359–360
  British terrorism laws, 442–443
  civil laws, 444
  definition of terrorism in Terrorism Act
    2000, 442
  United Kingdom, 13
  United States, 443–444
militant democracy
  Australia, 335, 337
  Canada, 407–408
  European Convention on Human Rights,
    57
  Israel, 108–110
  Lowenstein, 56
  Security Council Resolution 1624, 56, 94
  speech regulation, 109, 243–244, 257–258,
    335, 442–443
  United Kingdom, 94, 257–258, 307–308
  United States, 227–229
Military Commissions Act (MCA) 2006, U.S.,
  163, 165, 204–205, 210–214
military detention
  criminal prosecution *vs.*, U.S., 192–195
  Guántanamo, Obama and, 208–210
  Israel, 112–113
Military Intelligence, Section 5 (MI5), 278
Ministry of Public Safety 2003, Canada, 421
Miranda, 171, 216–218
Mohammed, Binyam, 224
Mohammed, Khalid Sheik (KSM), 212, 213,
  214, 291
Money Laundering Law 2002, Indonesia,
  145–146

money laundering, terrorism financing and, 34–36, 145–146, 158, 433–434
  Canada, 382–394
  Egypt, 88–89
  Indonesia, 145–146, 150
  Israel, 103–104
  Singapore, 136–137
  Syria, 98–99
  United Kingdom, 262–263
  United States, 179–180
Moro Islamic Liberation Front, 138
Mousa, Baba, 295
Moussaoui, Zacarias, 216
Mubarak, Hosni, 9, 80
  American renditions, 78
  fall of, Egypt and, 90–91
  Sudan, assassination attempt, 23
multiculturalism. *See* community relations
Munaf v. Geren, 210, 445
Munich Olympics 1972, 25
Murphy, Lionel, 315, 316–317
Muslim Brotherhood, 56, 83, 90, 93, 96
Muslim minorities, 207, 270, 451–452

Nasr, Osama Nustafa Hassan, 81
National Commission on Human Rights, Indonesia, 157
national security, 14
  activities, review of, Australia, 354–356
  activities, review of, Canada, 416–420
  all-risks policies, 420–423, 459, 460–461
  policies, Australia, 356–358
  policies, Canada, 365, 420–423
  policies, United Kingdom, 303–306
  policies, United States, 233–235
National Security Agency (NSA), warrantless spying controversy, 184–187
National Security Information Act 2004, Australia, 347–348
national security letters, Patriot Act, 178–179
National Terrorism Agency, Indonesia, 157–158
Newton Committee, U.K., 267, 271, 274–276
Ni Aolain, Fionnuala, 50–51, 70, 250
9/11 Commission, 11–12, 33, 34–35
9/11
  effects on criminal law, 438–440
  effects on United Nations, 432–436
  funding of, 35
  initial response (by country), 2–5
  terrorist attacks, 174

noise, interrogation and, 246–248
Northern Command of the Department of Defense, U.S., 196
Northern Ireland (Emergencies Provisions) Act 1973, U.K., 249
Northern Ireland (Sentences) Act 1998, U.K., 254
Northern Ireland, United Kingdom and, 238, 244–245
  Diplock courts, 248–250
  harsh interrogation, 249
  internment, 244–246
  legislation, 249–250, 252–254
  peace talks, 254
  speech restrictions, 251–252
notification orders, convicted terrorists, U.K., 324–325
Nurediin, Muayeed, 97–98, 412–413

Obama administration
  American response to 9/11, 4–5
  Bush administration, *vs.*, 208–209, 232, 235
  CIA, torture and, 221
  criminal prosecutions, 214
  extralegalism, 164
  extraordinary renditions, 225–227
  military commissions, 212–214
  military courts, terrorism cases and, 90
  military detention, 208–210
  national security policy, 235
  prosecution of Guantanamo detainees and, 213–216
  targeted killings, 73, 128, 231
October Crisis, Canada, 366–369, 372–373
Office of Critical Infrastructure and Emergency Preparedness, Canada, 421
Official Secrets Act, Canada, 388
Oklahoma City bombings 1995, response, 169–174
Omar, Abu, 81
ombudsperson 1267 listing process, 60–61, 62
Omnibus Anti-Terrorism Act 1986, U.S., 167
Operation TIPS program, U.S., 197
Osiel, Mark, 220

Padilla, Jose, 192–194, 201
Pakistan, U.S. targeted killings, 230
Palestine Branch, 97–98
Pam Am bombing, 26
Parker Committee 1972, U.K., 247
Parmar, Talwinder Singh, 371–372, 385

Parti Quebecois (PQ), 368
Pathogens Access Appeal Commission, U.K.,
 270
Patriot Act, 16, 161–162, 175–176
 criminal justice, changes to, 182–183
 definitions of terrorism, 180–182
 detention, grand jury material witness
  warrants and, 188–192
 detention, immigration law and,
  187–188
 FISA amendments, 176–178
 immigration law as antiterrorism law,
  183–184
 military detention, of citizens not
  authorized by, 192–195
 national security letters, 178–179
 NSA warrantless spying not authorized by,
  184–187
 terrorism financing, 179–180
Patriot Act II, 197–198
PIAs. *See* preparation of preliminary
 implementation assessments
police powers
 Canada, 390–392
 United Kingdom, 269
Posner, Eric, 228
Posner, Richard, 168, 229
Posse Comitatus Act 1878, U.S., 234–235
Powell, Colin, 30–31, 295
PQ. *See* Parti Quebecois
preparation of preliminary implementation
 assessments (PIAs), 49
Preservation of Public Security Ordinance
 1955, Singapore, 132
Prevention of Terrorism (Temporary
 Provisions) Act 1974, U.K., 249
Prevention of Terrorism (Temporary
 Provisions) Act 1979, Sri Lanka, 321
Prevention of Terrorism Act 2005, U.K.,
 280
Prevention of Terrorism Ordinance 1948,
 Israel, 102–103, 108–110
preventive detention
 Australia, 339–340
 Canada, 390–392
 grand jury material witness warrants, U.S.,
  188–192
 immigration law, U.S., 187–188
 Indonesia, 151–152
 material witness warrants, U.S., 188–192
 Singapore, 133

United Kingdom, 151, 192, 259–260
Proceeds of Crime Act 2002, U.K., 265–266
Prohibition on Terrorist Financing Law 2004,
 Israel, 103, 104–105
proportionality
 counter-terrorism laws, 6, 274–275
 efficacy concerns and 457–458
 starting points and, 398–399, 453–455
 targeted killing, Israel and, 127–128
 targeted killing, U.S. and, 232
Proscribed Organizations Appeal
 Commission, U.K., 258
proscription
 al Qaeda, 327
 Australia, initial response to 9/11, 325–327
 Hamas, 325
 Lashkar e Tayibba, 325
 Tamil Tigers, 320–322, 383
 Terrorism Act 2000, U.K., 257–259
Prost, Kimberly, 61
Protect America Act, 186
Protection of Freedoms Bill, U.K., 318–320
Public Committee against Torture in Israel,
 115, 116, 125
public inquiry. *See* inquiries
Public Order Act 1986, U.K., 251
Public Safety Act 2004, Canada, 421–422

Qatada, Abu, 276, 288
Quarantine Act, Canada, 421
questioning warrants, Australia, 328–332

Rabin, Yitzhak, 109
racial hatred, Anti-Terrorism Crime and
 Security Act 2001, U.K., 269–270
Radsan, John, 216
Rajeevan, Arumugen, 321
Ramraj, Victor V., 89
Rasul v. Bush, 198–200
RCMP. *See* Royal Canadian Mounted Police
Reagan administration
 extraordinary renditions, 167–168
 terrorism and, 167, 169
refugee status
 Anti-Terrorism Crime and Security Act
  2001, U.K., 273–274
 Security Council Resolution 1373, 40–41
Rehman v. Secretary of State, 277
Reid Commission 1957, 132
Reid, Richard, 274
Religious Harmony Act, Singapore, 141

religious hatred, Anti-Terrorism Crime and
  Security Act 2001, U.K., 269–270
religious rehabilitation programs
  Indonesia, 156–158
  Singapore, 140–142
*Report of the Security Legislation Review
  Committee*, 2006 328
Ressam, Ahmed, 374, 386
retroactive law, Indonesia, 153–154
review
  domestic, 456
  efficacy based, 419, 457–458
  national security activities, Australia,
    354–356
  parliamentary, 355–356
  propriety based, 419, 457–458
Reza, Sadiq, 90
rights-protection bodies, United Nations,
  70–72
Roche, Jack, 318
Ronen, Yael, 58
Roosevelt, Franklin D., extralegalism and,
  168–169
Royal Canadian Mounted Police (RCMP),
  362
Ruddock, Philip, 394
Russia, speech, terrorism and, 58

Saadi v. Italy, 288
Sadat, Anwar, 91
Saleb, Ahmed, 80
Salfafis, 96
Scheinin, Martin, 62–63
Scheppele, Kim Lane, 47, 441
Scheuer, Michael, 168
Sebastien, Leonard, 153
secrecy
  Australia, 330–332, 347–348
  Canada, 372, 387–389, 417
  United Kingdom, 240–241, 307–308
  United States, 229
secret evidence
  Canada, 397–399
  Egypt, 90
  Indonesia, 152
  Israel, 101–102, 117–124
  Diplock courts, U.K., 248
  United Kingdom, 240–241, 273, 282,
    290–292
  United Nations, 28, 36–38, 59–63
  United States, 183–184

Security Council Resolution 1267, 28
  criticism of, 37–38
  reform, of listing process, 1, 26–28, 59–63,
    74–75
Security Council Resolution 1368, 29–31
Security Council Resolution 1373, 1–3, 15–16,
    31–33, 63, 74
  criminal law, 44–45
  CTC, creation of, 45–51
  definition of terrorism and lack of
    guidance, 75–76
  enactment of, 21
  immigration law as antiterrorism law, 64,
    75
  intelligence sharing, 42–44
  terrorism financing, 33–39
Security Council Resolution 1540, 53–55,
    63–64, 76, 435
Security Council Resolution 1566, 51–53,
    75
Security Council Resolution 1624, 64–65
  definition of terrorism, 75–76
  speech, terrorism and, 55–59
Security Council Resolution 1730, 59–60
Security Council Resolution 1735, 59
Security Council Resolution 1822, 60
Security Council Resolution 1904, 60–61
Security Intelligence Review Committee
    (SIRC), Canada, 369
Security Legislation Amendment (Terrorism)
    Act 2002, Australia, 325
Security Legislative Review Committee 2006,
    Australia, 326
sedition
  hate speech and, Australia, 337–339
  war on terrorism and, Australia, 336–337
Seong, Patrick, 134
Shariff, Omar, 268
Sharm-el-Sheikh attacks 2005, 79
Sharon, Ariel, 115
Sheller Committee, 336
SIAC. *See* Special Immigration Appeal
    Commission
Simpson, A.W.B., 441
Sinai bombings 2004, 79
Singapore, 129–130, 142–143, 159
  British colonial emergency rule, ISA and,
    130–133
  initial response to 9/11, 3, 136–138
  ISA, overview of, 133–134
  ISA, use of, 134–136

Singapore (*cont.*)
  Jemaah Islamiyah arrests, 138–139
  rehabilitation programs, 140–142
  response to 9/11, 78
  white paper, 139–140
SIRC. *See* Security Intelligence Review
    Committee
sleep, interrogation and, 246–248
special courts
  Alien Terrorist Removal Court, United
    States, 171
  Diplock courts, United Kingdom
  Egypt, 90
  Federal Court, Canada, 371, 372
  Indonesia, 144
  military commissions, United States, 163,
    165, 204–205, 210–214
  Singapore, Internal Security Act, 133–134
  Special Immigration Appeal Commission
    (SIAC), U.K., 273, 276–277
  Syria, 95–97
Special Immigration Appeal Commission
    (SIAC), U.K., 273, 276–277
special rapporteur on the promotion of
    human rights and fundamental freedoms
    while countering terrorism, 24, 49,
    70–71
  harsh interrogation, 116
  Security Council Resolution 1373, 32
special rapporteur on torture, 71
special rapporteurs, United Nations, 70,
    456–457
speech
  Australia's regulation of, 319, 335–336
  Canada's regulation of, 393–395
  Egypt's regulation of, 87–88
  hate speech, 134, 337–339, 393–395
  Internal Security Acts and, 133–134
  Israel's regulation of, 108–110
  Security Council Resolution 1624 and,
    55–59
  Singapore's regulation of, 133–134
  Syria, prosecutions and, 95–97
  United Kingdom's regulation of, 241,
    251–252, 322–323
  United States First Amendment tradition,
    227–229
Sri Lanka, offences of terrorism, 321–322
states-secrets doctrine, U.S., 223–224
stop-and-search powers, U.K. and, 260–261,
    296–298

Suharto, 144
Sunstein, Cass, 200–201
Suresh, "exceptional circumstances" and, 288,
    401–403
Sweden, Agiza and Alzery, 81
Syria, 92–93, 99–100
  definition of terrorism, 93–94
  money laundering law, 98–99
  signs of change, 100
  special courts, speech prosecutions and,
    95–97
  speech, terrorism, laws and, 95
  torture, 97–98

Taliban
  Security Council Resolution 1267 and,
    26–28
  Security Council Resolution 1368 and,
    29–30
Tamil Tigers, 320–322, 383–384
Tampa, asylum seekers and, 333–334
targeted killings
  Alston, Philip and, 230
  bin Laden, killing of, 73, 230–231
  Israel, 124–128
  Koh, Harold and, 231–232
  judicial review, Israel, 128
  proportionality, Israel, 127–128
  United States, 128, 229–233
terrorism
  cause of, 68
  emergency response plans, 460
  financing of, 33–39, 179–180
  homegrown, 176–177, 228, 430
  international, 303–306, 426–427
  9/11, 174
  pre-9/11, 25–28, 143–145, 167, 244–255,
    314–317, 365–374
  prosecutions, Australia, 348–352
  prosecutions, Canada, 370–372
  prosecutions, United States, 173, 214–216
  relation with other risks, 460–461
  training for, 317–318, 322–323, 340
Terrorism Act 2000, U.K., 13, 241–242, 255,
    325–327
  Canada and, 51
  definition of terrorism, 255–257
  Indonesia and, 146–147
  Israel and, 103–104
  preventive arrest, investigative detention
    and, 259–260

proscription, 257–259
Singapore and, 136
speech and, 57
stop-and-search powers, 260–261
terrorism financing, 258–259
terrorism offenses, 261–262
Terrorism Act 2006, U.K., 243, 298–301
terrorism, definition of, 180–182
Australia, 318–320
Canada, 377–378
Counter-Terrorism Act 2008, U.K.,
323–324
Egypt, 84–87
Israel, 103–104
Patriot Act, 180–182
Security Council Resolution 1373,
75–76
Security Council Resolution 1566, 51–53
Syria, 93–94
Terrorism Act 2000, U.K., 255–257
U.N. General Assembly, 23–24, 25–26
United Nations and, 18
terrorism financing, 433–434
Anti-Terrorism Crime and Security Act
2001, U.K., 265–266
Australia, 320–322
Canada, 382–384
Egypt, 88–89
Indonesia, 145–146
Israel, 104
Terrorism Act 2000, U.K., 258–259,
265–266
Singapore, 136–137
Syria, 98–99
United Kingdom, initial response to 9/11,
262–263
United States, 179–180
terrorism offenses
Australia, 322–323, 327–328
Canada, 379–382
Egypt, 84–87
Indonesia, 150–153
Israel, 102–104, 108–113
Singapore, 136–137
Syria, 93–95
United Kingdom, 261–262
United States, 182, 196
Terrorism (United Nations Measures) Order
2001, U.K., 262
Terrorism Prevention and Investigative
Measures, U.K., 286, 290

Terrorist Bombing Convention 1997, U.K.,
261
terrorist, definition of, Anti-Terrorism Crime
and Security Act 2001, U.K., 272–273
Terrorist Financing Convention 1999, U.K.,
261
terrorist lists
Australia, 325–327
Canada, 375, 385–387
delisting procedure, 59–60
narrative summary, 60
ombudsperson, delisting requests and,
60–61
reform 1267 listing process, 59–63
terrorism financing and, 36–39
UN Global Counter-Terrorism Strategy, 69
terrorist organization
association offense, Australia, 327–328
membership offense, Australia, 327
Thambaithurai, Prapaharan, 381–382
Third model, as alternative to crime and laws
of war. *See also* administrative detention
control orders, Australia, 311, 340–342
control orders, United Kingdom, 242–243,
244, 280–287, 289–290, 333–334
failure of, 165
immigration detention, 395–396, 439
military detention, 112–113, 192–195, 208–210
security certificates, Canada, 242–243,
396–397, 400–403, 404–405, 424
Thomas, Jack, 342–344, 349, 350
control order, 311
proscription, 327
terrorism financing, 320
Al Timimi, Ali, 227–228
Tomkins, Adam, 264
Toronto 18 case, 408–410
torture
Canada, 272, 365, 411–413
CTC, Egypt and, 81–82
Egypt, 81–82
Israel, 113–117
Security Council Resolution 1373 and, 41
Suresh, "exceptional circumstances" and,
288, 401–403
Syria, 97–98
United Kingdom, 290–292
United States, 218–223, 236
torture memos, 219–220, 236
Total Information Awareness Program, U.S.,
197

Totten vs. United States, 223
transnational accountability, 458–459
transnational counter-terrorism investigations, 444–445
  Canada and, 424–425
  civil society groups, media and, 458–459
  United Nations and, 456–457
transnational responses, to terrorism, 19–20
treason, war on terrorism and, Australia, 324–325
Trudeau, Pierre, 368
1267 Taliban and al Qaeda Sanctions Committee, 28. *See also* security council resolution 1267

Uighurs, 207
UN. *See* United Nations
United Kingdom. *See also* Anti-Terrorism Crime and Security Act 2001, U.K.; Terrorism Act 2000, U.K.
  administrative detention, internment, pre-9/11, 244–246
  CONTEST, 244, 303–306
  Counter-Terrorism Act 2008, 301–303
  Diplock courts, criminalization and, 248–250
  Guantánamo, Britons held, 292–295
  immigration law, as antiterrorism law, pre-9/11, 250–251
  indeterminate detention, 107, 244
  initial response to 9/11, 262–263
  inquiries, 11
  interrogation, pre-9/11, 246–248
  legislative war on terrorism, 238–244
  migration of terrorism laws, 13
  national security strategy 2008, 304–305
  peace talks, counter-terrorism and, pre-9/11, 254–255
  response to terrorism, 17
  Security Council Resolution 1624, 57–58
  speech restrictions, 241, 251–252
  stop-and-search powers, discriminatory profiling and, 244, 296–298
  Terrorism Act 2006,
  torture, 290–292
  warrantless arrest, pre-9/11, 251
United Nations (UN), 22–25
  failure of, 432–436
  initial response to 9/11, 28–31
  pre-9/11 experience, 25–28
  rights-protection bodies, 70–72

  role of, 21–22
United Nations Act 1946, U.K., 36–37
United Nations Act 2001, 136
United Nations Committee against Torture, 116
United Nations Counter-Terrorism Implementation Task Force, 24–25, 50, 72–73
United Nations General Assembly, 23–24
  Counter-Terrorism Policy 2006, 21
  counter-terrorism strategy 2006, 67–70
  definition of terrorism, 75
  initial response to 9/11, 28–29
  intelligence, sharing of, 43
  post-9/11 record, 65
United Nations Global Counter-Terrorism Strategy, 67–70
United Nations Office on Drugs and Crime, 45
United Nations Security Council
  consensual treaty making, 65–66
  counter-terrorism committees, 65
  counter-terrorism policies and, 12–13
  as global legislator, 74–75
  human rights records, 21, 67
  legislation and, 66
  membership, 66–67
  post-9/11 records, 63–67
  reform, counter-terrorism work, 59–63
  response to 9/11, 14–15, 29
  structure, role of, 22–23
United States. *See also* extralegalism
  bin Laden, killing of, 73, 231
  counter-terrorism, *vs.* Egypt, 78
  criminal prosecutions, 214–218
  Detainee Treatment Act 2005, 203–204
  Egyptian antiterrorism policies, influence on, 3
  executive power, extralegalism and, 161–167, 235–237
  extraordinary renditions, 78, 167–169, 225–227
  habeas jurisdiction, judicial affirmation of, 200–201
  initial response to 9/11, 174–175
  legalism, 9
  national security policies, 233–235
  Oklahoma City bombings (1995), response, 169–174
  pre-9/11 experience, 167
  response to 9/11, 161–167

speech, terrorism and, 227–229
targeted killings, 229–233
torture, 218–223, 236
war model, 169
World Trade Center (1993), response,
  169–174
United States Defense Intelligence Agency,
  196
United States Department of Defense, 196
United States First Amendment, 58–59,
  162–163, 227–229
United States states-secrets doctrine, 223–224
United States Supreme Court,
  counter-terrorism and, 166–167
United States vs. Reynolds, 223
unlawful combatants, Israel, 119
Urwah, 157
U.S. Army Field Manual on Interrogation, 221

Vermeule, Adrian, 228
Viera de Mello, Sergio, 48

Walker, Clive, 250, 252–253
wall standing, 246–248
War Measures Act, Canada, 366–367
warrantless arrest, U.K., 251, 260

waterboarding, 219
weapons of mass destruction (WMD)
  Anti-Terrorism Crime and Security Act
    2001, U.K., 270–271
  Security Council Resolution 1540 and,
    53–55, 435
  whole of government responses, to terrorism,
    19–20
  accountability for, 11–12, 18, 19–20, 365,
    424–425
  integration, 18
  United Nations and, 24–25, 69
Wilkinson, Paul, 249–250
Williams, Daryl, 328–329
Williams, George, 336
wiretap warrants, Canada, 390–392
WMD. *See* weapons of mass destruction
Working Group on Arbitrary Detention, 71
World Trade Center 1993, response, 169–174

Yoo, John, 164, 184, 219, 222

Zabaydah, abu, 60
Zawahri, Ayman al, 91, 229
Zedner, Lucia, 280–281, 285
Zubayda, Abu, 219, 220

CPSIA information can be obtained
at www.ICGtesting.com
Printed in the USA
LVOW13s1943250817

546384LV00005B/368/P

9 780521 185059